Handbook of Research on Small and Medium Enterprises in Developing Countries

Noor Hazlina Ahmad
Universiti Sains Malaysia, Malaysia

T. Ramayah
Universiti Sains Malaysia, Malaysia

Hasliza Abdul Halim
Universiti Sains Malaysia, Malaysia

Syed Abidur Rahman
Universiti Utara Malaysia, Malaysia

A volume in the Advances in Business Strategy and Competitive Advantage (ABSCA) Book Series

IGI Global
DISSEMINATOR OF KNOWLEDGE

www.igi-global.com

Published in the United States of America by
IGI Global
Business Science Reference (an imprint of IGI Global)
701 E. Chocolate Avenue
Hershey PA, USA 17033
Tel: 717-533-8845
Fax: 717-533-8661
E-mail: cust@igi-global.com
Web site: http://www.igi-global.com

Library of Congress Cataloging-in-Publication Data

Names: Ahmad, Noor Hazlina, 1974- editor. | Ramayah, T., 1964- editor. | Halim, Hasliza Abdul, 1975- editor.
Title: Handbook of research on small and medium enterprises in developing countries / Noor Hazlina Ahmad, T. Ramayah, Hasliza Abdul Halim, and Syed Abidur Rahman, editors.
Description: Hershey : Business Science Reference, [2017]
Identifiers: LCCN 2016055825| ISBN 9781522521655 (hardcover) | ISBN 9781522521662 (ebook)
Subjects: LCSH: Small business--Developing countries. | Information technology--Developing countries. | Sustainable development--Developing countries.
Classification: LCC HD2346.5 .H356 2017 | DDC 338.6/42091724--dc23 LC record available at https://lccn.loc.gov/2016055825

This book is published in the IGI Global book series Advances in Business Strategy and Competitive Advantage (ABSCA) (ISSN: 2327-3429; eISSN: 2327-3437)

British Cataloguing in Publication Data
A Cataloguing in Publication record for this book is available from the British Library.

Advances in Business Strategy and Competitive Advantage (ABSCA) Book Series

Patricia Ordóñez de Pablos
Universidad de Oviedo, Spain

ISSN:2327-3429
EISSN:2327-3437

Mission

Business entities are constantly seeking new ways through which to gain advantage over their competitors and strengthen their position within the business environment. With competition at an all-time high due to technological advancements allowing for competition on a global scale, firms continue to seek new ways through which to improve and strengthen their business processes, procedures, and profitability.

The **Advances in Business Strategy and Competitive Advantage (ABSCA) Book Series** is a timely series responding to the high demand for state-of-the-art research on how business strategies are created, implemented and re-designed to meet the demands of globalized competitive markets. With a focus on local and global challenges, business opportunities and the needs of society, the **ABSCA** encourages scientific discourse on doing business and managing information technologies for the creation of sustainable competitive advantage.

Coverage

- Value Creation
- Ethics and Business Strategy
- Outsourcing
- Value Chain
- Foreign Investment Decision Process
- Entrepreneurship & Innovation
- Core Competencies
- Strategic management
- Differentiation Strategy
- Cost Leadership Strategy

IGI Global is currently accepting manuscripts for publication within this series. To submit a proposal for a volume in this series, please contact our Acquisition Editors at Acquisitions@igi-global.com or visit: http://www.igi-global.com/publish/.

The Advances in Business Strategy and Competitive Advantage (ABSCA) Book Series (ISSN 2327-3429) is published by IGI Global, 701 E. Chocolate Avenue, Hershey, PA 17033-1240, USA, www.igi-global.com. This series is composed of titles available for purchase individually; each title is edited to be contextually exclusive from any other title within the series. For pricing and ordering information please visit http://www.igi-global.com/book-series/advances-business-strategy-competitive-advantage/73672. Postmaster: Send all address changes to above address.

Titles in this Series

For a list of additional titles in this series, please visit: www.igi-global.com

Entrepreneurship and Business Innovation in the Middle East
Philippe W. Zgheib (Lebanese American University, Lebanon)
Business Science Reference • copyright 2017 • 357pp • H/C (ISBN: 9781522520665) • US $190.00 (our price)

Comprehensive Problem-Solving and Skill Development for Next-Generation Leaders
Ronald A. Styron, Jr. (University of South Alabama, USA) and Jennifer L. Styron (University of South Alabama, USA)
Business Science Reference • copyright 2017 • 389pp • H/C (ISBN: 9781522519683) • US $205.00 (our price)

Diasporas and Transnational Entrepreneurship in Global Contexts
Sanya Ojo (University of East London, UK)
Business Science Reference • copyright 2017 • 334pp • H/C (ISBN: 9781522519911) • US $200.00 (our price)

Integrating Art and Creativity into Business Practice
Giovanni Schiuma (University of Basilicata, Italy & University of the Arts London, UK) and Antonio Lerro (University of Basilicata, Italy)
Business Science Reference • copyright 2017 • 260pp • H/C (ISBN: 9781522520504) • US $170.00 (our price)

Sustainable Entrepreneurship and Investments in the Green Economy
Andrei Jean Vasile (Petroleum-Gas University of Ploiesti, Romania) and Domenico Nicolò (University Mediterranea of Reggio Calabria, Italy)
Business Science Reference • copyright 2017 • 339pp • H/C (ISBN: 9781522520757) • US $185.00 (our price)

CSR 2.0 and the New Era of Corporate Citizenship
Mark Anthony Camilleri (University of Malta, Malta)
Business Science Reference • copyright 2017 • 398pp • H/C (ISBN: 9781522518426) • US $190.00 (our price)

Managerial Strategies and Solutions for Business Success in Asia
Patricia Ordóñez de Pablos (University of Oviedo, Spain)
Business Science Reference • copyright 2017 • 376pp • H/C (ISBN: 9781522518860) • US $195.00 (our price)

Collective Creativity for Responsible and Sustainable Business Practice
Ziska Fields (University of KwaZulu-Natal, South Africa)
Business Science Reference • copyright 2017 • 385pp • H/C (ISBN: 9781522518235) • US $200.00 (our price)

IGI GLOBAL
DISSEMINATOR OF KNOWLEDGE
www.igi-global.com

701 E. Chocolate Ave., Hershey, PA 17033
Order online at www.igi-global.com or call 717-533-8845 x100
To place a standing order for titles released in this series, contact: cust@igi-global.com
Mon-Fri 8:00 am - 5:00 pm (est) or fax 24 hours a day 717-533-8661

List of Contributors

Ahmad, Noor Hazlina / *Universiti Sains Malaysia, Malaysia* 1,23,67,117,261
Amran, Azlan / *Universiti Sains Malaysia, Malaysia* 345
Chan, Donovan / *University of Malaya, Malaysia* 377
Gan, P. L. / *Universiti Sains Malaysia, Malaysia* 48
Ganesan, Yuvaraj / *Universiti Sains Malaysia, Malaysia* 345
Halim, Hasliza Abdul / *Universiti Sains Malaysia, Malaysia* 23,67,261
Hanifah, Haniruzila / *Universiti Sains Malaysia, Malaysia* 67,261
Haron, Hasnah / *Universiti Malaysia Pahang, Malaysia* 345
Hossain, Md. Mosharref / *Bangladesh Institute of Bank Management (BIBM), Bangladesh & Universiti Utara Malaysia, Malaysia* 137
Ibrahim, Yusnidah / *Universiti Utara Malaysia, Malaysia* 137
Indiran, Logaiswari / *University Technology Malaysia, Malaysia* 322
Ismail, Kamariah / *University Technology Malaysia, Malaysia* 322
Jaafar, Mastura / *Universiti Sains Malaysia, Malaysia* 82
Jalali, Alireza / *Universiti Sains Malaysia, Malaysia* 82
Jayapal, Pravina / *Universiti Sains Malaysia, Malaysia* 185
Kasemsap, Kijpokin / *Suan Sunandha Rajabhat University, Thailand* 233
Khalifah, Zainab / *University Technology Malaysia, Malaysia* 322
Koorsse, Melisa / *Nelson Mandela Metropolitan University (NMMU), South Africa* 159
Kumar, Sameer / *University of Malaya, Malaysia* 377
Loleka, Siyasanga / *Nelson Mandela Metropolitan University (NMMU), South Africa* 159
Mahmud, Imran / *Daffodil International University, Bangladesh* 1,48
Omar, Azizah / *Universiti Sains Malaysia, Malaysia* 185
Omiunu, Ojinga Gideon / *University of Ibadan, Nigeria* 208
Oni, Sola / *Pan-Atlantic University, Nigeria* 360
Ooi, Say Keat / *Universiti Sains Malaysia, Malaysia* 345
Rahman, Syed Abidur / *Universiti Utara Malaysia, Malaysia* 117,280
Ramanathan, Santhi / *Multimedia University, Malaysia* 322
Ramayah, T. / *Universiti Sains Malaysia, Malaysia* 48,67,280
Scholtz, Brenda / *Nelson Mandela Metropolitan University (NMMU), South Africa* 159
Taghizadeh, Seyedeh Khadijeh / *Universiti Tecknolgi PETRONAS, Malaysia* 117,280
Thongpoon, Siriluck / *Hatyai University, Thailand* 1
Thurasamy, Ramayah / *Universiti Sains Malaysia, Malaysia* 82

Table of Contents

Section 3
Recognising and Seizing Opportunities for SMEs

Detailed Table of Contents

basis for agropreneurship development among today's youth is based on training and inculcating an agropreneurship work culture at the university level, the authors proposed roles an academic institution could play in instilling positive an agropreneurial attitude among Gen Y graduates.

Bangladesh is a least developed country which ranks 131 out of 132 in the environment pollution index. Currently, small- and medium-sized enterprises (SMEs) provide 70–80 percent of job opportunities in Bangladesh. Information technology (IT) is one of the industries providing highest employment in the country. The IT professionals' expertise plays an important role in influencing the firms' decisions regarding sustainability. The objective of this chapter is to develop a theoretical model to measure attitude towards green IT usage among IT professionals in Bangladesh. The model will be grounded on self-determination theory.

There is a continuing debate among scholars concerning the existence of a fortune at the bottom of pyramid (BOP). While some scholars argue that there is a profitable market at the pyramid base, others argue that targeting poor people as customers could lead to unethical business practices. With the aid of preliminary study, this paper explains that there is a fortune to be made at the BOP if the community is treated as the entrepreneurs than as mere consumers. Nevertheless, for them to develop their own venture in order to reduce poverty is not an easy task due to various hindrances. Therefore, this paper provides insights into the under-researched area of comprehending the impediments that triggered the BOP community readiness to venture into business development. Converting the BOP into active entrepreneurs has become the agenda of the Malaysian government to eradicate the poverty by the year 2020 and thus this paper is expected to provide preliminary findings of the barriers that prohibit them to become entrepreneurs. A series of interview was conducted with a sample of ten BOP communities from Northern Region in Malaysia. In-depth, one-to-one interviews were conducted among them to probe into their outlook on this matter. The findings highlighted on the key factors that hamper the BOP community to create new ventures, new insights and experiences towards entrepreneurship. In sum, this study generates agenda for researchers to reach more conclusive evidence about the concept of entrepreneurship among the BOP community in Malaysia.

The importance of entrepreneurial orientation (EO), resource-based view (RBV), network types of social capital (SC) and small and medium enterprises (SMEs) have become the main focus in the manufacturing environment. The current study investigates 1. The relationship between EO and Manufacturing SMEs performance and 2. The moderating effect of intra- and extra-industry network in EO and manufacturing SMEs performance relationship. Quantitative method was done through survey. The population of this study was industrial SMEs in Tehran and Hamedan. Proportionate stratified random sampling was employed and out of 580 questionnaires sent out, only 150 questionnaires were returned. The result implies that the dimensions of EO positively improved manufacturing SMEs performance. In addition the result shows that the high intra-industry network strongly moderates the relationship between innovativeness and growth-profit ability and also strongly moderates the relationship between risk-taking and growth-profitability. Contributions and limitations of the study are also discussed accordingly.

Entrepreneurship has been deliberated as multidimensional and multidisciplinary study. From the economic point of view entrepreneurship is the central force for economic development for any nation. Scholars and policy makers now have started to see entrepreneurship as panacea for inclusive growth. Entrepreneurships are most widely popular and discussed area. Study on small and medium sized enterprises (SMEs) has been maturing for the last decade as it has been regarded as significant player for the social development along with the economic development. In Bangladesh, SMEs account for a large proportion of the total establishments in various sectors. Considering the importance of the SME sector in Bangladesh, this study intends to explore and sketch-out the landscape of current SME setting in Bangladesh. With this aim the study has extensively carried out literature review, observed and understood the secondary data obtained from various organizations, and finally presented a policy driven recommendation (micro and macro level) which would enable to develop the SME sector in a developing country like Bangladesh.

The proliferation of SMEs in Malaysia shows that a better understanding on this SMEs are needed. Even though the SME market is booming, these SMEs face difficulties in sustaining in the constantly evolving marketplace. In order to continuously flourish in this industry, the firms should understand the role of value co-creation in improving their market performance. The lack of value co-creation implementation has been found to act as a barrier for these SMEs. Moreover, SMEs are identified to have issues in establishing a strong brand image through value co-creation. Therefore, the book chapter develops a conceptual framework to improve the understanding on the contribution of value co-creation in the development of stronger brand image and greater market performance.

Beside the SMEs, families operate small and fragmented businesses due to poverty and unemployment to help cater for their needs and family needs. These small and fragmented businesses are common among the poor due to lack of credit to expand such businesses. In addition, with the mandate from the federal government of Nigeria, every business must be registered with the Corporate Affairs Commission of the federal republic of Nigeria and pay a certain amount of money every year depending on level of business growth and development. Suffice to note that despite the payment of these charges by businesses, nothing is done by the federal government to assist them.

This chapter explains the overview of internationalization; the aspects of internationalization in Small and Medium Enterprises (SMEs); internationalization, social capital, and Foreign Market Knowledge (FMK) in SMEs; internationalization and marketing capability; internationalization, innovation, and Research and Development (R&D); the implications of internationalization in SMEs; the overview of Entrepreneurial Orientation (EO); EO and firm performance; EO, organizational learning, and knowledge management; and the current trends and issues with EO in SMEs. Encouraging internationalization and EO is essential for SMEs that seek to serve suppliers and customers, increase business performance, strengthen competitiveness, and achieve continuous success in SMEs. The chapter argues that encouraging internationalization and EO has the potential to enhance organizational performance and reach strategic goals in SMEs.

Section 3
Recognising and Seizing Opportunities for SMEs

SMEs in Malaysia are dominated by Bumiputera that represent more than 50% of the Malaysian SME's population. However, there are many challenges faced by Bumiputera SMEs such as limited skilled workers, lack of creativity and knowledge. In this point of view, considering the specific human capital approach, the value, uniqueness, creativity, innovativeness and proactiveness are the most relevant features for innovation performance. To have an excellent innovation performance is to have an innovative culture where entrepreneurs needs to have creative employees which simultaneously improve the innovation performance in Bumiputera SMEs. This study focuses mainly on owner-manager of Bumiputera SMEs. It provides useful pointers to entrepreneurs and policy makers on the importance of specific human capital, innovative culture and enhancing innovation performance in Bumiputera SMEs.

Innovation requires an innovation mind-set derived from behavioural aspects of individuals. To realize such a notion, this paper introduces a framework and integrated theory of planned behaviour (TPB) in the line with the exploratory and exploitative innovations. Attitudes towards innovation, subjective norms for innovation and perceived control over innovation can influence on exploratory and exploitative innovations in SMEs. It is believed that through exploratory and exploitative innovations, entrepreneurs in SMEs may achieve subjective wellbeing. The approach of applying the TPB to exploratory and exploitative innovations will have few implications. First it allows SMEs to understand which factors are important in doing exploratory and exploitative innovations. Second, it will indicate that doing exploratory and exploitative innovations can bring the feeling of perceived wellbeing among entrepreneurs. Finally, the framework identifies a number of areas for future research that can verify the comprehensive understanding of successful innovations.

Small and medium enterprises (SMEs) which are dominated by non-state SMEs play an important role in economic growth, job creation and poverty reduction in Vietnam. However, most of non-state SMEs in Vietnam are young and contain several limitations in performance. Therefore, finding solutions and strategic orientations to enhance SMEs performance becomes the major concern of the policy makers and business practitioners. To generate the implications pertinent to firms for sustaining high organizational performance in long run, understanding the strategic situation of the firms is a vital step. Thus, based on strategic theory of SWOT and strategy formulation, this chapter aims to: (1) Explore the characteristics of dynamic macro environment for development of non-state SMEs in Vietnam; (2) identify the key firm's features; (3) examine firm performance to identify achievements and constraints; (4) suggest strategic implications for enhancement of SMEs performance toward long-run development of non-state SMEs in Vietnam.

The purpose of this chapter is to present the importance and contribution of business incubation programmes to Small and Medium Enterprises in Malaysia. Chapter starts with a brief review of the history and transition of major economic policies in Malaysia as well as the government responses towards achieving the status of fully developed nation by the year 2020. The policy review includes the Laissez-faire Policy, New Economy Policy, National Development Plan, National Vision Policy, and New Economy Model which were set to achieve nation's rapid economic growth. This review leads the paper towards the exploration of the major drivers of current economic growth in Malaysia. This chapter identifies Multimedia Super Corridor as the most important initiative and a key driver to global Information Communications Technology development as well as the major contributor to Small and Medium Enterprises establishment in Malaysia. In addition, it outlines the significant contribution of Small and Medium Enterprises to the economic growth in Malaysia, and finally identifies business incubators as a support mechanism to accelerate the SMEs success, especially the start-up firms. This chapter provides knowledge to the researchers and practitioners on the linkages among Multimedia Super Corridor, Small and Medium Enterprises and incubators that align with the economic policy development. As a conclusion, the chapter discusses the challenges faced by the incubation programmes in Malaysia and thus, highlights the prominence of business incubators as a niche subject to be explored in depth, in terms of their growth and potentials in Malaysia.

Given the increasing importance of the role played by small and medium-sized enterprises (SMEs) within the developing economy, this paper intends to provide further insight into corporate social responsibility (CSR) practices among SMEs. Within this context, the purpose is to propose the role of non-audit services (NAS), which contribute to the possible explanation of the SME adoption of CSR practices. A conceptual approach is taken whereby this paper is based on an extensive literature review of NAS and CSR practices in the SME context. Then, based on the knowledge-based view (KBV), this paper set to explain and highlight the role of NAS play to enhance CSR practices among SMEs. This paper provides a theoretical discussion on the importance of CSR in ensuring the survival of the SMEs. Although the proposition of NAS is relatively new, it provides an interesting and remarkable avenue for further research especially in the developing country. Overall, this paper draws attention to the importance of NAS in enhancing the survival and performance of the SMEs.

Research in the area of small and medium sized enterprises (SMEs) and coopetition has been ongoing for a considerable length of time. However, such studies have focused on SMEs in developed countries while there is very limited research in the same area with a focus on SMEs in Africa and developing countries. This research therefore aims to explore possible benefits and barriers that SMEs in Nigeria would experience in the adoption of coopetition. Considering the fact that it is a relatively new area of research, existing theories examining similar fields of study will be analysed with the aim of generating a theoretical framework through which factors affecting the phenomenon in the country may emerge.

Despite the current widespread adoption and use of social media as a marketing tool, very little empirical research focusing on local small and medium-sized enterprises (SMEs) is available. This study examines the usage of social media by small and medium-sized enterprises (SMEs) in Malaysia. The study assesses the impacts of age, educational attainment, and industry characteristics to the utilization, perceived benefits and barriers of SMEs. Results of the study indicate that social media is used by most SMEs for customer acquisition and its benefits are developing new business opportunities, reduced cost of advertising, 24 hours accessibility and decreased travelling time. The results however indicate that there is a lack of allocation of resources mainly in staffing and training when adopting the social media. Results also indicate that manager's age and educational attainment had significant impacts on social media strategies. The results did not reveal any evidence of different industry sectors relevance towards social media strategies. Implications for research are discussed.

Preface

This book, *Handbook of Research on Small and Medium Enterprises in Developing Countries*, is proposed for both academia and practitioners in the field of small and medium entreprises (SMEs) in developing countries. Chapters of this book were categorized into three sections. The first section titled "Understanding and Developing SMEs" presents a general overview of SMEs. This section contains five chapters that will familiarize the readers about the sustainable approach, agropreneurship intention, green IT usage intention in SMEs, the impediments to entrepreneurial ventures, entrepreneurial intention and SMEs performance. The second section titled "Realising the Strategies and Challenges of SMEs" discusses issues related to ways in which SMEs strategise to meet the various challenges posed by both the internal and external environment. Section two consists of six chapters representing challenges and opportunities of SMEs in Bangladesh, working capital financing, e-finance adoption by SMEs, market performance, ICT in SMEs and finally, internationalization related issues. The final section titled "Recognizing and Seizing the Opportunities" focuses on the application models of SMEs. Seven chapters of this section deliberate on the role of innovation culture on innovation performance, impact of innovation planned behaviour on well-being, the role of strategic situation on SME performance, business incubation, functions of non-audit service on corporate social responsibility, coopetition and finally, social media strategies for SMEs.

We hope that the publication of this book will enhance the spread of ideas and good practices among SMEs within the context of developing countries. This book will enrich knowledge and assist researchers or practitioners in the field of SMEs in developing countries to understand and solve issues related SMEs.

SECTION 1: UNDERSTANDING AND DEVELOPING SMEs

Chapter 1, "Sustainable Approach Towards Thai SMEs with Country Philosophy of 'Sufficiency Economy' and Government Support" by Siriluck Thongpoon of Hatyai University from Thailand, Noor Hazlina Ahmad from Universiti Sains Malaysia and Imran Mahmud from Daffodil International University, Bangladesh, examines the issues surrounding the sustainability of SMEs in the context of Thailand. Based on the findings, this research suggests that entrepreneurs, academicians, and policy-makers should be cognizant of the importance of sustainable development of SMEs through the lens of sufficiency economy philosophy, which is particularly derived from the Asian perspective. Additionally, the government institution can enhance the performance of SMEs by creating a healthy and appropriate business environment and infrastructure.

Chapter 2, "Agropreneurship Among Gen Y in Malaysia: The Role of Academic Institutions," by Asliza Yusoff, Noor Hazlina Ahmad, Hasliza Abdul Halim of Universiti Sains Malaysia provides a brief overview of the importance of the agriculture sector and agropreneurship and is followed by deliberation on the crucial involvement of the Gen Y segment the growth and development of this sector. This study suggests academic institutions should pay more attention to the curriculum development in enhancing entrepreneurial skills, capabilities and competencies relevant to agroventures. Adequate agropreneurship education coupled with extensive agropreneurship supports programs received, Gen Y graduates would be able to nourish creativity and innovation in developing viable agropreneurship products and ideas.

Chapter 3, "Understanding Attitude Towards Green IT Among Professionals in IT Service SMEs in Bangladesh," by Pei Leng Gan, T. Ramayah of Universiti Sains Malaysia and Imran Mahmud and Fatema Tuz Zuhora of Daffodil International University from Bangladesh, provide a theoretical framework to measure attitude towards green IT usage among IT professionals of SMEs in Bangladesh. The empirical evidence suggests that self-determination theory fits well in measuring the attitude towards green IT. More importantly, identified regulation is a very strong predictor to shape attitude towards using green IT, in the context of IT professionals of SMEs in Bangladesh.

Chapter 4, "The Impediments to Entrepreneurial Ventures Among the Bottom of Pyramid Community in Northern Malaysia," by Hasliza Abdul Halim, Noor Hazlina Ahmad, Haniruzila Hanifah, and T. Ramayah of Universiti Sains Malaysia explains that there is a fortune to be made at the BOP if the community is treated as the entrepreneurs than as mere consumers. Nevertheless, for them to develop their own ventures in order to reduce poverty is not an easy task due to various hindrances. Findings obtained from a series of interview on BOP communities from Northern Region in Malaysia revealed the key factors that hamper the BOP community to create new ventures, new insights and experiences towards entrepreneurship.

Chapter 5, "The Moderating Effect of Social Capital in Relation of Entrepreneurial Orientation and Firm Performance," by Alireza Jalali, T. Ramayah and Mastura Jaafar of Universiti Sains Malaysia emphasizes on the importance of entrepreneurial orientation (EO), resource-based view (RBV), network types of social capital (SC) and small and medium enterprises (SMEs).

SECTION 2: REALISING THE STRATEGIES AND CHALLENGES OF SMEs

Chapter 6, "On the Road to SME Sector Development in Bangladesh: A Guideline Based on Current Challenges and Opportunities," by Syed Abidur Rahman of Universiti Utara Malaysia, Noor Hazlina Ahmad of Universiti Sains Malaysia and Seyedeh Khadijeh Taghizadeh of Universiti Teknolgi PETRONAS, embarked upon exploring and sketching-out the landscape of current SME settings in Bangladesh. This study presents a policy driven recommendation (micro and macro levels) which would enable the development of SMEs in Bangladesh.

Chapter 7, "Working Capital Financing by Banks in Small Enterprises: Problems and Challenges for Bangladesh," by Md. Mosharref Hossain and Yusnidah Ibrahim of Universiti Utara Malaysia focuses on problems and challenges faced by banks while financing working capital. Based on the survey findings, a good number of solutions have been formulated for policy initiatives.

Chapter 8, "Understanding and Adoption of E-Finance in Small and Medium Enterprises (SMEs) in Developing Countries," by Brenda Scholtz, Melisa Koorsse and Siyasanda Loleka of Nelson Mandela Metropolitan University (NMMU) from South Africa investigates the extent of understanding and adoption of e-finance by SMEs in two developing countries: Bangladesh and South Africa. The results of the survey revealed that access to financial products and services was the highest rated benefit of e-finance to respondent SMEs, whereas regulatory environment and policy was the highest rated barrier.

Chapter 9, "The Role of Value Co-Creation on Brand Image: A Conceptual Framework for the Market Performance of SMEs in Malaysia," by Pravina Jayapal and Azizah Omar of Universiti Sains Malaysia develops a conceptual framework to improve the understanding on the contribution of value co-creation in the development of stronger brand image and greater market performance. The authors suggest that communication and the strong bond between customers and the firm is important for the firm to better understand the needs and wants of the customers. By co-creating value, firms would be able to enhance their brand image and reputation. When the brand image is strong, it would lead towards more purchase as well as increase in customer satisfaction that could subsequently enhance firm's market performance.

Chapter 10, "Deploying ICT to Enhance Small Businesses and Achieving Sustainable Development: A Paradigm to Reducing Poverty and Unemployment and Enhancing a Sustainable National Development in Nigeria," by Omine Ojinga Gideon of University of Ibadan from Nigeria provides current scenarios of ICT Deployment and Utilization Level by Small Business Development in Nigeria. Challenges and recommendations are also discussed.

Chapter 11, "Encouraging Internationalization and Entrepreneurial Orientation in Small and Medium Enterprises," by Kijpokin Kasemsap of Suan Sunandha Rajabhat University from Thailand explains the overview of internationalization; the aspects of internationalization in Small and Medium Enterprises (SMEs); internationalization, social capital, and Foreign Market Knowledge (FMK) in SMEs; internationalization and marketing capability; internationalization, innovation, and Research and Development (R&D); the implications of internationalization in SMEs; the overview of Entrepreneurial Orientation (EO); EO and firm performance; EO, organizational learning, and knowledge management; and the current trends and issues with EO in SMEs. The study argues that it is important for the SMEs to establish a strategic plan for internationalization to regularly check their practical advancements toward satisfying customer requirements.

SECTION 3: RECOGNISING AND SEIZING OPPORTUNITIES FOR SMEs

Chapter 12, "Innovation Culture as Mediator Between Specific Human Capital and Innovation Performance Among Bhumiputera SMEs in Malaysia," by Haniruzila Hanifah, Hasliza Halim, Noor Hazlina Ahmad and Ali Vafaei-Zadeh of Universiti Sains Malaysia investigates the mediating role of innovation culture in the relationship between specific human capital and innovation performance which focuses mainly on the Bumiputera SMEs in Malaysia. This study provides useful pointers to entrepreneurs and policy makers on the importance of specific human capital, innovative culture and enhancing innovation performance in Bumiputera SMEs.

Chapter 13, "Innovation-Driven Planned Behaviour Towards Achieving the Wellbeing of the Malaysian SMEs," by Seyedeh Khadijeh Taghizadeh of Universiti Teknology Petronas, Syed Abidur Rahman of Universiti Utara Malaysia and T. Ramayah of Universiti Sains Malaysia introduces a framework and integrated theory of planned behaviour (TPB) in the line with the exploratory and exploitative innovations. This study allows SMEs to understand which factors are important in doing exploratory and exploitative innovations and also indicates that doing exploratory and exploitative innovations can bring the feeling of perceived wellbeing among entrepreneurs.

Chapter 14, "Non-State SMEs in Vietnam Understanding Strategic Situation and Implications for Organizational Performance," by Nguyen Thi Uyen and Siti Rohaida Mohamed Zainal of Universiti Sains Malaysia from Malaysia provided the characteristics of dynamic macro environment for development of non-state SMEs, the key firm's features, firm's performance to identify achievements and constraints and suggested strategic implications for enhancement of SMEs performance toward long-run development of non-state SMEs in Vietnam.

Chapter 15, "Business Incubation in Malaysia: An Overview of Multimedia Super Corridor, Small and Medium Enterprises, and Incubators in Malaysia," by Logaiswari Indiran, Zainab Khalifah, Kamariah Ismail of Universiti Teknologi Malaysia and Santhi Ramanathan of Multimedia University presents the importance and contribution of business incubation programmes to Small and Medium Enterprises in Malaysia. This study provides knowledge to the researchers and practitioners on the linkages among Multimedia Super Corridor, Small and Medium Enterprises and incubators that align with the economic policy development. As well as the chapter discusses the challenges faced by the incubation programmes in Malaysia and thus, highlights the prominence of business incubators as a niche subject to be explored in depth, in terms of their growth and potentials in Malaysia.

Chapter 16, "Corporate Social Responsibility in SMEs: The Role of Non-Audit Services," by Yuvaraj Ganesan, Hasnah Haron, Azlan Amran and Say Keat Ooi of Universiti Sains Malaysia proposes the role of non-audit services (NAS), which contributes to the possible explanation of the SME adoption of CSR practices. This chapter also presents a theoretical discussion on the importance of CSR in ensuring the survival of the SMEs.

Chapter 17, "SMEs in Nigeria: Exploring Coopetition," by Sola Oni of Pan-Atlantic University from Nigeria explores the possible benefits and barriers that SMEs in Nigeria would experience in the adoption of coopetition. This study also generated a theoretical framework through which factors affecting the phenomenon in the country may emerge. May need to expand a bit on the findings/conclusion

Chapter 18, "Social Media Strategies for Small and Medium Scale Enterprise in the Klang Valley Region of Malaysia," by Donovan Chan and Sameer Kumar of University of Malaya, assesses the impacts of age, educational attainment, and industry characteristics to the utilization, perceived benefits and barriers of SMEs. The findings indicated that there is a lack of allocation of resources mainly in staffing and training when adopting the social media. Their study also revealed that manager's age and educational attainment had significant impacts on social media strategies.

Section 1
Understanding and Developing SMEs

Chapter 1
Sustainable Approach towards Thai SMEs:
The Effects of Country Philosophy of Sufficiency Economy and Government Support

Siriluck Thongpoon
Hatyai University, Thailand

Noor Hazlina Ahmad
Universiti Sains Malaysia, Malaysia

Imran Mahmud
Daffodil International University, Bangladesh

ABSTRACT

This study examines issues surrounding the sustainability of SMEs in the context of Thailand. Sufficiency economy philosophy and government support are seen as important covariates that could foster sustainable performance of SMEs. A sample of 119 SME entrepreneurs in the South of Thailand participated in this study. Exploratory factor analysis and hierarchical multiple regression were conducted and the results demonstrated that some dimensions of sufficiency economy philosophy and government support are critical predictors of economic and social performance. Moreover, knowledge and morality are found to promote the principle of sufficiency economy philosophy, as such SME entrepreneurs should be cognizant of the potential effects of this philosophy. The appropriate practices can be equipped and nurtured through the values of sufficiency economy philosophy, which shed light on means to achieve firm sustainability.

DOI: 10.4018/978-1-5225-2165-5.ch001

INTRODUCTION

The recent rise in sustainable development has attracted the attention of scholars, policymakers, business practitioners, and the community alike. The interest in sustainability, especially within the commercial sphere, is not only the focus of developed nations but also of developing countries like Thailand. SMEs are explicitly viewed as key players in promoting sustainability of the society. The importance of SMEs in both developed and developing countries is widely scrutinized, especially due to the fact their composition is huge, they create employment to the society as well as viewed as a source of income generation to the economy of a country (Tambunan, 2008). Researcher also mentioned, SMEs act as providers to the much-needed inter-firm linkages in supporting large enterprises to ensure that they remain competitive in the market. In the context of Thailand, all in all, approximately 99% of all enterprises can be classified as SMEs. Given the significant contribution of SMEs to the economy and social-well being of the society, SMEs are deemed to be the main actor to promote the economic and social sustainability.

In fact, the World Bank referred to Thailand as the fastest growing economy during 1986-1996 (Warr, 2009). Some key facts of Thailand economy are shown in Table 1.

However, the country plunged into severe economic crisis when the economic bubble collapsed in 1997. Big businesses were affected and most employers resorted to downsizing as a solution. The unemployment rate increased tremendously. Although this solution was deemed practical at that time, it could derail the effort towards enhancing economic and social sustainability in the long run. It is a worse scenario if one looks at Thai small- and medium-sized enterprises (SMEs). The available evidence indicates that Thai SMEs suffer from problems relating to lack of knowledge, ability, experience (OSMEP, 2006; Tambunan, 2008), moderate competencies among SMEs in Asian countries (Export-Import Bank of Thailand, 2012), insufficient capital, labour shortage, and marketing-related skills (Wiboonchutikula,

Table 1. Key facts of Thailand

Sector	Amount
Population	65 million
Literacy rate	96%
Minimum wage	300 baht per day
GDP (2014)	373.3 Billion US dollar
Trade Balance	US$ 24.6 billion
Current Account Balance (2014)	US$ 14.2 billion
International Reserves	US$ 157.1 billion
Capacity Utilization	60.48%
Manufacturing Production Index	168.2
Consumer Price Index (May 2015)	106.53
Corporate Income Tax	10-20%
Withholding Tax	0-15%
Value added Tax	7%
Currency rate 1 US$	33.55 baht

Source: Thailand Investment Review by Thailand Board of Investment (2015).

2002). These have resulted in instability of gross domestic product (GDP), imbalance of international trade, and fluctuation of the employment rate (Office of Small and Medium Enterprises Promotion [OSMEP], 2012), thereby putting the Thai economy in jeopardy.

In response to this problem, the philosophy of sufficiency economy, which is viewed as the values and norms embedded in Thai society, is reiterated by King Bhumibol Adulyadej as a remedy. This philosophy has been propagated to be re-applied at all levels, even at the business sector. Moreover, scholars have shown the significance of Thai values relating to sufficiency economy philosophy in determining balance and sustainability in Thai society, especially in the business setting (Kantabutra & Siebenhüner, 2011; Kusumavalee, 2010). Simultaneously, the Thai government has come to a resolution that SMEs should be at the fore front of the economy, given that they are crisis shock absorbers (Wiboonchutikula, 2002)—they help not only during a period of economic growth but also during economic recessions (Shariff & Peou, 2008). This resulted in the formulation of the SME master plan, which acted as Thailand's game changer. Therefore, in order to appreciate the contribution of informal rules (sufficiency economy philosophy) and formal rules (government support; North, 1990), these two factors have to be taken into account as important variables to promote sustainable performance of SMEs in Thailand. In 2010, SMEs accounted for 99 per cent of all enterprises in Thailand (OSMEP, 2012). Their significance has been widely scrutinized. They are obviously recognized as one of the key players in promoting sustainability in Thai society. Thailand's SMEs contribute significantly to the country's economic and social well-being.

A review of the literature on SMEs in the context of Thailand suggests that empirical research investigating the role of SMEs and others factors leading to sustainable performance is rather sparse. This study endeavours to delve into the sustainable performance of SMEs through the lens of sufficiency economy philosophy and government support. This study also bridges the gaps in data, or the dearth of it, on SMEs in Thailand (Wiboonchutikula, 2002).

BACKGROUND

Economically, the south region on the coast of the Gulf of Thailand and the border areas were agricultural base especially para rubber, palm oil, and fishery while most industries were the initial phase of agricultural processing industries. In the Andaman Sea coastal area, the main economy was tourism industry and business continuity. It could be highlighted that tourism in the south region was the major revenue for the region and the country. However, it was still concentrated in the popular areas such as Phuket, Krabi, and Samui. Border trade between the south region and Malaysia had the highest trade value compared to border trade in other areas. It accounted for 75 percent of the overall border trade of Thailand. Interestingly, it also had a rising trend. Most trades were through Sadao and Padang Besar checkpoint in Songkhla. Major products were agricultural products, vegetables, fruits, initial phase para rubber, industrial goods, and consumer goods. Besides, the economic structure also reflected that SMEs expanded throughout the region.

SMEs in Southern Andaman provinces (e.g. Phuket and Krabi) played important role in the service sector especially the tourism base, while SMEs in Southern border (e.g. Songkhla) played the important role in both agricultural industry and service industry, meanwhile SMEs in Southern Gulf of Thailand (e.g. Nakhon Si Thammarat and Surat-thani) played a key role in business which related to agriculture, trade and services sectors.

The majority of them operated in Bangkok, the capital of Thailand, and its five border provinces. In Thailand, SMEs are classified into three major categories which included 1) production sector including agricultural processing, manufacturing, and mining, 2) service sector, and 3) trading sector consists of wholesale and retail. The definition of SMEs in Thailand is based on either the number of employee or the total value of fixed assets that depended on the business sector as shown in Table 2.

Due to global economy problem and domestic political unrest, GDP of Thailand in 2014 increased 0.9%, a decelerate compare to that of 2.8% which was achieved in the year of 2013. It is computed that, in 2014, after attained 10.5% GDP, the overall GDP's value improved by 238, 563 million baht than the previous year. In non- agriculture sector, GDP value was worth 11,770,215 million baht.

Of the total business establishments, small enterprises and medium enterprises contributed 5,212,004 million baht which was 39.6% of Thailand's GDP. Among which, 27.8% attributable to small enterprises and 11.8% produced by medium enterprises. Overall, a small increase of 0.2% of the GDP value was observed in 2014.

Table 3 breaks down, economy activity, Thailand's overall GDP and, contribution of SMEs.

In Thailand, manufacturing industries, trade and maintenance sector and service sector contributed 27 per cent, 13.9 per cent and 32.6 per cent respectively. A detailed breakdown of contribution of those sectors is given below in Tables 4, 5 and 6.

Data from Table 4 indicates, in case of manufacturing SMEs, medium enterprises more than small enterprises and food and beverage category contributed 208,728 million baht on overall GDP in Thailand. In case of trade and maintenance sector, 1,242,015 million baht or 68.1% were from SEs and 214,270 million baht or 11.7% from MEs by two prime categories which are: wholesale and retail and

Table 2. The classification of small and medium enterprises

Type	Small Enterprise		Medium Enterprise	
	Number of Employees	Net Fixed Assets (Million Baht)	Number of Employees	Net Fixed Assets (Million Baht)
Production	≤ 50	≤ 50	51-200	> 50 – 200
Service	≤ 50	≤ 50	51-200	> 50 – 200
Wholesale	≤ 25	≤ 50	26-50	> 50 – 100
Retail	≤ 15	≤ 30	16-30	> 30 – 60

Source: Institute for Small and Medium Enterprises Development: ISMED (2008).

Table 3. Thailand's overall GDP and contribution of SMEs

	Country		SMEs	
	GDP (%)	Growth Rate (%)	GDP of SME (%)	Growth Rate (%)
Manufacturing	27.7	-0.4	23.5	-0.4
Trade	13.9	0.7	27.9	0.7
Service	38.8	2.4	41.3	0.8
Others	9.1	-1.1	7.3	-3.9

Source: The Office of the National Economic and Social development Board (NESDB).
Note: Agriculture sector is excluded and others include gas, water, construction, electricity and mining.

Table 4. Manufacturing SMEs and GDP

Overall GDP (OGDP)	27.7%	3,644,683 million baht
Contributed by SMEs on OGDP	33.7%	1,226,531 million baht
Size		
SEs	13.7%	496,533 million baht
MEs	20.0%.	729,998 million baht
Category		
Food and beverage	17.0% of OGDP	208,728 million baht
Furniture	13.0% of OGDP	159,349 million baht
Chemical	12.3% of OGDP	150,717 million baht

Source: White Paper on Small and Medium Enterprises of Thailand in 2015 by OSMEP (2015).

Table 5. Trade and maintenance SMEs and GDP

OGDP	13.9%	1,825,009 million baht
Contributed by SMEs on OGDP	79.8%	1,456,285 million baht
Size		
SEs	68.1%	242,015 million baht
MEs	11.7%	214,270 million baht
Category		
Whole sale and Retail	92.1% of OGDP	1,681,298 million baht
Maintenance	7.9% of OGDP	143,711 million baht

Source: White Paper on Small and Medium Enterprises of Thailand in 2015 by OSMEP (2015).

Table 6. Service oriented SMEs and GDP

OGDP	32.6%	4,281,173 million baht
Contributed by SMEs on OGDP	50.2%	2,150,924 million baht
Size		
SEs	39.4% of OGDP	1,688,078 million baht
MEs	10.8%. of OGDP	462,846 million baht
Category		
Real Estate	40.5%, contributed by SME	871,385 million baht
Hotel	21.1% contributed by SME	454,379 million baht
Transport and communication	16.1 % contributed by SME	345,453 million baht

Source: White Paper on Small and Medium Enterprises of Thailand in 2015 by OSMEP (2015).

maintenance (See Table 5). In concern of service oriented SMEs 1,688,078 million baht was generated by SEs accounting for 39.4% and 462,846 million baht by MEs equaling 10.8%. As concerns the role of SMEs, the service category with the highest GDP value was real estate acquiring a total of 871,385 million baht. Second and third position was achieved by hotel and transport respectively (see Table 6).

LITERATURE REVIEW

Sustainable Performance of SMEs

Although sustainable development has been discussed as a crucial concept for both business and policy, it has remained underexplored in the literature on entrepreneurship and small business (Hall, Daneke, & Lenox, 2010). A critical scrutiny of the previous studies demonstrates that the academic focus has mainly been on the economic performance of SMEs, but rarely on the sustainable performance of these ventures. The concept of sustainability emphasizes the triple bottom line, with SMEs being encouraged to engage in sustainability practices in their daily operations (Loucks, Martens, & Cho, 2010). However, it seems rather difficult for SMEs to apply these practices, for instance, in the environmental aspect (Labonne, 2006; Masurel, 2007; Schick, Marxen, & Freimann, 2002). Having highlighted this, the ultimate measure of SME performance is based on owner satisfaction (Reijonen, 2008)—especially through subjective self-report measures (Ahmad, Wilson, & Kummerow, 2011; Ahmad & Ramayah, 2012). Therefore, SMEs are deemed sustainable when they focus on satisfaction not only with their strong financial performance but also with their ability to contribute to social well-being. Gibb (2005) argues that an entrepreneur is the core of the firm as their actions and inactions contribute significantly to performance. Additionally, it is undeniable that their values play a crucial role in determining the sustainability of the firm. The present study explores the philosophy of sufficiency economy as the guiding principle of Thai SMEs.

Sufficiency Economy Philosophy

The term 'sufficiency economy philosophy', which is not a new concept for Thailand, was first coined in 1974. This philosophy is perceived as the panacea for various recent business and economic problems (Wattanasupachoke, 2009) because it leads to a balanced and sustainable development of the economy and society. It consists of three principal components—moderation, reasonableness, and self-immunity—that are overlapping and interlocking (See Figure 1).

Jairak, Praneetpolgrang and Subsermsri (2013) reported that the core essence of sufficiency economy was clearly expressed by Sufficiency Economy Movement Sub-Committee (2007) which was:

[…] The philosophy of sufficiency economy points the way for a recovery that will lead to a more resilient and sustainable economy that is better able to meet emerging challenges such as globalization. Sufficiency Economy stresses the middle path as an overriding principle for appropriate conduct by Thai people at all levels, from family to community to country. It calls for national development and administration to modernize in line with the forces of globalization.

Figure 1. Sufficiency economy philosophy model

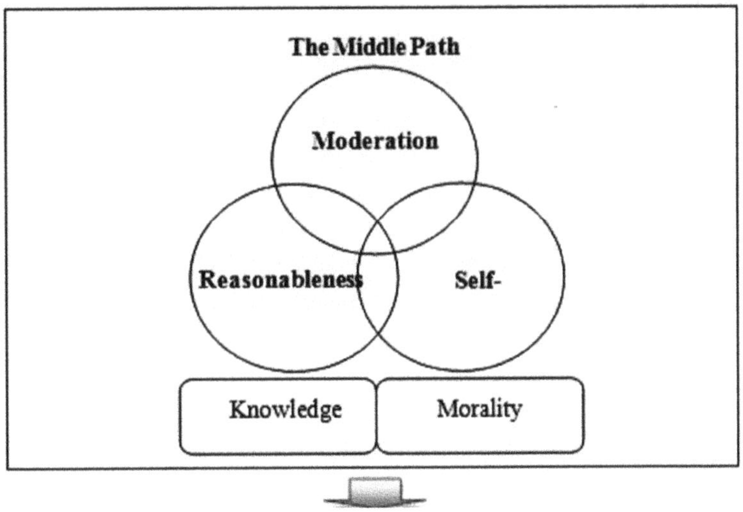

Boken and Short (2016) reported that Thailand Foreign Office (2014) illustrated "sufficiency economy" as a fundamental shift from over consumption towards sufficiency oriented view of consumption. Thai government included sufficient economy in their scheme to facilitate the community to maintain sufficient population size and protect eco system (UNEP, 2014).

Moreover, knowledge and morality are required to better practice these principles. The agricultural sector in Thailand has seen success by practicing the philosophy. Thereafter, it was suggested especially for the business sector. Empirical studies have shown the significant impact of sufficiency economy philosophy in predicting firm performance in the long run (e.g., Puntasen et al., 2003; Kantabutra & Siebenhüner, 2011; Kusumavalee, 2010; Ruenrom, 2009).

Sufficiency economy philosophy is perceived to reflect the values and norms that are desirable, contain trans-situational goals, and serve as guiding principles (with varying degrees of importance) in people's lives (Schwartz, 2005). In particular, it promotes the middle path and serves as the means to recovery. It leads to more resilient, balanced, and sustainable development, which is better able to meet challenges arising from globalization (Piboolsravut, 2004). Moreover, such norms and values are considered part of social capital, represented in institutions that can enhance economic performance (North, 1990). Mongsawad (2009) relates sufficiency economy philosophy to the strong social capital embedded in the Thai society. It determines individual behaviour and decision-making, resulting in the success of economic or non-economic activities. It could be applicable and scalable for every sector at all level (Bunyasrie, 2010; Piboolsravut, 2004). Therefore, it was expected that entrepreneurs who perceived sufficiency economy as values in running businesses would be likely to succeed and sustain performance in the long run. This was consistent with Bird (1988) and Parrish (2010) that success would be differed depending on values which entrepreneurs have. Importantly, Pruetipibultham (2010) indicated that sufficiency approach could develop core competency for community enterprise. This was because it focused on the strength of human's capabilities and potentials to benefit at all levels, individual, community, national and global (Indaratna, 2007).

Regarding to the application of sufficiency economy into business sector, (Sasin, 2010) analyzed that the moderation concerned business growth through prudent uses of available resources in order to sustain. The reasonableness referred to careful considerations of direct and indirect stakeholders when making business decisions. The self-immunity connoted a risk management policy that mitigated business economic, and social risk of the company. These components were claimed as the keys to sustainability and long-term performance (NESDB, 2007; Yoopetch & Chirapanda, 2008). In addition, there were empirical studies through the application of sufficiency economy philosophy into business sector (Chartrungruang, 2011; Kantabutra, 2005, 2006; Khunthongjan, 2009; Kusumavalee, 2005; Puntasen et al., 2003; Ruenrom, 2009; Wattanasupachoke, 2009). Empirical evidences had shown that sustainable organizations that went successfully through the 1997 economic crisis appeared to follow the identified business practices of the sufficiency economy philosophy (Puntasen et al., 2003), while many businesses collapsed.

Hypothesis 1: The principle of sufficiency economy philosophy is positively associated with sustainable performance among SMEs in Thailand.

Hypothesis 2: The underlying conditions of sufficiency economy philosophy are positively associated with the principle of sufficiency economy philosophy.

Intensity of Usage of Government Support

The studies on SME performance have pointed out that most SMEs lack resources, both tangible and intangible, and hence face many problems in operating their businesses. Small firms hardly access financial support due to several reasons like less credit and no data record, which prevent them from securing bank loans. Therefore, many of them do not have a secure growth curve and eventually fail to operate anymore. Since SMEs have already demonstrated their contribution to the development of Thailand, there needs to be more recognition from the formal institutions.

Previous studies have revealed the importance of government support in designing a business environment. It is seen as the critical success factor, especially for the developing countries. For example, it is a powerful predictor of firm performance in Malaysia (Zainol & Daud, 2011). Government support enhances the revenue growth rate in Vietnam (Hansen, Rand, & Tarp, 2009). As the consequences, government support had become the critical success factor; especially for the developing countries (Yusuf, 1995; Zainol & Daud, 2011). However, the result is inconsistent in case of Thailand (Sebora, Lee, & Sukasame, 2009) as entrepreneurs running SMEs in Thailand complain that government policies are unpredictable (World Bank, 2005), resulting in uncertainty in operating business. In particular to moderating effects, there were the interacting effects of governmental institution support with entrepreneurial values, firm practices (Mohd Shariff et al., 2010), strategy (Li & Atuahene-Gima, 2001) and firm performance. Moreover, the empirical found that quality of government-business coordination could make the performance difference (Rasiah, 2002). Government could provide the healthy environment for business activities. With the resources as accessible capital, information, technology, education and training, networks, business regulation, and so on, entrepreneur owner/manager might enhance their performance in the long run.

Since the economic crisis in 1997, the Thai government has put increasing importance on promoting SMEs. The Small and Medium Enterprises Promotion Act was promulgated in 1997. The Office of Small and Medium Enterprises Promotion (OSMEP) was established in 2001 to serve as the central agency in formulating policies and a master plan as well as to act as the coordinator for promotion of SMEs in Thailand. Promotion activities of SMEs span many areas including finance, marketing, geographical region, personal development, logistics, laws and regulations, science and technology, information, and an early warning system. The government creates a healthy environment for business activities, with resources like accessible capital, information, technology, education and training, networks, business regulations, and so on. This is done in the hope that entrepreneurs utilizing these resources will improve their performance in the long run. In particular, the Thai government offers eight direct support programmes to SMEs. However, the supply seems to be lesser than the demand. Based on this circumstance, the intensity of usage of government support could serve as a tool to comprehensively understand how frequently entrepreneurs running SMEs use these support programmes. The results may shed light on the importance of government institutions in supporting Thai SMEs.

Hypothesis 3: Intensity of usage of government support is positively associated with sustainable performance among SMEs in Thailand.

The proposed theoretical framework is shown in Figure 2.

METHODOLOGY

Sample and Data Collection

Questionnaires were distributed among the owners/managers of SMEs operating in southern Thailand. The focus on the south of Thailand can be attributed is due to several reasons such as the similarity of business infrastructure in each region (Nakhata, 2010) and the scantiness of SMEs phenomenon's disclosure in the whole region of the south (Runglertkrengkrai, 1999).

Figure 2. Theoretical framework

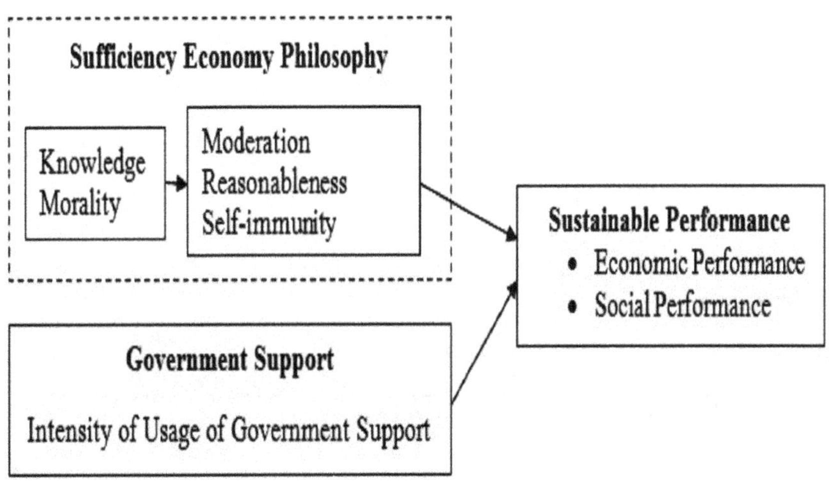

There are 397,718 SMEs operating in southern Thailand (OSMEP, 2010). Disproportionate and systematic sampling methods were employed to obtain a sample of 384 SMEs based on the sample calculation method proposed by Krejcie and Morgan (1970). Of the 384 questionnaires sent, 90 were returned, yielding the response rate of 23.4 per cent. However, only 56 of them were usable. The second wave of data collection yielded 63 more usable questionnaires, which made a total of 119 respondents. To check for response bias between the first wave and the second wave, T-test was employed (Armstrong & Overton, 1977). The results indicated that there is no difference between the two methods. Moreover, the common method variance (CMV) was tested to see the self-rating bias. The result revealed that self-rating bias is not a problem in this study.

The study found (see Table 7) that the age range of entrepreneurs conducting business in southern Thailand is largely between below 30 to above 50. Among 119 respondents, 48.7 per cent were male and the rest were female. The majority of entrepreneurs running SMEs hold bachelor's degrees (45.4 per cent). The firms sampled have been operational for three to five years (31.9 per cent), which is considerably younger than those studied by Runglertkrengkrai et al. (2007) and Aujirapongpan et al. (2005). Small enterprises were predominant over medium enterprises from our samples (the ratio was 22.8: 1). Moreover, service (46.2 per cent) and trade (41.2 per cent) among the firms was more popular than production.

Measurement

Twenty four questionnaire items on sufficiency economy philosophy were adapted and extracted from the previous studies (Chartrungruang, 2011; Kantabutra, 2007; Puntasen et al., 2003). The internal consistency was above 0.70. Eight items on the intensity of usage of government support were adapted from the eight support programmes offered by the Thai government (OSMEP, 2006). Sustainable performance has two dimensions. The first one is economic performance, which was reflected in five items

Table 7. Demographic profile of SMEs

Variables	Frequency	Percentage	Variables	Frequency	Percentage
Entrepreneur's Age			**Firm's Age**		
30 years or under	33	27.7	2 years or under	25	21.0
31 - 40 years	35	29.4	3 - 5 years	38	31.9
41 - 50 years	35	29.4	6 - 10 years	30	25.2
51 years or above	16	13.4	11 years or above	26	21.8
Gender			**Firm Size**		
Male	58	48.7	Small	114	95.8
Female	61	51.3	Medium	5	4.2
Educational Level			**Business Type**		
Secondary or less	31	26.1	Production	15	12.6
Diploma	16	13.4	Service	55	46.2
Bachelor's degree	54	45.4	Wholesale	14	11.8
Postgraduate	18	15.1	Retail	35	29.4

on satisfaction with financial performance, five items on performance relative to competitors, and three items on business growth— all adopted from Ahmad, Wilson, and Kummerow (2011) (See appendix 1 for details). The Cronbach's alpha value is .88 - .93. The second dimension is reflected in the five items on satisfaction with social performance, adapted from Ahmad and Ramayah (2012), with a reliability value of 0.76.

Analysis

In order to observe the importance of sufficiency economy philosophy, factor analysis was run separately on each of the three principals and the two underlying conditions of sufficiency economy philosophy, which explains sustainable performance. Then, exploratory factor analysis was separately conducted using principal component analysis with a fixed number of factors (See Appendix 2). Varimax was used for the rotation. Satisfactory results were based on communalities exceeding **0**.40 (Costello & Osborne, 2005), KMO exceeding 0.50, significant-cut-off point of 0.50 without cross-loadings, and total variance explained greater than 60 per cent (Hair et al., 2006). These procedures and criteria were also employed to extract the constructs of intensity of usage of government support, and sustainable performance. The results comprise five constructs of sufficiency economy philosophy, one construct of intensity of usage of government support, and four constructs of sustainable performance.

RESULTS

The correlation analysis indicates that there is no multicollinearity (Hair et al., 2006), since the inter-correlation among variables happens to be less than 0.80. The internal consistency of the variables in this study reports excellent results. All are between 0.81 and 0.96. Table 8 provides the related descriptive statistics.

Regression analysis was employed to test the hypotheses. For the first hypothesis, results demonstrate that the values of sufficiency economy philosophy and intensity of usage of government support are significantly associated with sustainable performance; in particular, moderation is positively significant with satisfaction with financial performance ($\beta = .25, p < 0.05$); reasonableness is positively related to business growth ($\beta = .27, p < 0.05$) and satisfaction with social performance ($\beta = .33, p < 0.001$); and self-immunity is positively related to performance relative to competitors ($\beta = .33, p < 0.001$), business growth ($\beta = .23, p < 0.05$), and satisfaction with social performance ($\beta = .19, p < 0.05$). Meanwhile, the intensity of usage of government support is positively significant with all dimensions of sustainable performance. It is related to satisfaction with financial performance ($\beta = .32, p < 0.001$), performance relative to competitors ($\beta = .20, p < 0.05$), business growth ($\beta = .20, p < 0.05$), and satisfaction with social performance ($\beta = .43, p < 0.001$).

Therefore, both Hypothesis 1 and Hypothesis 3 are supported. The results are also shown in Table 9.

Since this study would like to present the significance of sufficiency economy philosophy, the two underlying conditions were tested to see the relationship with the three principal components. The results confirmed that these two underlying conditions are positively and significantly related to the three principal components. Knowledge is significantly related to moderation ($\beta = .24, p < 0.05$), reasonableness ($\beta = .30, p < 0.001$), and self-immunity ($\beta = .76, p < 0.001$). Meanwhile, morality is positively related to moderation ($\beta = .40, p < 0.001$) and reasonableness ($\beta = .51, p < 0.001$).

Table 8. Descriptive, reliability, and correlation analysis

	Mean	S.D.	A	1	2	3	4	5	6	7	8	9	10
1. MOD	3.95	.75	.89	1									
2. REA	4.06	.68	.86	.65**	1								
3. SELF	3.82	.67	.82	.38**	.57**	1							
4. KNOW	3.92	.68	.81	.46**	.60**	.74**	1						
5. MOR	4.32	.66	.91	.53**	.68**	.47**	.66**	1					
6. GOV	2.68	1.10	.96	.03	-.03	.26**	.17	-.19*	1				
7. FIN	3.48	.77	.94	.37**	.34**	.39**	.37**	.28**	.37**	1			
8. REL	3.38	.80	.95	.32**	.33**	.47**	.43**	.26**	.29**	.59**	1		
9. GRO	3.65	.80	.93	.32**	.42**	.45**	.49**	.39**	.26**	.54**	.58**	1	
10. SOC	3.52	.89	.91	.29**	.42**	.49**	.45**	.27**	.47**	.45**	.40**	.44**	1

**. Correlation is significant at the 0.01 level (2-tailed).
*. Correlation is significant at the 0.05 level (2-tailed).
Note: 1= moderation, 2= performance relative to competitors, 3= self- immunity, 4=knowledge, 5=morality, 6= intensity use of government support, 7= satisfaction with financial performance, 8= performance relative to competitors, 9= business growth, 10= satisfaction with social performance. 1 = personal ability, 2 = learning ability, 3 = independence, 4 = extrinsic, 5 = moderation, 6 = self-immunity, 7 = morality, 12 = intensity of usage of government support, 13 = satisfaction with financial performance, 14 = performance relative to competitors, 15 = business growth, 16 = satisfaction with social performance

Table 9. Regression analysis-I

Variables	Financial Performance[a]		Relative Performance[b]		Business Growth		Social Performance[c]	
	β	*t*	*β*	*T*	*B*	*t*	*β*	*t*
Moderation	.25	2.47*	.14	1.38	.05	.50	-.01	-.12
Reasonableness	.19	1.65	.06	.50	.27	2.21*	.33	3.13***
Self-immunity	.10	1.03	.33	3.21***	.23	2.25*	.19	2.12*
Government[d]	.32	3.90***	.20	2.37*	.20	2.42*	.43	5.77***
R^2	.34		.28		.29		.44	
Adjusted R^2	.31		.25		.26		.42	
F value	14.23***		11.04***		11.39***		22.00***	

Note: $*p < 0.05$, $***p < 0.001$.
[a]satisfaction with financial performance,[b]performance relative to competitors, [c]satisfaction with social performance, [d]government = intensity of usage of government support

Therefore, Hypothesis 2 is supported. All results are demonstrated in Table 10.

DISCUSSION

As stated, this study is set to answer the call for greater scrutiny of Asian SMEs, given that they are in the vanguard of economic progress in most countries of the region. It provides an alternative approach to conducting business, namely embracing sufficiency economy philosophy in commercial dealings.

Table 10. Regression analysis-II

Variables	Moderation		Reasonableness		Self-Immunity	
	B	*t*	*B*	*T*	*β*	*t*
Knowledge	.24	2.34*	.30	3.70***	.76	9.11***
Morality	.40	4.00***	.51	6.30***	-.03	-.37
R^2	.34		.55		.55	
Adjusted R^2	.33		.55		.54	
F value	29.66***		70.97***		69.66***	

Note: *$p < 0.05$, ***$p < 0.001$.

The two underlying conditions, which are knowledge and morality, are prerequisites for sufficiency economy philosophy. Logically, when people accumulate knowledge and have a sense of morality, they are more moderate in conducting their lives. They adopt the middle path and are more reasonable instead of being given to excesses. Moreover, this philosophy also highlights self-immunity as the protection mechanism. For example, a business needs to promote innovation of products and services, plan for unexpected changes, encourage the participation of stakeholders, and to continuously develop human resources. This mechanism can help the business deal with external changes.

The results are consistent with previous studies (i.e., Puntasen et al., 2003; Kantabutra, & Siebenhüner, 2011; & Ruenrom, 2009), showing that sufficiency economy philosophy is a powerful predictor of SME performance in the long run. Additionally, the findings relating to the two underlying conditions—knowledge and morality—confirm that they are the necessary conditions of sufficiency economy philosophy (Wibulswasdi et al., 2010). External factors like government institutions also play a crucial role in predicting SME performance in the long run. This result is in line with previous studies (i.e., Zainal & Daud, 2011; Hansen et al., 2009). Furthermore, the findings are also consistent with the institutional theory (North, 1990), which states that both formal and informal rules can appropriately shape economic as well as non-economic activities.

THEORITICAL CONTRIBUTION AND PRACTICAL IMPLICATIONS

From theoretical point of view, the findings of this study were expected to provide additional understanding into the existing body of knowledge regarding intensity of usage of government support, sufficiency economy philosophy, and sustainable performance in the context of SMEs in Thailand.

From practical point of view, firstly, these findings would reflect the sustainable performance of SMEs. It showed the extent to which SME owners/managers could sustain their performance; especially throughout the entrepreneurial competencies. Therefore, this finding would be valuable and beneficial to the entrepreneurs. They could be enlightened of the critical competency areas which were essential to sustain their performance in the long run.

Secondly, the tendency of sustaining business performance in the long run would encourage the scholars to seek for the appropriate training and consultancy courses in developing entrepreneurial competencies.

Thirdly, government and its agencies could be the ones of the important players. They played the institutional role to provide the policy which neither directly or indirectly affects to the direction of

SMEs. Thus, these findings might help them to consider the appropriate policy as well as to promote the good business environment especially for the SMEs.

Finally, due to the scant empirical research on sustainable performance of SMEs in Thailand, the findings and limitations would be beneficial to provide avenue for the development of further study in the related area. Furthermore, this paper would like to call for both Thai and non-Thai researchers to delve into the sufficiency economy philosophy as the important values that would ultimately determine sustainable performance of business firms.

CONCLUSION

Entrepreneurship is a socio-economic process based on status and context. The combination of economic and sociological viewpoints can well guide SMEs to achieve sustainability, which, in turn, results in a healthy society. Based on the findings, entrepreneurs, academicians, and policymakers should pay more attention to sustainable development of the business community through the lens of sufficiency economy philosophy, which is particularly derived from the Asian perspective. Additionally, the government institutions can enhance the performance of SMEs by creating a healthy and appropriate business environment and infrastructure.

Based on the literature, there were not many studies available in the case of Thailand. The SMEs studies, which had been delved into, basically focused on the geographic location. Particularly Bangkok, the capital city of Thailand, was the most focused (Nakhata, 2007). It implied that there was less attention paying on SMEs in other parts. Thereby the main focus of this study was eventually the SME owner/manager who operated their businesses in the South of Thailand, due to the proportion of either number of SMEs to population or to workforce was inferior to those of the Central which included Bangkok.

However, since this paper is limited to a cross-sectional study and small sample size concentrated on one particular region, it may not be generalized too well. Therefore, future studies are encouraged to test the framework of this study in other contexts. In addition, it will be more beneficial if a future study can be conducted with the longitudinal approach.

REFERENCES

Ahmad, N. H., & Ramayah, T. (2012). Does the Notion of Doing Well by Doing Good Prevail Among Entrepreneurial Ventures in a Developing Nation? *Journal of Business Ethics*, *106*(4), 479–490. doi:10.1007/s10551-011-1012-9

Ahmad, N. H., Wilson, C., & Kummerow, L. (2011). Assessing the Dimensionality of Business Success: The Perspectives of Malaysian SME Owner-Managers. *Journal of Asia-Pacific Business*, *12*(3), 207–224. doi:10.1080/10599231.2011.586855

Armstrong, J. S., & Overton, T. S. (1977). Estimating Nonresponse Bias in Mail Surveys. *JMR, Journal of Marketing Research*, *14*(3), 396–402. doi:10.2307/3150783

Aujirapongpan, S., Dungtripop, W., & Jungkivinid, W. (2005). Cost Management Strategy of Small and Medium Factory Enterprises. *Songkhlanakarin Journal of Social Sciences and Humanities*, *11*(4), 409–420.

Bocken, N. M. P., & Short, S. W. (2016). Towards a sufficiency-driven business model: Experiences and opportunities. *Environmental Innovation and Societal Transitions*, *18*, 41–61. doi:10.1016/j.eist.2015.07.010

Chartrungruang, B.-o. (2011, 25 May). *The Model of Sufficiency Economy Philosophy Application for Tourism Industry in Chiang Mai, Thailand.* Paper presented at the Sustainability and Quality-of-Life in Tourism: Tasks for Consumers, Industry, Policy and Academia, Chiang Mai, Thailand.

Costello, A. B., & Osborne, J. W. (2005). Best Practices in Exploratory Factor Analysis: Four Recommendations for Getting the Most From Your Analysis. *Practical Assessment, Research & Evaluation*, *10*(7), 1–9.

Ex-Im Bank of Thailand. SMEs' Analysis. (2012). Retrieved July 6, 2012, from http://www.exim.go.th/doc/newsCenter/38795.pdf

Gibb, A. (2005). The Entrepreneur as the Core Competence of the Firm: Implications for Management Educators. *Entrepreneurship, Innovation and Small Business Network,* (2), 2.

Hair, J. F., Black, W. C., Babin, B. J., Anderson, R. E., & Tatham, R. L. (2006). *Multivariate Data Analysis* (6th ed.). Pearson.

Hall, J. K., Daneke, G. A., & Lenox, M. J. (2010). Sustainable development and entrepreneurship: Past contributions and future directions. *Journal of Business Venturing*, *25*(5), 439–448. doi:10.1016/j.jbusvent.2010.01.002

Hansen, H., Rand, J., & Tarp, F. (2009). Enterprise Growth and Survival in Vietnam: Does Government Support Matter? *The Journal of Development Studies*, *45*(7), 1048–1069. doi:10.1080/00220380902811025

Jairak, K., Praneetpolgrang, P., & Subsermsri, P. (2015). Information technology governance practices based on sufficiency economy philosophy in the Thai university sector. *Information Technology & People*, *28*(1), 195–223. doi:10.1108/ITP-10-2013-0188

Kantabutra, S. (2007). *Development of the Sufficiency Economy Philosophy in the Thai Business Sector: Evidence, Future Research & Policy Implications*. Retrieved 7 July, 2016, from http://www.sufficiencyeconomy.org/old/en/files/26.pdf

Kantabutra, S., & Siebenhüner, T. (2011). Predicting Corporate Sustainability: A Thai Approach. *Journal of Applied Business Research*, *27*(6), 123. doi:10.19030/jabr.v27i6.6471

Krejcie, R. V., & Morgan, D. W. (1970). Determining Sample Size for Research Activities. *Educational and Psychological Measurement*, *30*, 607–610.

Kusumavalee, S. (2010). Philosophy of Sufficiency Economy in the Large Scale Enterprise: A Case Study of Human Capital Management in the Siam Cement Group. *Human Resource and Organization Development Journal*, *1*(1), 80–90.

Labonne, J. (2006). *A Comparative Analysis of the Environmental Management, Performance and Innovation of SMEs and Larger Firms.* For the European Commission, Directorate-General Environment.

Li, H., & Atuahene-Gima, K. (2001). Product innovation strategy and the performance of new technology ventures in China. *Academy of Management Journal, 44*(6), 1123–1134. doi:10.2307/3069392

Loucks, E. S., Martens, M. L., & Cho, C. H. (2010). Engaging small- and medium-sized businesses in sustainability. *Sustainability Accounting. Management and Policy Journal, 1*(2), 178–200.

Masurel, E. (2007). Why SMEs invest in environmental measures: Sustainability evidence from small and medium-sized printing firms. *Business Strategy and the Environment, 16*(3), 190–201. doi:10.1002/bse.478

Mohd Shariff, M. N., Peou, C., & Ali, J. (2010). Moderating Effect of Government Policy on Entrepreneurship and Growth Performance of Small-Medium Enterprises in Cambodia. *International Journal of Business & Management Science, 3*(1), 57–72.

Mongsawad, P. (2009). Sufficiency Economy: A Contribution to Economic Development. *International Journal of Humanities and Social Science, 4*(2), 144–151.

Nakhata, C. (2010). The Relationship between Job Dimensions and Job Satisfaction of SME Entrepreneurs in Thailand. *Journal of American Academy of Business, Cambridge, 15*(2), 220–227.

North, D. C. (1990). *Institutions, Institutional Change and Economic Performance.* Cambridge, UK: Cambridge University Press. doi:10.1017/CBO9780511808678

OSMEP. (2006). *Small and Medium Enterprises Master Plan (2007-2011).* Retrieved 28 November, 2010, from www.sme.go.th

OSMEP. (2010). *The White Paper on Small and Medium Enterprises Of Thailand in 2010 and Trends 2011.* Retrieved 26 July, 2011, from www.sme.go.th

OSMEP. (2015). *Situation and Economic Indicators of SMEs in 2015.* The White Paper on Small and Medium Enterprises Of Thailand in 2015. Retrieved October 11, 2016 from http://www.sme.go.th/eng/images/data/SR/download/2015/report_year/ExecutiveSummary/Chapter%201.pdf

Piboolsravut, P. (2004). Sufficiency Economy. *ASEAN Economic Bulletin, 21*(1), 127–134. doi:10.1355/AE21-1H

Puntasen, A., Premchuen, S., & Keitdejpunya, P. (2003). *Application of the Royal Thought about the Sufficiency Economy in SMEs.* Bangkok: Thailand Research Fund.

Rasiah, R. (2002). Government-business coordination and small enterprise performance in the machine tools sector in Malaysia. *Small Business Economics, 18*(1-3), 177–194. doi:10.1023/A:1015139624218

Reijonen, H. (2008). Understanding the small business owner: What they really aim at and how this relates to firm performance. *Management Research News, 31*(8), 616–629. doi:10.1108/01409170810892172

Ruenrom, G. P. (2009). Applying the Philosophy of Sufficiency Economy to Form Business Policy and Marketing Plan of Small and Medium Enterprises in Thailand. *The Business Review, Cambridge, 13*(1), 326–331.

Runglertkrengkrai, S., Sirirat, J., Somboonkul, Y., Churirachaneekorn, S., Chulirachaneekorn, S., Samangsri, J., & Ruangsong, R. (1999). The Characteristics and Training Needs for Small and Medium Entrepreneurs in the Southern Thailand. *Songkhlanakarin Journal of Social Sciences and Humanities, 5*(3), 233–243.

Runglertkrengkrai, S., Sirirat, J., Somboonkul, Y., Churirachaneekorn, S., & Juligpong, S. (2007). *The Characteristics of Successful Entrepreneurs in Southern Region: Service Sector*. Retrieved from http://localinfo.tsu.ac.th/jspui/bitstream/123456789/24/1/article.pdf

Schick, H., Marxen, S., & Freimann, J. (2002). Sustainability Issues for Start-up Entrepreneurs. *GMI, 38*, 59–70.

Schwartz, S. H. (2005). Basic human values: Their content and structure across countries. In A. Tamayo & J. B. Porto (Eds.), *Values and behavior in organizations* (pp. 21–55). Vozes.

Sebora, T. C., Lee, S. M., & Sukasame, N. (2009). Critical Success Factors for E-commerce Entrepreneurship: An Empirical Study of Thailand. *Small Business Economics, 32*(3), 303–316. doi:10.1007/s11187-007-9091-9

Shariff, M. N. M., & Peou, C. (2008). The Relationship of Entrepreneurial Values, Firm Financing and the Management and Growth Performance of Small-Medium Enterprises in Cambodia. *Problems and Perspectives in Management, 6*(4), 55–64.

Sufficiency Economy Movement Sub-Committee. (2007). *Sufficiency economy implications and applications*. Retrieved 26 July, 2011, available at: www.nesdb.go.th/Md/book/booksuffwork_eng.pdf

Tambunan, T. (2008). Development of SME in ASEAN with Reference to Indonesia and Thailand. *Chulalongkorn Journal of Economics, 20*(1), 53–83.

Thailand Foreign Office. The Government Public Relations Department. (2014). *The New Theory and the Sufficiency Economy*. Retrieved June 30, 2014. From http://thailand.prd.go.th/ebook/king/new theory.html

UNEP. (2014). *Self Sufficiency Economy in Thailand*. Retrieved June 30, 2014. From http://ekh.unep.org/files/SELFSUFFICIENCY ECONOMY IN THAILAND.doc

Warr, P. (2009). *The Economics of Enough: Thailand's "Sufficiency Economy" Debate*. Paper presented at the Buddhist Economics: Theory and Practice, Thailand.

Wattanasupachoke, T. (2009). Sufficiency Economy Principles: Applications for Organisation Management Strategy. *Journal of American Academy of Business, Cambridge, 14*(2), 263–270.

Wiboonchutikula, P. (2002). Small and Medium Enterprises in Thailand: Recent Trends. *Small Business Economics, 18*(1), 211–224. doi:10.1023/A:1015143709196

Wibulswasdi, C., Piboolsravut, P., & Pootrakool, K. (2010). *Sufficiency Economy Philosophy and Development* (3rd ed.). Bangkok: Bureau of the Crown Property.

World Bank. (2005). *World Bank Report 2005: A Better Investment Climate for Everyone World Development Report*. Washington, DC: The World Bank and Oxford University.

Yusuf, A. (1995). Critical Success Factors for Small Business: Perceptions of South Pacific Entrepreneurs. *Journal of Small Business Management*, *33*, 68–73.

Zainol, F. A., & Daud, W. N. W. (2011). Indigenous ("Bumiputera") Malay Entrepreneurs in Malaysia: Government Supports, Entrepreneurial Orientation and Firms Performances. *International Business & Management*, *2*(1), 86–99.

KEY TERMS AND DEFINITIONS

Common Method Variance: CMV is a bias or measurement error caused in self-reported data set.

Entrepreneurship: Entrepreneurship is a process of identifying and initiating a business venture.

Intensity of Usage of Government Support: Degree of utilization of government support.

Multicollinearity: Multicollinearity is an event in statistics where two or more constructs are strongly correlated.

SME: Enterprises which corresponds less than 250 employees and assets less than 200 million bahts (approx. 6,000,000 USD).

Sufficiency Economy Philosophy: A belief on moderation, reasonableness, and self-immunity which will lead to a balanced and sustainable development of the economy and society.

Sustainable Performance: A strong financial performance by organization and its ability to contribute to social well-being.

APPENDIX 1

Table 11. Measurement items and reliability from previous studies

Measures	Items	Sources	Cronbach's Alpha	Objective
Sustainable Performance	Items: 1-5 Financial performance Items: 1-5 Performance relative to major competitors Items: 1-3 Business growth Items: 1-5 Social performance	Ahmad, Wilson, & Kummerow, (2011) Ahmad & Ramayah (2011)	.92 .93 .88 .76	To measure economic and social performance by using the multidimensional approach
Intensity of Usage of Government Support	Items: 1-8 • Finance • Marketing • Geographical region • Personal development • Logistics • Laws and regulations • science and technology • Information and early-warning system	SMEs Master Plan, Thailand (OSMEP, 2006)	-	To measure the intensity of usage of government support perceived by SME owner/ manager
Values of Sufficiency Economy Philosophy	Items: 1-24 • Moderation • Reasonableness • Self-immunity • Knowledge • Morality	Chartrungruang (2011) and additional extracted from Puntasen et al (2003) and Kantabutra (2007)	.70 - .83	To measure the values of sufficiency economy philosophy perceived by SME owner/manager
7. Personal Background Information	Self- developed			To obtain background information of SME owner/ manager
8. Business Information	Self-developed			To obtain background information of SME firm

APPENDIX 2: DETAILS OF FACTOR AND RELIABILITY ANALYSIS

Table 12. Factor and reliability analysis for sufficiency economy philosophy

Items	Factor Loadings		
	F1	F2	F3
Moderation			
SEP1: Hire only necessary staff.	.70	.24	.03
SEP2: Expect moderate profits, not excessive or less.	.85	.14	.03
SEP3: Use appropriate technology.	.82	.07	.24
SEP4: Expand business based on business actual growth.	.78	.19	.21
SEP5: Take order based on my business capability.	.68	.33	.10
SEP6: Ensure balance in business benefit sharing.	.80	.29	.24
Morality			
SEP20: Value sincerity with customers and investors.	.31	.79	.17
SEP21: Value honesty in doing business.	.19	.88	.17
SEP22: Am diligent in doing business successfully.	.13	.86	.16
SEP23: Treat staff as family members.	.30	.67	.30
SEP24: Am accountable for wide range of stakeholders.	.28	.72	.25
Self-immunity			
SEP11: Promote innovation in products/services.	.24	.28	.67
SEP12: Plan for unexpected changes.	.05	.21	.79
SEP13: Encourage participation of stakeholders.	.11	.05	.77
SEP14: Continuously develop human resources.	.16	.12	.83
SEP17: Adopt local wisdom in doing business.	.11	.32	.67
Eigenvalues	4.04	3.66	3.21
% of variance	25.23	22.86	20.04
Reliability (alpha)			
Total Variance Explained	68.13%		
Measure of Sampling Adequacy (KMO)	.87		
Barlett's Test of Sphericity Significant	1197.39***		

Note *** $p < 0.001$.

Table 13. Factor and reliability analysis for intensity of government support

Items	Factor
	F1
Gov2: Marketing (i.e. marketing exhibition, business negotiation, brand, export competitiveness, etc.)	.84
Gov3: Geographical region (i.e. establishing offices to assist SMEs in your province, business clusters, trade associations, business incubators, etc.)	.94
Gov4: Personal development (i.e. providing business training, NEC, mentors, consultants, etc.)	.89
Gov5: Logistics (i.e. training and consultation on effective warehouse, cost, transportation, etc.)	.93
Gov6: Laws and regulations (i.e. consultation, business registration, tax, intellectual property, etc.)	.84
Gov7: Science and technology (i.e. R&D, product development, etc.)	.93
Gov8: Information and early-warning system (i.e. providing economic and business information, early-warning information, etc.)	.89
Eigenvalues	5.59
% of variance	79.82
Reliability (alpha)	.96
Total Variance Explained	79.82%
Measure of Sampling Adequacy (KMO)	.91
Barlett's Test of Sphericity Significant	900.93***

Table 14. Factor and reliability analysis for economic performance

Items	Factor Loadings			
	F1	F2	F3	F4
Performance Relative to Competitors				
Return on sales	.82	.23	.16	.21
Cash flow	.81	.26	.20	.17
Net profit	.83	.28	.14	.26
Market share	.88	.20	.13	.16
Return on investment	.87	.27	.17	.23
Satisfaction with Financial Performance				
Profitability	.25	.82	.23	.12
Sales turnover	.16	.90	.08	.16
Sales growth	.29	.82	.14	.18
Return on investment	.26	.82	.25	.20
Market share	.338	.72	.27	.26
Satisfaction with Social Performance				
Contribution to projects that promote the well-being of the society.	.28	.07	.81	.10
Involvement in voluntary activities (i.e. donating money or giving materials for helping people from natural disaster such as flood)	.19	.09	.83	.11
Offering products that satisfy the local needs.	.07	.16	.83	.20

continued on next page

Table 14. Continued

Items	Factor Loadings			
	F1	F2	F3	F4
Contribution towards promoting social welfare.	.04	.21	.87	.08
Creation of job opportunities for local communities.	.14	.27	.77	.17
Business Growth				
Change in sales	.20	.29	.23	.84
Change in market share	.36	.20	.19	.82
Change in cash flow	.29	.21	.17	.86
Eigenvalues	4.30	3.98	3.85	2.60
% of variance	23.90	22.12	21.39	14.43
Reliability (alpha)	.95	.94	.91	.93
Total Variance Explained	81.84%			
Measure of Sampling Adequacy (KMO)	.89			
Barlett's Test of Sphericity Significant	2073.24***			

Note ***$p < 0.001$.

Chapter 2
Agropreneurship among Gen Y in Malaysia:
The Role of Academic Institutions

Asliza Yusoff
Universiti Sains Malaysia, Malaysia

Noor Hazlina Ahmad
Universiti Sains Malaysia, Malaysia

Hasliza Abdul Halim
Universiti Sains Malaysia, Malaysia

ABSTRACT

Despite great concerns regarding food security and the need to maintain a continuous food supply for an ever-increasing population, the agriculture sector remains an unattractive employment option, especially among younger generations. The big question is, "who should play a greater role in giving this sector young talents that are needed for successful agriculture and how it should it be acquired? Research has shown that this sector is dominated by an aging community of farmers who lack the innovative skills that is needed for running a new and modern agricultural industry. This chapter provides a brief overview of the importance of the agriculture sector and agropreneurship and is followed by why the involvement of the Gen Y segment is crucial for the growth and development of this sector. Since the basis for agropreneurship development among today's youth is based on training and inculcating an agropreneurship work culture at the university level, the authors proposed roles an academic institution could play in instilling positive an agropreneurial attitude among Gen Y graduates.

DOI: 10.4018/978-1-5225-2165-5.ch002

AGRICULTURE SECTOR AND WHY IT MATTERS?

In many parts of developing world, agriculture production is recognized as a strategy to improve a nation's standard of living, particularly to increase income, reduce hunger, and contribute to the improvement of other measures of well-being (Owens, Hoddinott, & Kinsey, 2003). Agriculture is also acknowledged to contribute significantly to economic growth in many countries (Bairwa, Lakra, Kushwaha, Meena, & Kumar, 2014; Diao, Hazell, Resnick, & Thurlow, 2007; Razak et al., 2015). Furthermore, agricultural growth is seen as precursor to the industrial revolutions that spread across the temperate world, from England in the mid-18th century to Japan in the late 19th century. Higher agricultural productivity that generates an agricultural surplus open to partial taxation and is used to finance industrial development as well as enabling lower food prices for the masses underpinned the success stories of industrial and structural transformation.

Agriculture also plays a substantial role in providing employment opportunity and poverty reduction. It accounts for 32 percent of total employment globally and 39 percent of employment in developing countries of Asia and the Pacific (International Labour Office, 2014). The sector has been acknowledged to be a major contributor to poverty reduction, as is found in countries such as Brazil, Cameroon, Chile, Costa Rica, Dominican Republic, Egypt, Mali, Mexico, Nicaragua, Panama, Tunisia and, not forgotten, Malaysia (Cervantes-Godoy & Dewbre, 2010) among others in Asia and the Pacific (International Labour Office, 2014; Kuldilok, Dawson, & Lingard, 2013). Similar scenario is also seen in many developed countries such as the United States, the United Kingdom, Japan, and Australia, where agriculture sector does not only play a significant role in contributing the countries' food supplies but also provides other benefits such as improved physical and mental health, improved aesthetics, community building, employment opportunities, improved local land prices, and etc. (Mok et al., 2014).

On reflection, agriculture today is no longer a sector for poor people only. For instance, Thailand has gained its competitive advantage by dominating world exports of canned tuna with a market share of around 40 percent, which is at least four times higher than any other exporter (Kuldilok et al., 2013). Many other developing countries have benefited from agriculture not only to have sufficient food to maintain normal health for a growing population but also to increase the nation's economic standing (Bairwa et al., 2014; Diao et al., 2007; Razak et al., 2015). There seems to be no compelling reason to argue for the economically inferior state of agriculture sector in shaping the country's economic condition. With agribusiness' increasing technological sophistication, as is found in developed countries, agriculture can appeal to younger generations.

OVERVIEW OF AGRICULTURE SECTOR IN MALAYSIA

For many years, agriculture sector has been standing high as the backbone of Malaysian economy through the production of agricultural products for domestic consumption and also as the earner of foreign exchange (Abu Dardak, 2015). Agriculture plays an important role in the development of the Malaysia's economy including providing employment opportunity, uplifting the income of the populations and ensuring national food security (Siwar, Yasar, Ghazali, & Mohd Idris, 2013). Since its independence in 1957, agriculture has become a significant contributor to Malaysia's economy. For example, agriculture has contributed 38 percent of the country's GDP in 1960 as compared to 9 percent contributed by the manufacturing sector in the same year. In mid-1980s however, agriculture contribution to GDP has declined significantly due to the slow growth in the production of commodity and fluctuations in agricultural commodity prices (Selamat & Nasir, 2013). The declining trend keeps on continuing for decades. Even though it went up to 10.09 percent in 2010, it went back down for years after (Malaysian Department of Statistics, 2016). Despite this unstable trend faced by Malaysia, the country has observed an increased in total agriculture value added from RM18.7 billion in 2000 to RM21.6 billion in 2005. Albeit the performance of Malaysian economy experienced a rapid growth where the GDP has increased from RM11.8 billion in 1970 to RM751.5 billion in 2012, the contribution of agriculture sector showed a declining trend since 1970 (30.8 percent) to 2012 (7.3 percent) (Abu Dardak, 2015; Malaysian Department of Statistics, 2016). Although its contribution increased to 3.0 in 2014 but it has decreased by 4.7 percent during the first quarter of the following year (Bank Negara Malaysia, 2015; Ministry of Finance, 2013).

The agriculture sector in Malaysia is an area where employment opportunity is offered to the population. In 1960, this sector contributed 60 percent of total employment in the country. The contribution however dropped in 2000 and 2005, where total employment contributed by the agriculture sector accounted only 15.3 and 12.9 percent, respectively. In 2010, agriculture, forestry and fishing has made up 13.3 percent of country's total employment and has provided employment for 11.1 million people in Malaysia (Jala, 2013, September 30). Even though its contribution to the country's total employment has been decreasing, the agriculture sector in Malaysia still continues to be a major contributor to the development of the country's economy (Selamat & Nasir, 2013). Because of this, the Malaysian government takes a serious attitude toward the decline in employment potential, where a total of RM6 billion is allocated for the agriculture sector in the 2014 national budget. Despite the growth in the services sector, which has taken over the manufacturing sector as the main contributor to the country's economic growth, the agriculture sector is not going to be ignored because it is the main source of income for many for farmers, fishermen and agro-based industries.

Recently there has been renewed interest in the agriculture sector as people begin to understand that the sector plays a crucial role in providing food and reducing the nation's poverty level, especially in rural areas. Against this background observation, the notion of sustainable agricultural development in relation to national food security and a continuous food supply is quickly gaining importance because the government has outlined it in the country's New Economic Model (NEM). A country's resourcefulness in developing its agricultural sector is an indication of its ability to provide sufficient food for its population. According to the Economic Planning Unit (EPU), agriculture consists of producing industrial and food commodities that include crops (plantation and food), horticulture (olericulture, pomology, floriculture, nursery crop culture and landscape horticulture), aquaculture (marine and freshwater), and livestock husbandry. In conjunction with the NEM, which has striven to reduce poverty among 40 percent Malaysians who earn less than RM1500 a month, agriculture and the agro-based sectors are seen to have potentials in realizing the government plan.

In Malaysia, agriculture stands as the third pillar of the country's economy and follows behind the service and manufacturing sectors (Selamat & Nasir, 2013). Entrepreneurship, on the other hand, is acknowledged as one of the best strategies for the development of economic growth for a country and is a useful tool to sustaining a country's competitiveness in today's increasing trend of globalization. This is because it indirectly creates political and social stability through the creation of job opportunities and initiates innovations that lead to technological change and productivity growth (Ahmad, Wan Yusoff, Mf Noor, & Ramin, 2012; Lim, Lee & Cheng, 2010). Therefore, an integration of both has given birth to the concept of 'agropreneurship', a new and promising dimension of the agriculture sector. Research findings show that agropreneurship has a profound impact on growth and survival (Baron & Shane,

2008; Poornima, 2009; Verhees, Kuipers, & Klopcic, 2011), not only on the individual, but also on the society and country altogether. The development of agropreneurship also contributes to the growth of small and medium-sized enterprises (SMEs) through the creation of small and medium-sized agro-based enterprises (SMAEs). Given the significant role played by SMEs in making a substantial contribution to the global economic growth (Jutla, Bodorik, & Dhaliwal, 2002), the development of agropreneurship is a worthy subject to be examined.

Comparing agriculture sector in Malaysia to that of the neighbouring countries such as Thailand, Vietnam and Indonesia, the agriculture sector's contribution to the Malaysian economy is still relatively low and lags behind these regional peers in percentage contribution to GDP due to lack of scale, production-driven farming and low-value products (Ramachandaran, 2010). For example, according to a report by the World Bank, agricultural contribution to the country's GDP in Thailand, Vietnam and Indonesia was 10.5 percent, 17.7 percent and 13.3 percent respectively. However, in Malaysia, the sector's contribution to the country's GDP in the same year was 8.9 percent only. This highlights that Malaysia need to strive hard to be at least at par with its closest neighbours.

Therefore, in view of the growing world population, it is imperative that sustainable agriculture and food security and nutrition be part of the new sustainable development agenda in 2016 and beyond. A way to achieve this plan is by encouraging Malaysians, especially the younger generation, to venture into agropreneurship business activities. With full and strong support from the government, the agriculture industry in Malaysia, with its enormous prospects and prosperous business potential, creates a large and attractive chance for entrepreneurs (D'Silva, Mohamad Shaffril, Uli, & Abu Samah, 2009). Slowly, Malaysians have immense investment prospects with quick and high returns in agropreneurship business activities (Abdullah & Naem Sulaiman, 2013).

AGROPRENEURSHIP: THE NEW DIMENSION IN AGRICULTURE SECTOR

The concept of agropreneurship, is gradually getting attention in both agriculture and entrepreneurship areas of study, especially in redefining new and modern agriculture. Recent studies show that agropreneurship as a concept and practice is not wishful thinking and exageration: it has a profound impact on business growth and survival (Verhees et al., 2011). According to Nagalakshmi and Sudhakar (2013):

Agricultural companies increasingly have to adapt to the vagaries of the market, changing consumer habits, enhanced environmental regulations, new requirements for product quality, chain management, food safety, sustainability, and so on. These changes have cleared the way for new entrants, innovation, and portfolio entrepreneurship.

This have conclusively shown that the emergence of the free market economies globally has resulted in the development of a new spirit of enterprise "Agropreneurship" and the increased individual need for responsibility for running their own businesses (Alex, 2011).

The concept of agropreneurship is being promoted to encourage setting up of enterprises related to the farm sector in the effort to modernise the agriculture sector. There are various definitions of agropreneurship in the literature. An early definition by Ahmed, Hasan, and Haneef (2011) refers to agropreneurship as an employment strategy that leads to economic self-sufficiency of rural people. Nagalakshmi and Sudhakar (2013), on the other hand, define agropreneurship as sustainable, community-oriented, and directly marketed agriculture. A more recent definition by Bairwa et al. (2014) indicates that agropreneurship is a profitable marriage between agriculture and entrepreneurship which turns a farm into an agribusiness establishment in agriculture and allied sectors. Similarly Azer, Mohamad, Abdullah, and Mustapha (2014) describe agropreneurs as individuals who involve the agricultural aspects into business. Agropreneurship could also be understood as the classification of all activities where farmers adjust a free market economy as entrepreneurial (Soumiya Devi, 2015). Despite the various definitions given to explain agropreneurship, the authors did agree on one aspect, which is that agropreneurship involves activities of producing, distributing and marketing of agricultural products to generate income and contribute to a sustainable community.

Agropreneurship is indeed seen to contribute at both individual and national levels. At the individual level, agropreneurship contributes to improving performance of an individual by reducing one's poverty level as a result of employment opportunity creation and allowing creativity and innovativeness to exist in meeting consumer demands (Bairwa et al., 2014; Nagalakshmi & Sudhakar, 2013; Osikabor, Adesope, Ibrahim, Babayemi, & Olatunji, 2011). At the national level on the other hand, agropreneurship has the power to improve economic viability (Osikabor et al., 2011) and to make agriculture a more attractive and profitable venture that contributes largely to national income by providing direct employment and income to the large, lower socioeconomic strata of society (Bairwa et al., 2014). Agropreneurship is now viewed to be an important agent of rural economic development (Mohd Yusof & Raja Abd Rahman, 2007). Agropreneurship's importance has also captured the attention of the country's important parties with the rise of the concept, 'agriculture is business' (Rezai, Mohamed, & Shamsuddin, 2011). With this concept, people in Malaysia are encouraged to become agropreneurs, not only to create wealth for themselves, but at the same time to contribute to the sustainability of society. This shows that communities also believe that agropreneurship indeed plays a significant role in contributing towards national economic growth and individual well-being. Therefore, future agropreneurs should be groomed, especially among youth.

THE IMPORTANCE OF AGROPRENEURSHIP IN ECONOMIC GROWTH AND DEVELOPMENT

Department of Statistics Malaysia revealed that in 2013, 76 percent of active companies in the agricultural sector were SMEs through the establishment of SMAEs. This shows that the success of agricultural projects depends largely on the success of SME's operation. Based on the findings, it is reported that SMEs and SMAEs play a significant role in and make substantial contributions toward national economies. This is evidenced by reports that 80 percent of global economic growth is attributable to SMEs (Jutla et al., 2002). In 2013, SMAEs drove 3 percent and 2.1 percent of Malaysian SME GDP growth and the country's overall GDP growth, respectively (SME Annual Report 2013/2014). Undoubtedly, agropreneurship activities play a significant role in contributing to the country's economic development by contributing to the supplies of food, job opportunities for people, earnings from exports and have also become major suppliers for agro-based industries (Hassan, Shaffril, Azril, Abu Hassan, & D'Silva, 2009; Okezie & Baharuddin, 2012; Siwar et al., 2013).

Even though the agriculture sector has recorded a more moderate growth (National SME Development Council, 2013), the country still expects the sector to improve, and this was supported by the higher output of crude palm oil from the maturing of new trees as well as being supported by food commodities, especially livestock and vegetables. The Third Industrial Master Plan (IMP3) highlights the need to push small entrepreneurs to become major players in agropreneurship and agro-based business activities with potential areas in resource based manufacturing SMAEs, such as herbal and traditional medicines, palm oil-based products, and food and beverages, including convenience foods for the halal market (Ministry of International Trade and Industry, 2006). Agro-based activities such as the agro-processing sector, which includes not only agro-related industries but also distribution services and trading activities, would roughly account for more than one-third of the GDP of Indonesia, Chile, Brazil and Thailand, and between 20 and 25 percent of GDP in sub-Saharan countries. The entire food system, including the production of primary goods and commodities, marketing and retailing, accounts for more than 50 percent of the GDP in developing countries (Jaffee, Kopicki, Labaste, & Christie, 2003). Furthermore, in developed countries such as in the United States of America (USA), agropreneurship activities contributes 13 times more to GDP than pure agricultural activities (Jaffee et al., 2003).

Due to the world's concerns about food security and continuous food supplies for people, agropreneurship has greatly captured the attention of multi-lateral organizations, policy makers and civil society (Food and Agriculture Organization of the United Nations, 2009). Hence, agropreneurship is a mechanism that provides an off-farm link in agrofood value chains. It supplies valuable inputs such as innovative information to the farm sector and at the same time connects the farm sector to the final consumers via the handling, processing, transportation, marketing, and distribution of agricultural products. These connections show strong cooperation between agropreneurship business activities and the performance of the agriculture sector. Indeed, vigorous agropreneurship business activities could encourage tremendous growth of this sector. At the same time, strong connection between agropreneurship and smallholders opens opportunity for the community to live a better life because it contributes to employment generation, poverty reduction and human resource development (Ahmed et al., 2011).

Agriculture today is no longer a sector for poor people only. Instead, given full and active supports from the government, it is now a sector where chances exist for businesses to prosper (D'Silva, Mohamad Shaffril, Uli, & Abu Samah, 2010). Hence, this offers significant opportunities for entrepreneurs to take advantage of opportunities and generate wealth. In fact, the focus of agropreneurship development is not only for the purpose of food security. Its importance also covers the transfer of knowledge, skills, techniques, expertise to the rest of the population via job creation and employment opportunity.

AGROPRENEURSHIP DEVELOPMENT IN MALAYSIA

Since the third era of industrialisation that took place between 1990 and 2005, it is only until recently that the focus on agropreneurship has started to regain momentum in Malaysia. Agropreneurship is now viewed to be an important agent for rural economic development (Mohd Yusof & Raja Abd Rahman, 2007). Because of that, the 9th Malaysian Plan outlined an RM 511.9 million budget allocation that aimed to produce 260,928 agropreneurs (Mohamed, Rezai, & Shamsudin, 2011). In this national development plan, the government placed great emphasis on the enrichment of the modern agriculture sector, outlining the way forward for it and to reenergize the sector to become one of the main contributors to the country's economic growth. The plan not only covers the commercial and biotechnology aspects of agriculture, but also on agriculture as a business. Consequently, small agricultural entrepreneurs in the country need to be pushed forward to become major players in SMAEs, as outlined in the Third Industrial Master Plan (IMP3). Based on the SME Annual Report 2012/2013, SMAEs that are run by agropreneurs rank number four of overall SMEs in this country. Table 1 summarizes the Malaysian SME establishment,

Table 1. Number of SME establishments by sector

Sector	Micro	Small	Medium	Total SME
Manufacturing	21,619	13,934	2,308	37,861
Services	462,420	106,061	12,504	580,985
Agriculture	3,775	1,941	992	6,708
Construction	8,587	6,725	3,971	19,238
Mining & Quarrying	57	126	116	299
Total SMEs	496,458	128,787	19,891	645,136

Source: Economic / SMEs Census 2011 by Department of Statistics, Malaysia.

as compared to other sectors in 2011. Even though SMAEs represent only 1 percent of the overall SME establishment in Malaysia, its contribution to GDP is still significant. As of 2012, SMAEs contribute 3.3 percent to Malaysia's GDP (Malaysian Department of Statistics, 2016).

In Malaysia, agropreneurship is becoming increasingly important. It offers opportunities for generating revenue and creating a future that straightforward subsistence farming often struggles to provide. In the 2003, the Ministry of Agriculture and Agro-Based Industry allocated and spent RM500 million on entrepreneurial development programs with aims to transform traditional farmers to visionary agropreneurs (Abdul Halim, Alias, Che Hamid, & Zakaria, 2011). Government's effort to promote agropreneurship did not just stopped there. The effort to promote modern agriculture and agropreneurship was also led by government agencies such as Department of Agriculture in collaboration with government linked companies (GLCs), such as Khazanah Nasional Berhad's subsidiary, Blue Archipelago. Realizing that agropreneurship is a very important activity among SMAEs specifically and its contribution to SMEs generally, the National Food Security Policy (FSP), which was approaching its expiration in 2011, was finally extended. Furthermore, the Fourth National Agricultural Policy (NAP4), a policy under which RM5.6 billion was allocated for agricultural development, was also executed in the same year (Adnan, 2011).

Moving forward, the government's support for agropreneurship and SMAEs was also clearly outlined in the national policies and development plans, such as Economic Transformation Program (ETP, 2011-2020), IMP3 (2006-2020), 10th Malaysian Plan (10MP) and SME Masterplan (2012-2020). In order to translate SME development strategy into reality, the National SME Development Council (NSDC) was established in 2004 to provide strategic direction for government policies on SME development and to ensure coordination and effectiveness of government programs. One of the key initiatives developed by NSDC is the National SME Development Blueprint, an annual action plan for SME development. Two types of government support for the development for agropreneurship and SMAEs are financial and non-financial support. Included under the first category are property loans, working capital and grants that are channelled through the Agro Bank with aims to provide agropreneurs a continuous working capital via overdraft facility. With the purpose to strengthen SMEs, the government has launched a Shariah-compliant SME Financing Fund of RM2 billion. The scheme is currently managed by 13 Islamic banks with the government providing a 2 percent profit rebate. Another initiative to assist agropreneurs with the capacity and potential to sustain their businesses is the SME Revitalisation Fund. The government also established an RM10 million SME Emergency Fund to assist SMEs that are affected by natural disasters. This fund channels soft loans up to a maximum of RM100 thousand to affected SMEs through the

Small and Medium Enterprise Corporation Malaysia (SME Corp. Malaysia) and the Malaysian Industrial Development Finance Berhad (MIDF). On the other hand, the latter category (non-financial) of support includes advisory, marketing, management, networking, research and development and technical support.

Equally important, various government agencies such as Palm Oil Research Institute of Malaysia (PORIM), Rubber Research Institute of Malaysia (RRIM), Malaysia Cocoa Board (MCB), Malaysia Agricultural Research & Development Institute (MARDI), Forest Research Institute Malaysia (FRIM) have also participated by expressing their support and commitment to grow agropreneurs and SMAEs to be economic champions by conducting research and development (R&D), activities in agriculture and providing agricultural training programs. Agencies like the Federal Agricultural Marketing Authority (FAMA) on the other hand, plays its role in securing market base and looking for market potential for local produce, particularly fruits and vegetables, as well as internationally promoting horticultural products such as fruits and flowers.

In order to promote the involvement of youth in producing modern agriculture and promoting the growth of agropreneurship, the government introduced the My *Kampung* My Future (MKMF) program. Huge amounts of funding were allocated for the success of this program with a goal of generating future agropreneurs. Today, as one of the government's effort to reduce graduate unemployment, RM50 million was allocated under the Graduate Entrepreneurship Fund, which is managed by SME Bank. The fund provides soft loans of up to RM500 thousand at an annual interest rate of 4 percent. To show that the government is very serious about building local agriculture industry, the sum of RM6 billion was allocated to implement high value-added and commercially-viable agriculture programs that requires human capital input from the youth sector ("Budget 2014: Support for SME plans," 2013). In order to further instil interest towards agriculture among the young segment and also to grow young agropreneurs with high income, the government has established the Young Agropreneur Unit through the aspirations of the Minister of Agriculture in September 2013. Mainly targeted for individuals under the age of 40, the aim of this program is to assist and encourage agropreneurship business activities among this group by involving in agricultural activities such as crops, livestock, fisheries, marketing, technology and innovation, as well as special projects such as agro-tourism and agro-based industry. Additionally, the implementation of this program is hoped to facilitate in shifting youth's paradigm towards this sector whereby the government is focussing in changing the traditional held belief regarding negative perception of agriculture sector.

As innovativeness was proven as being impacted by education (Yusoff, Ahmad, & Abdul Halim, 2016), the Agriculture Youth Entrepreneur Incubation Programme (AYEIP) with an aim to provide education, training and practices intended for youth who are interested in agriculture field was developed. The programme outlines provide agriculture coaching and offer a 'hands-on' experience on farming knowledge. The AYEIP programme was conducted in the Department of Agriculture (DOA) in four centres across the country. The programme was developed particularly for young (18-35 years old) agriculture institute graduates, university graduates, youth and any general Malaysian citizen, and police retiree or pension army personnel. The incubation consists of eight months full time programme which was fully funded by Malaysian government under the Ninth Malaysian Plan. At the end of the incubation programme, participants who passed stringent training together with good entrepreneurial qualities will be granted with a space for starting agropreneurship business activities.

Furthermore, to enhance youth agriculture interest and entrepreneurial skills, various activities and programs were provided by the Malaysian government through its agricultural departments. such as trainings that covers various business aspects that include production, marketing, advertising and promotion (Performance Management and Delivery Unit, 2010). The Malaysian Agriculture, Horticulture and Agro-tourism (MAHA), through its active promotion of agricultural products with its motto "Agriculture is business", was also one of the government's initiatives that opened important opportunities for youth to get ideas to create new products (Performance Management and Delivery Unit, 2010).

Finally, the government through its Ministry of Higher Education (MOHE) strives to assist SMEs in expanding their business through the introduction of Public-Private Research Network (PPRN) programme. Demand-Driven Innovation Project by PPRN endeavours to identify entrepreneurs with technological problems and researchers with viable research-based solution. Under PPRN programme, entrepreneurs who face difficulties in their venture could join the PPRN programme and begin describing their problems. In responding to that, PPRN subsequently develop a team of experts and scientists in the area to readily develop new technologies and taking appropriate action to assist in solving the entrepreneur's problem. Besides helping the entrepreneurs, this approach also aims to develop close cooperation between academics and entrepreneurs in producing innovative, high quality, competitive and unique products. Furthermore, in order to solve the problem, the entrepreneurs will be provided with a grant. A fund up to RM50,000 for every problem solved with the cooperation of entrepreneurs and academics will be granted.

AGROPRENEURSHIP SUPPORT THROUGH EDUCATION

Becoming an agropreneur is not a career path to be undertaken lightly. Agropreneurs have to prepare themselves to take calculated risks, be creative, innovative and resourceful, ready to put in long hours of hard work, cope with stress, and weather the bleak periods as well as the good ones. Realizing these needs, an agropreneur incubator program was established. It is a six-month course developed and aims to produce more agropreneurs with exposure to the realities of the entrepreneurial world who are confident and competitive. Agropreneurship training and education is actually not something new in Malaysia. Indeed, agropreneurship education: which is embedded in entrepreneurship education in Malaysia, began as early as lower secondary level in high school when the Integrated Living Skills (ILS) curriculum was introduced in 1991 (Mohamed, Rezai, Shamsudin, & Mahmud, 2012). Later when the students moved to the upper secondary level, students may choose subjects that relates to entrepreneurship such as Commerce as an elective course. At a much higher level, entrepreneurship education is even more emphasis. Through its Basic Student Entrepreneurial Program (BSEP) that started in 2003 and with early participation from 19 local and one private higher education institutions, the government aims to provide training to final year students who are interested in becoming entrepreneurs.

Subsequently, agropreneurship education and training in producing skilful agricultural talents cannot be given any less attention. Realizing the contribution of agriculture to the country's economic growth, the Malaysian government has been promoting both formal and informal agropreneurship education. For example, agropreneurship education has been promoted as early as primary school for children where most primary schools in the country encourage their students to sell foods during the *Canteen Day,* an entrepreneurship day of which students sell things during school hours. Other examples of government efforts to promote agropreneurship education can also be seen in common activities offered by various organizations, along with the formal entrepreneurship education offered at higher education institutions such as conferences, seminars, short courses and training on agropreneurship. Furthermore, realizing the importance of agropreneurship, the Malaysian government through its public and private universities and colleges has put in several academic programs and training at tertiary level to cultivate graduate feasibility and desirability for agropreneurship. At the university level, programs are typically offered by faculty of agro-based industries, faculty of agriculture or faculty of applied science.

WHY FUTURE GENERATION NEEDS TO CONCENTRATE ON AGROPRENEURSHIP?

In Malaysia, Chan, Selvadurai, and Hamid (2009) have raised concerns and highlighted the issue of small number of young entrepreneurs. According to the authors, the involvement of youth in entrepreneurship in Malaysia is not up to the expected level despite the huge efforts put forth by the government. The same issue was highlighted by Mohammad Nor, Nik Mohd Masdek, and Maidin (2015). The authors stressed that participation of youth in entrepreneurial activities was very low. Indeed, the growth percentage of entrepreneurs in Malaysia (youth and elderly) did not even exceed 26 percent (Mohammad Nor et al., 2015). Supporting this claim, a survey conducted by the Ministry of Education (MOE) in Malaysia revealed that among 22,016 working graduates, only 2.8 percent is self- employed and only 1.4 percent of 11,313 diploma holders are self-employed (Zainal Abidin and Irsyad, 2012).

Furthermore, a few of previous researchers have expressed their concern regarding youth unemployment in Malaysia (Abu Samah, D'Silva, Shaffril, & Uli, 2011; Mohammad Nor et al., 2015; Shamsuddin, Mohmad Isa, Aziz, Mohamed Mahfol, & Alagari, 2013). According to Abu Samah et al. (2011), the unemployment rate among youth was 4 percent in 2011. The rate kept on going up where in 2015, the youth unemployment rate was reported to be around 10 percent (Ministry of Finance, 2016; Mohammad Nor et al., 2015). Additionally, the current report by the Ministry of Finance showed that up to 40 percent of the total unemployed in Malaysia are youth especially the university graduates (Ministry of Finance, 2016). Furthermore, the report revealed that over 90 percent of those unemployed are aged between 15-29 years old.

Given this unfavourable situation, many researchers have called for agropreneurship activities as an approach in dealing with the overwhelming rate of youth unemployment as well as to increase the number of graduate entrepreneurs (Abdullah & Naem Sulaiman, 2013; Abdullah, Abu Samah, & Othman, 2012; Hock-Eam, Ahmad, & Jan, 2015; Mohammad Nor et al., 2015). Besides that, it was found that majority of graduate entrepreneurs were involved in wholesale and retail trade; services, real estate activities, and the manufacturing sectors (Hock-Eam et al., 2015). Hence, there is an urgent call for the involvement of young entrepreneurs to enhance and strengthen the agriculture sector in Malaysia via agropreneurship activities (Abdullah & Naem Sulaiman, 2013; Abdullah et al., 2012; D'Silva et al., 2009, 2010). Therefore, given the issue of small number of young entrepreneurs and an overwhelming rate of graduate unemployment in Malaysia, it is imperative for future generation to concentrate on agropreneurship as one of the tools to cater these issues.

THE CHALLENGE: GEN Y INVOLVEMENT IN AGROPRENEURSHIP

With the surge of interest in sustainable development, agropreneurship has now been earmarked as an important business activity for the country's economic development. However, the development of modern agriculture and agropreneurship endeavours will not be a success without an involvement of the young people, especially the Gen Y segment. Because of this, the Malaysian government endeavours to develop agropreneurial skills among this population. The local government has also placed great emphasis on encouraging and motivating them to become agropreneurs with the objectives of ensuring increasing and continuous supplies of food for the nation as well as decreasing the youth unemployment rate (Abdullah, Abu Samah & Othman, 2012; D'Silva et al., 2009). This can be seen through government highlights in the Third Industrial Master Plan (IMP3) to push small agropreneurs to become major players in the agro-based industries (Ministry of International Trade and Industry, 2006).

Yet, despite the considerable critical attention that was paid to the issue of food security and continuous food supplies in the country, Malaysians relatively show a lack of interest in agriculture sector when, compared to other sectors, only 11.8 percent of country's total employment comes from the agriculture sector (Abdullah et al., 2012). At the same time, the country is also facing the issue of an ageing agricultural community. The Performance Management and Delivery Unit (2010) reported that the average age of paddy farmers is above 60 years and 40 percent of fruit farmers are above 55 years of age. Supporting this report, a major finding in agriculture also showed that over 66 percent of people in agriculture are over 50 years old where the young are not interested and do not want to be involved in agriculture perhaps due to the view of low profitability held on this sector (Alam, Siwar, Murad, Molla, & Toriman, 2010; Jala, 2013, September 30; Zainal Abiddin & Irsyad, 2012). Later findings also showed the same phenomenon. It was revealed that 45 percent of farmers in Malaysia are 55 years old and above and this situation has caused retardation in production improvement (Abdullah & Abu Samah, 2014; Che Abdullah & Mustapha, 2009; Siwar, Idris, Yasar, & MOrshed, 2014). This phenomenon highlights that the agriculture sector in Malaysia is experiencing a shortage of young agricultural talent (Zainal Abiddin & Irsyad, 2012). Additionally, Movahedi, Latifi, and Sayyar (2013) emphasized that agropreneurship activities in Malaysia suffer from a lack of educated and skilful workforce and entrepreneurial spirit due to aging agricultural community. Until today, the issue of youth involvement in agriculture remains a big question mark. Their involvement in agropreneurship activities is still discouraging where young agropreneurs (aged 18 to 40 years) accounts for only 26 percent of all agricultural community (Abdullah et al., 2012). This figure is still far below despite the strong encouragement from the local government.

Notwithstanding the huge efforts put forth by the government, the involvement of youth in entrepreneurship in this country is still not up to the expected level (Chan et al., 2009). Possibly due to the instability of the agriculture sector, the youth in this country are more inclined to work in the manufacturing sector because they believe the sector brings them a better image, higher income and more advanced urban infrastructure (Che Abdullah & Mustapha, 2009). The great challenge therefore is to see how to get Malaysian youth, specifically the Gen Y segment, to venture into agriculture given the stigma associated with agriculture and farming. Researchers have expressed their concern regarding youth unemployment and suggesting venturing in agropreneurship and become agriculture self-employed as one of the solution (Abdullah & Naem Sulaiman, 2013; Abdullah et al., 2012). Hence, there is an urgent call for the involvement of young entrepreneurs to enhance and strengthen the agriculture sector in Malaysia via agropreneurship business activities (Abdullah & Naem Sulaiman, 2013; Abdullah et al., 2012; D'Silva et al., 2009, 2010).

WHY GEN Y INVOLVEMENT IN AGROPRENEURSHIP IS IMPERATIVE

Considering the significant role played by SMAEs in developing the country, Malaysian Gen Y are encouraged to become agropreneurs to meet both new career opportunities and also to ensure an increase and continuous supply of foods in the future (Abdullah et al., 2012; Zahrom, 2012, December 13). Besides its objective to enhance income distribution and reduce the nation's poverty level, many countries nowadays are gearing toward producing young entrepreneurs that possess many optimistic characteristics as one of the solutions to decrease the youth unemployment rate (Abdullah et al., 2012; D'Silva et al., 2009). Together with fast growing current technology and innovation, the agriculture sector definitely demands fresh and innovative ideas from the young segment, especially those with agropreneurship education, knowledge and skills.

Equally important, as SME Masterplan 2012-2020 outlines it's vision to develop globally competitive SMEs across all sectors that enhance wealth creation and contribute to the social well-being, the Malaysian Prime Minister encouraged high investment in youth as he believes "...the youth of today are an asset... who will take Malaysia to greater heights". Approximately, 38 percent of the Malaysian population consists of youth (SME Master Plan 2012-2020). In the same way, it has been suggested to create a "productive society" especially among the young population (those between the age of 18 to 40 years old) (Ahmad, Ramayah, & Tuan Muda, 2013). Agropreneurship activities should be cultivated among the young people because as individuals get older, they become less willing to invest time in activities that do not produce quick returns, including starting a new business (Lévesque & Minniti, 2006). In addition, the productivity level among this population must be kept high in order to spur economic growth and thus energize entrepreneurial spirit that drive first generation entrepreneurs (Ahmad et al., 2013).

Globally, the Gen Y population totals approximately 70 million, which is double the size of Gen X (Hewlett, Sherbin, & Sumberg, 2009). In Malaysia, Gen Y accounts for 40 percent of the country's total population and is the fastest growing segment of the workforce today. Even though there exists a contrary view that ageing or the third-age entrepreneurs (those between the age of 50 to 64) possess high working experience, know-how, and great financial means for entrepreneurship (Baucus & Human, 1994; Singh & DeNoble, 2003), and hence are better off in their entrepreneurial pursuits, the Gen Y cohort is more appropriate to be the key to drive a sustainable economy of long term growth that a nation can depend on because they are characterized by many optimistic values needed by agropreneurs in today's modern agriculture environment, such as being technology savvy, independent, self-reliant, entrepreneurial thinkers, well-educated, confident, passionate, upbeat, ambitious, result-oriented and socially conscious with high integrity (Geyzel, 2009; Martin, 2005; Sox, Kline, & Crews, 2014), as well as vibrant, energetic and high productivity (Joseph, Adanma, & Chinonso, 2012; Onwumere & Ukpebor, 2011). Evidence from the United States of America by the Kauffman Foundation (2012) reveals that 29.4 percent of entrepreneurs were 20 to 34 years old, and roughly 160,000 start-ups a month were led by Gen Y in 2011. Similarly, Pugh (2014) reports that more than half of Gen Y (54 percent) either want to start a business or have already started one. Thus, the Gen Y segment is the best candidate to venture in agropreneurship in order to realize the government plan in creating agriculture as a promising economic sector for the country's development. Based on those arguments, agropreneurship venturing among the Gen Y agropreneurs has recently grown in importance and is seen to be a practical concern to be investigated further in future research.

PROMOTING GEN Y AGROPRENEURSHIP: THE ROLE OF ACADEMIC INSTITUTIONS

It has been discussed extensively in the entrepreneurship literature that entrepreneurship is indeed a discipline of traits that can both be learned and taught (Vanevenhoven, 2013). Relying on the assumption that "entrepreneurs can be made", it is the role of academic institutions to take initiatives to promote agropreneurship among graduates by offering agropreneurship courses and programs and also via agropreneurship support mechanisms. Academic institutions emerged as a place where 'critical tools' for the development of future entrepreneurs are offered. The 'critical tools' here implies all efforts the institutions take in contributing to the development of future entrepreneurs. Furthermore, young agropreneurs have been postulated to have the risk taking and innovative attributes in undertaking a business enterprise (Mohamed et al., 2012; Zainal Abiddin & Irsyad, 2012). Therefore academic institutions are expected to produce young talents who are confident, motivated, proactive, innovative, take up entrepreneurship challenges as well as have a substantial skills to work in a team (Sánchez, 2013). The engines of agropreneurship development among youth are based in training and inculcating agropreneurship work culture (Mohamed et al., 2012) during their study at the university. Therefore, the role of academic institutions is paramount, as it is a centre that make contribution to the development of agropreneurship by creating an extent of business opportunities and equipping students with innovative business skills (Mohamed et al., 2012).

Specifically, in order to promote youth agropreneurship from academic institution perspective, the following suggestions are put forth.

1. **Stimulate Awareness and Positive Agropreneurial Attitude:** Firstly, academic institutions should stimulate students' awareness and form a mental picture and experience of the viability of agropreneurship as a career choice via formal agropreneurship courses and programs. Agropreneurship education must appear to enable students to acquire a set of knowledge and skills needed for successful performance along the entrepreneurial process (Matlay, 2008). This set of skills can facilitate future agropreneurs, especially for opportunity discovery and as well as promoting agroepreneurship desirability and feasibility and thus increase the formation of intention to become self-employed (Peterman & Kennedy, 2003; Saeed, Yousafzai, Yani-De-Soriano, & Muffatto, 2015; Solesvik, Westhead, & Matlay, 2014). Furthermore, young agropreneurs are postulated to have the risk-taking and innovative attributes needed in undertaking a business enterprise (Mohamed et al., 2012; Zainal Abiddin & Irsyad, 2012). Therefore, students who are supplied with agroepreneurship education and were enrolled in agroepreneurship courses are expected to be confident, motivated, proactive, innovative, and willing to face agroepreneurship challenges, as well as have the substantial skills to work in a team (Sánchez, 2013). Students who have participated in agropreneurship education are expected to be more entrepreneurially oriented, thus having a higher intention to become agropreneurs. This can be achieved by formulating detailed and meaningful curriculum and content that leads to students' adoption of appropriate attitudes that will cultivate their interest and desire in learning activities as well as developing their skills and competencies (Heinonen, 2007; Muhammad, Ismail, & Eh Rak, 2013).

2. **Provide Agropreneurship Education via a More Holistic Approach:** Secondly, academic institutions should provide agropreneurship education at the individual level with emphasis on the interaction between young agropreneurs and opportunity. It is true that developing positive attitude toward a certain behaviour is necessary, but positive attitude alone is insufficient. Students also need to be assured that the behaviour is feasible to achieve in real world (Baden & Parkes, 2013; Florin, Karri, & Rossiter, 2007). Notwithstanding positive outcomes derived from implementation of the entrepreneurship education programs that were reported, some however showed a contradictory discovery. Surprisingly, entrepreneurship education was found to exhibit negative outcomes too. For instance, students who engage in entrepreneurship education were found to show a somewhat declination in their intention to become entrepreneurs despite the significant positive effect on their self-assessed entrepreneurial skills (von Graevenitz, Harhoff, & Weber, 2010). This, possibly, is due to individuals' learning dissimilarities as students learn at different rates, have different motivations, start with different bases of knowledge and experience, and have access to different resource networks (Vanevenhoven, 2013). Therefore, what academic institutions could do is to pay more attention to finer variables such as pedagogical methods. In educating future agropreneurs, academic institutions could look at how individual interaction with the agropreneurship environment is emphasised. This approach is known as experiential learning. This technique is acknowledged to have the capability in producing entrepreneurs just the way it produces other people, such as professionals (Dhliwayo, 2008). Furthermore, in a different research setting, experiential learning in agricultural economics was revealed to be superior than traditional classroom learning (Parcell & Sykuta, 2003). An implementation of agropreneurship education with the presence of experiential learning in a supportive environment could affect students' perception of agropreneurship feasibility by allowing them to see themselves to be real agropreneurs. Rather than just learning theory, experiential learning is about action and thus it unlocks one's capabilities (Jennings & Wargnier, 2010) and give opportunities to students to see themselves as real entrepreneurs rather than pretending to be one (Vincett & Farlow, 2008). Experiential learning as an approach of discovery learning was acknowledged to have an ability to create the right learning atmosphere, allow articulations and interactions of ideas, offers synergistic learning among different participants and creates new meanings on students' knowledge, skills and experience (Smith, Collins, & Hannon, 2006) Additionally, Moore, Boyd, and Dooley (2010) indicated that true learning is the product of experiences which students collect throughout their learning process, as well as its evaluation and reflection.
3. **Create Large Agropreneurship Business Opportunities:** At the same time, agropreneurship education should also be tailored to contribute to the development of agropreneurship by creating large business opportunities (Mohamed et al., 2012). Hence, academic institutions could offer action-based agropreneurial programs. This is necessary for an acquisition of higher quality and quantity of education, relevance and current real-life experience from the external resources, network acquisition, and the availability of role models that can contribute to the movement of actual business start-up (Rasmussen & Sørheim, 2006). The reason for this is because effective entrepreneurial development programs must be based in a real work setting, encompassing a "learning-by-doing' element through outside classroom activities such as internships, so that the learning outcomes can be better implemented (Dhliwayo, 2008; Henry, Hill, & Leitch, 2005). Accordingly, academic institutions should extend their programs by offering more experiential programs such as internships to provide students with some exposure on the actual entrepreneurship environment as they learn

on the ground (Vanevenhoven, 2013). Besides that, real-life agropreneurship exposure can also be gained by allowing students to be trained by real agropreneurs who had encountered challenges, or even failure, during their enterprise founding journey (Kuratko, 2005). Agropreneurship education offered should allow students to be actively involved in real business opportunity because it could lead to a birth of an enterprise (Rasmussen & Sørheim, 2006). Through action-based agropreneurial programs, future agropreneurs as the experiential learners are able to establish multiple set of skills that are cognitive, emotional and physical and in which the learning experience is heightened while at the same time developing capabilities to solve real-world problems (Baden & Parkes, 2013). Experiential learning through internship or trial firms may develop relevant entrepreneurial skills and enhance the feasibility and desirability to become entrepreneurs (Davey, Plewa, & Struwig, 2011).

4. **Instil the Sense of Agropreneurship Desirability and Feasibility:** Next, offer opportunities for students to view agropreneurship more feasibly and desirably. Since an academic institution is the place where students formally acquire necessary entrepreneurial abilities and skills and systematically learn how to become successful agropreneurs, such institutions are also the right and best place in providing students with training and experiences to embark on an entrepreneurial career (Ghazali, Ibrahim, & Zainol, 2012), it should also be the place where students turn for support needed for initial agropreneurship venture creation. According to Ismail et al. (2013), the development of early entrepreneurial competencies is a significant result of the entrepreneurial role played by the educational institutions. Indeed, both the academic institutions and their instructors (i.e. professors) are important institutional key players in promoting entrepreneurial spirit, cultivating entrepreneurial capabilities and inspiring self-employment among the students through innovative programs and a research oriented culture (Ismail & Ahmad, 2013; Rae & Woodier-Harries, 2013; Souitaris, Zerbinati, & Al-Laham, 2007). Furthermore, students' intentions to become entrepreneurs was evidenced to positively and significantly relate with academic institutions environments (Md Rasli, Khan, Malekifar, & Jabeen, 2013; Trucker & Selcuk, 2009). In fact, many business enterprises, particularly in the developing world such as Malaysia, have been initiated at academic institutions (Ghazali et al., 2012). The supportive environment of an academic institution could lead to entrepreneurship development, particularly in intensifying students' entrepreneurial intention. The possibility of students to become self-employed is more likely to increase if the institutions provide adequate education and aspiration. By furnishing an entrepreneurially supportive environment and infrastructure, academic institutions are actually playing a part in increasing students' perceived self-efficacy and their involvement in entrepreneurial activities (Hashemi, Hosseini, & Rezvanfar, 2012) and thus changing students' perception on entrepreneurship feasibility.

Youth agropreneurial aspirations may be hindered due to inadequate preparation, such as insufficient business knowledge and lack of risk taking preparation. Because of this, agropreneurship may not be seen to be feasible or even desirable to students. In fact, stronger entrepreneurial promotion by academic institutions is needed by students to assist their enterprise foundation process (Venesaar, Kallaste, & Küttim, 2014). One way to supply adequate preparation to students is by fostering a supportive institutional environment, such as supplying resources like initial capital for business creation, inclusion of role models, and giving one-to-one support. With regard to a developing country such as Malaysia, academic institutions are expected by students to be supportive by providing networks, workshops, idea development for starting a business and entrepreneurship focus projects (Davey et al., 2011). These types of supports may increase students' confidence levels to take risk and thus initiate the new venture creation.

5. **Play an Active Role in Connecting Gen Y to the Network Circle:** Finally, since performing agropreneurial activities and founding an agropreneurship business cannot be done in isolation (Rutten & Boekema, 2007), academic institution should become an agent for networking development between students and potential suppliers, customers and capital providers. Indeed, it was found that the unavailability of social network and lack of resources were hurdles to entrepreneurship (Sandhu, Sidique, & Riaz, 2011) and contribute to hiccups along the agropreneurial process. Nascent agropreneurship businesses cannot be realized unless agropreneurs are able to acquire those resources (Sesen, 2013). In order for agropreneurs to successfully operate their business, the importance of resources available to them and knowledge is undeniable. Networks can be a source of necessary resources needed to start an entrepreneurial behavior (Fernández-Pérez, Alonso-Galicia, del Mar Fuentes-Fuentes, & Rodriguez-Ariza, 2014; Gutiérrez & Pérez, 2010; Najib & Kiminami, 2011; Quan, 2012; Rampersad, Troshani, & Plewa, 2012; Sequeira, Mueller, & Mcgee, 2007; Sesen, 2013; Slotte-Kock & Coviello, 2010), such as information regarding the applicable laws, necessary permits, reference, potential sources of financing and emotional support to provide agropreneurs with distinctive resources and knowledge (Sequeira et al., 2007). Valuable, distinctive and unique key resources supplied by networks improve the effectiveness of entrepreneurs (Slotte-Kock & Coviello, 2010) by greatly allowing them to experience positive outcomes as distinctive and unique resources contribute to greater and remarkable returns (Chiu & Lee, 2007; Rutten & Boekema, 2007). Since becoming an agropreneur, and also other kinds of entrepreneurs, they are challenged with limited resources (Sequeira et al., 2007) and uncertainty, encouragement, information, support, and access to key resources provided by networks greatly influence students' intention to become agropreneurs in a favorable manner. Agropreneurs who are capable of developing meaningful networking are entrepreneurs that gain rewards from networking, which enable them to make decisions quickly, build confidence, save lots of valuable time and necessary cost as well as learn greatly from the experiences of others (Liñán & Santos, 2007; Rampersad et al., 2012; Sequeira et al., 2007). At the initial state of the agropreneurship venture creation process, potential agropreneurs can benefit from networking in at least two ways. First, agropreneurs can make use of networks to recognize business opportunities and chances. Second, being surrounded by networking allows agropreneurs to get access to resources that can range from financial to human such as skilled labours. Therefore, an academic institution that is actively involved in arranging and introducing the students to the appropriate network circle will minimize the hiccups in the agropreneurship process. Academic institutions should take proactive actions to closely link students with potential business and social networks, which may be accomplished by conducting a seminar and providing focus group development with real world entrepreneurs, capital providers, and motivators.

CONCLUSION

In summary, the development of Gen Y creating a future that traditional subsistence farming often struggles to provide. Since an individual spends almost 18 years in getting formal education with 7 seven years at the tertiary level, an academic institution is undoubtedly a very salient agent in producing young agropreneurs. Academic institutions should pay more attention to what they could offer to develop more young agropreneurs by contributing to the development of integrated entrepreneurial skills, capabilities and competencies. With adequate agropreneurship education coupled with extensive agropreneurship supports programs received, it is believed to help Gen Y graduates to nourish creativity and innovation, especially in developing a novel agropreneurship product and useful ideas. Future research in agropreneurship area should focus on the impact of Gen Ys' skills and competencies developed by academic institution, and it is used along the agropreneurial business creation process as well as how these accumulated assets could impact the business performance. Another dimension that future research could focus is on the benefits the Gen Y could get from the network circle created by the academic institution in assisting the development of agropreneurhsip business activities among this unique cohort.

REFERENCES

Abdul Halim, M. A. S., Alias, M., Che Hamid, A., & Zakaria, Z. (2011). An inter-relationship of entrepreneurial personality, commitment and self-independent in a Terengganu agriculture industry. *International Journal of Business and Social Science*, *2*(23), 274–281.

Abdullah, A. A., & Naem Sulaiman, N. (2013). Factors that influence the interest of youths in agricultural entrepreneurship. *International Journal of Business and Social Science*, *4*(3), 228–302.

Abdullah, F. A., & Abu Samah, B. (2014). Factors influencing inclination toward agriculture entrepreneurship among students in agriculture learning institute. *Asian Social Science*, *10*(2), 273–278.

Abdullah, F. A., Abu Samah, B., & Othman, J. (2012). Inclination towards agriculture among rural youth in Malaysia. *Journal of Basic and Applied Scientific Research*, *2*(11), 10892–10894.

Abu Dardak, R. (2015). *Transformation of agricultural sector in Malaysia through agricultural policy*. Malaysia: MARDI.

Abu Samah, B., D'Silva, J. L., Shaffril, H. A. M., & Uli, J. (2011). The impact of female university students' acceptance towards agriculture contract farming on Malaysian economy. *African Journal of Business Management*, *5*(15), 6625–6631.

Adnan, H. (2011, April 9). Food security policy may be extended. *The Star Online*. Retrieved from http://www.thestar.com.my/story.aspx/?file=%2f2011%2f4%2f9%2fbusiness%2f8445971

Ahmad, A. R., Wan Yusoff, F. W., Md Noor, H., & Ramin, A. K. (2012). Preliminary study of rural entrepreneruship development program in Malaysia. *Journal of Global Entrepreneurship*, *2*(1), 1–8.

Ahmad, N. H., Ramayah, T., & Tuan Muda, S. A. D. (2013). Unlocking the entrepreneurial propensity among prime-age Malaysians: Multi-ethnic analysis. *Journal of Arts. Science & Commerce*, *4*(1), 1–6.

Ahmed, T., Hasan, S., & Haneef, R. (2011). Entrepreneurial characteristics of the agripreneurs under the Scheme of Agriclinics & Agri-business Centres. *Journal of Community Mobilization and Sustainable Development*, *6*(2), 145–149.

Alam, M. M., Siwar, C., Murad, M. W., Molla, R. I., & Toriman, M. E. (2010). Socioeconomic profile of farmer in Malaysia: Study on integrated agricultural development area in North-West Selangor. *Agricultural Economics and Rural Development. New Series*, *7*(2), 249–265.

Alex, L. (2011). *A review and analysis of policies on farmers' entrepreneurship development*. PELUM Association Retrieved from http://api.ning.com/files/mBFEJqp6LPA6uws0UOvKYJD594rw5TqjU-WCb6e5tQ*x02SZslAqcSAQNJIAirsnn3b6LLN7QbTlhi602siwc0PPbcR26h4v/Farmerentpolicystudy.pdf

Azer, I., Mohamad, S. A., Abdullah, N. S., & Mustapha, M. (2014). Agro-preneurial obstacles among students in the Faculty of Plantation and Agrotechnology, UiTM Pahang. *Social and Management Research Journal*, *11*(1), 1–8.

Baden, D., & Parkes, C. (2013). Experiential learning: Inspiring the business leaders of tomorrow. *Journal of Management Development*, *32*(3), 295–308. doi:10.1108/02621711311318283

Bairwa, S. L., Lakra, K., Kushwaha, S., Meena, L. K., & Kumar, P. (2014). Agripreneurship development as a tool to upliftment of agriculture. *International Journal of Scientific and Research Publication*, *4*(3), 1–4.

Bank Negara Malaysia. (2015). Economic and financial developments in Malaysia in the first quater of 2015. *Quaterly Bulletin*. Retrieved Jun 20, 2016, from http://www.bnm.gov.my/files/publication/qb/2015/Q1/1Q2015_fullbook_en.pdf

Baron, R. A., & Shane, S. A. (2008). Entrepreneurship: A Process Perspective (2nd ed.). Mason, OH: Thomson South-Western.

Baucus, D. A., & Human, S. E. (1994). Second-career entrepreneurs: A multiple case study analysis of entrepreneurial processes and antecedent variables. *Entrepreneurship Theory and Practice*, *19*(2), 41–71.

Budget 2014: Support for SME plans. (2013, October 26). *The Star Online*. Retrieved from http://www.thestar.com.my/Business/Business-News/2013/10/26/Support-for-SME-plans-Hafsah-says-activities-will-help-to-achieve-goals.aspx/

Cervantes-Godoy, D., & Dewbre, J. (2010). Economic importance of agriculture for poverty reduction. *OECD Food Agriculture and Fisheries Working Papers, 23*. doi: 10.1787/5kmmv9s20944-en

Chan, K. L., Selvadurai, S., & Hamid, B. A. (2009). Malay youth entrepreneurship in Malaysia: An empirical update. *Geografia: Malaysian Journal of Society and Space*, *5*(2), 61–68.

Che Abdullah, N., & Mustapha, R. (2009). Kajian kes usahawan tani industri kecil sederhana (IKS) bumiputera di Negeri Terengganu. *Jurnal Pendidikan Malaysia*, *34*(2), 143–165.

Chiu, S.-K., & Lee, Y.-I. (2007). Strategic resources, network competence, and sustainable competitive advantages - An empirical study on Taiwan led firms. *International Journal of Electronic Business Management*, *5*(1), 70–78.

D'Silva, J. L., Mohamad Shaffril, H. A., Uli, J., & Abu Samah, B. (2009). A review of contract farming and factors that impinge youth's acceptance to contract farming. *European Journal of Soil Science*, *11*(2), 328–338.

Davey, T., Plewa, C., & Struwig, M. (2011). Entrepreneurship perceptions and career intentions of international students. *Education+ Training, 53*(5), 335-352.

Dhliwayo, S. (2008). Experiential learning in entrepreneurship education: A prospective model for South African tertiary institutions. *Education+ Training, 50*(4), 329-340.

Diao, X., Hazell, P., Resnick, D., & Thurlow, J. (2007). The Role of agriculture in development: Implications for Sub-Saharan Africa. Washington, DC: International Food Policy Research Institute. Retrieved from http://www.ifpri.org/sites/default/files/pubs/pubs/abstract/153/rr153.pdf

DSilva, J. L., Mohamad Shaffril, H. A., Uli, J., & Abu Samah, B. (2010). Socio-demography factors that influence youth attitude towards contract farming. *American Journal of Applied Sciences*, *7*(4), 603–608. doi:10.3844/ajassp.2010.603.608

Fernández-Pérez, V., Alonso-Galicia, P. E., del Mar Fuentes-Fuentes, M., & Rodriguez-Ariza, L. (2014). Business social networks and academics entrepreneurial intentions. *Industrial Management & Data Systems*, *114*(2), 292–320. doi:10.1108/IMDS-02-2013-0076

Florin, J., Karri, R., & Rossiter, N. (2007). Fostering entrepreneurial drive in business education: An attitudinal approach. *Journal of Management Education*, *31*(1), 17–42. doi:10.1177/1052562905282023

Food and Agriculture Organization of the United Nations. (2009). *How to feed the world in 2050.* Retrieved from http://www.fao.org/fileadmin/templates/wsfs/docs/expert_paper/How_to_Feed_the_World_in_2050.pdf

Geyzel, M. V. (2009). Working with generation. Retrieved from http//vangeyzel.com/2009/08/20working-with-gen-y/

Ghazali, Z., Ibrahim, N. A., & Zainol, F. A. (2012). Factors affecting entrepreneurial intention among UniSZA students. *Asian Social Science*, *9*(1), 85–93. doi:10.5539/ass.v9n1p85

Gutiérrez, L. G., & Pérez, V. F. (2010). Managerial networks and strategic flexibility: A QM perspective. *Industrial Management & Data Systems*, *110*(8), 1192–1214. doi:10.1108/02635571011077834

Hashemi, S. M. K., Hosseini, S. M., & Rezvanfar, A. (2012). Explaining entrepreneurial intention among agricultural students: Effects of entrepreneurial self-efficacy, and college entrepreneurial orientation. *Research Journal of Business Management*, *6*(3), 1–9.

Hassan, M. S., Shaffril, M., Azril, H., Abu Hassan, M., & D'Silva, J. L. (2009). Developing agriculture in Malaysia: Internet utilization among Malaysian youth agro-businessman. *European Journal of Soil Science*, *11*(2), 215–224.

Heinonen, J. (2007). An entrepreneurial-directed approach to teaching corporate entrepreneurship at university level. *Education+ Training, 49*(4), 310-324.

Henry, C., Hill, F., & Leitch, C. (2005). Entrepreneurship education and training: can entrepreneurship be taught? Part I. *Education + Training, 47*(2), 98-111.

Hewlett, S. A., Sherbin, L., & Sumberg, K. (2009). How Gen Y & Boomers will reshape your agenda. *Harvard Business Review, 87*(7/8), 71–76. PMID:19630257

Hock-Eam, L., Ahmad, S. A., & Jan, S. J. (2015). *The inferring predisposed factors for graduate agropreneur in Malaysia: Mismatch?* Paper presented at the 9th Asia-Pacific Business Research Conference, Singapore.

International Labour Office. (2014). *Global employment trends 2014: Risk of a jobless recovery?* Geneva, ILO: Document and Publications Production, Printing and Distribution Branch (PRODOC), ILO. Retrieved from http://www.ilo.org/wcmsp5/groups/public/---dgreports/---dcomm/---publ/documents/publication/wcms_233953.pdf

Ismail, K., Ahmad Anuar, M., Wan Omar, W. Z., Aziz, A. A., Seohod, K., & Akhtar, C. H. (2013). *Entrepreneurial intention, entrepreneurial orientation of faculty and students towards commercialization.* Paper presented at the 3rd International Conference on Leadership, Technology and Innovation Management, Istanbul, Turkey.

Ismail, M. Z., & Ahmad, S. Z. (2013). Entrepreneurship education: An insight from Malaysian polytechnics. *Journal of Chinese Entrepreneurship, 5*(2), 144–160. doi:10.1108/JCE-02-2013-0003

Jaffee, S., Kopicki, R., Labaste, P., & Christie, I. (2003). *Modernizing Africa's agro-food systems: Analytical framework and implications for operations* (Africa Region Working Paper Series, No. 4). Retrieved from http://www.worldbank.org/afr/wps/wp44.pdf

Jala, I. (2013, September 30). Agriculture is a sector that is still important to Malaysia's economy. *The Star Online*. Retrieved from http://www.thestar.com.my/Business/Business-News/2013/09/30/Agriculture-is-a-sector-that-is-still-important-to-Malaysias-economy/

Jennings, C., & Wargnier, J. (2010). Experiential learning – A way to develop agile minds in the knowledge economy? *Development and Learning in Organizations, 24*(3), 14–16.

Joseph, O., Adanma, N. J., & Chinonso, E. H. (2012). Wealth allocation and determinants of venture capital among poultry agribusiness entrepreneurs in Abia State, Nigeria. *Journal of Economics and Sustainable Development, 3*(14), 188–196.

Jutla, D., Bodorik, P., & Dhaliwal, J. (2002). Supporting the e-business readiness of small and medium sized enterprises: Approaches and metrics. *Internet Research: Electronic Networking Applications and Policy, 12*(2), 139–164. doi:10.1108/10662240210422512

Kuldilok, K. S., Dawson, P. J., & Lingard, J. (2013). The export competitiveness of the tuna industry in Thailand. *British Food Journal, 115*(3), 328–341. doi:10.1108/00070701311314174

Kuratko, D. F. (2005). The emergence of entrepreneurship education: Development, trends, and challenges. *Entrepreneurship Theory and Practice, 29*(5), 577–598. doi:10.1111/j.1540-6520.2005.00099.x

Lévesque, M., & Minniti, M. (2006). The effect of aging on entrepreneurial behavior. *Journal of Business Venturing, 21*(2), 177–194. doi:10.1016/j.jbusvent.2005.04.003

Lim, Y.-M., Lee, T.-H., & Cheng, B.-L. (2012). Entrepreneurial inclination among business students: A Malaysian study. *The South East Asian Journal of Management, 6*(2), 113–127. doi:10.21002/seam.v6i2.1318

Liñán, F., & Santos, F. J. (2007). Does social capital affect entrepreneurial intentions? *International Advances in Economic Research, 13*(4), 443–453. doi:10.1007/s11294-007-9109-8

Malaysian Department of Statistics. (2016). Retrieved 2 April 2014, from http://www.statistics.gov.my

Martin, C. A. (2005). From high maintenance to high productivity: What managers need to know about Generation Y. *Industrial and Commercial Training, 37*(1), 39–44. doi:10.1108/00197850510699965

Matlay, H. (2008). The impact of entrepreneurship education on entrepreneurial outcomes. *Journal of Small Business and Enterprise Development, 15*(2), 382–396. doi:10.1108/14626000810871745

Md Rasli, A., Khan, S., Malekifar, S., & Jabeen, S. (2013). Factors affecting entrepreneurial intention among graduate students of Universiti Teknologi Malaysia. *International Journal of Business and Social Science, 4*(2), 182-188.

Ministry of Finance. (2013). *Gross domestic product by kind of economic activity at constant 2005 prices (RM million) 2013-2013*. Retrieved 21 June, 2016, from http://www.treasury.gov.my/pdf/ekonomi/dataekonomi/2013/timeseries/GDPbySector2013_2014.pdf

Ministry of Finance. (2016). *Economic performance and prospects Economic Report 2015/2016. Kuala Lumpur*. Malaysia: Ministry of Finance.

Ministry of International Trade and Industry. (2006). *IMP3: Third Industrial Master Plan 2006-2020, Malasia: Toward global competitiveness*. Retrieved from http://mset.org.my/myraig/pdf/Industry/MasterPlan3/Review-MITI%20IMP3.pdf

Mohamed, Z., Rezai, G., & Shamsudin, M. N. (2011). The effectiveness of entrepreneurship extension education among the FOA members in Malaysia. *Current Research Journal of Social Sciences, 3*(1), 17–21.

Mohamed, Z., Rezai, G., Shamsudin, M. N., & Mahmud, M. M. (2012). Enhancing young graduates' intention towards entrepreneurship development in Malaysia. *Education + Training, 54*(7), 605-618.

Mohammad Nor, N. A. A., Nik Mohd Masdek, N. R., & Maidin, M. K. H. (2015). Youth inclination towards agricultural entrepreneurship. *Economic and Technology Management Review, 10a*, 47–55.

Mohd Yusof, A. B., & Raja Abd Rahman, R. R. (2007). *Green lifestyle: Evaluating new business and income enhancement through agripreneurship development*. Paper presented at the The USM-UPM-PETA Conference, Penang, Malaysia.

Mok, H.-F., Williamson, V. G., Grove, J. R., Burry, K., Barker, S. F., & Hamilton, A. J. (2014). Strawberry fields forever? Urban agriculture in developed countries: A review. *Agronomy for Sustainable Development, 34*(1), 21–43. doi:10.1007/s13593-013-0156-7

Moore, C., Boyd, B. L., & Dooley, K. E. (2010). The effects of experiential learning with an emphasis on reflective writing on deep-level processing of leadership students. *Journal of Leadership Education, 9*(1), 36–52. doi:10.12806/V9/I1/RF3

Movahedi, R., Latifi, S., & Sayyar, L. Z. (2013). The factors affecting agricultural students' attitude towards self-employment and entrepreneurship. *International Journal of Agriculture and Crop Sciences, 5*(16), 1813–1819.

Muhammad, M., Ismail, A. A., & Eh Rak, A. (2013). Competency of agriculture graduates in Malaysian public universities. *International Journal of Enhanced Research in Educational Development, 1*(1), 1–9.

Nagalakshmi, T., & Sudhakar, A. (2013). Agri-preneurs: A case study of Dharmapuri farmers. *International Journal of Science and Research, 2*(8), 208–214.

Najib, M., & Kiminami, A. (2011). Innovation, cooperation and business performance: Some evidence from Indonesian small food processing cluster. *Journal of Agribusiness in Developing and Emerging Economies, 1*(1), 75–96. doi:10.1108/20440831111131523

National SME Development Council. (2013). *SME annual report 2013/2014: Transitioning for productivity-led and innovation-driven growth*. Sentral, Malaysia: SME Corporation Malaysia. Retrieved from http://www.smecorp.gov.my/vn2/node/1475

Okezie, C. A., & Baharuddin, A. H. (2012). Risk and poverty in agriculture: Expanding roles for agricultural cooperatives in Malaysia. *Geografia: Malaysian Journal of Society and Space, 8*(4), 1–11.

Onwumere, J., & Ukpebor, P. O. (2011). Evaluation of earning performance of female owned leather-based enterprises in Aba Metropolis, Abia State, Nigeria. *Journal of Agriculture and Social Research, 11*(2), 120–127.

Osikabor, B., Adesope, A. A., Ibrahim, A. G., Babayemi, O. F., & Olatunji, B. T. (2011). Animal-agriculture based entrepreneurship: Descriptive norms, perceived economic viability and behavioural intention among final year agriculture related students in Ibadan, Nigeria. *Asian Journal of Agricultural Sciences, 3*(2), 87–93.

Owens, T., Hoddinott, J., & Kinsey, B. (2003). The impact of agricultural extension on farm production in resettlement areas of Zimbabwe. *Economic Development and Cultural Change, 51*(2), 337–357. doi:10.1086/346113

Parcell, J., & Sykuta, M. (2003). *Undergraduate perceptions of the need for an agricultural entrepreneurship curriculum*. Paper presented at the Agricultural Economics Association Annual Meeting, Denver, CO.

Performance Management and Delivery Unit. (2010). *Economic transformation programme: A roadmap for Malaysia*. Putrajaya, Malaysia: Performance Management and Delivery Unit (PEMANDU). Retrieved from http://www.moa.gov.my/documents/10157/c65bb64f-da6c-4e83-bb51-40a1a55b9954

Peterman, N. E., & Kennedy, J. (2003). Enterprise education: Influencing students perceptions of entrepreneurship. *Entrepreneurship Theory & Practice, 28*(2), 129–144. doi:10.1046/j.1540-6520.2003.00035.x

Poornima, S. C. (2009). Motivating through satisfaction: An on-going effort of HR in organisations. *IUP Journal of Management Research, 8*(5), 26–37.

Pugh, M. (2014). Why millennials should become entrepreneurs now? *Entrepreneur.* Retrieved 28 April, 2014, from http://www.entrepreneur.com/article/230886

Quan, X. (2012). Prior experience, social network, and levels of entrepreneurial intentions. *Management Research Review, 35*(10), 945–957. doi:10.1108/01409171211272679

Rae, D., & Woodier-Harris, N. R. (2013). How does enterprise and entrepreneurship education influence postgraduate students' career intentions in the New Era economy? *Education + Training, 55*(8/9), 926-948.

Ramachandaran, G. (2010). Excerpts of the Government Transformation Programme (GTP) & Economic Transformation Programme (ETP): Key thrusts to power the nation towards 2020. *RSM Startegic Business Advisor.* Retrieved 22 April, 2014, from http://www.rsmi.com.my/WebLITE/Applications/productcatalog/uploaded/Docs/Government%20Transformation%20Programme%20&%20Economic%20Transformation%20Programme%20Article%205.10.10.pdf

Rampersad, G., Troshani, I., & Plewa, C. (2012). IOS adoption in innovation networks: A case study. *Industrial Management & Data Systems, 112*(9), 1366–1382. doi:10.1108/02635571211278974

Rasmussen, E. A., & Sørheim, R. (2006). Action-based entrepreneurship education. *Technovation, 26*(2), 185–194. doi:10.1016/j.technovation.2005.06.012

Razak, M. I. M., Abas, N. M., Yaacob, N. J. A., Rodzi, S. N. A. M., Yusof, N. M., & Azidin, R. A. (2015). An overview of primary sector in Malaysia. *International Journal of Economics. Commerce and Management, 3*(2), 1–13.

Rezai, G., Mohamed, Z., & Shamsuddin, M. N. (2011). Informal education and developing entrepreneurial skills among farmers in Malaysia. *International Journal of Social. Human Science and Engineering, 5*(7), 146–153.

Rutten, R., & Boekema, F. (2007). Regional social capital: Embeddedness, innovation networks and regional economic development. *Technological Forecasting and Social Change, 74*(9), 1834–1846. doi:10.1016/j.techfore.2007.05.012

Saeed, S., Yousafzai, S. Y., Yani-De-Soriano, M., & Muffatto, M. (2015). The role of perceived university support in the formation of students entrepreneurial intention. *Journal of Small Business Management, 53*(4), 1127–1145. doi:10.1111/jsbm.12090

Sánchez, J. C. (2013). The impact of an entrepreneurship education program on entrepreneurial competencies and intention. *Journal of Small Business Management, 51*(3), 447–465. doi:10.1111/jsbm.12025

Sandhu, M. S., Sidique, S. F., & Riaz, S. (2011). Entrepreneurship barriers and entrepreneurial inclination among Malaysian postgraduate students. *International Journal of Entrepreneurial Behaviour & Research, 17*(4), 428–449. doi:10.1108/13552551111139656

Selamat, Z., & Nasir, A. M. (2013). Efficiency measurement of Malaysian agriculture firms. *International Journal of Trade. Economics & Finance, 4*(2), 79–85.

Sequeira, J., Mueller, S. L., & Mcgee, J. E. (2007). The influence of social ties and self-efficacy in forming entrepreneurial intentions and motivating nascent behavior. *Journal of Developmental Entrepreneurship, 12*(03), 275–293. doi:10.1142/S108494670700068X

Sesen, H. (2013). Personality or environment? A comprehensive study on the entrepreneurial intentions of university students. *Education+ Training, 55*(7), 624-640.

Shamsuddin, A., Mohmad Isa, K. H., Aziz, M. N., Mohamed Mahfol, N. Z. N., & Alagari, T. (2013). Graduate unemployment: The awareness and perception of graduates towards government's initiatives. *International Journal of Business. Economics and Law*, *3*(1), 15–24.

Singh, G., & DeNoble, A. (2003). Early retirees as the next generation of entrepreneurs. *Entrepreneurship Theory & Practice*, *23*(3), 207–226. doi:10.1111/1540-8520.t01-1-00001

Siwar, C., Idris, N. D. M., Yasar, M., & Morshed, G. (2014). Issues and challenges facing rice production and food security in the granary areas in the East Coast Economic Region (ECER), Malaysia. *Research Journal of Applied Sciences, Engineering and Technology*, *7*(4), 711–722.

Siwar, C., Yasar, M., Ghazali, Z., & Mohd Idris, N. D. (2013). Vulnerability and sustainable livelihood of paddy farmers in the North Terengganu Integrated Agriculture Development Area (IADA KETARA), Malaysia. *Prosiding Perkem*, *8*(2), 778–789.

Slotte-Kock, S., & Coviello, N. (2010). Entrepreneurship research on network processes: A review and ways forward. *Entrepreneurship Theory & Practice*, *34*(1), 31–57. doi:10.1111/j.1540-6520.2009.00311.x

SME Annual Report. (2013/2014). Retrieved 17 November 2015, from http://www.smecorp.gov.my/vn2/sites/default/files/chapter2-SME%20Development%20and%20Outlook_0.pdf

SME Master Plan. (2012-2020). Retrieved 22 April, 2014, from http://www.chinesechamber.org.my/html/themes/chinesechamber/images/content/bulletin343/SME%20MASTERPLAN%202012-2020.pdf

Smith, A. J., Collins, L. A., & Hannon, P. D. (2006). Embedding new entrepreneurship programmes in UK higher education institutions: Challenges and considerations. *Education+ Training, 48*(8/9), 555-567.

Solesvik, M. Z., Westhead, P., & Matlay, H. (2014). Cultural factors and entrepreneurial intention: The role of entrepreneurship education. *Education+ Training, 56*(8/9), 680-696.

Souitaris, V., Zerbinati, S., & Al-Laham, A. (2007). Do entrepreneurship programmes raise entrepreneurial intentions of science and engineering students? The effect of learning, inspiration and resources. *Journal of Business Venturing*, *22*(4), 566–591. doi:10.1016/j.jbusvent.2006.05.002

Soumiya Devi, M. K. (2015). A study on the influencing factors for a literate youth to take up agricultural entrepreneurship. *International Journal of Management and Commerce Innovations*, *3*(1), 692–700.

Sox, C. B., Kline, S. F., & Crews, T. B. (2014). Identifying best practices, opportunities and barriers in meeting planning for Generation Y. *International Journal of Hospitality Management*, *36*, 244–254. doi:10.1016/j.ijhm.2013.09.009

Trucker, D., & Selcuk, S. S. (2009). Which factors affect entrepreneurial intention of university students? *Journal of European Industrial Training*, *33*(2), 142–159. doi:10.1108/03090590910939049

Vanevenhoven, J. (2013). Advances and challenges in entrepreneurship education. *Journal of Small Business Management*, *51*(3), 466–470. doi:10.1111/jsbm.12043

Venesaar, U., Kallaste, M., & Küttim, M. (2014). Factors influencing students venture creation process. *Procedia: Social and Behavioral Sciences, 110*, 678–688. doi:10.1016/j.sbspro.2013.12.912

Verhees, F. J. H. M., Kuipers, A., & Klopcic, M. (2011). Entrepreneurial proclivity and farm performance: The cases of Dutch and Slovenian farmers. *International Journal of Entrepreneurship and Innovation, 12*(3), 167–177. doi:10.5367/ijei.2011.0039

Vincett, P. S., & Farlow, S. (2008). Start-a-Business: An experiment in education through entrepreneurship. *Journal of Small Business and Enterprise Development, 15*(2), 274–288. doi:10.1108/14626000810871673

von Graevenitz, G., Harhoff, D., & Weber, R. (2010). The effects of entrepreneurship education. *Journal of Economic Behavior & Organization, 76*(1), 90–112. doi:10.1016/j.jebo.2010.02.015

Yusoff, A., Ahmad, N. H., & Abdul Halim, H. (2016). Entrepreneurial orientation and entrepreneurial intention among Malaysian agricultural students: The impact of entrepreneurship education. *Advances in Business-Related Scientific Research Journal, 7*(1), 77–92.

Zahrom, B. (2012, December 13). Generasi Y digalak sertai industry tani. *Berita Harian*. Retrieved from http://www.bharian.com.my/bharian/articles/GenerasiYdigalaksertaiindustritani/Article/index_html

Zainal Abiddin, N., & Irsyad, S. (2012). The involvement of graduates youth in commercial agriculture: Issues and challenges. *International Journal for Educational Studies, 5*(1), 15–24.

KEY TERMS AND DEFINITIONS

Academic Institutions: Higher educational institutions dedicated to education and research, which grants academic degrees the students.

Academic Institution Agropreneurship Support: The tangible and intangible assistance provided by the academic institution in fostering agropreneurship business activities among students including concept development support and perceived business development support.

Agriculture: The broad field that includes efforts of farming, planting, fisheries, and downstream agro-based and agro-processing industries. In Malaysia, agriculture involves plantation and food crops, horticulture, aquaculture, livestock husbandry and all other related activities.

Agropreneurship: Entrepreneurship activities practised by individuals who own goals to create wealth by applying innovative skills within the agriculture industry.

Agropreneurship Education: Formal pedagogical agribusiness programmes or process of education for agropreneurial attitude and skills which involves certain personal agropreneurial qualities.

Gen Y: Young people who were born between 1977 and 2000. Also known as Millennials, Nexters or the Nexus Generation, or Echo-Boomer.

Graduate Entrepreneurship: Entrepreneurship business activities that are run and managed by graduates who have graduated from higher education institutions.

Chapter 3
Understanding Attitude towards Green IT among Professionals in IT Service SMEs in Bangladesh

P. L. Gan
Universiti Sains Malaysia, Malaysia

T. Ramayah
Universiti Sains Malaysia, Malaysia

Imran Mahmud
Daffodil International University, Bangladesh

Fatema Tuz Zuhora
Daffodil International University, Bangladesh

ABSTRACT

Bangladesh is a least developed country which ranks 131 out of 132 in the environment pollution index. Currently, small- and medium-sized enterprises (SMEs) provide 70–80 percent of job opportunities in Bangladesh. Information technology (IT) is one of the industries providing highest employment in the country. The IT professionals' expertise plays an important role in influencing the firms' decisions regarding sustainability. The objective of this chapter is to develop a theoretical model to measure attitude towards green IT usage among IT professionals in Bangladesh. The model will be grounded on self-determination theory.

INTRODUCTION

The study of attitude towards green IT practice has emerged to be a dominant and driving field in current information system research. Many researchers suggest that the green IT perspective can be a partial solution to environmental problems According to Ansari et al. (2010), from the business point of view, "Green IT is part of a fundamental change in the economy and society. It is a subset of the larger green (sustainable) business trend, which reconciles sustainable business practices with profitable business operations." Molla et al. (2011) defined green IT attitude as sentiment, norms, and values with relation to eco sustainability and role of IT. Esfahani et al. (2015) tested green IT attitude by measuring the impact of argument quality, source credibility and green IT belief. By using value-belief-norm theory,

DOI: 10.4018/978-1-5225-2165-5.ch003

Huijts et al. (2013) measured the predictive power of personal norms on pro-environment behaviour. Akman and Misra (2015) investigated on technology acceptance model to explain the attitude towards using green IT. In this research, we primarily focus on green IT attitude, which will influence end users to adopt green IT practice. On individual level, limited researchers worked on self-determination theory (SDT). The objective of this study is to derive and empirically test a theoretically grounded model of the factors leading to green IT attitude.

BACKGROUND

Burning of fossil fuel, e-waste, deforestation and land clearing for agricultural purposes, and overexploitation of definite resources are some causes behind the increase of greenhouse gases in the atmosphere. According to The *Economist* (2015) special report on climate change, the earth's atmospheric carbon dioxide concentration increased from 361 parts per million in 1995 to 399 parts per million in 2014, with drastic increase between years 2000 and 2015.

Carbon dioxide, methane, CFCs – also commonly known as greenhouse gases – trap heat and warm the earth's surface, thus being the main culprits behind rising temperatures. The earth's temperature now is 0.9 degrees warmer than it was in 1880, that is, before the Industrial Revolution. The rising concern over climate change, pollution and ozone depletion has led to various treaties and agreements among the world leaders. With the Kyoto Protocol, participating countries agreed upon reducing greenhouse gas emissions by year 2020. In addition to the Kyoto Protocol, COP21, held in Paris recently, had participating nations achieve agreement that the global temperature increase should be kept below 2 degrees or 1.5 degrees Celsius above the industrial era (UNFCC, 2015). However, researchers argued reducing carbon emission or mitigating temperature is not achievable over a short period of time (Molla et al, 2009).

On the other hand, innovations in the last century have led to cheaper, better, and faster production. Modern technology has also changed business transactions from traditional business to e-business, and the economy to an e-economy. Information technology has taken an important role, both in business and daily human life. It has made the world closer and smaller, through eliminating global boundaries and creating economic opportunities. Sadly, such opportunities came with their own flaws, like increasing demand of energy, servers, and data centres. Older equipment or e-waste ended in landfills faster than we could imagine – all in order to make way for newer and higher-efficiency equipment (Srivastava & Srivastava, 2012). Although IT is one of the culprits behind environmental issues, Ruth (2009) argued that IT can also provide solutions to address the problem of the remaining 98 per cent of the carbon emission.

The mentioned effects are explained as first-order effects and second-order effects. First-order effects are the negative effects of IT, resulting from all phases of production from cradle to grave. Second-order effects refer to the positive effects of IT on the environment (Esfahani et al, 2014; Faucheux & Nicolaï, 2011). Hence, making greener and environmental friendly IT products is termed green IT, whereas using IT to tackle environmental issues is termed IT for green.

The IT Industry in Bangladesh

Bangladesh is a least developed country (LDC), located in South Asia, with a population of 160 million (Trading Economics, 2015) that has increased 211 per cent in 50 years. The country's vast population led it to becoming a country with large labour markets. Although Bangladesh Bureau of Statistics could not provide accurate data on the number of SMEs, Asian Development Bank reported that SMEs in Bangladesh create 70-80 per cent of all job opportunities in the country. It is estimated that SMEs in Bangladesh account for 90 per cent of employment in the industrial sector (Asian Development Bank, 2013). SMEs also contribute 25 per cent to national gross domestic product (GDP) and 75 per cent to the household income (Rahman et al, 2014).

The IT industry in Bangladesh is now expanding. It has a history of a few decades and is one of the mainstream contributors to the country's income. According to 2012 data from Bangladesh Association of Software and Information Services (BASIS), the information and communications technology (ICT) industry is growing at 20 to 30 per cent annually. The ICT market size is estimated at 350 million US dollars and it has increased 17 per cent compared to that in 2008. Software and IT Enabled Service (ITES) market amount to about 250 million US dollars, which is 70 per cent of the overall IT market in Bangladesh (JICA, 2015). Based on BASIS and other data, there are 800 to 1,000 software and IT service companies, and more than 30,000 IT professionals now working in Bangladesh. Every year, there are almost 6000 IT graduates joining the IT industry. BASIS aims to create 1 million IT professionals by year 2018 (Allmedialink, 2015; BASIS, 2012). According to the report (The New Age, 2015), very few software and IT firms hired a workforce of 300 people. Most IT firms in the country operate with a workforce of 30 people or less, which lead us to conclude that most of the software and IT service providers are SMEs (The New Age, 2015).

IT creates job opportunities alongside changing the business operations. For example, IBM pursues product innovation to improve their hardware energy efficiency, and cradle-to-cradle product life cycle to minimise environmental impact. Fuji Xerox has taken sustainability into their core business. According to their 2013 sustainability report, Fuji Xerox planned to reduce 30 per cent of their carbon emission by 2020, apart from practicing cradle-to-cradle product life cycle. Firms have taken various measures to incorporate sustainability in the business values, whereas IT professionals play an important role in ensuring that the objectives are met. Molla et al (2014) in their study believes that IT professionals play a big role in environmental sustainability. IT professionals stand on the front line in influencing the organisations to practise green initiatives and transformations. They are the ones able to provide technical expertise and solutions.

Green IT in Bangladesh

According to Bangladesh Air Pollution Management Project in 2015, Bangladesh was ranked 131 among 132 countries in the current environmental pollution index. Based on World Health Organization reports, Bangladesh was ranked fourth among 91 countries for the worst urban air quality (*The Daily Star*, 2015). Despite being one of the countries with highest pollution, Bangladesh takes environmental issues seriously. Several policies have been implemented over the years to curb environmental problems. Bangladesh's Ministry of Environment and Forest (MoEF) is formed in 1989 and there are two department fell under the ministry, Bangladesh Forest Department (BFD) and Department of Environment (DoE). MOEF oversees the planning, promotion, co-ordination and the implementation of environment and forestry programmes. BFD is in charge of the reservation of the forestry while DoE is the technical wing and responsible for the implementation of the Environment Conservation Act, 1995 (MOEF, 2016). The breakdown of government policies in Bangladesh are explained in Table 1.

Table 1. Policies in Bangladesh

Year	Policy Name	Task
1970	Water Pollution Control Ordinance	Adopt measures of prevention, control, and abatement of existing or potential pollution of any waters.
1977	Environmental Pollution Control Ordinance	Extends the control on prevention and abatement of pollution to air, water or soil.
1992	National Environmental Policy (NEP)	• Maintain ecological balance and overall development via protection and improvement of the environment. • Identify and regulate environmentally degrading activities. • Environmentally sound development. • Associate with all international environmental initiatives.
1995	National Environmental Management Plan (NEMAP)	• Programmes and intervention aim at implementing NEP. • Manage scarce resources and reduce environmental degradation. • Improve natural and man-made environment. • Conserve habitats and biodiversity. • Promote sustainable development. • Improve quality indicators of human life.
1995 and 1997	Environmental Conservation Act and Rules	• Conservation, improvement of quality standards and control by mitigating pollution. • Coordinate with other agencies relevant to the objectives of the act. • Adopt safety measures and determine abatement measures that may cause environmental degradation. • Advise on environmental use, storage, transportation, import and export of hazardous material or components. • Conduct research and assist other agencies in conservation and improvement of the environment. • Investigate locations, equipment, manufacture to ensure control and mitigation of pollution. • Publish and disseminate information regarding environmental pollution. • Advise government on pollution-causing manufacturing processes and materials. • Ensure potable water quality.
1999	National Water Policy	• Protection of water quality, sanitation and potable water. • Protection of fish and fisheries. • Participation of local communities in all water sector development.
2000	The Environmental Court Act	Support the Environment Conservation Act (1995) and Environmental Conservation Rules (1997).

Despite the importance, green IT is rather new, and least focused in Bangladesh. Ansari, et al(2010) reported that the idea of environmental conservation in Bangladesh focused more on preservation of forests and extinct wildlife, though there is increased interest in green IT issues.

Recently, the government agency, banks and industries are taking initiatives for green practice within the organisation. Sobhani et al. (2012) reported only 25 per cent of banks in Bangladesh provided disclosure for environmental sustainability. Sobhani's research identified various green practices like green promotion and marketing, green office, and green finance. But in case of green information technology usage, organisations are still falling behind.

Again, small-scale businesses and local financial intermediaries can play a crucial role by joining hands with the public sector to combat climate change. But accessing financial resources remains a challenge for most SMEs, particularly in least developed countries like Bangladesh. For that purpose, the United Nations proposes that the multi-billion dollar Green Climate Fund (GCF) engage the private sector, particularly SMEs, to combat climate change risks.

THEORETICAL BACKGROUND AND RESEARCH MODEL

The concept of green IT emerged in 2007, in CIO magazines. According to Gartner (2007), green IT manifested when firms wanted to sustain the triple bottom line. Yang et al (2013) argued that being green is regarded as a moral issue in the digital age and were supported by Murugesan. Murugesan (2008) defined green IT as environmentally sound IT. Green IT is the study and practice of designing, manufacturing, using and disposing of computers, servers and related subsystems efficiently and effectively with minimal or no impact to the environment (Murugesan, 2008). Four strategies were identified - green use, green disposal, green design, and green manufacturing. Green use aims to reduce energy usage of IT devices and promote energy efficiency; green disposal aims to minimise e-waste generated by extending the usability of computer equipment; green design aims to provide greener product via product innovation; and lastly, green manufacturing strives to manufacture computer equipment with minimal and or no impact to the environment. Therefore, green IT aims to improve the environmental sustainability via product stewardship, pollution prevention and sustainable development.

Nevertheless, researchers argue about the economic viability of green IT since it is believed that adopting green IT results in longer time to break even (Ambec & Lanoie, 2008). Over the years, the conceptualisation of green IT has been different in different studies – green IT, Green IS, IT for green, green by IT and so on. Bose and Luo (2011) explained that green IT implies three main research areas: namely, energy efficiency, end of life management of IT, and IT as enabler of green governance. The terms green IT and green IS have been used interchangeably in certain studies, while other researchers clearly define and separate green IT and green IS based on the idea that IT is both a cause of environmental problems and a means to solve them. In this study, we will assume both green IT and green IS share the same objective of tackling environmental sustainability.

Many researchers tried to measure green IT by incorporating various theories like belief-action-outcome, organisational motivation theory, process virtualisation theory, theory of planned behaviour, technological-organisational-environmental framework, technology acceptance model, resource-based view, innovation diffusion theory, stakeholder theory, institutional theory, absorptive capacity theory, stakeholder theory, technology acceptance model, inter-organisational knowledge transfer view, organisational information processing theory, theory of reasoned action, resource dependency theory, and transaction cost theory (Khor et al, 2015; Lei & Ngai, 2013). Lei and Ngai (2013) also clarify that most theories have only been used once. Moreover, the applied theories examine green IT differently, focusing on organisational, individual, environmental and technology perspectives (Esfahani et al, 2014).

However, very few researchers were interested to explore motivational factors of green IT usage attitude. Therefore, we plan to investigate the impact of motivational factors and institutional factors together, to measure the attitude. As a result, this research discovers one specific research question:

Is there any impact of external motivation factors like integrated, identified, introjected and external regulations on attitude towards green IT?

Based on the above research questions, our research objectives are:

RO1: To examine the effect of integrated regulations on attitude towards green IT.
RO2: To examine the effect of identified regulations on attitude towards green IT.
RO3: To examine the introjected regulations' impact on attitude towards green IT.
RO4: To examine the impact of external regulations on attitude towards green IT.

Self-Determination Theory

Self-Determination Theory (SDT) is an approach to human motivation and personality that uses traditional empirical methods, while employing organismic metatheory that highlights the importance of humans' evolved inner resources for personality development and behavioural regulations (Ryan & Deci, 2000). Three psychological needs of autonomy, competence, and relatedness need to be continuously satisfied through life in order for an individual to experience an ongoing sense of integrity and well-being. These three needs change through a person's life and are influenced by the culture she or he resides in.

SDT categorises motivation into several types – amotivation, intrinsic motivation, and extrinsic motivation. Amotivation refers to the results of not valuing an activity, not being competent to do it, or expecting it to harvest a desired outcome. Intrinsic motivation refers to doing an activity for the inherent satisfaction of the act itself. Extrinsic motivation refers to any activity performed in order to obtain separable types of outcomes. Intrinsic motivations are autonomous motivations, while extrinsic motivations are controlled motivations. According to Gagne and Deci (2005), autonomous motivation happens when people find that the activity they are involved in is interesting, and therefore, they involve in the activity on their own volition. Controlled motivation means performing a certain activity due to pressure, or a sense of feeling compelled to engage in the actions.

Extrinsic motivation is further explained by four sub categories – external regulations, introjected regulations, identified regulations, and integrated regulations. External regulations occur when an individual performs an action in order to avoid being punished or to gain a reward. Introjected regulations imply accepting a certain regulation, but not fully accepting it as one's own. External regulations and introjected regulations are identified as controlled motivations. Identified regulations reflect a conscious valuing of a behavioural goal. Integrated regulations occur when identified regulations are fully assimilated into the self. In the case of green IT, we would like to investigate if extrinsic motivations influence the IT professionals' intention to adoption green IT.

The importance of understanding adoption of green IT by individuals is critical. Practitioners and researchers may gain a better understanding of why people use green IT and predict how motivational factors influence users' attitudes.

Integrated Regulations (IR)

Integrated regulation means identifying so much with the value of doing an activity, that it becomes a habitual part of the self. People who are positively self-motivated have more interest, excitement, and confidence, which in turn enhance their performance, persistence, creativity (Deci and Ryan, 1991). IR has some relation with intrinsic motivation in the form of self-regulation. Intrinsic motivation is characterised by interest in the activity itself, whereas integrated regulation is characterised by the activity being personally important for a valued outcome. In our case, if any IT user believes that by practicing green IT he or she is contributing to conserve nature, then attitude towards green IT will improve. Higher level of IR will lead to higher level of positive attitude towards that activity. As a result, based on the research findings of Koo and Chung (2014), the researcher proposes the following hypothesis.

H1: Integrated regulation (IR) has positive effect on attitude towards using green IT.

Identified Regulations (IDR)

Identified regulation means that a person performs an activity solely because she or he identifies the value or meaning of that behaviour, and accepts the reason why it has to be done. Pelletier et al. (1998) posit that highly self-determined motivational subtypes are expected to lead to positive psychological and behavioural consequences. IDR allows the person to feel a sense of choice or volition about behaving. This is a kind of extrinsic motivation which allows users to act for the goal of improving nature because of its usefulness, rather than finding it interesting. This behaviour is relatively self-determined because the user acts in a certain way willingly for personal reasons, rather than due to external pressure.

In case of green IT, if the IT professionals recognise the values of green IT, that person will have a positive attitude towards green IT use. Koo and Chung (2014) observed identified regulations have positive impact on attitude towards green IT. Thus this researcher hypothesises:

H2: Identified regulation (IDR) has positive effect on attitude towards using green IT.

Introjected Regulations (ITR)

Taking in, but not accepting a regulation as one's own, is the basis of introjected regulations. Introjected regulations refer to behaviour motivated by feelings of self-worth, such as guilt and ego involvement. The IS field by its very nature is reliant on information and communication technologies. IT professionals have no option but to be highly dependent on technology, regardless of the impact on environment. An instance of being regulated by introjects would be a professional who feels like a bad person because she or he does not practise green IT. According to Watson et al (2010), people have a natural tendency to practise green. If IT professionals don't feel guilt while using technologies that effect environment, then attitude towards using green IT would be lower . Based on the findings of Koo and Chung (2014), we propose:

H3: Introjected regulation (ITR) has positive effect on attitude towards using green IT.

External Regulations (ER)

External regulations represent the least self-determined form of extrinsic motivation. External regulations refer to behaving in a certain way, solely to obtain a reward or to avoid a punishment. External regulation is referred to as controlled motivation because the motivation to perform comes from outside the self, or, is less determined by the self than autonomous motivations. If an organisation has no policy, reward or punishment for the employees, there is less possibility that the organisation will receive the desired behaviour from employees. In case of green IT, external regulations often identified the motivation of getting benefit from green IT usage. It implies that if external regulations are high then attitude towards green IT would be positive. Similar evidence was found in green IT research by Koo and Chung (2014). Thus, we propose the following hypothesis:

H4: External regulation (ER) has positive impact on attitude towards using green IT.

Attitude towards Green IT Adoption (ATT)

Attitude refers to a person's assessment of certain behaviour as favourable or unfavourable. Attitudes are learned dispositions and often result from experience. Molla et al (2011) explained green IT attitude as employees' sentiment, values and norms towards climate change, eco-sustainability, and IT roles. Molla et al. (2011) added that there are two attitudes towards climate change. The first is the belief that human activities are the culprits behind alarming climate change, while the second is skeptical about the change. In addition, Esfahani et al (2015) argued that the former group has positive influence on green IT adoption due to their pro-environment behaviour, while the latter has negative influence on green IT adoption. Hence we conclude that attitude has influence on green IT adoption. In another study by Gholami et al (2013), attitude is affective characteristic of senior managers, as the senior managers play an important role in decision-making in the firms. Attitude measures the extent to which they are aware of, and interested in, green IT.

The research model is shown in Figure 1.

METHODOLOGY

Study Design

In order to empirically test our hypotheses, data were collected via field survey. Purposive sampling method was used in this study. Participants of this study are individuals working in the IT field, across several SMEs, including software development companies, hardware sales and services, internet service providers, and network solution providers. Self-administered survey questionnaires were distributed to the respondents from eight different companies. Out of 250 individuals contacted, data from 108 were collected, generating response rate of 43.2 per cent. Based on the G*power calculation method, sample collected should have been 124. However, we only managed to collect data from 108 respondents, which is close to the targeted response.

Figure 1. Research model

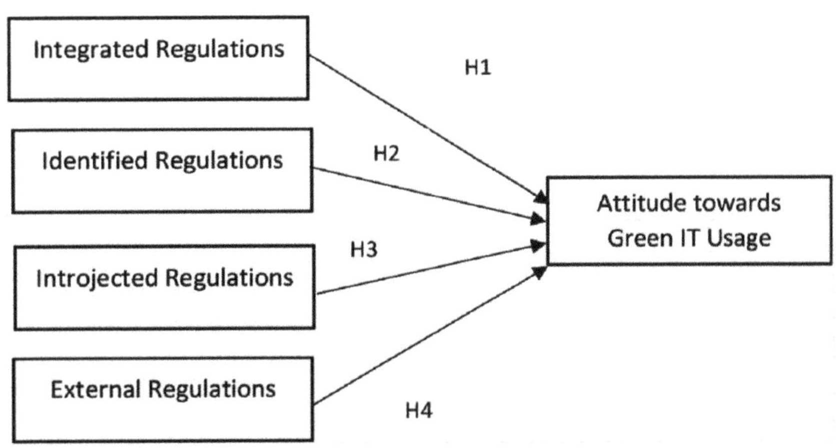

Table 2 provides the demographic information of the respondents. 65.7 per cent of respondents are between 26 and 30 years of age and 76.8 per cent are male. The survey participants represent various IT positions within their industries. 79.6 per cent of our respondents work with information technology from 5 to 8 hours.

Measures

Items of the questionnaire were adapted from valid instruments. The IT managers, who evaluated the questionnaire items, suggested necessary changes to make the questionnaire simpler and easier to understand. The survey questionnaire consists of three parts. The first part focuses on demographic information. The second part explains the basic information of green IT as many respondents might not understand about green IT usage, despite their use of green IT. The third part focuses on measurement items of the research model. All the items are adapted from the research of Koo and Chung (2014). Measurement items are given in Table 3.

Table 2. Demographic information

	Frequency	Percentage
	Gender	
Male	83	76.8
Female	25	23.2
	Age	
21-25	15	13.8
26-30	71	65.7
31-35	18	16.6
More than 35	4	3.7
	Use of Technology	
1-5 hrs	7	6.48
5 to 10 hrs	86	79.6
More than 10 hrs	15	13.8
Industry		
Software development company	2	33.3
Network solutions	1	16.6
Hardware sale and service	2	33.3
Internet service provider	1	16.6

Table 3. Items of the measurement questionnaire

Measurement Questionnaire
Integrated Regulations
Being green is part of my life
Being green has become a fundamental part of who I am
Being green has been a part of the way I have chosen to live my life
By using green technology, I take care of myself and, at the same time, I take care of my environment
Identified Regulations
Using green IT is a sensible thing to do
Using green IT is a way I have chosen to contribute to protecting the environment
Using green IT is a reasonable thing to do
Using green IT is a good idea to do
Introjected Regulation
I would regret it if I am not doing something for the environment and future generations
I would feel guilty if I did not do something for the environment and future generations
I would feel ashamed of myself if I was doing nothing to help the environment
External Regulations
This green technology device is of benefit to me
The advantages of this green technology device outweigh the disadvantages
Overall, using this green technology device is advantageous
Attitude
Using green technology is a good idea
Using green technology is a wise idea
I have a favour to the idea of using green technology
Using green technology would be pleasant

ANALYSIS AND RESULT

Analysis Technique

We adopted structural equation modelling, using partial least squares (PLS) to analyse the data. PLS has been widely used in theory testing. Of all other structural equation modelling techniques, PLS is best suited for testing a model with small sample size. (Koo and Chung, 2014; Cha, 2012; Haenlein and Kaplan, 2004). We have a small sample size, and therefore, PLS is a suitable analysis tool for the purposes of this study. We decided to use SmartPLS 3.0 to test the research model.

Measurement Model

Convergent validity is the degree to which the items that are used as indicators to a variable must cover high proportion of variance (Hair et al. 2011). According to Hair et al. (2011), factor loadings and average variance extracted (AVE) of more than 0.5 and composite reliability (CR) of 0.7 or above is deemed to be acceptable. Table 4 depicts that all loadings and AVE are above 0.5 and the composite reliability values are more than 0.7. Only IDR1 and IDR3 were removed due to poor loadings. Therefore, we can concluded that convergent validity has been established.

Next, we assessed the discriminant validity which reflects the distinction from one construct to other constructs (Hair et al. 2011). Fornell and Larcker (1981) suggested that to report the discriminant validity, the square root of the AVE should be compared with the correlation of the other constructs. Discriminant validity of the model is reported in Table 5, which shows discriminant validity is fully established in the data.

Multicollinearity is tested by calculating the variance inflation factor (VIF). Our VIF calculation is shown in Table 6.

According to Hair et al. (2011), VIF value of 5 and higher indicate a potential collinearity problem. Our study indicated VIF values of less than 5. Therefore we assume that there is no multicollinearity in our data set.

Structural Model

After analysing the AVE, reliability and validity of the data, we further analysed the structural model by using the evaluation coefficient of determination, and the significance level of each path coefficient. Focusing on the significance level of the path coefficients, our result indicated the following: Integrated regulation (IR) was found to be significantly related to attitude (ATT) towards using green IT ($\beta = 0.247$, $p < 0.01$). Similarly, identified regulation (IDR) was also found to have impact on attitude towards green IT use ($\beta = 0.457$, $p < 0.01$). External regulation (ER) also has significant positive relation with attitude

Table 4. Loadings, AVE, and composite reliability

	Loading	AVE	CR
ATT1	0.897		
ATT2	0.870	0.767	0.929
ATT3	0.872		
ATT4	0.864		
ER1	0.901		
ER2	0.828	0.751	0.900
ER3	0.868		
IDR2	0.913	0.852	0.920
IDR4	0.933		
ITR1	0.843		
ITR2	0.886	0.774	0.911
ITR3	0.910		
IR1	0.892		
IR2	0.890	0.780	0.914
IR3	0.868		

Table 5. Discriminant validity

	ATT	ER	IDR	IR	ITR
ATT	0.876				
ER	0.810	0.866			
IDR	0.847	0.809	0.923		
IR	0.789	0.710	0.764	0.883	
ITR	0.626	0.623	0.571	0.634	0.880

Table 6. Variance inflation factor of the constructs

	VIF
ER	3.317
IDR	3.663
IR	2.846
ITR	1.861

(β= 0.238, $p < 0.01$). However, introjected regulation (ITR) has positive, but not significant, relation with attitude (β= 0.051, $p < 0.01$). Thus, hypotheses H1, H2 and H4 are significant; and H3 is not supported. Path coefficients, t-values and results of hypotheses are reported in Table 7.

Blindfolding procedure was performed to measure the predictive relevance (Q^2) of the model fit. Q^2 represents a measure of how well observed values are reconstructed by the model and its parameter estimates. (Chin, 1998). Models with Q^2 greater than zero imply that the model has predictive relevance. In this case, $Q^2 = 0.558$ which indicates the model has predictive relevance. Table 8 represents the strength of effect of each construct to endogenous variable.

Importance Performance Map Analysis

The impact-performance analysis provides the variables which need to be improved in the areas of management and marketing. This kind of model measurement technique, based on index value, is for better interpretation of the model (Kirstensen et al. 2000). To improve the performance level of any specific variable, stakeholders should look at the variables with high performance and low performance.

Table 7. Hypothesis testing result

Hypothesis	Relationship	Path Coefficient	t value	Result
H1	IR -> ATT	0.247	2.640	Supported
H2	IDR -> ATT	0.457	3.871	Supported
H3	ITR -> ATT	0.051	0.506	Not Supported
H4	ER -> ATT	0.238	3.225	Supported

Table 8. Strength of effect

	Relation with	f^2	Strength
IR	ATT	0.105	Weak
IDR		0.218	Medium
ITR		0.015	No effect
ER		0.100	Weak

Cohen, 1988.
$f^2 > 0.35$, strong effect; $f^2 > 0.15$, medium effect; $f^2 > 0.02$, weak effect.

Figure 2. Final model
*$p < 0.01$***, $p > 0.05$ ns*

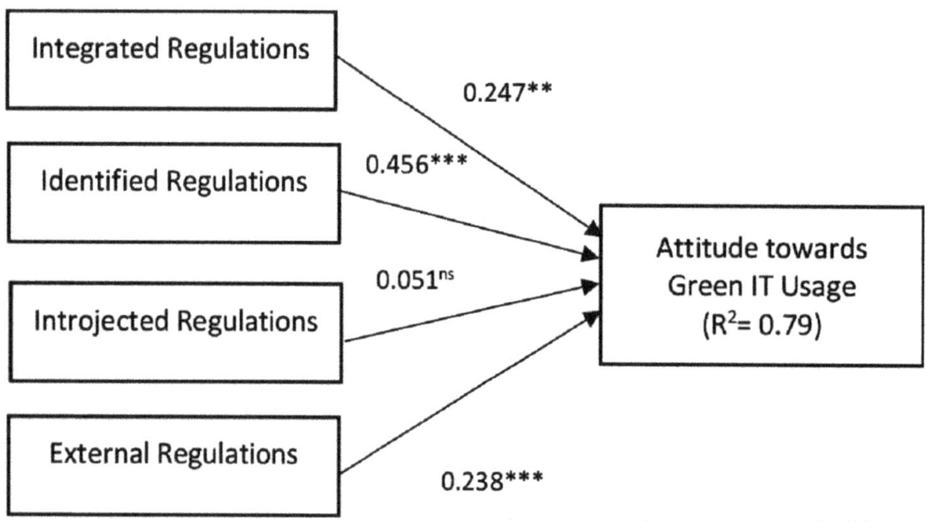

According to Slack (1994), the impact of variables on other variables can be derived from the total effects; and the calculation of these values can be derived by reformatting the scores from range 0 to 100 (Anderson and Fornell, 2000).

From Figure 3, identified regulation is highly relevant for increasing total effect on IT professionals' attitude towards green IT use. For example, in ceteris-paribus assessment of output, if the index value of the latent variable (identified regulation) increases one unit, the index value of the endogenous latent variable (attitude) should increase 0.404 points (See Table 9). The same applies as ITR has lower total effect, but IR and ER have comparatively higher performance level than other constructs, except IDR.

DISCUSSION

The purpose of our study was to test the self-determination theory (SDT) among the IT professionals of SMEs in Bangladesh. The study also examined the relationships of integrated regulations, identified regulations, introjected regulations, and external regulations, with attitude towards green IT use.

Figure 3. Importance-performance map analysis

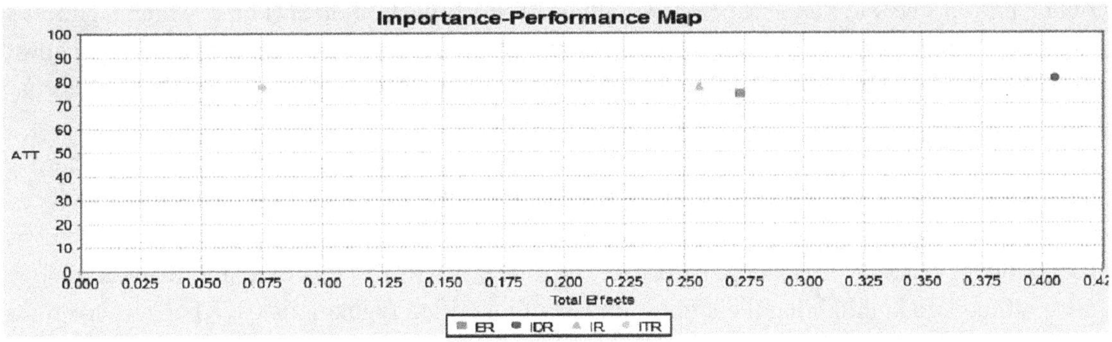

Table 9. Index value and total effects

Constructs	Index Value	Total Effect
IR	77.429	0.247
IDR	80.961	0.404
ITR	77.404	0.076
ER	74.313	0.260

The result of our study is similar to the previous green IT research of Koo and Chung (2014), where all the relationships were significant positive relations, except relation with introjected regulations. According to Ryan and Deci (2000), introjected regulations focus on the attitude of people when they perform certain acts to avoid guilt. In the context of Bangladesh, green IT is a new concept and the IT professionals are unaware of its importance. Although there are green IT practices in some cases, IT professionals are still not sure of its environmental impact. As a result, this relationship is not consistent in our study and result was not significant. The importance of using green IT, and its impact on environment, is crucial in the context of Bangladesh (Ansari et al. 2010). Since the variable identified regulations has the highest impact on attitude towards green IT usage, it implies that there is a need for further research to identify the antecedents that have highest variance and effect on identified regulations.

Overall, internal, external, identified, and introjected regulations explain 79 per cent variance on attitude towards using green IT. Results from the study also indicate that identified regulation has highest effect on attitude of IT professionals towards green IT usage.

IMPLICATIONS

This study marks two principal contributions to research and practice. The first contribution is that the paper sets out to revisit psychological behaviour from self-determination point of view. This deserves research attention. Most of the behavioural theories applied to predict behaviour rely on external influences to predict behaviour. For example, theory of planned behaviour (Azjen, 2002) depends on three types of belief to shape one's intention and actual behaviour. SDT, on the other hand, focuses on how one regulates herself or himself to behave through internalised regulations, that is, regulations that have become a part of one's life and shape one's attitude. The application of SDT in research signifies that one's motivational behaviour does not necessarily rely on surrounding influence, but rather on how one is perceived to behave in certain circumstances. Given as such, the application of SDT in this chapter provides new insights on aspects that influence human behaviour.

The second contribution is related to managers. If organisations can conduct several awareness programmes to improve users' attitude towards green IT, they could potentially maximise the likelihood of positive attitude towards green IT. An example would be a green IT photography contest among users on Facebook, or other social media platforms. These events will work as external regulations (ER) to improve attitude. In highlighting the highest impact of identified regulations (IDR) on attitude towards green IT, managers can arrange awareness programmes like green lifestyle. Green lifestyle may include practicing recycling both at work and home. Awareness programmes can motivate employees to take necessary steps willingly to practise green IT.

LIMITATIONS AND FUTURE DIRECTIONS

Despite the useful findings of this study, there are several limitations that need to be acknowledged. Firstly, due to time and resource constraints, the sample size of the study is only limited to 108 respondents. Secondly, the findings cannot be generalised in Bangladesh as the scope of this study only focused on SMEs, and more importantly, only on IT companies. Finally, this research focused only on measuring attitude, which does not represent the measurement of intention to use green IT. The researcher plans to test the theory of planned behaviour in this model in the future, by including two new variables — subjective norms and perceived behaviour control.

CONCLUSION

In this research, it was observed that self-determination theory fits to measure attitude towards green IT. More importantly, identified regulation is a very strong predictor to find out attitude towards using green IT, in the context of IT professionals in Bangladesh. The government, non-governmental organisations, and IT companies can focus to further develop identified regulations to improve attitude of IT professionals. This research, therefore, has meaningful implications for both theory and practice. It contributes to the literature on green IT projects, as well as to self-determination theory in the field of information systems.

REFERENCES

Ajzen, I. (2002). Residual effects of past on later behavior: Habituation and reasoned action perspectives. *Personality and Social Psychology Review*, *6*(2), 107–122. doi:10.1207/S15327957PSPR0602_02

Akman, I., & Mishra, A. (2015). Sector diversity in Green Information Technology practices: Technology Acceptance Model perspective. *Computers in Human Behavior*, *49*(0), 477–486. doi:10.1016/j.chb.2015.03.009

AllMediaLink. (2015). *BASIS will create 23000 IT skilled man power*. Retrieved on February 2, 2016, from https://allmedialink.com/basis-will-create-23000-it-skilled-manpower/

Ambec, S., & Lanoie, P. (2008). Does It Pay to Be Green? A Systematic Overview. *The Academy of Management Perspectives*, *22*(4), 45–62. doi:10.5465/AMP.2008.35590353

Anderson, E. W., & Fornell, C. (2000). Foundations of the American customer satisfaction index. *Total Quality Management*, *11*(7), 869–882. doi:10.1080/09544120050135425

Ansari, N. L., Ashraf, M. M., Malik, B. T., & Grunfeld, H. (2010). *Green IT awareness and practices: Results from a field study on mobile phone related e-waste in Bangladesh*. Paper presented at the Technology and Society (ISTAS), 2010 IEEE International Symposium on. doi:10.1109/ISTAS.2010.5514618

Asian Development Bank. (2013). *Asia's economic transformation: Where to, how, and how fast?* Retrived April 1, 2016, from http://www.adb.org/sites/default/files/publication/30358/ki2013.pdf

Basis. (2012). *Bangladesh software and IT service industry*. Retrieved on March 12, 2016, from http://www.basis.org.bd/resource/About_Industry.pdf

Bose, R., & Luo, X. (2011). Integrative framework for assessing firms potential to undertake Green IT initiatives via virtualization – A theoretical perspective. *The Journal of Strategic Information Systems*, *20*(1), 38–54. doi:10.1016/j.jsis.2011.01.003

Cha, H. S. (2012). Factors influencing the adoption of location-based smartphone applications: An application of the privacy calculus model. *Asia Pacific Journal of Information Systems*, *22*(4), 7–29.

Chin, W. W. (1998). The partial least squares approach to structural equation modeling. *Modern Methods for Business Research, 295*(2), 295-336.

Cohen, J. (1988). *Standard power analysis for the behavioral sciences*. Hillsdale, NJ: Erlbaum.

Deci, E. L., & Ryan, R. M. (1991). A motivational approach to self: Integration in personality. In R. Dienstbier (Ed.), *Nebraska Symposium on Motivation:* Vol. 38, *Perspectives on motivation* (pp. 237-288). Lincoln, NE: University of Nebraska Press.

Economist. (2015). Hot and Bothered. *The Economist*.

Esfahani, M. D., Azizah Abdul, R., & Nor Hidayati, Z. (2015). *Influence process for practicing green information technology: Elaboration likelihood model*. Paper presented at the Pacific Asia Conference on Information Systems.

Esfahani, M. D., Rahman, A. A., & Zakaria, N. H. (2014). The status quo and the prospect of green IT and green IS: A systematic literature review. *Journal of Soft Computing and Decision Support Systems*, *1*(1).

Faucheux, S., & Nicolaï, I. (2011). IT for green and green IT: A proposed typology of eco-innovation. *Ecological Economics*, *70*(11), 2020–2027. doi:10.1016/j.ecolecon.2011.05.019

Fornell, C., & Larcker, D. F. (1981). Evaluating structural equation models with unobservable variables and measurement error. *JMR, Journal of Marketing Research*, *18*(1), 39–50. doi:10.2307/3151312

Gagne, M., & Deci, E. L. (2005). Self determination theory and work motivation. *Journal of Organizational Behavior*, *26*(4), 331–362. doi:10.1002/job.322

Gartner. (2007). *Gartner estimates ICT industry accounts for 2 per cent of global CO2 Emissions*. Retrieved on February 2016, from http://www.gartner.com/newsroom/id/503867

Gholami, R., Sulaiman, A. B., Ramayah, T., & Molla, A. (2013). Senior managers perception on green information systems (IS) adoption and environmental performance: Results from a field survey. *Information & Management*, *50*(7), 431–438. doi:10.1016/j.im.2013.01.004

Haenlein, M., & Kaplan, A. M. (2004). A beginners guide to partial least squares analysis. *Understanding Statistics*, *3*(4), 283–297. doi:10.1207/s15328031us0304_4

Hair, J. F., Ringle, C. M., & Sarstedt, M. (2011). PLS-SEM: Indeed a silver bullet. *Journal of Marketing Theory and Practice*, *19*(2), 139–152. doi:10.2753/MTP1069-6679190202

Hock, C., Ringle, C. M., & Sarstedt, M. (2010). Management of multi-purpose stadiums: Importance and performance measurement of service interfaces. *International Journal of Services Technology and Management*, *14*(2-3), 188–207. http://newagebd.net/ doi:10.1504/IJSTM.2010.034327

Huijts, N. M. A., De Groot, J. I. M., Molin, E. J. E., & Van Wee, B. (2013). Intention to act towards a local hydrogen refueling facility: Moral considerations versus self-interest. *Transportation Research Part A, Policy and Practice*, *48*, 63–74. doi:10.1016/j.tra.2012.10.006

JICA. (2015). *Finding Diamond for IT industry: Information technology engineers examination in Bangladesh*. Retrieved March 23, 2016, from https://www.jica.go.jp/bangladesh/english/office/about/story_04.html

Khor, K.-S., Ramayah, T., Ahmad, N. H., Halim, H. A., & Lo, M.-C. (2015). Bridging the Gap of Green IT/IS and Sustainable Consumption. *Global Business Review*, *16*(4), 571–593. doi:10.1177/0972150915581101

Koo, C., & Chung, N. (2014). Examining the eco-technological knowledge of Smart Green IT adoption behavior: A self-determination perspective. *Technological Forecasting and Social Change*, *88*, 140–155. doi:10.1016/j.techfore.2014.06.025

Kristensen, K., Martensen, A., & Gronholdt, L. (2000). Customer satisfaction measurement at post Denmark: Results of application of the European customer satisfaction index methodology. *Total Quality Management*, *11*(7), 1007–1015. doi:10.1080/09544120050135533

Lei, C. F., & Ngai, E. W. T. (2013). *Green IT adoption: An academic review of literature*. Paper presented at the Pacific Asia Conference on Information System (PACIS).

Mines, C., & Davis, E. (2007). *Topic overview: Green IT*. Forrester Research.

Molla, A., Abareshi, A., & Cooper, V. (2014). Green IT beliefs and pro-environmental IT practices among IT professionals. *Information Technology & People*, *27*(2), 129–154. doi:10.1108/ITP-10-2012-0109

Molla., A., Cooper., V., & Pittayachawan., S. (2011). The green IT readiness(g-readiness) of organizations: An exploratory analysis of a construct and instrument. *Communication of Association of Information Systems, 29.*

Molla, A., Cooper, V. A., & Pittayachawan, S. (2009). IT and eco-sustainability: Developing and validating a green IT readiness model. *ICIS 2009 Proceedings, 141.*

Murugesan, S. (2008). Harnessing green IT: Principles and practices. *IT Professional, 10*(1), 24–33. doi:10.1109/MITP.2008.10

Pelletier, L. G., Tuson, K. M., Green-Demers, I., Noels, K., & Beaton, A. M. (1998). Why are you doing things for the environment? The motivation toward the environment scale (mtes) 1. *Journal of Applied Social Psychology, 28*(5), 437–468. doi:10.1111/j.1559-1816.1998.tb01714.x

Rahman, S. A., Amran, A., Ahmad, N. H., & Taghizadeh, S. K. (2014). GrameenPhone: Creating a Win-Win at the Base of the Pyramid in Bangladesh. *Global Business and Organizational Excellence, 33*(5), 41–53. doi:10.1002/joe.21562

Ruth, S. (2009). Green IT More Than a Three Percent Solution? *IEEE Internet Computing, 13*(4), 74–78. doi:10.1109/MIC.2009.82

Ryan, R. M., & Deci, E. L. (2000). Self-determination theory and the facilitation of intrinsic motivation, social development, and well-being. *The American Psychologist, 55*(1), 68–78. doi:10.1037/0003-066X.55.1.68 PMID:11392867

Slack, N. (1994). The importance-performance matrix as a determinant of improvement priority. *International Journal of Operations & Production Management, 14*(5), 59–75. doi:10.1108/01443579410056803

Sobhani, F. A., Amran, A., & Zainuddin, Y. (2012). Sustainability disclosure in annual reports and websites: A study of the banking industry in Bangladesh. *Journal of Cleaner Production, 23*(1), 75–85. doi:10.1016/j.jclepro.2011.09.023

Srivastava, S., & Srivastava, R. (2012). Adoption of green information technology (GIT) in India-A current scenario. *Journal of Information and Operations Management, 3*(1), 61–63.

The Daily Star. (2015). *Deteriorating air quality in Bangladesh.* Retrieved on March 12, 2016, from http://www.thedailystar.net/editorial/deteriorating-air-quality-bangladesh-197032

The New Age. (2015). *Not so digital after all.* Retrieved on March 2, 2016, from http://newagebd.net/38216/not-so-digital-after-all/#sthash.03ORQNWR.dpuf

Trading Economics. (2015). *Bangladesh Population.* Retrieved April 4, 2016, from http://www.tradingeconomics.com/bangladesh/population

UNFCC. (2015). *195 Nations set path to keep temperature rise well below 2 degrees Celsius.* Retrieved October 9, 2016, from http://newsroom.unfccc.int/unfccc-newsroom/finale-cop21/

Watson, R. T., Boudreau, M.-C., & Chen, A. J. (2010). Information systems and environmentally sustainable development: Energy informatics and new directions for the is community. *Management Information Systems Quarterly, 34*(1), 23–38.

Yang, X., Li, Y., & Tan, C.-H. (2013). *Drivers for green IT in organizations: Multiple case studies in China and Singapore.* Paper presented at the Pacific Asia Conference on Information Systems (PACIS).

KEY TERMS AND DEFINITIONS

External Regulations: Rules or behaviour being practiced in order to avoid punishment or to gain rewards.

Green IT: The practices of using computers and IT resources in environment-friendly manner.

Identified Regulations: Rules or behaviour that a person practices because of the value of such rules and behavior.

Integrated Regulations: Rules or behaviour being accepted as part of a person's life and routine.

Introjected Regulations: Rules or behaviour being practiced, but not being fully accepted.

Self Determination Theory: Theory that studies individual motivation and behaviour.

Chapter 4
The Impediments to Entrepreneurial Ventures among the Bottom of Pyramid Community in Northern Malaysia

Hasliza Abdul Halim
Universiti Sains Malaysia, Malaysia

Haniruzila Hanifah
Universiti Sains Malaysia, Malaysia

Noor Hazlina Ahmad
Universiti Sains Malaysia, Malaysia

T. Ramayah
Universiti Sains Malaysia, Malaysia

ABSTRACT

There is a continuing debate among scholars concerning the existence of a fortune at the bottom of pyramid (BOP). While some scholars argue that there is a profitable market at the pyramid base, others argue that targeting poor people as customers could lead to unethical business practices. With the aid of preliminary study, this paper explains that there is a fortune to be made at the BOP if the community is treated as the entrepreneurs than as mere consumers. Nevertheless, for them to develop their own venture in order to reduce poverty is not an easy task due to various hindrances. Therefore, this paper provides insights into the under-researched area of comprehending the impediments that triggered the BOP community readiness to venture into business development. Converting the BOP into active entrepreneurs has become the agenda of the Malaysian government to eradicate the poverty by the year 2020 and thus this paper is expected to provide preliminary findings of the barriers that prohibit them to become entrepreneurs. A series of interview was conducted with a sample of ten BOP communities from Northern Region in Malaysia. In-depth, one-to-one interviews were conducted among them to probe into their outlook on this matter. The findings highlighted on the key factors that hamper the BOP community to create new ventures, new insights and experiences towards entrepreneurship. In sum, this study generates agenda for researchers to reach more conclusive evidence about the concept of entrepreneurship among the BOP community in Malaysia.

DOI: 10.4018/978-1-5225-2165-5.ch004

INTRODUCTION

Many emerging countries such as China, India, Malaysia, Bangladesh, Indonesia, and other economies have moved forward very fast in terms of economies and often mentioned as 'heavyweights', or 'rising powers' (e.g. Bremmer, 2010; Sinkovics, et al. 2014). These countries become the central of attention for politicians, business practitioners and researchers alike, is due to their fast growing economy. Unexpectedly perhaps, these are the countries in which the majority of people in the so-called bottom or base of the pyramid (BOP) are struggling to work and live. This is quite intriguing and previous literature in entrepreneurship continually seeks to enhance understanding on how working with the BOP can generate fortune for both BOP ventures and their partners such as producers and sub-contractors (London, et al. 2010; Sinkovics, et al. 2014) particularly in the emerging countries.

The BOP community which is often located within least developed countries and the more rural and regions of developing and emerging countries are the potential market for new venture development (Prahalad & Hart, 2002). The popularity of BOP has not only spread into all developed countries but also in developing countries including Asian region. Asian countries, despite their impressive growth, have a huge population of poor people who lie at the bottom of the economic pyramid. The BOP comprises of three broad segments based on the income levels (Rangan et al. 2011), labelled as low income, subsistence and extreme poor. The top segment has received most academic attention due to their relative buying power compared to the other two segments that fight for survival. The BOP includes around four billion low-income people in which the majority of world's population, who survive on incomes below US$3000 per year in local purchasing power, or approximately US$8 per person per day (WEF, 2009). The income per day in Brazil is less than US$3.35, US$2.11 in China and US$1.56 in India. According WRI (2007), Asia countries has by far the largest BOP market in which 2.86 billion people with a total estimated income of US$3.47 trillion. In this respect, BOP community represents 83% of the region's population. According to initial assertion of BOP 1.0, large organisation would earn profit by providing goods and services to this community (Prahalad & Hart, 2002). Poor people are regarded as the potential opportunity to expand the market for profit oriented organisations. Nevertheless, many researchers criticize that by considering the BOP segment as the consumers particularly in developing countries is actually lead to exploitation of the poor (Ansari et al. 2012; Karnani, 2007; Rahman, Amran, Ahmad & Taghizadeh, 2016). In line with that, proposition of BOP 2.0 was proposed to create income opportunities for people who are at the pyramid base (London & Hart, 2004). In this respect, the BOP community should be encouraged and exposed to become active participant in the socio-economic development by providing more opportunities towards the practices of business venture development. Researchers have posited that the entrepreneurial opportunities for BOP community are an endeavour for inclusive growth, which improves the poverty situation (Hall et al., 2012; London & Anupindi, 2012; Azmat & Samaratunge, 2013).

From the context of Malaysia, enhancing the fortune at BOP is a key principle in the national socio-economic development agenda, to ensure all citizens enjoy the fruits of growth and development regardless of gender, ethnicity, socio-economic status and geographic location. The importance of balanced growth by providing access to education and skills training, infrastructure, and employment opportunities to boost outcomes for all segments of society, in particular the low-income group has long become the main agenda for Malaysia's economy. The emphasis has been put on ensuring more equitable access to economic growth opportunities while increasing wellbeing and quality of life across all segments (Eleventh Malaysia Plan, 2016-2020). The provision of rural basic infrastructure combined with entrepreneur development activities has enabled people in rural and remote areas to increase their participation in socio-economic development (Azmat & Samaratunge, 2013).

Moving forward, the Malaysian government embarked on several initiatives as efforts to provide supportive and conducive business environment for BOP community to start their own venture. One of the initiatives is Rural Economy Funding Scheme (SPED). The SPED is special funding schemes for BOP community to obtain capital for purchasing or procuring raw materials, and also to upgrade their business premises. By having this, the community is expected to become dynamic, competitive and resilient entrepreneurs. In addition, Rural Transformation Centre (RTC) is also one of entrepreneurial initiatives for BOP community or rural entrepreneurs. RTC is a site to implement integrated initiatives, which has been introduced by the government under the National Blue Ocean Strategy 4 (NBOS4). These initiatives have been executed in RTC and within 100km radius of RTC. The main aim of RTC is to reduce the extreme hard-core poor household to zero and also to halve the number of the BOP community. In this manner, RTC is to optimize the potential of rural areas as the generator and growth of new economy. Malaysian Government realized that by doing this, poverty eradication which has become the main agenda in Malaysia will be reduced. In fact, Malaysia has embarked on many poverty eradication programmes and evidenced by the sharp decline in the incidence of poverty from 52.4% in 1970 to 12.4% in 1992 and further decreased to 3.8% in 2009 (Tenth Malaysia Plan, 2011). On top of that, the government has put a lot of effort by investing in asset ownership and entrepreneurship programs such as cooperative-based community, enterprises through incentives on funding and facilities, and leadership and management programmes. Partnerships with large organisations will be initiated to provide more business opportunities for BOP. In fact, Entrepreneur development organisations (EDOs) such as SME Corporation Malaysia (SME Corp), SME Bank, and MTDC will continue to provide entrepreneurial training relevant to market needs (Eleventh Malaysia Plan, 2016).

PROBLEM STATEMENT

Although Malaysia has done remarkably well, there are challenges to serve this segment. They need specific interventions to increase attention and readiness in order to eliminate persistent inequalities between rich and poor, between those living in rural, remote areas or urban slums and better-off urban populations (Muhamed & Haron, 2011). The BOP community has been facing great significant problems and constraints for several years despite of government entrepreneurial initiatives to prepare them to start their own venture. In fact, the extent to which entrepreneurship improves the welfare of the BOP community remains unclear (Rahman, Amran, Ahmad & Taghizadeh, 2016). This indicates that the BOP communities are still struggling to develop their own ventures. Concurrently, many previous researches focus mainly on serving to the BOP community (London & Hart, 2011; Azmat & Samaratunge, 2013), while research on BOP as the significant sources for entrepreneurial activities are not well understood and this subject is limited within the entrepreneurship literature. Therefore, in order to gain a better insight into how business model can build a fortune among BOP community, it is very imperative to grasp the elements that hamper the BOP community to embark on new business development. In this respect, it is important to obtain fresh views on the concept of BOP community and what are the major factors for not venturing into business activities. This study embarks on the preliminary interviews with the selected BOP community in the rural areas around Northern Malaysia. This raises the following research questions that seek to explore in this paper: (1) in the context of BOP, what is their motivation and preparation to start own business? (2) in the context of BOP, what are the internal and external challenges that prohibit them to start their own entrepreneurial ventures?

LITERATURE REVIEW

As outlined in the introduction, this paper sets out to investigate the factors that hinder the BOP community to start their own entrepreneurial venture. For this reason, it is important to give a short overview of the debate on BOP entrepreneurs and factors impacting them to create their own business activities. The terms 'bottom of the pyramid" also known as the base of pyramid; refer to the largest and poorest socio-economic group in the economic chain (Pervez et al. 2013). The term was first introduced by Prahalad & Hart (2002) as the term in business strategy and subsequently this term has been used in strategic management (Munir et al., 2010) and marketing (Ireland, 2008). Prahalad & Hart (2002) argue that the BOP presents a huge opportunity for businesses, as there is a possibility of converting the BOP market into profitable business venture. Since this untapped market represents two-third of the world population, it would become multitrillion dollar industry. Nevertheless, Karnani (2007) postulates poor people as producers rather than consumers and London & Hart (2011) have suggested that creating fortune with BOP will benefit the development of the BOP community and may tackle the problem of poverty among them.

The BOP Entrepreneurs

As mentioned before, Karnani (2007) believes that it is a misapprehension that there are opportunities at the BOP to generate fortune for large organisations. This is because organisations should provide support in the creation of entrepreneurial businesses at the BOP community (Webb et al. 2010). Apparently, if people stop thinking of the poor or BOP community as a burden and start recognising them as resilient and creative entrepreneurs, a whole new world of opportunity will open up. In this manner, large organisations could transfer resources and knowledge to the BOP community, which facilitates business start-up success (Karnani, 2007; Rahman, Amran, Ahmad & Taghizadeh, 2015). On the other hand, serving the BOP as the consumers will require innovations in technology, products and services, and business model. Therefore, with the concept of BOP 2.0, market development at the BOP should be supported as it has the potential to create millions of new entrepreneurs at the grass roots level – from women working as distributors and entrepreneurs to village-level micro enterprises. These micro enterprises will be an integral part of the growth of the economy in the country (Prahalad and Hart, 1999; Jyoti et al. 2011). The opportunities at the BOP cannot be unlocked if large, medium and small organisations, government, external agencies and the BOP community themselves do work together with a shared agenda. Entrepreneurship on a massive scale is the key. In this scenario, the BOP community must also be willing to experiment, learn and change so that they could embark on their own business ventures (Jyoti et al. 2011; Anderson & Billou, 2007; Rahman et al. 2016).

Factors Affecting the BOP Community to Become Entrepreneurs

The studies on serving the world's poor are insurmountable (Prahalad & Hart, 1999; Simanis & Hart, 2006), but many past literatures have not analysed the potential of the BOP community to become resourceful entrepreneurs. Although, the concept of BOP 2.0 encourages the BOP community to become entrepreneurs, research has posed many challenges in increasing the entrepreneurial spirit among them. Apparently, past studies have indicated that poor infrastructure, corruption, non-existence distribution channel, lack of education and knowledge, lack of robust and enforceable legal framework, religious or racial conflicts and many other reasons are among the factors that hamper the BOP community to become entrepreneurs. The resources, skills and knowledge, which create entrepreneurship business success and support from large companies or government are still ambiguous. Simanis & Hart (2006) posit that enterprise-driven approach to poverty alleviation is important because it has empowered over 30,000 income-poor people to start or expand their own income-generating business on their own terms. Nevertheless, this approach may pose a daunting set of challenges. One of the main challenges is that the BOP community is not ready or prepared to run their own enterprises. Relative to wealthy and average consumer markets, BOP markets are characterized by a completely different set of geographic, structural (e.g. absence of roads, telecommunications network), institutional and cultural or life aspirations factors. With this in mind, there are a number of factors that are assumed to have an impact on encouraging them to become entrepreneurs.

Basically the potential constraints and barriers to the change readiness of the BOP to become entrepreneurs are elaborated from the internal and external factors. The internal factors include various forms of experience, superior networks and a stronger financial position (Hindle & Rushworth, 2002). Some of the theorized problems working against BOP community lower education levels, knowledge in entrepreneurship and the self-efficacy in which the BOP operates in their community. A final factor is the point of the attitude of the BOP towards the idea of creating the business venture. The cumulative body of knowledge, skill, practice and learning that is acquired over an extended period of time are said to be the most important resource that most entrepreneurs would possess. As argued by Joes-Evans (1996), one factor portrayed as having impact on entrepreneurial success is technical knowledge. Prior industry experience presents dual possibilities: on the one hand, prior experience of a market or industry assists in identifying potential gaps in the current business offerings; at the same time, such knowledge may blind the entrepreneur to other fresh perspectives or opportunities. Finally, extensive management experience may also be a useful asset, since it allows the mature entrepreneur to avoid many of the mistakes made by people unfamiliar with the task of organizing and managing a new or growing firm (Weber & Schaper, 2003; Simanis & Milstein, 2012).

Personal networks are another important asset. Formal and informal networks often help the process of new venture (Birley, 1985). Debruin & Mclaren (2002) have suggested that entrepreneurs usually gather a network of useful contacts during their professional lives. These personal contacts reduce the need for excessive promotion activities and help give rise to a ready-made customer base when launching a business (Curran et al. 1993). Baucus and Human (1994) also provide evidence of the impact of strong networks in assisting the start-up process, and suggests that such personal links can help older entrepreneurs gain both finance and marketing support. Many entrepreneurs discover that adequate capital to support venture formation and growth is a key contingency in the success of entrepreneurs at any age (Lussier & Pfeifer, 2001; Blanchflower & Oswald, 1998). In the context of BOP community lack of entrepreneurial capital may hinder them from running their own ventures (Simanis and Milstein, 2012).

External factors may provide pertinent elements that hinder the BOP community of venturing into their own business. Market accessibility in terms of distribution systems and communications provide barriers for the BOP community. Existing distribution systems mostly cater to urban areas and seldom to the rural poor (Baghai et al. 1996). The BOP community feels that lack access to market may hinder them to market and promote their products. Effective distribution systems facilitate the flow of products and services in the market and also build the competitiveness in the BOP markets. Harnessing local capabilities at the base of pyramid can help to link the poor to the rest of the world and generate the necessary income to become active participants in the market economy (Prahalad & Hart, 1999; Yaghoubi & Ahmadi, 2010). Communication links is important to inform the BOP community on learning and generate innovative new ways of becoming economic players and the communication links have altered the way BOP community works and how it is connected to the rest of the country (Pitroda, 1993). On top of market accessibility, the community support and encouragement for the BOP entrepreneurs in dealing with obstacles in the new venture creation supports the climate or the environment of BOP community (Plested et al. 2006).

A factor that will exert an impact upon the BOP community tendencies is availability of resources namely financial assistance, infrastructure and time. In order for this segment to encourage them to embark on enterprise-driven approach, creating commercial infrastructure tailored to the needs of BOP community must be seen as an investment (Yaghoubi & Ahmadi, 2010). Additionally, the financial assistance and commercial credit is frequently unavailable to the BOP community. Even if it was possible to access a bank, without collateral, it is hard to get credit from the banks and venture capitalists (Prahalad & Hart, 1999). Furthermore, support mechanisms in terms training and development, advisory support, mentoring and leadership may foster creativity, imagination, tolerance for ambiguity, stamina, passion, empathy and courage as well as analytical skill, intelligence and knowledge (Andeson & Billou, 2007). If a society is supportive of independent entrepreneurial endeavour as part of encouraging the BOP community to commence their own companies then more individuals are likely to start or run their own business than would otherwise be the case. Finally, it has become clear that the interventions of government and multinational companies must be put together. It is very critical for NGOs, MNCs, local and state government be involved in the development process of encouraging the BOP community embrace the concept of intrapreneurship (United Nations, 2004).

METHODOLOGY

The present study is undertaken to delve into the concept of BOP community and what are the factors that impede them from becoming entrepreneurs. It is important to have a better description of the BOP community inclination towards entrepreneurship and to comprehend of what elements that will ensure their readiness and how they operate their small ventures to ensure its sustainability. Interview protocols were prepared to understand on the BOP's motivation to start their own business and what are the elements that hinder them from starting their own business ventures.

The data were collected from the BOP community in the Northern areas (Penang, Kedah and Perak). Since this study is at the exploratory stage, snowball sampling method was employed. Altogether, 10 potential entrepreneurs volunteered to participate in the interview, in which the initial respondents recruit future respondents from among their acquaintances. This technique is used since the population of BOP is quite difficult to spot on. Semi-structured interviews were conducted on an individual, face-to face basis. In the interviews, respondents were asked to comment on various aspects of their concerns to starting their own business venture. The characteristics of the respondents are exhibited in Table 1.

Table 1 indicates that out of 10 respondents, 60 percent of the respondents were Malay as compared to Chinese with 40 percent. In term of gender, there is an equal percentage of the male and female respondents. Majority of the respondents received education at only high school level (50%) followed by bachelor degree of 30 percent and diploma level with 20 percent. Forty percent of the respondents were from Balik Pulau, Penang, 30 percent from Selama, Perak, 20 percent from Serdang, Kedah and only 10 percent from Jitra, Kedah. For current occupation, all the respondents are working in various jobs. In terms of types of business that they plan to establish, equally 30 percent of them plan to embark on food & beverages and manufacturing, followed by 20 percent to do online businesses (apparels, handbags) and finally only 10 percent for each of the respondents plan to venture into apparels and security accessories business.

FINDINGS

Based on the qualitative data gathered, participants in general perceived that there are many factors that hinder them to start their own entrepreneurial activities. The examples of internal and external factors reflecting the hindrances of new venture creation among BOP are summarised in Table 2.

Table 1. Characteristics of the respondents

Participants	Gender	Race	Current Age	Education Level	Location	Current Occupation	Types of Business Ventures (Plan)
A	Male	Chinese	42	High school	Balik Pulau	Involved in other business	Security accessories
B	Male	Malay	30	High School (SPM)	Balik Pulau	Employee in the hotel	Café
C	Female	Malay	35	Bachelor Degree	Balik Pulau	Working in a restaurant	Food industry
D	Male	Malay	25	High school (SPM)	Balik Pulau	Factory worker	Café and Restaurant
E	Male	Chinese	36	High school	Jitra	Factory worker	Retailer -Apparel
F	Male	Chinese	42	High school	Serdang	Government servant	Manufacturing
G	Female	Malay	24	Diploma	Serdang	Student & part time job	Online business - apparels, handbags
H	Female	Chinese	28	Bachelor degree	Selama	Employed in a private company	Manufacturing
I	Female	Malay	36	Bachelor degree	Selama	Employed in a private company	Manufacturing
J	Female	Malay	35	Diploma	Selama	Salesperson	Online business - apparels, handbags

$M = 33.3$

Table 2. Examples of internal and external factors of BOP new venture creation

Factors	Examples
Internal	• Personal factors such as attitude, personality • Knowledge and experience • Innovativeness and creativity • Lack of social networks • Lack of financial ability • High business risk
External	• Support mechanism from government for new creation • Support from external agencies, • Infrastructure • Financial assistance from banks, venture capitalist for new start-up • Climate of the environment – economy, globalisation, competition • High costs such as supplies, raw materials

The findings of this initial study highlight the basic issues pertaining to the concept of BOP and the factors that hinder tem from venturing into their own business. This will offer valuable preliminary insights on these attention-grabbing issues.

1. **Motivation to Start Own Business:** Motivation is very crucial in order for the community to have the initiatives to create their own ventures. In fact, there are supports for the argument that the poor must possess motivations in order to move themselves out of poverty region (Si et al., 2015). The respondents were asked on their motivation to start their own business. Three of them (A,C D) claimed that motivation is the ingredient of your success towards sustaining the business. As one of them mentioned (D):

Doing business is great because you can be independent and have your freedom to manage your own business (translation).

As also stated by another young person (G):

What motivates me to start business is that I can manage my own time and possess the flexible time as compared to working people. (translation)

The other two respondents (B, J) posited that doing own business can generate more money and you need to have higher level of motivation that you are able to sustain the business. One of respondents (B) described this as:

To excel in business we need to have a high sense of enthusiasm and motivation because once you have this it will bring serve as the foundation to generate more money..... (translation).

2. **Preparation to Start Own Business:** Many BOP communities realize that venturing into new business is not an overnight job. They have to consistently and continuously seeking for new ideas, knowledge and abilities in order to find what business to be in. In this respect, many of them have

agreed that they have to make thorough preparation before venturing into any business. A remark stated by three of the respondents (B, F, H) that they need to be fully prepared in creating their own entrepreneurial ventures. Respondent H mentioned that:

I am looking at the future and I have to be prepared for the obstacles that for sure will interfere in the middle. (translation)

Moreover, as mentioned by another respondent (I):

I plan to have big business but need to be more detailed on the preparation....mentally and physically. (translation).

The respondent further mentioned that:

Business venture requires a lot of money and I have to make a solid preparation on that (translation).

3. **The Internal Challenges to Start Business:** The internal challenges cover a lot of factors such as personal factor, attitude, knowledge, experience, social networks and a stronger financial position (Hindle & Rushworth, 2002). According to one of the respondents (E) that:

To embark on new business requires a lot of effort and involved with high risk. I like to take risk because if you do not take risk, you cannot see what you will get. But, risk is just like a gambling and if you are not careful they you will fail. (translation).

However, in the words of another participants (J),

Of course risk is one of the challenges because poor business decision will bring you down but you have to plan on the calculated risks... (translation).

Another interesting comment stated by the respondent (F) in terms of internal challenges is that:

You need to have knowledge about your business especially the nature of products you are selling. Your social networks need to strong also in order to assist you during difficult time. You need to be innovative and creative in order to compete with competitors especially big companies. Thus, to acquire new knowledge, skills and abilities are the greatest challenge for me. (translation).

4. **The External Challenges to Start Business:** External factors are also providing hurdles for the BOP community to begin their own start-up. There are many factors associated that limit them from venturing their own business namely support mechanism from government and external agencies, infrastructure, financial assistance, climate of the environment and many others. Majority of the respondents agreed that they need more support from government and external agencies for start up business. This is because, in general, support mechanisms are provided to the established business. Remarks made by respondent A.

The utmost problem is in terms of support and financial assistance. We heard that government gives a lot of assistance but we don't how to get there (translation).

This is echoed by one respondent (C):

Government and banks provide assistance but the process of getting the support is very bureaucratic and demanding. We just want seed money but it seems banks do not provide help for start-up business. They just give money to established business. (translation).

Furthermore, a remark made by another respondent (I):

... the cost of starting new venture is high. I need financial assistant especially for the start up. Money is always the greatest challenge. (translation).

Moreover, another respondent (D) uttered that:

... the cost of living is very high now. To start my own business I need to have upfront money. The cost of raw material, rental, bills are cutting my throat. Of course government has a lot of programs such as mentoring and training but what matter the most is money... (translation).

The remaining respondents did mention on other external factors such as general environment that is the economy situation, infrastructure and market accessibility also limit their readiness to start their own business start-up. As mentioned by one of them (B).

Economic situation is not good. Everything is high risk.... (translation)

The findings revealed that there are many internal and external factors that actually hindered them from starting their own business. Majority of them mentioned about risk taking, innovative and knowledge as the internal factors that limit their readiness while financial assistance play as an important role for the external challenges.

DISCUSSION AND CONCLUSION

The concept of BOP has becoming an important agenda in the Malaysia Government Transformation Programme and the BOP community must be ready to prepare themselves to face the challenges and build their capacity and capability to reap the benefits of new entrepreneurial ventures. However, it seems that this issue has escaped attention of many researchers. Therefore, it is assured that good research in the area of BOP community readiness to embrace the concept of entrepreneurship will add to the existing body of entrepreneurship knowledge, business fundamental, knowledge management and business innovation. It is important to have a better description of the BOP community inclination towards entrepreneurship and to comprehend of what elements that will hamper them in operating their small ventures as well as to ensure its sustainability. Subsequently, insights obtained from this research will further enhance the internal and external elements that impede the readiness of BOP community to start their own ventures.

This paper is concluded by first discussing the findings in relation to the two questions that motivated the research. Subsequently the implications of the findings for BOP community is discussed in the issues concerning internal and external factors that prohibit the creation of new business. In this paper, the research questions are (1) in the context of BOP, what is their motivation and preparation to start their own business? (2) in the context of BOP, what are the internal and external challenges that prohibit them to start their own entrepreneurial ventures?

With respect to the first question the findings highlight two points. The first point is that motivation to prepare for a new start-up is very crucial and it appears to be a necessary precondition for BOP community to develop enthusiasm in generating their interest for entrepreneurial ventures. Therefore, dismissing the motivation to start the new business activities may prohibit the establishment of new venture creation in a BOP context. Second and more importantly, perhaps, the findings also suggest that motivation should be accompanied with the readiness and preparation to turn their dreams into reality that is the development of new business. In this respect, they have to struggle to come out with innovative and creative ideas, knowledge and thorough preparation before venturing into any business operation. In fact, they have to consistently and continuously seeking for new opportunities and prospects in order to discover the types of new creation that suit them. In regards to second question, the trigger internal impediments were personal factors such as the attitude and personality of BOP, the knowledge and experiences that are deemed important in running the business operation as well as to emerge with new business innovation that will create a fortune among BOP community. Additionally, the impediment includes the lack of social networks among the BOP community with the government agencies, business mentors and competitors. Without business mentors it would be difficult for them to scout for opportunities as well as to understand the challenges in business operations. Importantly, many of the respondents agreed that to start their own ventures they must be able to manage the risks involved. Without proper plan and execution, any wrong business decision will lead to business failure among the new start-up. Reflecting on the above arguments, it seems clear that in the BOP context the internal factors need to be understood totally in order to prepare them for the development of new venture creation. The critical point seems to be whether these constraints act as a trigger for starting a business or whether constraints shape the business after its foundation. With respect to the second question, the findings clearly suggest that in order for BOP community to start running a business, they need to have strong support from the government and external agencies. Apparently, Malaysian government has provided many initiatives to encourage them to usher new opportunities and connect with the economic development of the local communities. However, it appears that BOP community has not realised the benefits initiated by the government. Obviously, it was understood that the existing infrastructure for them to develop their business is not appealing and in fact, the financial assistance provided by banks and venture capitalist are meant for established businesses. In this respect, new venture creation may have to struggle and strive in order to operate their business in the competitive environment. Without business resilient, they are not ready to come out with new business development.

Precisely, in this study, internal and external constraints appeared as the salient feature that need to be taken into account, when the BOP community decided to embark on business initiatives. While many entrepreneurs focus only on the impediments after a business has already been created, this study suggest that prospective entrepreneurs particularly in the context of BOP community needs to understand also the existence of constraints in response to which businesses are to be created.

IMPLICATION OF THE STUDY

The discussion in the previous section connects well with the emerging recognition in the entrepreneurship literature of the constraints that hamper the creation of entrepreneurial venture among the BOP community in Northern Malaysia. It is arguable that, in the BOP context, this study provides valuable knowledge to many parties such as governments, agencies, large organisations, SMEs and non-profit organisation. Policy makers and business advisory agencies will be able to better understand this BOP community to ensure that any targeted assistance programs, training and development can be effectively conveyed to this BOP community that poverty among them could be eradicated. Larger corporation that rely heavily on the strength of the small business sector, and financiers (such as banks and venture capitalists) could also benefit from a better understanding of the peculiarities of conducting business with the BOP community. In fact, the BOP community or the small business owners themselves will benefit from a better understanding of exactly what characteristics, knowledge and skills will best equip them to undertake a venture. For future research, it is essential to understand the nature and impact of trigger constraints, particularly in relation to what set of capabilities and strategies may enable the BOP community to realise on the development of venture creation. This is perhaps the most urgent question that future research needs to explore. Contextual studies of trigger constraints and their impact on business would be of value to develop a deeper understanding of entrepreneurial ventures among BOP. Furthermore, future research may wish to further explore the business model development and adaptation in the context of BOP.

ACKNOWLEDGMENT

We would like to thank to Ministry of Higher Education for funding this research under Fundamental Research Grant Scheme- FRGS 203/PMGT/6711398.

REFERENCES

Anderson, J., & Billou, N. (2007). Serving the worlds poor: Innovation at the base of the economic pyramid. *The Journal of Business Strategy*, *28*(2), 14–21. doi:10.1108/02756660710732611

Ansari, S., Munir, K., & Gregg, T. (2012). Impact at the bottom of the pyramid: The role of social capital in capability development and community empowerment. *Journal of Management Studies*, *49*(4), 813–842. doi:10.1111/j.1467-6486.2012.01042.x

Azmat, F., & Samaratunge, R. (2013). Exploring customer loyalty at bottom of the pyramid in South Asia. *Social Responsibility Journal*, *9*(3), 379–394. doi:10.1108/SRJ-09-2011-0077

Baghai, M., Coley, S. C., White, D., Conn, C., & McLean, R. J. (1996). Staircases to growth. *The McKinsey Quarterly*, *4*, 38–61.

Baucus, D., & Human, S. E. (1994). Second career entrepreneurs: A multiple case of entrepreneurial processes and antecedent variables. *Entrepreneurship Theory & Practice*, *19*(2), 41–71.

Birley, S. (1985). The role of networks in the entrepreneurial process. *Journal of Business Venturing*, *1*(1), 107–117. doi:10.1016/0883-9026(85)90010-2

Blanchflower, D., & Oswald, A. (1998). What makes an entrepreneur? *Journal of Labor Economics*, *16*(1), 26–60. doi:10.1086/209881

Bremmer, I. (2010). The fourth wave. *Foreign Policy*, *183*, 53–54.

Curran, J., Jarvis, R., Blackburn, R. A., & Black, S. (1993). Networks and small firms: Constructs, methodological strategies and some findings. *International Small Business Journal*, *11*(2), 13–25. doi:10.1177/026624269301100202

De Bruin, A., & McLaren, E. (2002). An Exploration of Networks of the Self-Employed. In *Proceedings of the 15th Conference of the Small Enterprise Association of Australia and New Zealand.* Adelaide, South Australia: SEAANZ.

Eleventh Malaysia Plan 2016-2020. (n.d.). T*he Economic Planning Unit, Prime Minister's Department.* Kuala Lumpur: EPU Retrieved from http:www. rmk11.epu.gov.my/index.php/en/

Hall, J., Matos, M., Severino, L., Sheehan, L., & Silvestre, B. (2012). Entrepreneurship and innovation at the base of the pyramid: A recipe for inclusive growth or social exclusion? *Journal of Management Studies*, *49*(4), 785–812. doi:10.1111/j.1467-6486.2012.01044.x

Hindle, K., & Rushworth, S. (2002). *GEM Australia 2002*. Hawthorn: Swinburne University of Technology.

Ireland, J. (2008). Lessons for successful BOP marketing from Caracas slums. *Journal of Consumer Marketing*, *25*(7), 430–438. doi:10.1108/07363760810915644

Jones-Evans, D. (1996). Technical entrepreneurship, strategy and experience. *International Small Business Journal*, *14*(3), 15–39. doi:10.1177/0266242696143001

Jyoti, J., Sharma, J., & Kumari, A. (2011). Factors affecting orientation and satisfaction of women entrepreneurs in rural india. *Annals of Innovation & Entrepreneurship*, *2*(1), 1–13. doi:10.3402/aie.v2i1.5813

Karnani, A. (2007). The mirage of marketing to the bottom of the pyramid: How the private sector can help alleviate poverty. *California Management Review*, *49*(4), 90–111. doi:10.2307/41166407

London, T., Anupindi, R., & Sheth, S. (2010). Creating mutual value: Lessons learned from ventures serving base of the pyramid producers. *Journal of Business Research*, *63*(6), 582–594. doi:10.1016/j.jbusres.2009.04.025

London, T., & Hart, S. (2004). Reinventing strategies for emerging markets: Beyond the transnational model. *Journal of International Business Studies*, *35*(5), 350–370. doi:10.1057/palgrave.jibs.8400099

Lussier, R., & Pfeifer, S. (2001). A crossnational prediction model of business success. *Journal of Small Business Management*, *39*(3), 228–239. doi:10.1111/0447-2778.00021

Muhamed, K., & Haron, S. (2011). *Poverty Mapping: An effective approach in determining the poor area- Case Study of Johor.* Retrieved June 20, 2013, from http://ww.statistics.gov.my

Munir, K., Ansari, S., & Gregg, T. (2010). Beyond the hype: taking business strategy to the bottom of the pyramid. In J. Baum & J. Lampel (Eds.), *The Globalization of Strategy Research* (pp. 247–276). Bingley, UK: Emerald. doi:10.1108/S0742-3322(2010)0000027012

Pervez, T., Maritz, A., & De Waal, A. (2013). Innovation and social entrepreneurship at the bottom of the pyramid – a conceptual framework. *South African Journal of Economic and Management Science, 16*(5), 54–66.

Pitroda, S. G. (1993). Development, democracy, and the village telephone. *Harvard Business Review, 71*, 66–79.

Plested, B. A., Edwards, R. W., & Jumper-Thurman, P. (2006). *Community Readiness: A handbook for successful change*. Fort Collins, CO: Tri-Ethnic Center for Prevention Research.

Prahalad, C. K., & Hart, S. (1999). *Strategies for the bottom of the pyramid: creating sustainable development*. Unpublished Draft Paper. Retrieved June 20, 2013, from http://www.nd.edu/~kmatta/mgt648/strategies.pdf

Prahalad, C. K., & Hart, S. (2002). The fortune at the bottom of the pyramid. *Strategy Business, 26*, 54–67.

Rahman, S. A., Amran, A., Ahmad, N. H., & Taghizadeh, S. H. (2015). Supporting entrepreneurial business success at the base of pyramid through entrepreneurial competencies. *Management Decision, 53*(6), 1203–1223. doi:10.1108/MD-08-2014-0531

Rahman, S. A., Amran, A., Ahmad, N. H., & Taghizadeh, S. H. (2016). Enhancing the wellbeing of base of the pyramid entrepreneurs through business success: The role of private organizations. *Social Indicators Research, 127*(1), 195–216. doi:10.1007/s11205-015-0951-4

Rangan, V.K., Chu, M. & Petkoski, D. (2011, June). Segmenting the base of the pyramid. *Harvard Business Review*.

Si, S., Yu, X., Wu, A., Chen, S., Chen, S., & Su, Y. (2015). Entrepreneurship and poverty reduction: A case study of Yiwu, China. *Asia Pacific Journal of Management, 32*(1), 119–143. doi:10.1007/s10490-014-9395-7

Simanis, E., & Hart, S. (2006). Expanding possibilities at the base of the pyramid: innovations case discussion: kick start. *Innovations: Technology, Governance, Globalization, 1*(1), 43–51. doi:10.1162/itgg.2006.1.1.43

Simanis, E., & Milstein, M. (2012). Back to business fundamentals: Making " bottom of the pyramid" relevant to core business. *Field Actions Science Reports, 4*, 82–88.

Sinkovics, N., Sinkovics, R. R., & Yamin, M. (2014). The role of social value creation in business model formulation at the bottom of the pyramid – Implications for MNEs? *International Business Review, 23*(4), 692–707. doi:10.1016/j.ibusrev.2013.12.004

Tenth Malaysia Plan 2011-2015. (n.d.). *The Economic Planning Unit, Prime Minister's Department*. Kuala Lumpur: EPU.

United Nation Development Programme. (2004). *Unleashing Entrepreneurship: Making Business Work for the Poor*. New York: UNDP.

Webb, J. W., Kistruck, G. M., Ireland, R. D., & Ketchen, D. J. Jr. (2010). The entrepreneurship process in base of the pyramid markets: The case of multinational enterprise/nongovernment organization alliances. *Entrepreneurship Theory and Practice*, *34*(3), 555–581. doi:10.1111/j.1540-6520.2009.00349.x

Weber, P., & Schaper, M. (2003). Understanding the grey entrepreneur: A review of the literature. In *Proceedings of the Small Enterprise Association of Australia and New Zealand 16th Annual Conference*. SEAANZ.

World Economic Forum. (2009). *The Next Billions: Unleashing Business Potential in Untapped Markets*. World Economic Forum.

World Resource Institute. (2007). The Next 4 Billion: Market Size and Business Strategy at the Base of the Pyramid. World Bank.

Yaghoubi, N. M., & Ahmadi, F. (2010). Factors affecting the women entrepreneurship in industrial section. *European Journal of Soil Science*, *17*(1), 88–101.

KEY TERMS AND DEFINITIONS

Bottom-of Pyramid Community: Poor people who received income below US$3000 per person per year.

Entrepreneurship Readiness: Entrepreneurs who are ready or prepared to run their own business.

Entrepreneurial Venture: The owner of organization who are attempts to make profit from businesses.

External Challenges: Outside constraints that may affect the entrepreneurial readiness.

Internal Challenges: The constraints and barriers factors within the individual.

Northern Malaysia: The northern region is made up of the states consisting of Perlis, Kedah, Penang and Perak in Malaysia

Small and Medium Enterprises: *For Manufacturing*: Sales turnover not exceeding RM50 million OR full-time employees not exceeding 200 workers. *For Services and Other Sectors*: Sales turnover not exceeding RM20 million OR full-time employees not exceeding 75 workers.

Chapter 5
The Moderating Effect of Social Capital in Relation to Entrepreneurial Orientation and Firm Performance

Alireza Jalali
Universiti Sains Malaysia, Malaysia

Ramayah Thurasamy
Universiti Sains Malaysia, Malaysia

Mastura Jaafar
Universiti Sains Malaysia, Malaysia

ABSTRACT

The importance of entrepreneurial orientation (EO), resource-based view (RBV), network types of social capital (SC) and small and medium enterprises (SMEs) have become the main focus in the manufacturing environment. The current study investigates 1. The relationship between EO and Manufacturing SMEs performance and 2. The moderating effect of intra- and extra-industry network in EO and manufacturing SMEs performance relationship. Quantitative method was done through survey. The population of this study was industrial SMEs in Tehran and Hamedan. Proportionate stratified random sampling was employed and out of 580 questionnaires sent out, only 150 questionnaires were returned. The result implies that the dimensions of EO positively improved manufacturing SMEs performance. In addition the result shows that the high intra-industry network strongly moderates the relationship between innovativeness and growth-profit ability and also strongly moderates the relationship between risk-taking and growth-profitability. Contributions and limitations of the study are also discussed accordingly.

DOI: 10.4018/978-1-5225-2165-5.ch005

INTRODUCTION

Nowadays, there is no doubt on the significance of the SMEs for development and the economic growth of the countries. Both developed and developing countries with the proper strategy try to solve the unemployment and produce better work environment and to utilize the SMEs in order to develop the entrepreneurship, and to increase the added value and industrial export. The SMEs are more changeable in comparison with the other larger enterprises and, innovation happens more in these enterprises. They could easily adopt themselves with the changeable environments and they showed a rapid reaction to the environmental factors such as economic, social, political, technical and legal factors (Saidi Kia, 2013). Since environment factors can be considered as unforeseen factors, this study focuses on internal resources and capabilities and also their industry network in improving the performance of SMEs in Iran.

the significance of SMEs in developing countries is broadly explained in the literature through their special characteristics that involve the followings: 1) their amount is extremely large, and they are dispersed extensively throughout the village areas and therefore they may have a special "local" significance for the village economy; 2) they attract different labour; 3) mainly involve agriculturally based activities; 4) these enterprises, especially small firms, finance their operations overwhelmingly by personal savings of the owners, supplemented by gifts or loans from relatives or from local informal moneylenders, traders, input suppliers, and payments in advance from consumers; and 5) provide an avenue for the development of entrepreneurship (. China's recent quick development is also related to the arrival of many new small firms in village townships and in littoral areas, often in new industries (Ratten, 2014; Hussain, Farooq, & Akhtar, 2012).

Generating employment is an overwhelmingly important issue in Iran since 2000. According to data released by the statistical Centre of Iran, national unemployment rate rose up to 11 per cent in 2015 to 750000 people entered the labour market each year in Iran, where more than half of the population of 79 million is under 30 (Statistical Centre of Iran [SCI], 2015). Statistics show that the share of added value of SMEs in Iran is less than the large enterprises. The added value of small and medium Iranian enterprises is just about 14.8% of the whole added value in the country (SCI, 2015). Table 1 shows that small and medium enterprises have the least share of value added in comparison with large Iranian enterprises between the years 2005 to 2009. The statistics proved that there is a need to pay more attention to SMEs in Iran.

Jalali, Jaafar, and Ramayah (2014) has identified that one of the most important problems in Iran which is related to the industry is internal barriers including existence of traditional structure in differ-

Table 1. The added value of enterprises in Iran according to the firm size

Large	Small and Medium	Firm Size
Value Added	**Value Added**	**Year**
385668	35094	2009
454229	40401	2010
569853	54480	2011
773439	74783	2012
1081186	82673	2013

Source: Institute for Trade Study and Research, 2015.

ent aspects of management, human power and machinery, inexperienced managers and employees and non-personal abilities of managers and owners such as entrepreneurial abilities and orientation. Another problem which is related to the Iranian industry is the inaccessibility to several kinds of information such as marketing data, information about SMEs technology and financial situation to help investors choose healthy work for investment, scientific and technical information and information about raw material providers and buyers (Jalali et al., 2014). These kinds of barriers prevent from fostering strong EO among organizations. However, social capital can be used to solve this problem by providing entrepreneurs with the access to the information to increase venture performance.

Previous research has identified the access and use of networks as essential to the success of small professional service firms (Gronum, Verreynne, & Kastelle, 2012). Building on such research, this paper identifies theories of capital, particularly social capital, as appropriate in exploring the impact, which relationships, networks and reputation have on the creation and subsequent development of SMEs. Since very little research has been conducted on this topic in Iran, there is undeniably a knowledge gap in the understanding of this issue with regard to the EO.

EO is the way of how strategies can be organized; it refers to a firm's strategic orientation, capturing specific entrepreneurial aspects of decision-making styles, methods and practices (Boso, Story, and Cadogan, 2013). Although a firm's entrepreneurial processes may facilitate the pursuit of new entry opportunities that enhance its performance, adopting a strong EO is increasingly considered as necessary but insufficient for wealth creation by new ventures (Jalali et al., 2014). A better understanding of the conditions which an EO enhances a firm's performance may thus require a contingency perspective that emphasizes on the importance of fit among a firm's strategic posture and other constructs of interest (Lumpkin & Dess, 1996).

Meihami, Varmaghani, and Meihami (2014) conceptualized social capital as the expectations for action within a group or organization that affects economic goals of its members. While business owners can build up social capital amongst themselves, it is the community aspect of social capital that is important in this study. Social capital may help to create competitive advantage for a firm, through the exchange of information among members (Klyver & Schenkel, 2013).Thus identifying the conditions under which particular relationships enhance or constrain entrepreneurial behaviours and performance represents an important research agenda (Jalali et al., 2014).

Previous entrepreneurship study demonstrates that studying multivariate configurations of an EO and other significant constructs may prepare a more complete understanding of the EO- performance relationship that bivariate contingency model (Wiklund & Sheperd, 2005). According to configured research, firms that are configured with systematic theory on multiple dimensions will achieve higher performance than firms that are consistent on only two dimensions (Dess, Lumpkin, & Covin, 1998). A superior judgment of the situations under which EO reinforcement may need a contingency perspective that emphasizes the significance of fit among a firm's strategic position and other compounds of interest (Lumpkin & Dess, 1996). In addition, Jalali et al. (2014) argued that although making ties may facilitate the performance of entrepreneurial firms, not all ties do so equally.

The majority of research has been directed towards the moderating role of environmental and organizational factors (Hu & Zhang, 2012), and only a few have examined the moderating role of social capital on the relationship between EO and firm performance (Simsek, Lubatkin, & Floyd, 2003). A research gap exists in understanding how social capital operates and endows benefits to firms that are beyond their start-up phase and are embarking in international activities (Ellis, 2010). Specifically, 'the RBV's lack of specificity have raised questions as to its status as a legitimate theory, and makes it difficult to design and test empirically' (Jalali et al, 2014).

The aim of the present study is to identify the effect of EO on SMEs enterprises performance in Iran. Specifically, the study attempts to explore whether the effect of EO on a firm's performance is stronger for the firm with intra industry network and extra industry network. This chapter is organized into three sections. First, the initial research that grounds this study is introduced. Second, the major literature on EO, SC and RBV is surveyed. These factors are then examined alongside the respondent group through an analysis of the data, to allow conclusions to be drawn.

BACKGROUND AND LITERATURE REVIEW

Entrepreneurship, RBV, and SC

The resourced-based view (RBV) of the firm posits that a firm's comparative advantage devolves from its ability to exploit the strategic resources under its control (Wills-Johnson, 2008). Resources can be tangible or intangible in nature. Tangible resources include capital, access to capital and location (among others). Intangible resources consist of knowledge, skills and reputation, EO, among others ((Perrigot, López-Fernández, & Eroglu, 2013). In this sense, this theory defends that under imperfection of markets, there exists a diversity of firms and variation in the specialization degrees that provokes a limited transfer of resources which present type, magnitude and different nature (Jalali et al., 2013). The RBV suggests that differences in performance among firms may be best explained through differences in firm resources and their accumulation and usage ((Lockett, Thompson, & Morgenstern, 2009).

The role of social capital to improve entrepreneurship has been emphasized by many researches. The social capital perspective consider that networks ties can help individuals or firms to improve their knowledge and access to different types of resources which can be useful to organizations (Robb & Robinson, 2014). Hence, social capital creates the networking between individuals inside the industry and between the firms and organizations outside of the industry as well as different kinds of resources can be concluded from these networks (Meihami et al., 2014). Moreover, networks affect entrepreneurial process by refreshing other actor's information to create new opportunities for organizations (Stam, Arzlanian, & Elfring, 2014). In this manner, investors are eager to invest in organizations with strong networks to reduce the risk of investment (Podolny, 2001). The research that was done by Kim and Aldrich (2005) revealed that entrepreneurs recognized that social networks can help them to establish new firms or finding the problems with regard to existing firms

EO and Firms Performance

EO defined as the processes, structures, and behaviours of firms that are characterized by innovativeness, proactiveness, and risk taking. It is therefore a psychological construct that reflects the intentions and inclinations of the organization's key players toward entrepreneurial tasks and behaviors (Lechner & Gudmundsson, 2014). Prior Studies have found a positive relationship between EO and firm performance (FP). However, this positive relationship is often not replicated in emerging economies, which may be explained by differences in constraints faced by firms operating in different contexts (Saeed, Yousafzai, & Engelen, 2014; Tang, Tang, Marino, Zhang, & Li, 2008).

Dibrell, Craig, and Neubaum (2014) identified that the innovativeness component of an EO is important to the success of new businesses. Of the three dimensions that integrate the EO construct, innovativeness is the one that meets with the greatest degree of consensus regarding its positive relationship with company growth (Rauch, Wiklund, Lumpkin, & Frese, 2009). Thus, Moreno and Casillas (2008) state that the strategy of innovation in new products and new processes has a positive and significant influence on the firm's growth rate.

If firms have risk-taking orientation, they may seize lucrative deals. Hence, risk-taking tendencies may be positively related to success. (Jalali et al., 2014). The ability to assume a risk enables a company to take on investment projects with less foreseeable results and such projects do not necessarily have to provide a substantial improvement in profits. However, Casillas, Moreno, and Barbero (2010), argued, if the management's organizational capabilities is taken to be constant and that the risk of any business activity is a general risk affecting all firms, then it would seem logical that those firms capable of taking on higher risk projects will tend to reap a larger reward in the form of greater performance.

Top management with high levels of EO proactively seek to learn about potential changes in their environments so as to take calculated risks on opportunities that arise from new technologies, new markets, or new ways of operating (Hu & Zhang, 2012). Lechner and Gudmundsson (2014) argue that proactive companies can develop competitive advantage by first move, plan novel requests and market, and charge high prices. Thus a positive relationship between proactiveness and firm performance is evident. According to the above discussion the first hypothesis of this research is as follows:

Hypothesis 1: There is a positive relationship between EO and firm performance.

- **H1a:** There is a positive relationship between proactiveness and growth-profitability.
- **H1b:** There is a positive relationship between innovativeness and growth-profitability.
- **H1c:** There is a positive relationship between risk-taking and growth-profitability.

Dimensions of Social Capital

This study is going to examine two important dimensions of social capital as a moderator between the relationship of EO and firm performance 1) intraindustry network centrality and 2) range of extraindustry bridging ties and these two dimensions show the difference between "internal" and "external" social capital (Adler & Kwon, 2002).

The Moderating Role of Intraindustry Network Centrality

Firms that develop an intra-industry network position are known as industry controllers, which can connect to the available resource providers from inside their industry, such as suppliers, customers, and shareholders interested in the entrepreneurial activities introduced by the firms (Stuart, Hoang, & Hybels, 1999). This type of network ties as "*prisms of the market*" (Podolny, 2001) suggests that high intraindustry network shows the capability and indicates the condition of a firm as an exchange partner (Stam & Elfring, 2008). Agents are more enthusiastic to assign a firm with high network centrality access to their resources and information because they identify it as more reliable and of superior characteristics than most minor firms. Particularly, firms with powerful EO gained advantage from the industry leadership position joined with high centrality, because these ventures need to acquire resources and mobilize institutional support from a different department to successfully make profit out of their innovations

(Aldrich & Fiol, 1994). Central firms are probably the first point of contact for concerned outsiders. Just so they will have better abilities to attract valuable resources from diverse social circles.

Intra-industry network centrality is defined as a firm's situation in the complete composition of ties including a network and shows the firm's relational proximity to all other agents in the network (Stam & Elfring, 2008). According to Bueno, Arrien, and Rodriguez (2003) the agents related to firm activities in a direct and prompt fashion are customer, supplier, alliances and shareholders.

Customer

Development in information technologies has empowered enterprises to gather more and comprehensive information about their customers and also to make that information useful for their strategic business missions (Saidi kia, 2013). There are several sources for collecting customer information that consists of information gathered from business dealings and interactions with customers (Garcia-Murillo & Annabi, 2002). The information obtained may be:

- Of the customer;
- For the customer; and
- By the customer information (Park & Kim, 2003).

Of-the-customer information (about) includes personal and business dealings data (e.g. sales volumes, profitability, frequency and preference); for-the-customer information is introduces products to the customers in order for them to make more knowledgeable decisions; by-the-customer information (from) includes, e.g. response information (Salomann, Dous, Kolbe, & Brenner, 2005). More yielding utilization of information has been considered as focal for being more market-oriented (Menon & Varadarajan, 1992). Information is also recognized to play an important role in initiating and maintaining customers' relationships (Jayachandran, Sharma, Kaufman, & Raman, 2005). Furthermore, the utilization of marketing information is seen to lead to organizational learning and, eventually, to improve performance of the firm (Piercy & Evans, 2014).

Supplier

SMEs can make a profit from engaging in expanding relationships with suppliers through intense interplay, personal visits, frequent communication and insights into the workings of foreign markets (Sinha, Akoorie, Ding, & Wu, 2011). As Martin, Mitchell, and Swaminathan (1995) pointed out, strategy theorists once tended to view suppliers and buyers primarily as antagonists seeking to appropriate the profits of existing business activities in an industry chain. Gomes-Casseres (1997) further argued that growing collaboration among firms generated new forms of rivalry. Involving suppliers in product development allows a firm to reduce its workload, to focus on the activities that take advantage of its areas of competence, and to capitalize on the supplier's competence and potential for scale economies. Nonaka and Takeuchi (2007), for example, observed that the extensive use of supplier networks had a positive effect on the speed and flexibility of product development in Japanese industries such as automobiles, copiers, cameras, and personal computers.

Alliances

Alliance ability is broadly viewed as a source of competitive advantage for firms (Schreiner, Kale, & Corsten, 2009). Alliance ability encounters the RBV theory for sustainable competitive advantage of being an asset that is precious, unique, imperfectly replaceable and imperfectly mobile (Ziggers & Henseler, 2009). Thus, there will be dissimilarity among firms, which is not a short-term experience, but rather a degree of dissimilarity that aims to be sustained over time (Peteraf, 1993). More recently the utilization of such a resource has been demonstrated to understand such a competitive advantage (Schreiner et al., 2009). Firms that have enough alliance experience often systematically and proactively scan and find partners that have the unique resources that are required to "develop" a relationship capacity or mix that complements existing competencies and provides them to hold positions of competitive advantage (Hunt, 1997).

Shareholders

Shareholders are generally classified as institutional investors and block holders. Institutional investors have plenty of amounts to invest, such as investment companies, mutual funds, brokerages, insurance companies, pension funds, investment banks and endowment funds. Block owners are persons or corporations that buy firm shares straight, not through an investment entity. While some research has shown a positive monitoring outcome for all large owners (Dahya, Lonie, & Power, 1998), the evolution of research models and conclusions indicates that there are differences in the outcome of institutional investors and large block owners and differences among the types of owners within these designations. Researchers have examined the monitoring outcome of both institutional investors and block holders in different settings. Early research studies partitioned large owners into institutional and block classifications and concluded that institutional investors were better monitors than block shareholders when measuring their effect on firm value (McConnell & Servaes, 1990) and risk taking. They also acknowledged that different types of institutional investors might have different motivations with respect to monitoring as well. According to the above discussion the second hypothesis of this study is as follows:

Hypothesis 2: High intra-industry network moderated the relationship between EO and firm performance.

- **H2a:** High intra-industry network moderated the relationship between proactiveness and firm performance.
- **H2b:** High intra-industry network moderated the relationship between innovativeness and firm performance.
- **H2c:** High intra-industry network moderated the relationship between risk-taking and firm performance.

The Moderating Role of Extra-Industry Network Bridging Ties

Extra-industry network bridging ties is defined as the extent to which a firm establishes ties outside of the central industry network to organizations from other fields (Jalali et al., 2014). Product development can benefit from cooperative relations with organizations outside the industry such as research communities. Extra-industry bridging ties are important for firms with strong EO as these ties may stimulate exposure to a diversity of approaches, perspectives, and ideas that are not well established in their industry

(Hargadon, 2002). Although firms with weak EO can depend on current industry capability regarding tried-and-true products and services, highly entrepreneurial firms improve new routines, proficiencies, and technologies and therefore need networks rich in bridging ties that "bring together new combinations of productive factors" (Boso, Story, & Cadogan, 2013).

Establishing a various set of bridging ties permits entrepreneurial ventures to generate an understanding of their innovative activities among exterior resources providers and increase their legitimacy by "piggybacking" on the validity of organizations from other industries (Starr & MacMillan, 1990). Extra-industry links with, for example, venture capitalists, educational curricula, and the media allow entrepreneurial ventures to demonstrate their proportion with current norms and practices, therewith facilitating approachability to precious resources that protect firm growth and survival (Zimmerman & Zeitz, 2002).

The outcomes of the literature show that the dimensions of social capital which are embedded in intra and extra-industry network provide the basis for all forms of organizational action, which can serve as facilitators of entrepreneurial behaviour and influence the specific form of entrepreneurship in which the company engages. Although previous research found the relationship between EO and firm performance in Iran, the moderating role of the SC theory was not considered as a crucial factor. The owners of SMEs in Iran may also sustain bridging ties to organizations outside their industry that are not available within industry boundaries. This study tries to fill this gap by examining the moderating role of bridging ties between entrepreneurial orientation and firm performance among Iranian SMEs. According to the above discussion the third hypothesis of the current study is as follows:

Hypothesis 3: High extra-industry network moderated the relationship between EO and firm performance.

- **H3a:** High extra-industry network moderated the relationship between proactiveness and firm performance.
- **H3b:** High extra-industry network moderated the relationship between innovativeness and firm performance.
- **H3c:** High extra-industry network moderated the relationship between risk-taking and firm performance.

Conceptual Framework

In relation to the explanation above, Figure 1 concludes the findings in a Conceptual framework.

RESEARCH METHODOLOGY

Research Design

This research is considered as a correlational rather than a causal study. A correlational study is a study whereby the researcher is interested in determining the important variables associated with the problem, whereas a causal study is conducted when the researcher wants to delineate the cause of one or more problems (Sekaran, 2006). This study is also conducted in order to examine the moderating effect of extra and intra- industry network on EO and SMEs performance. This cross-sectional study tested all hypotheses that are related to the research questions. This study was conducted in a non-contrived set-

Figure 1. Conceptual framework

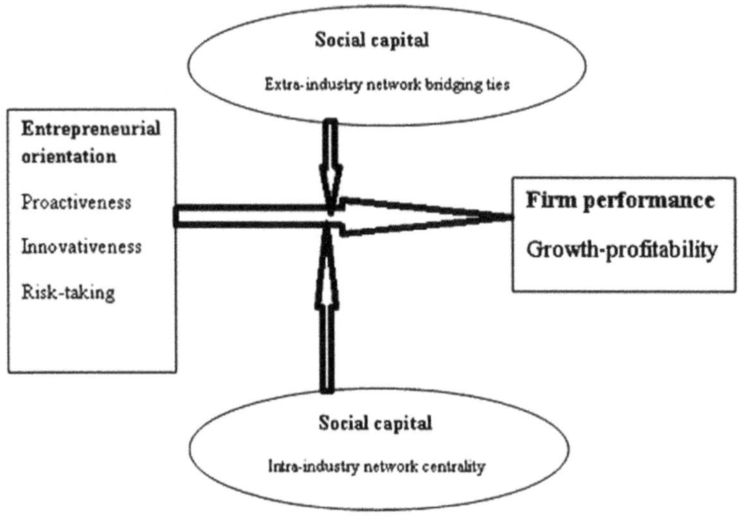

ting following Sekaran (2006, p.204) who states that:' correlational studies are always conducted in the non-contrived setting'.

Variables and Measures

Entrepreneurial Orientation

To measure dimensions of EO, we used nine –item 'EO' scale (Covin & Slevin, 1989), which has dominated research on EO. According to Kreiser,Marino, and Weaver (2002), the scale is the most commonly used instrument in operationalizing EO. For risk taking, we also add three items based on self-efficacy theory (Bandura, 1977) which measures an individual's belief that he or she is capable of mobilizing "the motivation, cognitive resources, and courses of action needed to exercise control over events in their lives" (Wood & Bandura, 1989, p.364). Chen, Tzeng, Ou, & Chang (2007) expanded self-efficacy theory by founding entrepreneurial self-efficacy and entrepreneurial intentions. Acknowledging the entrepreneurial orientation dimensionality debate (Lumpkin & Dess, 2001), we factor-analyzed the items and found that all of them loaded above 0.70 on a single factor. To assess the validity of this measure, we examined its correlation with objective indicators of an entrepreneurial strategy. Our entrepreneurial orientation measure was significantly correlated with the average percentage of sales spent on R&D and with the number of products and services introduced to the market during the past year ahead of competitors.

Extra Industry Networks Bridging Ties

We utilized the managerial ties scale created by Peng and Luo (2000) that was recognized to be a valid and trusted indicator of the extent to which a firm's entrepreneur develops personal ties to other organizations outside the industry. We provided the entrepreneurs with a list of 14 kinds of organizations that were distilled from the professional questionnaire and were expected to be significant sources of resources and legitimacy for SMEs. Examples of organizations are industry association, health institutes, media, special training centre, political parties and financial institutes. Respondents were requested to indicate the extent to which the owner of the firm created personal relations with each type of organization (1, "very low relation" to 5, "very high relation").

Intra-Industry Network Centrality

To measure intra-industry network centrality, we also used the same method as extra-industry network that was recognized to be a valid and trusted indicator of the extent to which a firm develops ties with other agents inside the industry. This approach enhances reliability of measurement and better captures weak ties that may be forgotten in studies using free-recall designs. We provided the entrepreneurs with a list of 9 kinds of agents that were distilled from the professional questionnaire and were expected to be significant sources of resources and legitimacy for SMEs. Examples of agents inside the industry are customers, competitors, suppliers and resource providers. Respondents were requested to indicate the extent to which the firms created relations with each type of agents inside the industry (1, "very low relation" to 5, "very high relation").

Firm Performance Measure

Respondents were asked to evaluate their firm's performance using financial information. According to Davidsson (1989) Compose dimension was used to measure firm performance, namely growth- profitability. Obtaining financial performance information from firms has always been a difficult exercise. Dess and Robinson (2006) suggest that, in the absence of objective data, self-report measures could serve as appropriate and reliable alternatives. Furthermore, in cases where comparisons of cross-industry organizational performance are influenced by external economic factors, subjective evaluations may be more appropriate than objective measures (Bamberger, Bacharach, & Dyer, 1989). All performance measures of the companies are subjective, i.e., according to the perception of the respondent. According to Davidsson (1989), he suggests growth-profitability as a performance measure.

Profit was assessed by two items, one asking about return on sales and another about net profit margin. In order to remain consistent with much of the previous research on entrepreneurship, performance was defined in terms of profitability. Specifically, measures of increase in average profitability from total sales and increase in profitability in relation to the competitors' profitability for the last three years were solicited as the measures of firm profitability. Profitability is considered to be the result of the policies and decisions chosen by an organization's managers. Company profitability was measured as the percentage of profitability over 3 years (Casillas et al., 2010). The response range is from 1= 10% to 20% to 8=90% to 100%. Profitability scores were calculated and higher scores represent better profitability.

Growth focuses on the increase in sales in comparison with competitors. In this study, the researcher uses the percentage growth in total sales in the last three years (labelled "sales growth rate") and the percentage growth in profit in the last three years (labelled as "profit growth rate") (Khatri, 2000). Company growth was measured as the percentage of sales over 3 years (Casillas et al., 2010). The response range from 1= 10% to 20% to 8=90% to 100% growth scores were calculated and higher scores represent better growth. In order to get the mean of firm performance, the percentage of profitability growth and sales growth merged from 8 scales to five scales (Casillas et al., 2010).

Population, Sample Size, and Sampling Process

The population of manufacturing SMEs in Tehran and Hamedan, according to Iranian statistical year book (2016), was 1774 companies. Therefore, according to Krejcie and Morgan (1970), if the population, N, is 4000, then, the sample size will be 351. Thus, the researcher decided to distribute a total of 351 questionnaires to cater for possibilities of questionnaires not being answered or returned. However, in order to ensure an equal distribution of industrial SMEs in the manufacturing sector for this study, proportionately stratified random sampling was used and illustrated as follows.

From the total number of 1774 manufacturing SMEs, 23 subgroups were classified accordingly as in Table 2.

Table 2. Classification of manufacturing SMEs in the population

Name of Industries	Value Added	Population (Percentage)	Sample
Total	100	100	NA
Non-metallic mineral products industry	20.46	25.58	140
Food products industry	21.56	18.82	100
Fabricated metal products industry	7.03	7.20	47
Textile industry	5.46	6.60	45
Rubber and Plastic products industry	8.46	7.62	50
Machinery and equipments products	5.36	6.09	35
Chemical products	10.12	5.75	34
Production of motor vehicles and trailer	3.14	3.52	20
Manufacture of basic metals	4.58	3.51	19
Production of furniture	1.66	3.04	21
Generators and power transmission products	3.25	2.66	13
Publication and printing	0.76	1.36	12
Paper production industry	1.86	2.15	11
Leather products industry	0.76	1.31	10
Clothing products industry	1.14	0.95	6
Production other transportation vehicles	0.69	0.74	5
Wood product industry	0.35	0.70	4
Coking coal production	2.13	1.09	3
Medical instrument manufacturing	0.57	0.73	2
Television and radio products industry	0.46	0.35	1
Manufacture of office machinery and calculating	0.09	0.11	1
Recycling metallic and non-metallic scraps	0.07	0.10	1
Tobacco industry	0.02	0.01	0
Total	100	100	580

Source: SCI, 2016.

Microsoft Office Excel was used to randomly select the sample. Firstly, all the companies in statistical year book of Iran directory were numbered accordingly. For example, for the manufacturing industry in Tehran and Hamedan, there were 1774 companies. From these 3127 companies, 351 companies were selected using the command RANDBETWEEN of Microsoft Office Excel, i.e. RANDBETWEEN (1, 1774). Then, the formula or command was copied to select, for example, 351 companies for the manufacturing industry which were based on the Iranian statistical year book 2016 directory.

Statistical Analysis

For the purpose of the data analysis, several statistical tools were utilized from the statistical package for the social sciences (SPSS). The analysis was conducted in five stages. Stage 1 was to examine the overall profile of the responding firms. Descriptive statistics such as means, standard deviations and frequencies for all variables used in the study were used. In stage 2, the researcher conducted factor analysis on these items to identify the structure of the interrelationships among a large number of variables by defining underlying factors. For the next stage, the measure of sampling adequacy (MSA) for factor analysis on both the overall basis and for each individual variable are tested.

In addition Harman's single factor test conducted to address common method bias. The test is the most widely utilized in the literature (Mat Roni, 2014). If the single factor will account for more than 50% of total variance among the measures then it is concluded that a substantial amount of common method bias is present (Mat Roni, 2014).

In stage 4, correlation analysis on all the variables was conducted to examine the degree of association among the study variables. The pearson product-moment correlation coefficient reflects accurately the relationships among variables. Besides that, high multi-co linearity independent variables can also be detected from the correlation analysis. The correlation matrix was examined to show how each of the item was associated with all the other items. Inspection of the correlation matrix for values exceeding .99 should reveal that the variables are redundant (Tabachnick & Fidell, 1996). In order for the regression results to be considered valid, an examination of the degrees of multicollinearity was determined by assessing the tolerance value and its inverse- the variance inflation factor (VIF). According to Hair et al. (1998), a cut off threshold is a tolerance value of .10, which corresponds to VIF of above 10.

Multiple regression analysis is a statistical technique that can be used to analyse the relationship between a single dependent (Criterion) variable and several independent (Predictor) variables. In order to test the hypothesis, this study employed two steps of multiple regression analysis to find out how much percentage of variance in financial performance is approximately explained by the constructs of EO. Hierarchical regression analysis is utilized to test the moderating effect of intra and extra industry network on the relationship between EO and firm performance. The moderated regression is used to test the anticipated regression effects.

ANALYSIS AND RESULTS

Factor Analysis for Entrepreneurial Orientation

Table 3 shows the "Total Variance Explained". The single factor component accounts less than 50% of all variables in the model, thus the instrument is clear from important common method bias. Table 4

Table 3. Total variance explained

Component	Initial Eigenvalues			Extraction Sums of Squared Loadings		
	Total	% of Variance	Cumulative %	Total	% of Variance	Cumulative %
1	14.407	35.139	35.139	14.407	35.139	35.139
2	6.789	16.559	51.698	6.789	16.559	51.698
3	3.274	7.986	59.683	3.274	7.986	59.683
4	2.098	5.117	64.800	2.098	5.117	64.800
5	1.848	4.507	69.307	1.848	4.507	69.307
6	1.635	3.988	73.295	1.635	3.988	73.295
7	1.283	3.129	76.424	1.283	3.129	76.424
8	.980	2.390	78.815			
9	.929	2.266	81.080			
10	.812	1.981	83.062			
11	.718	1.751	84.813			
12	.599	1.461	86.274			
13	.573	1.397	87.671			
14	.551	1.343	89.014			
15	.518	1.264	90.279			
16	.482	1.175	91.454			
17	.431	1.051	92.504			
18	.351	.857	93.361			
19	.317	.773	94.134			
20	.281	.684	94.819			
21	.269	.655	95.474			
22	.238	.579	96.053			
23	.212	.518	96.571			
24	.191	.465	97.036			
25	.169	.412	97.449			
26	.157	.384	97.832			
27	.137	.333	98.165			
28	.126	.307	98.473			
29	.094	.229	98.702			
30	.089	.216	98.918			
31	.077	.187	99.105			
32	.064	.157	99.262			
33	.061	.149	99.412			
34	.053	.129	99.540			
35	.043	.106	99.646			
36	.035	.086	99.732			
37	.033	.080	99.812			
38	.024	.059	99.871			
39	.022	.054	99.925			
40	.016	.040	99.965			
41	.015	.035	100.000			

shows the factor analysis for EO. The extraction method was principal component analysis. The rotation method was Varimax with Kaiser Normalization. Three factors were retrieved to represent the EO variable. The factors are proactiveness (PC), risk taking (RC) and innovativeness (IC). RC 2 was omitted in the rotated method of factor analysis. This is because of high cross loading between two factors. The values in bold and italic represent one factor. The loading values of PC range from 0.607 to 0.937 and 0.703 to 0.911 for RC. IC is slightly higher than PC and RC. The values range from 0.725 to 0.920. The eigenvalues value and variance are also reported in Table 4. Eigenvalues value and variance for PC are 4.073 and 27.150. RC are 3.814 and 25.428 as well as IC are 3.190 and 21.264. In total, the variance is 73.84 percent.

Table 4. Results of factor analysis for entrepreneurial orientation

	Item	Factor		
		PC	RC	IC
Proactiveness (PC)				
Identify new markets according to the customer demands related to the current products or services	PC1	.607	.162	.238
Try to find new technology for finalizing the farmer's knowledge related to sales techniques and relation with other sellers or marketing of new products or services	PC2	.741	.180	.133
Takes on a very competitive oriented "beat-the-competitor" position	PC3	.700	.232	.265
Our company is very often the first company to introduce new products or services	PC4	.878	.050	.205
Our company is very often the first company to introduce new administrative systems, methods of production etc.	PC5	.937	.065	.145
Normally we react upon initiatives taken by our competitors and initiate changes upon which our competitors react.	PC6	.835	.069	.136
Risk Taking (RC)				
A strong tendency towards getting involved in high risk projects (with a chance for high yield)	RC1	.205	.911	.120
Start a business without adequate human resources	RC3	.114	.703	.023
Live with uncertainty from return on investment	RC4	-.010	.847	.022
Live in high competitive risk environment (the speed of product to be saturated in the market and endurance against competitors)	RC5	.196	.932	.103
Endurance against market risk (number of customers greeting the new products or services)	RC6	.146	.858	.075
Innovativeness (IC)				
Our company strongly emphasizes R&D	IC1	.288	.066	.878
A lot of new products or services have been introduced by our company during the last few years	IC2	.219	.055	.920
There has been small changes of the present product/services during the last few years	IC3	.149	-.018	.889
Develop creative solutions to compete with other rivals to increase market share	IC4	.221	.189	.725
Eigenvalues Value		4.073	3.814	3.190
Total Variance (73.84%)		27.150	25.428	21.264

Factor Analysis for Social Capital of the Firm

Table 5 shows the factor analysis for social capital of the firms. The extraction method was principal component analysis. The rotation method was Varimax with Kaiser Normalization. Two factors were retrieved to represent the industry network of the firms. The factors are extra-industry network bridging tie (OID) and intra-industry network centrality (AID). Items AID 2 and AID 6 have been omitted from the table. This is due to high value of cross loadings and less than zero-point-five factor loading. The values in bold and italic represent one factor. The loading values of OID range from 0.629 to 0.936 and 0.723 to 0.900 for AID. Table 5 presents the eigenvalues value and variance. Eigenvalues value and variance for OID are 10.322 and 51.609. AID values are 4.933 and 24.664. A 76.27 percent is the total variance in this variable.

Table 5. Result of factor analysis for social capital of the firms

	Items	Factor	
		OID	AID
Extra-Industry Network Bridging Tie (OID)			
Industry association	OID1	.905	.176
Health institutes	OID2	.899	.181
Political parties/ Government	OID3	.819	.128
Specialized training and education centres	OID4	.898	.150
Media (e.g. newspaper, radio, television)	OID5	.841	.167
Foreign companies	OID6	.832	.186
The incubators (e.g. companies that assist in networking, marketing, high speed internet access, access to bank loans and funds, guarantee programmes, etc.)	OID7	0.936	.183
Open source software communities (i.e. focused on improving technical transfers between companies, generating social networks for collaboration among them)/ IT company	OID8	.810	.256
Law firms	OID9	.753	.112
Financial institutions	OID10	.877	.125
Research institutions/ Universities	OID11	.629	.178
Foreign open source organisations	OID12	.887	.210
Educational associations	OID13	.883	.203
Transport Industry	OID14	.888	.181
Intra-Industry Network Centrality (AID)			
Customers	AID1	.216	.876
Material Suppliers	AID3	.228	.723
Investors	AID4	.227	.888
Business partners	AID5	.128	.900
Individual members of firm such as directors, managers and employees	AID7	.124	.899
Different departments of the organization	AID8	.133	.890
Eigenvalues Value		10.322	4.933
Total Variance (76.27%)		51.609	24.664

Factor Loadings for Firm Performance

Table 6 shows the factor loadings for firm performance measure. The extraction method was principal component analysis. Based on the analysis, one component has been successfully extracted which named as firm performance measurement. The loadings range from 0.609 (FM3) to 0.889 (FM2). The Eigenvalues is 1.934 with 64.47 percent total variance.

Reliability Analysis

The internal consistency of all the variables were tested. The results are presented in Table 7 The Cronbach's Alpha for all independent; intervening and dependent variables are above 0.70 and thus sufficiently met the requirement for further use in the analysis. This shows that all of the variables have satisfactory results. The lowest Cronbach's Alpha value was firm performance (0.712) and the highest one is organizations outside the industry (0.969). According to the results, 2 items were deleted from intraindustry network and one item from risk taking because they have the Cronbach's Alpha of less than 0.7.

Descriptive Statistics

According to Table 8, risk taking has the lowest mean (3.569) and innovativeness (4.556) has the highest mean. Risk taking has the highest standard deviation (0.891) and the standard deviation value for innovativeness (0.589) is considered the lowest value compared to other variables.

Table 6. Result of factor loadings for firm performance

		Loadings
Increase in average profitability from total sales in the last 3 years	FM1	.879
Increase in total sales in the last 3 years	FM2	.889
Increase in profitability in relation to your competitors' profitability in the last 3 years	FM3	.609
Eigenvalues Value		1.934
Total Variance		64.47%

Table 7. Reliability test

	N of Items	Items Deleted	Cronbach's Alpha
Intra-industry network centrality	8		.942
Extra-industry network bridging tie	14	2	.969
Proactiveness	6		.900
Risk taking	6	1	.915
Innovativeness	4		.908
Firm performance	3		.712

Table 8. Descriptive statistics

	Mean	Minimum	Maximum	Std. Deviation
Intra-industry network centrality	4.33	1	5	.78
Extra-industry bridging tie	3.62	1	5	.82
Proactiveness	4.53	2.5	5	.66
Risk taking	3.57	1	5	.89
Innovativeness	4.56	2.25	5	.59
Firm performance	3.92	1	5	.85

Correlation Analysis

Table 9 shows the descriptive statistics among variables. High correlation exists between intra-industry network centrality and firm performance (r=0.597; p-value < 0.01). Therefore, small correlation exists between Extra-industry network bridging tie and firm performance (r=0.263; p-value < 0.01). Indeed other variables also show medium correlation between proactiveness and firm performance (r=0.482; p-value < 0.01); risk taking and firm performance (r=0.480; p-value < 0.01); and innovativeness and firm performance (r=0.460; p-value < 0.01). Based on the analysis, the correlation among variables are still in acceptable range (less than 0.80). There is no multicolenarity issue in this study.

Regression Analysis

EO is an independent variable that has regressed on firm performance. To assess the regression model, the R^2 was discussed. EO can explain 41.7% (R^2 = .417) of variance towards firm performance. The regression result is shown in Table 10. R squared is the proportion of variation in the dependent variable explained by the regression model. The values of R squared range from 0 to 1. The regression model is significant (F= 34.777, p<0.001).

Table 10 shows the result of regression analysis between EO and firm performance. Results of the regression analysis in this study show that all the dimensions of EO have positive and significant relationships on firm performance. The proactiveness (β = .250; t-value = 3.418; p<0.001), risk taking (β

Table 9. Descriptive statistics

	PC	RC	IC	OID	AID	FM
Proactiveness (PC)	1.000					
Risk taking (RC)	.299**	1.000				
Innovativeness (IC)	.457**	.194**	1.000			
Extra-industry network bridging ties (OID)	.378**	.048	.132	1.000		
Intra-industry network centrality (AID)	.598**	.321**	.496**	.409**	1.000	
Firm performance (FM)	.482**	.480**	.460**	.263**	.597**	1.000

**P<0.01.

Table 10. Result of regression analysis between EO and firm performance

	Standardized Coefficients Beta	t	Sig.
Proactiveness	.250	3.418	.001
Risk taking	.351	5.293	.000
Innovativeness	.277	3.894	.000
R^2		.417	
Adjusted R^2		.405	
F		34.777	.000

= .351; t-value = 5.293; p<0.001), and innovativeness (β = .277; 5.1t-value = 3.894; p<0.001) have been found to be positively significant on firm performance. Thus, the hypothesis H1.a, H1.b, and H1.c were supported.

Hierarchical Regressions: Intra-Industry Network Centrality

Intra-industry network centrality has been proven to play a moderating effect on the relationship between EO and firm performance. Table 11 shows results of the moderating effect of intra-industry network centrality on relationship between EO and firm performance. This analysis consists of three models. Model 1 looks at the inclusion of the independent variable. The F value = 34.777 (p<0.001) shows that

Table 11. Results of moderating effect of intra-industry network centrality on relationship between EO and firm performance

	Model 1	Model 2	Model 3
IV			
Proactiveness (PC)	.250***	.098	.970**
Risk taking (RC)	.351***	.303***	-.419
Innovativeness (IC)	.277***	.182*	-.507
Moderator			
Intraindustry network centrality (AID)		.351***	-.141
Interaction			
PCXAID			-1.706**
RCXAID			.966*
ICXAID			1.562*
R^2	.417	.486	.535
Adjusted R^2	.405	.472	.512
R^2 Change	.296	.002	.038
F	34.777***	34.298***	23.326***
F Change	34.777	19.581	4.955

Note: *p<0.05, **p<0.01, ***p<0.001.

the model is significant. It can be said that there is a significant model on relationship between EO and firm performance. The R^2 value denotes that 41.7% of variants are explained.

Model 2 looks at the inclusion of the moderating variable, with the model being significant (F value=34.298, p<0.001), with the R^2 value denoting 48.6% of the variants are being explained. Model 3 shows the results for the interaction effect of the moderating variable (intra-industry network centrality) and the independent variable (EO) on the dependent variable (firm performance). This was done by including the interaction effects of intra-industry network centrality between EO and firm performance. The model was found to be significant (F value=23.326, p<0.001), with the R^2 value denoting that 53.5% of the variants are explained, with 51.2% being attributed to the interaction terms. Thus, intra-industry network centrality has played a moderating role on independent variable (proactiveness, risk taking & innovativeness) and dependent variable (firm performance). This interaction is followed by a graph to examine the hypothesis testing.

Overall, model 1 was able to explain 41.7% of the variance on relationship between EO and firm performance. Model 2 was able to explain 48.6% of the variance on relationship between EO and firm performance with 47.2% attributed to a moderator effect. Finally, model 3 was able to explain 53.5% of variance on relationship between EO and firm performance with 51.2% attributed to the interaction terms.

Simple Slope of the Moderating Effect: Intra-Industry Network Centrality

The plot of intra-industry network centrality and independent variable (proactiveness, risk taking & innovativeness) shows a pattern that is consistent with the dependent variable (firm performance).

Figure 2 shows that intra-industry network moderated the proactiveness strategy to firm performance relationship. The proactiveness to firm performance relationship is stronger in the case of low intra-industry network and there is no difference in the case of high intra-industry network centrality. Stronger relationship is shown clearly by the slope of the low intra-industry network centrality compared to slopes of high intra-industry network centrality. Companies with low level of intra-industry network reported significantly higher levels of proactiveness.

Figure 3 shows that intra-industry network moderated the risk-taking to firm performance relationship. The risk-taking to firm performance relationship is stronger in the case of high intra-industry network and there is no difference in the case of low intra-industry network centrality. Stronger relationship is shown clearly by the slope of the high intra-industry network centrality compared to slopes of low intra-industry network centrality. Companies with high level of intra-industry network reported significantly higher levels of risk-taking.

Figure 4 shows that intra-industry network moderated the innovativeness to firm performance relationship. The innovativeness to firm performance relationship is stronger in the case of high intra-industry network and there is no difference in the case of low intra-industry network centrality. Stronger relationship is shown clearly by the slope of the high intra-industry network centrality compared to slopes of low intra-industry network centrality. Companies with high level of intra-industry network reported significantly higher levels of innovativeness.

Hierarchical Regressions: Extra-Industry Bridging Ties

The organization outside the industry has played a moderating effect on the relationship between EO and firm performance. Table 12 shows the results of the moderating effect of extra-industry bridging ties

Figure 2.

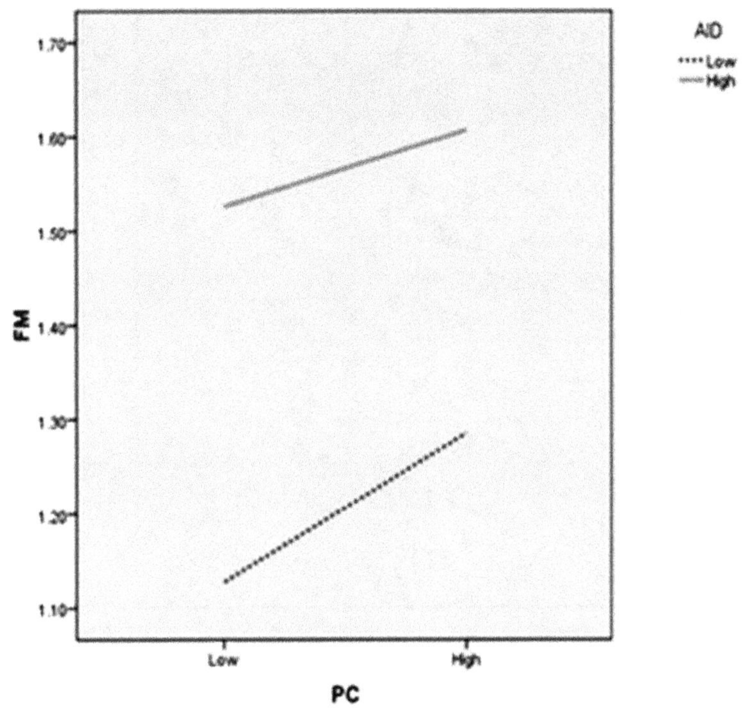

Figure 3.

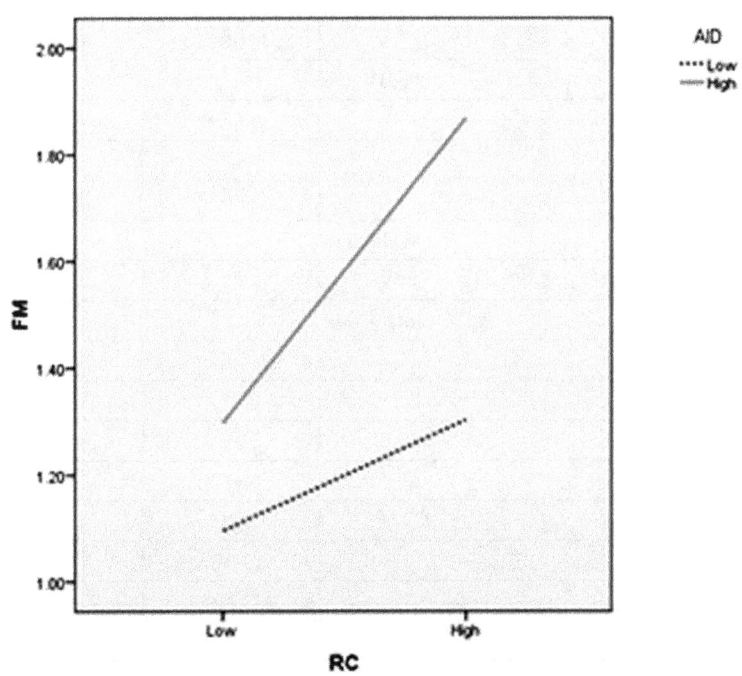

Figure 4.

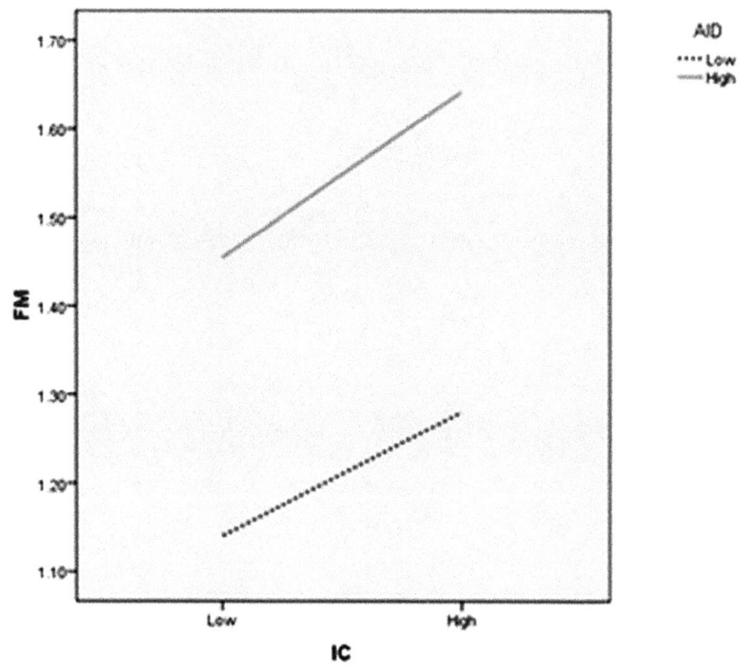

Table 12. Results of moderating effect of extra-industry bridging ties on relationship between EO and firm performance

	Model 1	Model 2	Model 3
IV			
Proactiveness (PC)	.250***	.194*	1.271*
Risk taking (RC)	.351***	.361***	.608
Innovativeness (IC)	.277***	.284***	.298
Moderator			
Extra-industry network bridging ties (OID)		.135*	2.071***
Interaction			
PCXOID			-2.339***
RCXOID			-.343
ICXOID			-.027
R^2	.417	.432	.506
Adjusted R^2	.405	.417	.482
R^2 Change	.417	.015	.074
F	34.777***	27.597***	20.770***
F Change	34.777	3.949	7.057

Note: *p<0.05, **p<0.01, ***p<0.001.

on the relationship between EO and firm performance. This analysis consists of three models. Model 1 looks at the inclusion of the independent variable. The F value = 34.777 ($p<0.001$) shows that the model is significant. It can be said that there is a significant model on the relationship between EO and firm performance. The R^2 value denotes that 41.7% of variants are explained.

Model 2 looks at the inclusion of the moderating variable, with the model being significant (F value=27.597, $p<0.001$), with the R^2 value denoting 43.2% of the variants being explained. Model 3 shows the results for the interaction effect of the moderating variable (Extra-industry network bridging ties) and the independent variable (EO) on dependent variable (firm performance). This was done by including the interaction effects of organizations outside the industry between EO and firm performance. The model was found to be significant (F value=20.770, $p<0.001$), with the R^2 value denoting that 50.6% of the variants are explained, with 48.2% being attributed to the interaction terms. Thus, extra-industry network bridging ties has played a moderating role on independent variable (proactiveness) and dependent variable (firm performance). This interaction is followed by a graph to examine the hypothesis testing.

Overall, model 1 was able to explain 41.7% of the variance on relationship between EO and firm performance. Model 2 was able to explain 43.2% of the variance on relationship between EO and firm performance with 41.7% attributed to a moderator effect. Finally, model 3 was able to explain 50.6% % of variance on relationship between EO and firm performance with 48.2% attributed to the interaction terms.

Simple Slope of the Moderating Effect: Extra-Industry Network Bridging Ties

The plot of extra-industry network bridging ties and independent variable (proactiveness) shows a pattern that is consistent with the dependent variable (firm performance).

Figure 5shows that extra-industry network bridging ties moderated the proactiveness to firm performance relationship. The proactiveness to firm performance relationship is stronger in the case of low extra-industry network bridging ties and there is no difference in the case of high extra-industry network bridging ties. The stronger relationship is shown clearly by the slope of the low extra-industry network bridging ties compared to slopes of high extra industry networks bridging ties. Companies with low level of extra-industry network bridging ties reported significantly higher levels of proactiveness.

CONCLUSION AND RECOMMENDATION

The study found support for the argument that EO has a positive and significant relationship with SMEs performance. EO is a kind of intangible resource for organizations including SMEs. Barney (1991), described resources as "*all assets, capabilities, organizational process, firm attributes, information, knowledge, etc, controlled by a firm that enables the firm to conceive of and implement strategies that improve its efficiency and effectiveness*". This statement is supported by the result of this study and it has been found that EO can affect firm performance by implementing suitable strategies for the organization. Specifically, the hierarchical regression analysis showed that risk taking, innovativeness and proactiveness are positively and significantly related to growth-profitability.

Figure 5.

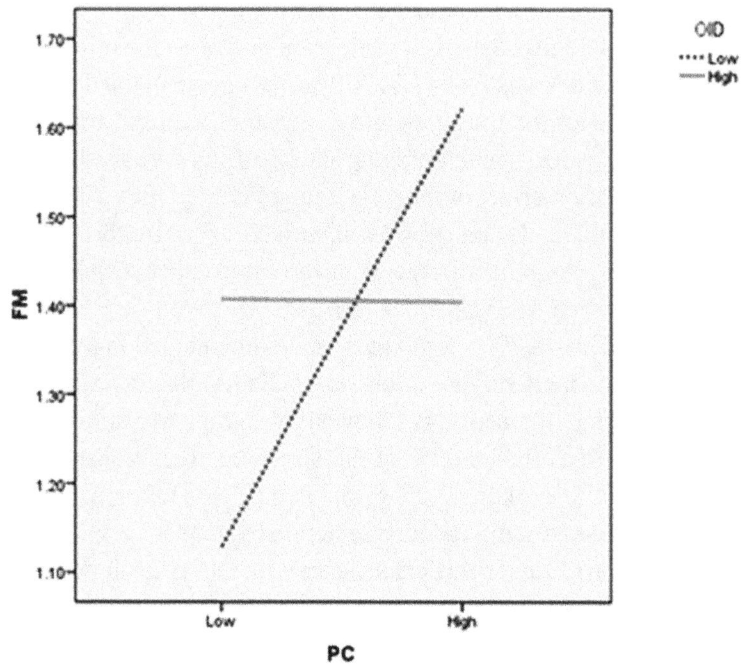

The Relationship between Risk Taking and Growth-Profitability

The present study firstly found that there is a positive and significant relationship between risk taking and growth-profitability. As Frese, Brantjes, & Hoorn (2002), found that, risk-taking tendency is positively related to success of the firm. Risk taking as a component of EO can help entrepreneurs not to be afraid of innovativeness due to producing new products or services. By risk taking, entrepreneurs can gather different kinds of resources to commit to in establishing the new products, to improve the business performance and to find international market.

The result of the study is also supported by covin and slevin (1989) finding, who found that entrepreneurial style, determines the extent to which entrepreneurs take risks to improve their business and compete proactively with other firms. As has been discussed in literature review, risk and risk management are the major interests for all companies specially SMEs. Important problems related to Iranian manufacturing sector are poor management and out-dated administrative infrastructures; the greatest portions comprise of unskilled workers and inadequate accounting and management processes. Iranian SMEs entrepreneurs should be trained in risk management principles, risk handling techniques that are available and risk control programmes which can be utilized, but attention must be taken in the application of risk management principles.

The Relationship between Innovativeness and Growth-Profitability

The result of the study shows that the innovativeness characteristic of Iranian entrepreneurs can lead to improve the firm performance in Iranian SMEs. This result is supported by previous studies that have been done by Dorenbosch, Engen, & Verhagen (2005), who found that individual innovative work behaviour has an important role in improving firm performance. Furthermore, Schumpeter and Backhaus (2003) found that one of the most important characteristic that distinguishes entrepreneurs from each other was their level of innovativeness.

In the past, many companies have been able to remain alive even with restricted amounts of innovation. They focus on the quality of the products and easily update them in order to maintain competitiveness in the market. This method is still being used to some special goods with long lifecycles. Nowadays, according to some elements such as globalization and outsourcing, there is an additional pressure to advance the efficiency and effectiveness of firms. Iranian manufacturing SMEs need more than good products to survive as they share the added value of equal to 30339.5 milliard Rial all over the country. They require innovative processes and entrepreneurs that can decrease costs and advance productivity.

To improve the level of innovation in the business, firstly, Iranian SMEs need to recognize where they stand. They should understand their strengths and weaknesses and know about the impact that they are able to gain. Secondly, Iranian SMEs need to recognize the potential within their team for innovation; they require ensuring that they have creative human resources, well-informed and motivated to improve new ideas.

The Relationship between Proactiveness and Growth-Profitability

Furthermore, the present study found that there is a positive and significant relationship between proactiveness and growth-profitability. Also according to the literature Lumpkin, and Dess (1996) conceptualize proactiveness as a pioneer posture of anticipating and acting on future consumer wants and new needs, thereby developing a first mover advantage. By being the first to enter a new market, the Iranian manufacturing SMEs gain an advantage over its actual and potential competitors. This is true whether the Iranian manufacturing SMEs is seeking to improve novel geographical or demographic markets or segments for existing products, or whether it is seeking to inset novel products to its present market segments. Due to the huge number of manufacturing SMEs in Iran, if the business is the first to go into a market, there will be a few advantages. Firstly, it can capture market share much more quickly without having to worry about competitors trying to capture identical customers. Secondly, when the competitors do advance, as they inevitably will be, the first mover and its operation team will have advantages in the ensuing competition, such as familiar products, brand loyalty and so on. By beating rivals into the market, the first-mover can strengthen its current position and rival more effectively, not only defending its previously acquired share but even persistent to develop.

The Moderating Effect of Intra-Industry Network on EO and SMEs Performance

The result of the moderating effects of intra-industry network centrality in this study is inconsistent with the finding of Stam and Elfring (2008) that concerned the lack of support for an independent moderating effect of network centrality. An unexpected outcome was related to the moderating effect of intra-industry network centrality between proactiveness and growth-profitability. We found that high network centrality weakens the relationship between proactiveness and growth-profitability. This finding underlines the significance of coordination between social capital resources and unique resources needs associated with an EO.

One possible explanation is the dominance of out-dated technology and machinery in Iranian manufacturing SMEs as mentioned in chapter 2, which has an impact on the advantages of the intra-industry network centrality. Using abolished technology does not allow SMEs to use the advantages of network centrality. Another explanation is that high network centrality and proactive actions, such as "constantly seeking new opportunities" may involve costs that do not pay off in many Iranian manufacturing SMEs. As mentioned before, the high level of concentration (monopoly power) in different branches of the industry is another problem related to the manufacturing industries in Iran, thus most of the SMEs prefer not to spend too much for high technology as it does not have an impact on firm growth.

As expected, it has been found that the high intra-industry network centrality strengthens the relationship between risk-taking and growth-profitability as well as innovativeness and growth-profitability. These findings are interesting because prior research have examined the moderating effects of centrality without investigating the impact of the dimensions of EO independently (e.g., Stam & Elfring, 2008). Iranian SMEs with high network centrality will be the first to learn about new market conditions, customers' expectations, strategies of competitors and partnership opportunities. This kind of information can help Iranian entrepreneurs to gather professional resources to innovate new products and services according to the needs of the customer.

The Moderating Effect of Extra-Industry Network on EO and SMEs Performance

The results of the study indicate that extra-industry network partially moderates the relationship between EO and firm performance. An unexpected outcome is related to the lack of support for the moderating effect of extra-industry network bridging ties between innovativeness, risk-taking and growth-profitability. One possible explanation is the nature of our sample and measures. Since innovativeness, risk-taking and extra-industry network bridging ties were positively correlated; the outcome may reflect limited variance in the bridging ties scores among SMEs manufacturing firms (Stam & Elfring, 2008). It could be that extra-industry in other types of industry networks applies stronger moderating effects.

Another possibility for the lack of moderation is that the use of an aggregated measure of firm performance, although supported by our factor analysis, may cover interactions among extra-industry network and innovativeness and risk-taking (Lumpkin & Dess, 2001). Extra-industry bridging ties may constrain innovativeness by limiting the emphasis on R&D in the firm and leading the firm to get information from outside the industry yet facilitate risk-taking by reducing the perceived uncertainty. Thus, future studies should examine precisely which network position influences firm performance.

This study also reveals that high extra-industry network bridging ties weakens the relationship between proactiveness and growth-profitability. One possible description is the lack of adaptability between a firm's strategic position and composition of factors such as environmental factors which leads to the worsening of the relationship between EO and firm performance (Lumpkin & Dess, 1996). The environmental factors such as the governmental financial aid and the protection of organizations outside the industry may affect the relationship between Iranian SMEs and organizations outside the industry. Making extra ties between Iranian firms and organizations outside the industry might be expensive for Iranian manufacturing firms and they may not be able to create these ties without governmental supports.

Theoretical Contribution

The resource-based view (RBV) is the underpinning theory to support the present study. Theoretically, we combined RBV and social capital theory that have been considered as central in the explanation of firm performance. The RBV has stressed a firm's unique proprietary assets, especially intangible assets such as patents and entrepreneurial orientation. The notion of social capital that have caused some theories on social networks shifted the attention away from the RBV-inspired question of 'what you know' to 'who you know' by taking stock of a firm's linkages with external networks. Furthermore, this research also makes a contribution by demonstrating how extra-industry network types of social capital channels form relationship between proactiveness and firm performance. Regarding the high expense of extra-industry network bridging ties, the commitment of the government to support Iranian SMEs may be as important as the prominence of the partners which is suggested by Podolny (2001), to encourage entrepreneurs for bridging ties with organizations outside the industry.

The research makes a theoretical contribution by demonstrating how different dimensions of social capital channels' interaction build the relationship between EO and SMEs financial performance. Based on the findings, the two dimensions of social capital, extra-industry network bridging ties and intra-industry network centrality have a partially and completely moderating role on the relationship between EO and SMEs financial performance. This prepares basic practical support for recent contentions that internal and external social capital may have interactive effects (Oh, Choi, & Kim, 2006) and supporting the idea that social capital has contingent value (Ahuja, 2000). The results emphasize the need to examine not only the interactions among different social capital channels, but also the contingencies that determine the maximum balance of ties, in future network study.

This study also improves the knowledge of the "dark side" of social capital (Gargiulo & Benassi, 2000). The results highlighted that by simultaneously examining internal and external social capital, we gained a better understanding of the conditions under which ties were destructive to performance. Too much networking however may eventually result in negative returns. Internal and external networking can only be of benefit to the enterprise's success if the enterprise has developed the absorptive capacity and ability to continually reconfigure its dynamic capabilities for value creation. The findings presented here strongly indicate that the owners' strategic objectives, and EO created within the Iranian SMEs, are crucial. If they are directed towards achieving sustainable growth in sales and profits, then the development and use of innovation, proactiveness and risk-taking will follow from the drive to compete successfully with other similar firms. Schumpeter saw this desire to win as the main driver of innovation just as he suggested that most entrepreneurs will eventually reach a point of personal and material satisfaction when they turn to other goals and become managers, not entrepreneurs.

The problems which are related to the Iranian industry such as inaccessibility to several kinds of information like marketing data, information about SMEs technology and financial situation to help investors choose healthy work for investment, scientific and technical information and information about raw material providers and buyers. These kinds of barriers prevent from fostering strong EO among organizations. However, social capital can be used to solve this problem by providing entrepreneurs with access to the information to increase venture performance, but it is insufficient. Also, no systematic effort by the Iranian government for the nationwide promotion of entrepreneurship has been made as yet.

Accordingly, firms may maximize their performance by achieving a mix of intra and extra-industry networks. We recommend that overused ties can be viewed as an imbalance between internal and external social capital. This idea also suggests that by considering a firm's participation only in a single network (intra-industry or extra-industry), it cannot lead the firm to a better performance, and implies the opposite. This study suggests that RBV and social capital theory need to be simultaneously considered and integrated to better account for entrepreneurial wealth creation.

Practical Contribution

The study revealed that linkage to industries outside the firms such as universities and research institutes do not have a main effect on the firms' performance and found that only firms with internal capabilities can effectively absorb knowledge and technologies that are cooperatively developed with universities and research institutes. One possible explanation is the lack of adaptability between the firm's strategic positions and composition of environmental factors, which worsens the relationship between EO and firm performance. In Iran, environmental factors, such as the government financial aid and the protection of organizations outside the industry, may affect the relationship between Iranian SMEs and organizations outside the industry.

Establishing extra ties between Iranian firms and organizations outside the industry may be expensive for Iranian manufacturing firms, and they may not be able to create these ties without government support. Another explanation is the contingent value of social capital. Maximum firm performance may result from the combination of its intra-and extra-industry ties. Creating relationships with other organizations outside the industry, without investing on networks, may have negative results on firm performance. Optimal firm performance results from the fit between a firm's strategic posture and the combination of its intra-and extra-industry ties.

Recommendation to Iranian Companies

The internal and external social capital moderated completely and partially the relationship between EO and SMEs performance. Without considering the moderating effect of internal and external social capital, entrepreneurs do not know which method they need to use to become a first mover in the market and how they can improve their R&D to innovate new products. However, in order for these linkages and networking to succeed, Iranian SMEs need to develop their absorptive capacity to continually reconfigure their dynamic capabilities for value creation. In Iranian SMEs, the entrepreneurs in the external network bridging ties with other industries and institutions should strengthen their proactiveness.

Extra-industry network did not have a moderating role between innovativeness and firm performance and also risk-taking and firm performance. It shows that in Iran, SMEs are not eager to connect with other industries to improve the level of their innovativeness and risk-taking, and this result is different from what we gained in literature review. Iranian entrepreneurs must improve their relationship with other institutes outside the industry such as the universities; and they should strengthen their relationship with the other firms to know how they can improve their products and become a first mover in the market. This relationship may be costly for Iranian SMEs and with regard to this problem; the government must support the SMEs in order to settle this expenditure and to not be afraid of making relationships with other industries outside the industry.

On the other hand, Iranian manufacturing companies should also emphasize a lot on the intra-industry network centrality in the proactiveness, innovativeness and the level of risk-taking and firm performance relationship. The moderating effect of intra-industry network centrality occurred in the proactiveness, innovativeness and risk-taking and performance relationship. Therefore, Iranian SMEs involved in the intra-industry network centrality should look closely to improve any activities related to EO. Iranian SMEs that are involved in extra-industry network bridging ties must focus more on the proactiveness activity.

Limitations and Suggestions for Future Research

As in any piece of research, there are some limitations in the present study. A single informant who was asked to evaluate EO may potentially increase the degree of subjectivity and bias in the responses. It is always highly desirable to get more than one respondent to the survey of each organization. Nevertheless, due to the high cost of including multiple respondents, many researchers choose a single respondent (Miller & Roth, 1994). In this study, one respondent was selected to answer each survey questionnaire, who was an entrepreneur.

Also, we only examined the SMEs which are working in manufacturing industries, the importance of the lack of big industries and the presence of many young firms are factors that may limit the generalizability of the result. We think that this will be a good chance for future research to cover up multiple industries that differ in life cycle, institutional and big manufacturing industries conditions that influence EO, RBV and social capital performance effects.

Future study would also benefit from better development in the measurement of the EO dimensions relying on richer, more fine-grained conceptualizations. In order to gain this goal, using multiple underlying components of the EO dimensions would be effective. For example, a former study suggested that innovativeness consists of both administrative and technological innovation (Ibarra, 1993). Similarly, business risks and financial risks are two components that could be utilized to depict the risk-taking EO dimensions, that is, the tendency to enter the new product-market which has not been examined before and propensity to use high levels of financial leverage, respectively. Future research utilizing other moderating variables might also brighten the performance results related to proactiveness, risk-taking and innovativeness under different organizational conditions.

REFERENCES

Adler, P. S., & Kwon, S.-W. (2002). Prospects for a New Concept. *Academy of Management Journal*, *27*(1), 17–40.

Aldrich, H. E., & Fiol, C. M. (1994). Fools Rush in? The Institutional Context of Industry Creation. *Academy of Management Review*, *19*(1), 645–670.

Bamberger, P., Bacharach, S., & Dyer, L. (1989). Human resources management and organizational effectiveness: High technology entrepreneurial startup firms in Israel. *Human Resource Management*, *28*(3), 349–366. doi:10.1002/hrm.3930280305

Bandura, A. (1977). Self-efficacy: Toward a unifying theory of behavioral change. *Psychological Review*, *84*(2), 191–215. doi:10.1037/0033-295X.84.2.191 PMID:847061

Barney, J. (1991). Firm resources and sustained competitive advantage. *Journal of Management*, *17*(1), 99–120. doi:10.1177/014920639101700108

Boso, N., Story, V. M., & Cadogan, J. W. (2013). Entrepreneurial orientation, market orientation, network ties, and performance: Study of entrepreneurial firms in a developing economy. *Journal of Business Venturing*, *28*(6), 708–727. doi:10.1016/j.jbusvent.2013.04.001

Bueno, E., Arrien, M., & Rodriguez, O. (2003). Modelo Intellectus: medición y gestión del capital intelectual. Intellectus Model: Model for the measurement and management of intellectual capital. Madrid: CIC-IADE (UAM).

Casillas, J. C., Moreno, A. M., & Barbero, J. L. (2010). A configurational approach of the relationship between entrepreneurial orientation and growth of family firms. *Family Business Review*, *23*(1), 27–44. doi:10.1177/0894486509345159

Chen, C. N., Tzeng, L. C., Ou, W. M., & Chang, K. T. (2007). The relationship among social capital, entrepreneurial orientation, organizational resources and entrepreneurial performance for new ventures. *Contemp. Manage. Res*, *3*(3), 213–232. doi:10.7903/cmr.90

Covin, J. G., & Slevin, D. P. (1989). *Empirical relationship among strategic posture environmental context variables, and new venture performance, Frontiers Entrepreneurship Research*. Wellesley, MA: Babson College.

Dahya, J., Lonie, A. A., & Power, D. M. (1998). Ownership structure, firm performance and top executive change: An analysis of UK firms. *Journal of Business Finance & Accounting*, *25*(9), 1089–1118. doi:10.1111/1468-5957.00228

Davidsson, P. (1989). *Continued entrepreneurship and small firm growth*. Stockholm: School of Economics Stockholm.

Dess, G. G., Lumpkin, G. T., & Covin, J. G. (1998). Entrepreneurial strategy making and firm performance: Tests of contingency and configurational models. *Strategic Management Journal*, *18*(9), 677–695. doi:10.1002/(SICI)1097-0266(199710)18:9<677::AID-SMJ905>3.0.CO;2-Q

Dess, G. G., & Robinson, R. B. (2006). Measuring organizational performance in the absence of objective measures: The case of the privately-held firm and conglomerate business unit. *Strategic Management Journal*, *5*(3), 265–273. doi:10.1002/smj.4250050306

Dibrell, C., Craig, J. B., & Neubaum, D. O. (2014). Linking the formal strategic planning process, planning flexibility, and innovativeness to firm performance. *Journal of Business Research*, *67*(9), 2000–2007. doi:10.1016/j.jbusres.2013.10.011

Dorenbosch, L., Engen, M. L., & Verhagen, M. (2005). On the job Innovation: The Impact of Job Design and Human Resource Management through Production Ownership. *Creativity and Innovation Management*, *14*(2), 129–141. doi:10.1111/j.1476-8691.2005.00333.x

Ellis, P. D. (2010). Social ties and international entrepreneurship: Opportunities and constraints affecting firm internationalization. *Journal of International Business Studies*, *42*(1), 99–127. doi:10.1057/jibs.2010.20

Frese, M., Brantjes, A., & Hoorn, R. (2002). Psychological success factors of small scale businesses in Namibia: The roles of strategy process, entrepreneurial orientation and the environment. *Journal of Developmental Entrepreneurship*, *7*(3), 259–282.

Gargiulo, M., & Benassi, M. (2000). Trapped in your own net? Network cohesion, structural holes, and the adaptation of social capital. *Organization Science*, *11*(2), 183–196. doi:10.1287/orsc.11.2.183.12514

Gomes-Casseres, B. (1997). *The alliance revolution: The new shape of business rivalry*. Boston, MA: Harvard University Press.

Gronum, S., Verreynne, M. L., & Kastelle, T. (2012). The role of networks in small and medium-sized enterprise innovation and firm performance. *Journal of Small Business Management*, *50*(2), 257–282. doi:10.1111/j.1540-627X.2012.00353.x

Hargadon, A. B. (2002). Brokering knowledge: Linking learning and innovation. *Research in Organizational Behavior*, *24*, 41–86. doi:10.1016/S0191-3085(02)24003-4

Hu, W., & Zhang, Y. (2012). New venture capability of the transformation from entrepreneurial orientation to new ventures performance: Theory model and empirical study in China. *Nankai Business Review International*, *3*(3), 302–325. doi:10.1108/20408741211264594

Hunt, S. D. (1997). Competing through relationships: Grounding relationship marketing in resource-advantage theory. *Journal of Marketing Management*, *13*(5), 431–445. doi:10.1080/0267257X.1997.9964484

Hussain, I., Farooq, Z., & Akhtar, W. (2012). SMEs development and failure avoidance in developing countries through public private partnership. *African Journal of Business Management*, *6*(4), 1581–1589.

Ibarra, H. (1993). Network centrality, power, and innovation involvement: Determinants of technical and administrative roles. *Academy of Management Journal*, *36*(3), 471–501. doi:10.2307/256589

Jalali, A., Jaafar, M., & Ramayah, T. (2014). Entrepreneurial orientation and performance: The interaction effect of customer capital. *World Journal of Entrepreneurship, Management and Sustainable Development*, *10*(1), 48–68.

Jayachandran, S., Sharma, S., Kaufman, P., & Raman, P. (2005). The role of relational information processes and technology use in customer relationship management. *Journal of Marketing*, *69*(4), 177–192. doi:10.1509/jmkg.2005.69.4.177

Khatri, N. (2000). Managing human resource for competitive advantage: A study of companies in Singapore. *International Journal of Human Resource Management*, *11*(2), 336–365. doi:10.1080/095851900339909

Kim, P., & Aldrich, H. (2005). Social Capital and Entrepreneurship. *Foundations and Trends in Entrepreneurship.*, *1*(2), 55–104. doi:10.1561/0300000002

Klyver, K., & Schenkel, M. T. (2013). From resource access to use: Exploring the impact of resource combinations on nascent entrepreneurship. *Journal of Small Business Management*, *51*(4), 539–556. doi:10.1111/jsbm.12030

Kreiser, P. M., Marino, L. D., & Weaver, K. M. (2002). Assessing the psychometric properties of the entrepreneurial orientation scale: A multi-country analysis. *Entrepreneurship Theory and Practice*, *26*(4), 71–94.

Lechner, C., & Gudmundsson, S. V. (2014). Entrepreneurial orientation, firm strategy and small firm performance. *International Small Business Journal*, *32*(1), 36–60. doi:10.1177/0266242612455034

Lockett, A., Thompson, S., & Morgenstern, U. (2009). The development of the resource-based view of the firm: A critical appraisal. *International Journal of Management Reviews*, *11*(1), 9–28. doi:10.1111/j.1468-2370.2008.00252.x

Lumpkin, G. T., & Dess, G. G. (1996). Clarifying the entrepreneurial orientation construct and linking it to performance. *Academy of Management Review*, *21*(1), 135–172.

Lumpkin, G. T., & Dess, G. G. (2001). Linking two dimensions of entrepreneurial orientation to firm performance: The moderating role of environment and industry life cycle. *Journal of Business Venturing*, *16*(5), 429–451. doi:10.1016/S0883-9026(00)00048-3

Martin, X., Mitchell, W., & Swaminathan, A. (1995). Recreating and extending Japanese automobile buyersupplier links in north America. *Strategic Management Journal*, *16*(8), 589–619. doi:10.1002/smj.4250160803

Mat Roni, S. (2014). *Introduction to SPSS*. Retrieved 10 August, 2016, from www.researchgate.net/publication/262151892_Introduction_to_SPSS

McConnell, J. J., & Servaes, H. (1990). Additional evidence on equity ownership and corporate value. *Journal of Financial Economics*, *27*(2), 595–612. doi:10.1016/0304-405X(90)90069-C

Meihami, B., Varmaghani, Z., & Meihami, H. (2014). Role of Intellectual Capital on Firm Performance (Evidence from Iranian Companies). *International Letters of Social and Humanistic Sciences*, (12), 43-50.

Menon, A., & Varadarajan, P. R. (1992). A model of marketing knowledge use within firms. *Journal of Marketing*, *56*(4), 53–71. doi:10.2307/1251986

Miller, J. G., & Roth, A. V. (1994). A taxonomy of manufacturing strategies. *Management Science*, *40*(3), 285–304. doi:10.1287/mnsc.40.3.285

Moreno, A. M., & Casillas, J. C. (2008). Entrepreneurial orientation and growth of SMEs: A causal model. *Entrepreneurship Theory and Practice*, *32*(3), 507–528. doi:10.1111/j.1540-6520.2008.00238.x

Nonaka, I., & Takeuchi, H. (2007). The knowledge-creating company. *Harvard Business Review*, *85*(7/8), 162–171.

Oh, W., Choi, J. N., & Kim, K. (2006). Coauthorship dynamics and knowledge capital: The patterns of cross-disciplinary collaboration in information systems research. *Journal of Management Information Systems*, *22*(3), 266–292. doi:10.2753/MIS0742-1222220309

Park, C. H., & Kim, Y. G. (2003). A framework of dynamic CRM: Linking marketing with information strategy. *Business Process Management Journal*, *9*(5), 652–671. doi:10.1108/14637150310496749

Peng, M. W., & Luo, Y. (2000). Managerial ties and firm performance in a transition economy: The nature of a micro-macro link. *Academy of Management Journal*, *43*(3), 486–501. doi:10.2307/1556406

Perrigot, R., López-Fernández, B., & Eroglu, S. (2013). Intangible Resources and Plural Form as Drivers of Franchise Internationalization: Examination within a Two-Country Perspective. *Journal of Small Business Management*, *51*(4), 557–577. doi:10.1111/jsbm.12006

Peteraf, M. A. (1993). The cornerstones of competitive advantage: A resource-based view. *Strategic Management Journal*, *14*(3), 179–191. doi:10.1002/smj.4250140303

Piercy, N., & Evans, M. (2014). *Managing Marketing Information (RLE Marketing)* (Vol. 17). New York, NY: Routledge.

Podolny, J. M. (2001). Networks as the Pipes and Prisms of the Market. *American Journal of Sociology*, *107*(1), 33–60. doi:10.1086/323038

Ratten, V. (2014). Future research directions for collective entrepreneurship in developing countries: A small and medium-sized enterprise perspective. *International Journal of Entrepreneurship and Small Business*, *22*(2), 266–274. doi:10.1504/IJESB.2014.062505

Rauch, A., Wiklund, J., Lumpkin, G. T., & Frese, M. (2009). Entrepreneurial orientation and business performance: An assessment of past research and suggestions for the future. *Entrepreneurship Theory and Practice*, *33*(3), 761–787. doi:10.1111/j.1540-6520.2009.00308.x

Robb, A., & Robinson, D. (2014). The capital structure decisions of new firms. *Review of Financial Studies*, *27*(1), 153–179. doi:10.1093/rfs/hhs072

Saeed, S., Yousafzai, S. Y., & Engelen, A. (2014). On cultural and macroeconomic contingencies of the entrepreneurial orientation–performance relationship. *Entrepreneurship Theory and Practice*, *38*(2), 255–290. doi:10.1111/etap.12097

Saidi Kia, M. (2013). *Business management and efficiency*. Tehran: Aha.

Salomann, H., Dous, M., Kolbe, L., & Brenner, W. (2005). Rejuvenating Customer Management. *European Management Journal*, *23*(4), 392–403. doi:10.1016/j.emj.2005.06.009

Schreiner, M., Kale, P., & Corsten, D. (2009). What really is alliance management capability and how does it impact alliance outcomes and success? *Strategic Management Journal*, *30*(13), 1395–1419. doi:10.1002/smj.790

Schumpeter, J., & Backhaus, U. (2003). The theory of economic development. *Joseph Alois Schumpeter*, *1*, 61–116. doi:10.1007/0-306-48082-4_3

Sekaran, U. (2006). *Research methods for business: A skill building approach*. New York, NY: Wiley-India.

Simsek, Z., Lubatkin, M. H., & Floyd, S. W. (2003). Inter-firm networks and entrepreneurial behavior: A structural embeddedness perspective. *Journal of Management*, *29*(3), 427–442. doi:10.1016/S0149-2063(03)00018-7

Sinha, P., Akoorie, M. E. M., Ding, Q., & Wu, Q. (2011). What motivates manufacturing SMEs to outsource offshore in China?: Comparing the perspectives of SME manufacturers and their suppliers. *Strategic Outsourcing: An International Journal*, *4*(1), 67–88. doi:10.1108/17538291111108435

Stam, W., Arzlanian, S., & Elfring, T. (2014). Social capital of entrepreneurs and small firm performance: A meta-analysis of contextual and methodological moderators. *Journal of Business Venturing*, *29*(1), 152–173. doi:10.1016/j.jbusvent.2013.01.002

Stam, W., & Elfring, T. (2008). Entrepreneurial orientation and new venture performance: The moderating role of intra-and extraindustry social capital. *Academy of Management Journal*, *51*(1), 97–111. doi:10.5465/AMJ.2008.30744031

Starr, J. A., & MacMillan, I. (1990). Resource cooptation via social contracting: Resource acquisition strategies for new ventures. *Strategic Management Journal*, *11*, 79–92.

Statistical Centre of Iran. (2015). *Iran statistical yearbook*. Retrieved April 18, 2011 from http:// www.amar.org.ir/

Statistical Centre of Iran. (2016). *Iran statistical yearbook*. Retrieved April 18, 2011 from http:// www.amar.org.ir/

Stuart, T. E., Hoang, H., & Hybels, R. C. (1999). Interorganizational endorsements and the performance of entrepreneurial ventures. *Administrative Science Quarterly*, *44*(2), 315–349. doi:10.2307/2666998

Tabachnick, B. G., & Fidell, L. S. (1996). Using Multivariate Statistics. New York: HarperCollins.

Tang, J., Tang, Z., Marino, L. D., Zhang, Y., & Li, Q. (2008). Exploring an Inverted U-Shape Relationship between Entrepreneurial Orientation and Performance in Chinese Ventures. *Entrepreneurship Theory and Practice*, *32*(1), 219–239. doi:10.1111/j.1540-6520.2007.00223.x

Wiklund, J., & Shepherd, D. (2005). Entrepreneurial orientation and small business performance: A configurational approach. *Journal of Business Venturing*, *20*(1), 71–91. doi:10.1016/j.jbusvent.2004.01.001

Wills-Johnson, N. (2008). The networked firm: A framework for RBV. *Journal of Management Development*, *27*(2), 214–224. doi:10.1108/02621710810849344

Wood, R., & Bandura, A. (1989). Social cognitive theory of organizational management. *Academy of Management Review*, *14*(3), 361–384.

Ziggers, G., & Henseler, J. (2009). Inter-firm network capability: How it affects buyer-supplier performance. *British Food Journal*, *111*(8), 794–810. doi:10.1108/00070700910980928

Zimmerman, M. A., & Zeitz, G. J. (2002). Beyond survival: Achieving new venture growth by building legitimacy. *Academy of Management Review*, *27*(3), 414–431.

KEY TERMS AND DEFINITIONS

Entrepreneur: A person who habitually creates and innovates to build something of recognized value around perceived opportunities.

Entrepreneurial Orientation: The construct involving organization's innovativeness, risk taking and proactiveness.

Entrepreneurship: The creation of new business enterprises by individuals or small groups, with the entrepreneur assuming the role of society's major agent of change, initiating the industrial progress that leads to wider cultural shifts.

Extra-Industry Bridging Ties: The extent to which a firm maintains ties beyond the focal industry network to organizations from other fields.

Innovativeness: The willingness to place strong emphasis on research and development, new products, new services, improved product lines and global technological improvement in the industry.

Intra-Industry Network Centrality: Firm's situation in the complete composition of ties including a network and shows the firm's relational proximity to all other agents in the network.

Proactiveness: Acting opportunistically in order to shape the environment by influencing trends and creating demand and becoming a first mover in a competitive market.

Risk Taking: The willingness to be bold and aggressive in pursuing opportunities, and having preference for high-risk projects with chances of very high returns over low-risk projects with lower and more predictable rates of return.

Section 2

Realising the Strategies and Challenges of SMEs

Chapter 6
On the Road to SME Sector Development in Bangladesh:
A Guideline Based on Current Challenges and Opportunities

Syed Abidur Rahman
Universiti Utara Malaysia, Malaysia

Noor Hazlina Ahmad
Universiti Sains Malaysia, Malaysia

Seyedeh Khadijeh Taghizadeh
Universiti Tecknolgi PETRONAS, Malaysia

ABSTRACT

Entrepreneurship has been deliberated as multidimensional and multidisciplinary study. From the economic point of view entrepreneurship is the central force for economic development for any nation. Scholars and policy makers now have started to see entrepreneurship as panacea for inclusive growth. Entrepreneurships are most widely popular and discussed area. Study on small and medium sized enterprises (SMEs) has been maturing for the last decade as it has been regarded as significant player for the social development along with the economic development. In Bangladesh, SMEs account for a large proportion of the total establishments in various sectors. Considering the importance of the SME sector in Bangladesh, this study intends to explore and sketch-out the landscape of current SME setting in Bangladesh. With this aim the study has extensively carried out literature review, observed and understood the secondary data obtained from various organizations, and finally presented a policy driven recommendation (micro and macro level) which would enable to develop the SME sector in a developing country like Bangladesh.

DOI: 10.4018/978-1-5225-2165-5.ch006

INTRODUCTION

Entrepreneurship is considered as multifaceted and multidisciplinary study. It has adopted different unit of analysis, theoretical standpoint and methodologies. (Low & MacMillan, 1988). From the economic point of view entrepreneurship is the central force for economic development for any nation (Ahmad, Halim, Ramayah, & Rahman, 2013). Scholars have observed increasing evidence that there is a substantial causal relationship between entrepreneurship, economic growth and poverty reduction (Chowdhury, 2007). It is believed that the growth of the entrepreneurship ventures increase the money flow in the economy, in other words triggers the circulation of money within the economy, create job opportunities, and ultimately enhance the living standard of the society and of an economy. Therefore, scholars and policy makers now have been started to see entrepreneurship as panacea for inclusive growth, where inclusive growth refers to the contributing to profit, as well as the society (Hall, Matos, Sheehan, & Silvestre, 2012). Considering the size of the entrepreneurship, Micro, Small and Medium Entrepreneurships are most widely popular and discussed area. Study on small and medium sized enterprises (SMEs) has been maturing for the last decade as it has been regarded as significant player for the social development along with the economic development. It is perhaps one of the major economic growth engine and backbone of the economic wellbeing for the developing countries. It has also been observed that SMEs are playing vital role on the rapid socio-economic growth of the developing countries and least developed countries.

In Bangladesh, one of the least developed countries, SMEs account for a large proportion of the total establishments in various sectors. Considering the importance of the SME sector in Bangladesh, this study embarked upon to explore and sketch-out the landscape of current SME setting in Bangladesh. The issues of entrepreneurship are complex and not enough and in-depth studies have been carried out in the context of Bangladesh (Chowdhury, 2007). This chapter book institutes a scope of further comprehensive study and expected to contribute to better apprehend the opportunities, challenges, dynamics, and future course of actions for the development of SME sector in Bangladesh. With this aim the study will extensively carry out literature review, observe and understand the secondary data obtained from various organizations, and finally present a policy driven suggestions for policy makers, researchers, and businesses which would enable to develop the SME sector in a developing country like Bangladesh.

OBJECTIVE AND RESEARCH METHODOLOGY

The critical and in-depth literature comprising a holistic picture of the entrepreneurship development in Bangladesh found to be rare (Chowdhury, 2007). Till now not enough significant studies have been conducted in the academic field which would give an inclusive illustration of the small-medium enterprises in Bangladesh. In addition, discussion on the opportunities, challenges, and possible guidelines also found to be sparse. Therefore, considering the frail state of studies conducted in Bangladesh, this study has made an attempt to provide a comprehensive sketch on the geo-politic and socio-economic portrait of the country. The snapshot on such areas has triggered to embark on the main objective of the study. The main objective of the study is to offer a policy guideline for the SME development in Bangladesh based on the prevailing challenges and opportunities of the SMEs. To fulfill the objective the study will carry out review from the extant literature on Bangladeshi SMEs, identify the challenges and opportunities for growth of the SME sector in Bangladesh.

The study is descriptive in nature. The study will also consider the secondary data available from various data bank such as, The World Bank, Asian Development Bank, United Nation Development Program (UNDP), International Monitory Fund, Global Entrepreneurship Monitor. The study will also highlight the information and recommendation from the renowned local research institutes such as, Bangladesh Institute of Development Studies (BIDS), Centre for Policy Dialogue. Combining and cross checking the obtained information, the study will offer a guideline for the SME development in Bangladesh.

BACKGROUND OF THE STUDY

Country Overview

Bangladesh is the country with ancient and historic events where civilization dates back over four millennia. During the 16th century British Empire ruled over the region and the country was part of British India till 1947. In 1947, the country was named as East Pakistan as part of Pakistan, which was basically partitioned based on the religious majority even though having completely different culture and territorial distance of 1,600 kilometres from West Pakistan. The country appeared in the global map as an independent nation in 1971 after the liberation war against Pakistan. Geographically, Bangladesh is located in the South Asia region. The Western, Northern and most of the Eastern part of the country have borders with India. The South-Eastern part of the country has a little border with the Eastern part of Myanmar.

In terms of size, Bangladesh Ranks at the 95th position in the world with the area of total 143,998 square kilometres. In comparison, the country is slightly smaller than the US state Iowa and almost 2.3 times smaller than Malaysia. The land area of the country occupies 130,168 square kilometres and water area is 13,830 square kilometres (The World Factbook, 2015).

Geographically, there are almost seven hundreds of rivers that have flown through the land of Bangladesh and the country is well known as "land of rivers". Therefore, there is abundance of reptiles, mammals, fish, bird, and duck throughout the riverine of Bangladesh. In fact, a large portion of the population is significantly dependent on the fisheries as major source of income.

Considering the formation of land from the geographic point, the country is composed of the world's largest Delta by Ganges-Brahmaputra-Meghna rivers. The existence of such number of rivers and delta land has augmented the fertility of approximately eighty per cent of the landmass and thus made the country depended on mostly in agriculture (National Encyclopedia of Bangladesh, 2015). Therefore the country's economic prosperity mainly depends on the agricultural development. According the Global Competitiveness Report (2015), Bangladesh is categorised as factor driven economy. Factor driven economy represents the economy which is mostly based on natural resources and unskilled labour. In addition, the country is still (after 44 years of independence) been considered as agro based economy, where most of the population lives in rural areas and dependence on agriculture.

Demography

With the population density of 1,222 per square kilometres, 10th in the world (The World Bank, 2015) Bangladesh stands on the world's 7th position (The World Factbook, 2015) in terms of population size. According to the United Nation Population Fund (UNFPA), in the year of 2015 the population Bangladesh has stood at 161 million where the world population touched at 7.3 billion (UNFPA, 2015).

Almost fifty per cent of the population (50.4%) consist of male and rest are females. In the population cohort, 65% of the population is aged between 15-64 years. This is perhaps a great opportunity for the country to turn the population in to productive human resources. In Bangladesh, people commonly live serenely together across religious divisions. The religious setting in Bangladesh and its subcontinent has always been multi-ethnic. In Bangladesh, the religious demography encompasses a broad majority of Muslims (approximately between 85 and 90 per cent of the population), Hindus as the second largest group (with around 8 per cent) as well as Buddhists (0.7 per cent) and Christians (0.3 per cent) (United Nations Human Rights Commission, 2015). The report prepared by the World Bank shows that sixty six per cent (66%) of the population resides in the rural areas of Bangladesh, while thirty four per cent (34%) lives in the urban areas of the country. Even though a rapid urbanization has been observed in the country in the last two decades, still the population in the rural areas are higher where such group of people are deprived of basic human needs and infrastructures. In the rural areas most of the population are engaged in agricultural activities with less technological advancement. Adult literacy rate for the population above 15 years of age is 60% for both the genders (The World Factbook, 2015). It is obvious notion that if the literacy could be improved further, the development of commercial activities, specifically the entrepreneurship venture would accelerate. Further, the statistics by UNFPA shows that the annual population growth rate in Bangladesh is 1.2 per cent in the year of 2015 (UNFPA, 2015), which is almost similar (1.2%) to the neighbouring country, Nepal. The annual population growth rate for other neighbouring countries are: India (1.3 per cent), Myanmar (0.8 per cent), Pakistan (2.1 per cent), Bhutan (1.5 per cent), and Sri Lanka 0.5 (per cent). Other Asian countries like China has average population growth of 0.5 per cent, Thailand 0.4 per cent, and Malaysia 1.5 per cent (UNFPA, 2015). Therefore, the present situation indicates that the population of the country is one of the major challenges for the development of the country.

Human Development

The setting of human development is critically associated with the entrepreneurship creation and development. Therefore, it is also important to have glance on the human development situation in Bangladesh. According to the Human Development Report (2015) Bangladesh ranks at the 142 out of 188 countries in the world, which indicates great challenges for the smooth economic activities and development. For the last 10 years in Bangladesh, the human rights have been severely violated by different stakeholders of the country. Strikingly, human rights violation initiated by the law enforcing agencies was spotted by the media and international community. Different human right activist, development agencies, and the civil society have pointed towards the ruling party and the law enforcing agencies for disappearance of citizens. On top, it has been clearly stated by the Human Rights Watch (2016), "The rights to freedom of speech and assembly are coming under sustained attack by Bangladesh's increasingly authoritarian government". However, considering the other indicators of the human development index is not also so impressive. Still in Bangladesh the inequality in terms of education and income persist. According to the latest Human Development Report (2015), inequality in education in Bangladesh is 38.6% and inequality in income is 28.3% as of 2014. The literacy rate of the country is 58.8 per cent, unemployment rate is 4.5 per cent, labour force participation is 70.8 per cent, participation of female in the labour force is 57.4 per cent, participation of male is 84.1 per cent, and employment to population is 67.8 per cent (Human Development Report, 2015). Another important indicator for human development is health care. In many developing countries people suffer from various diseases and also suffer from inadequate health care facilities. Many of the population receive less quality health related treatments due to insufficient infrastructure. The most recent report published by the World Economic Forum, shows that in Bangladesh, only 59% of the population are satisfied with the health care quality, whereas in the country like Vietnam 72% per cent, in Bhutan 90 per cent, and in Cambodia 79 per cent people are satisfied with the health care provided by the government as basic need and right of the citizen (Human Development Report, 2015).

Economy

Bangladesh has been considered as 44th largest economy in the world (The World Bank, 2015). It has been also identified as one of the Next-11 countries along with Egypt, Indonesia, Iran, Mexico, Nigeria, Pakistan, the Philippines, Turkey, South Korea and Vietnam which holds the potentiality to be in the largest economies club. This Next-11 would be another group of countries which is expected to grow beyond the BRICS (Brazil, Russia, India, China, and South Africa) (Goldman Sachs Investment Bank 2007).

The substantial contribution for such progress in the economic arena is due to the contribution of foreign remittance, and garments export to the Bangladesh economy. The scenario of foreign direct investment in the country is quite unpleasant till 2015 since the year of 2007, due to political instability. According to the The World Bank (2015) the foreign direct investment is only 1.4 per cent of the total GDP of the country. Whereas in country like Cambodia the foreign direct investment is 8.8 per cent, in Vietnam it is 5.2 per cent. The contribution of export and import to the gross domestic product of the country has been recently dived down. According to the Human Development Report (2015), progress of Bangladesh till 2005 in terms of economic and human development was remarkable and encouraging. However, due to political instability and government mismanagement and corruption, the researchers and political scientists in Bangladesh believe that the economic progress is weakening down. The data prepared by the The World Bank (2016) also validates such claims. According to the The World Bank (2016), 19 per cent of the GDP is contributed to the export of goods and services in Bangladesh, whereas country like, Bhutan the contribution of export of goods and services to the GDP is 36.3 per cent, in Vietnam it is 86.4 per cent, and in Cambodia 62.3 per cent.

The World Bank (2015) has grouped Bangladesh in the category of lower middle income country in the world as the gross domestic product (GDP) per capita is US$1086 and gross national income (GNI) per capita is US$1080 (The World Bank, 2016). It has been reported that Bangladesh has upheld a notable track record on economic growth and development. For last few decades the economy has experienced nearly on an average 6 per cent of economic growth per year. In spite of bright track record, around 47 million people are still below the poverty line (The World Bank, 2015) and improving access to quality services for this vulnerable group is a priority. In the global platform the country is mostly known as ground of millions of poor people who earned less than US$2 per day. However, fortunately, the level of poverty has dropped by nearly a third, coupled with increased life expectancy, literacy, and per capita food intake. According to World Bank's web site, currently the world holds in total more than two billions of poor people who live on equal or less than US$2 a day and south Asia contains half of those population (The World Bank, 2014, 2016). Therefore it is very important to alleviate the poverty level in this region. According to the databank of The World Bank (2015) the poverty rate in Sri Lanka is 8.9 per cent in 2010, Pakistan 22.3 per cent in 2006, India 29.8 per cent in 2010, and for Bangladesh in 2010, its poverty rate was at 31.5 per cent, comparing to the poverty rate of 58.8 per cent in 1991 (Imai & Azam, 2012). This indicates that from 1991 until 2010 poverty has been reduced by an average percentage of 1.43 per annum. The World Economic Forum published in their Human Development Report (2015) based on the data of 2011 that 49.5 per cent of the total population in Bangladesh suffers from multidimensional poverty. In this respect, Ghana which has an almost similar GNI per capita to Bangladesh, the holds 31.2 per cent population who suffers from multi-dimensional poverty, while Myanmar the percentage is 31.8.

Comparing the number of poor people of Bangladesh (56 million till 2011) with other countries the it brings out the fact that this figure (56 million) exceeded the total population of Korea Republic (48.8 million), Canada (34 million), Malaysia (27 million), or Australia (22 million) (The World Bank, 2011). As such, this data demonstrated the severity of poverty in Bangladesh. According to the General Economics Division Bangladesh (2010), poverty remains in the rural areas of the country due to inadequate access to technology and lack of infrastructural improvements. It has also been suggested that inequality in income, poor infrastructure, lack of education, poor health, inefficient public sector, lack of work opportunities, low wage rate, population growth, and lack of human resource development are among the major contributing grounds of poverty in Bangladesh (Hossain, 2005; Hye, 1996; Smith, Khan, Frankenberger, & Wadud, 2013).

In the effort to curb poverty, a number of poverty alleviation initiatives, e.g. micro-credit, development of health and education, infrastructural development, and social safety net have been carried out mostly by the government and donor agencies. All these stakeholders have been pursuing the alleviation poverty in Bangladesh since its independence in 1971. Moreover, apart from the traditional techniques, it is recognized that the private sector also contributes towards poverty alleviation, mainly through employment creation (Kolk, Rivera-Santos, & Rufín, 2013). In a similar vein, Davis (2011) surveyed on the life history of the poor in Bangladesh to explore the factor that will improve the people's life. It was revealed that 46% of the surveyed respondents gave credit to 'businesses' as their means to escape from poverty.

Small-Medium Entrepreneurship in Bangladesh

Speeding up socio-economic development, eradicating poverty, and reducing income disparity and regional inequality are the predominant objectives of the current strategic development paradigm of Bangladesh. One of the crucial and prolific strategies for achieving these goals is to create productive employment in the manufacturing and service sector by pulling out labour force out of the unproductive sectors. It is believed that nurturing the small and medium enterprises (SMEs) is the appropriate means to rightly address these national development agendas (Rahman, Amran, Ahmad, & Taghizadeh, 2015a). According to the researchers, achieving double digit growth in manufacturing and services the development of SMEs is considered as critical and obligatory. Developed micro, small and medium enterprise activities in the rural and backward regions comprise a vital constituent of the strategy for rural development and reduction of poverty and regional disparity (Bakht & Basher, 2015).

It has been a proven fact vowed by the scholars that entrepreneurship business especially the micro, small, medium enterprises (SMEs) is the key sector for the developing countries as they play a vital role in the national GDP (Shariff & Peou, 2008). In China, 99.8% of the total number of businesses are SMEs and contribute to 58.5% of total annual GDP, and also contribute 75% of new jobs (Sun, Buys, & Wang, 2011). In Bangladesh, the scenario is however less impressive, as micro, small, medium entrepreneurship business contributes only 25 percent of the total GDP (Rashid, 2012) though the country is having satisfactory upward GDP growth, which is 6.7 percent (The World Bank, 2012). Bangladesh 's SME sector contributed 40 per cent of gross manufacturing output, 80 per cent of industrial jobs, and around

25 per cent of the total labour force in 2003 (Chowdhury, 2007). Hence, it is important for country like Bangladesh to encourage the enhancement of entrepreneurship business in diverse range of ways. In the context of Bangladesh, the development of Small and Medium Enterprises (SMEs) can be considered as an important means of poverty alleviation and ensure the rapid industrialization (Rahman, Amran, Ahmad, & Taghizadeh, 2015b). It has been argued by the authors that the performance of SMEs of Bangladesh especially in terms of employee turnover rate, quality assurance, allocation of funds, marketing activities have been found significantly below the international standard (Rahman, Amran, Ahmad, & Taghizadeh, 2014; Rahman & Das, 2005).

Defining SMEs is one of major challenges. Due to the diverse socio-economic situation, different countries and organizations have defined SMEs differently. According to the European Union (2003), SMEs are illustrated as enterprises, which have at most 250 employees and an annual turnover not exceeding 50 million Euros. Further, there is the distinction of small enterprises which have fewer than 50 staffs and less than 10 million Euros turnover and micro-enterprises comprises of less than 10 employees and turnover of 2 million Euros per year.

According to the The World Bank (2010), micro-enterprises are those which have up to 10 persons and $100,000 turnover. The small enterprises have fewer than 50 staff members and up to 3 million US dollars turnover and medium enterprises are defined as enterprises, which have at most 300 employees and an annual turnover not exceeding 15 million US dollars.

The neighbouring country of Bangladesh, Vietnam, where the development of SMEs is striking, has classified and defined SMEs in their own way which aligns with their economic, social, and demographic context. For the categorization of micro-enterprises, the number of workers should be less 10. Small enterprises are those which have employees between 10-200 and total capital having less than 20 billion Vietnamese Dong. Enterprises which have employees between 200-300 and total capital more than 20 billion but less than 100 billion Vietnamese Dong are considered as medium enterprises.

The government of Bangladesh has categorises SME into two broad classifications, which are manufacturing enterprises and non-manufacturing enterprises. In the year of 2011, the central bank of Bangladesh has specifically numbered the classification of SMEs. According to the Bangladesh Bank (2015), in manufacturing sectors of the SMEs, medium enterprise would be those with assets worth US$14 to US$42 million (minus land and factory building, and including replacement value) and/or 100 to 250 of workers. In service industry, medium enterprises will be those which employ 50 to 100 employees and have assets (defined as above) worth of US$ 0.1 to US$ 2.1 million. In manufacturing, small enterprise would be those with assets worth US$71 thousand to US$1.4 million (defined as above) and/or 25 to 99 workers. In service industry, small enterprises will be those which employ 10 to 25 and have assets (defined as above) worth US$7 thousand to US$1.4 million.

Different consulting bodies and reports from different organization suggest that sub-sector of SMEs should be identifies and classified. According the report published by World Economic Forum (2013) various types of SMEs such as village handicraft makers (weaving, embroidery, etc.), potteries, dying, small machine shops, restaurants, knitting, small dairy process, etc. are becoming increasingly important to economic development of developing nations. In the same line, Bangladesh Bank has categorized 132 sub-sectors for the SMEs in Bangladesh such as, agro-processing, agro-based activities, horticulture, fisheries, Information technology, dry cell batteries, bio gas plant, light engineering, renewable energy, and handicrafts (Bangladesh Bank, 2015).

From the Global Entrepreneurship Monitor report, it has been revealed that total early-stage entrepreneurial activity which is the percentage of 18-64 population who are either a nascent entrepreneur or owner-manager of a new business is 12.8% in Bangladesh. In the country, 11.6 percentage of 18-64 population are currently an owner-manager of an established business for more than 42 months. 72 percentage of 18-64 population in Bangladesh (individuals involved in any stage of entrepreneurial activity excluded) have indicated that fear of failure would prevent them from setting up a business (Global Entrepreneurship Monitor, 2011). It has been also reported that Bangladesh couples with affirmative insights of opportunities to start a business with low perceived capabilities and high fear of failure. From the survey by the Global Entrepreneurship Monitor (2011), it has been noted that seven out of ten individuals see good opportunities to start a business while concurrently most of these individuals contend that fear of failure would preclude them to set up a business. In the human development index Bangladesh ranks 146 out of 187, Global Competitive Index 108 out of 142, in the doing business index Bangladesh ranks 122 out of 183 (Global Entrepreneurship Monitor, 2011). From the data it can be identified that the rate of perceived capabilities was the second lowest and the fear of failure was the highest in Bangladesh in global comparison. However, service sector is playing more roles in Bangladesh in both TEA and EBA in comparison to similar economies. Making a comparative analysis, it can be infer that Bangladesh still needs to go forward for the development of entrepreneurship activities for which SMEs sector should be given higher importance. The report published by the Global Entrepreneurship Monitor (2011), indicates that 64 per cent of the entrepreneurs in Bangladesh perceive that there is immense opportunities for the entrepreneurship ventures, which is higher than other Asian countries like Iran or Pakistan. On the contrary of seeing opportunities, 72 per cent of the entrepreneurs possess fear of failures of their venture. Perhaps this is one of the most important issues that need to be consider with attention and need to scrutinize. However, the entrepreneurial intention is one of the vital issues in the entrepreneurial domain as well as in the entrepreneurship research. It has been found that only 25 per cent of the surveyed responded embeds entrepreneurial intention. This could happen due to the setting of entrepreneurial environment, which is overshadowed by the fear of failure. Perhaps such fear of failures constitutes due to the impediments and limitations of the development of the entrepreneurship venture. The Table 1 shows an comparative picture of few entrepreneurship venture indicators of two countries (Iran and Pakistan) along with Bangladesh.

Table 1. Comparison of entrepreneurship indicators

	Bangladesh	Pakistan	Iran
Perceived Opportunities	64%	40%	32%
Perceived capabilities	24%	43%	46%
Fear of failure	72%	35%	33%
Entrepreneurial intentions	25%	23%	30%
Media attention for entrepreneurship	49%	48%	58%
Nascent entrepreneurship rate	7.1%	7.5%	10.8%
New business ownership rate	7.1%	1.7%	3.9%
Early-stage entrepreneurial activity (TEA)	12.8%	9.1%	14.5%
Discontinuation of business	2.5%	1.6%	6.4%
Female Necessity driven	34%	81%	24%
Male Necessity driven	26%	43%	56%

Source: Global Entrepreneurship Monitor (2011).

The participation of female in the entrepreneurship business is increasing in Bangladesh. Historical time shows that female population of the country were more inclined towards home making activities. But as the days are flowing through, capitalism is placing in the society with deep root; the incorporation of female population in the economic activities is becoming integral. In fact, it can be assert that the role of micro-credit program and Village Phone Program initiated by the Noble Laureate Professor Yunus have revolutionized the entrepreneurial setting of Bangladesh. The village phone program was supported by Grameen Bank, the mother institution of micro-credit and GrameenPhone, a leading telecommunication company in Bangladesh. The program facilitated the rural women of Bangladesh to be an entrepreneur. The program had impact the empowerment of the rural poor women in the country, which later contributed the overall national development. Under the VPP, the women entrepreneur could take out loans to buy a phone. Grameen Bank facilitated credit to the equivalent of US dollar 133 to each of these women, who were termed as Village Phone Operators or VPOs (Rashid & Rahman, 2009). GrameenPhone provided the technical and network support to the women entrepreneur. Each of the phones was under possession of the VPOs, who is responsible for expanding telecommunication services to village people and also adjacent areas. As part of the entrepreneurship business VPOs collects call charges according to the prescribed rate by GrameenPhone. This business model have facilitated both for the entrepreneurs and GrameenPhone to earn revenue (Rashid & Rahman, 2009). This has actually turned the entire community into the customer of GrameenPhone (Anderson, 2006). The VPP has significantly changed and contributed to the life of rural women in Bangladesh. It has opened up a way to earn their livelihood, increased the role in decision making, and enhanced their dignity relative to the rest of the community (Alam, Yusuf, & Coghill, 2010). From the societal perspective the VPP has able to eliminate the middlemen in trade and business of rural areas, once who were very powerful. It has also helped the rural micro-entrepreneurs to develop new business contacts (Alam et al., 2010). The concept of VPP is continuing its legacy but with different form. As reported by the Human Development Report (2015), in many villages in Bangladesh female entrepreneurs use their phones to provide paid services for neighbours. Many people sell phone cards or sell and repair mobile phones across developing countries, specifically in Bangladesh. Recently, in Kenya, an entrepreneurial initiative named M-Pesa has created much of interest and appreciation due to its effectiveness in the domain of social innovation. M-Pesa, a mobile money transfer service has created a scope to flourish entrepreneurship ventures in Kenya. Similarly, in Bangladesh a mobile money transfer services has emerged, which is not only a classic example of social innovation but also contributing a lot to create small scale entrepreneurship in Bangladesh.

Therefore, it can be comprehended that the scenario of SME sector in Bangladesh is mixture of challenge and great opportunities. To promote the development of entrepreneurship ventures, private organizations are playing important role in Bangladesh. However, as a principal stakeholder, the governed and other government related autonomous bodies have engaged themselves in the development process of SME sector in Bangladesh. To promote the development of the SME sector, there are indeed various financing scheme for the development of SME sector in Bangladesh initiated by Bangladesh Bank, SME foundation, and leading NGOs. Having said, still there are wide ranges of challenges for the development of SMEs in Bangladesh, which has been discussed in the following section.

CHALLENGES OF ENTREPRENEURSHIP DEVELOPMENT IN BANGLADESH

Policies, regulations, discussions, and initiatives have been taking place in Bangladesh by the all government during their tenure. Despite of the fact the SME sector is not flourishing in the way that it should have been. In fact, the entrepreneurs of SME sector in Bangladesh face a number of difficulties in their business. Though the promotion of SME development has been a stated objective of successive governments since 1971, the comprehensive macro policy system has sustained to keep on biased against SME development in numerous ways and distribution of public sector investments, trade and taxation policies in particular have mostly been anti-SME development in character and contents (Chowdhury, 2007).

According to Yusuf and Schindehutte (2000), there are some factors which push the entrepreneurship development specifically during the adverse economic condition of a country. These are mainly, the need for subsistence, the need to innovate to survive, need to quickly recognize and exploit the opportunities even in the declining economic situation. From different literatures it has been revealed that these nascent entrepreneurs in the developing countries need supports to make the business a successful one. Entrepreneurship throughout the world faces different challenges and barriers from different context. In a study on tourism conducted by Lordkipanidze, Brezet, and Backman (2005) found impediments of entrepreneurship such as lack of finance, high government tax, administrative barriers, negative social attitude towards entrepreneurship specifically in rural communities, low skill level, resistance to change, lack of awareness, and lack of information on market. In a developing country like Bangladesh micro, small, medium entrepreneurship business faces barriers such as access to appropriate information (Rahman & Yousuf, 2010), frequent harassment by government officials who extort money and regulatory barriers (Khan, Nazmul, Hossain, & Rahmatullah, 2012; Rashid, 2012), access to finance (Rahman & Yousuf, 2010; Rashid, 2012), poor infrastructure, including bad roads inadequate water shortage, erratic gas and electric supply, and a poor telecommunications system (Khan et al., 2012; Rashid, 2012). Further, scholars have noted that in Bangladesh SME is characterized by Low capitalization and limited assets, geographical diversity and high mortality, poor credit knowledge, very limited access to formal source of credit (Chowdhury, 2007). Miah (2007) stated that the foremost limitations for SMEs in Bangladesh are lack of adequate investment, lack of modern technology, irregular/inadequate supply of power, poor physical infrastructure and high transportation cost, poor information about market opportunities and requirements, inadequate availability of raw materials, lack of research & development facilities, absence of operative and transparent legal system, difficulties in accessing technology, credit constraints, and most importantly the political instability.

In a survey conducted by Chowdhury (2007), it has been revealed that infrastructure facilities are one of the significant impediment for the development of SME sector. Specifically, the respondents reported that frequent power failure, load shedding, poor transport facilities, inadequate telecommunication services are the major barriers for the entrepreneurship venture. The study shows that 83 per cent of the respondents were not at all satisfied with the required infrastructure for the development of the SME ventures (Chowdhury, 2007). According to the World Economic Forum (2015), Bangladesh ranks on 107 position out of 140 countries that they have surveyed. It has been reported by the World Economic Forum (2015), Institutional setting is ranked 132, Infrastructure is in 123, Business sophistication ranked 117 out of 140 countries in the world. Further, the report highlighted the most problematic factors of doing business in Bangladesh. The most problematic factors of doing business in Bangladesh are mainly: Corruption, Inadequate supply of infrastructure, Government instability/coups, and Inefficient government bureaucracy. However, there are other factors as well, which includes: Access to financing, Policy instability, Tax rates, Complexity of tax regulations, and so on. While focusing only on the infrastructure, it has also been revealed that Bangladesh ranks at 124 out of 140 countries in terms of quality of overall infrastructure. In quality of roads the country stands at 113, quality of railroad it is at 75th position, quality of air transport infrastructure the country stands at 121 out of 140 countries (World Economic Forum 2015). It has been also asserted by the scholars that Poor transport infrastructure or inefficient transport services mean higher transportation costs and longer time of delivery, which create bottlenecks to the development of healthy entrepreneurship since profit opportunities would become limited (Chowdhury, 2007). Further, supply of electricity is a major obstacle for the SME sector. Sufficient supply of electricity is vital for the inclusive development of the country. Without electricity it is in fact difficult to roll out the socio-economic activities in any given country. In Bangladesh, even after 45 years of independence, 40.4 per cent of the population still leaves without electricity (Human Development Report, 2015).

Legal and regulatory framework is one of the impediments for the development of SME sector in Bangladesh. According to the scholars, the lack of legal and regulatory framework, the ventures in Bangladesh either SME or large corporations are facing severe difficulties (Tsunoda, Ahmed, & Islam, 2013). From the study by Chowdhury (2007), it has been revealed that majority of the entrepreneurs reported that there is a prevalent lack of confidence in the legal and regulatory framework of the country, which is characterized by weak and non-transparent administrative and judicial systems, inconsistencies in enforcing laws, bureaucratic interpretation of rules, lack of firm political commitment, lack of accountability, hooliganism and political muscleman ship, lack of rule of law, and lack of control of corruption. For the last two decades there have been political turmoil continuing in the country. The credibility of the administration and to an extent the judicial system has been controversial. Specifically, the quality of the government administrative wings presumes to have deteriorated than earlier times. It happened mainly due to the political interference to the administration. Further, the rule of law in the country for the last decades is a major point issue. Local and international human rights organizations, political parties in the countries are questioning on the rule of law in the country. In fact, from the political view, currently, the country is turning to an authoritarian regime, where the government has set a puppet opposition party to legalise the parliamentarian system. During last few years, thousands billions of dollars have been looted from the public bank only by few persons who are alleged to have close connection with government leaders. Therefore, the in a sense, there is not rule of law, and no effective initiative to hold back the on-going race of corruption. Such situation is surely hindering the development of SME sector in Bangladesh.

Entrepreneurship is a multifaceted process that require for drive, vision, and tenacity for the development of business. The expansion of this route hinge on the educational system that is the most impelling factor for increasing human skills, knowledge, attitudes and values as well as encouraging creativity. The study by Chowdhury (2007), shows that 66 per cent of the total respondent have identified entrepreneurship education and training as a constraint for entrepreneurship development in Bangladesh.

Instable political climate is one of the major barriers for the SME development. A favourable and smooth political environment is essential for the development of any business in any country. Regrettably political environment in Bangladesh are too much contaminated. Political structures and the settings are still remaining hostile. Personal and political antagonism between political rivals, frequent strikes, lack of respect for elementary principles of democratic governance have become the principal characteristics of political system of the country. All these have raised the culture of corruption, bribery, and destructive attitudes of the politicians. Such situation has created an absenteeism of the rule of law and dispiriting the development of entrepreneurial talent and initiative in the country.

The balance of participation among male and female is also hindering the growth of the SME sector in Bangladesh. Specifically can say, gender discrimination is one of the reason that is discouraging the female populace to participate in the commercial activities in the country. Still, in many parts of the country female cohort of the population is in danger. Female are not encouraged to work or carry out entrepreneurial activities in the society. According to the scholars, Bangladesh's labour market is a typical in the extent to which women do not participate in the formal labour market (Bauchet & Morduch, 2013). That remains one of the challenges for the inclusive development of the SME sector in Bangladesh. The intense dearth of required capital to an extent is hindering the development of SME sector and small scale ventures. Inadequate personal and family savings and an absenteeism of financial innovation severely limit the growth prospects of promising start-ups in developing countries.

However, it is true that these challenges are not those which cannot be overcome. If there is serious intention of the government and the concern bodies, it is much of sure that SME sector in Bangladesh can flourish rapidly. Therefore, it is important to consider the challenges and capitalizes the existing opportunities for the development of the SME sector in Bangladesh.

OPPORTUNITIES OF ENTREPRENEURSHIP DEVELOPMENT IN BANGLADESH

Sarder, Ghosh, and Rosa (1997) found that firms which are receiving supports services significantly take hold of higher growth resulting in business success. However, the support services are mainly from the different organizations which are considered to have more institutionalized process such as: private organizations (Islam & Tsuji, 2011; Osmonalieva, 2011), Non-government organizations (Dahan, Doh, Oetzel, & Yaziji, 2010; Webb, Kistruck, Ireland, & Ketchen, 2010), government organizations (Ahmad, Ramayah, Wilson, & Kummerow, 2010; Hansen, Rand, & Tarp, 2009). Based on the research literatures and real business practices it has been found that these organizations support the entrepreneurs in different way, in different context, for example, providing financial assistance, training, information and technological support, infrastructural support etc. Ultimately all these supports collectively may contribute to the entrepreneurship business success in Bangladesh.

As mentioned earlier, Bangladesh holds a large number of populations which is an immense opportunity for the development of the SME sector. Due to the large population there are various ways to explore the opportunity to utilize the waste materials into renewable energy. According to Human Development Report (2015), a number of 129,000 of population has the employment potential of renewable energy. Renewable energy business venture not only will contribute to the development of SME sector, but also it will generate a large number of employments.

Bangladesh has coastline of 580 kilometers as the whole southern part is faced towards the Bay of Bengal. That gives an opportunity for the country to develop the ship breaking industry. Ship breaking is a multibillion-dollar industry in which large commercial vessels are recycled at the end of their operational lives, typically at 25–30 years. Rather than leave them to gradually weather away and release large volumes of harmful pollutants to the environment, there is an active business in recycling all fuel, oils, engine parts and fixtures, followed by the steel hull. Currently, the top five ship-breaking countries are Bangladesh, China, India, Pakistan and Turkey. Nurturing the ship breaking industry would give leverage to the SME sector to develop.

Handicrafts industry has long history of success and legacy in Bangladesh. The Moslin, Jamdani, and jute made products still are well attracted in the international markets. The design and the procedure of those products are unique therefore having great opportunities to flourish.

Most importantly, the young age cohort is the biggest opportunity for Bangladesh. It has been observed that this group of youth are doing immensely good in their own field. Young aged cohort is coming up with diverse range of innovative ideas, which actually are not nurtured properly. In many international competitions they have showed their talents and proved their competencies. This group of people could be potential opportunity for the development of SME sector in Bangladesh.

Innovativeness of the people in Bangladesh is one of the opportunities, which perhaps can be promoted and should be given priority. While people are lack of supports, they tend to come up with innovative solutions by own selves. In fact, it has been observed that poverty sometimes opens up the opportunity to innovative something unique that essentially solves the problems faced by the marginalised group. As, there are large number of people still under the poverty line, the poor people perhaps can be the source of further SME sector development.

The most interesting opportunities lies within the light engineering industry in Bangladesh. As said before, people in Bangladesh are innovative; therefore, the light engineering sector can be potential area for the overall SME sector development.

Based on the automobile industry in Bangladesh, SME sector could flourish. In fact, there is a place in Bangladesh, which is famous for theft car and automobile parts. Unfortunately the law enforcing agencies are indirectly supporting them to operate stealing cars and automobile parts. These people are truly talented as they can easily fix cars and replicate automobile parts. It is a contention that rather than considering them as group of social destructor, they can be considered as potential source for the automobile based SME sector in Bangladesh. In the following sections the possible recommendation would be provided.

The fertility of the soil in Bangladesh is well known due to the geographic structure and for the formation of land (delta land). The agro business thus possess a great opportunities for the development of SME sector in the country. Already, agro-products like strawberry have started to produce in the country for the first time. Similarly, other fruits and vegetable cultivation could be prospective for the entrepreneurial business in the country.

Bangladesh is well known for arts, culture, and literacy. Publishing house in Bangladesh are famous for publishing books, novels, text books, and etc. However, embracing the strong previous experience, this industry may join to the international publishing industry where, Bangladesh could be the back and production office for the academic and research journals. Due to the lower costing, international publishing agencies would be interested to bring in business in Bangladesh thus the scope of opening up publishing based SME sector will be instituted.

Bangladesh is a country of full potential with a large number of populations. If these opportunities are capitalized it is hoped that the SME sector in Bangladesh would be one of the strongest SME sector in the region. For that, it is important to have policies and a strong body which can implement those policies. Therefore, this chapter intends to provide some recommendation which would contribute to the development of the SME sector in Bangladesh.

RECOMMENDATION

Small-medium Enterprise (SME) sector development is the most important task for the government of Bangladesh. For long period of time this sector has been in the talk for the politicians and bureaucrats. Since the independence of the country citizens are continually been fed with hopes and aspiration that SME sector will be given highest priority. Nevertheless, for last few years, it seems that the pace of SME sector development is gearing up. Due to the high competitive environment, entrepreneurs are taking initiatives of their own to establish business venture. There have been less policy recommendation based studies have been carried out in context of Bangladesh. Based on the discussion in this chapter, the study intends to put up the following recommendations for the SME sector development in Bangladesh.

Micro Level Recommendation

- Entrepreneurship education is one of the vital means to develop the SME sector in Bangladesh. Still in the education system the entrepreneurship courses are not been made mandatory. The entrepreneurship education should start from the higher secondary level in the country. Entrepreneurship courses found to be taught only in business related programs in the country. However, it is important to include the entrepreneurship courses in the higher secondary level of the education system in Bangladesh. In addition, there should be separate courses as 'practical', where students need to create an entrepreneurship venture within their institutional premises and run the business for at least one year. Perhaps based on the running the business students will be evaluated in the exam.
- Entrepreneurship training program should be formalized in each district town of the country. Perhaps, entrepreneurship training course certification could be a pre-requisite to obtain financial assistance for the business. During the training program, entrepreneurs should be given information technology related training as well which will increase their technical competencies. From the study by Rahman et al. (2015b), it has been revealed that strategic competencies, technical competencies, conceptual competencies, and opportunity competencies are vital for the small scale venture entrepreneurs. Therefore, perhaps the government and the non-government organizations can come up with training program which would enhance the entrepreneurial competencies of the SMEs owners and managers. Such training program presumes to enhance the managerial capability of the SME entrepreneurs as well.
- There should be a strong well-built network among the SMEs in Bangladesh. SME foundation of Bangladesh should play more effective role to create a network among the SMEs. Unfortunately, still there no database for the SMEs in the country. To nurture the SMEs it is important to have detailed database for the SMEs operating in the country. Such data base would not only assist to build network, it will also open up the scope to get diverse range of benefits and business scheme for the business. SMEs should be connected with each other through the database which will allow to source and distribute product and services.
- A sturdy incubation centre based on sub sector is important for the development of the SME sector. This incubation centre will generate new business ideas for the particular sub-sector and source for potential market of the product and services.
- The SMEs business owner should be given certain level of priorities in doing banking and dealing with the government agencies. Perhaps the SMEs owner could be provided with special identity card which will allow them to get leverage for the purpose of their business.

Macro-Level Recommendation

- It is important to ensure a market-oriented economy based on sound legal and regulatory structures for the development of the SME sector in Bangladesh. For smooth functioning of the market economy, Bangladesh needs a sound legal and regulatory structure backed by the rule of law so that existing business can thrive and new businesses can emerge freely. A stable democratic system with binding rules and structures that govern all players is the best guarantor for political stability. Political and economic institutions must be built up in Bangladesh for practicing democracy geared at establishing a stable and a law enforcing government
- To create an entrepreneurial environment that is driven by friendly rules and regulations encourages the development of SMEs. And the foremost role in this scenario is played by government institutions. Effective government institutions must be open and decentralize their administrative structure which will allow a smooth flow of procedures. The government of Bangladesh should also be free from corruption and create conditions for all citizens to participate and compete in the market place without too much regulation.
- Intensifying markets for and nurturing competitiveness of SMEs (creating surroundings for SMEs to have access to information on markets and goods' prices and support them to develop markets and sell their products; supporting in presenting, introducing, promoting, and channelling their potential products; enabling participation in goods supply and service delivery under the plans on goods procurement with city corporation budget sources.
- Inspiring SMEs to accelerate export and build favourable conditions for the SMEs to collaborate with foreign partners, multiply goods and service export markets. The government of Bangladesh can come up with export promotion-support program, that will enable them meet up extra cost to create linkage with the foreign partners.
- Government should encourage to create a social entrepreneurship trend among the existing SME venture which will not only address the development of the SME but also it will assist to the development of the socio-economic sector of the country. Through the social entrepreneurship venture, the SME can achieve their financial success as well as address the need of the society and thus contribute to the social development in the country. Therefore, a spate scheme for the social entrepreneurship should be introduced in the country.
- In Bangladesh, the technology based entrepreneurial activities are popularizing. Therefore, the government should encourage to establish technological based business venture thus turn the existing entrepreneurs to techno-entrepreneur.
- The infrastructure facilities especially the, road communication, electricity, and internet should be given highest priority in order to boost up the SME sector.
- SMEs should be linked with the educational institution, particularly with the universities. This will create a win-win situation for universities and SME venture. Universities should be given additional budget to carry out research on SME sector, which can help to develop the SME sector. SMEs also can gain diverse knowledge from the universities.
- Research & Development centre should set up in every district of the country which will be under one university or highest educational institution of that particular district town,
- The government should also set up innovation centre in each district town of the country. From the Human Development Report (2015), it has been revealed that Bangladesh is far behind compare

with other countries in innovation. If the innovation centre is being set up in each district town, there will be a domino effect which will ultimately influence the SME development in Bangladesh.

- Large private organization should also be encouraged by the government to collaborate with small-medium enterprises for sourcing their supplies and raw materials. Large private organization may also create an environment which will enable to transfer of knowledge and skill to the SME ventures in the country.

CONCLUSION

SME is indeed a vital player for the overall development of the country like Bangladesh. Previous studies have offered different guidelines for the SME development in Bangladesh. However, time has been changed, new things, new issues are coming up in the current setting of SMEs in Bangladesh. Therefore, in the current context of Bangladesh, it is important to revise the landscape of SME in Bangladesh. With the available concurrent data, the study believes to contribute to knowledge building on SMEs in Bangladesh. The study will be helpful as guideline for the policy makers, entrepreneurs, other stakeholders, suppliers, researchers, and also academician for the further course of actions.

REFERENCES

Ahmad, N. H., Halim, H. A., Ramayah, T., & Rahman, S. A. (2013). Revealing an open secret: Internal challenges in creating an entrepreneurial university from the lens of the academics. *International Journal of Conceptions on Management and Social Sciences*, *1*(1), 2357–2787.

Ahmad, N. H., Ramayah, T., Wilson, C., & Kummerow, L. (2010). Is entrepreneurial competency and business success relationship contingent upon business environment? A study of Malaysian SMEs. *International Journal of Entrepreneurial Behaviour & Research, 16*(3), 182-203.

Alam, Q., Yusuf, M. A., & Coghill, K. (2010). Village Phone Program, Commodification Of Mobile Phone Set And Empowerment Of Women. *The Journal of Community Informatics*, *5*(3-4).

Anderson, J. L. (2006). A Structured Approach for Brining Mobile Telecommunications to the World's Poor. *The Electronic Journal of Information Systems in Developing Countries*, *27*(2), 1–9.

Bakht, Z., & Basher, A. (2015).*Strategy for Development of the SME Sector in Bangladesh*. Academic Press.

Bangladesh Bank. (2015). *SME activities*. Retrieved from https://www.bb.org.bd/sme/

Bauchet, J., & Morduch, J. (2013). Is micro too small? Microcredit vs. SME finance. *World Development*, *43*, 288–297. doi:10.1016/j.worlddev.2012.10.008

Chowdhury, M. S. (2007). Overcoming entrepreneurship development constraints: The case of Bangladesh. *Journal of Enterprising Communities: People and Places in the Global Economy*, *1*(3), 240–251. doi:10.1108/17506200710779549

Dahan, N. M., Doh, J. P., Oetzel, J., & Yaziji, M. (2010). Corporate-NGO collaboration: Co-creating new business models for developing markets. *Long Range Planning*, *43*(2), 326–342. doi:10.1016/j.lrp.2009.11.003

Davis, P. (2011). *Escaping poverty: Patterns and causes of poverty exits in rural Bangladesh* (978-1-906433-66-6). Retrieved from UK: http://www.environmentportal.in/files/Escaping%20poverty.pdf

General Economics Division Bangladesh. (2010). *Making vision 2021 a reality*. Dhaka: Government of Bangladesh.

Global Entrepreneurship Monitor. (2011). *Entrepreneurs and Entrepreneurial Employees Across the Globe*. Author.

Goldman Sachs Investment Bank. (2007). *Beyond the BRICS: A Look at the Next 11*. Author.

Hall, J., Matos, S., Sheehan, L., & Silvestre, B. (2012). Entrepreneurship and innovation at the base of the pyramid: A recipe for inclusive growth or social exclusion? *Journal of Management Studies*, *49*(4), 785–812.

Hansen, H., Rand, J., & Tarp, F. (2009). Enterprise Growth and Survival in Vietnam: Does Government Support Matter? *The Journal of Development Studies*, *45*(7), 1048–1069. doi:10.1080/00220380902811025

Hossain, N. (2005). *Elite perceptions of poverty in Bangladesh*. Dhaka, Bangladesh: University Press Limited.

Human Development Report. (2015). *Work for Human Development*. Author.

Human Rights Watch. (2016). *Country Profile- Bangladesh*. Retrieved from https://www.hrw.org/asia/bangladesh

Hye, H. A. (1996). *Below the line: Rural poverty in Bangladesh*. Dhaka: The University Press Limited.

Imai, K. S., & Azam, M. D. S. (2012). Does Microfinance Reduce Poverty in Bangladesh? New Evidence from Household Panel Data. *The Journal of Development Studies*, *48*(5), 633–653. doi:10.1080/00220388.2012.661853

Islam, M. A., & Tsuji, K. (2011). Bridging digital divide in Bangladesh: Study on community information centers. *The Electronic Library*, *29*(4), 506–522. doi:10.1108/02640471111156768

Khan, J. H., Nazmul, A. K., Hossain, M. F., & Rahmatullah, M. (2012). Perception of SME Growth Constraints in Bangladesh: An Empirical Examination from Institutional Perspective. *European Journal of Business and Management*, *4*(7), 256–272.

Kolk, A., Rivera-Santos, M., & Rufín, C. (2013). Reviewing a Decade of Research on the" Base/Bottom of the Pyramid"(BOP) Concept. *Business & Society*, 1–36.

Lordkipanidze, M., Brezet, H., & Backman, M. (2005). The entrepreneurship factor in sustainable tourism development. *Journal of Cleaner Production*, *13*(8), 787–798. doi:10.1016/j.jclepro.2004.02.043

Low, M. B., & MacMillan, I. C. (1988). Entrepreneurship: Past research and future challenges. *Journal of Management*, *14*(2), 139–161. doi:10.1177/014920638801400202

National Encyclopedia of Bangladesh. (2015). Banglapedia. In S. Islam (Ed.), *National Encyclopedia of Bangladesh* (2nd ed.). Dhaka, Bangladesh: The Asiatic Society.

Osmonalieva, Z. (Ed.). (2011). *Entrepreneurship Support*. Eskilstuna-Västerås, Sweden: Mälardalen University.

Rahman, J., & Yousuf, A. (2010). Economic growth in Bangladesh: Experience and policy priorities. *Journal of Bangladesh Studies*, *12*(1).

Rahman, S. A., Amran, A., Ahmad, N. H., & Taghizadeh, S. K. (2014). GrameenPhone: Creating a Win-Win at the Base of the Pyramid in Bangladesh. *Global Business and Organizational Excellence*, *33*(5), 41–53. doi:10.1002/joe.21562

Rahman, S. A., Amran, A., Ahmad, N. H., & Taghizadeh, S. K. (2015a). Enhancing the Wellbeing of Base of the Pyramid Entrepreneurs through Business Success: The Role of Private Organizations. *Social Indicators Research*, 1–22. doi:10.1007/s11205-015-0951-4

Rahman, S. A., Amran, A., Ahmad, N. H., & Taghizadeh, S. K. (2015b). Supporting entrepreneurial business success at the base of pyramid through entrepreneurial competencies. *Management Decision*, *53*(6), 1203–1223. doi:10.1108/MD-08-2014-0531

Rahman, S. A., & Das, D. K. (2005). The Development of Small and Medium Enterprises (SMEs) in Bangladesh. *Stamford Journal of Business Studies*, *1*(1), 108–123.

Rashid, A. T., & Rahman, M. (2009). Making profit to solve development problems: The case of Telenor AS and the Village Phone Programme in Bangladesh. *Journal of Marketing Management*, *25*(9-10), 1049–1060. doi:10.1362/026725709X479363

Rashid, M. M. (2012). Proposed research direction for sustainable SMEs in Bangladesh. *Bangladesh Research Publications Journal, 6*(3), 317-329.

Report, G. C. (2015). The Global Competitiveness Report 2015-2016. Author.

Sarder, J. H., Ghosh, D., & Rosa, P. (1997). The importance of support services to small enterprise in Bangladesh. *Journal of Small Business Management*, *35*(2), 26–36.

Shariff, M. N. M., & Peou, C. (2008). The relationship of entrepreneurial values, firm financing and the management and growth performance of small-medium enterprises in Cambodia. *Problems and Perspectives in Management*, *6*(4), 55–64.

Smith, L. C., Khan, F., Frankenberger, T. R., & Wadud, A. (2013). Admissible Evidence in the Court of Development Evaluation? The Impact of CAREs SHOUHARDO Project on Child Stunting in Bangladesh. *World Development*, *41*, 196–216. doi:10.1016/j.worlddev.2012.06.018

Sun, J., Buys, N., & Wang, X. (2011). *The Characteristics and Capabilities of New Chinese Entrepreneurs and their Emerging Small to Medium Size Enterprises.* Paper presented at the 8th SMEs in a Global Economy Conference 2011.

The World Bank. (2010). *Global economic prospects*. Author.

The World Bank. (2011). *World Development Indicators Database*. Retrieved 13 November from http://siteresources.worldbank.org/DATASTATISTICS/Resources/POP.pdf

The World Bank. (2012). *Bangladesh at glance*. Retrieved from http://www.worldbank.org/en/country/bangladesh

The World Bank. (2014). *Poverty and Equity Data*. Retrieved from http://data.worldbank.org/topic/poverty

The World Bank. (2015). *Indicators Data*. Retrieved from http://data.worldbank.org/indicator

The World Bank. (2016). *Indicators Data*. Retrieved from http://data.worldbank.org/indicator

The World Factbook. (2015). *Country Profile*. Retrieved from USA: https://www.cia.gov/library/publications/the-world-factbook/geos/bg.html

Tsunoda, J., Ahmed, M., & Islam, M. T. (2013). *Regulatory Framework and Role of Domestic Credit Rating Agencies in Bangladesh*. Academic Press.

UNFPA. (2015). *World Population Dashboard*. Retrieved from http://www.unfpa.org/world-population-dashboard

United Nations Human Rights Commission. (2015). *Preliminary findings of Country Visit to Bangladesh by Heiner Bielefeldt, Special Rapporteur on freedom of religion or belief* [Press release]. Retrieved from http://www.ohchr.org/en/NewsEvents/Pages/DisplayNews.aspx?NewsID=16399&LangID=E

Webb, J. W., Kistruck, G. M., Ireland, R. D., & Ketchen, J. D. J. Jr. (2010). The Entrepreneurship Process in Base of the Pyramid Markets: The Case of Multinational Enterprise/Nongovernment Organization Alliances. *Entrepreneurship Theory and Practice*, *34*(3), 555–581. doi:10.1111/j.1540-6520.2009.00349.x

World Economic Forum. (2013). The Global Competitiveness Report 2012–2013. Author.

World Economic Forum. (2015). The Global Competitiveness Report 2015–2016. Author.

Yusuf, A., & Schindehutte, M. (2000). Exploring entrepreneurship in a declining economy. *Journal of Developmental Entrepreneurship*, *5*(1), 41–56.

KEY TERMS AND DEFINITIONS

Grameen Bank: Grameen Bank is the mother institution of micro-credit and GrameenPhone. a leading telecommunication company in Bangladesh. The Grameen Bank facilitated the rural women of Bangladesh to be an entrepreneur and contributed the overall national development.

Poverty in Context of Bangladesh: In context of Bangladesh, poverty has been referred to the inequality in income, poor infrastructure, lack of education, poor health, inefficient public sector, lack of work opportunities, low wage rate, population growth, and lack of human resource development.

SMEs in Bangladesh: In manufacturing sectors of the SMEs, medium enterprise would be those with assets worth US$14 to US$42 million (minus land and factory building, and including replacement value) and/or 100 to 250 of workers. In service industry, medium enterprises will be those which employ 50 to 100 employees and have assets (defined as above) worth of US$ 0.1 to US$ 2.1 million. In manufacturing, small enterprise would be those with assets worth US$71 thousand to US$1.4 million (defined as above) and/or 25 to 99 workers. In service industry, small enterprises will be those which employ 10 to 25 and have assets (defined as above) worth US$7 thousand to US$1.4 million.

SMEs' Barriers in Bangladesh: Access to appropriate information, frequent harassment by government officials who extort money and regulatory barriers, access to finance, poor infrastructure such as bad roads inadequate water shortage, erratic gas and electric supply, and a poor telecommunications system, low capitalization and limited assets, geographical diversity and high mortality, poor credit knowledge, very limited access to formal source of credit, lack of modern technology, irregular/inadequate supply of power, poor physical infrastructure and high transportation cost, poor information about market opportunities and requirements, inadequate availability of raw materials, lack of research & development facilities, absence of operative and transparent legal system, difficulties in accessing technology, credit constraints, and most importantly the political instability.

Strategic Development Paradigm of Bangladesh: The predominant objective of strategic development paradigm of Bangladesh is speeding up socio-economic development, eradicating poverty, and reducing income disparity and regional inequality.

Chapter 7
Working Capital Financing by Banks in Small Enterprises: Problems and Challenges for Bangladesh

Md. Mosharref Hossain
Bangladesh Institute of Bank Management (BIBM), Bangladesh & Universiti Utara Malaysia, Malaysia

Yusnidah Ibrahim
Universiti Utara Malaysia, Malaysia

ABSTRACT

Among all the economic players, small enterprises (SEs), by number, dominate the whole world business segment. However, it is a very common problem for SEs, in every economy either developed or developing, to get access into formal financial sector. Working capital can be treated as the life blood for SEs to be operated. But unfortunately, most of the small enterprises face serious problem while obtaining such loan from banks. On the other hand, banks face a lot of problems to finance working capital to SEs. Therefore, this chapter intends to identify the problems faced by SEs in obtaining and by banks while financing working capital. A total of 413 small enterprises were interviewed through a structured questionnaire administrated directly by the researchers and selected purposively from the capital city (Dhaka) of Bangladesh. The major findings indicate that about 72% small enterprises got the access into banks for working capital loan although all of them face a lot of problems while obtaining such loan from banks. To identify the problems and challenges faced by banks while financing working capital to SEs, 34 commercial banks' officials working in SME department were interviewed through questionnaire and selected purposively based on their high involvement into SME sector lending. Bankers encountered different problems and challenges related to working capital financing in SEs. Based on the survey findings, a good number of solutions have been formulated for policy initiatives.

DOI: 10.4018/978-1-5225-2165-5.ch007

INTRODUCTION

Among all the economic players, small enterprises (SEs), by number, dominate the whole world business segment (EdinburghGroup, 2013). In consideration of the contribution to the world GDP, it varies from 16% (in low income countries) to 51% in high income countries (EdinburghGroup, 2013). In terms of employment creation worldwide, research suggests that small and medium enterprises are the dominant contributors in all the regions. Beyond the contribution towards the GDP and employment, small businesses are also significant for the society for building social network, ensuring life standard of poor people, export earnings, reducing social unrest, creating new entrepreneurs, satisfying consumers' needs with competitive price, fulfilling the requirements of many large businesses and others (Mamun, Hossain & Mizan, 2012).

Small and medium enterprises are considered as the backbone of the economies of Asia region. During 2007–2012, on an average SMEs account for 98% of all enterprises and constitutes more than 66% of the national labor force in Asia (ADB, 2013). This report also reveals that in the same period the sector contributed 38% (on average) of the GDP or manufacturing value added and 30% total export values. SEs are also the backbone of Bangladesh economy and their contributions can reduce poverty to a satisfactory level by creating jobs for the skilled and unskilled manpower in this sector. In Bangladesh, SME sector contribute 25% to the GDP, about 40% of gross manufacturing output, account for 90% of the private sector enterprises and about 70% to 80% of the non-agricultural workforce working in the sector which is around 25% of the country's total labor force (Alo, 2014, Februry 7).

Bangladesh economy is characterized by high population, low per capita income, high level of unemployment and underemployment, mass poverty and high income disparity (Mamun, Hossain & Mizan, 2012). In these circumstances, higher growth of SEs which is treated as an engine for economic growth and machine for job creation may reduce poverty of Bangladesh to a satisfactory level by creating employment for the skilled and unskilled manpower in this sector. Despite the high potentiality and remarkable contributions towards the economy, still the sector is facing severe financing problems almost all the Asian countries, along with other multidimensional problems depending on the countries, which are hindering their survival and jeopardizing potentiality of future growth.

As part of SEs financing requirements, working capital (WC) plays a significant role in the success of SEs. According to Kwenda (2015), working capital can be regarded as the reservoir of internal financial resources and can be used for supporting the growth or expansion of business. WC is that portion of a firm's capital which is employed in short term operations. It is a significant issue during financial decision making as this is a part of the investment in total assets that requires an appropriate financing investment (Bhunia, 2010). Although working capital problems can be experienced by organizations of any size, it is usually small businesses that experience most problems, especially during periods of start-up and expansion (McCosker, 2000). Too little of working capital will result in cash flow problem, failing to pay suppliers on time and being unable to claim discounts for prompt payment. On the other hand, too much resource tied-up in working capital will earn a lower-than-expected rate of return on capital employed. Proper management of working capital is important to guard the financing constraints (Ding, Guariglia & Knight, 2013). As a result, optimum investment in working capital is the precondition for the small business success. Therefore, Peel, Wilson and Howorth (2000) suggest that an efficient working capital management is particularly important for small and medium-sized firms due to the greater difficulties they have in obtaining funding on the long-term capital markets and, hence, their greater dependence on trade credit and bank credit as major sources of debt.

As SEs are heterogeneous in nature and lack proper business plan, required documents and formal business structure, they traditionally faced difficulty in obtaining working capital from formal sources (Mamun, Hossain & Mizan, 2012). Availability of required working capital in appropriate time is the significant problem for most of the SEs. For the day to day business operation, timely availability of working capital and its utilization is required. This kind of problem arises mainly due to delay in payments made by the debtors. In his study, Hossain (1998) reveals that SEs in Bangladesh encounter great difficulties while rising working capital because of the reluctance of banks to provide loans to SEs. On the other hand, WC financing in SEs is one of the key area for the banks where they face challenges. Most of the entrepreneurs in our country are illiterate and are unable to prepare proper business plan that may help them to get money from bank (Mamun, Hossain & Mizan, 2012). Lack of proper documentation, un-structured business record, on the other hand, create major problems for them.

The number of studies that have addressed the financing and capital structure of SMEs are mostly for developed countries (Hughes, 1997; Watson & Wilson, 2002; Zoppa & McMahon, 2002; Hussain & Matlay, 2007); only a few address for developing countries (Peterson & Shulman, 1987; Aidis, 2005; Abor, 2005; Bhaird & Lucey, 2011). Research into the area of working capital financing to SEs in Bangladesh is very scant, particularly research investigating the problems of WCF in SEs and banks. Therefore, this chapter focuses on the problems faced by SEs in obtaining and by banks while financing working capital.

OBJECTIVES OF THE CHAPTER

This chapter examines the problems faced by small enterprises in Bangladesh while obtaining working capital loan from banks and problems and challenges encountered by banks for financing working capital to SEs. Thus the specific objectives of the chapter are:

- To represent present scenario of working capital financing by banks to SEs and their existing mechanism.
- To identify the problems faced by SEs in obtaining working capital loans from banks.
- To point out the problems faced by banks while financing working capital to the SEs.
- To propose some solutions for policy initiatives.

PRESENT SCENARIO OF WORKING CAPITAL FINANCING BY BANKS

At present banks and financial institutions are coming forward to provide finance to the small enterprise sector. Different initiatives have already been taken and practiced by the financial institutions in order to facilitate small enterprise financing mostly for the behest of Bangladesh Bank (Mamun, Hossain & Mizan, 2012). The present scenario of working capital financing in SMEs has been analyzed in terms of percentage of total working capital financing by group of banks, bank group-wise total working capital financing, industry-wise working capital financing by group of banks, and working capital finance in small and medium industries by banks.

Table 1 shows the working capital financing by all banks in terms of percentage. It is evident that, the State Owned Banks' (SOBs) and Private Commercial Banks' (PCBs) working capital financing increased in 2014 compared to 2012. But the working capital financing by Specialize Banks (SBs) and Foreign

Table 1. Working capital financing by group of banks (in %)

	2012	2013	2014	CAGR*
SOBs	15.24%	9.91%	15.69%	20.49%
SBs	4.76%	5.95%	0.43%	-46.19%
FCBs	8.71%	10.71%	5.12%	0.16%
PCBs	71.29%	73.43%	72.80%	20.18%
All Banks	100.00%	100.00%	100.00%	19.35%

Source: Authors' calculation, Data: Scheduled Banks Statistics, Bangladesh Bank.
* CAGR stands for Compound Annual Growth Rate.
Note: SOB- State own Bank, SB- Specialized Bank, FCB- Foreign Commercial Bank, PCB- Private Commercial Bank.

Commercial Banks (FCBs) decreased from 4.76% to 0.43% and from 8.71% to 5.12% respectively. Among all, PCBs' financing was highest (72.80%) in 2014 followed by SOBs (15.69%). In terms of working capital financing, the compound annual growth rate (CAGR) of SBs was the lowest (- 46.19%) among all the banks in last three years (2012 to 2014). However, SOBs and PCBs achieved almost the same CAGR which are 20.49% and 20.18%. Therefore, the CAGR of all the banks shows the remarkable increase from year 2012 to 2014. This is a positive indication for accelerating the growth of economy.

Although the PCBs remained the major partner in working capital financing in 2014, the percentage of financing is slightly decreased from 2013. However, they are playing a significant role in fulfilling the working capital needs of the borrowers. Figure 1 depicts the bank group-wise working capital financing in terms of amount, which also shows that all the banks together increasing their contribution towards the working capital financing in different industries.

The industry-wise working capital financing by banks is shown in Table 2. The PCBs are playing the dominant role in working capital financing among all banks. In 2014, in all categories of industries except the cottage industries, the PCBs' working capital financing was highest. In large industries' PCBs provided 75.33% working capital in 2014, the SOBs' position was second (11.94%), followed by FCBs and SBs. Small and medium industries got maximum working capital financing from PCBs and SOBs. However, PCBs contribution towards the small and medium industries reduces from 69.56% to 63.15%

Figure 1. Group wise total working capital financing by banks (Tk. In Lacs)

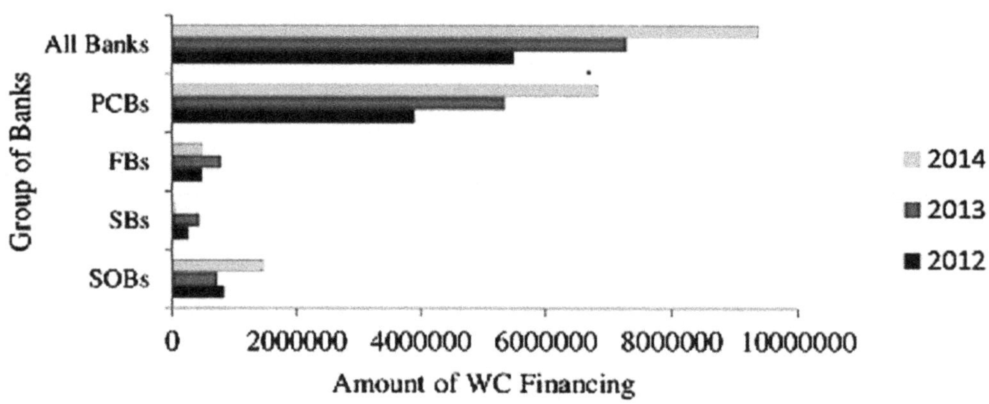

Table 2. Industry-wise working capital financing by banks (in %)

Size and Nature of Industrial Credit	2012				2013				2014			
	Large & Medium Industries	Small Scale Industries	Cottage Industries	Service Industries	Large Industries	Small and Medium Industries	Cottage /Micro Industries	Service Industries	Large Industries	Small and Medium Industries	Cottage /Micro Industries	Service Industries
SOBs	16.10 (1830)	6.92 (3261)	36.65 (3110)	4.51 (324)	12.79 (880)	8.69 (4309)	30.46 (2180)	1.10 (815)	11.94 (977)	28.29 (5914)	52.47 (1213)	1.57 (516)
PCBs	70.99 (32703)	68.54 (4125)	39.07 (1119)	79.25 (1541)	75.95 (19634)	69.56 (22706)	38.36 (1586)	72.06 (87043)	75.33 (25345)	63.15 (110922)	34.77 (1467)	85.37 (93496)
SBs	4.39 (5600)	23.22 (1936)	24.27 (5195)	0.22 (1122)	0.92 (44)	19.90 (24091)	30.96 (11063)	0.35 (121)	1.69 (125)	6.76 (6185)	12.70 (4996)	0.92 (525)
FCBs	8.52 (1603)	1.32 (58)	0.00 (0)	16.02 (78)	10.34 (1667)	1.85 (382)	0.21 (5)	26.49 (220)	11.05 (1522)	1.80 (373)	0.06 (4)	12.15 (181)
All Banks	100 (41736)	100 (9380)	100 (9424)	100 (3065)	100 (22225)	100 (51488)	100 (14834)	100 (88199)	100 (27969)	100 (123394)	100 (7680)	100 (94718)

Source: Authors' calculation, Data: Scheduled Banks Statistics, Bangladesh Bank.
*Parentheses indicate the number of account.

from the year 2013 to 2014 whereas the contribution of SOBs increases drastically for the same period from 8.69% to 28.29%. The contribution of FCBs in this regard is negligible and SOBs remained in moderate position.

In terms of the working capital financing in cottage/micro industries, SOBs played a pivotal role in 2014 which account for 52.47% followed by the PCBs (34.77%). However, in consideration of the service industries PCBs contribution was highest in 2014 which is 85.37% followed by the FCBs (12.15%). The stake of working capital finance by the SOBs and SBs is marginal in this regard.

Table 3 shows bank-wise amount of working capital finance and their compound annual growth rate (CAGR) in small and medium industries. All the groups of banks except the SBs show the positive trend in financing small and medium industries. The CAGR of SOBs shows the highest increase (121.35%) while SBs shows negative (-28.49%). The FCBs' and PCBs' CAGR also show the positive and almost similar. In aggregate, the CAGR for all banks is 22.67%, although the group of SBs' affects negatively. It is worthy to mention that the small enterprises' access to working capital finance in the SOBs, PCBs and FCBs are positive, meaning greater extent of financial inclusion in this segment.

Table 3. Working capital financing in small and medium enterprises by banks (Tk. in Lacs)

	2013	2014	CAGR
SOBs	165,453	810,682	121.35%
SBs	378,802	193,700	-28.49%
FCBs	35,264	51,485	20.83%
PCBs	1,324,360	1,809,301	16.88%
All Banks	1,903,879	2,865,168	22.67%

Source: Scheduled Banks Statistics, Bangladesh Bank.

EXISTING MECHANISM OF WORKING CAPITAL FINANCING BY BANKS

The SMEs of Bangladesh suffer from scarcity of working capital although day by day this portion is increasing as part of financial inclusion. However, these are not sufficient compared to the larger demand. Therefore, small businesses are using both formal and informal sources to finance their working capital needs. One of the important problems the entrepreneurs facing while financing from informal sources is the high interest rate. On the other hand, the absence of required documents and prior banking relationship mostly hiders those to get access in formal sources and also facing problems in getting finance on emergency basis.

Irrespective of many problems for the banks to provide funds to the SEs, most of the banks are providing working capital facilities to their SE clients. The banks follow different mechanism in providing finance to the SE clients. Usually the mechanism involves several steps. These are (i) Client selection based on the information furnished in the Know Your Customer (KYC) (ii) Assessment of the loan proposal by the credit officer (iii) forward it to the credit committee (including documentation and the comments based on the assessment) (iv) Re-assessment by the credit committee (v) Decision and Disbursement of the loan. The mechanism depends on the operational procedure (centralized or De-centralized), practices, risk management procedure of individual bank. The working capital financing mechanism also largely depends on the attitude of the individual banks to the SE clients. The current flow chart of working capital financing followed by different banks is shown in Figure 2.

The process shown in figure 2 for financing working capital to SEs is not a straight forward process rather it varies from bank to bank and even for client to client. For some clients, especially for the credit worthy firms, the mechanism may be pretty simple but for other cases it goes some rigorous process. While financing working capital, a few PCBs including some foreign banks operating in Bangladesh

Figure 2. Process flow chart of working capital loan disbursement

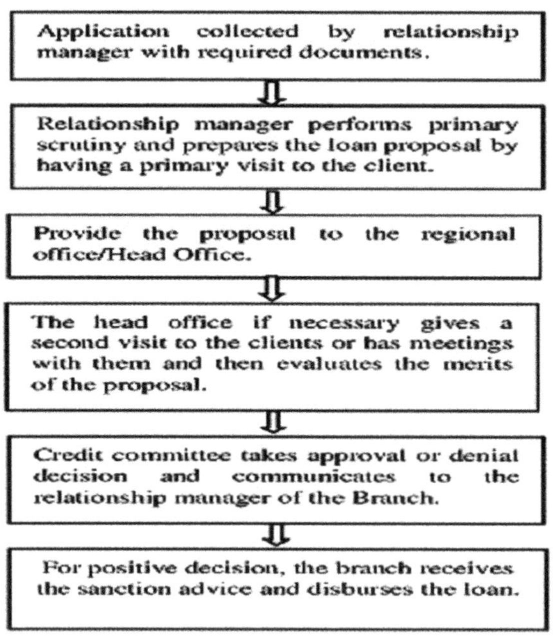

follow the best practices and emphasis more on cash flow of small business. But the other PCBs and SOBs are still heavily dependent on the traditional collateral based lending.

While appraising the proposal for working capital financing, the relationship manager or the credit officers of banks evaluate different factors. The selection depends on the strategic commitment of the individual banks towards the SEs. It is also very much dependent on the approach of the individual bankers related to working capital financing to the SEs. The common factors are the experience of the entrepreneur, the net worth of the business, security provided by the entrepreneur, the status of the banking relationship, cash-flow etc.

METHODOLOGY

The study emphasizes on the three broad sectors of small businesses operating in Bangladesh namely, manufacturing, trading and service sectors. It is evident from the SME Foundation cluster approach that out of 177 SME clusters, 38% small businesses are located in Dhaka division and most of them are concentrated in Dhaka city (Abdin, 2015, March 5). Therefore, the study considers Dhaka city as the study area. According to the census of Bangladesh Bureau of Statistics (2015), there are a total of 178,829 small business units are operating in Dhaka city. As the list of small enterprises including their addresses except the total number is not available in Bangladesh, the probabilistic sampling technique cannot be applied. Hence, the study considers non-probabilistic sampling technique to make the survey manageable but within reliable limits.

The study considers Krejcie and Morgan (1970) table to determine the total sample size. Based on the Krejcie and Morgan table 384 small businesses are selected as the sample size. However, to reduce the sampling error and to minimize the non response rate, the total sample size are multiplied by two (Hair, Wolfinbarger, Ortinau, & Bush, 2008). Therefore, the total 768 questionnaires are administered in Dhaka city those are purposively selected. Since the focus of the study is working capital financing problems faced by both small businesses and banks, the unit of analysis is small firms operating in Dhaka city and bank officials of SME department. Therefore, to collect the information about the firm, interview has been conducted through the structured questionnaire among the owners or the managers where owners are absent from their businesses operation and also from the bank officials of some selected banks in the same city. The total numbers of 768 questionnaires were distributed among the enterprises in Dhaka city. The researcher could able to receive 437 questionnaires (response rate 56.90%) from the interviewee. Out of the 437 questionnaire 24 were rejected by the researchers due to the insufficient information regarding specific answer. Finally, the total of 413 enterprises was selected and has been taken as the sample. Among 413 small enterprises, 114 (27.60%) enterprises are from manufacturing sector, 237 (57.39%) are from trading sector and the rest 62 (15.01%) are from the service sector.

For collecting the information from banks, a purposive sample survey has been conducted on 34 commercial banks considering their high involvement into SME sector. Among 34 banks, four state owned commercial banks (SOB), twenty-four private commercial banks (PCB) including six Islami banks, two specialized banks (SB), and four foreign banks (FCB) are selected. To justify the problems raised by the small entrepreneurs, both the accepted and rejected loan proposals of some particular banks were also reviewed. Published literature, research papers, different books were reviewed to complete the theoretical background and relevant websites were visited to collect secondary information.

This chapter is divided into six sections. After a brief background as part of introduction (section 1), section 2 highlights the present scenario of working capital financing by banks. Section 3 shows existing mechanism of working capital financing by banks. Section 4 presents the findings and discussion of survey results. Section 5 represents some proposed solutions for policy initiatives. Finally, section 6 and 7 present the scope of further research and chapter conclusion.

FINDINGS AND DISCUSSIONS OF SURVEY RESULTS

In order to identify the small enterprises access to working capital finance, problems faced by them while obtaining WC finance and the problems cited by banks to finance them, current study surveyed on 413 enterprises belonging in different sectors. The survey results are presented and discussed in below:

Survey Results of Small Enterprises

Small Enterprises' Access to Banks for Working Capital Loan

Access to finance has a beneficial impact on business start-ups and growth, which will ultimately contribute to the economic growth. It is the prerequisite for ensuring the overall growth of small businesses. A large body of literature on different countries shows that there is a good association between access to finance and the growth or performance of small firms. Some studies highlights that the availability of finance is the prime factor for the success and growth of SMEs (Cook, 2001; Ou & Haynes, 2006). Some studies conclude that financing constraints have negative influence on the firm growth (Ayyagari et al., 2008; Beck et al., 2005). For example, Beck et al. (2005) from their cross-country analysis reveal that firms bear a 3% growth penalty that face finance as a main constraint compared to the firms that do not face it. Study done by of Beck and Demirguc-Kunt (2006) finds that for SMEs the impact of financial constraint on their growth is highly severe. Another study in Eastern Europe reveals the interesting findings that firms with access to formal financial institutions exhibit 9% higher employment growth and 36% higher sales growth for the period of 2002 to 2005 (WB, 2009). Therefore, it is understandable that for the overall growth and contribution of small firms towards the economy, there access to the formal financial sector is the vital requirements.

In order to analyze the access to credit in formal sector, the study collected information through survey about the capital structure of small firms who took loan both from formal and informal financial institutions. A total of 349 (84.50%) enterprises got the access in both sources and their average capital structure is shown in Table 4. According to Table 4, the average debt/equity ratio of the manufacturing sector is the highest (41.67%) compared to other two sectors. This is because manufacturing sector needs working capital in different phases of their production including other requirements.

From the last column of Table 4 that describes for range of debt and equity position, it is clear that some of the firms are highly leveraged, while some are low leveraged. High leveraged enterprises are riskier for bank to finance further and the low leveraged small enterprises tend to be less risky. The manufacturing sector shows the highest range from 12.43% to 73.55% and the overall range of debt equity is from 4.63% to 73.55%. The lower debt equity ratio indicates that most of small business highly relied on their own financing due to the lack of greater access to formal financial sector or they do not need bank loan.

Table 4. Average capital structure of sample enterprises (group wise and total)

Business Type	Number[1]	Capital Structure		Range	
		Debt (%)	Equity (%)	(% of Debt)	
Manufacturing	93	41.67	58.33	12.43	73.55
Trading	209	27.33	72.67	7.44	62.49
Service	47	22. 71	77.29	4.63	69.85
Total Sample	349	31.94	68.06	4.63	73.55

Source: Authors' calculation based on survey questionnaire.

Figure 3 shows the overall scenario of sample small firms based on their access to banks for external financing. Although 84.50% firms got the access into the formal and informal sources for funds mobilization, the 71.91% got the access into banks only. The other 28.09% did not get access into banks and relied on their own or informal sources. Choudhury & Raihan (2000) conducted a survey on SME access to credit and found that, only 35.79% of SME stakeholders enjoy unrestricted access to the formal credit while 50.53% did not get any kind of access. Therefore, it is evident that the access to credit in formal sources increases highly due to different initiatives and programs of central banks and all the commercial banks operating in Bangladesh.

Enterprises those got the access to banks, 72.05% enterprises are satisfied in terms of loan covenants and, of them, 85.51% enterprises are willing to take further loan. But 14.48% enterprises were not willing to take further loan from banks mainly due to the fact that they do not need further loan. On the other hand, enterprises those received loan from banks, 27.94% enterprises are satisfied with the loan covenants and requirements. Although they are not satisfied with their banks, 62.65% enterprises are willing to take further loan which mean that there is a big gap between the demand of loan and the supply.

Figure 3. Summary of survey results on access to formal credit from banks

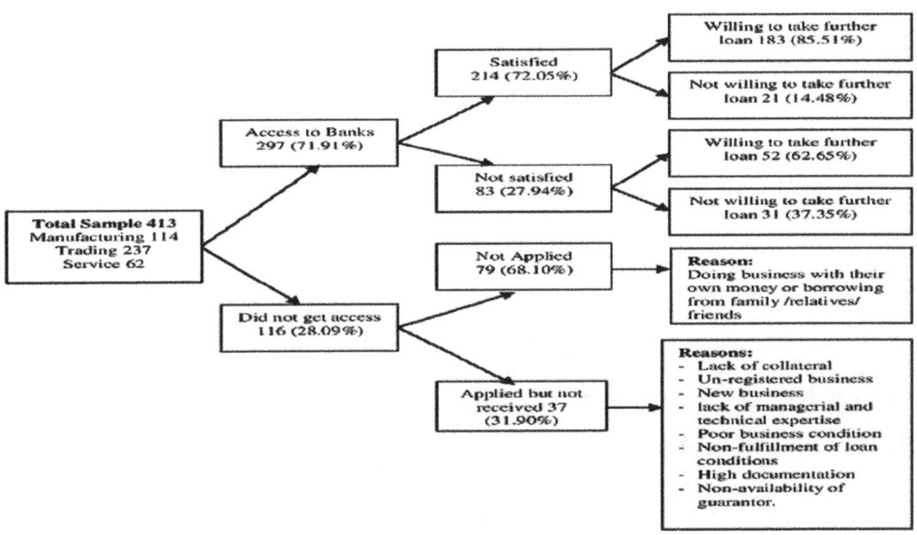

From figure 3 it is also evident that out of total enterprises who did not receive loan, 68.10% enterprises did not apply in banks for any loan since they do not need formal finance or do not want to involve with banks for financing needs rather borrowing from other informal sources like family, relatives and friends. On the other hand, 31.90% enterprises applied for the loan but they were rejected by banks. Some major reasons for that rejection also depicts in figure 3. The study also identifies that the trading sector got the highest access among the all sectors although the access of manufacturing sector should be more important as it acts as a catalyst of the economic growth of Bangladesh. Above all, it is evident that gradually the small enterprises access to the formal credit is improving due to the awareness of the customers as well as the eagerness of the banks and some regulatory compulsions of the central bank.

According to the survey result, many enterprises did not receive the full amount they applied for. In case of working capital, 63.87% firms obtained the full amount they applied and other 36.13% enterprises did not get the full amount they applied for. This kind of funds shortage may create problem for their business operation. Small enterprises generally receive working capital loan in different forms. Most of the funds they receive in the form of cash credit. Figure 4 shows different modes of working capital financing by banks and received by small enterprises.

From figure 4, it is evident that, the borrowers are availing a number of financing options such as cash credit, overdraft, letter of credit, bills financing, other short term loans, loan against imported merchandise (LIM), loan against trust receipt (LTR), export cash credit (ECC). Out of all the modes, they receive 68% through cash credit followed by bills financing (19%).

Small Enterprises' Sources of Working Capital Financing

While financing working capital, small enterprises generally use different sources. Among them internal financing is the most common source and includes owner investment, as well as funding through retained profits, and / or the sale of assets. On the other hand, more common external sources in Bangladesh are debt finance in the form of loans and overdrafts from bank and other financial institutions, micro credits, leasing and hire purchase, factoring and trade credit etc. More often, small firms need to use a combination of financing sources, depending on the sector, and the stage in their growth and development. Table

Figure 4. Different modes of working capital loan received by small enterprises

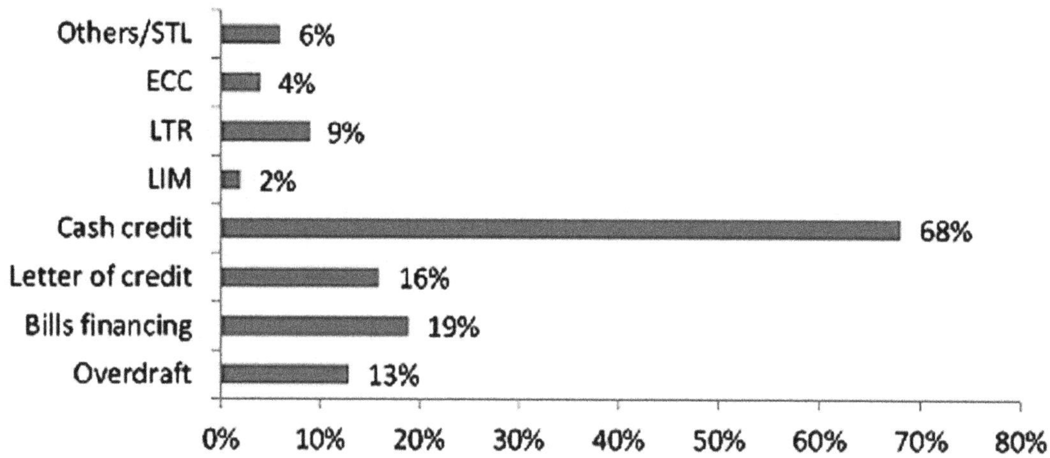

5 highlights the sources of finance for small business start-up and working capital needs. According to the table, at the start-up phase most of the enterprises (92%) finance their business with their own savings as formal lenders do not find much interest and are reluctant to finance the small business during the early stage of business cycle.

For business start-up, Small businesses use their family as one of the vital sources of finance and 52% of the respondents mentioned it as the second source. Supplier credit is the third and bank credit goes fourth one for financing their business start-up. In case of working capital financing, commercial banks are the important source for the small businesses. As shown in Table 5, 67% of the respondents are using banks as the prime source for their working capital needs. Now-a-days commercial banks are offering different types of products for serving their SE clients in respect to the working capital financing. Supplier credit is the second highest source for them as the working capital financing which is supported by the answer of 53% response. Supplier credit helps small business for effective management of their cash flow due to the delay payment facilities. This facility reduces the dependency on banks for short term credit.

Owner's savings for working capital financing is the most reliable and suitable for small businesses. About 38% of the respondents mentioned that they use their own savings for this purpose. They also use family borrowing for fulfilling these working capital needs. Sometime these sources help them to meet the gap they are demanding from formal sources and funds supplied by the institutions. Retained earnings are also the great source for their working capital financing tools. 47% of the respondents mentioned it as the source of working capital financing. Moreover, the respondents use some other sources for the same purpose like, factoring, other borrowing, government credit, etc.

Small Enterprises' Utilization of Working Capital Loan

Working capital are required to meet the needs of day-to-day expenses such as raw-materials, stores, power and fuel, salaries, wages, administrative expenses, interest, sales and distribution expenses and other expenses to produce the saleable goods, up-to the realization of the sale proceeds. Small businesses generally use most of their funds for fulfilling the working capital needs. In order to identify the utilization of working capital loan as well as fund diversion, a tentative list in the questionnaire is provided.

Table 5. Small enterprises' sources of working capital financing

Sources of Finance	% of Respondents	
	Working Capital	Business Start-Up
Bank credit	67	13
Gov. credit	05	01
Retained earning	47	12
Supplier credit	53	22
Owner's saving	38	92
Family borrowing Factoring	26 4	52 0
Other borrowing	17	9

Source: Authors' calculation based on survey questionnaire.

Respondents are asked to provide their response in a format measured through Likert type scale where 1 means 'not use' and 5 means 'mostly use'. Table 6 summarizes the responses of the small entrepreneurs.

It is evident from Table 6 that the mean value for using working capital to purchase raw materials is the highest (4.37) indicating that most of the loan they use for this purpose. The second highest mean value is 3.17 for the payment of wages. These two items are the clear evidence of proper utilization of working capital loan. Besides, it is also evident that many respondents utilized their fund in purchasing/modernization of machinery (2.92), and invested in factory building (2.74), meaning they are utilizing it in their business, but it should not be financed from the working capital loan rather it should be utilized from term loan. On the other hand, a number of respondents diverted a portion of their working capital loan by purchasing land (2.83), investing in another business (2.72), paying to other lenders (2.91) etc. Table 6 also evident that there are many other areas where the working capital loans are being partially diverted.

Major Problems Faced by Small Enterprises in Obtaining Working Capital Loan

In order to justify the severity of the problems small enterprises are facing while obtaining loan from banks, nine tentative problems are given in the questionnaire. Enterprises are asked to fill the questionnaire according to the Likert type scale where '1=No problem at all' and '5=Most severe problem'. Table 7 highlights the problems enterprises ranked base on the severity of the problems.

Collateral is typically an obligatory condition for granting a loan. Most of the financial institutions are reluctant to sanction credit to those firms who might fail to offer collateral. However, small businesses often have difficulty in providing sufficient and good-quality collateral to banks. Therefore, it is a major obstacle for obtaining loan from the formal financial sector. Survey result shows that the mean value for excessive security and guarantee requirement is highest (3.81) which is the most severe problem for obtaining loan from banks. The finding of this study is slightly differ with the study conducted by Mamun, Hossain and Mizan (2013) where they find the Security and guarantee is the second highest problems and interest rate is the prime barrier to get access in banks. The dimension is changed mainly due to increasing the ability of enterprises to repay but unable to offer suitable collateral, informal borrowing is costlier to them, high dependency on bank financing and so forth.

Table 6. Small enterprises' utilization of working capital loan

Parameters	Mean Value	Parameters	Mean Value
Raw material/Stock purchase	4.37	Investment in cooperative	2.11
Land Purchase	2.83	Improvement of personal land/building	2.48
Invest in another business	2.72	Purchase of valuables	1.86
Payment to other lenders	2.91	Personal use	2.53
Transportation	1.78	Medical treatment	1.36
Purchase/Modernization of machinery	2.92	Purchase of personal car/motor cycle	1.64
Payment of wages	3.17	Education / Marriage of children	1.24
Factory building	2.74	Sending children abroad	1.41
Investment in share market	1.68	Others (if any)	2.67

Source: Authors calculation from Survey Questionnaire.

Table 7. Severity of the problems for obtaining working capital loan from banks

Sl No.	Obstacle	Importance*
1	Excessive Security and Guarantee Requirement	3.81
2	Complexity of Documentation	3.62
3	High Interest Rate	3.48
4	Long Loan Processing Time	3.15
5	Banker's negligence or lack of interest	3.08
6	Fail to obtain loan on time	2.73
7	Fail to obtain required amount	2.68
8	High sunk cost for Obtaining Loan	1.51
9	Malpractices in Sanctioning Loan	1.46

Source: Authors' calculation based on survey questionnaire.
* Importance is ranked from 1 to 5, with 5 being the most significant.

Documentation is another obstacle for small businesses. Most of the businesses are family oriented and they do not maintain proper documents necessary for their business. On the other hand, banks require a standard set of documents to lend money. From the survey it is observed that complexity of documentation is the second highest problems with mean value 3.63 to get access in banks for working capital loan. Respondents also claim that they face a lot of problems while obtaining documents from different issuing authorities and even it takes much longer time.

Due to the fund shortage from their own, many small businesses are heavily relied on commercial banks for financing working capital. However, they consider interest rate as one of the prime barriers. The mean value of 3.48 indicates that the current interest rate for working capital loan is so high. Beside high interest rate, many banks impose different service charges and processing fees which ultimately increase their effective rate of interest.

Loan should be disbursed when needed. Some time it is found that, due to the time lag of loan requirement and disbursement many businesses cannot continue their operation in line with the market demand. In many cases especially for the businesses that are seasonal in nature face this problem seriously. As per the survey opinion, this is the number forth problem (mean value 3.15) for getting working capital loan. However, a few of the commercial banks in Bangladesh have reduced the loan processing time to one week or less than that. But still most of the banks need more than 15 days to process a loan even it requires a month to several months in some cases.

Generally, banks are very much reluctant to finance small enterprises with the perception that they are highly risky and not profitable to them. Most of the entrepreneurs opined that many officials of banks do not cooperate with them properly or timely, when they need financial services. Survey result shows that, the average rank score is 3.08 which reflect that the variable is marginally significant. As a result, due to the negligence of some bank official the small enterprises could not obtain working capital loan timely and when required.

Due to the long loan processing time, sometime small enterprises do not get the loan in time and cannot meet the requirement of customers. According to the survey, the mean value of respondents is 2.73 for 'fail to obtain loan on time'. Timely availability of working capital loan is one of the critical factors for sustainable business growth. If it is unavailable during the required time, they may be affected by seasonality. After this problem, enterprises rank the problem 'fail to obtain required amount' with a mean value of 2.68. Both over financing and under financing are the problems for small enterprises. When the enterprises do not receive loan amount they applied for, they cannot implement their business plan accordingly.

In order to enter into the formal credit sector small enterprises have to incur more sunk cost than their counterpart. Because, financial institutions do not easily provide their services to the small firms to fulfill their financial needs. Therefore, small businesses try to get the loan from different financial institutions one after another which increases their sunk cost in various forms. From the survey it is evident that the average rank score of this problem is 1.51 indicating the variable as marginally significant. Sometimes malpractices in sanctioning loan also hinder small enterprises to have access in the formal credit. Enterprises rank this problem with the score of 1.46. Although this is not a severe problem, it should be the concern of the policy makers. A few of the entrepreneurs claimed that some officials of banks demand extra money other than the stipulated fees or charges in order to get the required loan amount which they called bribe. Also, sometimes ineligible borrowers avail working capital loan from some corrupt bank officials.

Survey Results of Banks

Commercial banks are playing significant role in financing small enterprises although in some extent they are reluctant to accept the loan request from SEs. The increased involvement of banks in financing small enterprises, to the large extent, mainly due to the central bank's policy initiatives, directives and creation of business opportunities. Previous section highlights several problems of the small enterprises for their access to finance from banks. To identify the problems and challenges faced by banks, the study also conducted another survey cantering the banks that are supplying funds to small enterprises. The subsequent sections discuss the survey results.

Problems Faced by Banks in Sanctioning Working Capital Loan

Banks also face different problems while financing working capital to small enterprises. As a part of that the bankers were asked "what extent do you think following are the problems for financing working capital to small enterprises?" and a tentative list were given related to the problems they face during assessment and disbursement of working capital loan. Table 8 represents the problems banks ranked base on the severity of the problems.

Structured financial information is an important requirement for the banks to assess credit worthiness of borrowers. Unfortunately, most of the small businesses do not record financial information properly and fail to fulfill bank's loan requirements. From Table-8 it is evident that bankers ranked lack of proper and structured financial information with a mean value of 4.21 signifying the number one problem. Therefore, most of the respondents indicate that during working capital financing it is a challenge to get the real financial data about the enterprises and even if it is available in many cases there are some faulty representations and are not sufficient for assessment.

Most of the banks emphasized on proper documentation as one of the severe problems. There is a great dilemma that small enterprises claim banks require many documents and condition to get loan whereas banks claim small enterprises fail to produce the set of appropriate documents without those they cannot go for financing. Bankers ranked this item as the second highest problems where the mean

Table 8. Severity of the problems for financing working capital loan by banks to small enterprises

Sl No.	Obstacle	Importance*
1	Absence of structured financial information	4.21
2	Lack of proper documents	3.78
3	Non-disclosure of information	3.53
4	Lack of collateral and guarantee requirement	3.26
5	Absence of good business plan	3.12
6	Lack of business experience	2.86
7	Lack of previous banking relationship	2.72
8	Low banking literacy	2.31
9	High interest rate	2.29
10	Fund diversion tendency	1.66

Source: Authors' calculation based on survey questionnaire.
* Importance is ranked from 1 to 5, with 5 being the most significant.

value is 3.78 indicating that lack of proper documentation creates barriers in providing working capital loan to a small enterprise even if the enterprise is financially capable to pay the loans in due time.

Material information from the borrowers is important for the banks to assess their financial credibility. However, respondents rank this problem as the third major problem with a mean value of 3.53 that indicate borrowers do not like to disclose all the material information to the banks and sometimes request banks for working capital loans with fraudulent motives. Bankers also claim that, some of the good entrepreneurs sometime show reluctance to disclose financial information related to their businesses.

Collateral and guarantee become the next major problem (mean value is 3.26) identified by bankers. For smooth recovery of loan, banks require some collateral and guarantee form small businesses. According to the bankers' opinions, most of the small businesses operate in a rental house which is risky for them. However, collaterals offered by the small enterprises are either inadequate or inappropriate for a particular type of financing. Banks usually provide working capital financing against inventories as collateral. But it becomes very difficult for banks to value inventories offered by the client as collateral. On the other hand, in case of collateral free loan the borrowers face hurdle to get third party guarantee.

From a good business plan bankers get the idea about current and future movements of a business. Therefore, it is very important document the borrowers need to submit to get the loan from the commercial banks. Survey result shows that the mean value of this problem is 3.12 indicating the absence of business plan or borrowers cannot prepare proper plan of their business.

Banks usually consider small business having previous experiences for providing working capital loan. Previous track record helps them to justify future direction of the business. The mean score of the respondents for this problem is 2.86 that signify the medium level problem. Therefore, it is evident that prior business experience is necessary for small businesses to have working capital loan from banks. On the other hand, Banks can easily identify the behavior of small businesses if they have any previous banking relationship either depository or borrowing. Therefore, they consider this item as the moderate level problem where mean score is 2.72. Most of the small enterprises settle their transactions by cash. So, there is little or no evidence of banking transactions.

Beside the major problems banks face while lending working capital to small enterprises, respondents also consider low level of banking literacy (mean 2.31) among the entrepreneurs, the interest rate offered by banks (mean 2.29) and tendency of fund diversion by borrowers (mean 1.66).

Challenges Faced by Banks in Financing Working Capital

Recently banks are coming forward to finance SEs with a good number of products and services. However, these are not sufficient compared to the larger demand. In many cases bankers are facing a substantial amount of challenges for financing working capital. The common challenges banks face are shown in Figure 5.

According to Figure 5, most of the respondents (87%) encounter information asymmetry as the prime challenge for them. Bankers usually assess the borrower based on the information they disclose in loan proposal and from a short site visit. Besides, banks take some interview or even communicate personally with the proposed clients. However, respondents claim that in many cases small enterprises do not like to disclose some material information that leads them to take incorrect assessment. The second challenges they face is the competition among themselves. Majority of the respondents (74%) state that a very significant challenge they are facing now is the competition among banks. As the number of banks increases to 56, there is a great presence of unhealthy competition among banks. The third challenges they are facing is the un-supportive business environment. The total of 62% respondents opined that the current business environment, the political as well as the economic, is not supportive. Therefore, small enterprises do not like to invest money both in existing and new business.

Fund diversion tendency is another important challenge that banks are facing to lend working capital in small borrowers. Bankers response that, although there may have some lacking in ensuring proper monitoring, but the general tendency of the borrowers to divert funds has gradually increased. The 68% respondents claim in favor of fund diversion tendency. For small businesses, it is easy to enter or exit from the industry. As the small enterprises have easy entry and exit barriers, they can change the businesses frequently which create serious difficulty in ascertaining the use of fund by banks. This leads difficulty in collecting bad loans. Respondents (54%) claim that when the business condition is not good or favorable, some business owners stop operation and hide them to repay the loan amount. The next challenge

Figure 5. Challenges cited by banks in financing working capital

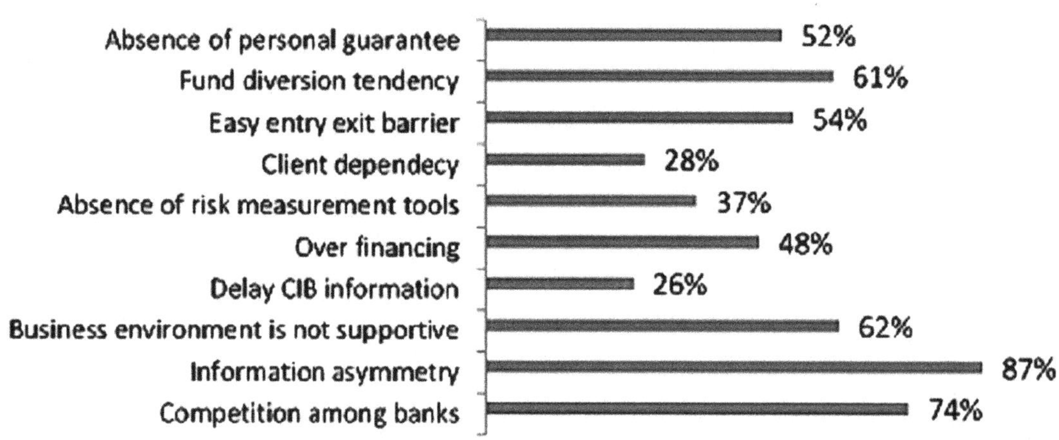

bankers are facing is the absence of personal guarantee. A total of 52% respondents encounter that due to the increase of nonperforming loan (NPL), no people would like to offer third party guarantee which make them reluctant to lend money.

Over financing is another important challenge for banks. Due to the unhealthy competition among banks, many small enterprises can get the access of more funds rather than the requirements. Respondents (48%) also state that the rejection of proposal by one bank may be accepted by another bank for financing. During the survey the bankers (37%) point out another important challenge which is absence of proper risk measurement tools which lead to select some disqualified borrower. The other challenges respondents identify are delay of Credit Investigation Bureau (CIB) information and few clients' dependency of many banks.

SOME PROPOSED SOLUTIONS FOR POLICY INITIATIVES

The study survey on both small enterprises and commercial banks in Bangladesh to identify the problems they are facing while obtaining and financing working capital. Based on the findings from the survey results, some proposed solutions those are shown in below have developed for the banks and policy makers.

1. Survey result evident that collateral and guarantee is the major problem both for bankers and borrowers. For small business it is difficult to manage the required amount of collateral and guarantee, but without sufficient collaterals banks are reluctant to finance working capital. To solve the problem, banks may introduce group guarantee or guarantee based on cluster for working capital financing. Credit guarantee scheme may be introduced although it has some limitations. Besides, financial institutions may take care for the collateral free loan where personal guarantee is strong and the project has good future prospects. Moreover, different collateral substitute such as, group based lending, frequent visit as part of strong monitoring, introduction of cash flow based lending, strong banker-customer relationship, development of credit products that automatically generates savings may be taken into consideration to provide working capital financing.
2. Regarding the required documentation both banks and small enterprises face serious problem. Bankers demand a set of required documentation without which they are reluctant to provide working capital, on the other hand, small firm in most of the cases fail to manage all the documents demand by banks. Therefore, it remains a challenge for the banks to complete the documentation during working capital financing. To address this problem, a coordinated effort is required among the Government, Bangladesh Bank and Commercial Banks to enhance market information availability and make the process easy for getting document from government office. Banks may circulate document checklists to make aware about the documents and may also provide consultancy services to the SEs in completing the documentation process. Moreover, the relationship officer should be very friendly in explaining the terms, documentation process and other aspects of the credit.
3. High interest rate as encounter by small enterprises is another significant problem for working capital financing. Although the prevailing interest rate of banks is not so high compared to the informal sources, the effective interest rate is slightly higher for some additional fees or service charges. Still banks may reduce the rate of interest by searching low cost funds. In this context, Bangladesh Bank, Government and other stakeholders can provide low cost fund to banks and enable them to finance small enterprises at a lower interest rate in consideration of economic development.

With a large number of clients in the portfolio along with standardized process, banks can reduce its administrative cost and thus the interest rate on loans. Bangladesh Bank may introduce more refinancing facility for working capital financing which will ensure a low cost source of fund for the commercial banks and thus enable them to reduce interest rate. In addition, banks may keep an SE database and should practice credit scoring model that may reduce their monitoring cost which ultimately help to reduce interest rate.

4. Sometime small enterprises do not get working capital loan when needed due to the long loan processing time. Long loan processing time may be reduced by adopting standard loan approving procedures based on information technology and maintaining better information management. For example, to ensure quick process of a loan requires support of accounting software, strong MIS, skilled and dedicated manpower along with good commitment from the top management.
5. The survey provides a few instances of banks' negligence in dealing with the SE clients. Although it is few, but the information is very significant for better access to working capital. In this case, bankers should change their mindset first, should have good customer relationship, and positive and caring attitude towards the small entrepreneurs. Bankers have to nourish the small entrepreneurs to become successful. This relationship should be like partnership. Moreover, banks should diversify their portfolio in SE segment for their own profitability as well as sustainability rather any compulsion from the central bank.
6. Many small enterprises claim that they do not get the required amount of loan as per their need. To minimize the problems related with insufficient working capital loan, banks should not consider the prior relationship with the borrower only rather they should also put emphasis on the business prospects of the borrowers. Banks should assess the need of borrower properly so that actual amount of working capital can be disbursed. Besides, banks should make them understand about the process of working capital assessment and the minimum time required for the approval of such capital.
7. Survey evident that frequent visits of the clients to the banks for getting working capital loans raise their sunk costs in terms of money, energy and time. In this regard, relationship officer should be very friendly in explaining the terms, documentation process and other aspects of the credit and should provide the prospective borrower a check list so that the borrower might visualize all the requirements of the loan clearly. Moreover, to reduce the knowledge gap of the borrower in fulfilling the loan requirements, banks should undertake extensive skill development program of their employees who will deliver services to the SE clients.
8. A few enterprises claim that sometime credit officer demand extra money from them to get working capital loan. To address the issue of such malpractices (taking bribe, nepotism etc.), banks may adopt better internal control and governance mechanism to identify such activities, and if found, involved officials must get exemplary punishment.
9. Unstructured financial information is a serious barrier for the entrepreneurs to get access to formal finance. Banks may encourage SE clients to provide accurate and authentic financial information for their analysis and assure them that the information will not be disclosed elsewhere for any other purposes. Beside, business owners should be encouraged to use proper accounting records on their business transactions by educating them to know the benefits of accounting and financial information and by setting up simple SEs accounting standards. In this regard, commercial banks can develop and circulate a simple customer friendly financial template in Bangla for the SEs so that they can record their financial transactions in an organized and structured manner.

10. In order to reduce the information asymmetry, a very good relationship between banks and its SEs should be established by which SEs can identify the potential suppliers of financial services and evaluate the cost of the financial services that are being offered by banks as well as the financial service providers can easily receive the feedback of managerial attributes and evaluate the risk and prospects of the SEs.
11. Bankers claim that most of the entrepreneurs have very low level of knowledge about banking norms and practices and cannot prepare a proper business plan as per banks requirement. In this regard, central bank can prepare a simple business plan template in bangle and circulate it among existing and potential SE borrowers. Bankers may educate the customers and provide consultancy services to help them for preparing good business plan.
12. Another important challenge banks face is the fund diversion tendency of small enterprises. As credits provided to SME clients are monitoring based credit, banks may create a dedicated monitoring team to ensure end use of the financing to avoid fund diversion. Bankers can reduce direct cash based credit and introduce transaction based credit so that the clients will not be able to use the fund at his will. Moreover, bankers may create awareness among the SE borrowers to avoid funds diversion.

FUTURE RESEARCH DIRECTIONS

Commercial banks in Bangladesh are coming forward to finance working capital in small enterprises with a good number of initiatives although these are not sufficient compared to larger demand. In this circumstance, if banks and other stakeholders follow the proposed solutions, in future financing in this sector may increase which will be the benefits both for banks and their clients. Current chapter focuses on the working capital financing problems faced by banks and also problems faced by small enterprises while obtaining working capital from banks. The sample selected from the capital city (Dhaka) of Bangladesh only. Therefore, further study can be done on easy financing mechanism, developing different products and services for working capital financing, how to finance through collateral substitute, business process reengineering for working capital finance considering the sample from both rural and urban areas.

CONCLUSION

Small enterprises sector is one of the major economic players in Bangladesh and contributor in the GDP. Hence, it is immense important to ensuring their access to formal credit like banks for greater economic benefits. The study has pointed out a number of demand side problems while obtaining working capital from banks and also identified the supply side problems and challenges for financing working capital. Small enterprises claim that they face severe problems with banks. On the other hand, banks claim most of the problems exhibit with SEs for financing working capital. Both SEs and banks encountered some common problems like documentation, collateral and guarantee, information asymmetry with a number of many other problems. To address these problems, this chapter recommended some solutions. It is highly expected that if banks and other stakeholders adopt the recommended solutions, these may reduce the current problems they are facing and will ensure a better access to banks for small enterprises to have working capital loan.

REFERENCES

Abdin, M. J. (2015). *SME cluster development key to speedy industrial growth*. The Financial Express.

Abor, J. (2005). The effect of capital structure on profitability: An empirical analysis of listed firms in Ghana. *The Journal of Risk Finance*, *6*(5), 438–445. doi:10.1108/15265940510633505

ADB. (2013). *Asia Small and Medium-sized Enterprise (SME) Finance Monitor 2013*. ADB Publishing.

Aidis, R. (2002). *Why Don't We See More Small-and Medium-sized Enterprises (SMEs) in Lithuania?* Institutional Impediments to SME Development.

Alo, J. N. (2014, February 7). SME credit grows 18% in 2013. *Dhaka Tribune*.

Ayyagari, M., Demirgüç-Kunt, A., & Maksimovic, V. (2008). How important are financing constraints? The role of finance in the business environment. *The World Bank Economic Review*, *22*(3), 483–516. doi:10.1093/wber/lhn018

Bangladesh Bureau of Statistics. (2015). *Economic Census 2013*. Retrieved from http://www.bbs.gov.bd/WebTestApplication/userfiles/Image/EcoCen13/FinalReport%20Part%201.pdf. Accessed at March 28, 2016.

Beck, T., & Demirguc-Kunt, A. (2006). Small and medium-size enterprises: Access to finance as a growth constraint. *Journal of Banking & Finance*, *30*(11), 2931–2943. doi:10.1016/j.jbankfin.2006.05.009

Beck, T., Demirgüç-Kunt, A., & Maksimovic, V. (2005). Financial and legal constraints to growth: Does firm size matter? *The Journal of Finance*, *60*(1), 137–177. doi:10.1111/j.1540-6261.2005.00727.x

Bhaird, C., & Lucey, B. (2011). An empirical investigation of the financial growth lifecycle. *Journal of Small Business and Enterprise Development*, *18*(4), 715–731. doi:10.1108/14626001111179767

Bhunia, A. (2010). A trend analysis of liquidity management efficiency in selected private sector Indian steel industry. *International Journal of Research in Commerce and Management.*, *1*(5), 618–628.

Choudhury, T. A., & Raihan, A. (2000). *Structural Adjustment Participatory Review Initiative, Bangladesh Study Theme 2(C): Implications of Financial Sector Reforms*. Retrieved from http://saprin.org/bangladesh/research/ban_finance.pdf

Cook, P. (2001). Finance and small and medium-sized enterprise in developing countries. *Journal of Developmental Entrepreneurship*, *6*(1), 17.

Ding, S., Guariglia, A., & Knight, J. (2013). Investment and financing constraints in China: Does working capital management make a difference? *Journal of Banking & Finance*, *37*(5), 1490–1507. doi:10.1016/j.jbankfin.2012.03.025

Edinburgh Group. (2013). *Growing the global economy through SMEs*. Retrieved May 21, 2015, from http://www.edinburgh-group.org/media/2776/edinburgh_group_research_growing_the_global_economy_through_smes.pdf

Hair, J. F., Wolfinbarger, M. F., Ortinau, D. J., & Bush, R. P. (2008). *Essentials of marketing research*: McGraw-Hill. *Higher Education.*

Hossain, N. (1998). *Constraints to SME Development in Bangladesh, JOBS project.* USAID.

Hughes, A. (1997). Finance for SMEs: A UK perspective. *Small Business Economics*, *9*(2), 151–166. doi:10.1023/A:1007971823255

Hussain, J., & Matlay, H. (2007). Financing preferences of ethnic minority owner/managers in the UK. *Journal of Small Business and Enterprise Development*, *14*(3), 487–500. doi:10.1108/14626000710773565

Krejcie, R. V., & Morgan, D. W. (1970). Determining sample size for research activities. *Educational and Psychological Measurement.*

Kwenda, F. (2015). Investment and financing constraints: Can working capital management make a difference in South Africa? *Banks and Bank Systems*, *10*(1), 24–33.

Mamun, A. A., Hossain, M. M. and Mizan A. N. K, (2012). *SME Financing: Demand Side Problems and Supply Side Responses.* Research Monograph 003. BIBM.

Mamun, A. A., Hossain, M. M., & Mizan, A. N. K. (2013). *Working Capital Financing in SMEs: Problems and Issues.* Bangladesh Institute of Bank Management.

Mc Cosker, P. (2000). *The effective management of Working Capital.* CIMA Management Accounting Magazine.

Ou, C., & Haynes, G. W. (2006). Acquisition of additional equity capital by small firms–findings from the national survey of small business finances. *Small Business Economics*, *27*(2-3), 157–168. doi:10.1007/s11187-006-0009-8

Peel, M. J., Wilson, N., & Howorth, C. (2000). Late Payment and Credit Management in the Small Firm Sector: Some Empirical Evidence. *International Small Business Journal*, *18*(2), 17–37. doi:10.1177/0266242600182001

Peterson, R., & Shulman, J. (1987). Capital structure of growing small firms: A 12-country study on becoming bankable. *International Small Business Journal*, *5*(4), 10–22. doi:10.1177/026624268700500401

Watson, R., & Wilson, N. (2002). Small and medium size enterprise financing: A note on some of the empirical implications of a pecking order. *Journal of Business Finance & Accounting*, *29*(3-4), 557–578. doi:10.1111/1468-5957.00443

WB. (2009). Doing Business 2009. Washington, DC: Amazon.com's Publishing.

Zoppa, A., & McMahon, R. G. (2002). Pecking order theory and the financial structure of manufacturing SMEs from Australias business longitudinal survey. *Small Enterprise Research*, *10*(2), 23–41. doi:10.5172/ser.10.2.23

KEY TERMS AND DEFINITIONS

Commercial Bank: Commercial bank is a licensed financial institution that act as an intermediary to provide variety of financial services.

Small Enterprises: A *manufacturing concern* with total assets at cost including installation of fixed asset and excluding land and building from Tk. 5 million to 100 million and/or number of employee ranges from 25 to 99. A *service concern* with total assets at cost including installation of fixed asset and excluding land and building from Tk. 0.5 million to Tk 10 million and/or number of employees ranges from 10 to 49. A *trading concern* with total assets at cost including installation of fixed asset and excluding land and building from Tk. 0.5 million to Tk 10 million and/or number of employees ranges from 6 to 10.

Working Capital: The actual amount of capital required for a business for its day-to-day operations and is measured as the current assets minus current liabilities.

ENDNOTE

1 Those who took the loan from both formal and informal sources.

Chapter 8
Understanding and Adoption of E-Finance in Small and Medium Enterprises (SMEs) in Developing Countries:
A Study of Bangladesh and South Africa

Brenda Scholtz
Nelson Mandela Metropolitan University (NMMU), South Africa

Melisa Koorsse
Nelson Mandela Metropolitan University (NMMU), South Africa

Siyasanga Loleka
Nelson Mandela Metropolitan University (NMMU), South Africa

ABSTRACT

The lack of access to finance is hindering growth and development to small and medium enterprises (SMEs), particularly in developing countries. Access to finance can be facilitated by ICT and e-finance, which can reduce the cost of financial services and increase access to international markets. However, in spite of the potential benefits of e-finance, developing countries have been reported to be lagging behind in terms of e-finance adoption as compared with developed nations. The reason for non-adoption could be due to barriers such as lack of ICT infrastructure, data privacy and security concerns. The purpose of this chapter is to investigate the extent of understanding and adoption of e-finance by SMEs. A survey of SMEs in two developing countries, South Africa and Bangladesh, was conducted. The results of the survey revealed that access to financial products and services was the highest rated benefit of e-finance to respondent SMEs, whereas regulatory environment and policy was the highest rated barrier.

DOI: 10.4018/978-1-5225-2165-5.ch008

INTRODUCTION

Small and medium enterprises (SMEs) play a vital role in the development of developing countries by raising employment and rational allocation of scarce resources (Srivastava, 2014). However, the growth of these SMEs in developing countries such as Bangladesh are constrained by a lack of capital (Khan, 2014; Su & Yuan, 2013). Access to finance has also been reported as a vital factor for SME sector development in Bangladesh (Bangladesh Bank, 2016; Hoque, Saif, AlBar & Bao, 2015). Access to finance can be facilitated by Information and Communication Technologies (ICTs), which can improve the probability of an organization's success (Bughin & Manyika, 2016) and in particular SMEs (Hoque *et al.*, 2015; Modimogale & Kroeze, 2009). ICT can enhance services and expand services beyond geographic boundaries (Gumbi & Mnkandla, 2015; Srivastava, 2014). The emergence of internet-based technologies such as social networks, cloud computing and mobile payments have resulted in a gradual shift in the paradigm of the financial sector (Agwu & Murray, 2014; Ping & Chuanwei, 2013). It is predicted that this paradigm shift will lead to a narrowing of the digital divide as basic financial services to a greater number of people will be provided as opposed to only a small group of elite wealthy individuals. However, in a study of SMEs in Bangladesh, it was revealed that ICT adoption has been lower than expected (Hoque *et al.*, 2015). One of the factors hindering this adoption was a lack of awareness of the benefits of ICT. According to Agwu and Murray (2014) the majority of SMEs in developing countries are lagging behind in the use of ICTs and the internet, especially for making transactions. One reason for this lag is perceived security issues by customers (Dewan & Nazmin, 2008).

The widely accepted definition of e-finance according to Allen, McAndrews and Strahan (2002:7) is: *The provision of financial services and markets using electronic communication and computation.* E-finance includes all financial products and services which are available to the consumers and businesses over the internet and includes online brokerage, banking, insurance, and other financial services. According to Agwu and Murray (2014), e-finance enables businesses and ordinary citizens to conduct various financial transactions on the internet, meaning greater availability of financial services. E-finance is classified as one type of e-service. Sorooshian, Onn and Yeen (2013) assert that services such as communication, financial, cultural and recreational that can be delivered with the aid of the internet and computerized systems, such as the web, information kiosks and mobile devices can be regarded as e-services. Whilst internet banking or online banking is one type of e-finance, it has also been classified as a category of e-commerce (Mohiuddin, 2014).

The adoption and use of e-finance can lead to a multitude of potential benefits for SMEs, such as reduced cost of services and transactions (Riyadh, Bunker & Rabhi, 2010; Srivastava, 2014), as well as increased access to products and services in international markets through PCs and mobile devices (Riyadh *et al.*, 2010; Srivastava, 2014; Su & Yuan, 2013). Another benefit of e-finance is improved access to financial information (Mubaraka, Momanyi & Jibia, 2013; Riyadh *et al.*, 2010; Shahrokhi, 2008; Srivastava, 2014).

In spite of the potential benefits of e-finance, the adoption of e-finance by SMEs in developing countries has been slow when compared with larger businesses or SMEs in developed countries (Riyadh *et al.*, 2010; Su & Yuan, 2013). Internet usage naturally impacts e-finance adoption and therefore it can be deduced that ICT and internet issues related to data privacy, security and safety are also barriers to e-finance adoption (Dewan & Nazmin, 2008; Koskosas, 2011; Nasri, 2011; Raza & Hanif, 2013; Susanto, Lee & Zo, 2013). ICT infrastructure (Agwu & Murray, 2014; Narayanasamy, Rasiah & Tan, 2011; Riyadh *et al.*, 2010) and the regulatory environment and policy can influence the adoption of e-finance by customers (Dewan & Nazmin, 2008; Narayanasamy *et al.*, 2011). A regulatory environment includes various rules, policies and regulations related to e-finance. Lastly the lack of ICT skills (Dewan & Nazmin, 2008) and insufficient training can negatively impact e-finance adoption (Riyadh *et al.*, 2010).

In most developing countries like Bangladesh there are problems with ICT infrastructure such as internet access (Ashta & Assadi, 2009), availability and speed (Dewan & Nazmin, 2008), as well as power shedding, which can negatively impact the growth of ICT and ultimately e-finance (Riyadh *et al.*, 2010). In the developing countries in Africa power shedding has also been reported as a barrier to adopting or implementing ICT and e-finance (Agwu & Murray, 2014).

The rapid increase of ICT use by SMEs across the globe has also led to an increase in research on how to utilize ICT in the provision of financial services and the performance of financial transactions (Agwu & Murray, 2014). A review of literature revealed that online financial services and e-finance for SMEs has received limited attention by researchers and that more studies are needed to understand the impact of technology adoption on the financial industry (Han, 2008; Tsai, Huang, Fan & Liu, 2006). In South Africa, research has been done on e-commerce (Kona, 2014), internet usage (Gillwald, Moyo & Stork, 2012), electronic banking also referred to as e-banking (Maduku, 2013; Masocha, Chiliya & Zindiye, 2011), as well as mobile phone banking (Maduku, 2013). In South Africa the adoption rate of certain e-banking services has been reported to be not as good as initially hoped for (Maduku & Mpinganjira, 2012). Whilst e-finance is a relatively new and emerging field of research it has gained great impetus in the business world, particularly in developing countries such as India, China and Brazil (Srivastava, 2014). However, in spite of the enormous growth in technology, the adoption rate of e-finance and in particular e-banking is low in many developing countries, including Pakistan (Khurshid, Rizwan & Tasneem, 2014). Whilst Pakistan is rich in technology adoption, with 20 million internet users and 100 million mobile phone users, e-banking adoption in Pakistan is reported to be still in an infant stage.

The purpose of this chapter is to report on the understanding and adoption of e-finance by SMEs and the types of e-finance currently being used by SMEs. The study investigated e-finance adoption in two developing countries, South Africa and Bangladesh. To give effect to the primary objectives of this study, the following secondary research objectives were formulated:

- To identify the most commonly used types of e-finance by SMEs;
- To establish the benefits of adopting e-finance by SMEs; and
- To establish the barriers to the adoption of e-finance by SMEs.

The structure of the chapter is as follows. The first section discusses the background to the adoption and benefits of ICT, particularly in SMEs and also introduces the concept of e-services. This is followed by an analysis of the benefits and barriers to e-finance adoption as identified by literature. In the next section, the characteristics of SMEs in two developing countries, South Africa and Bangladesh, are described. These two countries are used as participants in a survey and an analysis of these results are then provided. The chapter then highlights some issues encountered in the study and then presents some conclusions and recommendations.

BACKGROUND: ADOPTION OF ICT AND E-SERVICES IN DEVELOPING COUNTRIES

ICT makes a significant and meaningful contribution to economic growth since ICT in various forms, such as e-commerce and other tools, is known to boost productivity by improving the efficiency of individuals, businesses, and the economy as a whole. ICT adoption has recently been identified and recognized as one of the mechanisms that have the potential to stimulate the development and growth of SMEs (Gumbi & Mnkandla, 2015; Hoque et al., 2015; Modimogale & Kroeze, 2009). Those SMEs that are able to leverage and take advantage of ICT to achieve high levels of efficiency and effectiveness will be in a greater position than those that do not. Due to the accelerated global growth in internet and ICT usage, many businesses as well as governments around the world have made huge strides in transforming their services from traditional contact services to electronic means (Alanezi, Kamil & Basri, 2010). Many businesses, financial institutions in particular, have embraced e-services in order to make service accessibility easier for their customers.

In addition to ICT and internet usage, mobile device usage has grown radically and in 2014 reached 75 billion users globally (eMarketer, 2014). Africa has been reported to have the second largest mobile market worldwide after Asia (Phillips et al., 2011). In Sub-Saharan Africa smart phone usage is forecast to grow the most and it is predicted that by 2020 more than half of the connection base will have smart phones by 2020 (GSMA Intelligence, 2014).

However, in spite of the increase in ICT usage in some countries, Hoque et al. (2015) and Dewan and Nazmin (2008) identified several barriers to ICT adoption encountered by SMEs in developing countries such as Bangladesh. These barriers included attitude towards ICT, poor infrastructure, insufficient information and non-customized software. Several factors that could ultimately become barriers to adoption have been reported and of these, trust (Casaló, Flavián & Guinalíu, 2010) and quality (Alanezi et al., 2010) are the most commonly cited. E-service quality can be described as a user's perceptions of the outcome of the service delivery as well as service recovery perceptions should service fail. According to Alanezi et al. (2010), it includes dimensions such as security and privacy, design, reliability, responsiveness, information and ease of use or usability.

Singh and Chauhan (2012) reported that internet presence in remote areas remains a barrier to the adoption of any online service. Additionally, poor bandwidth and lack of trust compromise positive attitudes towards e-services. Conversely, trust, high bandwidth and broadband connectivity play a crucial role in delivering e-services to multiple users. Ashta and Assadi (2009) argue that in poorer countries, web-based lending is more difficult to implement and operate since most poor people are illiterate and have very limited access to the internet on a computer. In such countries, mobile financial applications are considered as an alternative. An Indonesian study revealed that perceived security was a primary factor for influencing trust towards internet banking services (Susanto et al., 2013). In a South African study (Maduku, 2013), low levels of trust in the system of banking through the use of mobiles, was revealed. However, in spite of these low trust levels, customers still have a positive attitude towards mobile banking. It is therefore important that banks investigate the factors that influence a customer's attitude to mobile banking or e-banking.

The focus on this chapter is on the adoption of e-finance by SMEs in developing countries. In particular, two countries South Africa and Bangladesh are investigated in more detail and reported on. The next section investigates the literature on the different types of of-finance and the benefits and barriers to e-finance adoption with a particular emphasis on developing countries such as South Africa and Bangladesh.

BENEFITS AND BARRIERS TO E-FINANCE ADOPTION

Benefits of E-Finance Adoption

The growing consumer demand and a fear of losing market share has driven banks to invest heavily in personal computer banking technology, mobile banking and internet banking (Murari & Tater, 2014). There are various types of e-finance and each of these has specific benefits (Figure 1). E-banking is an umbrella term that is used to describe the different types of services through which customers can request information and carry out most retail banking services such as balance reporting, inter account transfers and bill-payments with the use of technology (Daniel, 2000). Internet or online banking is the most prominent example of e-banking and allows SMEs to manage their current accounts, pay debts, collect credit as well as transfer funds over the internet (Maduku, 2013). The adoption of e-banking has resulted in cost savings (Riyadh *et al.*, 2010), reaching new population segments and enhanced reputation (Agwu & Murray, 2014).

Mobile banking is a technology that benefits banks and customers by allowing people to perform banking transactions anytime and anywhere, promoting efficiency and improved service quality (Malaquias & Hwang, 2016). However, as several studies surveyed by Malaquias and Hwang (2016) have shown, the adoption of mobile banking has been generally low despite the widespread adoption of mobile devices. A survey of banking customers in South Africa revealed that mobile banking was not as popular as expected; however customers still had a positive attitude towards mobile banking and positive intentions to start/continue using the service (Maduku, 2013; Maduku & Mpinganjira, 2012).

Figure 1. Types of e-finance

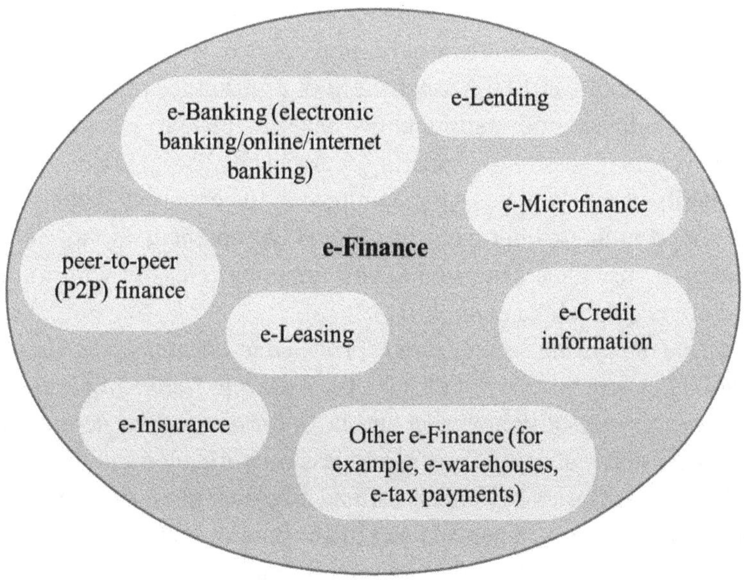

Wireless internet is the main type of broadband connectivity at household level in South Africa (World Wide Worx, 2013). According to Arthur Goldstuck, managing director of World Wide Worx, *the rapidly growing penetration of smartphones and the increased ease of use of the internet on feature phones has changed the way South Africa communicate.* The use of apps mobile phones in South Africa has increased to more than half (51%) of adult cellphone users in cities and towns in late 2013 from 24% in mid-2012. In rural areas, the growth has increased to a 27% usage level, surpassing the overall market of 18 months before and is still increasing rapidly. Both mobile network data use and internet access via hotspots is expected to boom.

According to a report produced by InfoDev, 71% of all South African internet users use a mobile phone in their individual capacity to browse the internet (Calandro, Gillwald, Deen-Swarray, Stork & Esselaar, 2012). This report also revealed that mobile phones are the primary method used for accessing information or for communicating by people at the base of the pyramid (BoP). The mobile phone is therefore the preferred medium to provide electronic ICT services to users at the BoP. Users at the BoP can be identified as private users or informal businesses. The report also stated that the majority of non-users of the internet state that they do not know how to use the internet, indicating that there is a need for initiatives that raise awareness of the benefits provided by internet access as well as of the various possible uses of the internet. Letsie, Kabanda and Chigona (2015) also argue that in disadvantaged families, mobile devices played a significant role, especially for communication.

E-lending is another type of e-finance and entails lending to entities using the internet and allows SMEs to apply for credit online or via mobile phones (text and voice) with reduced application costs and faster turnaround on loan approvals or rejections (Riyadh *et al.*, 2010). E-credit information allows businesses to have access to an online database of SMEs' credit histories for risk assessment purposes thus contributing to the reduction of information asymmetry and reducing collection costs for the business (Martinez Peria & Singh, 2014). Internet or other ICT mediated leasing is referred to as e-leasing and is known for the reduction of application costs and easy payments, ultimately providing SMEs with access to production assets at lower costs.

Research has shown that customers like to shop online for insurance products (Cata & Lee, 2006). Insurance companies are therefore moving more and more to "paperless" insurance and to doing business on the internet. E-insurance is the application of the internet and other ICT for the production and distribution of insurance services. The narrow definition refers only to the provision of insurance cover online (Sapa, Phunde & Godbole, 2014). A key benefit of e-insurance to the customer is the improved communications and marketplace information. Other benefits relate to increased transparency and the reduction in transaction costs (Grossman, McCarthy & Aronson, 2004; Odoyo & Nyangosi, 2011; Sapa *et al.,* 2014). The benefits of e-insurance to the country are the economic benefits associated with increased employment opportunities, improvement of local entrepreneurship as well as improved skills and awareness creation. E-insurance can provide customers more easily with information about new products and special offers (Mubaraka *et al.*, 2013).

Microfinance is a *type of banking service that is provided to unemployed or low-income individuals or groups who would otherwise have no other means of gaining financial services* (Ashta & Assadi, 2009). E-microfinance is the use of the internet and ICTs for designing micro-credit initiatives and is beneficial for SMEs because it reduces the costs to access microfinance and widens sources of finance. Peer-to-peer (P2P) lending platforms have been defined as online platforms where borrowers place requests for loans online and then private lenders can bid to fund these loans in a type of auction (Klafft, 2008). Online P2P lending has gained significant interest and relevance in recent years (Bachmann *et al.*, 2011; Klafft, 2008), even in developing countries like China (Su & Yuan, 2013). One of the main benefits of P2P platforms is the elimination of banks as intermediaries, thus resulting in a reduction in transaction costs. There are many other e-finance types such as e-tax payments and e-warehousing (Riyadh *et al.*, 2010). These are all beneficial to SMEs because they expand the sources of finances available.

E-finance has greatly transformed financial structures all over the world, and even more so in the context of developing and transitioning countries. E-finance delivers a wider selection of financial services and products to more individuals and SMEs in a speedier and timelier manner through (Shahrokhi, 2008):

- Real time access to financial services;
- Convenient access to financial services;
- Provision of sophisticated financial services to geographically remote areas; and
- Increasing number of financial services available at the retail level.

The primary benefits of e-finance to SMEs can be summarized into three categories (Table 1). The impact of e-finance on SMEs is that it allows them to have convenient access to finances and low cost financial services and this is beneficial in environments where resources are scarce and financial information is limited (Srivastava, 2014). Shahrokhi (2008) argues that e-finance delivers convenience to SMEs to enable them to access and perform financial transactions from anywhere at any time. The adoption of e-finance therefore provides access to a wider range of financial products and services (Mubraka, *et al.*, 2013; Riyadh *et al.*, 2010).

Su and Yuan (2013) state that e-finance may lead to lower costs and greater competition in financial services, through both new entries from outside the financial sector, and greater competition among institutions within the financial service sector. According to Riyadh *et al.* (2010) e-finance has made it easier for SMEs to access finance by lowering transaction costs and improving the quality of the financial service. Using e-finance is said to reduce costs of brokerage services as well as provide increased access to international securities markets.

One of the major problems for SMEs is the lack of reliable and validated business-related information, which is required for good investment decisions, efficient management and for gaining a competitive advantage (Raihan, 2001). Information that is required relates at least to the following areas: the procedure of business, legal issues, cost and process of products and services, market and industry average information and sensible business contact information. According to Shahrokhi (2008) e-finance has become a powerful medium for entrepreneurs in search of venture capital and for venture capitalists looking for investment opportunities. It is now possible to acquire data on the majority of venture firms and firms that are seeking new businesses to invest in. Agwu and Murray (2014) assert that SMEs have

Table 1. Benefits of e-finance to SMEs

Benefit	References
Improved access to financial products and services	Agwu and Murray (2014); Ashta and Asadi (2009); Mubaraka *et al.* (2013); Riyadh *et al.* (2010); Shahrokhi (2008); Srivastava (2014)
Decrease in transaction costs	Maduku (2013); Odoyo and Nyangosi (2011); Riyadh *et al.* (2010); Sapa *et al.* (2014); Srivastava (2014); Su and Yuan (2013)
Improved access to financial information	Agwu and Murray (2014); Mubaraka *et al.* (2013); Nasri (2011); Raihan (2001); Raza and Hanif (2013); Shahrokhi (2008)

access to extensive online information including information that can be utilized to make financial decisions. This information should be highly accurate, current and easy to understand in order to aid quality decision making.

In a study of internet banking in Pakistan, it was reported that customers believe that internet banking provides believable information, real time information, relevant information and at the right level of detail (Raza & Hanif, 2013). The increased information available regarding internet banking products, services and benefits has impacted the adoption rate of internet banking by customers (Nasri, 2011).

Banks therefore need to make customers aware of the availability of internet banking products and the benefits and value to the customer in comparison to competitive products. Improved marketing of these products and the provision of information regarding products and services can have a positive effect on the adoption of internet banking by customers.

Barriers to Adoption of E-Finance

Whilst there are several benefits to e-finance for both large organizations and SMEs, e-financing is not without its flaws and there are barriers to the use and adoption of e-finance. In a study done of banking customers in South Africa, only half of respondents were users of mobile phone banking (Maduku & Mpinganjira, 2012). Dewan and Nazmin (2008) found that ICT issues are the greatest perceived barriers for SMEs not to adopt e-finance. Three of the most commonly reported ICT issues that have been reported as barriers to the adoption of e-finance by customers are data privacy, security and safety (Dewan & Nazmin, 2008; Koskosas, 2011; Nasri, 2011). Dewan and Nazmin (2008) found that security issues (viruses & hackers) are the greatest perceived barriers for SMEs not to adopt e-finance. According to Raihan (2001) SMEs seek guarantees that they are protected against cyber-attacks and all other risks associated with transacting online that could lead to financial losses. Koskosas (2011) argues that security and safety are key concerns for both users and providers of e-finance. Safety and security issues include authentication of counterparts, no accountability transactions, inadequate customer support, guaranteed business continuity, data integrity and confidentiality. These issues are a reality for e-finance users and providers alike, and as such users need to safeguard against fraudulent service providers. Service providers on the other hand need to guarantee data integrity as well as the confidentiality of their customers' private information and user information needs to be protected from unauthorized parties. A study in Indonesia revealed that security and privacy impacted a customer's level of initial trust in internet banking. The results also showed that initial trust impacted a user's usage intention of internet banking (Susanto *et al.*, 2013). Initial trust was shown to be positively correlated with a user's usage intention of internet banking. From these studies it can be deduced that security and privacy are possible barriers to the adoption of e-finance by SMEs.

Another barrier to the adoption of e-finance is ICT infrastructure. In Bangladesh, like other developing countries, high speed broadband internet is not available in rural areas (Riyadh *et al.*, 2010). In addition, computer hardware and software costs are high and load shedding is a regular phenomenon (Mohiuddin, 2014). This lack of ICT infrastructure hinders the growth of e-business and e-finance. Integration of the economy to the global market, scale of business operations and technological developments are dependencies for the delivery of e-finance. According to Narayanasamy *et al.* (2011) there is a positive relationship between ICT infrastructure and growth of e-finance, which means that countries with a weaker ICT infrastructure (defined as organizations, personnel, procedures, facilities and networks used to transmit and receive information by electronic means) tend to experience slow e-finance growth.

In most developing countries a basic internet network exists; however, high speed broadband internet is not available in rural areas. Slow internet speeds in developing countries are a barrier to e-finance adoption. Most SMEs, especially those in rural areas, do not have a computer or access to the internet or related software in order to benefit from e-commerce (Dewan & Nazmin, 2008). According to the study of Gillwald *et al.* (2012), few informal businesses in South Africa maintain a website (estimated at four percent), with even fewer employees having access to an email address (estimated at three percent). Most informal businesses employ mobile phones more than any other ICT devices. Mobile phones are therefore more commonly used to conduct small business and make use of a combination of voice and internet services. This study also reported that availability of services on internet-enabled mobile phones was one of the biggest challenges faced by informal businesses. A Nigerian study of challenges and barriers to e-commerce adoption by SMEs revealed that small and medium scale online presence is unknown (Agwu & Murray, 2014). Technical skills were identified as some of the barriers to e-commerce adoption. In Malaysia, bad technology architectures were also a concern to e-finance customers and affected the growth of e-finance (Narayanasamy *et al.,* 2011). In Indonesia, even though there has been limited improvement in the ICT infrastructure situation, the existing infrastructure has created opportunities for the introduction of e-businesses, which are already being explored by many companies (Janita & Chong, 2013).

Telecommunications has been a high priority for the South African government and there have been ambitious goals set in this regard (Gillwald *et al.*, 2012). Although public access to the internet is increasing in major cities and metropolitan areas, affordable and reliable internet access remains poor amongst the rural areas of South Africa. The government has sought to create employment for citizens by creating opportunities with ICT. However, the cost of broadband access remains prohibitively high for most South Africans. In spite of this there has been a growth in data services whilst voice service usage in has declined. It is reported that the total number of broadband internet users in South Africa is 34% of the 15 years and older age group population.

Regulatory environment and policy is an additional barrier to e-finance adoption. According to Allen *et al.* (2002) legal risk arises from a violation or non-conformance with laws, rules and regulations and legal risks can further occur when the legal rights and obligations of the parties to a transaction are not well established. When SMEs adopt e-finance some rules and regulations must be in place; for example, Online Dispute Resolution, electronic signatures and e-business legislation. In developing countries the regulatory environment is more critical than in developed countries regarding the adoption of innovation (Riyadh *et al.*, 2010). A study of e-business in SMEs in Indonesia identified that regulation and policies are an important factor in influencing adoption (Janita & Chong, 2013). A regulatory environment for e-banking is usually provided by government. Another study in Indonesia revealed that the perceived level of government support influenced customers' initial trust in internet banking (Susanto *et al.*, 2013). Since initial trust was shown to be positively correlated with a user's usage intention of internet banking, a lack of perceived government support can be a barrier to e-finance adoption. The results of a Pakistan study confirmed the influence of government on internet banking adoption, since they encourage and promote the usage of internet banking and provide laws and regulations for internet banking (Raza & Hanif, 2013).

A lack of understanding, awareness or knowledge of the benefits of e-finance is another barrier to e-finance adoption (Nasri, 2011; Riyadh *et al.*, 2010). Awareness and training regarding the use and potential of ICT for profit enhancement, cost reduction and access to finance is important and should be provided to the community. Internet knowledge or skills can also influence a customer's adoption of e-banking, therefore improving training and skills and ultimately can improve adoption rates (Mohiuddin, 2014; Nasri, 2011). The barriers to e-finance for SMEs can therefore be summarized into four categories (Table 2).

SMEs IN DEVELOPING COUNTRIES (SOUTH AFRICA AND BANGLADESH)

In South Africa SMEs, also known as SMMEs (Small, Micro and Medium Enterprises), are defined as businesses that employ less than 200 full-time employees (Ndayizigamiye, 2014). Furthermore, the size of an SME (in terms of the number of full-time employees) differs according to the business sector it falls under. With the exception of the agricultural sector, it is noted that in all other sectors the limit to be classified as an SME is 200 full time employees, where the agricultural sector prescribes a limit of 100 full time employees. Small enterprises capture the upper end of the micro-enterprise market, and are often registered. Of these small businesses, 9% of them claim to have received or utilized some form of formal credit. The SME sectors in South Africa can be categorized as follows:

- A micro enterprise has up to 5 employees,
- A small enterprise has up to 50 employees, and
- A medium enterprise has from 51 to 200 employees.

According to Hoque *et al.* (2015), in Bangladesh the definition varies slightly from the South African definition in that small enterprise refers to a business which is not a public limited company and the limits with regards to employees are as follows:

- A micro enterprise has less than 10 employees,
- A small enterprise has up to 25 employees, and
- A medium enterprise from 50 to 100 employees.

Historically, banks and other formal financial institutions have avoided serving those in poverty since these institutions do not have practical solutions to overcome problems of high transaction costs, adverse selection and the risk of not being able to screen entrepreneurial projects effectively. Additionally, managing the disbursement of small loans efficiently is also problematic as proven methodologies for microfinance lending tend to be labor intensive (Bangladesh Bank, 2016; Centre for Inclusive

Table 2. Barriers to e-finance for SMEs

Barrier	Literature References
ICT privacy, security and safety	Dewan and Nazmin (2008); Koskosas (2011); Nasri (2011); Raza and Hanif (2013); Raihan (2001); Susanto *et al.* (2013)
ICT infrastructure	Agwu and Murray (2014); Dewan and Nazmin (2008); Narayanasamy *et al.* (2011); Riyadh *et al.* (2010); Singh and Chauhan (2012)
Regulatory environment and policy	Janita and Chong (2013); Murari and Tater (2014); Riyadh *et al.* (2010)
Training and skills	Janita and Chong (2013); Mohiuddin (2014); Nasri (2011); Raza and Hanif (2013); Riyadh *et al.* (2010)

Banking, 2013). In South Africa and Bangladesh, like most developing countries, micro-enterprises are underserved when it comes to the provision of microfinance. Some of the constraints for the provision of microfinance reported in Bangladesh (Bangladesh Bank, 2016) are:

- Transaction costs associated with processing loans are fixed,
- Difficulty in adopting new lending technologies;
- Microfinance institutions have not adopted innovative lending methodologies, and
- The high cost of obtaining credit information on micro-enterprises.

The estimated failure rate of SMEs in South Africa is between 70% and 80% (Adeniran & Johnston, 2011). Adcorp (2016) reported that around 440,000 small businesses in South Africa have closed in the last five years and that the reported number of new business start-ups is at an all-time low. Over the last decade, the number of small businesses in the country has stagnated. This situation needs addressing as SMEs are critical for large-scale job creation in South Africa. One of the obstacles when starting up a business is access to finance (Grundling & Kaseke, 2010). South Africa as a country exhibits characteristics of a developed and developing economy with regards to its technology accessibility trends. The country has been seen to adopt the advanced use of technology in research and educational institutions as well as in the private sector. It is noteworthy, however, that more than 25 million citizens in the country live below the poverty line. Millions of South Africans rely on social grants for their livelihood. A large portion of South Africans have low education levels and lack general skills and even more so computing skills, which leads to low employability (Calandro *et al.*, 2012).

E-FINANCE ADOPTION SURVEY

Methodology

In order to address the objective of this chapter, and to investigate if the literature surrounding e-finance adoption could be validated, a survey was undertaken of SMEs in two developing countries, Bangladesh and South Africa. A non-probability convenience sampling technique was used, based on the purposive sampling method (Saunders, Lewis & Thornhill, 2009). SMEs in the contact lists of the respective researchers in the two countries were contacted and invited to participate.

The survey questionnaire was designed to answer the following questions:

- What is the level of adoption of e-finance by SMEs?
- What are the most commonly used types of e-finance by SMEs?

Respondents could take either complete the questionnaire online of on paper. The majority (86%) of the Bangladesh respondents were employees, whereas only 36% of South African respondents were employees. The remaining respondents in South Africa were owners of SMEs (61%) or contractors (3%). In Bangladesh the remaining minority of respondents were owners of SMEs (13%) and contractors (1%). The main industries represented by respondents from the two countries were manufacturing, construction and tourism and catering. The business operations of the respondents' SMEs were a mixture of urban, rural, peri-urban and international.

Respondents were asked to rate the extent of their agreement regarding their experience with e-finance. It must be noted that the questionnaire was coded with five being Strongly agree and one being Strongly disagree. The results were analyzed in terms of mean ratings and frequency distributions. Seven e-finance factors of e-finance adoption were investigated, which consisted of the three benefits identified in literature (Table 1) and the four barriers (Table 2). In reporting on the analyses the Strongly agree and Agree categories will be referred to as "agreed" and the Disagree and Strongly disagree categories were combined into one category "disagreed" to make the analysis more meaningful. Furthermore, the mean ratings were categorized and interpreted as follows: Negative: $\mu = [1 - 2.6)$; Neutral: $\mu = [2.6 - 3.4]$ and Positive: $\mu = (3.4 - 5]$.

Results: E-Finance Usage

The survey results revealed that out of the respondents, e-banking (72%) and e-credit information (62%) are the most highly adopted types of e-finance in Bangladesh, when considering weekly or monthly usage (Figure 2). Conversely it should be noted that e-leasing (64%), e-insurance (62%) and e-microfinance (60%) have the lowest level of adoption when considering the response to e-finance types that are never used by SMEs.

The level of adoption of e-finance in South Africa (Figure 3) indicates that e-lending (51%), e-insurance (51%) and e-banking (30%) are the most highly adopted e-finance types when considering use on a weekly or monthly basis. It should be noted that all 100% of the South African respondents indicated that they use e-banking. E-microfinance (91%), other e-finance (85%), e-credit information (82%) and e-leasing (79%) have the lowest adoption levels in South Africa considering the e-finance types that are never used.

An analysis of the adoption patterns of the two developing countries reveals that, whilst South Africa has varied adoption levels (Figure 3), Bangladesh has more evenly distributed adoption levels (Figure 2). South Africa has a high adoption level for e-banking, however, there is very little adoption for other types of e-finance, whereas in Bangladesh the high adoption levels for the other types of e-finance are

Figure 2. Ranking of adopted e-finance types in Bangladesh (n = 105)

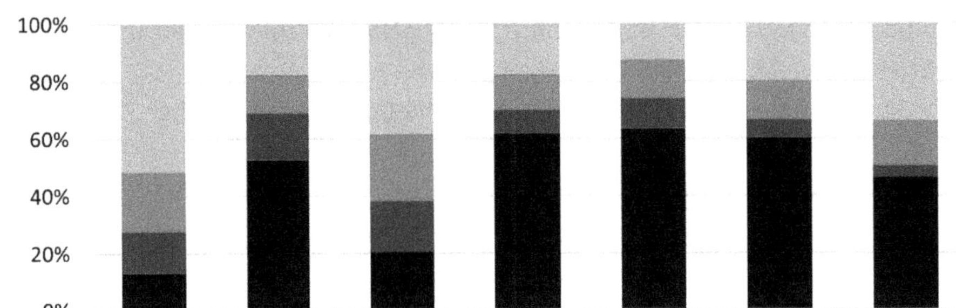

	E-Banking	E-Lending	E-Credit Information	E-Insurance	E-Leasing	E-Microfinanc e	Other E-Finance
Monthly	51%	18%	38%	18%	13%	20%	34%
Weekly	21%	13%	24%	12%	14%	14%	16%
Seldom	14%	16%	18%	8%	10%	6%	4%
Never	13%	53%	21%	62%	64%	60%	47%

Figure 3. Ranking of adopted e-finance types in South Africa (n = 33)

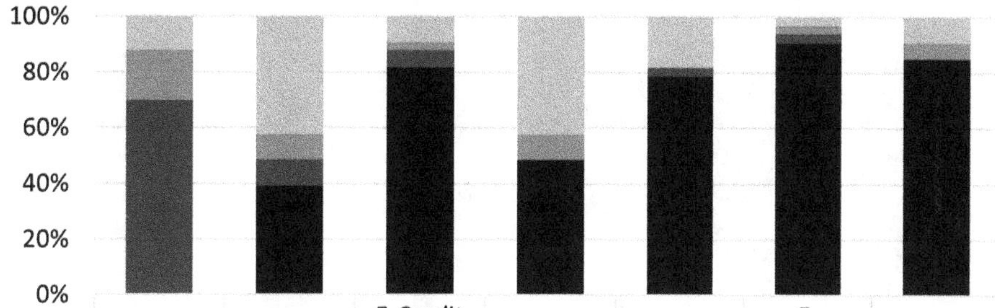

	E-Banking	E-Lending	E-Credit Information	E-Insurance	E-Leasing	E-Microfinance	Other E-Finance
Monthly	12%	42%	9%	42%	18%	3%	9%
Weekly	18%	9%	3%	9%	0%	3%	6%
Seldom	70%	9%	6%	0%	3%	3%	0%
Never	0%	39%	82%	48%	79%	91%	85%

observed. The majority of the respondents in South Africa (100%) and Bangladesh (86%) stated that they have adopted e-banking (Figure 4). However, only 61% of South African respondents and 47% of those in Bangladesh (54% average) have adopted e-lending. The greatest difference (61%) can be observed for e-credit information, since a larger percentage (79%) of Bangladesh respondents stated that they had adopted e-credit information than South African respondents (18%).

The respondents that were not using e-finance on at least a weekly basis were asked to indicate their future intentions to use the different e-finance types. In Bangladesh, 49% of respondents indicated that they had no intention to change their usage of e-banking in the future, while 39% indicated that they would likely increase their usage of e-banking (Figure 5). Similarly, for the other e-finance types, re-

Figure 4. Ranking of adopted e-finance types (n = 138)

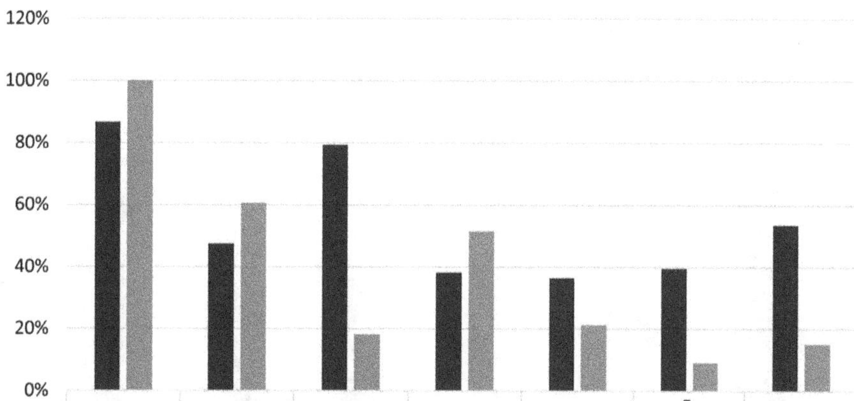

	E-Banking	E-Lending	E-Credit Information	E-Insurance	E-Leasing	E-Microfinance	Other E-Finance
Bangladesh	87%	47%	79%	38%	36%	40%	53%
South Africa	100%	61%	18%	52%	21%	9%	15%

Figure 5. Bangladesh SMEs' future intentions to use e-finance (n = [81,86])

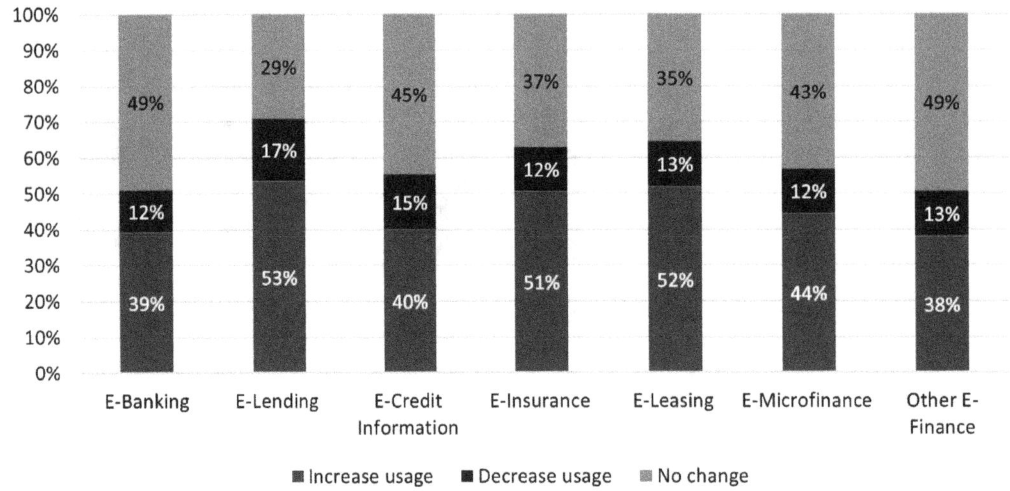

spondents indicated either maintaining their current usage or increasing their usage. E-lending showed the largest number of respondents wanting to decrease their usage (17%) but also the largest number of respondents wanting to increase their usage (53%).

South Africa shows an opposite trend (Figure 6), where 61% of the SMEs want to decrease their usage of e-banking and 67% want to decrease their usage of e-lending. South African SMEs would like to increase their usage of e-microfinance (45%) and e-leasing (39%), while remaining largely unchanged in the adoption of e-credit information (76%) and other e-finance (70%). E-credit information and other e-finance types remain services that South African SMEs are not interested in based on current adoption (Figure 3) and future adoption (Figure 6). The general trend depicted in Figure 5 shows that Bangladesh SMEs have greater intentions to increase their usage of different e-finance types in the future compared

Figure 6. South African SMEs' future intentions to use e-finance (n = 33)

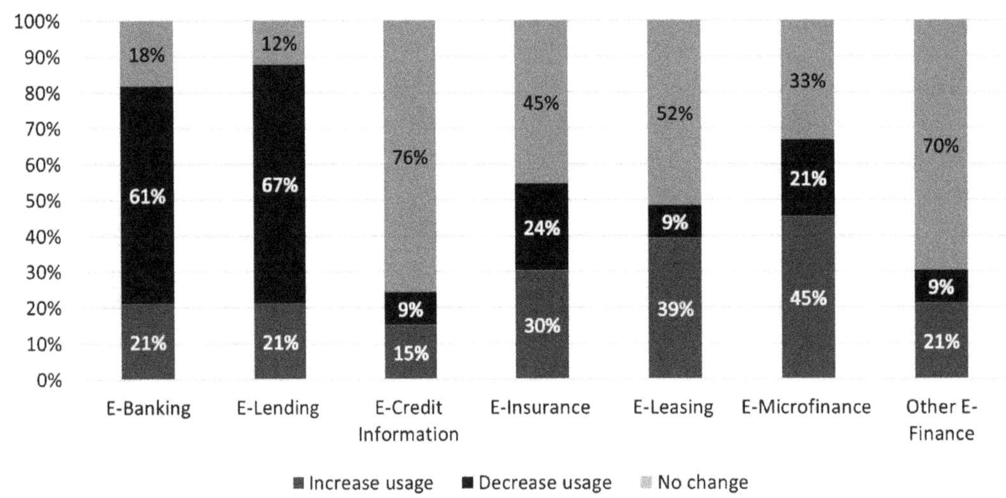

to South African SMEs (Figure 6). This difference in intention is evidenced by the proportionally lower average of South African SMEs that intend to use e-finance in the future.

Results: Benefits of E-Finance Adoption to SMEs

Two of the three benefits listed in the questionnaire had a mean rating in the positive range (Table 3). The benefit that had the highest rated mean ($\mu = 4.34$) for adopting e-finance was "Access to financial products and services". The lowest rated reason for adopting e-finance was "Reduced transaction costs", which was in the neutral range. This could be seen to contradict literature stating that the reduced cost of transactions is a primary benefit of e-finance adoption. Each of these benefits were analyzed in terms of secondary benefits (Table 4, 5 and 6).

Table 3. Benefits of e-finance (n = 138)

Benefit	Mean (μ)	Agree and Strongly Agree (%)	Category
Access to financial products and services	4.34	90.33	Positive
Access to financial information	4.00	71.00	Positive
Transaction costs	2.83	37.66	Neutral

Table 4. Access to financial products and services benefit (n = 138)

E-Finance Enables the Business to Perform Financial Transactions...	Strongly Disagree	Disagree	Neutral	Agree	Strongly Agree	Mean (μ)	Standard deviAtion
From anywhere on computer/mobile with internet.	2%	1%	3%	38%	55%	4.43	0.81
Any time of the day on a computer/ mobile with internet.	1%	1%	7%	41%	50%	4.38	0.74
Required by the business on a computer/ mobile with internet.	1%	4%	9%	43%	43%	4.25	0.83
On a computer/mobile with internet without having to leave the business.	3%	4%	14%	39%	40%	4.09	0.99

Table 5. Results of the transaction costs benefit (n = 138)

E-Finance Enables the Business to Pay Less...	Strongly Disagree	Disagree	Neutral	Agree	Strongly Agree	Mean (μ)	Standard Deviation
For financial transactions completed online	26%	15%	15%	27%	16%	2.92	1.46
In fees for a loan completed online	23%	26%	19%	15%	17%	2.77	1.40
In interest for a loan completed online	22%	28%	13%	23%	14%	2.80	1.38

Table 6. Results of the access to financial information benefit (n = 138)

E-Finance Enables the Business to Access Information on...	Strongly Disagree	Disagree	Neutral	Agree	Strongly Agree	Mean (μ)	Standard Deviation
Improving my finances of the business online	1%	5%	17%	43%	35%	4.06	0.89
Funding my business online	1%	7%	22%	36%	34%	3.96	0.96
Other financial products and services online	1%	7%	21%	33%	38%	4.02	0.96

All the mean ratings were in the positive range for the access to financial products and services benefit, meaning that respondents agree that e-finance provides better access to financial products and services (Table 4). At least 91% of the respondents confirm that e-finance enables their businesses to perform financial transactions from anywhere, during any time of the day on a computer or mobile device that is connected to the internet. The respondents also "agree" that e-finance enables the business to perform financial transactions required by the business (86%) without having to leave the business (79%).

All the mean ratings were in the neutral range for the transaction costs benefit (Table 5), indicating that respondents were generally neutral regarding the statement that e-finance lowers the cost of financial products and services. The standard deviations indicate that there was much variation in the responses for all statements, as most exceed the value of one. Respondents were evenly split regarding the transaction costs benefit of e-finance with 41% that "disagree" and 43% that "agree" that e-finance enables the business to pay less for financial transactions completed online.

The majority (78%) of the respondents "agree" that e-finance enables their businesses to access information on improving their finances online (Table 6). Most of the respondents (68%) also "agree" that e-finance enables them to access information on funding their business online, with a further 71% confirming that e-finance enables access to information on other financial products and services online. The mean scores of the respondents regarding the benefits of access to financial information are all positive ($3.96 \leq \mu \geq 4.06$).

Results: Barriers to E-Finance Adoption for SMEs

Table 7 shows that the barrier to the adoption of e-finance that had the highest rated mean was "Regulatory environment and policy" ($\mu = 3.8$). The second rated barrier to e-finance based on the mean value was "Training and skills" ($\mu = 3.8$). However, in terms of percentage agreement, more respondents "agreed"

Table 7. Barriers of e-finance (n = 138)

Barrier	Mean (μ)	Agree and Strongly Agree (%)	Category
Regulatory environment and policy	3.80	63.66	Positive
Training and skills	3.60	52.33	Positive
Privacy, security and safety	3.59	57.75	Positive
ICT infrastructure	3.58	56.80	Positive

with the privacy, security and safety barrier than with the training and skills barrier. The barrier with the lowest mean is ICT infrastructure.

The mean ratings for all items in the privacy, security and safety barrier were all positive, which indicates that respondents tend to agree with the statements with regards to privacy, security and the safety barrier (Table 8). The standard deviations indicate there was much variation in responses for all statements, as all values exceed one. It can be seen that the highest rated barrier of respondents was that unauthorized parties could access their financial information ($\mu = 3.83$) and that there are no guarantees should there be associated financial losses during a financial transaction ($\mu = 3.81$). Respondents are less concerned about the limited support for e-finance and the uncertainty of the continuity of e-finance.

The overall mean rating for the ICT infrastructure barrier is positive ($\mu = 3.59$) and all of the five items in this barrier had mean positive ratings, which indicates that the respondents were on average all in agreement with regards to the ICT infrastructure barrier (Table 9). The highest rated barrier in the ICT infrastructure category was *"Power cuts interrupting access to online financial services"* ($\mu = 3.83$). The standard deviations indicate there was much variation in responses for all statements, as all values exceed 1.20. The mean ratings for the regulatory and policy barrier were all in the positive range (Table 10). The positive ratings indicate that the respondents were on average mostly in agreement with this barrier, with most of the respondents agreeing or strongly agreeing with the statements. Both barriers in the training and skills category had mean positive ratings, indicating that respondents supported this barrier to e-finance (Table 11).

Table 8. Results of the privacy, security and safety barrier (n = 138)

	Strongly Disagree	Disagree	Neutral	Agree	Strongly Agree	Mean (μ)	Standard Deviation
Unauthorized parties could access financial information	4%	14%	13%	34%	35%	3.83	1.16
No guarantees should the business lose money during a financial transaction	7%	8%	19%	31%	36%	3.81	1.19
Little support is provided for e-finance	10%	13%	32%	30%	16%	3.28	1.17
Uncertainty about the continuity of e-finance	7%	13%	31%	23%	25%	3.45	1.21

Table 9. Results of the ICT infrastructure barrier (n = 138)

	Strongly Disagree	Disagree	Neutral	Agree	Strongly Agree	Mean (μ)	Standard Deviation
Poor internet access	5%	13%	22%	26%	34%	3.71	1.21
High internet costs	7%	12%	29%	25%	27%	3.51	1.22
Power cuts interrupting access to online financial services	4%	15%	13%	28%	39%	3.83	1.23
Software to access online financial services is too expensive	7%	18%	22%	28%	25%	3.46	1.24
Hardware to access online financial services is too expensive	9%	17%	22%	27%	26%	3.44	1.28

Table 10. Results of the regulatory and policy barrier (n = 138)

	Strongly Disagree	Disagree	Neutral	Agree	Strongly Agree	Mean (μ)	Standard Deviation
Lack of laws that protect consumers	5%	8%	27%	31%	29%	3.71	1.12
Laws, regulations and policies regarding online finance that are uncertain and ambiguous	1%	4%	26%	33%	36%	3.99	0.95
Online contracts are hard to enforce	5%	5%	26%	38%	26%	3.74	1.06

Table 11. Results of the training and skills barrier (n = 138)

	Strongly Disagree	Disagree	Neutral	Agree	Strongly Agree	Mean (μ)	Standard Deviation
Lack of knowledge about some of the online financial services available	3%	8%	45%	26%	18%	3.49	0.98
The business has adequate skill to perform online financial transactions	2%	7%	35%	30%	25%	3.70	1.00

Ranking of E-Finance Factors

The mean ratings of the factors (benefits and barriers) identified for e-finance were ranked in descending order (Table 12). It is evident that that the two factors that respondents ranked the highest are the two highest ranked benefits. These are followed by the barriers, with regulatory policy being the highest ranked barrier. Finally, the respondents rated the benefits of decreased transaction costs when using e-finance lowest in terms of mean rating. It must be noted that both transaction cost and IT telecommunications infrastructure had the most variation in responses based on the standard deviation, indicating that some respondents had agreed more than others for these issues.

Issues and Problems

Several types of e-finance have been adopted in developing countries. In South Africa e-banking, e-lending and e-insurance were the top three types of e-finance adopted, whereas in Bangladesh it was e-banking,

Table 12. Ranking of e-finance factors

Factors	Mean	Std. Deviation
Access to financial products and services benefit	4.35	0.65
Access to financial information benefit	4.00	0.71
Uncertain regulatory and policy barrier	3.80	0.81
Low ICT training and skill barrier	3.60	0.74
Low ICT privacy, security and safety barrier	3.59	0.80
Low ICT telecommunications infrastructure barrier	3.58	1.03
Improved transaction costs benefit	2.83	1.21

e-insurance and other e-finance. Whilst 100% of the South African respondents used e-banking, only 87% of respondents in Bangladesh. However, one must consider that the profile of respondents between the two countries were possibly not the same and therefore direct comparisons may not be accurate reflections. Future studies could investigate this phenomenon further.

The reviewed literature reported that the adoption of e-finance has the potential to provide many benefits to an SME in a developing country. The main benefits reported in literature are decreased transaction costs as well as improved access to financial information, products and services. The survey results confirmed the literature reporting that e-finance can improve access to financial information that is useful for SMEs. This information can be used to facilitate growth and/or sustainability for the SME. However, regarding the benefit of reduced transaction costs, the respondents were neutral. This is an unexpected result and it is not evident what the reasons for this could be. One reason could be that perceptions could be different to the real cost of e-services compared to traditional services. This study did not examine actual cost incurred by the SMEs, but rather perceptions of SMEs. Future research could examine this in more detail and possibly investigate if decreased transaction costs are experienced as a benefit in other developing countries as compared with South Africa and Bangladesh.

The benefits of e-finance adoption cannot be achieved to their full potential due to several barriers that are encountered by SMEs, particularly in poorer countries. The literature reviewed identified four categories of barriers to e-finance adoption, namely: privacy, security and safety; ICT infrastructure; regulatory environment/policy and training. All four of these barriers were confirmed by the survey results, implying that these barriers are experienced by SMEs in both South Africa and Bangladesh. The results from the survey confirms that privacy, security and safety in the online environment is a barrier for SMEs using and adopting e-finance. The survey results also confirm studies (Agwu and Murray, 2014; Dewan and Nazmin, 2008); Riyadh *et al.*, 2010) which argue that a low ICT infrastructure is a barrier to e-finance use and adoption. It was found that developing country populations do not have easy access to affordable and reliable internet services. Furthermore, power supply issues as well as expensive hardware and software to access financial services are a major issue for SMEs. The regulatory environment and training categories were also both supported as a barrier to e-finance adoption by respondents. It is evident that government and other policies need to be put into place to support the adoption of e-finance. Training and awareness campaigns should be conducted in order to improve the understanding of the benefits of e-finance adoption. In order to improve e-finance adoption governments, the banking community and other stakeholders need to investigate these barriers and find ways to address them.

The limitations of the study relate to the relatively small sample size and uneven distribution of owners and employees in the respondents. There was also an uneven number of respondents between the two countries, thus making it difficult in most cases to do a direct comparison. It is also important to note therefore that the sample may not be representative of the population. The analysis of results revealed that further investigation is required with additional countries and larger sample sizes. More detailed qualitative research should also be undertaken in order to reveal a more in depth understanding of SME perceptions and behavior with regards to e-finance.

SOLUTIONS AND RECOMMENDATIONS

The following recommendations are suggested for government, employees or owners of SMEs and other stakeholders:

- Governments of developing countries need to urgently prioritize ICT infrastructure so as to ensure lower internet costs and better connection to the web as well as provision of a consistent supply of energy for SMEs.
- Hardware and software that is used to access e-finance should be made more affordable for SMEs. This can be made possible by a collaboration between e-finance providers and respective government through subsidies.
- Guarantees should be made for SMEs in the event that they lose money during a financial transaction.
- The laws governing ICT should be strengthened in order to restore the confidence of the SMEs as well as protecting them from potential exploitation.
- Any and all ambiguities should be explained to SMEs with regards to online contracts, such that the rights and the responsibilities of each transacting party are well understood.
- SME employees or owners should access financial information online in order to improve operational finances; funding growth or expansion of their businesses and to seek suitable financial products and services.
- Greater emphasis should be placed on ensuring that unauthorized parties cannot access financial information of SMEs. This should not only be done in the background but highly publicized in order to alleviate negative perceptions.

CONCLUSION

The survey results revealed that e-banking is adopted widely amongst the respondents in both Bangladesh and South Africa. However, other types of e-finance such as e-leasing had much lower levels of adoption. The results also revealed that access to financial products and services was the highest rated benefit of e-finance to SMEs, whereas regulatory environment and policy was the highest rated barrier. Awareness of the different types and uses of e-finance were also found to be low. The literature reviewed and the survey results both revealed that government and stakeholders need to improve education around the benefits of e-finance as well as the available types and uses of e-finance. In addition, ICT infrastructure needs urgent attention and improvement in developing countries. It is also critical that the digital divide be narrowed. If governments and banking stakeholders prioritize on improving the underlying ICT infrastructure and make education and awareness around e-finance and the benefits thereof a priority, SMEs will be better equipped to adopt e-finance. This adoption of e-finance by SMEs can ultimately improve their access to finance and SME sector development.

REFERENCES

Adcorp. (2016). *New business start-ups slump to all-time low*. Retrieved January, 2016, from http://www.adcorp.co.za/NEws/Pages/Newbusinessstart-upsslumptoall-timelow.aspx

Adeniran, T. V., & Johnston, K. A. (2011). Investigating the level of Internet capabilities of South African small and medium enterprises in changing environments. In *Proceedings of the 13th Annual Conference on World Wide Web Applications* (pp. 5–21). Cape Town, SA: Cape Peninsula University of Technology.

Agwu, M. E., & Murray, J. P. (2014). Drivers and inhibitors to e-commerce adoption among SMEs in Nigeria. *Journal of Emerging Trends in Computing and Information Sciences*, *5*(3), 192–199.

Alanezi, M. A., Kamil, A., & Basri, S. (2010). A proposed instrument dimensions for measuring e-government service quality. *International Journal of u- and e- Service. Science and Technology*, *3*(4), 1–18.

Allen, F., McAndrews, J., & Strahan, P. (2002). E-finance: An introduction. *Journal of Financial Services Research*, *22*(1), 5–27. doi:10.1023/A:1016007126394

Ashta, A., & Assadi, D. (2009). An analysis of European online micro-lending websites. *Cahiers du CEREN*, *29*, 147–160.

Bachmann, A., Becker, A., Buerckner, D., Hilker, M., Kock, F., Lehmann, M., & Tiburtius, P. (2011). Online peer-to-peer lending – A literature review. *Journal of Internet Banking and Commerce*, *16*(2), 1–18.

Bangladesh Bank. (2016). *Small and Medium Enterprise (SME) Credit Policies & Programmes*. Retrieved January 2016, 2016, from https://www.bb.org.bd/sme/smepolicye.pdf

Bughin, J., & Manyika, J. (2016). *Measuring the full impact of digital capital*. Retrieved January, 2016, from http://www.mckinsey.com/industries/high-tech/our-insights/measuring-the-full-impact-of-digital-capital

Calandro, E., Gillwald, A., Deen-Swarray, M., Stork, C., & Esselaar, S. (2012). *Mobile usage at the base of the pyramid in South Africa: An infoDev publication prepared by Research ICT Africa and Intelecon*. Washington, DC: International Bank for Reconstruction and Development / The World Bank.

Casaló, L. V., Flavián, C., & Guinalíu, M. (2010). Generating trust and satisfaction in e-services: The impact of usability on consumer behavior. *Journal of Relationship Marketing*, *9*(4), 247–263. doi:10.1080/15332667.2010.522487

Cata, T., & Lee, S. M. (2006). Adoption of web-based applications in the financial sector: The case of online insurance. *Journal of Internet Commerce*, *5*(2), 41–61. doi:10.1300/J179v05n02_03

Centre for Inclusive Banking. (2013). *The microfinance review 2013 - From microfinance to financial inclusion: A review of the South African microfinance sector trends, successes, challenges and policy issues*. Pretoria: University of Pretoria.

Daniel, E. (2000). The provision of electronic banking services in the UK and Scandinavia. *Journal of Financial Services Marketing*, *4*(4), 319–330.

Dewan, A. M., & Nazmin, S. A. (2008). The opportunities and barriers of using ICT by small and medium enterprises in Bangladesh: Case of SMEs in BSCIC industrial estates. In *Proceedings of the International Conference on Computer and Communication Engineering* (vol. 1, pp. 656–661). Kuala Lumpur, MY: International Islamic University Malaysia.

eMarketer. (2014). *Smartphone Users Worldwide Will Total 1.75 Billion in 2014*. Retrieved February 5, 2015, from http://www.emarketer.com/Article/Smartphone-Users-Worldwide-Will-Total-175-Billion-2014/1010536#sthash.dwESSnqk.dpuf

Gillwald, A., Moyo, M., & Stork, C. (2012). *What is happening in ICT in South Africa: A supply-and demand-side analysis of the ICT sector.* Evidence for ICT Policy Action, Policy Paper 7.

Grossman, M., McCarthy, R. V., & Aronson, J. E. (2004). E-commerce adoption in the insurance industry. *Issues in Information Systems*, *5*(2), 467–473.

Grundling, I., & Kaseke, T. (2010). *FinScope South Africa small business survey 2010*. Retrieved May 2015, from http://www.finmark.org.za/wp-content/uploads/2016/01/FS-Small-Business_-reportFNL2.pdf

GSMA Intelligence. (2014). *The Mobile Economy: Sub-Saharan Africa 2014*. Retrieved April 20, 2014, from http://www.gsmamobileeconomyafrica.com/GSMA_ME_SubSaharanAfrica_Web_Singles.pdf

Gumbi, L. N., & Mnkandla, E. (2015). Investigating South African vendors' cloud computing value proposition to small, medium and micro enterprises : A case of the city of Tshwane Metropolitan Municipality. *The African Journal of Information Systems*, *7*(4), 1–16.

Han, L. (2008). Bricks vs clicks: Entrepreneurial online banking behaviour and relationship banking. *International Journal of Entrepreneurial Behavior & Research*, *14*(1), 47–60. doi:10.1108/13552550810852820

Hoque, R., Saif, A. N. M., AlBar, A. M., & Bao, Y. (2015). Adoption of information and communication technology for development: A case study of small and medium enterprises in Bangladesh. *Information Development*, 1–15.

Janita, I., & Chong, W. K. (2013). Barriers of B2B e-business adoption in Indonesian SMEs: A literature analysis. *Procedia Computer Science*, *17*, 571–578. doi:10.1016/j.procs.2013.05.073

Khan, A. S. (2014). *The SME missing middle problem in developing countries and its link to lack of financing: The case of Bangladesh* (Master's Thesis). University of Ottawa, Ottawa, ON, Canada.

Khurshid, A., Rizwan, M., & Tasneem, E. (2014). Factors contributing towards adoption of e-banking in Pakistan. *International Journal of Accounting and Financial Reporting*, *4*(2), 437–455. doi:10.5296/ijafr.v4i2.6584

Klafft, M. (2008). Online peer-to-peer lending: A lenders' perspective. In *Proceedings of the International Conference on E-Learning, E-Business, Enterprise Information Systems, and E-Government* (pp. 371–375). Las Vegas, NV: CSREA Press.

Kona, O. T. (2014). *Website interface design: A study on the status quo of South African e-commerce website interfaces*. Retrieved April 2015, from http://www.web-visibility.co.za/0069-working-paper-2014-kona-weideman-interface-design-e-commerce.pdf

Koskosas, I. (2011). The pros and cons of internet banking : A short review. *Business Excellence and Management*, *1*(1), 49–58.

Letsie, M., Kabanda, S., & Chigona, W. (2015). Economically disadvantaged families domesticating mobile devices: Case of South African. *Proceedings of the 9th IDIAConference*, 72–83.

Maduku, D. K. (2013). Predicting retail banking customers' attitude towards internet banking services in South Africa. *Southern African Business Review*, *17*(3), 76–100.

Maduku, D. K., & Mpinganjira, M. (2012). An empirical investigation into customers' attitude towards usage of cell phone banking in Gauteng, South Africa. *Journal of Contemporary Management*, *9*, 172–189.

Malaquias, R. F., & Hwang, Y. (2016). An empirical study on trust in mobile banking: A developing country perspective. *Computers in Human Behavior*, *54*, 453–461. doi:10.1016/j.chb.2015.08.039

Martinez Peria, M. S., & Singh, S. (2014). *The impact of credit information sharing reforms on firm financing?* World Bank Policy Research, Working Paper No 7013.

Masocha, R., Chiliya, N., & Zindiye, S. (2011). E-banking adoption by customers in the rural milieus of South Africa: A case of Alice, Eastern Cape, South Africa. *African Journal of Business Management*, *5*(5), 1857–1863.

Modimogale, L., & Kroeze, J. H. (2009). Using ICTs to become a competitive SME in South Africa. In *Proceedings of the 13th International Business Information Management Association Conference* (pp. 504–513). Norristown, PA: International Business Information Management Association.

Mohiuddin, M. (2014). Overview the e-commerce in Bangladesh. *IOSR Journal of Business and Management*, *16*(7), 1–6.

Mubaraka, C. M., Momanyi, W. K., & Jibia, M. S. (2013). Integrating ICT in insurance management : Design & development of an online insurance system for E. Africa insurance company. *Journal of Information Engineering and Applications*, *3*(5), 10–20.

Murari, K., & Tater, B. (2014). Employees attitude towards adoption of IT-based banking services: A case of Indian private sector banks. *Competitiveness Review*, *24*(2), 107–118. doi:10.1108/CR-01-2013-0005

Narayanasamy, K., Rasiah, D., & Tan, T. M. (2011). The adoption and concerns of e-finance in Malaysia. *Electronic Commerce Research*, *11*(4), 383–400. doi:10.1007/s10660-011-9081-5

Nasri, W. (2011). Factors influencing the adoption of internet banking in Tunisia. *International Journal of Business and Management*, *6*(8), 143–160. doi:10.5539/ijbm.v6n8p143

Ndayizigamiye, P. (2014). The influence of SMMEs internal factors on e-commerce adoption: A South African perspective. *Mediterranean Journal of Social Sciences*, *5*(23), 246–253.

Odoyo, F. S., & Nyangosi, R. (2011). E-insurance : An empirical study of perceived benefits. *International Journal of Business and Social Science*, *2*(21), 166–171.

Phillips, T., Lyons, P., Page, M., Viviez, L., Molina, M., & Ensor, T. (2011). *African Mobile Observatory 2011: Driving Economic and Social Development through Mobile Services.* Retrieved May 10, 2013, from http://www.gsma.com/spectrum/wp-content/uploads/2011/12/Africa-Mobile-Observatory-2011.pdf

Ping, X., & Chuanwei, Z. (2013). The theory of internet finance. *China Economist*, *8*(2), 1–15.

Raihan, A. (2001, October). *The state of e-finance in developing countries: Bangladesh perspective*. Paper presented in Expert Group Meeting on "Improving Competitiveness of SMEs in Developing Countries: Role of Finance, including E-finance to Enhance Enterprise Development", Geneva, Switzerland.

Raza, S. A., & Hanif, N. (2013). Factors affecting internet banking adoption among internal and external customers: A case of Pakistan. *International Journal of Electronic Finance*, *7*(1), 82–96. doi:10.1504/IJEF.2013.051746

Riyadh, A. N., Bunker, D., & Rabhi, F. (2010). Barriers to e-finance adoption in small and medium sized enterprises (SMEs) in Bangladesh.*Proceedings of the 5th International Conference on Qualitative Research in IT & IT in Qualitative Research*, 1–10. doi:10.2139/ssrn.1726262

Sapa, S. G., Phunde, S. B., & Godbole, M. R. (2014). Impacts of ICT application on the insurance sector (e-insurance). *IBMRD's Journal of Management and Research*, *3*(1), 311–320.

Saunders, M., Lewis, P., & Thornhill, A. (2009). *Research Methods for Business Students* (5th ed.). Sussex, UK: Pearson Education Limited.

Shahrokhi, M. (2008). E-finance: Status, innovations, resources and future challenges. *Managerial Finance*, *34*(6), 365–398. doi:10.1108/03074350810872787

Singh, A. J., & Chauhan, R. (2012). Technology challenges in e-service accessibility. *Journal of Engineering and Technology*, *2*(1), 32–40. doi:10.4103/0976-8580.93233

Sorooshian, S., Onn, C. W., & Yeen, C. W. (2013). Malaysian based analysis on e-service. *International Journal of Academic Research*, *5*(4), 62–64. doi:10.7813/2075-4124.2013/5-4/B.8

Srivastava, A. (2014). The status and impact of e-finance on developing economy. *Golden Research Thoughts*, *3*(11), 1–3.

Su, C., & Yuan, H. (2013). New exploration - The role of e-finance in small business financing. In *Proceedings of the 2013 6th International Conference on Information Management, Innovation Management and Industrial Engineering* (Vol. 1, pp. 501–504). IEEE. Retrieved from www.ieee.org

Susanto, A., Lee, H., Zo, H., & Ciganek, A. P. (2013). User acceptance of internet banking in Indonesia: Initial trust formation. *Information Development*, *29*(4), 309–322. doi:10.1177/0266666912467449

Tsai, W.-H., Huang, B.-Y., Fan, Y.-W., & Liu, J.-Y. (2006). Trends and developments in electronic lending: A preliminary research in Taiwan. *International Journal of Electronic Finance*, *1*(2), 241–259. doi:10.1504/IJEF.2006.010318

World Wide Worx. (2013). *The time of the App*. Retrieved January 12, 2016, from http://www.worldwideworx.com/mobileinternet2014/

KEY TERMS AND DEFINITIONS

Developing Country: A country with a slow rate of industrialization and lower per capita income than a developed country.

E-Commerce: Economic transactions using the internet or electronic means to conduct business. Transactions include business-to-business, business-to-consumer, consumer-to-consumer and consumer-to-business.

E-Finance: The provision of, implementation and allocation of financial services and resources using electronic means such as the Internet.

E-Services: Delivery of services using ICT.

Finance: Money used for funding a business, project or purchase.

ICT: Information and Communications Technologies (ICT) consist of the hardware, software, network and media used to collect, store, process, transmit and present information in the form of text, images, data and voice.

Mobile Banking: Using mobile devices such as smartphones, tablets and laptops to perform banking activities from anywhere at any time. Smartphones and tablets may have specific mobile banking apps installed.

Online Banking: Use of the Internet to perform banking activities is called online banking, also known as Internet banking or Web banking.

Small and Medium Enterprises (SMEs): A small to medium-sized business which is small by nature in terms of either employees, capital or turnover when compared to larger businesses. SMEs are also single owner or single product enterprises which are generally located in a specific area of business. Different countries may have their own definition of SMEs based on number of employees and annual turnover.

APPENDIX

Table 13. Cronbach's alpha for survey items

Items	E-Finance Enables the Business to Pay Less...	Cronbach's Alpha after Deletion
COST1	for transactions completed online	0.82
COST2	in fees for a loan completed online	
COST3	in interest for a loan completed online	
Items	**E-Finance Enables the Business to Perform Financial Transactions...**	**Cronbach's Alpha after Deletion**
PERF1	from anywhere on computer/mobile with internet.	0.76
PERF2	any time of the day on a computer/mobile with internet.	
PERF4	required by the business on a computer/mobile with internet.	
ACCS1	E-finance enables the business to access information on improving my finances of the business online	0.76
ACCS2	E-finance enables the business to access information on funding my business online	
ACCS3	E-finance enables the business to access information on other financial products and services online	
SECU1	Unauthorized parties could access financial information	0.63
SECU 2	No guarantees should the business lose money during a financial transaction	
SECU 3	Little support is provided for e-finance	
SECU 4	Uncertainty about the continuity of e-finance	
INFR1	Poor internet access	0.89
INFR2	High internet costs	
INFR3	Power cuts interrupting access to online financial services	
INFR4	Software to access online financial services is too expensive	
INFR5	Hardware to access online financial services is too expensive	
LAWS1	Lack of laws that protect consumers	0.67
LAWS2	Laws, regulations and policies regarding online finance that are uncertain and ambiguous	
LAWS3	Online contracts are hard to enforce.	
SKLL1	Lack of knowledge about some of the online financial services available	0.58
SKLL2	The business has adequate skill so perform online financial transactions	

Chapter 9
The Role of Value Co-Creation on Brand Image:
A Conceptual Framework for the Market Performance of SMEs in Malaysia

Pravina Jayapal
Universiti Sains Malaysia, Malaysia

Azizah Omar
Universiti Sains Malaysia, Malaysia

ABSTRACT

The proliferation of SMEs in Malaysia shows that a better understanding on this SMEs are needed. Even though the SME market is booming, these SMEs face difficulties in sustaining in the constantly evolving marketplace. In order to continuously flourish in this industry, the firms should understand the role of value co-creation in improving their market performance. The lack of value co-creation implementation has been found to act as a barrier for these SMEs. Moreover, SMEs are identified to have issues in establishing a strong brand image through value co-creation. Therefore, the book chapter develops a conceptual framework to improve the understanding on the contribution of value co-creation in the development of stronger brand image and greater market performance.

INTRODUCTION

The existence of Small Medium Enterprises (SMEs) plays an important role in the socioeconomic development of the country. In recent years, the SMEs in Malaysia have been continuously booming. According to SME Corp. Malaysia, among the business entities in Malaysia, approximately 97.3% are SMES based on the year 2014, which contributed about 33.1% towards the Gross Domestic Product (GDP) and 57.5% of employment (Rosley, 2015). Up to the year 2015, the Malaysian government has allocated RM11.34 billion towards the development of these SMEs (SME Annual Report, 2015). This allocation is expected to boost the productivity as well as encourage new businesses to embark into the

DOI: 10.4018/978-1-5225-2165-5.ch009

SME industry. The major focus of these firms is to improve their market performance which depends on the capability and ability of the SMEs' market orientation. Thus, firms have come up with various strategies in order to improve their market performance. One of the recent strategies of firms are collaborating with customers in terms of value co-creation.

Firms have evolved from the goods-dominant logic (G-D) which focuses solely on the activities performed by the company to the service dominant logic (S-D), giving importance to the involvement of the consumers in the process chain and the relationship between the firms and consumers. Value co-creation has been identified to provide various benefits to the firms as well as consumers. According to Badurdeen and Liyanage (2011), value co-creation contributes to the betterment and sustainability of the products whereby, firms get to understand and meet the consumers' needs and preferences. Therefore, firms are able to modify and implement the decision making process which is more efficient and saves time and resources (Chen et al., 2012). This shows that value co-creation is able to encourage competitive advantage and improve its market performance.

One of the organization that successfully practice value co-creation is IKEA, one of the popular retail furniture company in the world. In IKEA, consumer value is implemented through the co-creation of personalized customer experiences in the store itself in terms of testing and trying the home design which are available. Different themes of rooms are provided based on the customers' preferences. Moreover, IKEA also uses value co-creation where consumers are required to conduct their own assembly operation. By doing so, IKEA manages to have high turnover of products while consumers benefit from the lower cost. Another company that uses value co-creation is LEGO. LEGO has an online platform called Lego Ideas which allow Lego users to come up with their own ideas and share them here. Other users are allowed to vote on these ideas and the ideas which are the most popular will receive a small amount from the net revenue from LEGO. Since the G-D logic has transitioned into the S-D logic, SMEs are also moving into the value co-creation process in order to sustain within their highly competitive industry. Value co-creation is vital for SMEs as it would be able to train them to utilize their limited resources efficiently and effectively while sustaining their brand in the marketplace.

In addition, value co-creation also plays a role in the field of new product development. Here, consumers come into the picture in providing useful information and ideas on the products and services that they need and want. These products and services might not be available in the market currently but is considered to be useful in the nearest future. Therefore, the firms which practice value co-creation would have the competitive advantage of introducing a new product which will meet the demand of consumers. However, even though SMEs have difficulties in terms of budget and resources, investing in product development would benefit the firm in terms of sustainability and increase in sales revenue. Through value co-creation, SMEs can expect to have more involvement in the product development which will subsequently improve their brand image.

In the current business world, the brand image of the organization plays an important role. Brand image is defined as the combinations of different brand names in terms of the brands' characteristics (Keller, 1993). Brands are an important asset for every firm because it determines the value of the particular firm and drives the entire marketing activity of the firm. Moreover, the brand serves as a competitive advantage for the firm. For SMEs, creating a strong brand image would ensure its sustainability in the marketplace. Having a strong brand image would help the SME in terms of spending lesser budget on promotions of the brand. This is because brands which are reputable, trusted and well known provide assurance and confidence to consumers in purchasing its products.

Building a good business image takes a long time to establish and it can be further improved by identifying the strengths and overcoming the weaknesses of the particular brand. SMEs which are able to establish their brand among customers will have many advantages. Consumers would trust and purchase the products which are provided by firms with the positive brand image. Moreover, a well communicated brand image would be able to help consumers to recognize the needs and wants that can be satisfied by the brand as well as distinguishing it from its competitor brands (Huang & Cai, 2015). As mentioned in previous literature, brand image has a positive impact on the firms' market performance in terms of customer satisfaction, customer loyalty, market share, expanding into a new market and customer retention. However, establishing and creating a well-known brand consumes a lot of time and fund. SMEs have been identified to face problem in maintaining their brand image. To gain the trust of customers as well as retaining them, SMEs would have make sure that the quality of the products manufactured and sold is consistent and reliable. Positive brand image requires the hard work of every actors of the firm to maintain it.

As we know, value co-creation requires a huge amount of investment and expertise to be created and implemented within the firms' process chain. Larger firms have been successfully implementing value co-creation by interacting with their customers. Technology plays an important role in value co-creation in terms of having access to latest resources, knowledge on systems and new products, supply chain management and keeping track of the competitors (Möller & Törrönen, 2003). As been expected, technology implementation and advancement has been continuously taking place within the larger firms.

SMEs on the other hand, encounter difficulties in survival and growth in value co-creation because of the lack of financial strength (Desouza & Awazu, 2006). Moreover, SMEs need to compete in gaining the knowledge on value co-creation and implementing it to enhance their competitive advantage. Having limited resources such as capital, labour force and land serves as its major hurdle. In order to improve their market performance, efficient use of resources is required (Desouza & Awazu, 2006). Other than that, SMEs have been facing issues in the field of technology and value co-creation. The advancement of technology has provided various ways for consumers to communicate with firms such as the Internet, social networks, emails and websites (Hoyer et al., 2010). Realizing on the importance of technology in improving business performance as well as creating a strong brand image, SMEs in Malaysia are beginning to embark into the Internet. However, the lack of budget has held them back in pursuing their business activities in the online platform. Moreover, with the vast growth of technology, SMEs will soon be forced to take up the online environment for their business activities especially through value co-creation. Having a strong brand image could help SMEs in establishing themselves in the industry. However, this brand image needs the hard work and perseverance of the firms.

A strong brand image is achieved only when the customers have a better impression of the firms' brand and are more confident to associate with it. As more customers purchase products from the firm, strong brand image would be established. Firms believe that brand image acts as a guide to the identity of the brand, targeted market and benefits that it has to offer to customers. The improvement of the firms' brand image results in more profit and better market performance. However, the problem arises when the SMEs need to implement and develop their brand image. In order to do so, the brand needs to be known, communicated and shared which will be efficient with the help of value co-creation between the firm and customers (Payne et al., 2009).

Payne et al. (2009) further added that even though scholars have been focusing on the service-dominant logic area, very few have embarked into the role of brand in value co-creation. Other studies also agree that previous literature has only been indirectly discussing branding in the value co-creation context (Brodie et al., 2006). Moreover, Vargo and Lusch (2004) also briefly pointed out on the concept of branding in their paper. Bell and Loane (2010) stressed that many studies have focused on huge companies with strong brand while limited attention have been given to SMEs and their value co-creation. Only a few recent studies have begun to investigate on the branding of SMEs. Gilmore et al. (1999) and Merrilees (2007) also supports that there is considerable quantity of SMEs studies in the marketing literature but only a limited number embarks into branding. This is because SMEs are also facing problems in establishing and sustaining brand image (Mäläskä et al., 2010). This creates a need for studies on branding within SMEs in Malaysia.

In addition, more research on the effects of value-co-creation on firm's performance are required (Hoyer et al., 2010) as SMEs have been booming and gaining importance in the Malaysian business market. Mäläskä et al. (2010) further supported that actors of a business are considered to be useful in providing information and advice on improving the brand image of the SMEs which will eventually increase the firm's profit and sales. However, how the brand image of SMEs can enhance the market performance through integrating consumers into the value chain has remains unclear. Thus, this study proposes that the application of value co-creation with consumers of SMEs in Malaysia will have a positive impact on brand image which in turn leads to a higher level of market performance. Based on these issues, the objective of this study is to propose a conceptual framework on the relationship between value co-creation, brand image and market performance.

BACKGROUND

Value Co-Creation

Over the years, many definitions of value have emerged within the literature (Sánchez-Fernández & Iniesta-Bonillo, 2007). Value was initially being conceptualized as unidimensional but later on evolved into a multi-dimensional construct. Value has a vast range of definitions, i.e. value as a symbolic meaning, value added concept (Woodruff & Flint, 2006), relativistic preference experience (Holbrook, 1999) and value-in-use (Vargo & Lusch, 2004). According to Moore et al. (2014), consumer value is what the consumers want or believe that they would gain from the purchase of a product or service. These values might differ between consumers as different consumers have different value propositions from the same product or purchase. For example, one consumer might emphasize on the functionality of product while another would consider the design and colour. This study uses the definition of Ulaga and Eggert (2006), which describes value co- creation as the value which exists between the firm and the customer as well as produced from the relationship between them.

Based on previous literature, value and value creation are divided into two categories which are: "value-in-exchange" and "value-in-use" (Vargo & Lusch, 2008). Value-in-exchange is related to the goods-dominant logic (G-D) (Lin et al., 2010). Based on Vargo and Lusch (2008), value-in exchange refers to the value which is quantifiable whereas, value-in-use is heterogeneous because the definition varies according to individuals. According to the G-D approach, value is created by the activities which are executed by the firm alone such as designing the products, creating manufacturing processes, developing the marketing cues and controlling the sales without the involvement of the consumers (Prahalad, 2004), which later leads to the distribution of value into the market in the form of goods exchange and monetary transactions (Vargo et al., 2008). The role of both actors are distinct whereby the firms act as the value producer and distributor while consumers are the end users of the value. However, from the 1980s, literature started to focus on different areas within the marketing field such as market orientation, relationship marketing, service marketing, quality management and brand relationship (Smit et al., 2007). Later on, the goods-dominant logic started to reflect limitations which urged firms to question the approach and begin venturing into a new solution for better market performance, reaching diverse markets and fulfil customers' needs and wants (Tanev et al., 2011).

The evolvement of the market can be identified through the introduction of value co-creation. Value co-creation represents the S-D logic from the previous G-D logic in terms of products and services personalization (Vargo & Lusch, 2008). The S-D logic was beginning to be utilized when the exchange of products was replaced with exchange of intangible products such as knowledge and expertise. S-D logic is associated with the value-in-use whereby service refers to individual usage of the knowledge and skills in order to provide value to others (Vargo & Lusch, 2008). According to Barrett et al. (2015), the S-D logic is conceptualized as the process of utilizing an individual's resources for the benefit of others. The process of co-creation is frequently expressed in the literature as dyadic, two-way, continuous, voluntary, active, open and voluntary (Zwass, 2010). According to S-D logic, firms cannot provide value, however they can only give value proposition. This is because the consumers will be the ones deciding on the final value of the product or service (Vargo & Lusch, 2008). S-D logic offers a suitable framework to explain creative exchange forms (Lusch & Vargo, 2014). As the logic of branding has moved from a firm-centric to a collective, value co-creation activity, SDL and branding related research can boost and inform each other (Payne et al., 2009)

Recently, firms marketing strategy evolved into collaboration with customers and working hand-in-hand with their partners for improving their market performance. Some of the areas studied were customer and market orientation, value and supply chain management, relationship marketing, network analysis, quality management, services marketing and resource management (Vargo & Lusch, 2004) (As displayed in Figure 1). The transformation works in understanding the needs and wants of market,

Figure 1. The evolution of marketing
Source: Vargo and Lusch (2004).

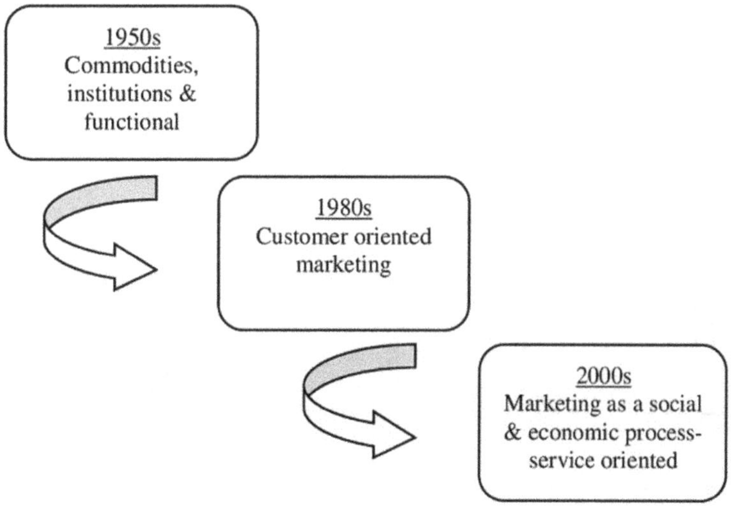

customizing the products and services offered and co-creating with the stakeholders to improve their market performance (Payne et al., 2008).

These changes have played a major impact on the firm's organizational structure and its daily activities. Consumers opinions and ideas became important inputs that could help the firms' market performance tremendously (Payne et al., 2008). Other stakeholders such as employees, stockholders and government organizations also play a role as the co-creator of value, but the value is decided by the consumers (As displayed in Figure 2). Therefore, it can be assumed that the firm and consumer relationship has changed by the involvement of all other actors of the value co-creation who work together in creating the value which is favourable to the consumers (Vargo & Lusch, 2008).

From the value co-creation perspective, Grönroos (2011) and Korkman et al. (2010) claimed that consumers are the ones who create value and it is supported by the communication between the customer and firms. Various benefits could be experienced by firms as well as consumers through value co-creation in terms of product development, consumers communicate with the firm on the suitable design for the product, production activities, logistics as well as consumption behaviour. Other than that, through communication with customers, firms are able to introduce new product or service which are needed (Lin et al., 2010). Value co-creation is important because firms identify and acknowledge the customers' value creation and this approach gives priority to the activities which are co-created as a result of a business relationship rather than the activities performed by the firm on its own. Hence, the S-D logic transformed from consumers to co-creators of value, value chain to value network, product value to network value, simple co-operation or competition to complex co-opetition, individual firm strategy to strategy in relation to the total value ecology (Juscius & Jonikas, 2013).

The significance of consumers in the value co-creation process is undeniable. Prahalad and Ramaswamy (2001) described that consumers represent a new source of competitive advantages. They further introduced the DART model in order to reduce the traditional information imbalance between consumers and the firm. It also acts as a foundation for the value co-creation process (Prahalad, 2004). Four components have been found to act as the building blocks in describing the interaction between consumers and firms. These factors are dialogue (D), access (A), risk-benefits (R) and transparency (T) (DART). This DART model has been found to assist in value co-creation by creating innovation strategies and providing a system for value co-creation. Numerous literatures have explained the relationship between these four factors and value co-creation. Dialog (D) refers to the communication between both parties which is essential in value co-creation. Dialog assist in the interactivity, commitment, capability and willingness of both parties in engaging with each other (Prahalad, 2004). For example, firms will be

Figure 2. Value co-creators in a business organization

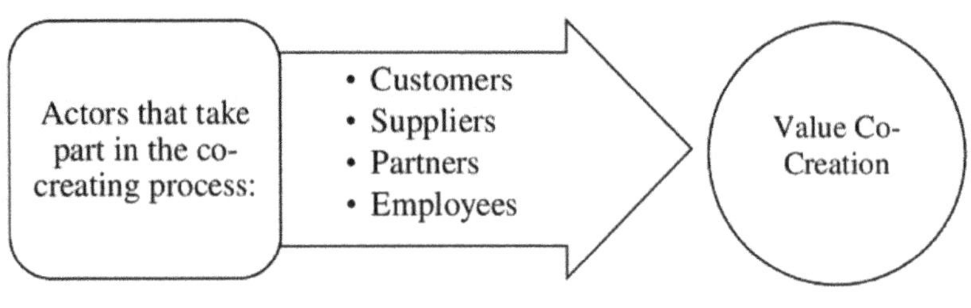

required to be transparent on the financial statements and information sharing which are confidential to the organization. Moreover, dialogue helps in understanding the emotional, social and cultural needs of consumers. Other than that, it develops trust between the stakeholders and firms which enables them to share information and ideas that are important to them. It also assists consumers and firms to communicate and work together in improving the product or services that are provided by the firm (Taghizadeh et al., 2016).

However, dialogue will only be fruitful when consumers are given the access and transparency to the firm's information. By providing access and being transparent to the stakeholders, it will provide a better understanding and develop honest relationship between both parties. Through the advancement of technology, consumers are able to gather information about the firm through stakeholders and online community of other consumers which is easily and conveniently accessible these days. Consumers who have the exact information about the brand and firm would be able to have a stronger bond with the organization which will provide more satisfaction and loyal consumers. The dialog, access and transparency results in risk-assessment which is the trade-off between the risks and benefits involved in the value co-creation process.

Access is defined as how alliances provide strength to consumers in gaining knowledge and information through value co-creation (Spena et al., 2012). According to Islam et al. (2015), access portrays the facilities and information that are available for consumers. Risk assessment describes the likelihood of risk to consumers. The stakeholders who go through value co-creation require firms to provide them with details on the risks that they might be exposed to and this makes them more responsible in dealing with the possible risks (Prahalad & Ramaswamy, 2013). Other than that, risk assessment also relates to the evaluation of the risks and advantages that the stakeholders will obtain through value co-creation (Islam et al., 2015). Lastly, transparency helps in providing shared information on the products, technologies available in the firm and business systems (Prahalad & Ramaswamy, 2013).

DART model has been focusing on the interaction facets of the value co-creation activity. Moreover, the dimensions explained by this model would be able to provide a better way of decision making after evaluating the risk and benefits of the value co-creation (Prahalad & Ramaswamy, 2004). It also helps in simplifying the value co-creation process. In addition, Skaržauskaitė (2013) also supported that the usage of DART model would enable firms to engage better with their consumers. Through the DART model, firms can co-create mutual values and improve on their current collaborations too. Other than that, the firm would be able to learn about the consumer's behaviour directly through the consumer's feedback on their preferences. Therefore, it is agreeable that the DART model provides a guideline which eases the firms in value co-creation with their consumers. By practising the DART model, SMEs would be able to have a proper guideline in developing and monitoring their innovation strategies. The transformation to value co-creation is deemed important for every SMEs in order to them to sustain in the marketplace. Ramaswamy and Gouillart (2010) mentioned that value co-creation is a process building the activities of the firm with the stakeholders which is in contrast to the traditional way of creation whereby firm carries the responsibility of building the firm solely and wait for the stakeholders to come to them. As a result, firms are open to more business advantages, growth and more opportunities towards innovation. Therefore, firms need to change their approach in terms of the firms' practices and management if they would want to adapt to the value co-creation environment (Ramaswamy, 2009).

BRAND IMAGE

Brand image is an important component in the marketing field. Different definitions and conceptualizations have emerged from past literatures. Kotler (2001) defined image as "the set of beliefs, ideas, and impression that a person holds regarding an object". Low and Lamb (2000) stated that brand image represents consumers' attachment on the rational or emotional aspects of a brand. Brand plays its role during the decision making process of consumers whereby it helps in differentiating products and services. Moreover, Ataman and Ülengin (2003) explained brand image as to how consumers' choose between brands after the information gathering in the buying decision making process. Brand image represents the perceptions, beliefs and expectations of consumers on a brand based on the value that it can provide to them and the firm (Nandan, 2005). Besides that, brand image also refers to the stakeholder's idea or perception of the brand. In the organization perspective, some studies have provided differing definitions for brand image. Besides that, Vukasovic (2009) claimed that brand image is the overall perception and associations that the consumer has in his/ her mind. This book chapter uses the widely used definition of brand image from Keller (1993) which describes brand image as the perception of consumers on a particular brand which is developed through brand association in the consumer's memory and experiences. It was further added that the brand image within consumers are from the experiences that they have been through when purchasing or using the product.

The various definition and concepts of brand image was found to be possible due to the lack of the foundation theory which explains the brand image in detail (Dobni & Zinkhan, 1990). Brand image has been used interchangeably with terms such as brand identity. However, Aaker (1996) had clarified on the differences between these two concepts. "Brand identity is a unique set of brand associations that the brand strategist aspires to create or maintain", whereby the brand identity is the idea that firms want the consumers to relate the brand to. It further explains on the assurance of what the brand provides to the consumers. However, brand image represents the way the brand is perceived by the consumers which has been developed through the consumers past experience or memories.

Apéria and Back (2004) claimed that brand image is derived through the mental image or the way that the brand is perceived by the consumers. This is because brand image is mainly influenced by those who consume the final brand which are the end users. Thus, it is understood that brand image is formed from the way stakeholders interpret the signs that are deriving through the firm's products or services (Aaker, 2003). Brand image is found to be highly influenced by symbolic interpretations that are gained through the product's characteristics or the benefit that the consumers perceive to receive when consuming the product. By understanding brand image, SMEs are able to identify the strength and weakness of their brand as well as the perception of consumers towards their brand. This is because brand image differs based in the consumer's perception. Therefore, brand image is an essential component that SMEs need to focus on.

In the organizational perspective, brand image determines the reputation of a particular firm (Mudambi, 2002). According to Kapferer (2012), brand image comprises of the name of the product, logo, physical attributes and functionality. Leek and Christodoulides (2011) explained brand image as "a combination of stakeholders" evaluation of the firms' ability to reach their desired goals and expectations which should also parallel with the brand identity. Brand image is different than brand identity in the sense that identity represents the firms' values and culture (Michel & Rieunier, 2012) while brand image describes the mental image of the firm and goes beyond the status and identity (Schmitt, 2012).

There are different ways to identify the brand image of a firm or product. Ataman and Ülengin (2003) provided further clarification that brand image is commonly portrayed through the name of the product, the attributes and exterior of the product such as the design and packaging, the functionality which helps in determining the consumer's choice of brand. These aspects are examined by the consumers during the information searching process before purchasing a product or service. Aaker (1991) explained that brand image is significant in assisting consumer in processing information, providing valid reason for purchase, distinguishing the brand from its competitors' and ensuring consumers feel happy and satisfied at the end of the purchase. For SMEs, patenting their brand name, logo and trademark would be able to improve their brand image. By having a strong brand image, SMEs would be able to compete with their competitors as well as other established brands.

However, a particular brand image might be favourable to only a certain group of consumers. This is because brand image can be formed from the information that a consumer receives from their social group or through the positive relationship that the consumer has developed with the firm and its brand. Through branding, firms can produce, cultivate and innovate their products or services. Based on this, SMEs can market the product to the targeted customers by segmenting their market. These consumers will continuously be loyal to the brand and brand switching is unlikely to take place. This can be done through understanding the needs of each target market and deciding which target market will be suitable for their brand. The inability to focus on the right consumer market might lead to less sales revenue and profit margin. As a result, the brand will not be able to sustain with the competing brands due to their lack of knowledge on the consumers buying behaviour. Therefore, having a strong and successful brand image is important to firms especially SMEs.

A successful brand should be able to attract its targeted consumers based on its distinct attributes and benefits (Jalilvand & Samiei, 2012; Keller, 1993). Attributes refer to characteristics of a brand that describes a brand. It focuses on the product-related attributes and non-product-related attributes. Product-related attributes describe the characteristics of the product which helps in delivering the function of the product while non product-related attributes describes the external aspects of the product or service (Keller, 1993). Besides that, benefits describe the values that consumers see in a particular brand or product and how the brand can add value to their life. For example, what a consumer perceives about a brand and what they can gain when they purchase the brand. These brands have such a strong brand image that when features such as high quality or price saving are mentioned, consumers could immediately associate it with a particular brand. This displays the success of the firm in positioning its brand. This distinctiveness is able to set the brand apart from the competing brand (Webster & Keller, 2004). The benefits have been divided into the components in previous studies namely, functional, experiential and symbolic benefits. Functional represents the intrinsic advantages of the product such as the quality and price. Experiential discusses the feelings and emotional characteristics that consumers feel when utilizing the product while symbolic benefits refer to the need for self-expression and social approval. SMEs are able to attract customers through any of these benefits. Therefore, sufficient planning and emphasis should be provided to the brand image in order to secure a permanent position within their targeted group of customers.

According to Hsieh et al. (2004), a strong brand image is displayed when consumers could satisfy their needs with it and able to distinguish it from other competing brand which increases the probability of consumer's purchase behaviour. A particular brand image might be favourable to only a certain group of consumers. Therefore, SMEs have to segment their market in order to identify their target market. This can be done through understanding the needs of each target market and deciding which target market will be suitable for their brand. The inability to focus on the right consumer market might lead to less sales revenue and profit margin. The brand will also not be able to sustain with the competitive brand due to their lack of knowledge on the consumers buying behaviour.

Furthermore, Solomon et al. (2009) suggested the use of marketing strategies and marketing mix to ensure a strong brand image. This could help in the product positioning for the suitable targeted market. Customers who are receiving the brand have the power to determining their perceptions of brand image. Kapferer (2012) supported that the sender-receiver model relies on perception of the customers on brand, product and firm. Moreover, Bengtsson and Servais (2005) mentioned that brand image is related to the relationship between all the actors related to a firm. In addition, Keller (1993) stressed on the importance of positive brand image among firms to encourage the loyalty of consumers. It is also understood that favourable brand image leads to positive impression on the brand which enables firms to charge premium prices for their products. This is because the consumers are loyal to the particular brand and would encourage positive word-of-mouth to others (Dennis et al., 2007).

Strong brand images need time to be established. Firms have to build a long term relationship with customers if they would want to retain their customers and create brand loyalty. The value for the particular brand can be determined by the strength of the bond with its customers (Nandan, 2005). Through value co-creation, firms are able to establish a strong bond with customers. Leek and Christodoulides (2011) supported this by explaining that firms require skills and ability to understand the needs of the customers through active communication in order to provide better product or service. By doing so, the firms will be more trustworthy and reliable. Therefore, customers' confidence, satisfaction and loyalty will increase which leads towards better market performance.

Additionally, Ojasalo et al. (2008) suggested that brand image can also be built by developing a good relationship with their business partners. The business partners also play an important role in the establishment of a strong brand image. They are able to promote the brand to other actors in the network which helps in promoting the brand. Moreover, actors in the business system will start developing their trust on the brand based on the positive word-of-mouth from the partners. Therefore, partners act as the intermediaries between the firm and other players in the business chain.

Besides that, brand image is significant due to it being the deciding factor when a consumer decides whether the particular brand is suitable for themselves or vice versa. This will later on affect the next decision making and buying behaviour of the consumer and subsequently brand equity. According to Keller (1993), brand equity is described as the distinctive differences of brand knowledge towards consumer's reaction the marketing of the particular brand. Strong brand image would be able to provide better brand position which helps in standing out from the competing brand, improving the market performance as well as shaping the brand equity of the product which will determine the future of the brand and the firm (Bian & Moutinho, 2011; Keller, 1993). Research on brand image has begun as early as the 1950s which signifies the important role that it plays in businesses. However, there is a lack of clarity and agreement on the conceptualization of brand image. Therefore, a comprehensive understanding on brand image is absent.

MARKET PERFORMANCE

In the dynamic business world, firms have to constantly compete with each other to create its unique competitive advantage and improve its market performance to sustain in the market. This is also found to be relevant in the SME industry. Most of the SMEs are striving to appear unique in the eyes of their customers and achieve higher market shares. Market performance can be determined by many different aspects such as image, customer satisfaction, customer loyalty and ability to attract new customers (Storey & Easingwood, 1999). Based on Laukkanen et al. (2013), market performance is defined as the firm's success in gaining new customers and maintaining existing ones. Other than that, Griffin and Page (1993) identified that profitability, revenue of sales and market share can also determine market performance. This book chapter describes firms' market performance through the number of products or services that are successfully sold, customer loyalty, new customers, attaining the targeted market share and growth rate (Homburg et al., 2010).

Even though performance measures such as customer satisfaction, customer acceptance and degree of competitive advantage is found to be useful if applied, in the practical world, it is seldom utilized (Griffin & Page, 1993). The development in market performance is possible through creating new products and services while constantly understanding the demand and evolvement of the consumers' needs and wants. This serves as an issue in SMEs due to the lack of funding and facilities. Firms try their best to identify, understand and satisfy the needs and wants of consumers. However, firms that are able to meet the needs of the consumers remain at the top of their industries. For SMEs, it is important for them to be able to sustain their consumers in terms of their satisfaction and loyalty. Those consumers who are loyal would spread word of mouth which would help in gaining new consumers. As it is known, maintaining existing customers cost lesser than acquiring new ones (Storbacka et al., 1994). Nevertheless, successful firms are those that could gain new customers and maintaining their existing ones.

The market performance of the firm is very important in order for the firm to sustain in the business. One of the way to increase market performance is by co-creating with customers. By doing so, customers get to express their needs and preferences while the firms will be able to serve the customers better. The fulfilment of the consumers' needs would improve sales of the firms' products as well as provide satisfaction for consumers which leads towards brand loyalty as well as recommendation to other consumers (Mokhtar et al., 2014), As the competition between SMEs are stiff, having the co-creation with customers serves as a competitive advantage for these organizations. Therefore, the SMEs that are practicing value co-creation would be able to perform better in the market compare to their competitors.

However, in order to achieve higher market performance, SMEs are trying to embark in new innovations to promote their brand to potential customers. Through technology, SMEs are able to reach their customers faster and it appears to be more convenient for the firm as well as the customers. being able to penetrate into the Internet and social media helps firms to bring their brand to the next level of innovation while increasing their market performance. Customers are also feeling comfortable with the new approach due to the ease of communicating and co-creating with firms through the new platform.

PROPOSED RESEARCH MODEL

Research focusing on branding have been found to give little importance to brand relationships and co-creation. This was supported by Arnould et al. (2006) who suggested that more research should be conducted on branding within the service-dominant logic (S-D). Moreover, Keller and Lehmann (2006) also emphasized on the relationship between brand and customer experience. Customer experience which falls under value-co creation is deemed to be related to brand image. In addition, Beverland et al. (2007) described value to be present when there is a mutual understanding between the firms and its stakeholders. Value co-creation can be identified in activities such as co-designing, co-production, co-production and co-branding. Hence, the incorporation of value co-creation in every process of the firm helps in the enhancement of its brand image. As an example, Intel improved its brand image by collaborating with its manufacturers and assemblers as well as displaying its logo clearly on the products that are promoted.

In addition, with value co-creation, firms are able to influence the rest of the stakeholders, and the stakeholders in turn are also utilizing this opportunity to communicate with firms (Håkansson & Snehota, 2006). Value co-creation acts as a way for the firm and its stakeholders to work together in providing a positive and enhance brand image for the company (Mäläskä et al., 2010). Thus, the brand image is influenced by the value co-creation process. Subsequently, various literatures have been found the influence of different stakeholders on brand image such as consumers (Merrilees, 2007), employees (Wong & Merrilees, 2005), resellers (Ojasalo et al., 2008) and business partners (Beverland et al., 2007).

Besides that, as SMEs have limited resources, other stakeholders assist and provide guidance on the business strategies of these SMEs. By focusing on value co-creation, the stakeholders are able to give suggestions on the firms operation and brand image which will be very useful to these SMEs (Mäläskä et al., 2010). In addition, Ojasalo et al. (2008) supported that branding in SMEs can be improved through the value co-creation with other stakeholder, thereby creating a supportive brand relationship.

Other than that, studies on brand has been found to be focusing on value co-creation recently (Hatch & Schultz, 2010). Another study by Ind and Coates (2013) also justified that brands should be built through value co-creation. Moreover, Merz et al. (2009) explains that brands are now being created through collaboration with stakeholders and the firm itself. Ojasalo et al. (2008) further described that the internal and external stakeholders of the firm play an important role in the brand's success. The commitment of the stakeholders is essential since SMEs have limited resources to establish their brand through huge branding activities. These stakeholders could assist by providing their knowledge and expertise in improving the SMEs brand image. Therefore, it is proposed that:

P1: Value co-creation is positively related to brand image.

Other than that, according to previous scholars, there is a positive, significant relationship between brand image and customer loyalty (Esch et al., 2006; Zins, 2001) Customer loyalty, satisfaction and purchase behaviour are often found as a measurement for market performance (Kim et al., 2009). Thus, brand image is a positive predictor to market performance. Moreover, Wong and Merrilees (2008) seconded that a strong brand image would be able to create a good reputation for the brand and encourage product purchase which will satisfy the needs and wants of the consumer. Strong brand image also leads towards more satisfaction and continuous satisfaction and consequently towards consumer loyalty. When consumers are satisfied, they would repeat their purchase, as well as introduce the particular brand to other consumers. Rundle-Thiele et al. (2005) further added that brand image plays a role in influencing consumer's satisfaction which later develops into loyalty. This word of mouth recommendation by existing consumers are able to reduce the cost of the firm in acquiring new consumers. As a result of the positive brand image, the sales, market share and profit of the firm will increase.

Furthermore, Park et al. (1986) explained that well communicated brand image is able to distinguish the brand from its competing brands, helps in positioning the brand and improves the brand's market performance. When the brand image of the firm is strong, the firm will be able to reduce the cost in establishing their brand among consumers. They only need to sustain the brand image that they have created. Besides that, Malhotra et al. (1999) found that brand image is related to market performance such market share and sales. This leads to the next proposition:

P2: Brand image is positively related to market performance.

In addition, value co-creation is deemed essential for the firm to sustain in the continuously evolving business world. Lusch and Harvey (1994) found that the strong bond between consumers and firms resulted in higher revenue and better financial stability for the firm. Coopetition approach has been identified to lead to better market performance (Grant & Baden-Fuller, 2004). Ahuja (2000) also supported that the capability of the firm increases when collaboration with partners take place. Coopetition benefits the firm in terms of joining forces for a certain technology or innovation that would help improve the market performance of each of the players involved in the co-creation activity. Besides that, value co-creation would also help in gathering the resources which could assist in the betterment of the firms performance (Ritala, 2012). Those firms that are not able to sustain a strong brand image are likely to be left behind by their competitors (Laukkanen et al., 2013).

According to Prahalad (2004), value co-creation has been predicted to influence the market performance of the firm. Through value co-creation, the firm would gain competitive advantages compared to the other firms (Payne et al., 2008). By having the competitive advantage, the firm has already secured loyal consumers who would continue purchasing the product. However, the firm needs to have the knowledge and capability to sustain these consumers. This is only possible through understanding the needs of consumers which can be performed effectively through value co-creation. By implementing value co-creation, firms will gain many advantages. One of the advantage is the increase in production and reduction in cost of production. The reduction of cost is possible for the firm in terms of gaining information from consumers in new product development which costs lesser compared to through their employees and market researchers (Evans & Wolf, 2005). Therefore, the employment cost will be reduced and firms would also receive valuable details on the latest need of the consumer market from the consumer itself which will be more reliable.

Next, the firm would be able to improve its efficiency. This would be through the improvement of the product value, innovation ideas for new products and fulfilling the needs and wants of consumers (Hoyer et al., 2010). Therefore, firms would be able to cater the needs of consumers earlier than their competitors. When they are able to receive the new ideas from consumers in advance, therefore, they have the advantage of satisfying this need before other firms (Sawhney et al., 2005). Value co-creation has also been found to significantly influence the firm's performance in terms of the reduced product and service turnover, increase in employee and consumer satisfaction, sales revenue and profit (Hoyer et al., 2010; Vega-Vazquez et al., 2013).

Besides, value co-creation gives the firms the competitive advantage in embarking into innovation. Innovation is important if the firm wants to remain in the market for long term. According to Prahalad and Ramaswamy (2013), firms that are successful in value creating innovation and are able to protect their innovation from being replicated by their competitors would perform better in the market. When the firm dominates the market, it would be hard for other firms to compete with them. This is further supported by Taghizadeh et al. (2016) who claimed when consumers co-create with the firms in the process of innovation, a stronger bond is formed between the firm and its customers. It was also added that innovation has the ability to improve the market performance of the firm. Firms that have been continuously providing innovative products would create a positive image for the firm.

From the stakeholders perspective, Ritter and Gemünden (2003) stated that firms do not have the power to control the stakeholders and the market. However, the stakeholders have the ability to influence and change the market as well as determining the firm's success or failure. The value co-creation between the stakeholders and firm serves as a great way for the stakeholders to convey their needs to the firms. This interdependency between all the players in the market is able to determine future of the firm (Mäläskä et al., 2010). Therefore, the next proposition is recommended:

P3: Value co-creation is positively related to market performance.

As a contribution to the existing theory, a concept of the value co-creation was proposed. In this study, value co-creation is studied in relation to brand image which incorporates all stakeholders that co-create an SME's brand identity and image, both directly and indirectly which in turn increases its market performance. In this respect, a firm's capability to acquire resources through exchange with the actors in its brand co-creation will have a significant impact on its brand success and market performance. Furthermore, Tung (2012) explained that in terms of product innovation, consumers would be able to have a wide range of products to select from which will ensure better market performance as well as consumer satisfaction. Therefore, this explains the next proposition which is:

P4: Brand image mediates the relationship between value co-creation and market performance.

Based on the findings and models from prior studies, a conceptual model on the influence of value co-creation towards market performance is proposed in Figure 3. The Figure 3 proposes that the market performance is influenced by value co-creation and brand image.

PROPOSED METHODOLOGY

This research will utilise the quantitative research method to collect the data as suggested by Creswell and Clark (2011). Self- administered questionnaire will be distributed to Malaysian SMEs via purposive sampling. The respondents will consist of business owners of SMEs operating in Malaysia. The inclusion criteria for the organisations are (1) the organization must have less than 150 employees for the manufacturing sector and less than 50 employees for the service sector, and (2) the organization must be a stand-alone firm, not a franchise or part of a larger organization. The survey will be designed in two languages namely English and Malay.

Figure 3. Proposed conceptual model

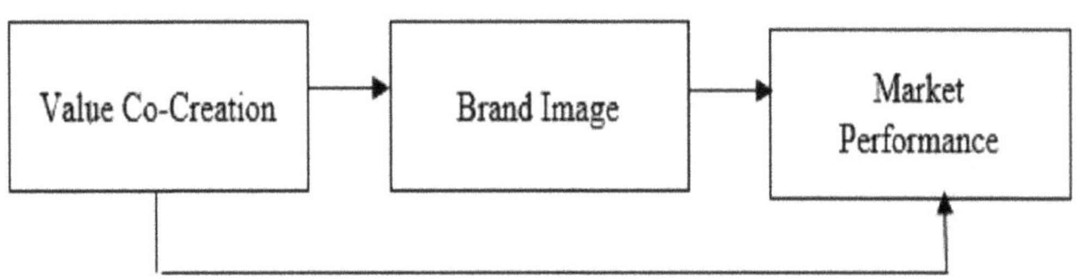

The instruments that will be utilized for this study are adapted from Ulaga and Eggert (2006) for value co-creation, brand image from Keller (1993) and Homburg et al. (2010) for market performance. The data will be analysed using the Partial Least Squares (PLS) 3.0.

STUDY IMPLICATIONS

The primarily purpose of this study was to contribute to the body of knowledge in the importance of value co-creation for SMEs. This study also hopes sought to provide better understanding on the theoretical and practical understanding of the role of brand image in improving the market performance of SMEs which has been understudied especially in Malaysia. By conducting this research, we will be able to understand how crucial value co-creation and brand image are for SMEs. By engaging in value co-creation, firms will be able to understand the needs of consumers better as they will be able to communicate and share their preferences. Other than that, this study will also provide SMEs with the importance of value co-creation in new product development and advancement. The feedback and suggestions that are received from the consumers could help in enhancing the product's quality as well as its brand image. The improved product would be able to satisfy the consumers better and attract new ones too.

Brand image is crucial for firms especially SMEs. By establishing a strong brand image, firms will be able to penetrate their target market easily. Brand image is built by gaining the trust and loyalty of consumers which require lots of time and effort. In order to achieve this, firms have to put in consistent and continuous effort. Firms should also understand that consumer's brand image perception differs among individual. Therefore, providing a personalized and more variety of products would be able to cater the needs of the consumers.

Stakeholders are also an important actor in the value co-creation process. The inputs and ideas from these stakeholders would be useful for the firm in improving their business. Firms should utilize the expertise, knowledge as well as experiences of these stakeholders to flourish in their business. In the context of SMEs whereby resources are known to be limited, firms are able to use the stakeholders to their advantage. Some of the ways of collaborating includes joint recognition, training workshops and developing a positive relationship with suppliers.

Moreover, this study would be able to provide an interconnection between value co-creation, brand image and market performance which has been scarcely studied in the past. As all the actors in a SME collaborate, communicate and co-create, better products could be manufactured. These products which are good in functional and experiential factors would be able to attract more consumers. Therefore, a strong brand image has been formed. This strong brand image will further lead to consumer satisfaction, repurchase and loyalty. Consumers who are loyal will introduce these products to new consumers. This explains the importance of having a strong brand image. The successful brand will then lead to better sales, more revenue and profit.

FUTURE RESEARCH DIRECTIONS

This research reveals that various studies have been conducted on value co-creation, brand image and market performance. However, studies on value co-creation within SMEs remain scarce. SMEs particularly in Malaysia have not been investigated thoroughly by researchers. As a result, the current proposed research model is expected to further explore SMEs market performance. Future studies could be carried out by expanding the current model through adding relevant variables to better explain market performance. Furthermore, future study could re-examine the relationships among the constructs in the existing model in different contexts. Other than that, with the increasing popularity social media, further research could be carried out on the impact of social communities on SMEs market performance. A focused and systematic effort on this proposed framework can lead to a meaningful impact on the market performance of SMEs in Malaysia.

CONCLUSION

The objective of the book chapter was to review and propose a framework on the influence of value co-creation and brand image on market performance. The framework shown in Figure 3 gives an overview of the factors influencing market performance. The proposed framework is believed to help researchers to identify the role and importance of value co-creation on the market performance of SMEs. The authors propose that the practice of value co-creation is able to improve the image of the brand which consequently enhances the market performance of SMEs.

The study also proposes a framework that could be utilised further in future studies. As explained, value co-creation explains that customers and other actors in the value chain are given the priority in assisting the firm on its products and services. The authors suggest that communication and the strong bond between customers and the firm is important for the firm to better understand the needs and wants of the customers. By co-creating value, firms would be able to enhance their brand image and reputation. When the brand image is strong, it would lead towards more purchase, as well as increase in customer satisfaction. Customers' who are satisfied will continue purchasing the brand which will result in customer loyalty. This would further improve the firm's market performance.

SMEs need to be studied further to improve the knowledge that the market has on this industry. Understanding the SMEs is deemed important because of the increasing number of SMEs in Malaysia. These SMEs have the knowledge to implement the value co-creation. However, the problem that they face is in terms of the monetary support. Due to this, very few SMEs are involved in value co-creation activities. SMEs should expand their business into the value co-creation system in order to increase their market performance and sustain in the market. The government and financial institutions should provide the help needed for these SMEs to invest in value co-creation activities. By doing so, the SMEs would be able to compete with their competitors as well as larger firms.

REFERENCES

Aaker, D. (1991). *Managing brand equity*. New York: The Free Press.

Aaker, D. (1996). Measuring brand equity across products and markets. *California Management Review*, *38*(3), 102–120. doi:10.2307/41165845

Aaker, D. (2003). The power of the branded differentiator. *MIT Sloan Management Review*, *45*(1), 83.

Ahuja, G. (2000). Collaboration networks, structural holes, and innovation: A longitudinal study. *Administrative Science Quarterly*, *45*(3), 425–455. doi:10.2307/2667105

Apéria, T., & Back, R. (2004). *Brand relations management: bridging the gap between brand promise and brand delivery*. Copenhagen Business School Pr.

Arnould, E. J., Price, L. L., & Malshe, A. (2006). Toward a cultural resource-based theory of the customer. In R. F. Lusch & S. L. Vargo (Eds.), The service-dominant logic of marketing: Dialog, debate and directions (pp. 320-333). M. E. Sharpe.

Ataman, B., & Ülengin, B. (2003). A note on the effect of brand image on sales. *Journal of Product and Brand Management*, *12*(4), 237–250. doi:10.1108/10610420310485041

Badurdeen, F., & Liyanage, J. P. (2011). Sustainable value co-creation through mass customisation: A framework. *International Journal of Sustainable Manufacturing*, *2*(2-3), 180–203. doi:10.1504/IJSM.2011.042151

Barrett, M., Davidson, E., Prabhu, J., & Vargo, S. L. (2015). Service innovation in the digital age: Key contributions and future directions. *Management Information Systems Quarterly*, *39*(1), 135–154.

Bell, J., & Loane, S. (2010). 'New-waveglobal firms: Web 2.0 and SME internationalisation. *Journal of Marketing Management*, *26*(3-4), 213–229. doi:10.1080/02672571003594648

Bengtsson, A., & Servais, P. (2005). Co-branding on industrial markets. *Industrial Marketing Management*, *34*(7), 706–713. doi:10.1016/j.indmarman.2005.06.004

Beverland, M., Lindgreen, A., Napoli, J., Ballantyne, D., & Aitken, R. (2007). Branding in B2B markets: Insights from the service-dominant logic of marketing. *Journal of Business and Industrial Marketing*, *22*(6), 363–371. doi:10.1108/08858620710780127

Bian, X., & Moutinho, L. (2011). The role of brand image, product involvement, and knowledge in explaining consumer purchase behaviour of counterfeits: Direct and indirect effects. *European Journal of Marketing*, *45*(1/2), 191–216. doi:10.1108/03090561111095658

Brodie, R. J., Glynn, M. S., & Little, V. (2006). The service brand and the service-dominant logic: Missing fundamental premise or the need for stronger theory? *Marketing Theory*, *6*(3), 363–379. doi:10.1177/1470593106066797

Chen, L., Marsden, J. R., & Zhang, Z. (2012). Theory and Analysis of Company-Sponsored Value Co-Creation. *Journal of Management Information Systems*, *29*(2), 141–172. doi:10.2753/MIS0742-1222290206

Creswell, J., & Clark, V. (2011). *Designing and Conducting Mixed Methods Research* (2nd ed.). Sage Publications Inc.

Dennis, C., King, T., & Martenson, R. (2007). Corporate brand image, satisfaction and store loyalty: A study of the store as a brand, store brands and manufacturer brands. *International Journal of Retail & Distribution Management*, *35*(7), 544–555. doi:10.1108/09590550710755921

Desouza, K. C., & Awazu, Y. (2006). Knowledge management at SMEs: Five peculiarities. *Journal of Knowledge Management*, *10*(1), 32–43. doi:10.1108/13673270610650085

Dobni, D., & Zinkhan, G. M. (1990). In search of brand image: A foundation analysis. *Advances in Consumer Research. Association for Consumer Research (U. S.)*, *17*, 110–119.

Esch, F.-R., Langner, T., Schmitt, B. H., & Geus, P. (2006). Are brands forever? How brand knowledge and relationships affect current and future purchases. *Journal of Product and Brand Management*, *15*(2), 98–105. doi:10.1108/10610420610658938

Evans, P., & Wolf, B. (2005). Collaboration rules. *IEEE Engineering Management Review*, *33*(4), 50–57. doi:10.1109/EMR.2005.27015 PMID:16028820

Gilmore, A., Carson, D., O'Donnell, A., & Cummins, D. (1999). Added value: A qualitative assessment of SME marketing. *Irish Marketing Review*, *12*(1), 27.

Grant, R. M., & Baden-Fuller, C. (2004). A knowledge accessing theory of strategic alliances. *Journal of Management Studies*, *41*(1), 61–84. doi:10.1111/j.1467-6486.2004.00421.x

Griffin, A., & Page, A. L. (1993). An interim report on measuring product development success and failure. *Journal of Product Innovation Management*, *10*(4), 291–308. doi:10.1016/0737-6782(93)90072-X

Grönroos, C. (2011). Value co-creation in service logic: A critical analysis. *Marketing Theory*, *11*(3), 279–301. doi:10.1177/1470593111408177

Håkansson, H., & Snehota, I. (2006). No business is an island: The network concept of business strategy. *Scandinavian Journal of Management*, *22*(3), 256–270. doi:10.1016/j.scaman.2006.10.005

Hatch, M. J., & Schultz, M. (2010). Toward a theory of brand co-creation with implications for brand governance1. *Journal of Brand Management*, *17*(8), 590–604. doi:10.1057/bm.2010.14

Holbrook, M. B. (1999). *Consumer value: a framework for analysis and research*. Routledge. doi:10.4324/9780203010679

Homburg, C., Klarmann, M., & Schmitt, J. (2010). Brand awareness in business markets: When is it related to firm performance? *International Journal of Research in Marketing*, *27*(3), 201–212. doi:10.1016/j.ijresmar.2010.03.004

Hoyer, W. D., Chandy, R., Dorotic, M., Krafft, M., & Singh, S. S. (2010). Consumer cocreation in new product development. *Journal of Service Research*, *13*(3), 283–296. doi:10.1177/1094670510375604

Hsieh, M.-H., Pan, S.-L., & Setiono, R. (2004). Product-, corporate-, and country-image dimensions and purchase behavior: A multicountry analysis. *Journal of the Academy of Marketing Science*, *32*(3), 251–270. doi:10.1177/0092070304264262

Huang, Z. J., & Cai, L. A. (2015). Modeling consumer-based brand equity for multinational hotel brands–When hosts become guests. *Tourism Management*, *46*, 431–443. doi:10.1016/j.tourman.2014.07.013

Ind, N., & Coates, N. (2013). The meanings of co-creation. *European Business Review*, *25*(1), 86–95. doi:10.1108/09555341311287754

Islam, M. A., Agarwal, N. K., & Ikeda, M. (2015). Conceptualizing value co-creation for service innovation in academic libraries. *Business Information Review*, *32*(1), 45–52. doi:10.1177/0266382115573155

Jalilvand, M. R., & Samiei, N. (2012). The effect of electronic word of mouth on brand image and purchase intention: An empirical study in the automobile industry in Iran. *Marketing Intelligence & Planning*, *30*(4), 460–476. doi:10.1108/02634501211231946

Juscius, V., & Jonikas, D. (2013). Integration of CSR into Value Creation Chain: Conceptual Framework. *The Engineering Economist*, *24*(1), 63–70.

Kapferer, J.-N. (2012). *The new strategic brand management: Advanced insights and strategic thinking* (5th ed.). Kogan Page.

Keller, K. L. (1993). Conceptualizing, measuring, and managing customer-based brand equity. *Journal of Marketing*, *57*(1), 1–22. doi:10.2307/1252054

Keller, K. L., & Lehmann, D. R. (2006). Brands and branding: Research findings and future priorities. *Marketing Science*, *25*(6), 740–759. doi:10.1287/mksc.1050.0153

Kim, E. Y., Knight, D. K., & Pelton, L. E. (2009). Modeling brand equity of a US apparel brand as perceived by Generation Y consumers in the emerging Korean market. *Clothing & Textiles Research Journal*, *27*(4), 247–258. doi:10.1177/0887302X08327085

Korkman, O., Storbacka, K., & Harald, B. (2010). Practices as markets: Value co-creation in e-invoicing. [AMJ]. *Australasian Marketing Journal*, *18*(4), 236–247. doi:10.1016/j.ausmj.2010.07.006

Kotler, P. (2001). *A framework for marketing management*. Upper Saddle River, NJ: Prentice-Hall.

Laukkanen, T., Nagy, G., Hirvonen, S., Reijonen, H., & Pasanen, M. (2013). The effect of strategic orientations on business performance in SMEs: A multigroup analysis comparing Hungary and Finland. *International Marketing Review*, *30*(6), 510–535. doi:10.1108/IMR-09-2011-0230

Leek, S., & Christodoulides, G. (2011). A literature review and future agenda for B2B branding: Challenges of branding in a B2B context. *Industrial Marketing Management*, *40*(6), 830–837. doi:10.1016/j.indmarman.2011.06.006

Lin, Y., Wang, Y., & Yu, C. (2010). Investigating the drivers of the innovation in channel integration and supply chain performance: A strategy orientated perspective. *International Journal of Production Economics*, *127*(2), 320–332. doi:10.1016/j.ijpe.2009.08.009

Low, G. S., & Lamb, J. C. W. Jr. (2000). The measurement and dimensionality of brand associations. *Journal of Product and Brand Management*, *9*(6), 350–370. doi:10.1108/10610420010356966

Lusch, R. F., & Harvey, M. G. (1994). Opinion: The Case for an Off-Balance-Sheet Controller. *Sloan Management Review*, *35*(2), 101.

Lusch, R. F., & Vargo, S. L. (2014). *The service-dominant logic of marketing: Dialog, debate, and directions*. New York: Routledge.

Mäläskä, M., Saraniemi, S., & Tähtinen, J. (2010). *Co-creation of Branding by Network Actors.* Paper presented at the 10th annual EBRF conference on Co-Creation as a Way Forward, Co-creation of Branding by Network Actors.

Malhotra, N. K., Peterson, M., & Kleiser, S. B. (1999). Marketing research: A state-of-the-art review and directions for the twenty-first century. *Journal of the Academy of Marketing Science*, *27*(2), 160–183. doi:10.1177/0092070399272004

Merrilees, B. (2007). A theory of brand-led SME new venture development. *Qualitative Market Research: An International Journal*, *10*(4), 403–415. doi:10.1108/13522750710819739

Merz, M. A., He, Y., & Vargo, S. L. (2009). The evolving brand logic: A service-dominant logic perspective. *Journal of the Academy of Marketing Science*, *37*(3), 328–344. doi:10.1007/s11747-009-0143-3

Michel, G., & Rieunier, S. (2012). Nonprofit brand image and typicality influences on charitable giving. *Journal of Business Research*, *65*(5), 701–707. doi:10.1016/j.jbusres.2011.04.002

Mokhtar, S. S. M., Yusoff, R. Z., & Ahmad, A. (2014). Key elements of market orientation on Malaysian SMEs performance. *International Journal of Business and Society*, *15*(1), 49.

Möller, K. K., & Törrönen, P. (2003). Business suppliers value creation potential: A capability-based analysis. *Industrial Marketing Management*, *32*(2), 109–118. doi:10.1016/S0019-8501(02)00225-0

Moore, K., Berger, P. D., & Weinberg, B. D. (2014). *Issues for Exploration of Differing Values among Sub-groups of Young-Adult Consumers* (Vol. 1). Global Journal of Business and Social Science.

Mudambi, S. (2002). Branding importance in business-to-business markets: Three buyer clusters. *Industrial Marketing Management*, *31*(6), 525–533. doi:10.1016/S0019-8501(02)00184-0

Nandan, S. (2005). An exploration of the brand identity–brand image linkage: A communications perspective. *The Journal of Brand Management*, *12*(4), 264–278. doi:10.1057/palgrave.bm.2540222

Ojasalo, J., Nätti, S., & Olkkonen, R. (2008). Brand building in software SMEs: An empirical study. *Journal of Product and Brand Management*, *17*(2), 92–107. doi:10.1108/10610420810864702

Park, C. W., Jaworski, B. J., & Maclnnis, D. J. (1986). Strategic brand concept-image management. *Journal of Marketing*, *50*(4), 135–145. doi:10.2307/1251291

Payne, A., Storbacka, K., Frow, P., & Knox, S. (2009). Co-creating brands: Diagnosing and designing the relationship experience. *Journal of Business Research*, *62*(3), 379–389. doi:10.1016/j.jbusres.2008.05.013

Payne, A. F., Storbacka, K., & Frow, P. (2008). Managing the co-creation of value. *Journal of the Academy of Marketing Science*, *36*(1), 83–96. doi:10.1007/s11747-007-0070-0

Prahalad, C. K. (2004). The cocreation of value. *Journal of Marketing*, *68*(1), 23.

Prahalad, C. K., & Ramaswamy, V. (2001). The value creation dilemma: New building blocks for co-creating experience. *Harvard Business Review*, *18*(3), 5–14.

Prahalad, C. K., & Ramaswamy, V. (2004). Co-creation experiences: The next practice in value creation. *Journal of Interactive Marketing, 18*(3), 5–14. doi:10.1002/dir.20015

Prahalad, C. K., & Ramaswamy, V. (2013). *The future of competition: Co-creating unique value with customers*. Harvard Business Press.

Ramaswamy, V. (2009). Leading the transformation to co-creation of value. *Strategy and Leadership, 37*(2), 32–37. doi:10.1108/10878570910941208

Ramaswamy, V., & Gouillart, F. J. (2010). *The Power of Co-Creation: Build It with Them to Boost Growth, Productivity, and Profits* (1st ed.). New York: Free Press.

Ritala, P. (2012). Coopetition strategy–when is it successful? Empirical evidence on innovation and market performance. *British Journal of Management, 23*(3), 307–324.

Ritter, T., & Gemünden, H. G. (2003). Network competence: Its impact on innovation success and its antecedents. *Journal of Business Research, 56*(9), 745–755. doi:10.1016/S0148-2963(01)00259-4

Rosley, F. (2015). Faster SME Growth. *The Star*. Retrieved from http://www.thestar.com.my/business/business-news/2015/10/19/faster-sme-growth/

Rundle-Thiele, S., Russell-Bennett, R., & Dann, S. (2005). The Successful Preperation and Development of Future Marketing Professionals: A Recommended Methodological Framework. *Journal for Advancement of Marketing Education, 7*, 27–35.

Sánchez-Fernández, R., & Iniesta-Bonillo, M. Á. (2007). The concept of perceived value: A systematic review of the research. *Marketing Theory, 7*(4), 427–451. doi:10.1177/1470593107083165

Sawhney, M., Verona, G., & Prandelli, E. (2005). Collaborating to create: The Internet as a platform for customer engagement in product innovation. *Journal of Interactive Marketing, 19*(4), 4–17. doi:10.1002/dir.20046

Schmitt, B. (2012). The consumer psychology of brands. *Journal of Consumer Psychology, 22*(1), 7–17. doi:10.1016/j.jcps.2011.09.005

Skaržauskaitė, M. (2013). Measuring and managing value co-creation process: overview of existing theoretical models. *Socialnės Technologijos,* (1), 115-129.

Smit, E., Bronner, F., & Tolboom, M. (2007). Brand relationship quality and its value for personal contact. *Journal of Business Research, 60*(6), 627–633. doi:10.1016/j.jbusres.2006.06.012

Solomon, M. R., Bamossy, G., Askegaard, S., & Hogg, K. (2009). *Consumer Behaviour: A European Perspective* (4th ed.). Prentice Hall.

Spena, T. R., Caridà, A., Colurcio, M., & Melia, M. (2012). Store experience and co-creation: The case of temporary shop. *International Journal of Retail & Distribution Management, 40*(1), 21–40. doi:10.1108/09590551211193586

Storbacka, K., Strandvik, T., & Grönroos, C. (1994). Managing customer relationships for profit: The dynamics of relationship quality. *International Journal of Service Industry Management*, *5*(5), 21–38. doi:10.1108/09564239410074358

Storey, C., & Easingwood, C. J. (1999). Types of new product performance: Evidence from the consumer financial services sector. *Journal of Business Research*, *46*(2), 193–203. doi:10.1016/S0148-2963(98)00022-8

Taghizadeh, S. K., Jayaraman, K., Ismail, I., & Rahman, S. A. (2016). Scale development and validation for DART model of value co-creation process on innovation strategy. *Journal of Business and Industrial Marketing*, *31*(1), 24–35. doi:10.1108/JBIM-02-2014-0033

Tanev, S., Bailetti, T., Allen, S., Milyakov, H., Durchev, P., & Ruskov, P. (2011). How do value co-creation activities relate to the perception of firms' innovativeness? *Journal of Innovation Economics & Management,* (1), 131-159.

Tung, J. (2012). A study of product innovation on firm performance. *International Journal of Organizational Innovation (Online)*, *4*(3), 84.

Ulaga, W., & Eggert, A. (2006). Value-based differentiation in business relationships: Gaining and sustaining key supplier status. *Journal of Marketing*, *70*(1), 119–136. doi:10.1509/jmkg.2006.70.1.119

Vargo, S. L., & Lusch, R. F. (2004). Evolving to a new dominant logic for marketing. *Journal of Marketing*, *68*(1), 1–17. doi:10.1509/jmkg.68.1.1.24036

Vargo, S. L., & Lusch, R. F. (2008). Service-dominant logic: Continuing the evolution. *Journal of the Academy of Marketing Science*, *36*(1), 1–10. doi:10.1007/s11747-007-0069-6

Vargo, S. L., Maglio, P. P., & Akaka, M. A. (2008). On value and value co-creation: A service systems and service logic perspective. *European Management Journal*, *26*(3), 145–152. doi:10.1016/j.emj.2008.04.003

Vega-Vazquez, M., Ángeles Revilla-Camacho, M., & Cossío-Silva, J., F. (2013). The value co-creation process as a determinant of customer satisfaction. *Management Decision*, *51*(10), 1945–1953. doi:10.1108/MD-04-2013-0227

Vukasovic, T. (2009). Searching for competitive advantage with the aid of the brand potential index. *Journal of Product and Brand Management*, *18*(3), 165–176. doi:10.1108/10610420910957799

Webster, F. E., & Keller, K. L. (2004). A roadmap for branding in industrial markets. *The Journal of Brand Management*, *11*(5), 388–402. doi:10.1057/palgrave.bm.2540184

Wong, H. Y., & Merrilees, B. (2005). A brand orientation typology for SMEs: A case research approach. *Journal of Product and Brand Management*, *14*(3), 155–162. doi:10.1108/10610420510601021

Wong, H. Y., & Merrilees, B. (2008). The performance benefits of being brand-orientated. *Journal of Product and Brand Management*, *17*(6), 372–383. doi:10.1108/10610420810904112

Woodruff, R. B., & Flint, D. J. (2006). Marketing's service-dominant logic and customer value. In R. F. Lusch & S. L. Vargo (Eds.), *The service-dominant logic of marketing: Dialog, debate, and directions* (pp. 183–195). New York: Taylor and Francis.

Zins, A. H. (2001). Relative attitudes and commitment in customer loyalty models: Some experiences in the commercial airline industry. *International Journal of Service Industry Management, 12*(3), 269–294. doi:10.1108/EUM0000000005521

Zwass, V. (2010). Co-creation: Toward a taxonomy and an integrated research perspective. *International Journal of Electronic Commerce, 15*(1), 11–48. doi:10.2753/JEC1086-4415150101

KEY TERMS AND DEFINITIONS

Brand Image: The perception of consumers on a particular brand based on the characteristics of the brand itself and the consumer's experience.

Goods-Dominant Logic: An approach whereby the process chain activities are solely planned by the firm.

Market Performance: The performance of a firm which can be measured through sales revenue, market share, profitability, competitive advantage, customer satisfaction and loyalty.

Service-Dominant Logic: An approach which focuses on the customer's involvement and communication with the firm in the process chain activities.

Small-Medium-Enterprise (SME): A stand-alone firm which has lesser than 150 employees.

Value Co-Creation: The value which results from the collaboration of all stakeholders and the firm.

Value-In-Exchange: Value that is gained from the trade-off between cost and benefits of a product/service.

Value-In-Use: Value that consumers perceive to obtain from consumption of a product or service.

Chapter 10
Deploying ICT to Enhance Small Businesses and Achieving Sustainable Development:
A Paradigm to Reducing Poverty and Unemployment and Enhancing a Sustainable National Development in Nigeria

Ojinga Gideon Omiunu
University of Ibadan, Nigeria

ABSTRACT

Beside the SMEs, families operate small and fragmented businesses due to poverty and unemployment to help cater for their needs and family needs. These small and fragmented businesses are common among the poor due to lack of credit to expand such businesses. In addition, with the mandate from the federal government of Nigeria, every business must be registered with the Corporate Affairs Commission of the federal republic of Nigeria and pay a certain amount of money every year depending on level of business growth and development. Suffice to note that despite the payment of these charges by businesses, nothing is done by the federal government to assist them.

INTRODUCTION

In the past, less attention was given to SMEs development as the major contribution to GDP and sustenance of the economy was oil. Nevertheless, in recent years, due to high level of poverty, unemployment and the inability of the oil sector to meet the economic demand for national development, attention has been drawn towards SMEs development. It is very obvious that, in Nigeria, individuals and families, in trying to break out of the yoke of poverty and unemployment bewildering individuals and the nation indulge in one or more businesses or the other so as to meet individuals and family needs. These busi-

DOI: 10.4018/978-1-5225-2165-5.ch010

ness are so fragmented and so small because of access to vital resources, there turnovers are so small that they can't be fitted into the micro and small enterprises categories of the nation, yet the businesses are so important to the various individuals and families in meeting their needs.

According to the Central Bank of Nigeria (1989) quoted by the Nigeria Vision 2020 (2009), small scale enterprises should have an annual turnover not exceeding 500,000 naira. In addition, in section 37 (2) of the Companies and Allied Matters Decree of 1990, small company should have at least annual turnover of 2 million naira. Ekpenyong & Nyong (1992) had used both limits to draw conclusion in classifying small scale enterprises- not lower than 500,000 naira and not higher than 2 million naira. However in a more recent classification, the Vision 2020 (2009) also provide its own small scale classification. Small scale enterprise should have employees between 10-49 and also have an asset of between 5-50 million naira. Howbeit, it seems the Vision 2020 perceived a wide gap of other businesses whose gap was farfetched from the small enterprise perspective, this brings about the micro enterprise. The micro enterprise, which a lower level than the small enterprise should have less than 10 employees and have assets not less than 5 million naira. This shows a higher upgrade than the limit provided by the Central Bank of Nigeria and the Companies and Allied Matters Decree. This could be due to the depreciating value of the naira and the Nigeria economy.

However, to an average Nigerian, living in a country with average poverty of 70% (NEEDS, 2006) and with approximately 24% of unemployment rate (although various sources have stated that in recent years it has reduced however, obviously the rate of unemployment has sky rocketed as one could notice in every nook and craning of the nation unemployed individuals and graduates rooming the streets with no jobs and searching for menial jobs just to keep living) and with no government support for its citizens, such annual return or turnover and asset based limit might be a mirage. Omiunu (2014) found that, average turnover of SMEs was 375,356 naira which is much more lower as compared to the 500,000 naira of the Central Bank of Nigeria of 1989 and also far from more recent standard of the vision 2020 (2009) which should have an asset of between 5-50 million naira for micro enterprises. This implies that most small businesses in Nigeria are far from achieving the annual turnover and the standard assets possession and may not be among the categories stated by the Central Bank of Nigeria, Companies and Allied Matters Decree and the Vision 2020. Thus, this category of businesses are not acknowledged and recognized in the Nigeria economy, yet they constitute a higher percentage but fragmented businesses of the businesses in Nigeria. Also of importance is their incapability to grow and reach other higher businesses levels in the economy.

This incapability has been caused by so many factors such as lack of planning, poor marketing strategies, lack of availability and accessibility to credit (Ekpenyong & Nyong, 1992); lack of finance and lack of business ethnics (Omiunu, 2014); shortage and inadequacy of financial institutions for SMEs support, high rate of collateral requirements and restriction of collateral to specific assets, lack of effective coordination mechanism to centralise information on possible sources of finance and other resources, misuse of government sources, concentration of finance sources in urban areas (UNEP, 2007); lack of infrastructural facilities, corruption, lack of awareness of necessary information for SMEs development among owners, lack of skills and training, cultural factors, lack of government policies that support SMEs (Apulu & Latham, 2009).

In addition, the lack of effective deployment of Information Communication Technology (ICT) could be another important factor. In addition, studies such as Croteau & Bergeran (2001), Laudon, Laudon & Dass (2006), Ajiferenu & Olatokun (2009), Omiunu (2014), among others have revealed the importance of ICT to business enterprises. However, Omiunu (2014) and Ajiferune & Olatokun (2009) among others have shown that business enterprises in Nigeria do not use ICT or use it at a low level to enhance their performance, and that the benefits of ICT are not experienced in their fullest by businesses in Nigeria. This scenario is worse among small business as Onugu (2005) affirmed that, small businesses mostly believed that innovations which include ICT innovation and use are for larger organizations. Major problems that a led to lack of deployment in ICT as stated by Onugu (2005) and Omiunu (2014) are ignorance of lack of awareness of ICT user to business, lack of skills high cost of ICT, credits electricity failure, lack of experience and competence in using ICT, among others. Also, of importance are the low of ICT and information literacy among business owners. From these, perceptible arguments, one can affirmed that, although ICT can benefit businesses, nevertheless, businesses in Nigeria are facing several challenges that are reducing their potential to deploy ICT and this would at the long run limit their performances. To this end, there is need to deploy strategies to make it possible for small business to deploy ICT and tap into the benefits it brings for enhanced development which include personal, business, community and national development.

Luftman (1996) and Gartlan & Shanks (2007) stated that deploying ICT by businesses is a function of business scope, distinctive, competencies business governance, administrative structure, administrative processes administrative skills, technological scope, systematic competencies, IT governance, IT architecture, IT processes and it skills. These twelve functions are important variables needed to be inculcated by businesses especially in developing countries with and ever changing and stochastic environment.

The Vision 2020 (2009) clearly states that, the micro enterprises are widely spread in Nigeria and are numerous, in most cases with time, they tend to develop into the small scale enterprises and may also with time develop into medium scale enterprise. In addition, this will create impetus and a multiplier effect on employment generation, poverty reduction and also national development.

It could also be important to note that, if attention is given and drawn to these small businesses which are not up to the micro and small enterprises by the governments and various private investors and organisations/agencies to train, mentor/monitor, develop and provide necessary resources such as financial resources, they may also develop into the micro and small business enterprises, thereby reducing poverty, increasing employment and also national development. Thus, achieving a sustainable development if well maintained and sustained. Thus far, in the Nigeria economy, achieving sustainable development in the SME sector has been a mirage as many programmes (such as Small Scale Industries Credit Scheme; Nigerian Bank for Commerce and Industries; Nigerian Industrial Development Bank; SME Apex Unit of Central Bank; National Economic Reconstruction Fund; Nigerian Export Import Bank; National Directorate of Employment; Industrial Development Co-ordinating Centre; Family Economic Advancement programmes, State Ministry Industries Equity Investment Scheme; Small and Medium Enterprises Developing Agency of Nigeria; Credit Guarantee Scheme for SMEs among others) that are been introduced and established by the federal, state and local government and other private agencies to enhance growth and development in the SME sector had not have lasting impact on businesses in this sector. Yet various researches still provided evidences of numerous problems and challenges militating businesses and reducing their potentials to grow and develop, living the small and fragmented business that could not meet up with the micro and small enterprises standards to their fate, thereby leading to increase poverty and unemployment and also influencing national development negatively (Hashim, 1999; Basil, 2005, Altenburg and Eckhardt, 2006; and Omiunu, 2014). To this end, this paper tends to provide a paradigm to reducing poverty and unemployment and enhancing national development through concentrating on and developing the small and fragmented businesses in Nigeria.

LITERATURE REVIEW

Micro, Small, and Medium Enterprises and the National Economy

The impact of small and medium enterprises in the nation cannot be overemphasised. Micro small and medium enterprise has been a major sector in both developed and developing nations and can form the bedrock on which all activities are built and can also be the mainstay of any economy (UNEP, 2007). Mahmood & Hanafi (2013) states that, small and medium enterprises (SMEs) play an increasingly important role in the economic growth of most nations and are also important as a major source of employment and job creation for the nation's work force. Also, SMEs are known to represent over 90% of businesses in Africa, account for approximately 63% of employment and also contribute to over 50% of nation's employment and GDP. There had been an increasing recognition of SMEs as major tool for economic development, a chief source of employment, revenue generation, innovation and technological advancement in both developed and developing nations. Apulu & Latham (2009) have stated that, researches have shown that, SMEs play a major role in poverty alleviation, and also stimulate domestic and regional economic growth in both national and regional economies. In addition, Ongori (2009) in Apulu & Latham (2009) notes that, they can also help to diversify economic activities and are flexible to changing market demands.

In Nigeria, about 97% of the enterprises are SMEs and employ an average of 50% of the work force and contributes approximately 50% to its industrial output (Ihua, 2009). Okpara & Kumbiadis (2008) clearly states that, several nations including developing nations such as Nigeria have recognised the importance of SMEs and have formulated policies to encourage, support and fund them. He further outlines the various benefits that SMEs can bring to the economy. These include job creation, development of skill and semi skilled workers among others. Other benefits may also include providing experiences, skills and training for the nation's work force that could be needed by bigger companies and industries, poverty reduction, enhancing quality of lives among others.

SMEs and Sustainable Development in Nigeria

The concept of sustainable development has been approached from different perspectives. Although, it can be self defined without channelling it to the various sectors of the economy such as oil, agriculture, education, telecommunication among others, howbeit, other times, its definition becomes more meaningful when it is channelled towards these sectors in the economy. Sustainable development is defined as the development that is stable, endurable, and consistent (Omiunu, 2012).

The World Commission on Environment and Development (1987) states that, sustainable development has nine important objectives. These include: reviving growth; changing the quality of growth; meeting essential needs for jobs, food, energy, water, and sanitation; ensuring a sustainable level of population; conserving and enhancing the resource base; reorienting technology and managing risk; merging environmental considerations and economics in decision making; reorienting international economic relations; and making development more participatory. It will be unreasonable to try to neglect the important aspects of the definition of sustainable development provided by WCED (1987) with regards to SMEs development.

ICT Deployment and Utilization Level by Small Business Development in Nigeria

Information Communication Technology deployment involves the way small businesses plan, manage and use ICT to benefit from its potential and effectiveness (Omiunu, 2014). ICT refers to technology such as computers, laptops mobile phones, internets, emails, wireless communication devices social network sites, flashes CD/VCD/DVD. etc. (Ministry of Economic Development, 2004). ICT is perceived as a tool that makes business activities easier (Van Akkeran & Harker, 2003) and can improve critical thinking, information handling skills, increase problem-solving capacity in businesses among owners (Branford et al., 2000). Van Akkeran and Harker (2003) outlined four stages in ICT deployment and use by businesses. These four stages include “no ICT”, “basic ICT”, “intermediate ICT” and “advanced ICT” adoption groups. Businesses that belong to the “no ICT” adoption group are businesses that do not use ICTs at all. The “basic ICT” groups are those businesses that have adopted ICTs such as internet for collecting information, use email or use latest phones such as the 3rd generation, 3G, among others. The “intermediate ICT” adoption group include businesses that have a basic or static website or information systems and are also engaged in electronic commerce. The “advanced ICT” adoption group are those businesses that conduct business-to-business transactions electronically, business-to-customers transactions and/or have any other complex ICT integration in their business processes.

Putting into consideration the study of the National Agency for Information and Communication Technologies (2008) that although there have been substantial efforts to increase the use if ICT especially by businesses however, the level of ICT mastery and use especially in Sub-Sahara Africa which Nigeria is a part is very low and poor. Also Omiunu (2014) found that, majority of businesses in Nigeria do not use ICT nevertheless, a few percentage (less than 40%) that used ICTs only use mobile phone for their businesses. Thus, majority of Nigerian businesses belong to the “No ICT” adoption group while the very few that use ICT belong to the ‘basic ICT’ adoption group. This situation is more ambiguous and severe for the small businesses in Nigeria.

It is expedient at this point to also draw attention to the fact that, if more businesses belonged to the “no ICT” adoption group and only a very few belong to the ‘basic ICT” adoption group, then it is very impossible for these business to deploy businesses information strategy and management information system to enhance their business development. According to Durodoye (2005), business information strategy is a top dog between business strategy and information system strategy. This implies that business information comprises of two important variables, business strategy and information and communication system and strategy (Omiunu, 2014). Usually for a business to deploy and adapt an effective business information strategy, such must have passed the “No ICT” adoption stage, the “basic ICT” adoption stage, and must have passed to the “intermediate ICT” and “advanced ICT” adoption stage. This makes the state of ICT use by business in Nigeria infinitesimal and thus businesses in Nigeria could not stand their counterparts in other developed and/or developing countries. This at the long run may lead to under-development. In addition, SMEs in developing countries such as Nigeria are incapable to deploy business information strategies less the small business. To this end, it is important to pay cognizance to the deployment of ICT among businesses especially in developing countries such as Nigeria to enhance business growth and development and thus increasing the net possible outcome of the national Gross Domestic product.

Challenges of ICT Use and Deployment in Nigeria

These barriers that the influence the successful implementation of ICTs in SMEs which could also include small businesses includes (Igbaria and Tan, 1997): the cost of ICTs—this is perhaps not so much of an issue these days (well, in developed countries anyway); lack of time to devote to the implementation and maintenance of ICT; a lack of ICTs knowledge combined with difficulty in finding useful, impartial advice; lack of use of external consultants and vendors; short-range management perspectives; a lack of understanding of the benefits that ICTs can provide and how to measure those benefits; and a lack of formal planning or control procedures. In addition to this, many SMEs are unaware of the potential of e-commerce to enhance their business; some SMEs occupy clearly defined (and small) niche markets that they are satisfied with; there are still perceptions of unresolved security and privacy issues related to use of the Internet; many SMEs lack the necessary skill base to engage in the digital economy; the perceived high initial and ongoing costs associated with ICTs and e-business can be seen as a barrier; and many SMEs cannot experiment with ICT investments like larger businesses. They need to be sure that there will be returns for the e-commerce investments they make. In addition, lack of understanding of the benefit of ICT by SMEs owners can also serve as barrier to ICT deployment and use (Apulu & Latham, 2009).

The drivers of ICT use are broad, as they are very important because they influence the tendency for SMEs to deploy and use ICTs. According to Thong, Yap & Raman (1997), they include: the involvement of owner/managers in the implementation of ICTs; the involvement of users (employees) in development and installation; the training of users; the use of disciplined planning methodologies in setting up applications; the number of analytical/strategic (versus transactional) applications being run; the level of ICTs expertise within the organisation; and the role of the external environment (especially consultants and vendors). Also, Mehrtens, Cragg, and Mills (2001) stated some other factors SMEs must identify to be able to use and deploy ICT. These are: Identifying perceived benefits, Organisational readiness and dealing and coping with external pressure. In addition, of importance to ICT deployment and use in an SME is the owner/managers perception and exposure, the location of the business, the differences between industries and employee skill levels and training.

According to Van Akkeren & Cavaye (1999) in Manueli, Latu & Koh (2007), the factors that influence IT adoption are divided into three: Owners/managers characteristics, firms; characteristics and the firms return on investment. The firm/business characteristics include: the organisation's ICT readiness; external pressure to adopt; customer/supplier dependency; structural sophistication of the business; size, sector and status; and its information intensity. The business's ICT readiness refers to its current level of technology use in its business processes. Little or no technology use reflects low ICT readiness and a strong reluctance for ICT adoption. External pressure may come from suppliers and/or customers for ICT adoption. Consequently, customer/supplier dependency may arise from the external pressure, whereby a small business tows the line to ensure its continuous survival. The structural sophistication of the firm/business refers to its ability to incorporate ICT into its existing business processes.

A complex structure may encourage ICT adoption because ICT is perceived as a tool for making work easier, whereas a simple structure may not readily adopt ICT because of the perception that everything is working smoothly and there is no need to change it. The size, sector and status of a firm/business influence its ICT adoption. If competitors, suppliers, customers in a certain sector have adopted ICT, a firm/business is inclined to do so because are already in it. Finally, the level of information intensity within the firm/business can be a contributing factor for ICT adoption. For example, if a firm/business

Figure 1. Factors affecting ICT adoption by SMEs

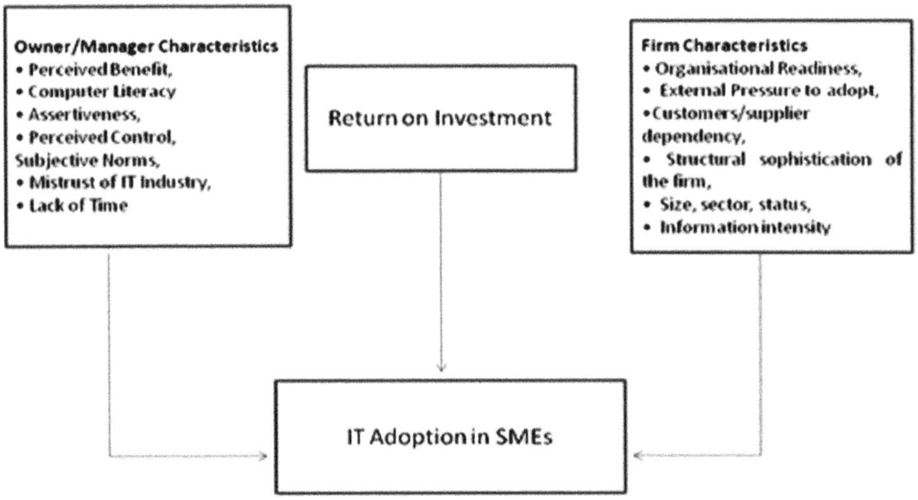

handles large amounts of information, it is most likely that ICT adoption will be undertaken to improve its efficiencies (Van Akkeren and Harker, 2003 in Manueli, Latu & Koh (2007).

Also, Windrum and de Berranger (2002), in his own view outlined the contributing factors that influence ICT adoption and that these can be categorised into five major clusters that include: the business characteristics; business action; system characteristic; internal expertise; and external expertise. Business characteristics such as size, determines the business structure that in turn strongly influence the business's ICT uptake. Small businesses have simple business structures when compared to larger businesses and have less internal requirements for extensive communication technologies. Small businesses communicate and store smaller volumes of information and as a result far lesser need to use ICT.

Typically, business action is driven from the top management. In this case, if the business owner or top management establishes appropriate ICT goals, identifies critical ICT business needs, and allocates financial resources then ICT adoption is possible. For small businesses, age and the experience of the owner strongly influences ICT adoption. System characteristics within a business assist in ICT adoption. For instance, small businesses with a large number of administrative applications readily support management control, operational control and administration. In addition, access to ICT expertise within a business and externally is another contributing factors to ICT adoption. If the business owner or employees are ICT literate, there is a strong tendency to adopt ICT for business processes. In the event that they face difficulties, the availability of external expert will provide support and motivation to succeed (Windrum and de Berranger, 2002 in Manueli, Latu & Koh 2007).

How ICT Can Affect Small Business Development in Nigeria

Studies such as Croteau & Bergeran (2001), Laudon, Laudon & Dass (2006) Ajiferenu & Olatokun (2009), Omiunu (2014), among others have revealed the importance of ICT to business enterprises. However, Omiunu (2014) and Ajiferune & Olatokun (2009) among others have shown that the use of ICT by business enterprises in Nigeria is low where many businesses do not use it at all and that the benefits of ICT are not experienced in their fullest by businesses in Nigeria. This scenario is worse among small business as Onugu (2005) affirmed, businesses in Nigeria believed that such innovations which include ICT innovation and use is for larger organizations.

Major problems that led to the lack of deployment of ICT as stated by Onugu (2005) and Omiunu (2014) are ignorance or lack of awareness of ICT use to business, lack of skills, high cost of ICT, credits, electricity failure, lack of experience and competence in using ICT, among others. From these perceptible arguments, one can affirmed that, although ICT can benefit businesses nevertheless, businesses in Nigeria are facing several challenges that are reducing their potential to deploy and use ICT and this would at the long run limit their performances. To this end, there is need to addressing these challenges and make it possible for small business to deploy and use ICT thereby are able to tap into the benefits it brings for enhanced development which include personal, business, community and national development. Luftman 1996 and Gartlan & Shanks (2007) state that deploying ICT by businesses is a function of business scope, distinctive competencies business governance, administrative structure, administrative processes administrative skills, technological scope, systematic competencies, IT governance, IT architecture, IT processes and it skills. Thus one can come up with the following nested relationship between the deployment/use of ICT and Businesses characteristics. These can be represented in Figure 2.

Putting into cognizance the studies of Luftman 1996 and Gartlan & Shanks (2007) that deploying ICT by businesses is a function of business scope, distinctive competencies business governance, administrative structure, administrative processes administrative skills, technological scope, systematic competencies, IT governance, IT architecture, IT processes and it skills; and of the problems faced by small businesses in Nigeria, it can be noted that making businesses enjoy the benefits that ICT brings in Nigeria would involves providing resources and materials for businesses by governments and other interested agencies such as non-government organisations and international organisations with regard to their businesses function thus, achieving development that can be sustainable at the long run. This is because a certain ICT of benefit to one type or category of business may not fit well into another type of business.

Figure 2. A nested relationship between the deployment/use of ICT and Businesses characteristics
Source: The Author (A Re-visitation on Luftman (1996) and Gartlan & Shanks (2007) of ICT Deployment by Businesses).

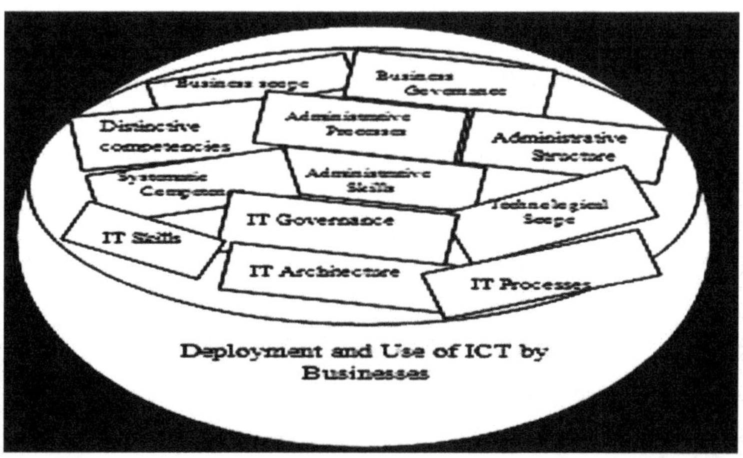

Challenges and Problems Militating Small Businesses Growth and Development in Nigeria

Despite SMEs significant role in the economy, studies have detected various problems militating against their growth and development. From early to recent studies, there are proofs of the undying problems and challenges facing SMEs especially in developing countries such as Nigeria. Despite the continuous effort of the government and other interested organisations, SMEs are still plagued by high failure rates and poor performance levels despite their recognition as major contributor to nations' economy. These problems seem perennial as one observes their trends, dynamics and elastic spread of setbacks they cause on SMEs.

Hashim (1999) had earlier discovered that the recurring problems of SMEs included a lack of capital and credit facilities; shortage of skilled workers and raw materials; inadequate infrastructure; lack of managerial, marketing and technical expertise; and limited applications of new technology. In addition, external environmental factors, such as fast changing technology, competition, economics, socio-cultural and international factors also have a significant effect on the success and failure of SMEs.

The Liberal feminist theory by Fischer et al. (1993) suggests that SMEs run by women exhibit poorer performances than those run by men because women are overtly discriminated against (by lenders, for example) and/or because of other systematic factors that deprive women of important resources (for example: business education and experience). By way of contrast, social feminist theory (Fischer et al. 1993) suggests that men and women are inherently different due to differences in their early and ongoing socialization. Nevertheless, these differences do not imply that women will be less effective in business than men, but only that they may adopt different approaches which may, or may not, be equally as effective as the approaches adopted by men (Watson, 2003).

Attention has also been expanded into other variables affecting SMEs performances and growth. Moorthy, Tan, Choo, Wei, Ping, and Leong (2012) outlined factors that can influence growth and performance of SMEs. They include lack of effective entrepreneurship in the nation, bad human resource management lack of the use of or no marketing information, and lack or low level of application of IT. In addition to this, Neneh & van Zyl (2012) also outlined problems faced by SMEs. They include lack of planning, improper financing, poor management, lack of skilled labour, brain drain, unavailability of financial skills, lack of performance analyses of business operations and incompetent senior managers. Studies have also revealed that, another major challenge to SMEs is gender inequality to access to vital resources which are important to their development. Other problems may also include poor knowledge and information consciousness culture among SMEs owners, poor reading culture, poor or bad regard for information, lack of awareness of the importance of information to SMEs development, poor information environment, among others. Omiunu (2014) found that, infrastructural problems such as electricity failure, faulty machines, among others, lack of skills, experience and competence, network problems, lack of credit, economic meltdown, etc. are major problems facing businesses in Nigeria.

The Increased Nigeria Population Trap

It is not a story that Nigeria has a population of 140,003,542, which most often has been approximated to 150 million, with male population of 71,709,859 and a female population of

68,293,683 (Nigeria Population Census, 2006). Also, the Nigeria population is placed at an average growth rate of 3.3%, and known to be the fastest growing population especially in Africa (Daily News, Sunday, August 05, 2012 in Omiunu, 2014). According to Omiunu (2014), with this estimate in mind, the Nigeria population was 88,992,201 in 1991 (NPC, 1991), increased to 140,003,542 in 2006 (NPC, 2006) by 51,111,341, which shows a 57.4% increase of the Nigerian population of 1991. However, the estimate of the Nigeria population by the Federal Ministry of Agriculture and Natural Resources (1997), was that, by 2013, Nigerian population will double the 1991 population with the growth rate increase of 3.2% assumed, which will show a 100% increase from 1991-2013. However, there is no accurate data for the recent data of Nigerian population because of the fact that census count is done every ten years and the next census in Nigeria would be in 2016.

However, according to estimate, the Nigerian population would produce an estimated population of 177,984,402 at 2013 and this would have increased by 2015. In addition, there is a 7-year lag between 2006 to 2013 compared with the 15-year lag between 1991-2006. This implies that, between 2006-2013, an addition of 37,980,860 average would be added to the Nigerian 2006 population of 140,003,542 to give a total of approximately 177,984,402. Although, looking at the population growth rate and dynamics, by 2013, the Nigeria population might even be greater than the assumed forecasted 177,984,402 (Omiunu, 2014). However, with the advent of child reduction and spacing may put the figure between ±177,984,402. This high population will also have significant effect on the resource allocation which also include the use of ICT and the access to resources (such as ICT) to maintain livelihood and thus will increase competition of resources (which may also include in businesses) where it would be the survival of the fittest. This however poses a big problem to the sectoral and national development.

Poverty and Unemployment: The Two Great Monsters of National (Nigerian) Development

With a geometric progression of the Nigerian population, the two great monsters for national development are poverty and unemployment. Economic stagnation, deepening poverty and weakening human development are known to be major problems of Sub-Sahara Africa which Nigeria is part and there have been progress in governance and regional collaboration, and concerted international endeavours to achieve sustainable development in this region (Aboderin, 2005). These features are pivotal in shaping the policy developments and emerging challenges for to achieving sustainable development in the region (Aboderin, 2005). In addition, poverty is been felt and has been a major issue in both rural and urban areas (Heeks, 2009). In addition, Heeks (2009) stated that for any problem especially in developing countries, It is the poor who are suffered it the most. And, of course, they suffer from that other blot on the world's conscience – poverty – with more than half the global population living on less than two US dollars per day. Alexander (2014) stated that in Nigeria, over 75% of the citizens are living below 1 dollar per day while the microscopic few kleptocrats living in corridor of power cart away our money in billions of dollars

According to United Nations Development Programme (UNDP) (2002; 2004) and the Commission for Africa (CfA) (2005), over the last decade, economic growth in most of sub-Saharan Africa including Nigeria did not outstrip the increase in its population. In contrast to all other developing world regions (which have seen drastic improvements in their fortunes in recent times), therefore, sub-Saharan Africa ended the Millennium poorer than it was in 1990. Also, 23 countries in the region are now poorer than they were in 1975. Today, over 50% of sub-Saharan Africa's inhabitants live under $1 per day which also include Nigeria, the great majority under $2, and it is globally the only region where the proportion of people living in poverty is expected to grow with their drastic geometrically increasing population. This has for a long time has effect and impetus of the development of this region and thus the sustainable development.

Poverty is a condition characterized by severe deprivation of basic human needs including food, safe drinking water, sanitation facilities, health, shelter, education and information (World Summit for Social Development, 1995). It includes people who earn and spend less than one US Dollars per Day and it is lack of, or inadequate access to social services (Agba, Ushie, Bassey & Agba 2009). Nigeria over the past five decades has embarked on various health, economic, educational, political, cultural and social reforms that are either home initiated or as a response to international agreed on poverty reduction. Despite government efforts, the incidence of poverty in Nigeria has been galloping since the 1980s (Agba et al, 2009). Statistics shows that poverty level on Nigeria move from 28.1 percent in 1980 to 46.3 percent in 1985; it escalated to 65.6 percent in 1996 and 71.3 percent in 2005 (Central Bank of Nigeria, 2005; Onyeagba, 2008). According to Agba, Ocheni and Nkpoyen (2014), stated that plethora of literature continue to show that over 70 percent of Nigerians live on less than one US Dollar per day only better than Mali 73 percent, compared to Ghana 45 percent and Brazil 8 percent. In 2002 according to Ekong (2003), NEEDS (2006), Vision 2020 (2009), over 70 percent of Nigerians were still living below the international poverty line despite government's multiple poverty alleviation programmes. Till date, this data of over 70% poverty level in Nigeria has not changed and thus, gives birth to other monsters of development such as unemployment. Alexander (2014) added that critically looking at Nigeria, malnutrition, poverty, illiteracy, diseases, and joblessness (unemployment) are still prevalent which proves Nigeria is an underdeveloped nation.

Unemployment covers persons (aged 15–64) who during the reference period were currently available for work, actively seeking for work but were without work. A person is regarded as employed if he/she is engaged in the production of goods and services, thereby contributing to the Gross Domestic Product (GDP) in a legitimate manner, which is a component of the national accounts and receives any form or amount of compensation for that activity (National Bureau of Statistics, 2015). The category of persons considered not in the labour force include those not between 15-64 (economic active population) as well as those within the economically active population (15-64 years), who are unable to work, not actively seeking for work or choose not to work and/or are not available for work.

When one conceptualizes the effect and burden of this population on the economic, one will realize that the nation's dependency ratio is high. Dependency ratio refers to the number of population of a nation who are not working, are unemployed and are not able to work to contribute their quota to national development, therefore these sets of people depend on any actively unemployed person. This is why nations and developmental indices use the per capita income to measure poverty- which is the ratio of the total income of any household divided by the number of persons in such household. In developing countries such as Nigeria, dependency ratio is very high and perfectly elastic.

Alexander (2014) stated that in Nigeria, over one million unemployed youths are readily applying for jobs where less than five thousand people are needed. The country is in the verge of revolution which undoubtedly will be triggered by this terrible economic menace called unemployment. It has been stated that unemployment is one of the most critical socio-economic problems facing Nigeria (Atufe, Okojie, Echenim, Ogunmola and Bello, 2014). According to the National Bureau of Statistics (NBS), the unemployment rate in Nigeria increased to 23.90 per cent in 2011 from 21.10 per cent in 2010 while the unemployment rate averaged 14.60 percent from 2006 until 2011, reaching an all time high of 23.90 percent in 2011 and a record low of 5.30 per cent in 2006 (Atufe et al., 2014).

Unemployment also has social consequences as it increases the rate of crime. School graduates consist of the principal fraction of the unemployed accounting for nearly 35 per cent to 50 per cent of the unemployed group. The rate of unemployment within the age group of 20 to 24 years is 40 per cent and between 15 to 19 years it is 31 per cent. The statement by Comrade Issa Aremu, vice president, Nigeria Labour Congress (NLC) and General Secretary, Textile Workers' union, Federal Republic of Nigeria that with 50 per cent unemployment, Nigeria is not just seating on time bombs but as we can see the bombs are exploding in scores through murderous insurgencies (Alexander, 2014) shows that the level of unemployment in Nigeria has reached climax where it can destroy the Nigerian economy. Therefore, there is need to address poverty and unemployment in Nigeria to enhance development which include individual, community and national development.

THEORETICAL UNDERPINNING

Restriction of Opportunities Theory of Poverty (ROTP) was introduced Appadurai (2004) and Chakravarti (2006) developed upon it. ROTP posit that poverty is caused by unstable environmental conditions and lack of social and economic capital. Lack of social and economic capital can be lack of small business development because it is a social and economic activity that requires social and economic capital. Restriction of Opportunities Theory of Poverty emphasized the influence of human environment on people's daily lives; and since people's lives are condition by their environment, the individual's daily decisions/actions are dependent upon what is present or what is not in the environment (Agba et al. 2014). As the poor continue to navigate within the environment of poverty, they develop fluency within the environment, but a near illiterate in the larger society or environment (Chakravarti, 2006).

Lack of capacities, such as include the development of small businesses among household families could cause an individual to enter the environment of poverty. This implies that, an individual who is poor lack adequate capacities with which to change his/her position (Agba et al. 2014). The capacity to inspire is paramount in this regard; the individual through social interactions develops aspirations that would change his/her socio-economic environment. It suggests that, a person's aspiration is conditioned by his/her environment. It therefore holds that, the better one is placed in his/her environment, the more chances he/she has to not only aspire but to fulfill his/her aspiration (Appadurai, 2004).

ROTP posit that the capacity to aspire required practice in a stable environment and that the environment of poverty is unstable with a high prevalence of unemployment. The unstable life of poverty as defined by unstable environment, often limits the poor's aspiration to basic necessities of life such as food, cloth and shelter; and this reinforces lowered aspiration levels and could significantly obstruct change of environment or condition (Agba et al. 2014). It implies that the way out of poverty is to expand the aspiration horizon of the poor such as given attention to the small businesses they are involved in and helping to grow such businesses through then deployment and use of ICT, to escape the reinforcement that perpetuate the poor in the environment of poverty. It entails creating programmes or making policies that provide the poor and household small businesses with an arena that enables he/she to practice and boost his/her aspiration. It includes designing schemes that enables the poor to meet his/her basic needs; and motivate him/her to higher aspirations (Appadurai, 2004; Chakravarti, 2006).

This Restriction of Opportunities Theory of Poverty differs from the neoclassical growth model proposed by Solow (1956) which argues that low capital cannot explain underdevelopment and contends that the particular set of institutions in an economy does not matter. This position rests on three points: (a) outcomes are determined by fundamental forces (reflecting resources, preferences, and technology), (b) these forces lead to Pareto-efficient outcomes, and (c) institutions do not even influence the choice of the equilibrium. Solow (1956) also stated that it is government impediments to markets (such as small businesses or SMEs) that prevent the economy from working smoothly. However, such theories are inherently unsatisfactory and in most versions, the government failures are assumed to be exogenous, leaving unexplained why they should be larger in some societies than in others and why some other institutions should come to play to stabilize the economy.

The theory of Solow (1956) may have to be re-worked to fit into the environment of Nigeria- bringing together the government, the people and other institutions that may be interested in developing small businesses in Nigeria. For example, apart from government failures, market failures in other institutions such as the banks, SMEs, telecommunications, among others are pervasive, especially in developing countries and these can affect the economy (e.g. Stiglitz, 1989; Floro and Yotopoulos, 1991 and Hoff, Braverman and Stiglitz, 1993). This was why Omiunu (2012) noted that theories imbibed into new environment such as developing economies) are like square pegs in round holes until they are reshaped to fit in such holes (developmental plans and strategies). Although, technology deployment in Solow (1956) is important, however, ICT deployment should be done in a way that such ICT introduced could fit in the business activities and could be useful to such businesses both at the short and long run. Therefore, theoretical work that focused on institutional issues and the scope for policy in development attempted to identify specific institutional characteristics of developing countries such as related to SMEs and small business among the poor and unemployed and incorporated them as features of models are of interest to development theories (Hoff and Stiglitz, 2000).

Also, of importance is the Endogenous growth or the new growth theory which emerged in the 1990s to explain the poor performance of many less developed countries thus can be used to explain sectoral poor performance also. Unlike the Solow model that considers technological change as an exogenous factor, the new growth model notes that technological change has not been equal nor has it been exogenously transmitted in most developing countries (World Bank, 2000). The new growth theorists such as Romer (1986), Lucas (1988), Aghion and Howitt (1992), among others linked the technological change to the production of knowledge thus making it endogenous. Such knowledge can be an enhancer of development among households small business. The new growth theory emphasizes that economic growth results from increasing returns to the use of knowledge (which could include both tacit and explicit) in addition to labour and capital. The theory argues that the higher rate of returns as expected in the Solow model is greatly eroded by lower levels of complementary investments in human capital (education which include conducting training and workshops), infrastructure such as ICT, or research and development (R&D). Meanwhile, knowledge is different from other economic goods because of its possibility to grow boundlessly. Knowledge or ICT innovation can be reused at zero additional cost. Investments in knowledge creation therefore can bring about sustained growth in SMEs and small business among households. Moreover, the knowledge could create the spillover benefits to other firms once they obtained the knowledge.

Bringing in the "Big Push" theory of Rosenstein-Rodan (1943), until there is need in a particular market system, the need to produce a product for the population does not arise. To this end, there have been continuous needs to give attention to reducing poverty and unemployment and also enhance small business development thus, the "Big Push" theory.

Also, with regards to the framework of National Economic Empowerment Development Strategies (NEEDS) (2006), it focuses on four key strategies: reorienting values; reducing poverty; creating wealth, and generating employment. NEEDS is about the Nigerian people: their welfare, health, employment, education, political power, physical security, and empowerment.

NEEDS gives special support to all types of businesses such as agriculture, industry, small and medium-scale enterprises, and oil and gas. Under the plan, the government will seek long-term capital for investment. NEEDS strategy consists of:

- **Empowering People:** By allowing the private sector to thrive which include small business of the poor people operating in a fragmented and small form, NEEDS creates opportunities for employment and wealth creation. It empowers people to take advantage of these opportunities by creating a system of incentives that reward hard work and punish corruption, by investing in education, and by providing special programmes for the most vulnerable members of society. This could cut across providing ICT for various businesses and organizing workshop training for them on how they can deploy ICT to enhance their business productivity.
- **Promoting Private Enterprise:** The private sector will be the engine of economic growth under needs. It will be the executor, investor, and manager of businesses. The government will play the role of enabler, facilitator, and regulator, helping the private sector grow, create jobs, and generate wealth. Deregulation and liberalization will diminish governmental control and attract private sector investment.
- **Changing the Way the Government Does Its Work:** NEEDS aims to restructure the government to make it smaller, stronger, better skilled, and more efficient at delivering essential services. It seeks to transform the government from a haven of corruption to an institution that spurs development and serves the people. The number of government jobs will decline, and the cost of running the government will fall dramatically, as in-kind benefits for civil servants, such as subsidized housing, transport, and utilities, are monetized. Reforms and regulations will be implemented to ensure greater transparency and accountability, and corrupt practices will be outlawed. Government activities and budgeting will be informed by a framework that connects policy with government income and expenditure.

The NEEDS document articulates the strong commitment of the federal government to a programme of collaboration with and strengthening of the private sector. Therefore, the NEEDS aims to alter the strategy for industrial development and make it less import- dependent, more local resource - based and more related to local research and development, particularly in the area of small medium enterprises (SMEs). Economic empowerment of indigenous SME businesses which include small businesses through patronage of their products by improved tendering and procurement processes that stipulates minimum levels of local content would be encouraged.

Figure 3. NEEDS at a glance
Source: NEEDS (2006).

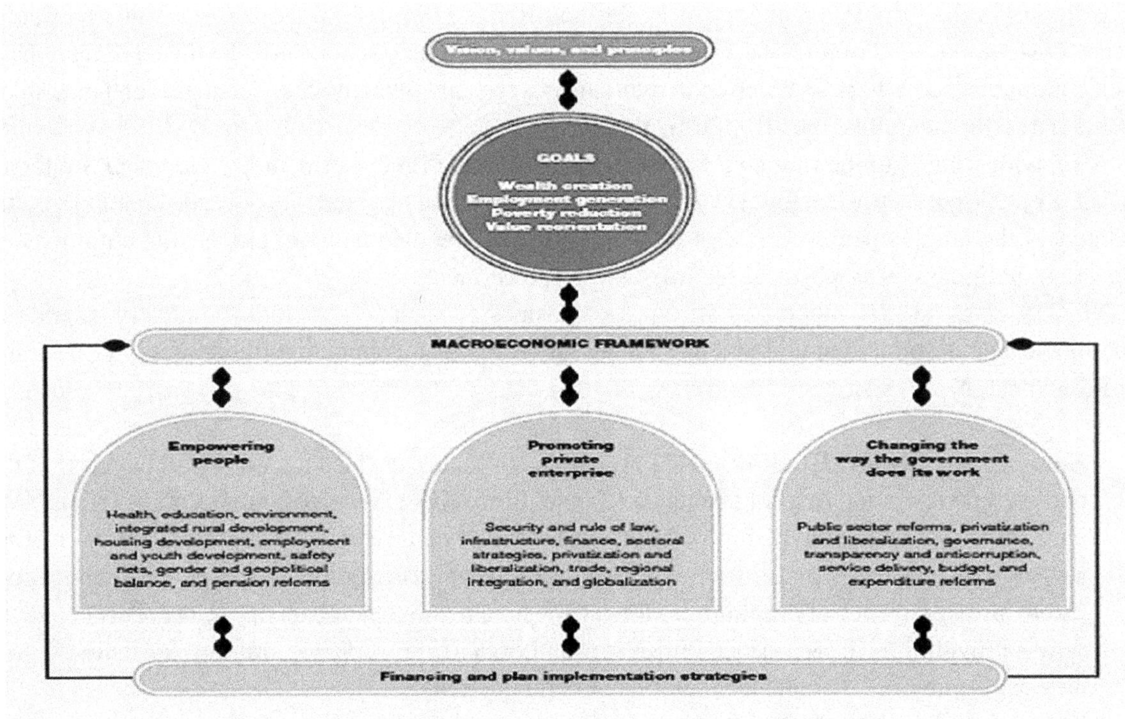

Developing Small Businesses to Achieving Sustainable Development

Small businesses are less able to address weaknesses in the investment climate and also in their environment as they have less competitive advantage over the larger ones. Attentions have been placed on small, medium and large business enterprises and have been drawn away from the minute or smaller businesses in the nation. This has caused a lot of damaged to those smaller and minute businesses. Of the strategies to develop the small, medium and large business enterprises in Nigeria, they are still plagued by so many problems, less the smaller businesses.

Onugu (2005) had revealed that, only 5% of SMEs survived and between 20-25 struggled to survive within the first five years of their initiation. It shows that, approximately 95% of SMEs were either between struggling to survive or dead. This would be more conceptualize when one noticed that, as great as the potential of SMEs are to contribute to national development, only 5% of SMEs survived and nothing are being done for the 95% to be revived and stand. In addition, the smaller businesses are not given attention to fill in the gap of the potential dead SMEs in the nation. Major reasons for the inability for the dead of SMEs and the inability for small businesses to be able to grow to fill in the gaps of the dead SMEs can also be attributed to lack of capital and credit facilities; shortage of skilled workers and raw materials; inadequate infrastructure; lack of managerial, marketing and technical expertise; and limited applications of new technology which also include major ICTs that could enhance their growth and productivity as provided by Hashim (1999) in early study. This is a tragedy scenario and if not tackled will eventually lead to increase in unemployment, poverty and draw back in the national development. This is because the dependency ratio of the population of Nigeria will increase as their source of income which is either the SMEs or the smaller businesses are gone.

To tackle this problem, it is necessary for attentions to be drawn to both the approximately 95% of the either struggling to survive or dead SMEs and the smaller business which do not have access to resources to develop themselves or metamorphose to SMEs as they grow. Rather they are been limited by various problems which, could also be the same problems militating against the dead or surviving SMEs but could be in a higher dimension because of their little capability to pave way for growth and development in the face of all these challenges.

Drawing attention to smaller businesses could be a vital tool to achieving and enhancing sustainable development in Nigeria. If sustainable development has been defined as the development that is stable, endurable, and consistent, it revealed that, various developmental programmes that has been embarked on by governments and other private agencies had not been sustainable because of the consistent and perennial problems and challenges militating against SMEs including small businesses in Nigeria. In addition, in view of the World Commission on Environment and Development's (1987) definition of sustainable development, important aspect in respect to SMEs development are the reviving growth (which could be reviving the growth and development of SMEs which also include small businesses in the nation); changing the quality of growth (this could also be the transition of the fragmented smaller businesses into the micro, small and medium enterprises in the Nigerian economy); meeting essential needs for jobs, food, energy, water, and sanitation (thereby reducing unemployment, poverty levels and providing infrastructures for the use and development of these smaller businesses); ensuring a sustainable level of population (this could be sustaining the level of smaller business population in the country so as not cause easy exit out of the businesses by putting higher pressure, demand, standard and criteria on this businesses that they cannot meet, however encouraging increase in their population); conserving and enhancing the resource base (this could cut across the human and natural resource base of the nation made available for SMEs); reorienting technology and managing risk, merging environmental considerations and economics in decision making, reorienting international economic relations and making development more participatory (that will be conducive for and influence positively SMEs development in the nation).

In addition, in respect to business enterprises, sustainable development refers to the adoption of business strategies and activities that meet the needs of the enterprise (the SMEs sector) and its stakeholders today while protecting, sustaining and enhancing the human and natural resources that will be needed in the future (International Institute for Sustainable Development, 1992). Stakeholders in this context refer to shareholders, lenders, customers, employees, suppliers, and communities who are affected by the business's or organisation's activities.

Using ICT to Enhance Small Business Development to Address Poverty and Unemployment Issues in Nigeria

Heeks (2009) affirmed that poverty is the mother to invention and innovation. The epidemics of poverty have made various governments and international bodies to collaborate to curtailing its effect on the populace and the development of such nation such as Nigeria. In Nigeria, to enhance SMEs development, reduce poverty and unemployment, various strategies and agencies have been instituted such as include Small and Medium Enterprises Development Agency (SMEDAN), National Economic Summit Group (NESG), National Association of Small-Scale Industrialists (NASSI), Manufacturers Association of Nigeria (MAN), Small Scale Industries Credit Scheme (SSICS) 1971), Nigerian Bank for Commerce and Industries (NBCI) (1973), Nigerian Industrial Development Bank (NIDB) (1964), SME Apex Unit of Central Bank (1989), National Economic Reconstruction Fund (NERFUND) (1989), The African Development Bank/ Export Stimulation Loan (ADB/ESL) (1989), Nigerian Export Import Bank (NEXIM), National Directorate of Employment (NDE), Industrial Development Co-ordinating Centre (IDDC), Community Banks, People's Bank, Family Economic Advancement Programme (FEAP), State Ministry of Industry SME Schemes, Small and Medium Industries Equity Investment Scheme (SMIEIS), Bank of Industry (BOI), Credit Guarantee Scheme for SMEs, among others. Others include Operation Feed the Nation (OFN). National Directorate of Employment, The Family Support Programme (FSP), The national poverty eradication programme (NAPEP), The Youth Empowerment Scheme (YES), National Economic Reconstruction Fund (NERFUND), among others (Emmanuel and Daniya, 2012). However, despite all these developmental plans and strategies to ameliorate poverty, unemployment and also enhance SMEs growth and development, studies such as Onugu (2005), and Altenburg and Eckhardt (2006), Agba et al. (2014), Alexander (2014), Atufe et al. (2014) still revealed that the level of poverty, unemployment are still high and SMEs are still facing considerable challenges militating against their growth and development, thus development in this sector has not been achieved. This could be worse among the small businesses in Nigeria.

It showed that much still need to be done and attention need to be drawn to small businesses to fill in the gap of dead SMEs which according to Onugu (2005) that, only 5% of SMEs survived and between 20-25 struggled to survive and 75% died within the first five years of their initiation which implied that approximately 95% of SMEs were either between struggling to survive or dead. If nothing is done to revive this 95%, and nothing is done for the small neglected businesses in the economy especially among the poor, and unemployed thus, one can affirm that the statement of the time bomb issue by Comrade Issa Aremu, vice president, Nigeria Labour Congress (NLC) and General Secretary, Textile Workers' union, Federal Republic of Nigeria as stated by Alexander (2014) is not far-reached in Nigeria.

In addition, to fill in this gap, there is need to deploy ICT for businesses which include the SMEs and these small businesses. Heeks (2009), added that ICTs can be deployed to deliver information and services that might address poverty, health, education and gender equality – the four areas that form the bulk of the Millennium Development Goals (MDGs). In addition, Omiunu (2014) has stated that ICT can also be deployed and used to enhance the performance, growth and development of businesses which include small businesses in Nigeria. Thus, the neglect of ICT may further aggravate the present problems of SMEs and small businesses in the Nigerian economy because these business cannot compete with international businesses and standards from developed economies such as the UK, US, Japan, among others. To this end, ICT deployment and innovations can be a source of emergence from the long time confusion and problems of poverty, unemployment and problems militating against SMEs including small businesses in Nigeria.

Drawing attention to small business to addressing the issue of poverty and unemployment through the help of ICT is of paramount importance. This could be achieved by the following strategy below:

According to Sofowora (2009), the assumption of the Nigerian government is that if there is a conducive environment for business to thrive and when the people are empowered (which in this context may include empowerment with respect to business development), to take the advantages of the new opportunities, then poverty and unemployment problem will be curtailed in the nation. Mchombu and Mchombu (2014) stated that sustainable development is a very important factor in the provision of information and knowledge support for poverty eradication. Talisayon and Suministrado (2008) noted that the sustainability movement which began in 1992 concluded that sustainability depends on preservation and enhancement of three forms of capital: social capital (which include community cohesiveness and trust, relationships, local values and local support system); natural capital (which refers to the natural environment), and economic and financial capital (which refers to economic benefits, participation and control and ownership).

Talisayon and Suministrado (2008) argue that successful knowledge for poverty alleviation interventions should make use of both the tangible and intangible assets found in a poor community. To this end, Omiunu (2012) affirmed that sustainable development should be participatory, people centred, and Mchombu and Mchombu (2014) added that such development should be in line with what the community already has in the form of financial, human, social and physical and natural assets and structures which affect livelihoods of the dwellers. Suffice to note that most of the livelihoods of Nigerians are small and minute businesses due to their incapability to raise capital and the lack of capital to enrich their businesses. To this end, any sustainable development plan coming from the government to enhance small businesses such as the deployment and use of ICT must match the kind of businesses they do which could include subsistence farming, provisions, stores including medical stores, fish farming, snacks and drinks, salon which include hair and barbing salon, tailoring, sales of food items, canteens, and other consumables, shoes, clothes, and jewelries, and other telecommunication-like small businesses such as sales of recharge cards, phone repair, electricians, computer operators, typesetting and engineering, graphic designs, photo editing, photocopies, etc. It is also expedient to draw attention to the major fact that most of these businesses operate is a very small and minute scale and do not have capital to grow their businesses.

Therefore, to enhance their sustainability and growth, it is expedient to take a complete census of these businesses and then have a database for them, and deploy and provide ICTs that can help them to maximize their sales and growth. According to FAO (2006) and Mchombu and Mchombu (2014) stated that to achieve sustainable developments in businesses which include small and family businesses, governments and other responsible bodies which include national and international should give attention to these five categories of assets or capital:

- **Natural Capital:** Access to land and to other resources such ICT resources to allow people to invest in productive processes.
- **Social Capital:** Relations among people are shaped by histories of interactions which regulate further interaction, including their understanding of their rights over national resources.
- **Human Capital:** Development and poverty eradication requires good health, nutrition and access to medicine, among others. Moreover, development require skills and knowledge, which are in short supply when access to and information or other ICTs is weak or non-existent.
- **Financial Capital:** People need money to make long-term investments and also to acquire some resources such as ICT and other infrastructure that may be helpful for their businesses but access to financing is often problematic for Nigerians mostly for those who live in rural and remote areas. Most commercial banks will not lend money without collateral.
- **Physical (Built) Capital:** Buildings, roads and tools provide the security, mobility and capability that allow people to produce, transform, exchange and consume goods.

Each one of these dimensions has an information and knowledge implication and can use ICT to enhance their achievement. For example, for social capital- enable knowledge sharing; human capital which refers to capacity to acquire and absorb knowledge; and financial capital which is a frequent constraint in development situations where the poorest do not have sufficient information and no or low availability of financial resources thus, unable to utilize the limited collateral at their disposal. To this end, ICT can be provided by the government and other various bodies (nationally and internationally based) interested in the development of businesses among the poor either for free or for a subsidized price. First, to achieve this, the government has to have all businesses at local, state and federal level at its database. The corporate affair commission could be deployed and registered businesses with this federal government organization should be used to obtain the information of various businesses. In addition, year in-year out, these various businesses pay a certain amount to the federal government, it won't be a gain saying to state that the government should try to use part of this money also to provide such ICT that could be of benefit to these businesses in Nigeria.

CONCLUSION AND RECOMMENDATION

To ensure the developing of smaller business and achieving sustainable development, it has been revealed that attention should be drawn to them providing for them access to resources that will enhance their potential to grow and develop to becoming micro, small, medium and even large business enterprises so as to reduce poverty, increase employment and enhance sustainable development in Nigeria. In addition, the following recommendations would be of importance from this study:

1. Various governments at all tiers should be encouraged and involved in conducting research that will benefit both the SMEs and smaller businesses in Nigeria. Such researcher will outlined the needs of SMEs and smaller businesses in Nigeria through owners oriented study and such needs should be directed to them to enhance their growth and development.
2. Governments should increase the access of private agencies to support small business either within or outside the country so as to enhance their growth and development.
3. Programmes and workshop to provide skills, training and mentoring and monitoring services (consultancy services) should be geared by the governments and various private agencies to enhance the growth, performance and development of small businesses in Nigeria.
4. The provision of grants for business development should be encouraged by governments and other private agencies interested in their development and reward entrepreneur in Nigeria.
5. Organisational body spread in all round the state, local and federation should be instituted and established which can be a vital point of access for help for small business owners. This may be controlled by either government or private agencies.
6. Also, of importance is the provision of loan by banks with a reduced interest rate and provision with very little or no collateral and access to loan by smaller business owners to help them develop.
7. In addition, access to information and various information system should be design for smaller businesses and even the SMEs to ensure that, they tap into the benefits of ICT to developing their businesses and also enhancing the Nigeria economy when those information and information system are been used.

8. Also, the federal government can use some of the money paid in by various businesses to provide ICTs for them with regard to their activities. This could boost commitment from the side of the business owners to be faithful in paying taxes and other dues.
9. Infrastructural problems in Nigeria should be addressed by the federal government so as to enhance SMEs growth, development and performance, because small business development is highly dependent on infrastructure availability.

REFERENCES

Aboderin, I. (2005). Understanding and responding to ageing, health, poverty and social change in Sub-Saharan Africa: A strategic framework and plan for research. In *Research on Ageing, Health and Poverty in Africa: Forging Directions for the Future*. Oxford.

Agba, A. M. O., Ocheni, S., & Nkpoyen, F. (2014). Microfinance credit scheme and poverty reduction among low-income workers in Nigeria. *Journal of Good Governance and Sustainable Development in Africa.*, *2*(1), 1–13.

Agba, A. M. O., Ushie, M. A., Bassey, A. O., & Agba, M. S. (2009). Human development trend in Nigeria: The need for concrete implementation of the seven point agenda. *Nigerian Journal of Social Development*, *6*(1), 15–28.

Aghion, P., & Howitt, P. (1992). A model of growth through creative destruction. *Econometrica*, *60*(2), 323–351. doi:10.2307/2951599

Ajiferuke, I., & Olatokun, W. (2009). Sectoral Analysis of ICT Use in Nigeria. In Encyclopedia of Information Science and Technology (2nd ed.). Information Resources Management Association. doi:10.4018/978-1-60566-026-4.ch534

Alexander, O. S. (2014). *Unemployment In Nigeria: A Factor For Revolution!* Retrieved from http://saharareporters.com/2014/03/25/unemployment-nigeria-factor-revolution-osobu-suuru-alexander

Altenburg, T., & Eckhardt, U. (2006). *Productivity enhancement and equitable development: Challenges for SME development*. United Nations Industrial Development Organization.

Appadurai, A. (2004). The Capacity to Aspire: Culture and Terms of Recognition. In V. Rao & M. Walton (Eds.), *Culture and Public Action* (pp. 59–84). Stanford, CA: Standford University Press.

Apulu, I., & Latham, A. (2009). Information and communication technology adoption: Challenges for Nigerian SMEs. *TMC Academic Journal*, *4*(2), 64–80.

Atufe, F., Okojie, G., Echenim, S., Ogunmola, T., & Bello, O. (2014). Tackling Unemployment In Nigeria. *Leadership Online Newspaper*. Retrieved from http://leadership.ng/business/379110/tackling-unemployment-nigeria

Bransford, J. D., Brown, A. L., & Cocking, R. R. (2000). *How People Learn: Brain, Mind, Experience, and School Committee on Developments in the Science of Learning*. Washington, DC: National Academy Press.

Central Bank of Nigeria. (2005). *CBN Bullion: Micro Finance Policy as a Strategy for Poverty Reduction*. Abuja: CBN.

Chakravarti, D. (2006). Voices unheard: The psychology of consumption in poverty and development. *Journal of Consumer Psychology*, *16*(4), 363–376. doi:10.1207/s15327663jcp1604_8

Clements-Hunt, P. (2007). *Innovative Financing for Sustainable Small and Medium Enterprises in Africa, International Workshop*. Geneva, Switzerland: Meeting Report, A forward, United Nation Environment Programme.

Commission for Africa (CfA). (2005). *Our Common Interest. Report of the Commission for Africa*. London: Commission for Africa Secretariat.

Croteau, A., & Bergeron, F. (2001). An information technology triology: Business strategy, technological deployment and organisational performance. *The Journal of Strategic Information Systems*, *10*(2), 77–99. doi:10.1016/S0963-8687(01)00044-0

Durodoye, K. K. (2005). Strategic planning of information systems: Research concepts and framework. In M. A. Tiamiyu (Ed.), *Information Science concepts, models and application*. University of Ibadan.

Ekong, E. (2003). *An Introduction to Rural Sociology*. Dove Educational Publishers.

Ekpenyong, D. B., & Nyong, M. O. (1992). *Small and Medium Scale Enterprise in Nigeria: Their characteristics, problems and sources of finance*. African Economic Research Consortium, Nairobi, Kenya.

Emmanuel, O. O., & Daniya, A. A. (2012). Development of small and medium Scale enterprises: The role of government and other financial institutions. *Arabian Journal of Business and Management Review*, *1*(7), 16–29.

Federal Ministry of Agriculture and Natural Resources. (1997). Nigeria: National Agricultural Research Strategy Plan 1996-2010. Department of Agricultural Sciences, Federal Ministry of Agriculture and Natural Resources, Federal Republic of Nigeria, Nigeria.

Fischer, E. M., Reuber, R. A., & Dyke, L. S. (1993). A theoretical overview and extension of research on sex, gender, and entrepreneurship. *Journal of Business Venturing*, *8*(2), 151–168. doi:10.1016/0883-9026(93)90017-Y

Floro, S., & Yotopoulos, P. (1991). *Informal Credit Markets and the New Institutional Economics: The Case of Philippine Agriculture*. Boulder, CO: Westview Press.

Food and Agricultural Organisation. (2006). *Better Forestry, less poverty. A practitioners guide*. Rome: FAO.

Gartlan, J., & Shanks, G. (2007). The alignment of business and information technology strategy in Australia. *Australasian Journal of Information Systems*, *14*(2), 113–139. doi:10.3127/ajis.v14i2.184

Hashim, M. K. (1999). SMEs in Malaysia: Past, present and future. Malaysian Management Review, 35.

Heeks, R. (2009). *The ICT4D 2.0 Manifesto: Where Next for ICTs and International Development?* Development Informatics, Working Paper Series, Paper No. 42, Development Informatics Group, Institute for Development Policy and Management, University of Manchester, UK.

Hoff, K., Braverman, A., & Stiglitz, J. E. (Eds.). (1993). *The Economics of Rural Organization: Theory, Practice, and Policy*. New York: Oxford University Press.

Hoff, K., & Stiglitz, J. E. (2000). *Modern economic theory and development*. The World Bank. Retrieved from http://www8.gsb.columbia.edu/faculty/jstiglitz/sites/jstiglitz/files/2000_Modern_Economic_Theory_and_Development.pdf

Igbaria, M., & Tan, M. (1997). The consequences of information technology acceptance on subsequent individual performance. *Information & Management*, *32*(3), 113–121. doi:10.1016/S0378-7206(97)00006-2

Ihua, U. B. (2009). SMEs, key failure-factors: A comparison between the UK and Nigeria. *Journal of Social Sciences*, *18*(13), 199–207.

International Institute for Sustainable Development. (1992). *Business Strategies for Sustainable Development; Leadership and accountability for the 90's*. IISD in conjunction with Deloitte and Touche and the World Business Council for Sustainable Development.

Laudon, K., Laudon, J., & Dass, R. (2006). *Management Information System*. Prentice Hall, Azimuth Interactive Inc.

Lucas, R. E. Jr. (1988). On the mechanics of economic development. *Journal of Monetary Economics*, *22*(1), 3–42. doi:10.1016/0304-3932(88)90168-7

Luftman, J. (1996). *Competing in the information age: strategic alignment in practice*. New York: Oxford University press.

Mahmood, R., & Hanafi, N. (2013). Entrepreneurial orientation and business performance of women-owned small and medium enterprises in Malaysia: Competitive advantage as a mediator. *International Journal of Business and Social Science*, *4*(1), 82–90.

Manueli, K., Latu, S., & Koh, D. (2007). *ICT Adoption Models*. Paper presented at the 20th Annual Conference of the National Advisory Committee on Computing Qualifications (NACCQ 2007), Nelson, New Zealand.

Mchombu, K. J., & Mchombu, C. M. (2014). *The Role of Information and Knowledge in Poverty Eradication in Africa: a case study of Namibia*. Retrieved from http://library.ifla.org/996/1/189-mchombu-en.pdf

Mehrtens, J., Cragg, P. B., & Mills, A. M. (2001). A model of Internet adoption by SMEs. *Information & Management*, *39*(3), 165–176. doi:10.1016/S0378-7206(01)00086-6

Ministry of Economic Development. (2004). *Digital strategy: A draft New Zealand digital strategy for consultation*. Wellington: Ministry of Economic Development.

Moorthy, M. K., Tan, A., Choo, C., Wei, C. S., Ping, J. T. Y., & Leong, T. K. (2012). A study on factors affecting the performance of SMEs in Malaysia. *International Journal of Academic Research in Business and Social Sciences*, *2*(4), 224–239.

National Agency for Information and Communication Technologies. (2008). *Cameroon national ICT Policy 10-03-2008*. Retrieved 05 30, 2009, from www.antic.com: http://www.antic.cm/IMG/pdf/Cameroun_National_ICT_Policy_10-03-2008.pdf

National Bureau of Statistics. (2015). *Unemployment/Under-Employment Watch, Q1- 2015*. Federal Republic of Nigeria.

National Economic Empowerment Strategy. (2006). The Federal Government of Nigeria.

National Population Census (NPC). (1991). Federal Bureau of Statistics, The Federal Government of Nigeria.

National Population Census (NPC). (2006). Federal Bureau of Statistics, The Federal Government of Nigeria.

Neneh, N. B., & Vanzyl, J. (2012). Towards establishing long term surviving small and medium enterprises (SMEs) in South Africa: An entrepreneurial approach. *African Journal of Business Management*, *6*(28), 8327–8343.

Okpara, J. O., & Kumbiadis, N. (2008). SMEs export orientation and performance: Evidence from a developing economy. *International Review of Business Research Papers*, *4*(5), 109–119.

Omiunu, O. G. (2014). *ICT deployment, business environment information and information strategy as correlates of Women-owned SMEs performance in Oyo State, Nigeria* (Masters dissertation). Africa Regional Centre for Information Science, University of Ibadan, Nigeria.

Omiunu, O. G. (2014). Towards a sustainable higher education for an increasing population and information technology dynamics. *Journal of Education Research and Behavioral Sciences.*, *3*(5), 116–121.

Omiunu, O. G. (n.d.). Deploying indigenous knowledge for sustainable development. *African Journal of Sustainable Development, 2*(1), 149-170.

Ongori, H. (2009). Role of Information communication technologies in SMEs: Evidence from Botswana, *Research. Journal of Information Technology*, *1*(2), 79–85. doi:10.3923/rjit.2009.79.85

Onugu, B. A. N. (2005). *Small and medium enterprises (SMEs) in Nigeria: Problems and prospects* (Doctoral dissertation). St. Clements University.

Onyeagba, J. B. C. (2008). Micro-finance and micro financing as strategy for poverty reduction in Nigeria the emerging global technology. *Journal of International Politics and Development Studies*, *4*(1&2), 160–176.

Romer, P. M. (1986). Increasing returns and long-run growth. *Journal of Political Economy*, *94*(5), 1002–1037. doi:10.1086/261420

Rosenstein-Rodan, P. N. (1943). Problems of industrialisation of Eastern and South-Eastern Europe. *The Economic Journal*, *53*(210/211), 202–211. doi:10.2307/2226317

Sofowora, O. (2009). The potential of using information and communication technology for poverty alleviation and economic empowerment in Osun State, Nigeria. *International Journal of Education and Development using Information and Communication Technology, 5*(3), 131-140.

Solow, R. M. (1956). A contribution to the theory of economic growth. *The Quarterly Journal of Economics*, *70*(1), 65. doi:10.2307/1884513

Stiglitz, J. (1989). *More instruments and broader goals: Moving toward the post-Washington consensus*. Helsinki: Wider Annual Lecture United Nations University—World Institute for Development Economics Research.

Talisayon, S., & Suministrado, J. (2008). *Knowledge for Poverty Alleviation: A framework for design and evaluation of development projects in low income countries*. Paper presented at the conference on 'Knowledge Architecture for Development', Singapore.

Thong, J. Y., Yap, C. S., & Raman, K. S. (1997). Environments for information systems implementation in small businesses. *Journal of Organizational Computing and Electronic Commerce*, *7*(4), 253–278. doi:10.1207/s15327744joce0704_1

United Nation Environment Programme (UNEP). (2007). *Innovative Financing for Sustainable Small and Medium Enterprises in Africa*. Meeting Report presented at the International Workshop, Geneva, Switzerland.

United Nations Development Programme (UNDP). (2002). *UNDP in Africa. Supporting Africa as it Meets the Challenges of the 21st Century*. UNDP.

United Nations Development Programme (UNDP). (2004). *Human Development Report 2004*. UNDP.

Van Akkeren, J., & Harker, D. (2003). The mobile Internet and small business: An exploratory study of needs, use and adoption with full-adopters of technology. *Journal of Research and Practice in Information Technology*, *35*(3), 205–220.

Vision 2020. (2009). *Report of the vision 2020*. National Technical Working Group on SMEs, Federal Republic of Nigeria.

Watson, J. (2003). *SME Performance: Does Gender Matter?* A paper for the Small Enterprise Association of Australia and New Zealand 16th Annual Conference, Ballarat, Australia.

Windrum, P., & de Berranger, P. (2002). *The adoption of e-business technology by SMEs*. Retrieved from http://www.merit.unimaas.nl/publications/rmpdf/2002/rm2002-023.pdf

World Bank. (2000). *Entering the 21st century—World development report 1999/2000*. New York: Oxford University Press.

World Commission on Environment and Development (WCED). (1987). *Our Common Future*. Oxford, UK: Oxford University Press.

World Summit for Social Development. (1995). *Report of the World Summit Social Development Copenhagen 6-12 March, 1995* (United Nations Publication, Salcs No. E. 96. Iv.8). Author.

KEY TERMS AND DEFINITIONS

ICT: Tools that can be used to enhance the various activities of small business to enhance productivity in businesses.

Poor: Individuals in the society or economy who are deprived from the resources of the nation and are not able to meet up with the demands of the society.

Poverty: The lack of resources to meet the demands of life and the society by individuals in the economy.

Small Businesses: Business that do not fall into the category of Small and medium enterprises but are operated as fragments in the economy and are mostly owned by the poor in the society.

Small Business Development: The development that is geared towards small businesses in the economy to enhance their productivity and development in the long run.

Sustainable Development: The development that is geared to enhancing the livelihood and wellbeing of the poor in the economy and which could be sustained over time.

Sustainable National Development: The development that is geared towards the enhancement of individuals in the economy and which would also enhance the development of the nation and such development should be sustainable over time.

Unemployment: The inability of individuals to be able to get a job or such individual is living without a job.

Chapter 11
Encouraging Internationalization and Entrepreneurial Orientation in Small and Medium Enterprises

Kijpokin Kasemsap
Suan Sunandha Rajabhat University, Thailand

ABSTRACT

This chapter explains the overview of internationalization; the aspects of internationalization in Small and Medium Enterprises (SMEs); internationalization, social capital, and Foreign Market Knowledge (FMK) in SMEs; internationalization and marketing capability; internationalization, innovation, and Research and Development (R&D); the implications of internationalization in SMEs; the overview of Entrepreneurial Orientation (EO); EO and firm performance; EO, organizational learning, and knowledge management; and the current trends and issues with EO in SMEs. Encouraging internationalization and EO is essential for SMEs that seek to serve suppliers and customers, increase business performance, strengthen competitiveness, and achieve continuous success in SMEs. The chapter argues that encouraging internationalization and EO has the potential to enhance organizational performance and reach strategic goals in SMEs.

INTRODUCTION

Small and medium enterprises (SMEs) now have access to new technology and their ability to embrace risk and uncertainty allows them to take advantage of their entrepreneurial and human capabilities, improving their ability to enter challenging new business environments (Javalgi & Todd, 2011). The internationalization of SMEs has attracted growing attention as a subject of academic inquiry and a goal of public policy (Child & Hsieh, 2014), and is a major perspective for sustaining innovation, employment, and economic renewal (Greene & Mole, 2006). The institutional network relationships have a positive effect

DOI: 10.4018/978-1-5225-2165-5.ch011

on the internationalization process of SMEs (Oparaocha, 2015). Business growth and knowledge-related perspectives are the most influential factors in driving SMEs toward internationalization (OECD, 2009).

Entrepreneurial orientation (EO), learning orientation, and market technology have attracted major scholarly interest within their specific streams of literature for some decades (Hakala, 2011). With today's complexity in conducting business transactions, EO can be considered as a critical factor to ensure the success of a business (Arshad, Rasli, Arshad, & Zain, 2014). EO is representative of a strategic organizational posture that encourages the acquisition, structuring, and exploitation of organizational resources that facilitate competitive advantage (Wiklund & Shepherd, 2011). SMEs can capitalize on business-related scanning and planning processes because of their international EO (Swoboda & Olejnik, 2016).

SMEs play an important role for national economies. Internationalization can have implications for SMEs as for any companies in terms of cost reduction (relocation), market differentiation (export), and development of key strengths, such as competitive advantages. Internationalization is the significant factor for entrepreneurial success and business growth. Despite trade barriers and technical difficulties, internationalization represents an essential step to grow the businesses and secure the market demand toward promoting the growth of SMEs. In order to excel in innovativeness, SMEs should be market-oriented, proactive, and willing to take risks, as well as have access to superior technological assets and capabilities (Renko, Carsrud, & Brännback, 2009).

This chapter aims to bridge the gap in the literature on the thorough literature consolidation of internationalization and EO in SMEs. The extensive literatures of internationalization and EO provide a contribution to practitioners and researchers by explaining the current issues and approaches of internationalization and EO in order to maximize the business impact of internationalization and EO in SMEs.

BACKGROUND

The research regarding SMEs internationalization began in the early 1970s in the Nordic countries and produced gradualist models (Johanson & Vahlne, 1977). The main output is the Uppsala model (Johanson & Vahlne, 1977). Regarding Uppsala model, the internationalization of the firm is considered as a process of the firm's international involvement increasing as a result of different types of learning (Ruzzier, Hisrich, & Antoncic, 2006). SMEs are able to internationalize more rapidly than the gradualist models predict (Oviatt & McDougall, 2005). The two major sources in such a rapid internationalization process are knowledge and international networking (Oviatt & McDougall, 2005). The international network helps the entrepreneurs in emphasizing the opportunities, establishing the international relationships, and accessing the information (Kalinic & Forza, 2012).

Nowadays, competition among firms is becoming fiercer (Felício, Caldeirinha, & Ribeiro-Navarrete, 2015). SMEs make sizeable contributions to the economic success of nations (Javalgi & Todd, 2011). Traditional SMEs are able to expedite their internationalization process by rapidly catching up with the increasing global competition (Kalinic & Forza, 2012). Internationalization of the firms significantly concerns the relationship among the firms and their international environments, derives its origin from the development and utilization process of the individual's cognitive and attitudinal readiness, and is exhibited in the development process of different international activities (Lehtinen & Penttinen, 1999). The significant role played by decision makers in SMEs means that their personal characteristics and interpretations are likely to affect their strategic decisions, including those on internationalization (Hsu, Chen, & Cheng, 2013).

Long-term survival requires firms to engage in entrepreneurial activities in order to revitalize their business and stay competitive (Cruz & Nordqvist, 2012). EO has become a central concept in the domain of entrepreneurship that has received a substantial amount of theoretical and empirical attention (Covin, Green, & Slevin, 2006). EO represents the policies and practices that provide a basis for entrepreneurial decisions and actions (Mintzberg, Raisinghani, & Theoret, 1976). Firms need to be entrepreneurial in order to survive in fast-changing industries (Teece, 2007). EO and growth orientation are positively related with each other (Moreno & Casillas, 2008). Firms with EO are more likely to develop both driving markets and market driven innovations, while firms with market orientation are more likely to develop market driven innovations (Zortea-Johnston, Darroch, & Matear, 2012).

EO is a significant contributor to the profitable business performance (Mahmood & Hanafi, 2013) and successful venture creation (Lim, Trimi, & Lee, 2010). EO is positively related to a wide variety of key performance outcomes including sales growth (Covin et al., 2006), profitability (Baker & Sinkula, 2009), and non-financial performance measures (Marino, Strandholm, Steensma, & Weaver 2002), market share (Rodrigues & Raposo, 2011), technology commercialization (Li, Guo, Liu, & Li, 2008), and investors' valuation (Colombelli, 2010). Marketing is the set of strategies, allowing entrepreneurs to make their business ideas intelligible and accessible (Bettiol, Di Maria, & Finotto, 2012). EO reflects the degree to which firms' growth objectives are driven by the identification and exploitation of untapped market opportunities (Baker & Sinkula, 2009).

INTERNATIONALIZATION AND ENTREPRENEURIAL ORIENTATION IN SMALL AND MEDIUM ENTERPRISES

This section emphasizes the overview of internationalization; the perspectives of internationalization in SMEs; internationalization, social capital, and FMK in SMEs; internationalization and marketing capability; internationalization, innovation, and R&D; the implications of internationalization in SMEs; the overview of EO; EO and firm performance; EO, organizational learning, and knowledge management; and the current trends and issues with EO in SMEs.

Overview of Internationalization

Internationalization is defined as the mobilization of human, material, technological, and organizational resources for international markets (Spowart & Wickramasekera, 2012). Buckley and Casson (2009) viewed internationalization as a general principle that explicates the boundaries of organization. The accelerated internationalization is related to the phenomenon of international entrepreneurship (Ramos, Acedo, & Gonzalez, 2011). Internationalization has a positive impact on firms' performance (Gupta, Wilson, Gregoriou, & Healy, 2014). Firms willing to take the risks about the venturing abroad are exposed to the new learning and growth opportunities (Zahra & Hayton, 2008).

Firm's technological intensity affects the internationalization process through the specific characteristics of the product and the environment in which firm operates (Golovko & Valentini, 2011). Internationalization can enhance the development of suitable products to meet customer needs and can avoid the competition with large multinational companies (Knight, Madsen, & Servais, 2004). However, small firms are typically constrained by a narrower set of capabilities, limited access to comprehensive market research, and their inability to hire the business experts who can assist them in their internationalization efforts (Musteen, Francis, & Datta, 2010).

The effective connection with customers significantly contributes to the rapid internationalization concerning knowledge sharing (Soriano & Dobon, 2009). Optimal market knowledge and ability to integrate information are essential for internationalization (Kyvik, Saris, Bonet, & Felício, 2013). The development of networks with different partners (e.g., universities, companies, industrial associations, and experts) enhances the opportunities in foreign markets (McDougall, Shane, & Oviatt, 1994) and promotes the development of knowledge-intensive products (Smith, Collins, & Clark, 2005). The utilization of networks considerably fosters knowledge acquisition and resource development (Nerkar & Paruchuri, 2005).

Aspects of Internationalization in SMEs

During the past two decades, the number of studies focusing on SMEs operating in high-tech markets has rapidly grown (Gassmann & Keupp, 2007). SMEs are known to face the barriers which limit their ability to grow (Hessels & Parker, 2013). The access of international newcomers in the entrepreneurial provision of internationalization strengthens local economies and make them more globally competitive (Kasemsap, 2016a). SMEs often make use of business relationship networks to reduce information asymmetry by acquiring information relevant to their international business growth (Ellis, 2011), and that this is likely to be the rapidly internationalizing new ventures (Coviello, 2006). Business relationship networks play a significant role in the observed patterns of internationalization across industries (Sui, Morgan, & Baum, 2015). In high-tech industries, the ability of the established small firms to internationalize is attributed to their access to knowledge, technology, and other resources in business relationship networks (Coviello, 2006).

Many SMEs must internationalize and engage in international entrepreneurship as a crucial concern for survival and growth (Oparaocha, 2015). Many governments proactively strive to support the engagement of firms in international entrepreneurship as a way to ensure the survival of local industries and the international competitiveness (Greene & Mole, 2006). Internationalization can provide a competitive advantage to SMEs and can enhance the economic strength of industrial sectors, particularly within manufacturing and knowledge-intensive industries (Lu & Beamish, 2006). Offshore outsourcing enhances international competitiveness by enabling SMEs to reduce costs, increase relational ties, and serve customers more effectively (Di Gregorio, Musteen, & Thomas, 2008).

SMEs face many internationalization-related difficulties regarding how to effectively manage the international opportunities and the need to mitigate risks, competition, and other challenges on the international business frontiers (Bretherton & Chaston, 2005). Although international SMEs face higher credit risk, they are more financially transparent to lenders and suppliers than their domestic counterparts (Beck & Demirguc-Kunt, 2006). International SMEs have better access to finance than their domestic counterparts, and fewer problems of financial distress (Gupta et al., 2014).

Impediments to the internationalization of SMEs in the perspective of international entrepreneurship can involve the internal and external barriers (Leonidou, 2004). Internal barriers to internationalization may include inadequate human capital, financial constraints, a lack of foreign market exposure, and limited technical expertise. External barriers to internationalization may include a country's policies and regulatory environment, its competitive dynamics, a lack of access to network resources, and the liabilities of foreignness (Zucchella & Servais, 2012).

Internationalization, Social Capital, and Foreign Market Knowledge in SMEs

Foreign market knowledge (FMK) is defined as the important resource obtained from foreign market operations (Sharma & Blomstermo, 2003) and financial resources (Spence, 2003). Internationalization is an incremental process because the existing FMK positively affect decision making (Lindstrand, Melen, & Nordman, 2011). The importance of FMK is obvious in the internationalization of manufacturing firms (Lindstrand, Eriksson, & Sharma, 2009) and high-tech SMEs (Zou & Ghauri, 2010). FMK can enhance SMEs' internationalization and performance (Blomstermo, Eriksson, Lindstrand, & Sharma, 2004). FMK helps managers effectively perform under the highly demanding international business conditions (Stoian, Rialp, & Rialp, 2011).

Social capital is the network of relationships among people, firms, and institutions in a society, together with the associated norms of behavior, trust, and cooperation that enable a society to effectively function (Kasemsap, 2014). Social capital theory explains how firms generate the value from the network of relationships in which they are embedded, emphasizing the role of relationship building for young firms seeking to go abroad (Nahapiet & Ghoshal, 1998). Institutional theory suggests that firms based in emerging markets may be more likely to rely on social and relational capital than firms based in developed economies (Khanna & Palepu, 2010). International business opportunities can be found through a wide variety of network-supported mechanisms (Ciravegna, Lopez, & Kundu, 2014). Firms can compensate for market failures by relying more on the personal contacts of the entrepreneur and senior management, often defined as social and relational capital (Ciravegna, 2011). Social capital-related geographically diverse networks contribute to superior business performance (Musteen et al., 2010).

Encouraging diverse international networks can help entrepreneurs reach a broader number of markets (Felzensztein, Ciravegna, Robson, & Amorós, 2015). To acquire FMK, high-tech SMEs utilize their networks (Coviello, 2006), especially the personal networks of founders and managers (Moen, Gavlen, & Endresen, 2004). The use of personal networks for resource acquisition has been merged with the notion of social capital while investigating the internationalization processes of high-tech SMEs (Coviello & Cox, 2006). Freeman et al. (2010) indicated that the use of personal network relationships allows managers of smaller firms to develop new knowledge for rapid commercialization of their products. High-tech SMEs' social capital affects their acquisition of FMK and financial resources during their internationalization (Lindstrand et al., 2011).

Internationalization and Marketing Capability

Marketing is an important factor to evaluate when investigating the success of SMEs in their efforts to enter and compete in the global markets (Ren, Eisingerich, & Tsai, 2015). Regarding marketing, the commercialization of new products and services is recognized by the firms' marketing efforts (Ren et al., 2015). Shah et al. (2006) stated that marketing can help firms obtain the useful intelligence on customers, competitors, and market trends. Marketing focuses on the attention of the firms and their members through maximizing the business value from customer relationships and generating revenue streams from the existing and new customers, which are the crucial elements of the firms' innovation efforts (Rust, Lemon, & Zeithaml, 2004).

Marketing capability refers to the integrative process in which the firms utilize their tangible and intangibles resources to understand market needs, enable product differentiation, enhance customer cooperation (Prahalad & Ramaswamy, 2000), and achieve superior financial performance (Nath, Nachiappan, & Ramanathan, 2010). Marketing capability can positively affect the internationalization strategies of firms (Kotabe & Helsen, 2004). Identifying new market opportunities internationally and exploiting accessible resources from the beginning of internationalization are the major approaches to the success of new ventures while competing in the global markets (Jones & Coviello, 2005).

The growing literature on international new ventures (INVs) establishes the importance of the SMEs' resources and capabilities for their internationalization performance (Zhou, Wu, & Barnes, 2012). Firms' marketing capabilities are managed by their capacity to integrate the Internet technology (Prasad, Ramamurthy, & Naidu, 2001). Firms using electronic business (e-business) take advantage of being market leaders to increase revenues before their competitors can enter the market (Kasemsap, 2016b). The development of e-business capabilities is found to positively affect the SMEs' internationalization performance (Raymond & Bergeron, 2008).

Internationalization, Innovation, and Research and Development

The innovation process for SMEs is based on the firms' ability to activate their internal knowledge, and depends on the firms' ability to gain knowledge from the external sources through imitation strategies, licensing acquisition, and partnerships (Kunday & Sengüler, 2015). There is a positive relationship between internationalization and innovation (Cassiman & Golovko, 2011). Exporters can learn from their foreign contacts, adopt new production technologies, and consequently enhance productivity (Garcia, Avella, & Fernandez, 2012). Internationalization can provide the firms the opportunity to gain the benefits from exposure to new technological knowledge and foreign markets (Salomon & Jin, 2010).

Research and development (R&D) capability has emerged as the significant issue in the international new ventures and rapid internationalization literature, and is recognized as a strategically significant source of competitive advantage (Golovko & Valentini, 2011). R&D spending affects the firm's innovation (Wang & Kafouros, 2009). R&D and innovation activities play an important role in explaining the firm's decision to export (Cassiman & Golovko, 2011). Promoting R&D activities among international organizations importantly reduce the entry barriers into foreign markets (Wang & Kafouros, 2009). Internationalization tends to be related to the type of innovation, much more than to R&D intensity or other measures of novelty, such as radical or incremental perspectives (Denicolai, Hagen, & Pisoni, 2015).

Implications of Internationalization in SMEs

The scope of international operations is the significant element of the internationalization strategies of SMEs (Baum, Schwens, & Kabst, 2011). Many studies in the international entrepreneurship and SMEs-related internationalization perspectives indicated that entrepreneurial firms effectively pursue different internationalization strategies (Kuivalainen, Saarenketo, & Puumalainen, 2012), and that both resources and capabilities have a positive impact on the selected internationalization strategies (Baum, Schwens, & Kabst, 2015). Explosive growth of low-cost technology, better information processing and communication technology, and reducing trade barriers, along with financial deregulation, are the key perspectives to enhance the internationalization of SMEs (Acs, Morck, & Yeung, 2001).

The ability to internationalize has become a competitive necessity for SMEs, thus enabling their survival and access to the larger markets (Dutot, Bergeron, & Raymond, 2014). Firms that intend to internationalize must strategically decide whether to adopt a regional or global internationalization strategy (Rugman & Verbeke, 2004). Internationalization brings about greater uncertainty and complexity in the environmental and strategic context of SMEs (Westhead, Wright, & Ucbasaran, 2004). The prior international experience of export managers is a driver of SME internationalization by influencing the firm's involvement in the export activities (Ibeh & Young, 2001).

Organizations aiming to increase business performance and achieve business goals should focus on developing information technology (IT), technical alignment, and information system capabilities (Kasemsap, 2015a). Project-based organizations should develop and maintain the systems of IT and knowledge management in order to meet specific business, project requirement, and customer satisfaction (Kasemsap, 2015b). The applications of virtual team and IT are necessary for modern organizations toward achieving continuous success in global business (Kasemsap, 2016c). SMEs have much less access to the necessary management and financial resources to correct situations arising from an unsuccessful IT investment (Zhang, Sarker, & Sarker, 2007). SMEs whose internationalization strategy and IT are aligned should be less vulnerable to the external changes and internal inefficiencies, and should perform better (Dutot et al., 2014). IT capability plays on the performance of born-global firms (Zhang, Sarker, & Sarker, 2013).

Many studies have emphasized the differences in the internationalization strategies of SMEs or entrepreneurial firms by indicating that a large proportion of born-global firms pursues the regionalized internationalization rather than expanding globally (Lopez, Kundu, & Ciravegna, 2009). Sui and Baum (2014) stated that on the selected internationalization strategy, firms' internal resources are of significance for the survival of SMEs in a given export market. The internationalization-related decision is essential for SMEs because their ability to exploit commercial opportunities in the global markets considerably depends on how well business owner's capabilities are matched with the different business environments in the global markets (Olejnik & Swoboda, 2012).

Overview of Entrepreneurial Orientation

Entrepreneurial orientation (EO) is described as the involvement of the firm to enter a new market (Lee & Peterson, 2000). The original EO scales include autonomy, innovativeness, risk taking, proactiveness, and competitive aggressiveness (Zellweger & Sieger, 2012). Three dimensions frequently used to describe EO are innovativeness, proactiveness, and risk taking (Wiklund & Shepherd, 2003). Innovativeness refers to the supporting creativity, introducing new products and services and developing new processes (Lumpkin & Dess, 1996). Proactiveness refers to the opportunity-seeking perspective that involves introducing new products, services, and processes ahead of the competition (Lumpkin & Dess, 1996).

Risk taking deals with a tendency to take actions, such as entering into new foreign markets (Lumpkin & Dess, 1996). Naldi et al. (2007) stated that risk taking is positively associated with proactiveness and innovativeness. Innovativeness is related to the importance of marketing strategies, such as developing new products and process technologies (Eggers, Hansen, & Davis, 2012). Tang et al. (2009) indicated that the innovative and risk-taking behaviors are fundamentally driven by proactiveness and the perceived availability of opportunities in SMEs. Autonomy is an important component of EO (Lumpkin, Cogliser, & Schneider, 2009).

Many researchers have used the EO-related three dimensions (i.e., innovativeness, proactiveness, and risk taking) in the international context in order to explore the performance of SMEs (Todd & Javalgi, 2007). Regarding innovativeness and risk-taking perspectives, the SME's act of attempting to participate in the international market significantly constitutes entrepreneurship (Ibeh, 2003). Innovativeness and proactiveness have positively moderated the relationship between market orientation and firm performance

(Li, Zhao, Tan, & Liu, 2008). Market orientation is the main determinant of EO in SMEs (Sciascia, Naldi, & Hunter, 2006). The international activities are entrepreneurial as they represent a combination of acceptance of risk and the ability to innovate, which are necessary to create the business value in the global markets (Fletcher, 2004).

The dynamic capabilities theory argues that the firms' strategies for organizing their resources considerably affect their value-creation potential (Liu, Ding, Guo, & Luo, 2014). The dimensions of EO have a positive effect on the dynamic capabilities to different extents, and firms can establish the dynamic capabilities through the different levels of organizational learning in the context of innovative and proactive perspectives (Jiao, Wei, & Cui, 2010). Firms that have higher levels of social capital and EO tend to enhance the effects of intellectual capital on innovativeness (Wu, Chang, & Chen, 2008). EO and social capital of entrepreneurs can promote their SME internationalization efforts (Zhang, Ma, & Wang, 2012).

Individualism is found to positively moderate the relationships between innovativeness-performance and proactiveness-performance (Kreiser, Marino, Kuratko, & Weaver, 2013). Middle managers' disposition toward proactiveness and innovativeness is positively related to their creative performance, and their internal bonding networks and upper management networks are found to strengthen the effects of EO on the creative performance (Chen, Chang, & Chang, 2015). Uncertainty avoidance and power distance are both found to have a negative impact on risk taking (Kreiser, Marino, Dickson, & Weaver, 2010).

Entrepreneurial Orientation and Firm Performance

EO is recognized as an antecedent of growth, competitive advantage, and superior firm performance (Kraus, Rigtering, Hughes, & Hosman, 2012). The firm's performance is positively related to EO and network resources, which significantly increases the enhancement of EO to firm performance (Yao, Wen, & Ren, 2009). New ventures often encounter a strategic dilemma of whether to differentiate themselves from or to conform to other businesses in the industry (Guo, Tang, & Su, 2014). The relationship between EO and firm performance is inverse U-shaped in new ventures but positive in established firms (Su, Xie, & Li, 2011). International entrepreneurship research maintains that firms with high EO can expand to international markets in order to enhance firm performance (Brouthers, Nakos, & Dimitratos, 2015).

Competitive intensity and demand volatility affect the impact of EO on firm performance in both the short term and the long term (Gupta & Gupta, 2015). The impact of EO on firm performance is moderated by environmental hostility (Grimmer, Miles, & Grimmer, 2015). Self-efficacy and EO are positively and directly associated with firm performance, whereas creativity and firm performance are fully mediated by EO (Khedhaouria, Gurău, & Torrès, 2015).

Entrepreneurial Orientation, Organizational Learning, and Knowledge Management

EO can enhance the acquisitive and experimental learning (Kreiser, 2011) and strategic learning capability (Anderson, Covin, & Slevin, 2009). Learning orientation must be in place to maximize the effect of EO on firm performance (Wang, 2008). Organizational learning capability and innovativeness should be enhanced by managers in order to boost the positive EO-performance relationship (Alegre & Chiva, 2013). Organizational learning partially mediates the relationship between EO and firm performance and fully mediates the relationship between learning orientation and firm performance (Real, Roldán, & Leal, 2014).

There are the positive relationships among EO, entrepreneurial cognition, and firm capability (Chaston & Sadler-Smith, 2012). EO provides the mobilizing vision to utilize the knowledge and experiences offered by the generational involvement toward entrepreneurship (Chirico, Sirmon, Sciascia, & Mazzola, 2011). EO and environmental hostility are positively related to the SMEs' cultivation of tacit knowledge (Pérez-Luño, Saparito, & Gopalakrishnan, 2016). Higher levels of internal knowledge sharing relate to stronger EO, and such knowledge sharing results from higher levels of trust and goal congruence (de Clercq, Dimov, & Thongpapanl, 2013).

Absorptive capacity refers to the firm's ability to acquire, assimilate, transform, and exploit the new knowledge (Wales, Parida, & Patel, 2013). EO moderates the absorptive capacity-performance relationship, thus enhancing financial gains at lower levels of absorptive capacity and mitigating the decline in financial performance at higher levels of absorptive capacity (Wales et al., 2013). Potential absorptive capacity enhances the effects of EO on the variability in innovation outcomes, whereas realized absorptive capacity helps transform and exploit the variability in innovation outcomes to enhance firm performance (Patel, Kohtamäki, Parida, & Wincent, 2015).

Current Trends and Issues with Entrepreneurial Orientation in SMEs

SMEs are assumed to be more likely to adopt EO when it is considered as a legitimate response and aligned with the normative, regulative, and cognitive aspects of the institutions that create the environment of the firm (Dickson & Weaver, 2008). Ripollés-Meliá et al. (2007) indicated that rapid entry into foreign markets is positively related to the development of EO in established firms, and that firms with a marked EO have higher relative international sales and operate in a greater number of foreign countries. Firms with high EO are more committed to the Internet and have better export performance than firms with low EO (Mostafa, Wheeler, & Jones, 2005). The firm's EO significantly affects product innovation within a vertical alliance (Bouncken, Plüschke, Pesch, & Kraus, 2016), and this relationship is stronger among firms implementing strategic human resource management (HRM) practices to a greater extent (Tang, Chen, & Jin, 2015).

EO scale has become the most widely used measure of entrepreneurial behavior (Runyan, Ge, Dong, & Swinney, 2012). Jantunen et al. (2005) indicated that entrepreneurial behavior combined with organizational capabilities constitutes a potential source of competitive advantage. EO constitutes an organizational phenomenon that reflects a managerial capability by which firms establish the proactive initiatives to alter the competitive scene to their competitive advantage (Avlonitis & Salavou, 2007). Younger firms are better able to capture the value from entrepreneurial strategies in the form of higher organizational growth rates than their older peers (Anderson & Eshima, 2013).

Entrepreneurial activities usually occur as a result of individuals' entrepreneurial behaviors (Fini, Grimaldi, Marzocchi, & Sobrero, 2012). Entrepreneurs must plan the strategies and be able to communicate the vision, goals, and strategies in order to sustain the SMEs' performance and operational excellence which have been widely accepted as central to the long-term economic stability around the world (Hafiz & Ismail, 2015). For entrepreneurs with stronger EO, the effect of network ties on speed of entrepreneurial success is superior to those without EO (Huang, 2016). CEOs whose personalities reflect higher core self-evaluations have a stronger positive influence on their firms' EO (Simsek, Heavey, & Veiga, 2010). van Doorn et al. (2013) stated that senior team's shared vision has a positive impact for firms operating in dynamic environments, providing a premium for firms aiming to realize the inherent value of EO.

EO has been recognized as an essential attribute of high performing firms, and the role of culture has been highlighted for generating strong EO (Lee, Lim, & Pathak, 2011). Early development of an entrepreneurial culture positively affects the firm's international intent, allowing the firm to pursue the international opportunities (Zucchella, Palamara, & Denicolai, 2007). Organizational culture is positively related to organizational climate (Kasemsap, 2016d). Organizational culture that is an adhocracy is most effective in advancing EO, especially in national cultures that are characterized by strong individualism and low power distance, whereas a hierarchical organizational culture is a barrier to EO (Engelen, Flatten, Thalmann, & Brettel, 2014). The developmental, group, and rational culture has a strong positive impact on EO (Brettel, Chomik, & Flatten, 2015).

FUTURE RESEARCH DIRECTIONS

The classification of the extensive literature in the domains of internationalization and EO in SMEs will provide the potential opportunities for future research. The essence of entrepreneurship education is recognized within academia because it aims to create independent entrepreneurs, and it has the general objective of preparing organizational individuals where they need to manage their own careers in an entrepreneurial way (Kasemsap, 2015c). Entrepreneurship education is designed to facilitate strategic entrepreneurs and the entrepreneurial programs emphasize radical innovation and the models of entrepreneurial process that deliver innovation, new business ventures, and disruptive business models (Kasemsap, 2016e). Successful knowledge management efforts are focused on the ideal outcomes that help organizations meet the critical business objectives in global business (Kasemsap, 2016f).

The use of social media has created the highly effective communication platforms where any user, virtually anywhere in the world, can freely create the content and disseminate this information in real time to a global audience (Kasemsap, 2017a). Promoting internationalization and EO through entrepreneurship education, knowledge management, and social media platforms would be beneficial for future research directions. Consumer attitude influences the way consumer thinks and behaves and it is important for the marketers who study it to understand how consumer behaves toward increasing business profit (Kasemsap, 2017b). Sustainability is the business strategy that drives the long-term corporate growth and profitability by mandating the inclusion of environmental and social issues in the business model (Kasemsap, 2017c). An examination of linkages among internationalization, EO, consumer attitude, and sustainability in SMEs would seem to be viable for future research efforts.

CONCLUSION

This chapter highlighted the overview of internationalization; the aspects of internationalization in SMEs; internationalization, social capital, and FMK in SMEs; internationalization and marketing capability; internationalization, innovation, and R&D; the implications of internationalization in SMEs; the overview of EO; EO and firm performance; EO, organizational learning, and knowledge management; and the current trends and issues with EO in SMEs. SMEs are confronted with international competition and are forced to play a role in international markets. The changing business environment creates new opportunities and incentives for SMEs to internationalize. Internationalization is accompanied by improved performance and competitiveness of SMEs. Internationalization in SMEs can take various forms, such as import, export, foreign direct investment (FDI), and international collaboration.

Regarding internationalization in SMEs, exporting can lead to the increasing productivity, through economies of scale. FDI can provide SMEs with new know-how and technologies, which can be combined to develop new competitive strengths. As large firms increasingly outsource parts of their supply chain, opportunities for SMEs arise to internationalize through cooperation with large firms. The internationalization provides SMEs with opportunities to improve productivity and increase their chances of survival. The advances in telecommunication and other technologies have considerably reduced the costs and risks involved in internationalization. This perspective makes it possible for an increasing number of SMEs to exploit opportunities in foreign markets. Government policy can play an important role in encouraging SMEs in their internationalization process.

EO is the strategy making practices that firms make to identify and launch business ventures. Firms are described as having greater EO when they have demonstrated a sustained pattern of behavior over time which may be considered as entrepreneurial in nature characterized by innovativeness, proactiveness, and risk taking. EO allows for distancing the intentions and attitudes of members from the firm's overall behavioral orientation toward entrepreneurship. Encouraging internationalization and EO is essential for SMEs that seek to serve suppliers and customers, increase business performance, strengthen competitiveness, and achieve continuous success in SMEs. Therefore, it is essential to understand their internationalization and EO and establish a strategic plan to regularly check their practical advancements toward satisfying customer requirements. Encouraging internationalization and EO has the potential to enhance organizational performance and reach strategic goals in SMEs.

REFERENCES

Acs, Z. J., Morck, R. K., & Yeung, B. (2001). Entrepreneurship, globalization, and public policy. *Journal of International Management*, *7*(3), 235–251. doi:10.1016/S1075-4253(01)00046-1

Alegre, J., & Chiva, R. (2013). Linking entrepreneurial orientation and firm performance: The role of organizational learning capability and innovation performance. *Journal of Small Business Management*, *51*(4), 491–507. doi:10.1111/jsbm.12005

Anderson, B. S., Covin, J. G., & Slevin, D. P. (2009). Understanding the relationship between entrepreneurial orientation and strategic learning capability: An empirical investigation. *Strategic Entrepreneurship Journal*, *3*(3), 218–240. doi:10.1002/sej.72

Anderson, B. S., & Eshima, Y. (2013). The influence of firm age and intangible resources on the relationship between entrepreneurial orientation and firm growth among Japanese SMEs. *Journal of Business Venturing*, *28*(3), 413–429. doi:10.1016/j.jbusvent.2011.10.001

Arshad, A. S., Rasli, A., Arshad, A. A., & Zain, Z. M. (2014). The impact of entrepreneurial orientation on business performance: A study of technology-based SMEs in Malaysia. *Procedia: Social and Behavioral Sciences*, *130*, 46–53. doi:10.1016/j.sbspro.2014.04.006

Avlontis, G. J., & Salavou, H. E. (2007). Entrepreneurial orientation of SMEs, product innovativeness, and performance. *Journal of Business Research*, *60*(5), 566–575. doi:10.1016/j.jbusres.2007.01.001

Baker, W. E., & Sinkula, J. M. (2009). The complementary effects of market orientation and entrepreneurial orientation on profitability in small businesses. *Journal of Small Business Management*, *47*(4), 443–464. doi:10.1111/j.1540-627X.2009.00278.x

Baum, M., Schwens, C., & Kabst, R. (2011). A typology of international ventures: Empirical evidence from high-technology industries. *Journal of Small Business Management*, *49*(3), 305–330. doi:10.1111/j.1540-627X.2011.00328.x

Baum, M., Schwens, C., & Kabst, R. (2015). A latent class analysis of small firms' internationalization patterns. *Journal of World Business*, *50*(4), 754–768. doi:10.1016/j.jwb.2015.03.001

Beck, T., & Demirguc-Kunt, A. (2006). Small and medium-size enterprises: Access to finance as a growth constraint. *Journal of Banking & Finance*, *30*(11), 2931–2943. doi:10.1016/j.jbankfin.2006.05.009

Bettiol, M., Di Maria, E., & Finotto, V. (2012). Marketing in SMEs: The role of entrepreneurial sensemaking. *The International Entrepreneurship and Management Journal*, *8*(2), 223–248. doi:10.1007/s11365-011-0174-3

Blomstermo, A., Eriksson, K., Lindstrand, A., & Sharma, D. D. (2004). The perceived usefulness of network experiential knowledge in the internationalizing firm. *Journal of International Management*, *10*(3), 355–373. doi:10.1016/j.intman.2004.05.004

Bouncken, R. B., Plüschke, B. D., Pesch, R., & Kraus, S. (2016). Entrepreneurial orientation in vertical alliances: Joint product innovation and learning from allies. *Review of Managerial Science*, *10*(2), 381–409. doi:10.1007/s11846-014-0150-8

Bretherton, P., & Chaston, I. (2005). Resource dependency and SME strategy: An empirical study. *Journal of Small Business and Enterprise Development*, *12*(2), 274–289. doi:10.1108/14626000510594656

Brettel, M., Chomik, C., & Flatten, T. C. (2015). How organizational culture influences innovativeness, proactiveness, and risk-taking: Fostering entrepreneurial orientation in SMEs. *Journal of Small Business Management*, *53*(4), 868–885. doi:10.1111/jsbm.12108

Brouthers, K. D., Nakos, G., & Dimitratos, P. (2015). SME entrepreneurial orientation, international performance, and the moderating role of strategic alliances. *Entrepreneurship Theory and Practice*, *39*(5), 1161–1187. doi:10.1111/etap.12101

Buckley, P. G., & Casson, M. C. (2009). The internationalization theory of the multinational enterprise: A review of the progress of a research agenda after 30 years. *Journal of International Business Studies*, *40*(9), 1563–1580. doi:10.1057/jibs.2009.49

Cassiman, B., & Golovko, E. (2011). Innovation and internationalization through exports. *Journal of International Business Studies*, *42*(1), 56–75. doi:10.1057/jibs.2010.36

Chaston, I., & Sadler-Smith, E. (2012). Entrepreneurial cognition, entrepreneurial orientation and firm capability in the creative industries. *British Journal of Management*, *23*(3), 415–432.

Chen, M. H., Chang, Y. Y., & Chang, Y. C. (2015). Entrepreneurial orientation, social networks, and creative performance: Middle managers as corporate entrepreneurs. *Creativity and Innovation Management*, *24*(3), 493–507. doi:10.1111/caim.12108

Child, J., & Hsieh, L. H. Y. (2014). Decision mode, information and network attachment in the internationalization of SMEs: A configurational and contingency analysis. *Journal of World Business*, *49*(4), 598–610. doi:10.1016/j.jwb.2013.12.012

Chirico, F., Sirmon, D. G., Sciascia, S., & Mazzola, P. (2011). Resource orchestration in family firms: Investigating how entrepreneurial orientation, generational involvement, and participative strategy affect performance. *Strategic Entrepreneurship Journal*, *5*(4), 307–326. doi:10.1002/sej.121

Ciravegna, L. (2011). Social ties and technological learning in new Silicon Valley clones. *The Journal of Development Studies*, *47*(8), 1178–1198. doi:10.1080/00220388.2010.547935

Ciravegna, L., Lopez, L., & Kundu, S. (2014). Country of origin and network effects on internationalization: A comparative study of SMEs from an emerging and developed economy. *Journal of Business Research*, *67*(5), 916–923. doi:10.1016/j.jbusres.2013.07.011

Colombelli, A. (2010). Alternative investment market: A way to promote entrepreneurship. *Journal of Industry, Competition and Trade*, *10*(3), 253–274. doi:10.1007/s10842-010-0079-9

Coviello, N. E. (2006). The network dynamics of international new ventures. *Journal of International Business Studies*, *37*(5), 713–731. doi:10.1057/palgrave.jibs.8400219

Coviello, N. E., & Cox, M. P. (2006). The resource dynamics of international new venture networks. *Journal of International Entrepreneurship*, *4*(2/3), 113–132. doi:10.1007/s10843-007-0004-4

Covin, J. G., Green, K. M., & Slevin, D. P. (2006). Strategic process effects on the entrepreneurial orientation-sales growth rate relationship. *Entrepreneurship Theory and Practice*, *30*(1), 57–81. doi:10.1111/j.1540-6520.2006.00110.x

Cruz, C., & Nordqvist, M. (2012). Entrepreneurial orientation in family firms: A generational perspective. *Small Business Economics*, *38*(1), 33–49. doi:10.1007/s11187-010-9265-8

de Clercq, D., Dimov, D., & Thongpapanl, N. (2013). Organizational social capital, formalization, and internal knowledge sharing in entrepreneurial orientation formation. *Entrepreneurship Theory and Practice*, *37*(3), 505–537. doi:10.1111/etap.12021

Denicolai, S., Hagen, B., & Pisoni, A. (2015). Be international or be innovative? Be both? The role of the entrepreneurial profile. *Journal of International Entrepreneurship*, *13*(4), 390–417. doi:10.1007/s10843-015-0143-y

Di Gregorio, D., Musteen, M., & Thomas, D. E. (2008). Offshore outsourcing of international competitiveness for SMEs. *Journal of International Business Studies*, *40*(6), 969–988. doi:10.1057/jibs.2008.90

Dickson, P. H., & Weaver, K. M. (2008). The role of the institutional environment in determining firm orientations towards entrepreneurial behavior. *The International Entrepreneurship and Management Journal*, *4*(4), 467–483. doi:10.1007/s11365-008-0088-x

Dutot, V., Bergeron, F., & Raymond, L. (2014). Information management for the internationalization of SMEs: An exploratory study based on a strategic alignment perspective. *International Journal of Information Management*, *34*(5), 672–681. doi:10.1016/j.ijinfomgt.2014.06.006

Eggers, F., Hansen, D. J., & Davis, A. E. (2012). Examining the relationship between customer and entrepreneurial orientation on nascent firms' marketing strategy. *The International Entrepreneurship and Management Journal*, *8*(2), 203–222. doi:10.1007/s11365-011-0173-4

Ellis, P. D. (2011). Social ties and international entrepreneurship: Opportunities and constraints affecting firm internationalization. *Journal of International Business Studies*, *42*(1), 99–127. doi:10.1057/jibs.2010.20

Engelen, A., Flatten, T. C., Thalmann, J., & Brettel, M. (2014). The effect of organizational culture on entrepreneurial orientation: A comparison between Germany and Thailand. *Journal of Small Business Management*, *52*(4), 732–752. doi:10.1111/jsbm.12052

Felício, J. A., Caldeirinha, V. R., & Ribeiro-Navarrete, B. (2015). Corporate and individual global mind-set and internationalization of European SMEs. *Journal of Business Research*, *68*(4), 797–802. doi:10.1016/j.jbusres.2014.11.031

Felzensztein, C., Ciravegna, L., Robson, P., & Amorós, J. E. (2015). Networks, entrepreneurial orientation, and internationalization scope: Evidence from Chilean small and medium enterprises. *Journal of Small Business Management*, *53*(Suppl. 1), 145–160. doi:10.1111/jsbm.12188

Fini, R., Grimaldi, R., Marzocchi, G. L., & Sobrero, M. (2012). The determinants of corporate entrepreneurial intention within small and newly established firms. *Entrepreneurship Theory and Practice*, *36*(2), 387–414. doi:10.1111/j.1540-6520.2010.00411.x

Fletcher, D. (2004). International entrepreneurship and small business. *Entrepreneurship & Regional Development*, *16*(4), 289–305. doi:10.1080/0898562042000263267

Freeman, S., Hutchings, K., Lazaris, M., & Zyngier, S. (2010). A model of rapid knowledge development: The smaller born-global firm. *International Business Review*, *19*(1), 70–84. doi:10.1016/j.ibusrev.2009.09.004

Garcia, F., Avella, L., & Fernandez, E. (2012). Learning from exporting: The moderating effect of technological capabilities. *International Business Review*, *21*(6), 1099–1111. doi:10.1016/j.ibusrev.2011.12.001

Gassmann, O., & Keupp, M. M. (2007). The competitive advantage of early and rapidly internationalising SMEs in the biotechnology industry: A knowledge-based view. *Journal of World Business*, *42*(3), 350–366. doi:10.1016/j.jwb.2007.04.006

Golovko, E., & Valentini, G. (2011). Exploring the complementarity between innovation and export for SMEs' growth. *Journal of International Business Studies*, *42*(3), 362–380. doi:10.1057/jibs.2011.2

Greene, F., & Mole, K. (2006). Defining and measuring the small business. In S. Carter & D. Jones-Evans (Eds.), *Enterprise and small business: Principles, practice and policy* (pp. 7–29). Harlow, UK: Financial Times/Prentice Hall.

Grimmer, L., Miles, M. P., & Grimmer, M. (2015). A research note on the effect of entrepreneurial orientation on small retailer performance: A resource-advantage perspective. *The International Entrepreneurship and Management Journal*, *11*(2), 409–424. doi:10.1007/s11365-013-0279-y

Guo, H., Tang, J., & Su, Z. (2014). To be different, or to be the same? The interactive effect of organizational regulatory legitimacy and entrepreneurial orientation on new venture performance. *Asia Pacific Journal of Management*, *31*(3), 665–685. doi:10.1007/s10490-013-9361-9

Gupta, J., Wilson, N., Gregoriou, A., & Healy, J. (2014). The effect of internationalisation on modelling credit risk for SMEs: Evidence from UK market. *Journal of International Financial Markets, Institutions and Money*, *31*, 397–413. doi:10.1016/j.intfin.2014.05.001

Gupta, V. K., & Gupta, A. (2015). Relationship between entrepreneurial orientation and firm performance in large organizations over time. *International Journal of International Entrepreneurship*, *13*(1), 7–27. doi:10.1007/s10843-014-0138-0

Hafiz, M. R., & Ismail, K. (2015). The propensity of adapting strategic reactiveness and entrepreneurial management amongst SMEs. *Procedia: Social and Behavioral Sciences*, *181*, 356–365. doi:10.1016/j.sbspro.2015.04.898

Hakala, H. (2011). Strategic orientations in management literature: Three approaches to understanding the interaction between market, technology, entrepreneurial and learning orientations. *International Journal of Management Reviews*, *13*(2), 199–217. doi:10.1111/j.1468-2370.2010.00292.x

Hessels, J., & Parker, S. C. (2013). Constraints, internationalization and growth: A cross-country analysis of European SMEs. *Journal of World Business*, *48*(1), 137–148. doi:10.1016/j.jwb.2012.06.014

Hsu, W. T., Chen, H. L., & Cheng, C. Y. (2013). Internationalization and firm performance of SMEs: The moderating effects of CEO attributes. *Journal of World Business*, *48*(1), 1–12. doi:10.1016/j.jwb.2012.06.001

Huang, H. C. (2016). Entrepreneurial resources and speed of entrepreneurial success in an emerging market: The moderating effect of entrepreneurship. *The International Entrepreneurship and Management Journal*, *12*(1), 1–26. doi:10.1007/s11365-014-0321-8

Ibeh, K. I. N. (2003). Toward a contingency framework of export entrepreneurship: Conceptualisations and empirical evidence. *Small Business Economics*, *20*(1), 49–68. doi:10.1023/A:1020244404241

Ibeh, K. I. N., & Young, S. (2001). Exporting as an entrepreneurial act an empirical study of Nigerian firms. *European Journal of Marketing*, *35*(5/6), 566–586. doi:10.1108/03090560110388114

Jantunen, A., Puumalainen, K., Saarenketo, S., & Kyläheiko, K. (2005). Entrepreneurial orientation, dynamic capabilities and international performance. *Journal of International Entrepreneurship*, *3*(3), 223–243. doi:10.1007/s10843-005-1133-2

Javalgi, R. G., & Todd, P. R. (2011). Entrepreneurial orientation, management commitment, and human capital: The internationalization of SMEs in India. *Journal of Business Research*, *64*(9), 1004–1010. doi:10.1016/j.jbusres.2010.11.024

Jiao, F., Wei, J., & Cui, Y. (2010). An empirical study on paths to develop dynamic capabilities: From the perspectives of entrepreneurial orientation and organizational learning. *Frontiers of Business Research in China*, *4*(1), 47–72. doi:10.1007/s11782-010-0003-5

Johanson, J., & Vahlne, J. E. (1977). The internationalization process of the firm: A model of knowledge development and increasing foreign market commitment. *Journal of International Business Studies*, *8*(1), 23–32. doi:10.1057/palgrave.jibs.8490676

Jones, M. V., & Coviello, N. E. (2005). Internationalization: Conceptualizing an entrepreneurial process of behavior in time. *Journal of International Business Studies*, *36*(3), 284–303. doi:10.1057/palgrave.jibs.8400138

Kalinic, I., & Forza, C. (2012). Rapid internationalization of traditional SMEs: Between gradualist models and born globals. *International Business Review*, *21*(4), 694–707. doi:10.1016/j.ibusrev.2011.08.002

Kasemsap, K. (2014). The role of social capital in higher education institutions. In N. Baporikar (Ed.), *Handbook of research on higher education in the MENA region: Policy and practice* (pp. 119–147). Hershey, PA: IGI Global. doi:10.4018/978-1-4666-6198-1.ch007

Kasemsap, K. (2015a). The role of information system within enterprise architecture and their impact on business performance. In M. Wadhwa & A. Harper (Eds.), *Technology, innovation, and enterprise transformation* (pp. 262–284). Hershey, PA: IGI Global. doi:10.4018/978-1-4666-6473-9.ch012

Kasemsap, K. (2015b). The roles of information technology and knowledge management in project management metrics. In G. Jamil, S. Lopes, A. Malheiro da Silva, & F. Ribeiro (Eds.), *Handbook of research on effective project management through the integration of knowledge and innovation* (pp. 332–361). Hershey, PA: IGI Global. doi:10.4018/978-1-4666-7536-0.ch018

Kasemsap, K. (2015c). Mastering entrepreneurship education in global business. In A. Szopa, W. Karwowski, & D. Barbe (Eds.), *Competitive strategies for academic entrepreneurship: Commercialization of research-based products* (pp. 1–28). Hershey, PA: IGI Global. doi:10.4018/978-1-4666-8487-4.ch001

Kasemsap, K. (2016a). Exploring the roles of entrepreneurship and internationalization in global business. In L. Carvalho (Ed.), *Handbook of research on entrepreneurial success and its impact on regional development* (pp. 481–512). Hershey, PA: IGI Global. doi:10.4018/978-1-4666-9567-2.ch021

Kasemsap, K. (2016b). Advocating electronic business and electronic commerce in the global marketplace. In S. Dixit & A. Sinha (Eds.), *E-retailing challenges and opportunities in the global marketplace* (pp. 1–24). Hershey, PA: IGI Global. doi:10.4018/978-1-4666-9921-2.ch001

Kasemsap, K. (2016c). Examining the roles of virtual team and information technology in global business. In C. Graham (Ed.), *Strategic management and leadership for systems development in virtual spaces* (pp. 1–21). Hershey, PA: IGI Global. doi:10.4018/978-1-4666-9688-4.ch001

Kasemsap, K. (2016d). A unified framework of organizational perspectives and knowledge management and their impact on job performance. In A. Normore, L. Long, & M. Javidi (Eds.), *Handbook of research on effective communication, leadership, and conflict resolution* (pp. 267–297). Hershey, PA: IGI Global. doi:10.4018/978-1-4666-9970-0.ch015

Kasemsap, K. (2016e). Advocating entrepreneurship education and knowledge management in global business. In N. Baporikar (Ed.), *Handbook of research on entrepreneurship in the contemporary knowledge-based global economy* (pp. 313–339). Hershey, PA: IGI Global. doi:10.4018/978-1-4666-8798-1.ch014

Kasemsap, K. (2016f). The roles of e-learning, organizational learning, and knowledge management in the learning organizations. In E. Railean, G. Walker, A. Elçi, & L. Jackson (Eds.), *Handbook of research on applied learning theory and design in modern education* (pp. 786–816). Hershey, PA: IGI Global. doi:10.4018/978-1-4666-9634-1.ch039

Kasemsap, K. (2017a). Professional and business applications of social media platforms. In V. Benson, R. Tuninga, & G. Saridakis (Eds.), *Analyzing the strategic role of social networking in firm growth and productivity* (pp. 427–450). Hershey, PA: IGI Global. doi:10.4018/978-1-5225-0559-4.ch021

Kasemsap, K. (2017b). Mastering consumer attitude and sustainable consumption in the digital age. In N. Suki (Ed.), *Handbook of research on leveraging consumer psychology for effective customer engagement* (pp. 16–41). Hershey, PA: IGI Global. doi:10.4018/978-1-5225-0746-8.ch002

Kasemsap, K. (2017c). Advocating sustainable supply chain management and sustainability in global supply chain. In M. Khan, M. Hussain, & M. Ajmal (Eds.), *Green supply chain management for sustainable business practice* (pp. 234–271). Hershey, PA: IGI Global. doi:10.4018/978-1-5225-0635-5.ch009

Khanna, T., & Palepu, K. G. (2010). *Winning in emerging markets: A road map for strategy and execution*. Boston, MA: Harvard Business Review Press.

Khedhaouria, A., Gurău, C., & Torrès, O. (2015). Creativity, self-efficacy, and small-firm performance: The mediating role of entrepreneurial orientation. *Small Business Economics*, *44*(3), 485–504. doi:10.1007/s11187-014-9608-y

Knight, G. A., Madsen, T. K., & Servais, P. (2004). An enquiry into born global firms in Europe and the US. *International Marketing Review*, *21*(6), 645–665. doi:10.1108/02651330410568060

Kotabe, M., & Helsen, K. (2004). *Global marketing management*. Hoboken, NJ: John Wiley & Sons.

Kraus, S., Rigtering, J. P. C., Hughes, M., & Hosman, V. (2012). Entrepreneurial orientation and the business performance of SMEs: A quantitative study from the Netherlands. *Review of Managerial Science*, *6*(2), 161–182. doi:10.1007/s11846-011-0062-9

Kreiser, P. M. (2011). Entrepreneurial orientation and organizational learning: The impact of network range and network closure. *Entrepreneurship Theory and Practice*, *35*(5), 1025–1050. doi:10.1111/j.1540-6520.2011.00449.x

Kreiser, P. M., Marino, L. D., Dickson, P., & Weaver, K. M. (2010). Cultural influences on entrepreneurial orientation: The impact of national culture on risk taking and proactiveness in SMEs. *Entrepreneurship Theory and Practice*, *34*(5), 959–983. doi:10.1111/j.1540-6520.2010.00396.x

Kreiser, P. M., Marino, L. D., Kuratko, D. F., & Weaver, K. M. (2013). Disaggregating entrepreneurial orientation: The non-linear impact of innovativeness, proactiveness and risk-taking on SME performance. *Small Business Economics*, *40*(2), 273–291. doi:10.1007/s11187-012-9460-x

Kuivalainen, O., Saarenketo, S., & Puumalainen, K. (2012). Start-up patterns of internationalization: A framework and its application in the context of knowledge-intensive SMEs. *European Management Journal*, *30*(4), 372–385. doi:10.1016/j.emj.2012.01.001

Kunday, O., & Sengüler, E. P. (2015). A study on factors affecting the internationalization process of small and medium enterprises (SMEs). *Procedia: Social and Behavioral Sciences*, *195*, 972–981. doi:10.1016/j.sbspro.2015.06.363

Kyvik, O., Saris, W., Bonet, E., & Felício, J. A. (2013). The internationalization of small firms: The relationship between the global mindset and firms' internationalization behavior. *Journal of International Entrepreneurship*, *11*(2), 172–195. doi:10.1007/s10843-013-0105-1

Lee, S. M., Lim, S. B., & Pathak, R. D. (2011). Culture and entrepreneurial orientation: A multi-country study. *The International Entrepreneurship and Management Journal*, *7*(1), 1–15. doi:10.1007/s11365-009-0117-4

Lee, S. M., & Peterson, S. J. (2000). Culture, entrepreneurial orientation, and global competitiveness. *Journal of World Business*, *35*(4), 401–416. doi:10.1016/S1090-9516(00)00045-6

Lehtinen, U., & Penttinen, H. (1999). Definition of the internationalization of the firm. In U. Lehtinen & H. Seristoe (Eds.), *Perspectives on internationalization* (pp. 3–19). Helsinki, Finland: Helsinki School of Economics and Business Administration.

Leonidou, L. C. (2004). An analysis of the barriers hindering small business export development. *Journal of Small Business Management*, *42*(3), 279–302. doi:10.1111/j.1540-627X.2004.00112.x

Li, Y., Guo, H., Liu, Y., & Li, M. (2008). Incentive mechanisms, entrepreneurial orientation, and technology commercialization: Evidence from Chinas' transitional economy. *Journal of Product Innovation Management*, *25*(1), 63–78. doi:10.1111/j.1540-5885.2007.00283.x

Li, Y., Zhao, Y., Tan, J., & Liu, Y. (2008). Moderating effects of entrepreneurial orientation on market orientation-performance linkage: Evidence from Chinese small firms. *Journal of Small Business Management*, *46*(1), 113–133. doi:10.1111/j.1540-627X.2007.00235.x

Lim, S., Trimi, S., & Lee, H. H. (2010). Web 2.0 service adoption and entrepreneurial orientation. *Service Business*, *4*(3/4), 197–207. doi:10.1007/s11628-010-0097-z

Lindstrand, A., Eriksson, K., & Sharma, D. D. (2009). The perceived usefulness of knowledge supplied by foreign client networks. *International Business Review*, *18*(1), 26–37. doi:10.1016/j.ibusrev.2008.11.002

Lindstrand, A., Melen, S., & Nordman, E. R. (2011). Turning social capital into business: A study of the internationalization of biotech SMEs. *International Business Review*, *20*(2), 194–212. doi:10.1016/j.ibusrev.2011.01.002

Liu, H., Ding, X. H., Guo, H., & Luo, J. H. (2014). How does slack affect product innovation in high-tech Chinese firms: The contingent value of entrepreneurial orientation. *Asia Pacific Journal of Management*, *31*(1), 47–68. doi:10.1007/s10490-012-9309-5

Lopez, L. E., Kundu, S., & Ciravegna, L. (2009). Born global or born regional? Evidence from an exploratory study in the Costa Rican software industry. *Journal of International Business Studies*, *40*(7), 1228–1238. doi:10.1057/jibs.2008.69

Lu, J. W., & Beamish, P. W. (2006). SME internationalization and performance: Growth vs. profitability. *Journal of International Entrepreneurship*, *4*(1), 27–48. doi:10.1007/s10843-006-8000-7

Lumpkin, G. T., Cogliser, C. C., & Schneider, D. R. (2009). Understanding and measuring autonomy: An entrepreneurial orientation perspective. *Entrepreneurship Theory and Practice*, *33*(1), 47–69. doi:10.1111/j.1540-6520.2008.00280.x

Lumpkin, G. T., & Dess, G. G. (1996). Clarifying the entrepreneurial orientation construct and linking it to performance. *Academy of Management Review*, *21*(1), 135–172.

Mahmood, R., & Hanafi, N. (2013). Entrepreneurial orientation and business performance of women-owned small and medium enterprises in Malaysia: Competitive advantage as a mediator. *International Journal of Business and Social Science*, *4*(1), 82–90.

Marino, L., Strandholm, K., Steensma, H. K., & Weaver, K. M. (2002). The moderating effect of national culture on the relationship between entrepreneurial orientation and strategic alliance portfolio extensiveness. *Entrepreneurship Theory and Practice*, *26*(4), 145–160.

McDougall, P. P., Shane, S., & Oviatt, B. M. (1994). Explaining the formation of international new ventures: The limits of theories from international business research. *Journal of Business Venturing*, *9*(6), 469–487. doi:10.1016/0883-9026(94)90017-5

Mintzberg, H., Raisinghani, D., & Theoret, A. (1976). The structure of "unstructured" decision processes. *Administrative Science Quarterly*, *21*(2), 246–275. doi:10.2307/2392045

Moen, Ø., Gavlen, M., & Endresen, I. (2004). Internationalization of small, computer software firms: Entry firms and market selection. *European Journal of Marketing*, *38*(9), 1236–1251. doi:10.1108/03090560410548951

Moreno, A. M., & Casillas, J. C. (2008). Entrepreneurial orientation and growth of SMEs: A causal model. *Entrepreneurship Theory and Practice*, *32*(3), 507–528. doi:10.1111/j.1540-6520.2008.00238.x

Mostafa, R. H. A., Wheeler, C., & Jones, M. V. (2005). Entrepreneurial orientation, commitment to the Internet and export performance in small and medium sized exporting firms. *Journal of International Entrepreneurship*, *3*(4), 291–302. doi:10.1007/s10843-006-7857-9

Musteen, M., Francis, J., & Datta, D. K. (2010). The influence of international networks on internationalization speed and performance: A study of Czech SMEs. *Journal of World Business*, *45*(3), 197–205. doi:10.1016/j.jwb.2009.12.003

Nahapiet, J., & Ghoshal, S. (1998). Social capital, intellectual capital, and the organizational advantage. *Academy of Management Review*, *23*(2), 242–266.

Naldi, L., Nordqvist, M., Sjöberg, K., & Wiklund, J. (2007). Entrepreneurial orientation, risk taking, and performance in family firms. *Family Business Review*, *20*(1), 33–47. doi:10.1111/j.1741-6248.2007.00082.x

Nath, P., Nachiappan, S., & Ramanathan, R. (2010). The impact of marketing capability, operations capability and diversification strategy on performance: A resource-based view. *Industrial Marketing Management*, *39*(2), 317–329. doi:10.1016/j.indmarman.2008.09.001

Nerkar, A., & Paruchuri, S. (2005). Evolution of R&D capabilities: The role of knowledge networks within a firm. *Management Science*, *51*(5), 771–786. doi:10.1287/mnsc.1040.0354

OECD. (2009). *Top barriers and drivers to SME internationalisation*. Paris, France: Organisation for Economic Co-operation and Development.

Olejnik, E., & Swoboda, B. (2012). SMEs' internationalisation patterns: Descriptives, dynamics and determinants. *International Marketing Review*, *29*(5), 466–495. doi:10.1108/02651331211260340

Oparaocha, G. O. (2015). SMEs and international entrepreneurship: An institutional network perspective. *International Business Review*, *24*(5), 861–873. doi:10.1016/j.ibusrev.2015.03.007

Oviatt, B. M., & McDougall, P. P. (2005). Defining international entrepreneurship and modelling the speed of internationalization. *Entrepreneurship Theory and Practice*, *29*(5), 537–553. doi:10.1111/j.1540-6520.2005.00097.x

Patel, P. C., Kohtamäki, M., Parida, V., & Wincent, J. (2015). Entrepreneurial orientation-as-experimentation and firm performance: The enabling role of absorptive capacity. *Strategic Management Journal*, *36*(11), 1739–1749. doi:10.1002/smj.2310

Pérez-Luño, A., Saparito, P., & Gopalakrishnan, S. (2016). Small and medium-sized enterprises' entrepreneurial versus market orientation and the creation of tacit knowledge. *Journal of Small Business Management*, *54*(1), 262–278. doi:10.1111/jsbm.12144

Prahalad, C. K., & Ramaswamy, V. (2000). Co-opting customer competence. *Harvard Business Review*, *78*(1), 79–87.

Prasad, V. K., Ramamurthy, K., & Naidu, G. M. (2001). The influence of Internet-marketing integration on marketing competencies and export performance. *Journal of International Marketing*, *9*(4), 82–110. doi:10.1509/jimk.9.4.82.19944

Ramos, E., Acedo, F. J., & Gonzalez, M. R. (2011). Internationalisation speed and technological patterns: A panel data study on Spanish SMEs. *Technovation*, *31*(10/11), 560–572. doi:10.1016/j.technovation.2011.06.008

Raymond, L., & Bergeron, F. (2008). Enabling the business strategy of SMEs through e-business capabilities: A strategic alignment perspective. *Industrial Management & Data Systems*, *108*(5), 577–595. doi:10.1108/02635570810876723

Real, J. C., Roldán, J. L., & Leal, A. (2014). From entrepreneurial orientation and learning orientation to business performance: Analysing the mediating role of organizational learning and the moderating effects of organizational size. *British Journal of Management*, *25*(2), 186–208. doi:10.1111/j.1467-8551.2012.00848.x

Ren, S., Eisingerich, A. B., & Tsai, H. T. (2015). How do marketing, research and development capabilities, and degree of internationalization synergistically affect the innovation performance of small and medium-sized enterprises (SMEs)? A panel data study of Chinese SMEs. *International Business Review*, *24*(4), 642–651. doi:10.1016/j.ibusrev.2014.11.006

Renko, M., Carsrud, A., & Brännback, M. (2009). The effect of a market orientation, entrepreneurial orientation, and technological capability on innovativeness: A study of young biotechnology ventures in the United States and in Scandinavia. *Journal of Small Business Management*, *47*(3), 331–369. doi:10.1111/j.1540-627X.2009.00274.x

Ripollés-Meliá, M., Menguzzato-Boulard, M., & Sánchez-Peinado, L. (2007). Entrepreneurial orientation and international commitment. *Journal of International Entrepreneurship*, *5*(3), 65–83. doi:10.1007/s10843-007-0016-0

Rodrigues, R. G., & Raposo, M. (2011). Entrepreneurial orientation, human resources information management, and firm performance in SMEs. *Canadian Journal of Administrative Sciences*, *28*(2), 143–153. doi:10.1002/cjas.205

Rugman, A. M., & Verbeke, A. (2004). A perspective on regional and global strategies of multinational enterprises. *Journal of International Business Studies*, *35*(1), 3–18. doi:10.1057/palgrave.jibs.8400073

Runyan, R. C., Ge, B., Dong, B., & Swinney, J. L. (2012). Entrepreneurial orientation in cross-cultural research: Assessing measurement invariance in the construct. *Entrepreneurship Theory and Practice*, *36*(4), 819–836. doi:10.1111/j.1540-6520.2010.00436.x

Rust, R. T., Lemon, K. N., & Zeithaml, V. A. (2004). Return on marketing: Using customer equity to focus marketing strategy. *Journal of Marketing*, *68*(1), 109–127. doi:10.1509/jmkg.68.1.109.24030

Ruzzier, M., Hisrich, R. D., & Antoncic, B. (2006). SME internationalization research: Past, present and future. *Journal of Small Business and Enterprise Development*, *13*(4), 476–497. doi:10.1108/14626000610705705

Salomon, R., & Jin, B. (2010). Do leading or lagging firms learn more from exporting? *Strategic Management Journal*, *31*(10), 1088–1113. doi:10.1002/smj.850

Sciascia, S., Naldi, L., & Hunter, E. (2006). Market orientation as determinant of entrepreneurship: An empirical investigation on SMEs. *The International Entrepreneurship and Management Journal*, *2*(1), 21–38. doi:10.1007/s11365-006-7087-6

Shah, D., Rust, R. T., Parasuraman, A., Staelin, R., & Day, G. S. (2006). The path to customer centricity. *Journal of Service Research*, *9*(2), 113–124. doi:10.1177/1094670506294666

Sharma, D. D., & Blomstermo, A. (2003). The internationalization process of born globals: A network view. *International Business Review*, *12*(6), 739–753. doi:10.1016/j.ibusrev.2003.05.002

Simsek, Z., Heavey, C., & Veiga, J. F. (2010). The impact of CEO core self-evaluation on the firms' entrepreneurial orientation. *Strategic Management Journal*, *31*(1), 110–119. doi:10.1002/smj.800

Smith, K. G., Collins, C. J., & Clark, K. D. (2005). Existing knowledge, knowledge creating capability, and the rate of new product introduction in high-technology firms. *Academy of Management Journal*, *48*(2), 346–357. doi:10.5465/AMJ.2005.16928421

Soriano, D. R., & Dobon, S. R. (2009). Linking globalization of entrepreneurship in small organizations. *Small Business Economics*, *32*(3), 233–239. doi:10.1007/s11187-008-9155-5

Spence, M. (2003). International strategy formation in small Canadian high-technology companies: A case study approach. *Journal of International Entrepreneurship*, *1*(3), 277–296. doi:10.1023/A:1024162823079

Spowart, M., & Wickramasekera, R. (2012). Explaining internationalisation of small to medium sized enterprises within the Queensland food and beverage industry. *International Journal of Business and Management*, *7*(6), 68–80. doi:10.5539/ijbm.v7n6p68

Stoian, M. C., Rialp, A., & Rialp, J. (2011). Export performance under the microscope: A glance through Spanish lenses. *International Business Review*, *20*(2), 117–135. doi:10.1016/j.ibusrev.2010.07.002

Su, Z., Xie, E., & Li, Y. (2011). Entrepreneurial orientation and firm performance in new ventures and established firms. *Journal of Small Business Management*, *49*(4), 558–577. doi:10.1111/j.1540-627X.2011.00336.x

Sui, S., & Baum, M. (2014). Internationalization strategy, firm resources and the survival of SMEs in the export market. *Journal of International Business Studies*, *45*(7), 821–841. doi:10.1057/jibs.2014.11

Sui, S., Morgan, H. M., & Baum, M. (2015). Internationalization of immigrant-owned SMEs: The role of language. *Journal of World Business*, *50*(4), 804–814. doi:10.1016/j.jwb.2015.04.002

Swoboda, B., & Olejnik, E. (2016). Linking processes and dynamic capabilities of international SMEs: The mediating effect of international entrepreneurial orientation. *Journal of Small Business Management*, *54*(1), 139–161. doi:10.1111/jsbm.12135

Tang, G., Chen, Y., & Jin, J. (2015). Entrepreneurial orientation and innovation performance: Roles of strategic HRM and technical turbulence. *Asia Pacific Journal of Human Resources*, *53*(2), 163–184. doi:10.1111/1744-7941.12053

Tang, Z., Kreiser, P. M., Marino, L., Dickson, P., & Weaver, K. M. (2009). A hierarchical perspective of the dimensions of entrepreneurial orientation. *The International Entrepreneurship and Management Journal*, *5*(2), 181–201. doi:10.1007/s11365-008-0097-9

Teece, D. (2007). Explicating dynamic capabilities: The nature and microfoundations of (sustainable) enterprise performance. *Strategic Management Journal*, *28*(13), 1319–1350. doi:10.1002/smj.640

Todd, P., & Javalgi, R. (2007). Internationalization of SMEs in India: Fostering entrepreneurship by leveraging information technology. *International Journal of Emerging Markets*, *2*(2), 166–180. doi:10.1108/17468800710739234

van Doorn, S., Jansen, J. J. P., van den Bosch, F. A. J., & Volberda, H. W. (2013). Entrepreneurial orientation and firm performance: Drawing attention to the senior team. *Journal of Product Innovation Management*, *30*(5), 821–836. doi:10.1111/jpim.12032

Wales, W. J., Parida, V., & Patel, P. C. (2013). Too much of a good thing? Absorptive capacity, firm performance, and the moderating role of entrepreneurial orientation. *Strategic Management Journal*, *34*(5), 622–633. doi:10.1002/smj.2026

Wang, C., & Kafouros, M. I. (2009). What factors determine innovation performance in emerging economies? Evidence from China. *International Business Review*, *18*(6), 606–616. doi:10.1016/j.ibusrev.2009.07.009

Wang, C. L. (2008). Entrepreneurial orientation, learning orientation, and firm performance. *Entrepreneurship Theory and Practice*, *32*(4), 635–657. doi:10.1111/j.1540-6520.2008.00246.x

Westhead, P., Wright, M., & Ucbasaran, D. (2004). Internationalization of private firms: Environmental turbulence and organizational strategies and resources. *Entrepreneurship & Regional Development*, *16*(6), 501–522. doi:10.1080/0898562042000231929

Wiklund, J., & Shepherd, D. (2003). Knowledge-based resources, entrepreneurial orientation, and the performance of small and medium-sized businesses. *Strategic Management Journal*, *24*(13), 1307–1314. doi:10.1002/smj.360

Wiklund, J., & Shepherd, D. (2011). Where to from here? EO-as-experimentation, failure, and distribution of outcomes. *Entrepreneurship Theory and Practice*, *35*(5), 925–946. doi:10.1111/j.1540-6520.2011.00454.x

Wu, W. Y., Chang, M. L., & Chen, C. W. (2008). Promoting innovation through the accumulation of intellectual capital, social capital, and entrepreneurial orientation. *R & D Management*, *38*(3), 265–277.

Yao, X., Wen, W., & Ren, Z. (2009). Corporate entrepreneurship in the enterprise clusters environment: Influence of network resources and entrepreneurial orientation on firm performance. *Frontiers of Business Research in China*, *3*(4), 566–582. doi:10.1007/s11782-009-0027-x

Zahra, S. A., & Hayton, J. C. (2008). The effect of international venturing on firm performance: The moderating influence of absorptive capacity. *Journal of Business Venturing*, *23*(2), 195–220. doi:10.1016/j.jbusvent.2007.01.001

Zellweger, T., & Sieger, P. (2012). Entrepreneurial orientation in long-lived family firms. *Small Business Economics*, *38*(1), 67–84. doi:10.1007/s11187-010-9267-6

Zhang, M., Sarker, S., & Sarker, S. (2007). *Drivers and effects of IT capability in "born-global" firms: A cross-national study*. Paper presented at the 28th International Conference on Information Systems (ICIS 2007), Montreal, Canada.

Zhang, M., Sarker, S., & Sarker, S. (2013). Drivers and export performance impacts of IT capability in "born-global" firms: A cross-national study. *Information Systems Journal*, *23*(5), 419–443. doi:10.1111/j.1365-2575.2012.00404.x

Zhang, X., Ma, X., & Wang, Y. (2012). Entrepreneurial orientation, social capital, and the internationalization of SMES: Evidence from China. *Thunderbird International Business Review*, *54*(2), 195–210. doi:10.1002/tie.21451

Zhou, L., Wu, A., & Barnes, B. R. (2012). The effects of early internationalization on performance outcomes in young international ventures: The mediating role of marketing capabilities. *Journal of International Marketing*, *20*(4), 882–905. doi:10.1509/jim.12.0076

Zortea-Johnston, E., Darroch, J., & Matear, S. (2012). Business orientations and innovation in small and medium sized enterprises. *The International Entrepreneurship and Management Journal*, *8*(2), 145–164. doi:10.1007/s11365-011-0170-7

Zou, H., & Ghauri, P. N. (2010). Internationalizing by learning: The case of Chinese high-tech new ventures. *International Marketing Review*, *27*(2), 223–244. doi:10.1108/02651331011037539

Zucchella, A., Palamara, G., & Denicolai, S. (2007). The drivers of the early internationalization of the firm. *Journal of World Business*, *42*(3), 268–280. doi:10.1016/j.jwb.2007.04.008

Zucchella, A., & Servais, P. (2012). The internationalisation process of small- and medium-sized firms and the liability of complexity. *International Journal of Entrepreneurship and Small Business*, *15*(2), 191–212. doi:10.1504/IJESB.2012.045204

ADDITIONAL READING

Anderson, B. S., Kreiser, P. M., Kuratko, D. F., Hornsby, J. S., & Eshima, Y. (2015). Reconceptualizing entrepreneurial orientation. *Strategic Management Journal*, *36*(10), 1579–1596. doi:10.1002/smj.2298

Clarke, J. E., Tamaschke, R., & Liesch, P. W. (2013). International experience in international business research: A conceptualization and exploration of key themes. *International Journal of Management Reviews*, *15*(3), 265–279. doi:10.1111/j.1468-2370.2012.00338.x

Covin, J. G., & Miller, D. (2014). International entrepreneurial orientation: Conceptual considerations, research themes, measurement issues, and future research directions. *Entrepreneurship Theory and Practice*, *38*(1), 11–44. doi:10.1111/etap.12027

Etemad, H. (2015). The promise of a potential theoretical framework in international entrepreneurship: An entrepreneurial orientation-performance relation in internationalized context. *Journal of International Entrepreneurship*, *13*(2), 89–95. doi:10.1007/s10843-015-0157-5

Fernhaber, S. A., & Li, D. (2013). International exposure through network relationships: Implications for new venture internationalization. *Journal of Business Venturing*, *28*(2), 316–334. doi:10.1016/j.jbusvent.2012.05.002

Grünhagen, M., Wollan, M. L., Dada, O., & Watson, A. (2014). The moderating influence of HR operational autonomy on the entrepreneurial orientation–performance link in franchise systems. *The International Entrepreneurship and Management Journal*, *10*(4), 827–844. doi:10.1007/s11365-013-0270-7

Hohenthal, J., Johanson, J., & Johanson, M. (2014). Network knowledge and business-relationship value in the foreign market. *International Business Review*, *23*(1), 4–19. doi:10.1016/j.ibusrev.2013.08.002

Huang, K. P., & Wang, K. Y. (2013). The moderating effect of social capital and environmental dynamism on the link between entrepreneurial orientation and resource acquisition. *Quality & Quantity*, *47*(3), 1617–1628. doi:10.1007/s11135-011-9614-y

Jalali, A., Jaafar, M., & Ramayah, T. (2014). Entrepreneurial orientation and performance: The interaction effect of customer capital. *World Journal of Entrepreneurship. Management and Sustainable Development*, *10*(1), 48–68.

Jansen, R. J. G., Curseu, P. L., Vermeulen, P. A. M., Geurts, J. L. A., & Gibcus, P. (2013). Information processing and strategic decision making in small and medium-sized enterprises: The role of human and social capital in attaining decision effectiveness. *International Small Business Journal*, *31*(2), 192–216. doi:10.1177/0266242611406762

Karmann, T., Mauer, T., Flatten, T. C., & Brettel, M. (2016). Entrepreneurial orientation and corruption. *Journal of Business Ethics*, *133*(2), 223–234. doi:10.1007/s10551-014-2305-6

Kollmann, T., & Stöckmann, C. (2014). Filling the entrepreneurial orientation–performance gap: The mediating effects of exploratory and exploitative innovations. *Entrepreneurship Theory and Practice*, *38*(5), 1001–1026. doi:10.1111/j.1540-6520.2012.00530.x

Lehto, I. (2015). International entrepreneurial selling as construction of international opportunities. *Journal of International Entrepreneurship*, *13*(3), 277–302. doi:10.1007/s10843-015-0147-7

Moss, T. W., Neubaum, D. O., & Meyskens, M. (2015). The effect of virtuous and entrepreneurial orientations on microfinance lending and repayment: A signaling theory perspective. *Entrepreneurship Theory and Practice*, *39*(1), 27–52. doi:10.1111/etap.12110

Norbäck, P. J., Persson, L., & Douhan, R. (2014). Entrepreneurship policy and globalization. *Journal of Development Economics*, *110*, 22–38. doi:10.1016/j.jdeveco.2014.04.006

Omri, W., & Becuwe, A. (2014). Managerial characteristics and entrepreneurial internationalization: A study of Tunisian SMEs. *Journal of International Entrepreneurship*, *12*(1), 8–42. doi:10.1007/s10843-013-0119-8

Popescu, N. E. (2014). Entrepreneurship and SMEs Innovation in Romania. *Procedia Economics and Finance*, *16*, 512–520. doi:10.1016/S2212-5671(14)00832-6

Raymond, L., & St-Pierre, J. (2013). Strategic capability configurations for the internationalization of SMEs: A study in equifinality. *International Small Business Journal*, *31*(1), 82–102. doi:10.1177/0266242610391325

Saeed, S., Yousafzai, S. Y., & Engelen, A. (2014). On cultural and macroeconomic contingencies of the entrepreneurial orientation–performance relationship. *Entrepreneurship Theory and Practice*, *38*(2), 255–290. doi:10.1111/etap.12097

Sciascia, S., Mazzola, P., & Chirico, F. (2013). Generational involvement in the top management team of family firms: Exploring nonlinear effects on entrepreneurial orientation. *Entrepreneurship Theory and Practice*, *37*(11), 69–85. doi:10.1111/j.1540-6520.2012.00528.x

Spillecke, S. B., & Brettel, M. (2014). Antecedents and performance implications of a sales departments learning and entrepreneurial orientation in SMEs. *Journal of Small Business Management*, *52*(3), 407–426. doi:10.1111/jsbm.12041

Su, Z., Xie, E., & Wang, D. (2015). Entrepreneurial orientation, managerial networking, and new venture performance in China. *Journal of Small Business Management*, *53*(1), 228–248. doi:10.1111/jsbm.12069

Tang, Z., & Hull, C. (2012). An investigation of entrepreneurial orientation, perceived environmental hostility, and strategy application among Chinese SMEs. *Journal of Small Business Management*, *50*(1), 132–158. doi:10.1111/j.1540-627X.2011.00347.x

Vissak, T., & Zhang, X. (2014). Chinese immigrant entrepreneurs' involvement in internationalization and innovation: Three Canadian cases. *Journal of International Entrepreneurship*, *12*(2), 183–201. doi:10.1007/s10843-014-0128-2

Wales, W., Gupta, V., & Mousa, F. (2013). Empirical research on entrepreneurial orientation: An assessment and suggestions for future research. *International Small Business Journal*, *31*(4), 357–383. doi:10.1177/0266242611418261

Wolfe, M. T., & Shepherd, D. A. (2015). "Bouncing back" from a loss: Entrepreneurial orientation, emotions, and failure narratives. *Entrepreneurship Theory and Practice*, *39*(3), 675–700. doi:10.1111/etap.12057

Yener, M., Doğruoğlu, B., & Ergun, S. (2014). Challenges of internationalization for SMEs and overcoming these challenges: A case study from Turkey. *Procedia: Social and Behavioral Sciences*, *150*, 2–11. doi:10.1016/j.sbspro.2014.09.002

Yu, L., Orazem, P. F., & Jolly, R. W. (2014). Entrepreneurship over the business cycle. *Economics Letters*, *122*(2), 105–110. doi:10.1016/j.econlet.2013.10.036

KEY TERMS AND DEFINITIONS

Entrepreneur: A person who organizes, operates, and assumes the risk for a business venture.

Entrepreneurship: The capacity and willingness to organize and manage a business venture along with any of its risks in order to make a profit.

Innovation: The process of translating an idea or invention into a product or service that creates value.

Internationalization: The growing tendency of companies to operate across national boundaries.

Knowledge Management: The strategies and processes designed to identify, capture, value, and share an organization's intellectual assets to enhance the competitiveness.

Marketing: The strategic functions involve in identifying and appealing to the particular groups of consumers, often including activities such as advertising, branding, pricing, and sales.

Market Orientation: The business approach or philosophy that focuses on identifying and meeting the stated or hidden needs or wants of customers.

Organizational Learning: The organization-wide continuous process that enhances its collective ability to accept, make sense of, and respond to the internal and external change.

Research and Development: The systematic activity combining both basic and applied research, and aimed at discovering the solutions to problems or creating the new products and knowledge.

Section 3
Recognising and Seizing Opportunities for SMEs

Chapter 12

Innovation Culture as a Mediator Between Specific Human Capital and Innovation Performance Among Bumiputera SMEs in Malaysia

Haniruzila Hanifah
Universiti Sains Malaysia, Malaysia

Noor Hazlina Ahmad
Universiti Sains Malaysia, Malaysia

Hasliza Abdul Halim
Universiti Sains Malaysia, Malaysia

Ali Vafaei-Zadeh
Universiti Sains Malaysia, Malaysia

ABSTRACT

SMEs in Malaysia are dominated by Bumiputera that represent more than 50% of the Malaysian SME's population. However, there are many challenges faced by Bumiputera SMEs such as limited skilled workers, lack of creativity and knowledge. In this point of view, considering the specific human capital approach, the value, uniqueness, creativity, innovativeness and proactiveness are the most relevant features for innovation performance. To have an excellent innovation performance is to have an innovative culture where entrepreneurs needs to have creative employees which simultaneously improve the innovation performance in Bumiputera SMEs. This study focuses mainly on owner-manager of Bumiputera SMEs. It provides useful pointers to entrepreneurs and policy makers on the importance of specific human capital, innovative culture and enhancing innovation performance in Bumiputera SMEs.

INTRODUCTION

Small and medium enterprise (SME) plays an important role in Malaysia economic development. The government of Malaysia has constantly recognized that SMEs is a major factor in injecting investment and transforming Malaysia into a developed nation by 2020. According to Small and Medium Industries Development Corporation, the sectors in SME is based on the annual sales turnover or number of full

DOI: 10.4018/978-1-5225-2165-5.ch012

time employees. There are two sectors which divided into; manufacturing, manufacturing related services and agriculture industries; and services (including ICT) and primary agriculture (SMECorp., 2015).

According to SMECorp, 98.1% (591,883 of total business establishments) of the SMEs are in the services sector, 95.4% in the manufacturing sector and only 76% is in the agricultural sector (SMECorp., 2015). The SME provides 59.5% of the nation's employment and despite having 99.2 percent of the total number of business establishments in Malaysia it contributes to merely 1/3 or 32% of the nation's GDP (National SME Development Council, 2012). In year 2010, according to National SME Development Council (2012), SMEs performance showed many positive indicators such as increase in sales, increase in new orders, introduction of new products, business expansions within the country and even expansion to other countries. Based on technical analysis by Malaysia data from SME Masterplan 2012-2020, six key areas influence the SMEs performance. These six performance keys are:

1. Innovation and technology adoption.
2. Human capital development.
3. Access to financing.
4. Market access.
5. Legal and regulatory environment.
6. Infrastructure.

These keys serve as the benchmark that would encourage SMEs to enhance their productivity and performance (Masterplan S.M.E, 2013). However, SMEs in Malaysia dominant by Bumiputera where represented more than 50% of the Malaysian SME's population because Bumiputera is known as a son of the soil in Malaysia as compared to Chinese, India and other races (Awang et al, 2009). According to 11th Malaysia Plan, only 37.4% or 241,281 of the total 645,136 SMEs were owned by Bumiputera and 90.7% or 218,930 of Bumiputera SMEs are micro enterprises (11MP). Unfortunately, Bumiputera SMEs continually fail to secure larger share and they only can manage to share less than 20% of the Malaysian economy as well as the GDP of Bumiputera SMEs in 2015 was only about 16% (ETP Annual Report, 2014). Based on EPU (2015), There is a need to grow Bumiputera SMEs to match non-Bumiputera SME contribution to the GDP by year 2020 to at least a 50:50 ratio.

In order to continuous effort to increase the growth and to achieve the contribution of 20% GDP by year 2020 as well as includes encouraging the participation of Bumiputra SME's in the 12 National Key Economic Areas (NKEAs). Therefore, TERAJU launched a programme known as TERAS which is aims to increase the Bumiputera SMEs' participation in the economy by enabling SMEs to scale up, accelerate their growth and could compete in the open market (ETP Annual Report, 2014). In addition, the promotion of Bumiputera into business is often seen as a socioeconomic initiative engineered by the Malaysian government. The respective policies under the New Economic Policy (NEP) and National Development Policy (NDP) sought to enhance and intensify the participation of Bumiputera economic and business ventures (Zainol & Daud, 2011). Therefore, 11th Malaysian Plan aims to strengthening the Bumiputera socio-economic development focusing on areas such as equity ownership in the corporate sector as well as asset ownership (11MP). It was intended to work in concert with New Economic Model (NEM) as a comprehensive development approach that is based on growth in equity to ensure all communities in Malaysia will obtain the benefits from economic development and the nation's riches (NEM, 2012). Apparently, government efforts to inculcate and inspire Bumiputera SMEs to become a game-changer and a risk-taker by exploring new possible platforms (Hashim, 2013). Against this backdrop, Malaysia government encourage Bumiputera SMEs to be innovative, creative and proactive in order to move towards innovation-centred economy.

This is because innovation performance in Malaysia SMEs very low which proven by The global innovation index showed that Malaysia was ranked 33 in 2014 compared 31 in 2011, 28 in 2010 and 26 in 2008 (Rasiah & Yap, 2014). This indicated that Malaysia rung down from the previous year. Malaysia's innovation performance has declined compared to other countries and is lower than Singapore, Hong Kong and China. Nevertheless, Malaysia's ranking as reported by the Global Index for the past five years has been stagnant. In terms of innovation output index, Malaysia was ranked 35, creative output was ranked 39 and innovation efficiency index was ranked 72 (Rasiah & Yap, 2014). Why this happened? One of the reason is lack of skilled workers (Omar & Azmi, 2016). They do not have skilled manpower because they could not afford to pay high salaries and unable to develop career development programmes for their employees. Thus, entrepreneurs seen to be less creative, lack of originality, and innovativeness (Omar & Azmi, 2016). Also, they lack experience of technological capability due to insufficient capital to acquire technology that may actually be very pertinent for them to be competitive and have a strong market position (Gilroy, 2013).

In that vein, Malaysia has to strengthen its capability to innovate, adapt and create indigenous technology, design, develop and market new products (MOSTI, 2010). The question is how to innovate? Study by Shafirad and Atei (2012) said that, creativity and innovative thinking are crucial to encourage innovation and this situation is driven by the culture of the organizations. It implies that culture is the core of innovation. In order to do so, Malaysia government needs to promote the innovative culture among Bumiputera SMEs since innovation is considered as a seed that needs to be cultivated. It is because innovative culture plays an important role for SMEs to expand their business growth in both local and global market. As many SMEs are facing with the same problem which is low innovativeness among employees, organization culture could advocate them to focus on which dimension of culture that would further stimulate high-end product innovation and results in higher competitive advantage (Abdullah et al., 2014). Many successful SMEs relies on their strong innovative culture that gives them direction to what they want to achieve. Top SMEs usually engraves and highly value their company's mission and vision, employees' performance and consistency, as well as active employees' participation in company's activities (Hsieh, 2010). Compared to ordinary SMEs, SMEs with innovative culture accelerates much faster in product differences and dimension (Voon, 2014). Therefore, to be successful in business, SMEs Bumiputera need to cultivate the culture of innovation which may encourage them to be more creative and innovative in operating their daily businesses. To have the innovative culture, Bumiputera SME must have the specific human capital where it can enhance the innovation performance as well as need to boost their research and development (R&D) spending to promote competitive advantage among employees (Al-Amin, 2013). Therefore, Malaysian Government plays an important role to develop specific human capital in Bumiputera entrepreneurs.

Challenges in Bumiputera SMEs

Notwithstanding the increase in the number of the SME establishments' and many other positive indicators such as improvement in product quality, enhance productivity of output, boost profit and market share, increase the business performance, strengthen networking of Bumiputera SMEs and create competitive advantage (Kohar, 2013). Nevertheless, there are still several challenges in Bumiputera SMEs which preventing them from growing further and putting them in a desperate position to face the new challenges arising from globalization, liberalization and extensive organizational, institutional and technological change.

Based on Omar and Azmi (2016), most of Bumiputera entrepreneurs failed in business because of weakness in management which make they cannot survive and cannot afford to be greater even though they are being so long in business arena. This is because of less effective performance management function, particularly with regards to decision making. Decision making is need to be on entrepreneurs who have tacit knowledge towards business. Unfortunately, Bumiputera SMEs still lack of creativity and knowledge, limited skilled workers, and produce low productivity (Talebi & Tajeddin, 2010).

One of the reason why SME sector is still lack of creative and skill employees because Malaysian SMEs they are not able to offer salaries and condition of service as well as unable to provide training schemes for employees. This is the challenges faced by Bumiputera SMEs where large firms offer better employment condition, however, leaving SME with less educated, low skill employees and lack of employee's commitment to handle business operation will affect SME sector (Omar & Azmi, 2016).

Other than that, Bumiputera SME still faces many challenges from high cost of raw materials, rising overhead costs, financing and credit issues, no access to latest technology tools, high regulatory costs and lack of managerial capabilities, lack of state government support (Omar & Azmi, 2016; National SME Development Council, 2012; Muhammad et al., 2010; Samad, 2007; Aris, 2007). This will turn them to low creativity and innovative performance.

Besides, to achieve an objective to be innovation led-economy, they need to be innovative. However, the objectives of small enterprises will also vary therefore continuous growth cannot be assumed as an objective. The only objective common to the whole small business sector seems to be that of survival, as the risk of failure is high (Rohra & Junejo, 2009). These constraints will contribute to Bumiputera SME inability to compete in cost and in a long term may lead to their business failure. Therefore, by having excellence knowledge, specific skill and innovative of entrepreneurs can lead to innovation performance.

LITERATURE REVIEW

Bumiputera SMEs

In today's quickened world, with its gushing information, uncertain global economy, confounding options and ever-morphing culture, SMEs must be able to move in-line with ever-growing technology and consistently educating their organization for technology changes. In global market, lots of business industries start to form due to correlation of innovation and technology (Aris, 2007). In Malaysia, among notable increasing business venture in that particular area are online retails, halal bio-technology, and animation production. Online retails are new and the trend is expanding among general SMEs because of ever increasing number of consumers to online shopping platforms at an exponential speed (Chow et al., 2014). Compared to traditional and stagnant business operation, technology offers a much more flexibility to modern SMEs in managing their business. Furthermore, SMEs can gain access to enormous amount of free advice and resources which could assist them to reach bigger market (Bridge, 2012).

Moreover, rather than spending money on creating website, SMEs also could take advantage on the use free web-based platforms such as Facebook and blog to promote their business (Hairuddin et al., 2012). On the other side, halal bio-technology specifically receives full support from Malaysia government since year 2001 because it holds a large captured market which is Muslim society (Bakar et al., 2014). For Malaysia is known as an Islamic country and a leader in Organization of Islamic Country (OIC), this new business industry could bring Malaysia a step closer to becoming a new halal-hub for global market demand (Bakar et al., 2014). Furthermore, halal bio-technology also act as another approach by the government to expand Bumiputera SMEs business growth. Although development of halal bio-technology is still on the early stage of maturation, but it is a promising sector which could be led by Bumiputera SMEs due to Muslim majority in Bumiputera category (Siaw & Rani, 2012). In relation to Bumiputera SMEs development, government began to encourage Bumiputera participation in animation industry when it made its breakthrough to local market in year 1683. However, the progress of animation industry in Malaysia is extremely slow until year 2009, when a Bumiputera SME company known by Les' Copaque Production Sdn Bhd made a major leap by penetrated global market through animation film "Geng: The Adventure Begins" (Yee, 2009). Les Copaque is one of among successful Bumiputera SMEs in Malaysia who managed to adopt, align, and deliver splendid business performance through creativity and innovation. Starting with just a few employees, Les' Copaque expands rapidly in terms of growth. Along the expansion road, Les' Copaque faced several difficulties including lack of resources, limited equipment, and technical skills. However, they managed to get through by maximizing whatever resources they had, using local equipment rather than outsource from neighbor country, and also came out with a 'pipeline' workflow for the production (Yee, 2009). Their success also had a strong link with government's aid during the animation production. Government provided assistance and support in terms of financial grant and privileges access to high-end equipment at Ministry of Science, Technology, and Innovation (MOSTI) for Les Copaque's animation purposes. Government believes that Bumiputera entrepreneurs should be participate in these strategic sectors which can promise them high returns (Hamidon, 2009)

Innovation Performance

Today's business environment is dynamic and changing extremely. In order to compete and sustain in business, an organizations have to introduce innovative product continuously. It is an idea, which has the purpose of changing an actual state. Innovations can be embodied through products, processes or services and can incorporate something that in its present form has not been available before (Galbraith, 1982). There is a fundamental distinction between radical innovations and incremental innovations. These two kinds of innovation can, considering some research findings, be complemented by architectural innovations (O'Reilly & Tushman, 2004). Definition of radical innovation is a complete change from the existing product and service (Damanpour 1991; Pohl & Elmquist, 2010) where it includes reorientation of activities and nonroutine innovation that differ significantly from current practices. According to Banu Goktan & Miles (2011), radical innovation occurred within longer time-frame for at least 50 years. Therefore, borrowing previous innovation, as in the form of shared core technology, ancillary components, shared functional (application) or shared-look-and feel, can shorten the time taken due to the reduction of activities. However, the definition of incremental innovation is involved exploitation of new opportunities by performing improvements on the existing products in order to align it with the arising opportunities (Farooquie et al, 2012; Bhaskaran, 2006; and Damanpour, 1991). Thus, the outputs of incremental innovation are almost similar to firms' existing products or services. Therefore, this study focuses on the innovation performance among Bumiputera SMEs in which the SMEs owners need to pursue incremental innovation (exploitation). Why Bumiputera SME needs to apply incremental innovation rather than radical innovation? As stated by Chang, Hughes and Hutho (2011) said that radical innovation is a research aspect of the R&D process while incremental innovation captures the development element for product and services so that through radical activities SMEs can maximize the result of today and to secure their survival tomorrow they need to do incremental practices. On the contrary, based on McDermott and Prajogo (2012), radical innovation and incremental innovation are suitable for large and multi-unit firms. This is because large organizations have significant budgets and formal R&D centers to execute major changes in the products and services. In fact, the used of radical innovation is very uncertain and not applicable among SMEs. Supported by Oke et al. (2007), SMEs tend to adopt incremental innovation rather than radical innovation in their business operations.

Realizing the importance of innovation performance among Bumiputera SME as it has a promising future particularly to drive Malaysia towards Vision 2020 to become innovation led-economy (11MP, 2016). They are encouraged to develop new products and services, organisational structure, culture, strategic and managerial concepts when determine the innovative performance. Notably, by developing these elements, Bumiputera SMEs have the ability to achieve a solid and competitive position in the market. In fact, innovative performance is an important aspect which allows the Bumiputera SMEs to improve their flexibility and competitive position (Halim et al., 2015)

Innovative Culture

To succeed today, organizations are challenged to infuse the kind of innovativeness which not only ensure the organization survival but develop an excellence in the global marketplace (Seen, Singh, & Jayasingam, 2012). Studies have found innovation has a positive effect on performance in SME and underline the importance for entrepreneurs in SME to develop innovation diligently (Rosenbusch et al., 2011). Besides, innovation being an element of organizational culture where it helps to build a proactive and entrepreneurial organization (Naranjo-Valencia, Jiménez-Jiménez, & Sanz-Valle, 2011; Johannessen et al., 2001) that has become widely recognized as a key to competitive success and maintain competitive advantage (Francis and Bessant, 2005). Most entrepreneurs are aware of the organization culture that has become well established in the Malaysia over the past two decades (Ismail & R. Abdmajid, 2007). Thus, organizations have been aggressively instilling innovation in its culture where it is to steer the organization to maintain competitive advantage (Zeng & Saixing, 2016).

Previous study by Morgan (1997) has stated that organizations can be retain and improve their innovative, competitiveness and capabilities by fusing a culture sharing to the employees into the overall strategic direction of the organization. It is because organizational culture is a powerful determinant of the innovative potential and ability to sustain an innovative-supportive culture (Durendez et al, 2011). According to Martins and Terblanche (2003) and Deshpande and Webster (1989) define organizational culture as "the pattern of shared values and beliefs that help individuals understand organizational functioning and thus provide them with norms for behavior in the organization".

In that manner, culture plays an important role in enhancing innovation within organizations which can improve organization performance (Zeng & Saixing, 2016). For example, excellence cultures ranked higher in producing new product and expected to grow more in the future, based on growth assumptions in their stock prices. On the other hand, a balanced culture also can help an organization to be innovative (Ashley and Bryan, 2009). With this standpoint, Malaysian government has put an extra effort to encourage the innovativeness among Bumiputera SMEs specially to move Malaysia into the innovation-led economy. This is clearly highlighted by the Prime Minister of Malaysia, Dato Seri Najib Tun Razak, Malaysia aspires to reach the highest standards with regard to the entrepreneurs' skills, knowledge and abilities to reach the innovation-centred economy (11MP, 2016).

In order to become more creative, productive, competitive and avoid being left behind from the progress and innovations at par with world standards, SMEs Bumiputera need to search business success recipe in exploring changes in products, services, process or business models (Mohd Nasir, 2012). Therefore, to be successful in business, SMEs Bumiputera need to cultivate the culture of innovation which may encourage them to be more creative and innovative in operating their daily businesses. Kanter (1983) suggested organizations to embrace a "culture of pride and climate of success" to enhance employees' innovative culture within the organization and at the same increase the organization's performance.

Specific Human Capital

As global business environment is gradually transformed into knowledge-based economy, human capital becomes increasingly visible to affect business performance (Crook et al., 2011). According to Sharabati et al (2010), human capital defined as it is embedded in the mind of individuals that comprises of the accumulated knowledge, creativity, and innovativeness of employees in organization which can be used to extract the best solution for the organization. In addition, human capital is also related to the willingness of individual in sharing their knowledge, abilities that allow for changes in action, experience as well as skills in organization to enhance performance of the firm and economic growth (Baron, 2011; Coleman, 1988). The previous study of Wang et al (2009), categorized human capital into general and specific human capital which refer to explicit or implicit knowledge. Tacit knowledge is related to entrepreneurs' general knowledge about business, while tacit knowledge is related to specific knowledge, skills and experience in conducting the business.

Therefore, according to Wang et al (2009), specific human capital can be associated with the specific industry knowledge, experience, training, and skills and possible to be obtained through learning process. Prior researcher has proposed that specific human capital play an important role in the generation of innovative activity within an industry if it characterized by high quality knowledge exchange among employees in the organization.

As entrepreneurs in SMEs they need to attend industrial related training, seminar and professional advice which will provides them with guidelines to start and run particular business and ascertain firms what they need to know and what is the best approach for them to market their products (Lampadarios, 2015). Considering the specific human capital approach, the value, uniqueness, creativity, innovativeness and proactiveness are the most relevant features for innovation performance (De Jong & Wennekers, 2008). These assumptions raise issues on which characteristics of knowledge enable innovation in organization. This is because creative entrepreneurs must deal with novel, fresh and ambiguous problem, they tend to display strong, valuable and irreplaceable knowledge and skills (Halim et al, 2014; Mumford, 2000). These conditions can only be produced by specific human capital, which is positively associated with innovations. Employees with abilities are willing to experiment and apply new knowledge (Halim et al, 2014; Taggar, 2002).

HYPOTHESES DEVELOPMENT

Figure 1 exhibits the conceptual framework in this study. This is advanced for further empirical investigation where it is mainly probed into relationship between the specific human capital, innovation culture and innovation performance.

Specific Human Capital and Innovative Culture

Culture influences the behavior of the employees, which paves the way towards accepting innovation as a significant asset of the firm and the employees feel more committed to their organization (Jan, Shah & Khan, 2014). Employees is the variable asset of the companies especially talented employees. Talent can be defining as an innate capacity, which enables people to give an extra-ordinary high performance in a particular area that demands some specific skills and training (Simonton, 1999). Specific human capital pertains to specific skills and knowledge that are valuable only within a specific firm. Although specific skills may give firms an advantage over their competitors as these skills are not transferable to other firms and advantage over their competitors.

Lund Vinding (2006) stated that highly educated employees through their daily tasks will increase their knowledge of the organization and this is a main contributor to know-how which implies that they will be in the better position to recognize and value new external knowledge. Formalized knowledge, tacit knowledge is an important component of innovation (Halim et al, 2014). Therefore, they found that specific knowledge has a positive influence on employees or managers innovative behaviour.

Previous studies investigated the relationship between organisational culture and intellectual capital (Lai, 2002; Wang, 2012; Santos- Rodrigues et al., 2013) in which they have posited that a high efficiency, supportive culture will lead to enhancement of intellectual capital such as human capital, innovation capital and process capital. These assumptions raise issues on which characteristics of culture that promotes knowledge which enable innovation. This is because creative people must possess specific knowledge that deal with novel, fresh and ambiguous problems and they tend to display strong, valuable and irreplaceable knowledge and skills (Mumford, 2000). These conditions can only be produced by specific human capital, which is positively triggered by positive innovative culture. Hence, it is hypothesized that:

Figure 1. Conceptual framework

Hypothesis 1: There are positive relationship between specific human capital and innovative culture among Bumiputera SMEs.

Innovative Culture and Innovation Performance

Innovation is a key driver for organization's performance and now universally accepted. In this respect, innovation plays an important role in organization but beyond their enthusiasm for bright ideas, most entrepreneurs know that to be successful over the long term they have to develop a strong innovative culture (Dobni, 2008; Hacioglu et al, 2012). To achieve innovation performance, organization can have a set of organization-wide shared beliefs, ideas, behaviors, and their past experience (Morris, 2007). In addition, organization that inculcate culture in their organization for future survival will have useful incremental innovation in doing business (Shafirad & Ataei, 2011; O'cass & Ngo, 2007).

For the purpose of this research, innovation culture has been considered as a multi-dimensional context which encompasses the intention to be innovative, the infrastructure to support innovation, innovation influence on market orientation and value orientation as well as environment to implement innovation (Dobni, 2008, Halim et al 2014; Halim et al 2015). Taking this into account, to develop and sustain a culture of innovation, Bumiputera SMEs need to have a more organizational constituency and innovation propensity which trust, communication and network are optimal, structural flexibility, empowered employee's creativity, risk taking, orientation, learning and knowledge are tolerated. In that vein, with the right mix of these factors, innovative culture has the potential to prosper in organization (Halim et al., 2014; Halim et al., 2015). Moreover, it is imperative for the organizations to improve the innovative culture so that all the employees can become alert, creative and innovative to drive the organisation (Skerlavaj et al. 2010, Halim et al., 2015).

From this vintage point, organization that an adapt innovative culture has a positive influence on performance (Ngo & Loi, 2008; Tushman & O'Reilly, 2013). Hence, successful operation in business environment is required to understand the culture of the organisations. As the innovative culture plays a crucial role in performance development, the current study proposes that Bumiputera SMEs innovative performance can be enhanced through the innovative culture of the organizations. Hence,

Hypothesis 2: Innovative culture has a positive relationship on innovation performance among Bumiputera SMEs.

Innovative Culture Mediates the Relationship Specific Human Capital and Innovation Performance

Specific human capital is important to the firm-level innovation. For example, employees who have better training are usually more efficient and can develop a new skill effectively, an essential part of firm-level innovation (Al-Laham et al, 2011). The influence of specific human capital on innovation performance has been proved in the previous studies (Jan et al., 2014). Thus, the current study believes that innovative culture plays as mediating role in the relationship.

Specific human capital may result in enhancing innovative culture for instance, sharing specific knowledge, willingness or attitudes towards the creativity, specific skills and innovativeness of their tasks and apply to its organization (Halim, Ahmad, Ramayah, & Hanifah, 2014). In turn, the organisation may be able to enjoy higher organisational competitiveness and innovative performance (Asplund,

2003). It shows that owner-manager in organizations with high pool of specific knowledge and specific skills can transform the employees' knowledge, and ideas into products and services tailored to customer needs. These innovations are then manifested into a new product, service, technology or administrative practice. In short, innovative performance is enhanced by leveraging on the innovative culture through specific human capital. In line with the discussion above, the following hypothesis is postulated:

Hypothesis 3: Innovative culture mediates the relationship between specific human capital and innovation performance.

METHODOLOGY

Research Design

This empirical research is quantitative method strategy which is phase to test and generalize the initial findings (Cresweel & Plano Clark, 2011). The data will be collect by means of self-administered questionnaires which will be distribute to Malaysian small and medium entreprises (SMEs). The subjects in this study will consists of business owners-managers of SMEs operating in Peninsular Malaysia. This study is a cross-sectional design in which it is implemented only once and represents a snapshot of one point in time in an uncontrolled setting (Sekaran & Bougie, 2010; Cooper & Schindler, 2008). A cross-sectional design is appropriate for this study because the data collected reflects the phenomenon of the situation and the behaviour of the individual; and the organisation environment is assumed to be constant at different point in time (Cooper & Schindler, 2008). Since this study focus mainly on Bumiputera entrepreneurs, the definitions of SMEs provided by Small and Medium Industries Development Corporation Malaysia will be used to identify appropriate business for inclusion in this study. The criteria meet the following specifications for inclusion: (1) only active, current and registered Bumiputera SMEs in TERAS database from the year 2011-2014. An active and current Bumiputera SMEs which are listed in the database of Program Syarikat Bumiputera Berprestasi Tinggi (TERAS). It is because TERAS aims to increase Bumiputera SMEs' participation in the economy by enabling SMEs to scale up, accelerate their growth and compete in the open market (11MP); (2) the organisation is classified as belonging to an innovative sector; (3) the business must have less than 150 employees for manufacturing sector and less than 50 employees for service sector.

Data Collection

A structured set of questionnaires is the instrument used in this study to gather the relevant data to answer the research questions. To lessen any response biasness, the questionnaire will be designed in two languages—English and Malay. Participants will be invited to respond to the questionnaire in the language that they are most comfortable with and that they commonly used in their daily work life. Respondents are given within seven (7) days to complete the questionnaire and return them back to the sender. If there is no response has been made by the owners or managers, a friendly call will be made to alert the respondent about returning the complete questionnaires.

In operationalizing specific human capital questions, the study adapted the items of human capital from Sharabati et al. (2010). There are nine items that will be used for this study and will be assessed based on 7-point Likert scale (1=Strongly disagree and 7=strongly agree). For innovation culture which is adapted from Dobni (2008), five-point Likert scale ranging from 1=strongly disagree to 5=strongly agree will be used to measure the extent to which respondents agree or disagree to each of the statement. There are six questions to measure the innovative performance. A five point Likert type-scale ranging from "Strongly Disagree" to "Strongly Agree" will be use and adapted from Denan, Ismail, & Ishak (2009).

Pre testing will be implement and the feedback provide to help in refining the questionnaires. This is because pre-testing is conduct to check the questionnaire for face and content validity, content relevance, readability, and to proof read the comprehensiveness, syntax errors and the general format layout. The instruments will be validating by the experts and once the instrument is finalized the actual data collection will be done. Thus, the questionnaires will be send to respondents which is Bumiputera SME business owner-manager from services and manufacturing sectors. These respondents were excluded from the sample size of this study. Feedbacks from two academicians will be seek for their feedback and comments. After considering their comments and suggestions obtained from the experts, the items of the questionnaires will be edit and interpret before collect the data.

Data Analysis

This study will apply two kinds of software: the SPSS 22 and SmartPLS 3.0 which were developed by Ringle, Wende, and Will (2005). SPSS will be used for data screening, demographic profiling, and descriptive statistics whereas the SMartPLS is use for hypothesis testing by means of Structural Equation Model (SEM) utilising the Partial Least Square approach.

The testing is divided into 2 parts:

1. Measurement Model (Instrument validation).
2. Structural Model (Hypothesis testing).

The measurement model in PLS is assessed in terms of item loadings and reliability coefficients (composite reliability), as well as the convergent and discriminant validity. The discriminant validity of the measures (the degree to which items differentiate among constructs or measure distinct concepts) will be assessed by examining the correlations between the measures of potentially overlapping constructs. The structural model in PLS is assessed by examining the path coefficients (standardized betas). T statistics are also calculated to assess the significance of these path coefficients. In addition, R2 is used as an indicator of the overall predictive strength of the model (Haenlein & Kaplan, 2004; Hair, Hult, et al., 2014; Henseler, Ringle, & Sinkovics, 2009; Urbach & Ahlemann, 2010).

DISCUSSION

The present study aims to examine the relationship between specific human capital on innovative culture as well as innovation performance among Bumiputera SMEs. Innovation is a key driver for organization to be successful in their business organization. It is because innovation can develop and sustain their competitive edge to continue to be successful. The concept of innovation has been closely studied in recent years, with strong interest shown by Malaysian Government Transformation Program and practicing managers due to its promise of providing enhanced competitiveness. Nonetheless, it seems that attention of innovation in Bumiputera SMEs still has been overlooked by previous researchers. It is certain that good research in the expanse of specific human capital, innovative culture and innovation performance will contribute to the existing literature on innovation management, business management and knowledge management.

In this respect, owners/managers need create innovative culture among employees and improve innovativeness in Bumiputera SMEs which particularly to move Malaysia into high income level by year 2020 because Bumiputera SME is considered as a backbone of the national economy. Moreover, owners/managers need to be more innovative and make more effective use of their organizational resource. It is because SMEs need to constantly acquire information on effective strategies to compete with large organizations and survive by being innovative and creative. Therefore, this study proposes to fill the gap in the body of knowledge in the practices of an innovative culture mediates relationship between specific human capital and innovation performance among Bumiputera SMEs. It is to investigate the impact of innovative culture on Bumiputera SMEs which can help employees to create more ideas, new products and services in Malaysia SMEs.

In this point of view, this study intends to facilitate the development and implementation of government to assist owners/managers to stay competitive in the marketplace. Government will be able to provide support for Bumiputera SMEs in their effort to stimulate the culture of innovation to enhance innovation performance. In this regards, the context of innovative culture among Bumiputera SME could be cultivated and furthered improved via structured programs and strategically crafted plan of actions to boost and create more innovative Bumiputera owners/managers amongst Malaysian SME. In this sense, the understanding of the specific human capital, innovative culture and innovation performance will add to the body of knowledge in innovation management literature, business management and knowledge management.

REFERENCES

Abdullah, N. H., Shamsuddin, A., Wahab, E., & Hamid, N. A. A. (2014). The relationship between organizational culture and product innovativeness. *Procedia: Social and Behavioral Sciences, 129*, 140–147. doi:10.1016/j.sbspro.2014.03.659

Al-Amin, M. (2013). *SMEs urged to adopt culture of innovation, boost R&D spending*. Retrieved January 10, 2016, from http:// www.smecorp.gov.my

Al-Laham, A., Tzabbar, D., & Amburgey, T. L. (2011). The dynamics of knowledge stocks and knowledge flows: Innovation consequences of recruitment and collaboration in biotech. *Industrial and Corporate Change*, *20*(2), 555–583. doi:10.1093/icc/dtr001

Aris, N. M. (2007). SMEs: Building blocks for economic growth. *Journal of Department of Statistics, Malaysia*, *1*(1), 1–14.

Ashley, G. M., & Bryan, A. (2009). Organizational culture and innovation: exploring the link. 11th Annual Best of Organizational Development Summit, Chicago, IL.

Asplund, R. (2003). *Flexibility and Competitiveness: Labour Market Flexibility, Innovation and Organisational Performance*. Helsinki: ETLA, The Research Institute of the Finnish Economy Discussion Paper, 875.

Awang, A., Khalid, S. A., Kassim, K. M., Ismail, M., Zain, R. S., & Madar, A. R. S. (2009). Entrepreneurial orientation and performance relations of Malaysian Bumiputera SMEs: The impact of some perceived environmental factors. *International Journal of Business and Management*, *4*(9), 84. doi:10.5539/ijbm.v4n9p84

Bakar, S. A., Sulaiman, M., & Osman, I. (2014). Exploring the relationship between business factors and performance in the Malaysian halal biotechnology SMEs context. *Procedia: Social and Behavioral Sciences*, *121*, 243–252. doi:10.1016/j.sbspro.2014.01.1125

Banu Goktan, A., & Miles, G. (2011). Innovation speed and radicalness: Are they inversely related? *Management Decision*, *49*(4), 533–547. doi:10.1108/00251741111126477

Baron, A. (2011). Measuring human capital. *Strategic HR Review*, *10*(2), 30–35. doi:10.1108/14754391111108338

Bhaskaran, S. (2006). Incremental innovation and business performance: Small and medium-size food enterprises in a concentrated industry environment. *Journal of Small Business Management*, *44*(1), 64–80. doi:10.1111/j.1540-627X.2006.00154.x

Bridge, R. (2012). *How to start a business without any money?* Virgin Books.

Chang, Y. Y., Hughes, M., & Hotho, S. (2011). Internal and external antecedents of SMEs innovation ambidexterity outcomes. *Management Decision*, *49*(10), 1658–1676. doi:10.1108/00251741111183816

Chow, E., Voon, S., Lim, S., Yong, Y., & Dimyati, N. I. (2014). Higher growth, less spending power. *Personal Money*, *160*, 32–47.

Coleman, J. S. (1988). Social capital in the creation of human capital. *American Journal of Sociology*, *94*, S95–S120. doi:10.1086/228943

Cooper, D. R., & Schindler, P. S. (2008). *Business research methods* (10th ed.). New York: McGraw-Hill Irwin.

Crook, T. R., Todd, S. Y., Combs, J. G., Woehr, D. J., & Ketchen, D. J. Jr. (2011). Does human capital matter? A meta-analysis of the relationship between human capital and firm performance. *The Journal of Applied Psychology*, *96*(3), 443–456. doi:10.1037/a0022147 PMID:21244126

Damanpour, F. (1991). Organizational innovation: A meta-analysis of effects of determinants and moderators. *Academy of Management Journal*, *34*(3), 555–590. doi:10.2307/256406

De Jong, J., & Wennekers, S. (2008). *Intrapreneurship; conceptualizing entrepreneurial employee behaviour*. Research Report H200802. Zoetermeer: EIM.

Denan, Z., Ismail, N., & Ishak, N. A. (2009). The Impact of Environmental Dynamism on Knowledge Absorptive Capacity-Innovation Performance Relationship Amongst Manufacturing SMEs in Malaysia. *Social and Management Research Journal, 6*(1), 63–85.

Deshpande, R., & Webster, F. E. Jr. (1989). Organizational culture and marketing: Defining the research agenda. *Journal of Marketing, 53*(1), 3–15. doi:10.2307/1251521

Díez, J. M., Ochoa, M. L., Prieto, B., & Santidrián, A. (2010). Intellectual capital and value creation in Spanish firms. *Journal of Intellectual Capital, 11*(3), 348–367. doi:10.1108/14691931011064581

Dobni, C. B. (2008). Measuring innovation culture in organizations: The development of a generalized innovation culture construct using exploratory factor analysis. *European Journal of Innovation Management, 11*(4), 539–559. doi:10.1108/14601060810911156

Duréndez, A., Madrid-Guijarro, A., & García-Pérez-de-Lema, D. (2011). Innovative culture, management control systems and performance in small and medium-sized Spanish family firms. *Innovar, 21*(40), 137–154.

EPU. (2015). *The Malaysian Economy in Figures (EPU)*. Retrieved July 25, 2016, from http://www.epu.gov.my

ETP Annual Report. (2014). *Narrowing siparity*. Retrieved From July 25, 2016, from http://etp.pemandu.gov.my/annualreport2011

Farooquie, P., Gani, A., Zuberi, A. K., & Hashmi, I. (2012). An empirical study of innovation-performance linkage in the paper industry. *Journal of Industrial Engineering International, 8*(23), 1–6.

Francis, D., & Bessant, J. (2005). Targeting innovation and implications for capability development. *Technovation, 25*(3), 171–183. doi:10.1016/j.technovation.2004.03.004

Galbraith, J. R. (1982). Designing the innovating organization. *Organizational Dynamics, 11*(1), 5–25. doi:10.1016/0090-2616(82)90033-X PMID:10256769

Gilroy, K. (2013). *The link fostering cultural of innovation and plugging the SME skills gap*. Retrieved February 14, 2016, from http: www.blogs.sap.com

Hacioglu, G., Eren, S. S., Eren, M. S., & Celikkan, H. (2012). The effect of entrepreneurial marketing on firms innovative performance in Turkish *SMEs. Procedia: Social and Behavioral Sciences, 58*, 871–878. doi:10.1016/j.sbspro.2012.09.1065

Haenlein, M., & Kaplan, A. M. (2004). A beginners guide to partial least squares analysis. *Understanding Statistics, 3*(4), 283–297. doi:10.1207/s15328031us0304_4

Hair, J. F. Jr, Sarstedt, M., Hopkins, L., & Kuppelwieser, V. G. (2014). Partial least squares structural equation modeling (PLS-SEM) An emerging tool in business research. *European Business Review, 26*(2), 106–121. doi:10.1108/EBR-10-2013-0128

Hairuddin, H., Noor, N. L. M., & Ab Malik, A. M. (2012). Why do microenterprise refuse to use information technology: A case of batik microenterprises in Malaysia. *Procedia: Social and Behavioral Sciences, 57*, 494–502. doi:10.1016/j.sbspro.2012.09.1216

Halim, A. H., Ahmad, N. H., Ramayah, T., Hanifah, H., Taghizadeh, S. K., & Mohamad, M. N. (2015). Towards an Innovation Culture: Enhancing Innovative Performance of Malaysian SMEs. *Academic Journal of Interdisciplinary Studies*, *4*(2), 85–94. doi:10.5901/ajis.2015.v4n2p85

Halim, H. A., Ahmad, N. H., Ramayah, T., & Hanifah, H. (2014). The Growth of Innovative Performance among SMEs: Leveraging on Organisational Culture and Innovative Human Capital. *Journal of Small Business and Entrepreneurship Development*, *2*(21), 107–125.

Hamidon, S. (2009). *The development of Malay entrepreneurship in Malaysia.* ITBM. Retrieved May 20, 2016, from http://mro.massey.ac.nz

Hashim, H. (2013). *Propelling Malaysian SMEs into a Higher Economic Contributor*. Saudi International SMEs Forum 2013.

Henseler, J., Ringle, C. M., & Sinkovicks, R. R. (2009). The use of partial least square modeling in international marketing. *New Challenges to International Marketing Advances in International Marketing*, *20*, 277–319.

Hsieh, T. (2010). *Delivering happiness: A path to profits, passion, and purpose*. New York: Business Plus.

Ismail, W. K. W., & Abdmajid. R. (2007). Framework of the culture of innovation: A revisit. *Jurnal Kemanusiaan, 9*.

Jan, M. A., Shah, S. M. A., & Khan, K. U. (2014). The Impact of Culture on Innovation: The moderating role of Human Capital. *International Journal of Accounting and Financial Reporting*, *4*(2), 607. doi:10.5296/ijafr.v4i2.6871

Johannessen, J., Olsen, B., & Lumpkin, G. T. (2001). Innovation as newness: What is new, how new, and new to whom? *European Journal of Innovation Management*, *4*(1), 20–31. doi:10.1108/14601060110365547

Kanter, R. M. (1983). *The change masters: Innovation for productivity in the American corporation.* New York: Simon & Schuster.

Kohar, U. H. A. (2013). *The factors that influence the sustainability of Malaysian Bumiputera (indigenous) new technology-based small firms* (Doctoral dissertation). RMIT University, Melbourne, Australia.

Lai, K. Y. (2002). *A Study on the Relationship between Corporate Culture and Types of Knowledge Management versus Formation of Corporate Intellectual Capital Accumulation* (Master Thesis). Taiwan: Department of Accounting, National Chengchi University

Lampadarios, E. (2015). *Critical Success Factors (CSFs) for Small Medium Enterprises (SMEs): An Empirical Study in the UK Chemical Distribution Industry* (Doctoral dissertation). Leeds Beckett University.

Lund Vinding, A. (2006). Absorptive capacity and innovative performance: A human capital approach. *Economics of Innovation and New Technology*, *15*(4-5), 507–517. doi:10.1080/10438590500513057

Martins, E. C., & Terblanche, F. (2003). Building Organizational Culture that Stimulates Creativity and Innovation. *European Journal of Innovation Management*, *6*(1), 64–74. doi:10.1108/14601060310456337

McDermott, C. M., & Prajogo, D. (2012). Service innovation and performance in SMEs. *International Journal of Operations & Production Management, 32*(2), 216–237. doi:10.1108/01443571211208632

Morgan, G. (1989). *Creative Organization Theory: A Resource Handbook*. London: Sage Publications.

Morris, L. (2007). *Creating the innovation culture: Geniuses, champions, and leaders*. White Paper, Innovation Labs, retrieved February 25, 2016, from http://www. innovationlabs. com/innovation_culture2. html

MOSTI. (2010). *Malaysian science and technology incubator report 2010*. Retrieved April 16, 2016, from http://www.mosti.gov.my/

11. MP. (2016). *Eleventh Malaysia Plan 2016-2020: Anchoring growth on people*. Retrieved May 17, 2016, from http://rmk11.epu.gov.my/book/eng/Elevent-Malaysia-Plan/RMKe-11 Book.pdf

Muhammad, M. Z., Char, A. K., Yasoa', M. R., & Hassan, Z. (2010). Small and medium enterprises (SMEs) competing in the global business environment: A case of Malaysia. *International Business Research, 3*(1), 66–75.

Mumford, M. (2000). Managing creative people: Strategies and tactics for innovation. *Human Resource Management Review, 10*(3), 313–351. doi:10.1016/S1053-4822(99)00043-1

Naranjo-Valencia, J. C., Jiménez-Jiménez, D., & Sanz-Valle, R. (2011). Innovation or imitation? The role of organizational culture. *Management Decision, 49*(1), 55–72. doi:10.1108/00251741111094437

Nasir, M. (2012, December). Innovative accountants the key to success. *Malaysia SME., 15*, 32.

National SME Development Council. (2012). *SME annual report 2010/11*. SME Corp. Malaysia. Retrieved April 16, 2016, from http://www.smecorp.gov.my/

New Economic Model. (2012). *New Economic Model for Malaysia*. Retrieved April 16, 2016, from http://www.epu.gov.my/en/new-economic-model

Ngo, H.-Y., & Loi, R. (2008). Human resource flexibility, organizational culture and firm performance: An investigation of multinational firms in Hong Kong. *International Journal of Human Resource Management, 19*(9), 1654–1666. doi:10.1080/09585190802295082

O'Reilly, C. A., & Tushman, M. L. (2004). The ambidextrous organization. *Harvard Business Review, 82*(4), 74–81. PMID:15077368

OCass, A., & Viet Ngo, L. (2007). Market orientation versus innovative culture: Two routes to superior brand performance. *European Journal of Marketing, 41*(7/8), 868–887. doi:10.1108/03090560710752438

Oke, A., Burke, G., & Myers, A. (2007). Innovation types and performance in growing UK SMEs. *International Journal of Operations & Production Management, 27*(7), 735–753. doi:10.1108/01443570710756974

Omar, C. M. Z. C., & Azmi, N. M. N. (2016). Factors Affecting the Success of Bumiputera Entrepreneurs in Small and Medium Enterprises (SMEs) in Malaysia. *International Journal of Management Science and Business Administration, 1*(9), 40–45. doi:10.18775/ijmsba.1849-5664-5419.2014.19.1004

Pohl, H., & Elmquist, M. (2010). Radical innovation in a small firm: A hybrid electric vehicle development project at Volvo Cars. *R & D Management*, *40*(4), 372–382. doi:10.1111/j.1467-9310.2010.00608.x

Rasiah, R., & Yap, X. S. (2014). *Innovation Performance of the Malaysian Economy*. Academic Press.

Ringle, C. M., Wende, S., & Will, A. (2005). *SmartPLS 2.0 (M3) Beta*. Retrieved from http://www.smartpls. De

Rohra, C. L., & Junejo, M. A. (2009). Strategies for developing the success of Small Medium Enterprises in Pakistan. *International Journal of Business and Management*, *4*(6), 171. doi:10.5539/ijbm.v4n6p171

Rosenbusch, N., Brinkmann, J., & Bausch, A. (2011). Is innovation always beneficial? A meta-analysis of the relationship between innovation and performance in SMEs. *Journal of Business Venturing*, *26*(4), 441–457. doi:10.1016/j.jbusvent.2009.12.002

Samad, N. A. (2007). *Positioning Malaysian SMEs in the global. Proceedings of Persidangan Kebangsaan IKS 2007*. Kota Kinabalu: Universiti Utara Malaysia.

Santos-Rodrigues, H., Pereira-Rodrigues, G., & Cranfield, D. (2013, April). Human Capital and Financial Results: A Case Study. In *Proceedings of the 5th European Conference on Intellectual Capital: ECIC 2013* (p. 384). Academic Conferences Limited.

Seen, N. Y., Singh, S. K. G., & Jayasingam, S. (2012). Organizational Culture and Innovation among Malaysian Employees. *The Journal of Human Resource and Adult Learning*, *8*(2), 147.

Sekaran, U., & Bougie, R. (2010). *Research methods for business: A skill building approach* (5th ed.). Chichester, UK: John Willey & Sons Ltd.

Sharabati, A. A. A., Naji Jawad, S., & Bontis, N. (2010). Intellectual capital and business performance in the pharmaceutical sector of Jordan. *Management Decision*, *48*(1), 105–131. doi:10.1108/00251741011014481

Sharifirad, M. S., & Atei, V. (2012). Organizational culture and innovation culture: Exploring the relationships between constructs. *Leadership and Organization Development Journal*, *33*(5), 494–517. doi:10.1108/01437731211241274

Siaw, C., & Rani, N. S. A. (2012). A critical review on the regulatory and legislation challenges faced by halal start-up SMEs food manufacturers in Malaysia. *Procedia: Social and Behavioral Sciences*, *57*, 541–548. doi:10.1016/j.sbspro.2012.09.1222

Simonton, D. K. (1999). Creativity from Historiometric Perspective. In R. J. Stenberg (Ed.), *Handbook of Creativity* (pp. 116–134). Cambridge, UK: Cambridge University Press.

Skerlavaj, M., Song, J. H., & Lee, Y. (2010). Organizational learning culture, innovative culture and innovations in South Korean firms. *Expert Systems with Applications*, *37*(9), 6390–6403. doi:10.1016/j.eswa.2010.02.080

SME Annual Report. (2012). Retrieved February 8, 2013, from http://www.smecorp.gov.my/v4/sites/default/files/Section1_0.pdf

SME Corporation Malaysia. (2011). *Financial guide for smes. SME Corporation Malaysia.* Retrieved March 13, 2015, from http://www.smecorp.gov.my/vn2/

SME Masterplan (2013). *SME Master Plan 2012-2020: Catalysing growth and income*. Author.

SMECorp. (2015). *SME Corporation Malaysia - SME Definition*. Retrieved May 18, 2016, from http://www.smecorp.gov.my/index.php/en/policies/2015-12-21-09-09-49/sme-definition

SMIDEC. (2007). *SME development programme*. Retrieved March 13, 2015, from http://www.smidec.gov.my/detailpage.jsp?section=defsme&level=1

Taggar, S. (2002). Individual creativity and group ability to utilize individual creative resources: A multilevel model. *Academy of Management Journal*, *45*(2), 315–330. doi:10.2307/3069349

Talebi, K., & Tajeddin, M. (2011). The adoption of new and innovative knowledge by small and medium enterprises of Iran: Opportunities and constraints for growth. *African Journal of Business Management*, *5*(1), 39–49.

Tushman, M. L., & OReilly, C. A. III. (1996). Ambidextrous organizations: Managing evolutionary and revolutionary change. *California Management Review*, *38*(4), 8–30. doi:10.2307/41165852

Urbach, N., & Ahlemann, F. (2010). Structural equation modeling in information systems research using partial least squares. *Journal of Information Technology Theory and Application*, *11*(2), 5.

Voon, S. (2014). Insurance. *Personal Money*, *160*, 14–15.

Wang, G. L. (2012). A Study of How the Organizational Culture of International Tourist Hotels Affects Organizational Performance: Using Intellectual Capital as the Mediating Variable. *The Journal of Global Business Management*, *8*(1), 189–201.

Wang, H. C., He, J., & Mahoney, J. (2009). Firm-specific knowledge resources and competitive advantage: The roles of economic- and relationship-based employee governance mechanisms. *Strategic Management Journal*, *30*(12), 1265–1285. doi:10.1002/smj.787

Yee, Y. P. (2009). Daring adventures. *The Star*. Retrieved January 04, 2015, from http://www.thestar.com.my

Zainol, F. A., & Daud, W. N. W. (2011). Indigenous ("Bumiputera") Malay entrepreneurs in Malaysia: Government supports, entrepreneurial orientation and firms performances. *International Business and Management*, *2*(1), 86–99.

Zeng, X. X., & Saixing, Y. W. (2016). A theory of multi-dimensional organizational innovation cultures and innovation performance in transitional economies: The role of team cohesion", Chinese Management Studies. *Chinese Management Studies*, *10*(3). doi:10.1108/09564230910978511

KEY TERMS AND DEFINITIONS

Bumiputera: In Malaysia, by convention, it is generally considered that all Malays are Bumiputeras. This official definition which is widely used in Malaysia whereby it taking up ethnic Malays and other indigenous ethnic groups such as the Orang Asli in Peninsular Malaysia and the tribal people in Sabah and Sarawak.

Bumiputera SMEs: The firm is owned by the Bumiputera entrepreneurs.

Innovation: An idea that is new to the organization. It can be a new product, a new service or a new technology.

Innovation Culture: The behaviour to shared creativity or ideas within groups, or adoption of innovativeness significantly benefit the individual, the group, organization, or wider society.

Innovation Performance: The use of an ideas or creativity to improve the products, processes, procedures that increase the significance, usefulness and performance of the products and services.

Small Medium Enterprises (SME): An enterprise is classifies as micro, small or medium which will depends on the two criteria, i.e. full-time employees and annual sales turnover as per the definition by the National SME Development Council.

Specific Human Capital: It is specific individual abilities, specific knowledge, talent, skills and experience of the employees in organization in order to enhance the organization performance.

Chapter 13
Innovation-Driven Planned Behaviour Towards Achieving the Wellbeing of the Malaysian SMEs

Seyedeh Khadijeh Taghizadeh
Universiti Teknology Petronas, Malaysia

Syed Abidur Rahman
Universiti Utara Malaysia, Malaysia

T. Ramayah
Universiti Sains Malaysia, Malaysia

ABSTRACT

Innovation requires an innovation mind-set derived from behavioural aspects of individuals. To realize such a notion, this paper introduces a framework and integrated theory of planned behaviour (TPB) in the line with the exploratory and exploitative innovations. Attitudes towards innovation, subjective norms for innovation and perceived control over innovation can influence on exploratory and exploitative innovations in SMEs. It is believed that through exploratory and exploitative innovations, entrepreneurs in SMEs may achieve subjective wellbeing. The approach of applying the TPB to exploratory and exploitative innovations will have few implications. First it allows SMEs to understand which factors are important in doing exploratory and exploitative innovations. Second, it will indicate that doing exploratory and exploitative innovations can bring the feeling of perceived wellbeing among entrepreneurs. Finally, the framework identifies a number of areas for future research that can verify the comprehensive understanding of successful innovations.

DOI: 10.4018/978-1-5225-2165-5.ch013

INTRODUCTION

There has been noticeable shift in comprehending the innovation and its trail. Coupling with the shift, one of the key questions whirling around academicians' thoughts and minds is how to best measure the impact of innovation (Dolan & Metcalfe, 2012). According to Martin (2013), the globe is now witnessing the shift from 'innovation for *economic growth*' to 'innovation for *sustainable development*'. In addition, researchers have highlighted few challenges for innovation, such as, shift from 'innovation for *wealth creation*' to 'innovation for *wellbeing*'. Despite of the view as challenge, wellbeing has become an important consideration among all sections of the society. The significance of wellbeing further has been thrived and echoed by the global leaders, resulting in inclusion in the post-2015 global development agenda (UNDP, 2015). Other than the initiatives of global leaders and development agencies, different stakeholders of the society may play instrumental role in ensuring wellbeing of the individuals as well as the society. Business organizations as an entity also play a role in avowing wellbeing of the people. In a study, Rahman et al. (2015) revealed that financial and non-financial performance of small-medium enterprise business strongly predicts the subjective wellbeing of the entrepreneurs in Bangladesh. However, with vision to move forward as developed country at the end of year 2020, Malaysia is unremittingly endeavouring to develop itself in all respect. In the country, small-medium enterprises (SMEs) sector plays important role in the economy, and thereby the wellbeing of the businesses and the entrepreneurs is a necessity for the country's future achievement. In Malaysia the SMEs sector employ over 65 per cent of the total workforce and contributes 35.9 per cent to the country's GDP, and makes up 17.8 per cent of the nation's total export (SME Corporation Malaysia, 2016b). The extent of this sector's economic consequence is highlighted by the fact that 99.2 per cent of the total business establishments in Malaysia are SMEs (Singh & Mahmood, 2014). Nonetheless, notwithstanding impressive picture, the contribution of Malaysian SME to the national Gross Domestic Product (GDP) is comparatively stumpy as compared to other countries (Halim et al., 2015). As a developing country, SMEs of Malaysia are facing constricted coerce and multidimensional confronts. Researchers have also noted that for last few years, Malaysian economic progression is decelerating for various reasons along with financial crisis (Rasiah et al., 2015). Furthermore, the competition in the SME sector is very high and such stiff competition requires the SMEs to offer facilitating and supporting products/services driven by innovation based behaviour (Luoma-aho et al., 2012).

Despite the increased attention paid to this sector, comparatively little attention has been given to the issue of wellbeing of the SMEs which perhaps fostered by innovation. Even in the extant literatures and among the scholars there is paradoxical stand with regard to relationship of innovation and wellbeing. Famous economist and Noble laureate Stiglitz (2014) put forward that innovation might not necessarily generate wellbeing for individual and society as whole. On the other hand, innovation has been attributed as a means to improve people's lives (Dolan & Metcalfe, 2012). Further, it is also important to consider the influential factors of innovation in context SMEs, particularly in Malaysia. Scholars have earlier indicated that innovation requires an innovation mind-set which can be derived from behavioural aspects of individuals. Therefore, it is also remaining a dilemma that whether, the elements of planned behaviour instigates to pursue for innovation. On this context, the current study will embark upon to propose a conceptual framework, which demonstrates that attitudes towards innovation, subjective norms for innovation and perceived control over innovation could have possible relationship with two types of innovation (i.e. exploratory innovation, exploitative innovation). Further, the study stands on the quest to reveal that exploratory innovation and exploitative innovation should influence to enhance the wellbeing. In light of the discussion outlined above, our proposed chapter will:

1. Reveal the relationship for certain elements of theory of planned behaviour towards exploratory and exploitative innovation among SMEs in Malaysia.
2. Ascertain the possible predictive relationship exploratory and exploitative innovation with wellbeing.

The study will assist to understand the state of wellbeing of the SME entrepreneurs and the possible impact of exploratory and exploitative innovation on SME entrepreneur's wellbeing. Further, the role of attitudes towards innovation, subjective norms for innovation and perceived control over innovation will also be determined. Holistically, the study may be used as guideline for Malaysian SME entrepreneurs.

CONTEXTUAL BACKGROUND

Small medium enterprises (SMEs) are acknowledged as the most important base for the economic development and employment growth (Ramayah et al., 2016). In the same line, previously also Audretsch and Keilbach (2004) vowed that the role of small and medium enterprises (SMEs) in creating jobs and economic growth in both developed and developing countries is noteworthy. From every segments of the society around the world are now recognising the significance of small and medium enterprises (SMEs) to improve the distribution of income and to redesign economic structures that are dependent on large organizations (Abdullah, 1999; Ahmad, 2007; Savlovschi & Robu, 2011; Yu, 2001). Given the important role of SMEs in the developing countries, it is crucial to identify how SMEs can utilize their resources (i.e. innovation) and owner's personal behaviour to achieve long-term competitiveness and survival in the business environment. In the developing countries it has been reported that SMEs takes in the major portion of the gross domestic product (GDP) (Beck et al., 2005; Chowdhury et al., 2015). According to the latest date from the Economic Census 2011, SMEs in Malaysia account for 97.3% or 645,136 of total business establishments in 2010 (SME Corporation Malaysia, 2016b). However, researcher claimed that the number of SMEs in Malaysia increased and occupied the 99.2% of the country's total businesses (Singh & Mahmood, 2014).

According to the SME Corporation Malaysia (2016b), SME GDP growth has consistently outpaced the country's overall economic growth since 2004. In the period of 2005 to 2014, the average compounded annual growth rate (CAGR) of SMEs was 7.1%, which was higher than the 4.9% CAGR of the overall economy. As a result, SME contribution to GDP increased from 29.6% in 2005 to 35.9% in 2014 and also contributed 65% of total employment and 17.8% of total exports (SME Corporation Malaysia, 2016b). This large portion in the economy has eventually powered economic growth, assisting Malaysia to become one of the Asian dragons (Taghizadeh et al., 2014). The SME sector in Malaysia plays a vital role in the country's industrialization program and represents the mainstay of industrial development in the country (Saleh & Ndubisi, 2006; Yeoh, 2014). In view of the imperative role occupied by SMEs, the government of Malaysia endures to be steadfast on the way to the progression of a strong and competitive SME sector and contemplates its welfare as a key national development strategy (Ramayah et al., 2016).

It has also been acknowledged by the scholars that the Malaysian government has recognized SMEs as a vital sector that would possibly catalyse the economic investment in the country. The SME sector has been also deemed to play a role in transfiguring Malaysia into a developed nation by 2020 (Halim et al., 2015). However, in the academic area there has been a confusion existing regarding the definition of small-medium enterprises (SMEs) as the definition of the SMEs varies across the countries and also over time. Ever since 2005, a general explanation for SMEs validated by the National SME Development Council (NSDC) 1 has been embraced by the government ministries, bureaus, and all the public and private institutions involved in SME development of the country. According to the definition, manufacturing (including agro-based) and manufacturing-related services having sales turnover of less than RM25 million or comprising full-time employees of less than 150 are considered as SMEs. Further, primary agriculture and services (including ICT), which have sales turnover of less than RM5 million or encompassing full-time employees of less than 50 are defined as SMEs (SME Corporation Malaysia, 2011). However, due to the price inflation, transformation in business trends, and structural alterations, a review of the classification was commenced in 2013 and a new SME definition was permitted by the Malaysian agencies. According to the new definition (SME Corporation Malaysia, 2016a), small enterprise in the manufacturing sector will be considered those which have sales turnover from RM300, 000 to less than RM15 million or have employees from 5 to less than 75. In the services and other sectors, small enterprise are considered those which have sales turnover from RM300, 000 to less that RM3 million or have employees from 5 to less than 30.

On the other hand, medium enterprise in the manufacturing sector has been considered those which have sales turnover from RM15 million to not exceeding RM50 million or have employees from 75 to not exceeding 200. In the services and other sectors, medium enterprise are considered those which have sales turnover from RM3 million to not exceeding RM20 million or have employees from 30 to not exceeding 75 (SME Corporation Malaysia, 2016a). However, another categorization has been added in defining the SMEs in Malaysia, which includes micro-enterprises. According to the SME Corporation Malaysia (2016a), micro enterprises has been defined to have sales turnover of less than RM300, 000, or less than 5 full-time employees in the manufacturing, services and other sectors. Table 1 shows the details. However, in the determination of new product/service introduction, diversified business expansion, SMEs are playing positive role in the Malaysian businesses (The National SME Development Council, 2011).

SMEs' concentration are in the services sector with 90% or 580,985 establishments. Meanwhile, 6% of total SMEs (37,861) are in the manufacturing sector, followed by 3% in the construction sector (19,283) and the remaining 1% (6,708) in the agriculture sector and 0.1% in the mining and quarrying sector (SME Corporation Malaysia, 2016b).

Table 1. Definition of Micro enterprise and SMEs

Category	Micro Enterprise	Small Enterprise	Medium Enterprise
Manufacturing	Sales turnover of less than RM300,000 OR employees of less than 5	Sales turnover from RM300,000 to less than RM15 mil OR employees from 5 to less than 75	Sales turnover from RM15 mil to not exceeding RM50 mil OR employees from 75 to not exceeding 200
Services and Other Sectors	Sales turnover of less than RM300,000 OR employees of less than 5	Sales turnover from RM300,000 to less than RM3 mil OR employees from 5 to less than 30	Sales turnover from RM3 mil to not exceeding RM20 mil OR employees from 30 to not exceeding 75

Source: SME Corporation Malaysia (2016a)

CONCEPT DEVELOPMENT

Theory of Planned Behaviour

The Theory of Planned Behaviour (TPB) has been efficaciously smeared to a wide range of behaviours, including individual behaviour and also complex behaviour such as managerial decision making (Sommer, 2011). It has also become one of the most dominant models for the prediction of human social behaviour (Ajzen, 2011). Till to date the Theory of Planned Behaviour (TPB) has received substantial attention in the literature (Armitage & Conner, 2001). The theory is considered as one of the best-supported social psychological theories that enable to predict human behaviour (Sommer, 2011). The fundamental assumption of the theory is that behavioural decisions are the result of a reasoned process in which the behaviour is influenced by attitudes, norms and perceived behaviour control. These constructs influence the behaviour primarily through the impact on behavioural intention (Smith et al., 2007).

The model employed in the current proposed research is basically grounded on the theory of planned behaviour (TPB) (Ajzen, 1985, 1991). The theory of planned behaviour is an extension of theory of reasoned action (TRA) that includes measures of control belief and perceived behavioural control (Armitage & Conner, 2001; Gopi & Ramayah, 2007). The theory was principally established to answer the limitation in the theory of reasoned action (Ajzen & Fishbein, 1977; Fishbein & Ajzen, 1975). The theory of planned behaviour deals with behaviour where individual have partial ability of utilizing distinct determination or situation where they possess lack of control of their behaviour (Ajzen, 2005). The extension of theory of reasoned action, TPB is comprised of attitude en route for the behaviour, social factor called subjective norm and an added variable which is the degree of perceived behavioural control (PBC) (Ajzen, 1985, 1991). Attitude, subjective norms, and perceived behavioural control are shown to be related to appropriate sets of salient behavioural, normative, and control beliefs about the behaviour (Ajzen, 1991). The theory of planned behaviour is the individual's intention to accomplish a given behaviour (Ajzen, 1991). According to TPB, a person's concrete behaviour in execution specific actions is directly predisposed by his or her behavioural intention and, in turn, is mutually determined by his or her attitude, subjective norms and perceived behavioural controls en route for performing the behaviour (Lee, 2009).

Attitude refers to the degree to which a person has favourable or unfavourable evaluation or appraisal of the behaviour in question (Shah Alam & Mohamed Sayuti, 2011). According to Hagger et al. (2002), attitude mirrors a personal inclination toward involving in certain behaviour. It signifies a person's evaluation of his or her beliefs concerning the target behaviour's efficacy in generating outcomes and an assessment of these outcomes. For long time, attitude has been identified as a construct that directs future behaviour or the basis of individual intention that eventually leads to a specific behaviour (Gopi & Ramayah, 2007). In the theory of reasoned action, attitude has been considered as the judgmental consequence of positive or negative feeling of each individual in carrying out a specific behaviour (Fishbein & Ajzen, 1975). However, Ajzen and Fishbein (2000) came up with revised version for the defining the attitude. According to Ajzen and Fishbein (2000), attitude is the degree of favourableness and unfavourableness of an individual sensing, which is headed for a psychological entity.

The construct 'subjective norm' has been used as one of the original construct embedded in the theory of reasoned action. Subjective norm represent the individual's behaviour that they perform, even if they are not inclined toward the behaviour and its consequences (Venkatesh & Davis, 2000). Subjective norms denote the effect of social pressure or social environment on the individuals and thus on behavioural intention (Fishbein & Ajzen, 1975). Scholars have defined subjective norms as individual's view of the possibility that the potential referent group or individuals approve or disapprove of performing the given behaviour (Ajzen, 1991; Fishbein & Ajzen, 1975). In the theory of reasoned action (TRA) and theory of planned behaviour (TPB), and technology acceptance model (TAM2) 'subjective norms' has been included as predictor of behavioural intention. According to Venkatesh and Davis (2000), an individual would carry out the behaviour even though the individual is not in support of acting out the behaviour, while there is presence of noteworthy social influence and social pressure. However, researchers have revealed that 'subjective norms' has inconsistent result with intention (Gopi & Ramayah, 2007; Mathieson, 1991; Venkatesh & Davis, 2000)

Perceived behavioural control (PBC) has been included in the theory of planned behaviour, from the fundamental ground of theory of reasoned action (TRA) by Ajzen and Madden (1986). PBC is demarcated as, given the presence or absence of necessary means and prospects, the individual's view of the easiness or strain in performing the behaviour of interest (Ajzen, 1991). In a more simplified manner, PBC has been defined as an individual's approximation of how easy or difficult it will be for the those individual to express certain the behaviour (Ajzen & Madden, 1986). The control belief in theory of planned behaviour is epitomized by PBC. The construct of PBC was included into the model to get the answer of limitations in theory of reasoned action (Ajzen & Fishbein, 1977; Fishbein & Ajzen, 1975) in order to deal with circumstances where a person may lack comprehensive control over the behaviour (Ajzen, 1991). Perceived behavioural control (PBC) is supposedly to create instrumental role on both intention and behaviour. Scholars believe that inclusion of PBC into the TPB was more psychological in nature and concerns the motivational impact (Ajzen & Madden, 1986). It has been argued in the literature that individuals who consider themselves as possessing a comparatively higher degree of control over the behavior should be able to do things in better way (Manstead & Eekelen, 1998). Provided with the surge in resources and opportunities, it is assumed by the scholars that the greater is the perceived control of the particular behaviour (Ajzen, 1991) and thus the more likely is the performance of the behaviour (Gopi & Ramayah, 2007).

Exploratory and Exploitative Innovations

March (1991) conceptualized the notion of exploitation and exploration which later has developed as an underlying theme in research on innovation (Jansen et al., 2006; Rothaermel & Deeds, 2004), entrepreneurship (Kollmann & Stöckmann, 2014; Shane & Venkataraman, 2000), and organizational learning and strategy (Vera & Crossan, 2004). Exploitation is defined as "such things as refinement, choice, production, efficiency, selection, implementation, execution" and exploration is defined as "things captured by terms such as search, variation, risk taking, experimentation, play, flexibility, discovery, innovation" (March, 1991, p. 71).

The strategy of exploitative innovation is basically built on improvements, refinements, efficiency, and implementation of current skills and processes in organization (Mueller et al., 2013; Schamberger et al., 2013). It has incremental character and focus on the needs of existing customers and lead to incremental product changes (Amason et al., 2006; Schamberger et al., 2013). Exploitative innovation respond to the real-time environmental conditions through accompanying advances in processes and technologies (Jansen et al., 2006; Kollmann & Stöckmann, 2014). Cost reduction as well as superior satisfaction of customers and markets are targeted in exploitative innovation activities (Abernathy & Clark, 1985). According to Schamberger et al. (2013), exploitative innovation activities are less risky which lead to new adapted products while requiring small investments. Typically, exploitative innovation build on existing knowledge and extend existing products and services for the existing customers (Benner & Tushman, 2003; Jansen et al., 2006). Abernathy and Clark (1985) define that exploitative innovation broaden existing knowledge and skills, expand existing products and services, improve established designs, and increase the efficiency of existing distribution channels. Thus, it can be conclude that exploitative innovations form on existing knowledge and reinforce existing skills, processes, and structures.

In contrast, exploratory innovations respond to and affect latent environmental trends through creating new products or services and new markets (Jansen et al., 2006; Kollmann & Stöckmann, 2014). Exploratory innovations deals with offering innovative designs and creative ways to satisfy customer and market needs (Lubatkin et al., 2006). According to Schamberger et al. (2013) and March (1991), exploratory innovations are characterized by processes such as variation, experimentation, flexibility and discovery which these activities are riskier and require investments. Exploratory innovations are radical novelties targeting at serving both current and future customers (Schamberger et al., 2013). Characteristically, exploratory innovations are radical innovations and firms engaged in exploratory innovation pursue new knowledge and develop new products or services for emerging customers or markets (Benner & Tushman, 2003; Jansen et al., 2006). It requires new knowledge or departure from existing knowledge (Benner & Tushman, 2003). Thus, Exploratory innovations offer new designs, create new markets, and develop new channels of distribution (Abernathy & Clark, 1985; Benner & Tushman, 2003).

According to March (1991), in many aspects exploratory and exploitative innovation differ significantly such as in their antecedents and the conditions required for their success. For example, exploratory innovation mainly involves the challenging of existing approaches in the organization (Mueller et al., 2013). As exploratory innovation is a high-risk strategy, organizational actors must be willing and be able to allocate resources to high-risk projects whose outcomes are unpredictable (Mueller et al., 2013). In contrast, exploitative innovations require in-depth knowledge and skills at all organizational levels (Mueller et al., 2013), hence, employees' education levels, their knowledge, and their skills could be keys to success for such innovations. Jansen et al. (2006) stated that both exploratory and exploitative innovations need various organizational setting like different skills, resource, and capabilities. Thus, firm resources which are influenced by the values may not trigger to go for exploratory and exploitative innovations (Mueller et al., 2013).

Subjective Wellbeing

Wellbeing commonly drawn on philosophy to pronounce what is good for a person eventually (Crisp, 2008) and concern about the optimal functioning (Ryan & Deci, 2001). According to Ryan and Deci (2001), wellbeing is comprehended as fulfilment of pleasure and evading of pain which refers to the happiness, and degree of functioning which refers to the self-realization. Raz (2004) has also claimed that a good life is more related with individual personal value. According to Alkire (2005) functionings are valuable activities and conditions that make up people wellbeing. The functionings that have been proposed so far are: being adequately nourished, escaping morbidity and mortality, having mobility, being happy, achieving self-respect, taking part in the life of the community, appearing in public without shame (Nussbaum et al., 1993; Oosterlaken, 2009). Ensuring the well-being through functioning actually depicts the capability development (Nussbaum et al., 1993; Sen, 1999).

Owners of the entrepreneurship business usually assert greater freedom, flexibility, and opportunity for self-fulfilment (Parasuraman & Simmers, 2001). This can be used as tool to achieve the wellbeing of the society. In the domain of wellbeing studies, a large number of researches have been concentrated on subjective well-being especially in measuring quality of life. Subjective well-being measures happiness through asking how individuals have felt about their life. On the other hand, Objective wellbeing measures the observable variables, such as life expectancy. However, as there is no objective measure of happiness, it is useful to employ subjective measures of happiness towards ones' own life (Argyle, 2001). The literature on the subjective wellbeing mostly concern with the approach and the reasons of experiencing a life in positive way including the cognitive judgments and affective reactions (Diener, 2009). The area of subjective well-being roams around three hall-marks, such as: it is subjective, it includes positive measures, and it includes global assessment of all aspects of a person's life (Diener, 2009).

PROPOSITION DEVELOPMENT

TPB and Exploratory Innovation and Exploitative Innovation

Unsworth et al. (2009) introduced innovation TPB model, which suggest that attitudes towards innovation, subjective norms for innovation and perceived control over innovation can influence on innovation adoption behaviour. Within the organizational innovation literature, attitudes towards innovation have been demonstrated in a number of forms (Unsworth et al., 2009). For example, Damanpour (1991) found that managers' attitude towards innovation has significant relationship with the adoption of innovation in organization. Further, attitudes towards risk taking in organization have a positive relationship with innovation adoption (Nystrom et al., 2002). As innovation is risky in nature, it may be seen as state of attitudes towards innovations (Unsworth et al., 2009). Scholars also believed that the perceived benefits of doing innovation indicates attitudes towards innovation because they expose the cognitive component of the attitude, hence such benefits have relationship with innovation adoption (Mehrtens et al., 2001).

Subjective norms denote the effect of social pressure or social environment on the individuals (Fishbein & Ajzen, 1975) which can effect on individual intention for innovation. Scholars also noted that subjective norms is defined as perceived pressures applied by significant others in adoption of innovations (Unsworth et al., 2009). Further, according to the past studies, subjective norms have usually derived from customers, suppliers, competitors, and government departments (Drazin & Schoonhoven, 1996; Mehrtens et al., 2001). Thus, as subjective norms examined the perceived external pressure from suppliers, customers, competitors, technology diffusion agencies, universities, and government departments, it may bring the behaviour of doing innovation.

In addition, perceived behavioural control (PBC) is defined as the perceived ease or perceived difficulty of adopting as well as implementing an innovation within an organization (Unsworth et al., 2009). When the process of innovations is easy, the people of organization feel that they have control. Previous study found that factors like knowledge, technical, staff readiness (Snyder-Halpern, 2001) and financial resource (Bates & Flynn, 1995) can be as indicators of ease of innovation adoption. If an organization has resources for innovations, the decision-makers can perceive that the process is relatively easy and therefore, they feel greater control over innovation (Unsworth et al., 2009).

Proposition 1: Attitudes towards innovation, subjective norms for innovation and perceived behavioural control over innovation can influence on exploratory and exploitative innovations in SMEs.

Exploratory Innovation and Exploitative Innovation and SWB

After introducing exploratory innovation to the market, firms usually shift to a new path (Mueller et al., 2013). Along with this path, as opportunities for improvement and refinement exist (Mueller et al., 2013), it may bring the feeling of well-being among people as well. Because organizational learning happens along with the new path, people in organization can build on experience, existing knowledge, competencies, and market linkages (Henderson, 1993). Innovation is meant to enhance people lives and standard of living. Since the emergence of the civilization, innovation is contributing towards the development of the society. The impact of the innovation is playing vital role for the betterment of the lives. However, such betterment perhaps can be referred as wellbeing. The links made between innovation and subjective wellbeing (SWB) have, however, rarely been made, amongst of the few exceptions, such as, the study of Dolan and Metcalfe (2012). The study of Dolan and Metcalfe (2012) presumed the influence of innovation on subjective wellbeing. The innovation made in the medical sector has been proven improve the subjective wellbeing of the study context. Currently, the domain of wellbeing appears to be established on an understanding that the perceptive assessment of one's life satisfaction is considerably and positively impacted by increases in living standard. However, innovation can be a means to improve individuals' living standard. Scholars have identified different types of innovation, of which exploitation innovation and exploration innovation have been considered appropriate in the current contextual background.

Proposition 2: Through exploratory and exploitative innovation, entrepreneurs in SMEs can achieve subjective wellbeing in a greater level.

Based on the above discussion, this paper proposes a framework (Figure 1) which can be applied in SMEs. In this framework, dimensions of TBP regarding innovation namely attitude towards innovation, subjective norm for innovation, and perceived behavioural control over innovation are proposed to have

Figure 1. A proposed framework of TPB and innovation towards wellbeing

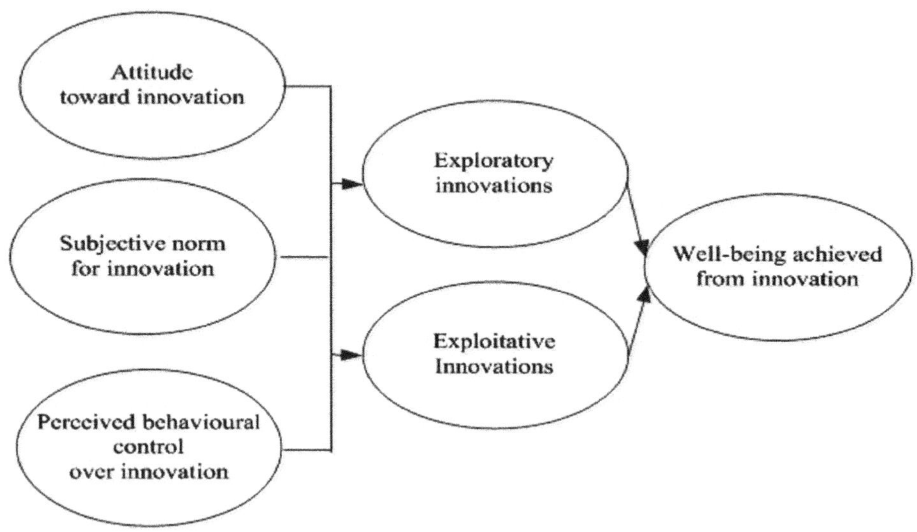

influence on exploratory and exploitative innovations. In addition, it suggests that having exploratory and exploitative innovations, the desired outcome such as subjective wellbeing will be achieved.

DISCUSSION

In this paper, we introduced a framework and integrated theory of planned behaviour (TPB) with exploratory and exploitative innovations resulting in subjective wellbeing of SMEs entrepreneurs. The framework proposes that attitudes towards innovation, subjective norms for innovation and perceived behavioural control over innovation can influence on exploratory and exploitative innovations in SMEs. In addition, it suggests that through exploratory and exploitative innovations, entrepreneurs in SMEs can perceive subjective wellbeing. The approach of applying the TPB to exploratory and exploitative innovations will have few implications. First, it allows SMEs to understand which factors are important in doing exploratory and exploitative innovations. Second, it will indicate that doing exploratory and exploitative innovations can bring the feeling of perceived wellbeing among entrepreneurs. As scholars highlighted exploratory innovations as an example, are linked with a number of advantages such as price premium, the generation of sales in new or emerging markets, and even positive spill over effects on nonfinancial goals (Benner & Tushman, 2003; Salomo et al., 2008; Schmidt & Calantone, 1998). Scholars have asserted that there may also be important intangible inputs to innovation that probably might have an impact upon SWB (Dolan & Metcalfe, 2012).

Wellbeing generally drawn on philosophy to pronounce what is eventually good for a person (Crisp, 2008). Nevertheless, from the philosophical point of view, a contradiction exists to comprehend it clearly. In this manner, it has been considered that there is a significant philosophical metamorphosis in happy life, good life, and quality life. There are in fact several factors which enhances the wellbeing. Innovation presumed to be factors achieve wellbeing as innovation leads to economic growth, while such growth have causal consequences for wellbeing (Dolan & Metcalfe, 2012). However, innovation can be categorized into exploratory and exploitative innovations. Exploratory innovations are radical innovations and are designed to meet the needs of emerging customers or markets. They offer new designs, create new markets, and develop new channels of distribution. Exploratory innovations require new knowledge or departure from existing knowledge. Conversely, exploitative innovations are incremental innovations and are designed to meet the needs of existing customers or markets. Therefore, it is of interest to comprehend the relationship of exploratory and exploitative innovations with the wellbeing of the SME entrepreneur's in Malaysia.

However, while measuring the extent of innovation amongst SME entrepreneurs in achieving wellbeing, the obvious and associated queries arise as to what are the determinants that push forward exploratory and exploitative innovation. In the previous study, scholars have noted that some of the elements contained in the theory of planned behaviour play significant role innovation adoption mind set and thus establishes innovation adoption behaviour model (Weigel et al., 2014). Theory of Planned Behaviour has been shown in several studies to predict behaviour in diversified context (Ajzen et al., 2011; Chang & Zhu, 2011). In a study, Pierce and Delbecq (1977) vowed that attitude play a critical role in predicting innovation. According to Kim et al. (2009), subjective norms perform significant functions in the adoption of decision. However, such decision perhaps can be related with the taking up the approach of exploratory and exploitative innovation. Perceived behavioural control refers to the perceived ease or difficulty of performing the behaviour and it is assumed to reflect past experience as well as anticipated impediments and obstacles (Ajzen, 1991). However, it is believed that the more complimentary the attitude and subjective norm with respect to behaviour, and the better the perceived behavioural control, individual's intention to perform the behaviour under certain consideration i.e. innovation would be better and effective.

Finally, the framework identifies a number of areas for future research that can verify the comprehensive understanding of successful innovations.

DIRECTION OF FUTURE RESEARCH

The current research has mainly embarked with the objective to propose a conceptual research framework which adjoins the three main domains in the entrepreneurship study, namely: elements of theory of planned behaviour, innovation, and subjective wellbeing. The current study intended to connect these domains and proposed a framework, which can be considered as the founding base of future empirical research. It is expected that this conceptual framework, can be tested and validated in context of SMEs in Malaysia as well as other countries. The proposed framework will encourage the researchers to delve into the empirical investigation with regard to the influence of theory of planned behaviour on the exploratory and exploitative innovation as well as the impact of such innovations on the subjective wellbeing of the SMEs entrepreneurs in Malaysia and also in other countries. The empirical study can also be tested across the industry such as technology, agriculture, manufacturing, and service oriented SMEs in countries. Further, researchers who are interested on the base of pyramid segment of the society can also take up the framework and test among the entrepreneurs of such vulnerable group. It is hoped that such empirical test and validation across the country, industry, and societal segment would make the proposed framework more robust.

CONCLUSION

Research on small-medium enterprises (SMEs) surely is a subjugated domain but still believe to have wide range of scope for probe from diverse perspectives. Particularly, in country like Malaysia, with the significance of SMEs and its wide range of potentials, it is worthwhile to carryout research on the individual behaviour, innovation, and the subjective wellbeing. The theory of planned behaviour (TPB) is a very established model to comprehend behavioural aspects of individuals. In addition, innovation is such a matter, which needs elements of behavioural aspects along with resources and competencies. It is expected that coming up with new things which contributes to the betterment of the living standard would certainly improve the subjective wellbeing of the individuals. The proposition made in this study will however believe to have contribution to the theoretical domains in the business academia. The study may be considered as the seminal work for adjoining theory of planned behaviour, innovation, and subjective wellbeing. It is hoped that the current propositions would widen up the scope of research among the entrepreneurship, innovation researchers. The proposition made in the current paper also expected to benefit the private and public entities, policy-makers, and researchers to formulate strategies and policies for the development of the small-medium enterprises (SMEs) in Malaysia and also other countries.

REFERENCES

Abdullah, M. A. (1999). *Small and medium enterprises in Malaysia: Policy issues and challenges*. Ashgate.

Abernathy, W. J., & Clark, K. B. (1985). Innovation: Mapping the winds of creative destruction. *Research Policy*, *14*(1), 3–22. doi:10.1016/0048-7333(85)90021-6

Ahmad, N. H. (2007). *A cross cultural study of entrepreneurial competencies and entrepreneurial success in SMEs in Australia and Malaysia*. University of Adelaide.

Ajzen, I. (1985). *From intentions to actions: A theory of planned behavior*. Springer.

Ajzen, I. (1991). The theory of planned behavior. *Organizational Behavior and Human Decision Processes*, *50*(2), 179–211. doi:10.1016/0749-5978(91)90020-T

Ajzen, I. (2005). *Attitudes, personality, and behavior*. McGraw-Hill International.

Ajzen, I. (2011). The theory of planned behaviour: Reactions and reflections. *Psychology & Health*, *26*(9), 1113–1127. doi:10.1080/08870446.2011.613995 PMID:21929476

Ajzen, I., & Fishbein, M. (1977). Attitude-behavior relations: A theoretical analysis and review of empirical research. *Psychological Bulletin*, *84*(5), 888–918. doi:10.1037/0033-2909.84.5.888

Ajzen, I., & Fishbein, M. (2000). Attitudes and the attitude-behavior relation: Reasoned and automatic processes. *European Review of Social Psychology*, *11*(1), 1–33. doi:10.1080/14792779943000116

Ajzen, I., Joyce, N., Sheikh, S., & Cote, N. G. (2011). Knowledge and the prediction of behavior: The role of information accuracy in the theory of planned behavior. *Basic and Applied Social Psychology*, *33*(2), 101–117. doi:10.1080/01973533.2011.568834

Ajzen, I., & Madden, T. J. (1986). Prediction of goal-directed behavior: Attitudes, intentions, and perceived behavioral control. *Journal of Experimental Social Psychology*, *22*(5), 453–474. doi:10.1016/0022-1031(86)90045-4

Alkire, S. (2005). *Valuing freedoms: Sen's capability approach and poverty reduction*. Oxford University Press.

Amason, A. C., Shrader, R. C., & Tompson, G. H. (2006). Newness and novelty: Relating top management team composition to new venture performance. *Journal of Business Venturing*, *21*(1), 125–148. doi:10.1016/j.jbusvent.2005.04.008

Argyle, M. (2001). *The psychology of happiness*. New York: Routledge.

Armitage, C. J., & Conner, M. (2001). Efficacy of the theory of planned behaviour: A meta-analytic review. *The British Journal of Social Psychology*, *40*(4), 471–499. doi:10.1348/014466601164939 PMID:11795063

Audretsch, D. B., & Keilbach, M. (2004). Does entrepreneurship capital matter? *Entrepreneurship Theory and Practice*, *28*(5), 419–429. doi:10.1111/j.1540-6520.2004.00055.x

Bates, K. A., Flynn, E. J. (1995). Innovation History and Competitive Advantage: A Resource-Based View Analysis of Manufacturing Technology Innovations. *Academy of Management Proceedings, 1995*(1), 235-239.

Beck, T., Demirguc-Kunt, A., & Levine, R. (2005). SMEs, growth, and poverty: Cross-country evidence. *Journal of Economic Growth, 10*(3), 199–229. doi:10.1007/s10887-005-3533-5

Benner, M. J., & Tushman, M. L. (2003). Exploitation, exploration, and process management: The productivity dilemma revisited. *Academy of Management Review, 28*(2), 238–256.

Chang, Y. P., & Zhu, D. H. (2011). Understanding social networking sites adoption in China: A comparison of pre-adoption and post-adoption. *Computers in Human Behavior, 27*(5), 1840–1848. doi:10.1016/j.chb.2011.04.006

Chowdhury, M. S. A., Azam, M. K. G., & Islam, S. (2015). Problems and Prospects of SME Financing in Bangladesh. *Asian Business Review, 2*(2), 51–58. doi:10.18034/abr.v2i2.304

Crisp, R. (2008). Well being. In E. N. Zalta (Ed.), The Stanford Encyclopedia of Philosophy (Winter ed.). Stanford University Press.

Damanpour, F. (1991). Organizational innovation: A meta-analysis of effects of determinants and moderators. *Academy of Management Journal, 34*(3), 555–590. doi:10.2307/256406

Diener, E. (2009). Subjective well-being. In E. Diener (Ed.), *The science of well-being* (Vol. 37, pp. 11–58). New York: Springer. doi:10.1007/978-90-481-2350-6_2

Dolan, P., & Metcalfe, R. (2012). The relationship between innovation and subjective wellbeing. *Research Policy, 41*(8), 1489–1498. doi:10.1016/j.respol.2012.04.001

Drazin, R., & Schoonhoven, C. B. (1996). Community, population, and organization effects on innovation: A multilevel perspective. *Academy of Management Journal, 39*(5), 1065–1083. doi:10.2307/256992

Fishbein, M., Ajzen, I. (1975). *Belief, attitude, intention and behavior: An introduction to theory and research.* Academic Press.

Gopi, M., & Ramayah, T. (2007). Applicability of theory of planned behavior in predicting intention to trade online: Some evidence from a developing country. *International Journal of Emerging Markets, 2*(4), 348–360. doi:10.1108/17468800710824509

Hagger, M. S., Chatzisarantis, N. L., & Biddle, S. J. (2002). A meta-analytic review of the theories of reasoned action and planned behavior in physical activity: Predictive validity and the contribution of additional variables. *Journal of Sport & Exercise Psychology, 24*(1), 3–32. doi:10.1123/jsep.24.1.3

Halim, H. A., Ahmad, N. H., Ramayah, T., Hanifah, H., Taghizadeh, S. K., & Mohamad, M. N. (2015). Towards an Innovation Culture: Enhancing Innovative Performance of Malaysian SMEs. *Academic Journal of Interdisciplinary Studies, 4*(2), 85.

Henderson, R. (1993). Underinvestment and incompetence as responses to radical innovation: Evidence from the photolithographic alignment equipment industry. *The Rand Journal of Economics, 24*(2), 248–270. doi:10.2307/2555761

Jansen, J. J., Van Den Bosch, F. A., & Volberda, H. W. (2006). Exploratory innovation, exploitative innovation, and performance: Effects of organizational antecedents and environmental moderators. *Management Science*, *52*(11), 1661–1674. doi:10.1287/mnsc.1060.0576

Kim, H., Kim, T., & Shin, S. W. (2009). Modeling roles of subjective norms and eTrust in customers acceptance of airline B2C eCommerce websites. *Tourism Management*, *30*(2), 266–277. doi:10.1016/j.tourman.2008.07.001

Kollmann, T., Stöckmann, C. (2014). Filling the entrepreneurial orientation–performance gap: The mediating effects of exploratory and exploitative innovations. *Entrepreneurship Theory and Practice*, *38*(5), 1001-1026.

Lee, M.-C. (2009). Factors influencing the adoption of internet banking: An integration of TAM and TPB with perceived risk and perceived benefit. *Electronic Commerce Research and Applications*, *8*(3), 130–141. doi:10.1016/j.elerap.2008.11.006

Lubatkin, M. H., Simsek, Z., Ling, Y., & Veiga, J. F. (2006). Ambidexterity and performance in small-to medium-sized firms: The pivotal role of top management team behavioral integration. *Journal of Management*, *32*(5), 646–672. doi:10.1177/0149206306290712

Luoma-aho, V., Vos, M., Lappalainen, R., Lämsä, A.-M., Uusitalo, O., Maaranen, P., & Koski, A. (2012). Added value of intangibles for organizational innovation. *Human Technology*, *8*(1), 7–23. doi:10.17011/ht/urn.201205141650

Manstead, A. S., & Eekelen, S. A. (1998). Distinguishing between perceived behavioral control and self-efficacy in the domain of academic achievement intentions and behaviors. *Journal of Applied Social Psychology*, *28*(15), 1375–1392. doi:10.1111/j.1559-1816.1998.tb01682.x

March, J. G. (1991). Exploration and exploitation in organizational learning. *Organization Science*, *2*(1), 71–87. doi:10.1287/orsc.2.1.71

Martin, B. R. (2013). Innovation studies: an emerging agenda. In Innovation Studies: Evolution and Future Challenges. Academic Press.

Mathieson, K. (1991). Predicting user intentions: Comparing the technology acceptance model with the theory of planned behavior. *Information Systems Research*, *2*(3), 173–191. doi:10.1287/isre.2.3.173

Mehrtens, J., Cragg, P. B., & Mills, A. M. (2001). A model of Internet adoption by SMEs. *Information & Management*, *39*(3), 165–176. doi:10.1016/S0378-7206(01)00086-6

Mueller, V., Rosenbusch, N., & Bausch, A. (2013). Success patterns of exploratory and exploitative innovation a meta-analysis of the influence of institutional factors. *Journal of Management*, *39*(6), 1606–1636. doi:10.1177/0149206313484516

Nussbaum, M. C., Sen, A., & Sugden, R. (1993). *The quality of life*. Oxford, UK: Clarendon Press Oxford. doi:10.1093/0198287976.001.0001

Nystrom, P. C., Ramamurthy, K., & Wilson, A. L. (2002). Organizational context, climate and innovativeness: Adoption of imaging technology. *Journal of Engineering and Technology Management*, *19*(3), 221–247. doi:10.1016/S0923-4748(02)00019-X

Oosterlaken, I. (2009). Design for Development: A Capability Approach. *Design Issues*, *25*(4), 91–102. doi:10.1162/desi.2009.25.4.91

Parasuraman, S., & Simmers, C. A. (2001). Type of employment, work–family conflict and well-being: A comparative study. *Journal of Organizational Behavior*, *22*(5), 551–568. doi:10.1002/job.102

Pierce, J. L., & Delbecq, A. L. (1977). Organization structure, individual attitudes and innovation. *Academy of Management Review*, *2*(1), 27–37.

Rahman, S. A., Amran, A., Ahmad, N. H., & Taghizadeh, S. K. (2015). Enhancing the Wellbeing of Base of the Pyramid Entrepreneurs through Business Success: The Role of Private Organizations. *Social Indicators Research*, 1–22. doi:10.1007/s11205-015-0951-4

Ramayah, T., Ling, N. S., Taghizadeh, S. K., & Rahman, S. A. (2016). Factors influencing SMEs website continuance intention in Malaysia. *Telematics and Informatics*, *33*(1), 150–164. doi:10.1016/j.tele.2015.06.007

Rasiah, R., Crinis, V., & Lee, H.-A. (2015). Industrialization and labour in Malaysia. *Journal of the Asia Pacific Economy*, *20*(1), 77–99. doi:10.1080/13547860.2014.974327

Raz, J. (2004). The role of well-being. *Philosophical Perspectives*, *18*(1), 269–294. doi:10.1111/j.1520-8583.2004.00029.x

Rothaermel, F. T., & Deeds, D. L. (2004). Exploration and exploitation alliances in biotechnology: A system of new product development. *Strategic Management Journal*, *25*(3), 201–221. doi:10.1002/smj.376

Ryan, R. M., & Deci, E. L. (2001). On happiness and human potentials: A review of research on hedonic and eudaimonic well-being. *Annual Review of Psychology*, *52*(1), 141–166. doi:10.1146/annurev.psych.52.1.141 PMID:11148302

Saleh, A. S., & Ndubisi, N. O. (2006). An evaluation of SME development in Malaysia. *International Review of Business Research Papers*, *2*(1), 1–14.

Salomo, S., Talke, K., & Strecker, N. (2008). Innovation field orientation and its effect on innovativeness and firm performance. *Journal of Product Innovation Management*, *25*(6), 560–576. doi:10.1111/j.1540-5885.2008.00322.x

Savlovschi, L. I., & Robu, N. R. (2011). The Role of SMEs in Modern Economy". *Economia. Seria Management*, *14*(1), 278–281.

Schamberger, D. K., Cleven, N. J., & Brettel, M. (2013). Performance Effects of Exploratory and Exploitative Innovation Strategies and the Moderating Role of External Innovation Partners. *Industry and Innovation*, *20*(4), 336–356. doi:10.1080/13662716.2013.805928

Schmidt, J. B., & Calantone, R. J. (1998). Are really new product development projects harder to shut down? *Journal of Product Innovation Management*, *15*(2), 111–123. doi:10.1016/S0737-6782(97)00074-X

Sen, A. (1999). *Development as Freedom*. New York: Alfred A. Knopf Inc.

Shah Alam, S., & Mohamed Sayuti, N. (2011). Applying the Theory of Planned Behavior (TPB) in halal food purchasing. *International Journal of Commerce and Management*, *21*(1), 8–20. doi:10.1108/10569211111111676

Shane, S., & Venkataraman, S. (2000). The promise of entrepreneurship as a field of research. *Academy of Management Review*, *25*(1), 217–226.

Singh, H., Mahmood, R. (2014). Combined Effect of Competitive and Manufacturing Strategies on Export Performance of Small and Medium Enterprises in Malaysia. *Global Journal of Management and Business Research, 14*(1).

SME Corporation Malaysia. (2011). *Financial guide for SMEs.* SME Corporation Malaysia. Retrieved from http://www.smecorp.gov.my/vn2/

SME Corporation Malaysia. (2016a). *Definition of Micro Enterprises and SMEs.* Retrieved from http://www.smecorp.gov.my/index.php/en/

SME Corporation Malaysia. (2016b). *Profile and Importance to the Economy.* Retrieved from http://www.smecorp.gov.my/index.php/en/policies/2015-12-21-09-09-49/profile-and-importance-to-the-economy

Smith, J. R., Terry, D. J., Manstead, A. S., Louis, W. R., Kotterman, D., & Wolfs, J. (2007). Interaction Effects in the Theory of Planned Behavior: The Interplay of Self-Identity and Past Behavior. *Journal of Applied Social Psychology*, *37*(11), 2726–2750. doi:10.1111/j.1559-1816.2007.00278.x

Snyder-Halpern, R. (2001). Indicators of organizational readiness for clinical information technology/systems innovation: A Delphi study. *International Journal of Medical Informatics*, *63*(3), 179–204. doi:10.1016/S1386-5056(01)00179-4 PMID:11502432

Sommer, L. (2011). The theory of planned behaviour and the impact of past behaviour. *International Business & Economics Research Journal, 10*(1).

Stiglitz, J. E. (2014). The Innovation Enigma. Project Syndicate.

Taghizadeh, S. K., Jayaraman, K., Ismail, I., & Rahman, S. A. (2014). A Study of Service Innovation Management in the Malaysian Telecommunications Industry. *Global Business and Organizational Excellence*, *34*(1), 67–77. doi:10.1002/joe.21585

The National SME Development Council. (2011). *SME annual report.* Retrieved from http://www.smecorp.gov.my/vn2/node/113

UNDP. (2015). *Post-2015 Sustainable Development Agenda.* Retrieved July 1, 2015, from http://www.undp.org/content/undp/en/home/mdgoverview/post-2015-development-agenda.html

Unsworth, K. L., Sawang, S., Murray, J., Sorbello, T. (2009). Developing An Integrative Model For Understanding Innovation Adoption. *Academy of Management Proceedings, 2009*(1), 1-6.

Venkatesh, V., & Davis, F. D. (2000). A theoretical extension of the technology acceptance model: Four longitudinal field studies. *Management Science*, *46*(2), 186–204. doi:10.1287/mnsc.46.2.186.11926

Vera, D., & Crossan, M. (2004). Strategic leadership and organizational learning. *Academy of Management Review*, *29*(2), 222–240.

Weigel, F. K., Hazen, B. T., Cegielski, C. G., & Hall, D. J. (2014). Diffusion of Innovations and the Theory of Planned Behavior in Information Systems Research: A Metaanalysis. *Communications of the Association for Information Systems*, *34*(1), 31.

Yeoh, P. L. (2014). Internationalization and Performance Outcomes of Entrepreneurial Family SMEs: The Role of Outside CEOs, Technology Sourcing, and Innovation. *Thunderbird International Business Review*, *56*(1), 77–96. doi:10.1002/tie.21597

Yu, T. F.-L. (2001). The Chinese family business as a strategic system: An evolutionary perspective. *International Journal of Entrepreneurial Behaviour & Research*, *7*(1), 22–40. doi:10.1108/13552550110385736

KEY TERMS AND DEFINITIONS

Attitude: Attitude refers to the degree to which a person has favourable or unfavourable evaluation or appraisal of the behaviour in question.

Exploitative Innovation: Exploitative innovation is built on improvements, refinements, efficiency, and implementation of current skills and processes in organization. It has incremental character and focus on the needs of existing customers and lead to incremental product changes.

Exploratory Innovation: Exploratory innovations respond to and affect latent environmental trends through creating new products or services and new markets. It deals with offering innovative designs and creative ways to satisfy customer and market needs.

Perceived Behaviour Control: Perceived behaviour control has been defined as an individual's approximation of how easy or difficult it will be for the those individual to express certain the behaviour.

Subjective Norm: Subjective norm represent the individual's behaviour that they perform, even if they are not inclined toward the behaviour and its consequences.

Subjective Wellbeing: Subjective wellbeing encompasses people's long term view of how pleased or satisfied they are with their life. It has mostly considered the reasons for experiencing a life in a positive way, including the cognitive judgments and affective reactions of one's own life.

Theory of Planned Behaviour: The fundamental assumption of the theory is that behavioural decisions are the result of a reasoned process in which the behaviour is influenced by attitudes, norms and perceived behaviour control.

Chapter 14
Non-State SMEs in Vietnam:
Understanding Strategic Situation and Implications for Organizational Performance

Nguyen Thi Uyen
Universiti Sains Malaysia, Malaysia

Siti Rohaida Mohamed Zainal
Universiti Sains Malaysia, Malaysia

ABSTRACT

Small and medium enterprises (SMEs) which are dominated by non-state SMEs play an important role in economic growth, job creation and poverty reduction in Vietnam. However, most of non-state SMEs in Vietnam are young and contain several limitations in performance. Therefore, finding solutions and strategic orientations to enhance SMEs performance becomes the major concern of the policy makers and business practitioners. To generate the implications pertinent to firms for sustaining high organizational performance in long run, understanding the strategic situation of the firms is a vital step. Thus, based on strategic theory of SWOT and strategy formulation, this chapter aims to: (1) Explore the characteristics of dynamic macro environment for development of non-state SMEs in Vietnam; (2) identify the key firm's features; (3) examine firm performance to identify achievements and constraints; (4) suggest strategic implications for enhancement of SMEs performance toward long-run development of non-state SMEs in Vietnam.

INTRODUCTION

For nearly three decades, Vietnam has gained one of the highest rates of economic growth and poverty reduction in the world. There are several factors supported this achievement of which two central determinants are the positive innovation of economic policy and the growth of private sector largely composed of non-state SMEs in Vietnam (ADB, 2013). The effective adoption and implementation of Doi moi (revolution) in 1986 are recognized in Vietnam's economic history as a turning point because

DOI: 10.4018/978-1-5225-2165-5.ch014

the renovation boosts the development of non-state SMEs and enables them to be a key part in Vietnam's economy. The renovation was started with a series of the reforms that effectively ended the central planning system of resource allocation in 1989. Reforms, therefore, generated a multi-stakeholder economy under socialist-oriented market mechanism. And the private sector is officially considered as a legal component of Vietnam's economy. Hence, this significant revolution has created a lot of opportunities for non-state sector in Vietnam than ever before.

Following this positive movement was the presence of the Enterprise Law in 2009 that took effect in 2010. This is the second turning-point in Vietnam policy revolution that allows non-state enterprises to do business in all lawful economic industries instead of restrictions placed under central planning mechanism. The legal regulations of procedures for business start-up are also much simpler, that has fostered significantly the development of non-state SMEs in Vietnam.

Besides creating more favorably legal framework for opening market and setting up new business, Vietnamese government also put strong effort in implementing several national action plans and support services. These initiatives stimulate the firm SMEs performance. The deeper engagement in international market of Vietnam also enables local entrepreneurs to be more active. These above movements have created a dynamic development of non-state SMEs which become one of the most important components of Vietnam's economy (ADB, 2013). According to the White Paper 2014 launched by Vietnam Ministry of Planning and Investment, the number of active enterprises has increased rapidly, in just 5 years from 1993 to 1997 there were nearly 20 thousand enterprises established and then increased from 98,833 firms in 2000 to nearly 325,000 in 2008, and to 347,000 firms in 2012 that increased by around 16% per year (VMPI, 2014b). Especially, around 97% of which are non-state enterprises (consists of private enterprise, collective name, limited company, joint-stock company composed of less than 50% from government capital, and join-stock company without government capital) (*VGSO, 2013*). In addition, according to statistics of VGSO (2012), the large sized enterprises in the non-state sector account for less than 1% (0.81%). It means that SMEs contributes to more than 99% in total number of non-state enterprise. Furthermore, employment in non-state sector contributes increasingly from 29% in 2000 to 59% of total employment in 2011 (ADB, 2013). Therefore, Vietnam's non-state sector in general and non-state SMEs in particular is truly crucial to economic growth of the country.

It is really a huge achievement to reach such development for SMEs but keeping growth for development in long-run of the whole country is the bigger question. Vietnam SMEs grew rapidly at the beginning stage of positive changing policy and opening market but they are now facing a lot of difficulties. Besides, some favourable drivers from macro-environment and expansion of non-state sector, SMEs especially the non-state SMEs are facing several obstacles from external environment such as administrative procedures, limited access to support services, limited access to finance, poor skilled human resource market and other internal constraints as well. Large number of non-state SMEs has been operating with very poor organizational performance, a lot of them are unprofitable and even dissolved and halted-production (VMPI, 2014a). To find the solution for these raising problems, understanding strategic situation to identify the opportunities, threats, achievements and weaknesses in the light of long–run orientation is a vital step of formulating strategic orientation for both firm and policy makers. With the full landscape of external and internal environment, the solid implications will be generated for both policy makers and business practitioners in stimulating firm performance toward long-term development of non-state SMEs in Vietnam.

STATEMENT OF PROBLEM, LITERATURE GAP, AND OBJECTIVES

It is great success of SMEs in Vietnam in the past decades. However, the development mostly on wide expansion which seems not stable and sustained for long run (VMPI, 2014b). Consequently, in recent years of 2009-2012, there were up to 60,737 SMEs which mostly are non-state SMEs were dissolved and halted-production in 2013, increased by 11,9% as compared to 2012 and 12,5% as compared to 2011 (VMPI, 2014a). Especially, VMPI (2014a) indicated that the dominant number of enterprises are doing business unprofitably since 2010 that continuously increased to nearly 70% in 2013. In this context, the topic of finding solutions for enhancing SMEs performance especially for non-state SMEs toward long-run development becomes the central concern in many economic forums and scientific conferences in Vietnam.

Most of Non-state SMEs in Vietnam have established after the effect of Enterprise Law in 2000 so they are almost in their infant stage of development. So many constrains such as small scale, lack of management skills, poor human resource management, limited capital are the key weaknesses of private SMEs explored partly in different previous researches (Tran, Le, & Nguyen, 2008; VGSO, 2013; VMPI, 2014a; Xuan Nha & Quan, 2014, Cuong 2007). In addition, the effect of external drivers such as legal regulations, business competition, financial market, government service support, infrastructure ...on SMEs performance is also remarkable and needs to be considered.

Nevertheless, up far now there is no study that focuses on identifying and illustrating a current landscape of strategic situation of SMEs in light of stimulating SMEs performance toward long-term growth. Most of previous research have focused on evaluating single constraints such as top leader, human resource management (Quan, 2015; Xuan Nha & Quan, 2014) and organizational performance or influence of HRM practices with organizational performance (Thang & Quang, 2013), training (Hang, 2015). There was a study of T. Cuong, Sang, & Anh, (2007) which emphasized on characteristics of SMEs in 2007. This study was conducted before financial crisis in 2008 with several changes from macro environments. This study targeted to the whole SMEs, not emphasized on non-state SMEs. It was also not analyzed with strategic approach in scanning environment and formulating strategic orientation for the firm. Therefore, there are no studies interpreted the full landscape of strategic situation of SMEs and generated strategic orientation for non-state SMEs.

From strategic theory of SWOT analysis, it is necessary to understand strategic situation of both external and internal perspective. Several studies asserted the influence of external factors on the outcomes of small business such as governmental support in creating business environment, in providing financial and training programs, in upgrading infrastructure or even in creating protection (Yusuf, 1995); education and training programs (Robertson & Collins, 2003); favourable loans and export assistance (Mahajar, Binti, & Yunus, 2006). While other studies found the significance of internal factors such as managerial and planning skill (Gaskill & Auken, 1993), organizational features of monetary, equipment, personnel capabilities, production, market resources.., and individual features (Covin & Slevin, 1991). Based on scanning these internal and external variables, strategy formulation need to exploit opportunities, avoid threats from external environment, take advantage of strengths and overcome the weaknesses from internal environment.

Thus, based on previous literature and practical requirement form Vietnam, this study fills this gap by revealing a full picture of strategic situation through environment scanning for non-state SMEs in Vietnam in order to sustain high organizational performance for long run. The following objectives are targeted: (1) to present insights from the dynamic macro environment for development of non-state

SMEs in Vietnam in both opportunities and challenging problems perspectives; (2) Identify characteristics of non-state SMEs development (3) Examine the organizational performance of SMEs to identify achievements and weaknesses associated to constraints in generating high organizational performance for long term; (4) suggest strategic implications for enhancement of firm performance toward long-run development of non-state SMEs in Vietnam. With the important role and dominant portion of non-state SMEs in Vietnam as well the similarity to SMEs in other developing countries, the current study which fills up above gaps becomes more valuable in both theory and practices.

MACRO ENVIRONMENT FOR DEVELOPMENT OF NON-STATE SMES IN VIETNAM

Opportunities for Development of Private SMEs In Vietnam

Positive Movement in Legal Framework and Regulations

As mentioned above, Vietnam has gained one of the highest rates of economic growth and poverty reduction in the world. And the central driver of this result is positive economic policy innovations. Therefore, the biggest opportunities of SMEs in Vietnam are the economic transition as well as the regime reforms of all business regulations. It has started since 1986 with a series of the reforms that effectively ended the central planning system of resource allocation and opening great opportunities for non-state enterprises to do business in both local and international market. This significant movement in policy reforms could be summarized briefly as shown in Table 1.

Table 1. Vietnam's key market – oriented economic reforms since 1986

Areas	Content
Agricultural reforms	• Since 1981: introduction of farming contract system replaced for single dominance of collective ownership in agriculture in the past. This allows households join as the basic decision-making units in production and security of tenure for farm families. • Since 1987: Applying policy of using durable land for farmers. • In 1993, enacting Land Law and subsequent revision in 2003, creating a more solid legal background for agriculture development.
Macroeconomic/price stabilization (during second half of 1980s and first half of 1990s)	• Completion of several regulations on price liberalization, elimination of dual price system (1989-1991). • Large devaluation and unification of the exchange rate (1991). • Adjusting interest rates to positive levels in real terms (positive real interest rates) to curb hyperinflation (1989).
Foreign trade and WTO-driven reforms	• Creating liberalization in international trading: eradicating SOEs monopoly in international trade; abolishing licenses requirement in international trading and so on) (1989-1998). • Building a more transparent and stable regulations on export-import (2001). • Enabling simplification in customs services. • Partly removing non-tariff barriers (NTBs), reducing tariff rates to implement commitments in AFTA, VN-US BTA and so on). • Since 2005, intensive efforts in amendment and new promulgation of a huge number of legal documents to conform to WTO rules and provisions. • Became WTO member since December 2006, started to implement WTO commitments in 2007.

continued on next page

Table 1. Continued

Areas	Content
Investment environment reforms	• Promulgation of Foreign Investment Law (1987) and making subsequent revisions in 1996, 2000 and 2002. • Granting different kinds of incentives (especially taxation) to attract FDI inflows. • Improving FDI environment significantly (streamlining administrative procedures; licensing, fairer treatment; enlarging permission for scope of business; easing land clearance; enhancing stock market). • Promulgation of Law on Promotion of domestic investment (for domestic companies) in 1999. • Provision investment incentives provided by provinces for attraction of investment inflows.
Financial markets reforms	• Establishment of two foreign exchange trading centers in Hanoi and HCMC (1991), inter-bank money market (1993) and inter-bank foreign exchange (1994). • Liberalization of VND interest rate and foreign interest rates (2001). • April 2001, commencement programs of state-owned commercial bank (SOCB) restructuring, dealing with nonperforming loans (NPLs) by gradual reduction of lending policy practices to SOEs, increasing lending to private sector, and strengthening supervision and risks management. • Establishment of official securities market in HCM in 2000, and second board (planned to be OTC) for SMEs in Hanoi in 2005. • In 2006, promulgation of Securities Law creating firm legal ground for the market development. • Gradual opening domestic market for foreign bank subsidiaries, especially as committed by Vietnam – US Bilateral Agreement and WTO accession. • Amending a number of articles in the Law enterprise Income Tax and the Law on Value Added Tax during the 5th session in May 2013. Accordingly, the corporate income tax rate of 22% is applied from 01/2014 and then further reduced to 20% from 01/2016. • The Vietnamese government issued Directive No. 14/CT-TTg dated 28/6/2013 to strictly control the formulation appraisal and approval of investment projects using state budget and Government bonds and strengthen management in order to minimize outstanding debts in basic infrastructure construction. • Improving credit information system through the Government's Decree No. 10/2010/ND-CP dated 12/02/2010 setting up the legal framework for the establishment of private credit information centres. Vietnam has also strengthen investor protection by introducing stricter requirement on information disclosures for listed companies. • Government issued Resolution 02/NQ-CP; 01/NQ-CP dated 07/01/2013 focusing on major solutions directing the implementation of the socioeconomic development plan – and State budget estimates in 2013 and number of measures to remove difficulties for production and business, market support and bad debt settlement; new policies on tax intensives, lending rates, credit funds with comprehensive, accurate, clear content that strengthen legal framework and favorable, fair business environment.
Non-state sector reforms	• Since 1986: recognition multi-stakeholder economy; since 1989, encouragement of the private sector as an economic component; revision of the Constitution 1992 to protect private capital. • In 1997, enacting Cooperative Law to revitalize cooperatives as one pillar of market economy with socialist orientation. • In 1999, promulgation of Enterprise Law (1999), allowing non-state enterprises to do business in all lawful economic sectors/domains. • In 2005, promulgation of (Common) Enterprise Law and (Unified) Investment Law creating the common legal regulations for all forms of enterprises (non-state, state-own, FDI enterprises). • Decree 66/2008 to ensure that the rights of enterprises to conduct business are protected. • The communist Party of Vietnam adopted the Socio-Economic Development Strategy for 2011-2020. Consequently, The Government issued Resolution No. 10/NQ-CP dated 24/04/2012 on the Government's Action Plan implementing the Socio-Economic Development Strategy in 2011-2020, and the country's development orientations and tasks in 5 years from 2011 to 2015. This regulations focus on renew growth model, restructure the economy toward socialist-oriented market and economy development which enhance the development of enterprises that including SMEs.
Administrative reforms	• In 2001, the Government established its Public Administration Reform Master Program 2001-2010, with key reforms on legal and institutional framework, public organization, human resources, and public finance. These reforms, together with the application of one-stop-shop model for business registration streamlined significantly public administrative procedures and enabled non-state, especially private sector to shorten significantly business registration time and costs. • Since 2006, application of one-stop-shop model for business registration to shorten business registration time. • Decision 74/2010 and The Government's Administrative Procedures Simplification Scheme (Scheme 30) has been implemented since 2010 in order to: Reform the tax billing procedures; applying electronic customs declaration, implementing a national single window mechanism connecting ministries, branches; scrap regulation of collecting construction fee, controlling construction progress and regulation of real estates as well.

Source: Adapted from 'Vietnam's Small and Medium Sized Enterprises Development: Characteristics, Constraints and Policy Recommendations'' by Tran, T. C., X. S. Le and K. A. Nguyen (2008) and from White Paper 2014 by Vietnam Ministry of Planning and Investment - VMPI (2014a).

All above constant efforts from government have not only changed the economic regimes, provided larger opportunities for non-state sector but also created a simpler administrative procedures and higher productive business environment. According to ADB (2013), one of the significant results of the government's effort in improving administrative procedures is that the Prime Minister has approved 25 resolutions for simplification of 4,800 administrative procedures. In addition, the regulation on business registration is also handling procedures with shorter time of a maximum of 5 days now, from around 6-12 months in the 1990s. The business registration files can be submitted at one-stop shops since 2008 with the fee about VND 200,000 (US$10) to obtain the business registration (ADB, 2013).

National Action Programs and Support Institutions

The second opportunities come from the national action plan and support institutions that directly stimulate the SMEs growth with strong support from government. There are 2 key national SME development programs described as follows (Table 2).

In addition, on 7th September 2012, the prime minister issues Decision No.1231/QD-TTg approving the 2nd SME development Plan, 2011-2015 targeted to set up 350,000 new enterprises and reached

Table 2. The five-year SME development plan 2006-2010

I. SME Development viewpoints	1. Realize consistently the policy of building a multi-stakeholder economy. Economic sectors that do business in compliance with legal regulations are all important constituent parts of a socialist oriented market economy with a vision of long term development, cooperation and healthy competition; 2. The State creates a sound policy, legal and institutional environment that ensures fair and healthy competition for SMEs and service providers of all economic sectors so as to mobilize all internal and external resources for development investment; 3. Develop SMEs in an active but sustainable way, enhancing the quality, increasing the quantity to have economic efficiency and realize the goal of contribution to employment generation, poverty reduction, ensuring social safety and security; SME development objectives are also to be integrated into national goals, and specific socioeconomic goals of every region and locality, encouraging agricultural industries, traditional trade villages with a focus on SME development in mountainous areas and regions having socioeconomic difficulties; SMEs owned by people of ethnic minority groups, women and the disabled...should be prioritized and supported, priorities should also be given to SMEs having production and investment in sectors that can be competitive; 4. State support will gradually shift from direct support to indirect support to enhance the capacity of SMEs; 5. The State will link business activities with environmental protection and assurance of social security and safety; 6. Raise awareness of governments of all levels about the role played by SMEs in socioeconomic development.
II. Goals of SME development	1. Overall objective: Boost the progress rate of SME development, creating environment for healthy competition, strengthening the national competitiveness, SMEs are to contribute more and more to the growth of the national economy. 2. Specific objectives: a) The number of newly established SMEs will be 320,000 (annual growth rate of 22 percent); b) The number of newly established SMEs in disadvantaged provinces will have increased by 15 percent by 2010; c) The ratio of SMEs having direct export is 3-6 percent; d) SMEs will create about 2.7 million new jobs in the period 2006-2010; e) There will be additionally 165,000 technical workers in SMEs.

continued on next page

Table 2. Continued

III. Main tasks	1. The stability of the legal framework and the reform of the administrative procedures will be continued to be improved to create a transparent, stable, and equal business and investment environment for SME development; 2. Assess new policies' impacts on SMEs, organize periodical dialogues between public authorities and SMEs to give instructions and answers to pressing demands for business development; 3. The tax system is to be adapted to encourage start-ups, conduct the reform of the accounting system, and reporting requirements to simplify them and encourage the tax self-assessment system that is both convenient to the enterprises and against the tax losses; Improve the lack of work premises, and enhance the environment protection by formulating and publicizing the land master planning and land use plan; facilitate the development of industrial zones, industrial clusters of appropriate size with suitable land lease price for SMEs; support the relocation of polluting SMEs from residential and urban areas to industrial zones and industrial clusters; 5. Revise regulations to boost the establishment of SME credit guarantee funds at the local level; Take steps to restructure the state-owned banking sector, encourage the emergence of different forms of banking services, joint stock commercial banks for SMEs, including the development of the leasing service and the extension of non-collateralized finance for SMEs that have feasible business plans in order to satisfy the need of finance for investment and business; 6. Boost the implementation of support programs disseminating and applying modern technologies and advanced techniques for SMEs, enhancing technology management capacity; encourage the cooperation and sharing in technology among enterprises of different sizes; develop effectively research program that can be developed in reality; study, revise and issue the system of technical standards, quality assurance system and quality certification system in conformity with international standards. Encourage SMEs to participate in programs for industry linkages, regional linkages and developing supporting industry; 7. Accelerate the development of the business information system to have the background for the assessment of this sector's state, for the process of policy making and at the same time to provide business information to enterprises; 8. Conduct general information and awareness raising activities to disseminate entrepreneur spirit and the awareness of legal wealth creation to all. Carry out pilot projects of integrating specific enterprise-related training modules into education schemes at high schools, colleges and universities, technical high schools, vocational schools in order to foster entrepreneurial spirit and entrepreneur culture and create supporting social attitude towards legal business activities; 9. Develop market (both supply and demand) for business development services; improve the legal environment of business development services, with the focus on the management of service quality. Encourage associations to have business development services; implement actively SME support programs; participate in the policy making process of SME support policies and support programs in order to strengthen the supporting role of these associations and to make them really become the legal representative for SMEs' interests; 10. Improve the effectiveness in coordinating SME development support activities, enhance the role played by the SME Promotion Council; enhancing capacity at the local level in the management, promotion and development of SMEs.

Source: Retrieved from 'Vietnam's Small and Medium Sized Enterprises Development: Characteristics, Constraints and Policy Recommendations'' by Tran, T. C., X. S. Le and K. A. Nguyen, 2008, SME in Asia and Globalization, ERIA Research Project Report 2007-5, pp.323-364.

600,000 business by 31/12/2015 *VMPI (2014b)*. And to realize the goals, the plan has employed 8 groups of favourable policies as indicated in Table 3.

To implement above action plans, besides reforms taken in legal regulation, Vietnam government has allowed to set up a multi-level system of support institutions for SMEs such as SME promotion council, Agency for SMEs development (ASMED), Provincial Industry Promotion Agency, Provincial Investment Promotion Agency, Trade Promotion Agency, Technical Assistant Centre in Hanoi and Ho Chi Minh... (Tran et al., 2008; VMPI, 2014b). These institution focus on enhancing development of SMEs at both central and provincial levels in term of different fields such as to build effective business environment (BEE: Business enabling Environment), to create better Assess to Finance (ATF), and to enhance Busi-

Table 3. The 2nd SME development plan, 2011-2015

No.	Content
1	Improve the legal frame work for enterprises to complete business registration, do business or withdraw from market
2	Support for access to finance and credit, improve the efficiency of using capital for SMEs
3	Support technological innovation and new technology application in SMEs
4	Develop human resources for SMEs
5	Promote the formation of industrial clusters, improve the access to land for SMEs.
6	Provide information to SMEs and promote market expansion for SMEs.
7	Build a System of SME development agencies
8	Manage the implementation of the Plan

Source: Adapted from "Vietnam SMEs White Paper" by Vietnam Ministry of Planning and Investment (2014b) retrieved from http://en.business.gov.vn/tabid/179/catid/572/item/13807/white-paper-on-vietnam-sme-2014.aspx

ness Development Services (BDS) of consulting in legal issues, accounting, finance, marketing, training, business linkages, market information, technology transfer and so on.

Especially, along with the effort of the Government in creating the system of support institutions, the community of business practitioners also set up their own support system (N. Cuong, 2007; VMPI, 2014b). This system is created by the different business associations, clubs which provide support services in training, sharing information, consultancy and facilitation for the members. There are around 200 major business associations which are currently active in Vietnam (Cuong, 2007). Among of which, Vietnam Chamber of Commerce and Industry (VCCI), Union of Associations of Industries and Commerce (HUAIC) in Ha Noi and Ho Chi Minh City, Young Entrepreneurs Association (YEA) are playing important role in supporting SMEs especially the non-state SMEs in Vietnam.

These above national action plans as well as the support institutions directly influenced the development of SMEs. This brought the significant opportunities for development of SMEs in Vietnam and enabled SMEs to become the key component and to be "contributing to the growth of the national economy, job creation, poverty alleviation and hunger eradication" (Vietnam National Assembly, 2002).

Fund Financed by Government and Donors

The SMEs' support funds from government and the donors are also important parts which have been creating favourable finance for SMEs. The grants from aid agencies and non-government organizations was estimated around USD 840 million over a 10-year period (2001-2010) and generated a lot of chances for SME (N. Cuong, 2007). In addition, SMEs also have the Fund for SMEs Credit Guarantee which is financed by government. Especially the Supporting Program on Human Resource Training for SMEs granted total amount of VND 93.143 million in 3 years from 2011-2013 (Table 4). There are up to 72,448 SMEs leaders trained and VMPI (2014a) also indicated that, this training program had gained a positive improvement in planning, HRM management, the leadership competency.

Table 4. Report on national program of HR development for SMEs leaders, 2011-2013

Year	Number of Course	Number of Trainees	Government Grant (Million VND)
2011	189	7.636	10.814
2012	928	38.974	41.258
2013	900	35.838	41.071
Total	2.017	72.448	93.143

Source: Adapted from "Report on Enterprise and Plan for Social and Economic Development 2014-2015" by Vietnam Ministry of Planning and Investment (2014a).

Stable Political Climate and Potential Context of National Economic Development

Vietnam is among a few transitional economies that have been sustained quite high economic growth rates over the recent 3 decades. Especially, since financial crisis of 2008, Vietnam's economy still remained annual growth rate around 5.5-6.5% (Table 5). Furthermore, the political climate and reforms in legal regulations are also considered as favorably factor for business development (ADB, 2013; ERIA, 2014; VMPI, 2014b). Therefore, the political stability as long as the potential context of national economic growth have significantly been creating a favorably groundwork for fostering SMEs development and vice versa.

CHALLENGES OF NON-STATE SMES IN VIETNAM

Policy Index

Despises that Vietnamese government has put huge effort in creating market-orientated legal framework since 1986 as mentioned above but this system remained many shortcomings especially in comparison with other countries' systems in the same area. According to ERIA (2014), an appropriate SME policy framework plays a fundamental role in fostering the growth of the private sector. And the ASEAN SME Policy index is created to measure 5 main priorities: (i) capacity building and human resource development; (ii) stimulating SME marketing capabilities; (iii) Finance access; (iv)Technology access; and (v) Building a conducive policy environment. Hence, the country ranked with higher index scores has better performance and practices. However, based on this average index, Vietnam is ranked at quite modest position of 3.7, lower than the index of many other countries in the region such as Singapore (5.4),

Table 5. Key macroeconomic indicators

Index	2008	2009	2010	2011	2012	2013
GDP growth rate (% year)	6.2	5.4	6.42	6.24	5.25	5.42
Inflation (Change in CPI, % year)	23.1	6.9	9.19	18.58	9.21	6.6
Credit growth (% year)	25.4	37.7	27.65	12	8.91	12

Source: Adapted from "Vietnam SMEs White Paper" by Vietnam Ministry of Planning and Investment (2014b) retrieved from http://en.business.gov.vn/tabid/179/catid/572/item/13807/white-paper-on-vietnam-sme-2014.aspx

Malaysia (4.7), Indonesia (4.1), Thailand (4.1), and even Philippines (3.8) (*ERIA, 2014).* These figures reflect the shortage of SMEs policy system in meeting requirement of enhancing SMEs development and it becomes the challenge that SMEs in Vietnam have to face in doing business.

From other perspective, Doing Business Report-Smarter Regulations for Small and Medium-Size Enterprises of World Bank (2003) has also ranked Vietnam at 99 that belongs to middle level. Especially, there are some fields was ranked low as electricity access (155/185), investor protection (169/185), tax payment (138/185), and handling insolvent businesses (149/185) (White paper 2014). Although policy makers in Vietnam have took a lot of efforts in policy simplification especially in tax policy but the time for completing tax payment is still long (872 hours/year) and the gross tax rate is still high at 34.5%. And the insolvent business even takes 5 years to be completed. ADB (2013) also suggests that Vietnam needs to improve legal texts quality and SME access to legal services. Especially, the ADB report stressed on the inconsistencies in large number of regulations for business growth. Despite improvements since 2000, the legal framework remains overlapping, being complexity, being contradictions, lagging in implementation, and lacking an effective reliable mechanisms for commercial disputes (Tran et al., 2008). These shortcomings prevent the development of SMEs in Vietnam. Hence the white paper 2014 launched by Vietnam Ministry of Planning and Investment concluded that "the administrative reform and creating effective business environment need to be continued with further efforts".

Limited Access to Support Services and Capital

As mentioned above, the national action plan in Vietnam has enhanced support services through multi-level institution at both central and local level but the real access still limited and does not sufficient to meet demand of business communities. Hence, in ASEAN, Vietnam is ranked at modest level in term of policy framework for supporting service and this becomes the obstacle for SME sectors (ADB, 2013; ERIA, 2014). Especially, in term of access to legal services, ADB (2013) indicated that, SMEs have been dealing with this problem as the main constraint in business development.

In term of e-service which is considered as a creative and powerful instrument in upgrading several service, the e-government is better exploited, several e-government services are introduced to the public and business practitioners in many fields such as taxation, export/import, custom, business registration and bidding services (ERIA, 2014). Then in this term, Vietnam is ranked at 4 compared to 3.7 on average. However, according to ERIA (2014) the online portal for enterprises (including SMEs) is not regularly updated. The content on this portal is still poor and does not meet the requirements of SMEs. The enhancement of this portal to SMEs is also limited and just a few SMEs can access this portal.

In term of access to capital, the dynamic growth in financial sector in Vietnam has not stimulated all group of the economy equally. In reality, there are up to 45% of small firms have main constraint in access to finance that are significantly higher than larger enterprises' (ADB, 2013). The report of ADB also indicated that in manufacturing sector, there are up to 65% of enterprises laid on retained earnings to finance their investment. There is a few, estimated at 5%–10% of SMEs, having loans from banks. This figure is even lower with the enterprises without the land use certificates. While this certificate has not mostly been fully documented and the land without land use certificates accounted for 70-75 percent of land ownership (ERIA, 2014). The annual growth of credit seriously has fallen down for recent years, from 53.9% in 2008 to 8.83% in 2013 (Figure 1) and there is only about 30% of current total credit accounted by SMEs sector, while SMEs contribute to nearly 50% of GDP.

Figure 1.

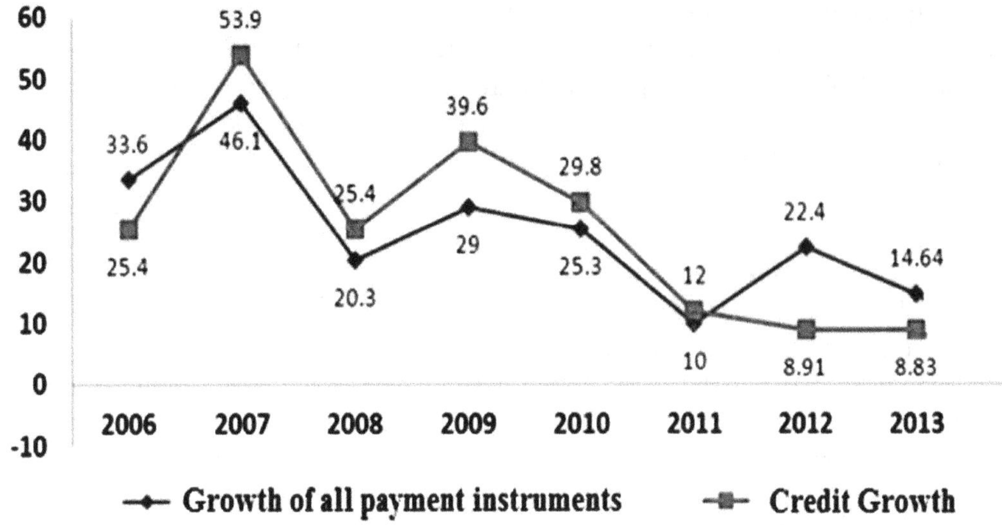

Thus, SMEs in Vietnam have to diversify their financial resources from microfinance for business development. The fund for microfinance institutions raised from public, donor and private sources. Especially, the private source accounted for 82.5 percent of total amount of funds. This reflects the limitations of the unprofessionally financial market in Vietnam.

Competition From Foreign Firms

SMEs are facing the major problems relating to rapid trade liberalization (ERIA, 2014). To sustain their market even in local market, non-state SMEs who have less direct support from government need to strengthen their capacities to deal with the challenges from harder competition. However, most of non-state SMEs in Vietnam have small size and they still "have difficulties in fully exploiting opportunities arising from globalization and regional trading agreements" (ERIA, 2014). Because they have limited knowledge about foreign languages and cultures. Especially SMEs have poor knowledge in the legal and bureaucratic issues of global market and global supply chain networks. The skills of dealing with customers especially in foreign market markets are also limited. So, with current capacity of non-state SMEs in Vietnam, global integration context is one of the hard challenges for SMEs in many industries such as banking, retailing and automobile.

Poor Skilled Labor Market

OECD (2014) indicated that the economic development requires higher skilled labor but increased demand for skilled labor currently is not satisfied by current workforce of Vietnam. The proportion of untrained labor almost does not change during the 2007-2012 period with around 83%. There is up to 30.7% of unskilled labor need to be trained at work by employers (OECD, 2014). A survey of Viet Nam's Central Institute for Economic Management (CIEM) in 2012 under the grant from World Bank indicated that around 47% of enterprises claimed that a lot of skills such as cognitive skill, interpersonal skill, and problem-solving and other required by work place are not satisfied by the education system (OECD, 2014). It is truly a shortage in human resource in term of quality even the quantity is quite abundance in Vietnam. This even becomes bigger threat in current context because the competition for hunting skilled workforces among FDI and local enterprises are extremely tougher than ever before.

Underdeveloped Infrastructure, Poor Support Industries

Last but not least, other factors such as underdeveloped infrastructure, poor supporting industries are the two other bottlenecks of SME growth. This factors threatened the production cost and competitiveness which is inherent less advantages in non-state SMEs (Tran et al., 2008; VMPI, 2014b). Therefore, improving infrastructure and leveraging support industries are taken into account of the national plan in coming years (VMPI, 2014b). However, it is such a long journey to make a significant improvement for these sectors. Thus, the underdeveloped infrastructure, poor support industries are still two major challenges for many non-state SMEs which have no advantage in production cost and economy of scale.

CHARACTERISTICS OF NON-STATE SMES IN VIETNAM

As other countries, Vietnam also has created the official definition for SMEs. And the SMEs system also has their own characteristics in term of ownership, capital size, and employment structures. Thus, the following parts will present more detail about these elements.

SMEs and Non-State SMEs in Vietnam

In term of SMEs, the formal SMEs definition widely accepted in Vietnam is provided by the formal Vietnam Government Decree 90/2001/ND-CP that promulgated in November 2001. According to this definition, SMEs are defined as "a business establishment with registered capital of no more than VND 10 billion (equivalent to USD 630,000) or with an annual average workforce of no more than 300 employees". In addition, the term of non-state enterprises in Vietnam is generated from typical characteristics of transition economy, Vietnam's economy includes several types of ownership. Beside the state ownership enterprise, the economy also consists other participants from other non-state and FDI sector. Officially, non-state enterprises are defined as "enterprises are set up by domestic capital. The capital may be owned by private with 1 or individual group or the government when capital of the government is equal or less than 50% of registered capital. There are following types of non-state enterprises: (1) Private enterprises; (2) Cooperative name companies; (3) Private limited companies; (4) Joint stock companies without capital of State (5) Joint stock companies with 50% and less than of charter capital shared by the government" (VGSO, 2013).

Non-State SMEs Distribution by Criteria

According to Statistical Yearbook of VGSO (2013), the number registered enterprises has increased rapidly since 2000, increased from 98.833 firms in 2000, to nearly 347.000 firms in 2012 and 359,794 in 2013 (VGSO, 2014), increased by around 16% per year, and the non-state enterprises remains dominant proportion of around 97% (Table 6).

Table 6. Number of active enterprises as of annual 31 December by types of enterprise

	2005	2009	2010	2011	2012
TOTAL	106616	236584	279360	324691	346777
State owned Enterprise	**4086**	**3360**	**3281**	**3265**	**3239**
Central	1825	1806	1779	1798	1792
Local	2261	1554	1502	1467	1447
Non-State Enterprise	**98833**	**226676**	**268831**	**312416**	**334562**
Private	34646	47840	48007	48913	48159
Collective name	37	69	79	179	312
Limited Co.	52505	134407	163978	193281	211069
Joint Stock Co. Having capital of state	1096	1738	1710	1751	1761
Joint Stock Co. Without capital of state	10549	42622	55057	68292	73261
Foreign investment enterprise	**3697**	**6548**	**7248**	**9010**	**8976**
100% Foreign capital	2852	5414	5989	7516	7523
Join Venture	845	1134	1259	1494	1453

Note. Adapted from "Statistical Yearbook of Vietnam 2013" by VGSO (2013) retrieved from www.gso.gov.vn/default.aspx?tabid=512&idmid=5&ItemID=14080

According to statistics of VGSO (2012), there is a significant difference in proportion of each type of enterprises. While the state sector is dominated by 39.6 of large sized enterprises, the non-state sector is accounted for less than 1% (0.81%) by large sized enterprises in. It means that SMEs contribute to more than 99% in total non-state enterprises. Especially, the enterprises with less than 10 labors are the majority which account for around 64% (Table 7).

Especially, on average, the Figure 2 shows that the private sector has the lowest average number of labor per enterprise, it is merely around 20 employees. This size is smallest compared to other sectors. The average number of labor of FDI enterprise was 297 in 2010, and increased to 303 in 2012, average number of employees in state enterprise decreased slightly but still remains at 496 in 2012. These reflects the features of SMEs in Vietnam that are in early stage of development and mostly have small size.

ORGANIZATIONAL PERFORMANCE OF NON-STATE SMES: ACHIEVEMENTS AND CONSTRAINTS

Achievements of Non-State SMEs

The non-state SMEs have rapid development after a series of renovation on legal frame works and business regulation since 1986 especially after the effect of Enterprise Law since 2000. This development has enabled the private sector to be dominated by non-state SMEs to play a key role in Vietnam's economy (ADB, 2013).

First of all, in term of investment, the non-state sector has contributed a dominant proportion in total investment of the countries over the past few years. This sector has increased the total investment from 3514.8 trillion dongs in 2009 to 8735.3 trillion dongs in 2013 (Table 8). As a result of global integra-

Table 7. Number of active enterprises by labor size

Labor Size	Total	Number of Enterprises			Percentage (%)		
		State Enterprises	Non-state enterprises	Foreign Invested Enterprises	State Enterprises	Non-State Enterprises	Foreign Invested Enterprises
Less than 5 employees	105,925	36	104,931	958	1.10	33.59	10.63
From 5 to 9 employees	96,165	81	95,108	976	2.48	30.44	10.83
From 10 to 49 employees	92,912	655	89,534	2,723	20.06	28.66	30.22
From 50 to 199 employees	21,853	1,211	18,395	2,247	37.09	5.89	24.94
From 200 to 299 employees	2,841	343	1,951	547	10.51	0.62	6.07
From 300 to 499 employees	2,162	333	1,306	523	10.20	0.42	5.80
From 500 to 999 employees	1,628	315	779	534	9.65	0.25	5.93
From 1000 to 4,999 employees	1,087	252	392	443	7.72	0.13	4.92
Over 5,000 employees	118	39	20	59	1.19	0.01	0.65
Total	**324,691**	**3265**	**312,416**	**9,010**	**100.00**	**100.00**	**100.00**

Note. Adapted from "Vietnam SMEs White Paper" by Vietnam Ministry of Planning and Investment (2014b) retrieved from http://en.business.gov.vn/tabid/179/catid/572/item/13807/white-paper-on-vietnam-sme-2014.aspx_

Figure 2.

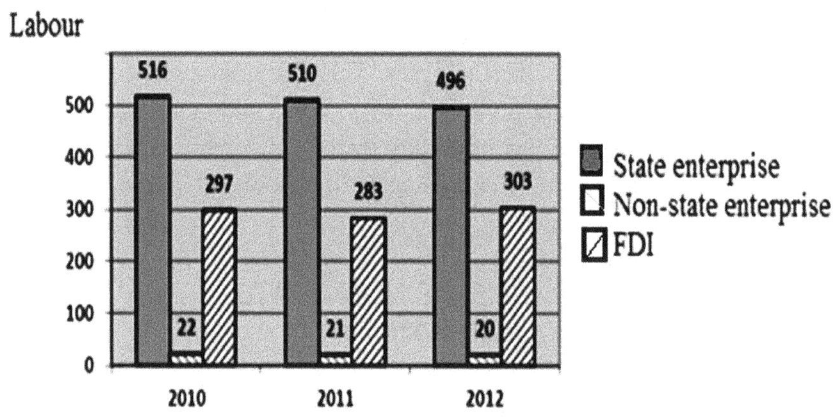

tion, FDI enterprises have raised their investment almost triple after 4 years, from 1221.8 trillion dongs in 2009 to 3342.9 trillion dongs in 2013 (Table 8). However, the state enterprises which are holding the most important business in Vietnam have lower investment proportion in total investment. Even though, with dynamic movement, the non-state sector has contributed to 50% of total national investment by enterprises in Vietnam since 2010. In the context of developing countries and limited access to finance, this figure becomes more meaningful in government's effort to leverage the economy development.

Table 8. Annual average capital of enterprises by types of enterprise

	2009	2010	2011	2012	2013
TOTAL	**7936.7**	**10841.1**	**13622.8**	**15189.8**	**17486.6**
State owned Enterprise	**3200.1**	**3701.8**	**4568.6**	**4908.4**	**5408.4**
Central	2930.8	3397.6	4181.2	4464.1	4939.4
Local	269.3	304.2	387.4	444.3	469.0
Non-State Enterprise	**3514.8**	**5451.8**	**6875.0**	**7711.7**	**8735.3**
Private	188.8	323.9	205.5	297.2	303.7
Collective name	3326.0	5127.9	6669.5	7414.5	8431.6
Foreign investment enterprise	**1221.8**	1687.5	2179.2	2569.7	3342.9
100% Foreign capital	847.6	1050.3	1603.8	1927.6	2477.5
Join Venture	374.2	637.2	575.4	642.1	865.4

Note. Adapted from "Statistical Yearbook of Vietnam 2014" by Vietnam General Statistics Office (2014) retrieved from gso.gov.vn/?tabid=628&ItemID=14277

Similar to level of investment, the non-state enterprises have a large share in total business revenue, which increased almost double from 3,224.9 trillion dongs in 2009 to 6203.6 trillion dongs in 2013 (Table 9). Thus, this non-state sector has accounted for more than 50% of total business revenue from all 3 sectors, and the rest 50% is composed of state companies and FDI enterprises. This reflects the dominance in market of non-state SMEs and their significant contribution to GDP because non-state enterprises is accounted up to 99% by non-state SMEs in Vietnam.

Last but not least, in the context of labour abundance in developing countries as Vietnam, the non-state enterprises has reached a huge achievement in providing a largest number of jobs compared to other sectors. Figure 3 shows that the total business employment increased from 9.83 million in 2010 to 11.08 million in 2012. Especially, the non-state sector absorbed the largest portion with 5,98 million

Table 9. Net turnover of enterprises by types of enterprise

	2009	2010	2011	2012	2013
TOTAL	**5900.3**	**7487.7**	**10302.0**	**11167.8**	**12235.0**
State owned Enterprise	**1603.1**	**2033.6**	**2695.7**	**2941.3**	**2977.0**
Central	1327.0	1653.5	2189.1	2482.8	2546.3
Local	276.1	380.1	506.6	458.5	430.7
Non-State Enterprise	**3224.9**	**4068.2**	**5574.3**	**5797.4**	**6203.6**
Private	320.8	391.4	486.1	468.7	496.8
Collective name	2904.1	3676.8	5088.2	5328.7	5706.8
Foreign investment enterprise	1072.3	1385.9	2032.0	2429.1	3054.4
100% Foreign capital	706.7	943.5	1479.7	1877.4	2435.0
Join Venture	365.6	442.4	552.3	551.7	619.4

Note. Adapted from "Statistical Yearbook of Vietnam 2014" by Vietnam General Statistics Office (2014) retrieved from gso.gov.vn/?tabid=628&ItemID=14277

Figure 3.

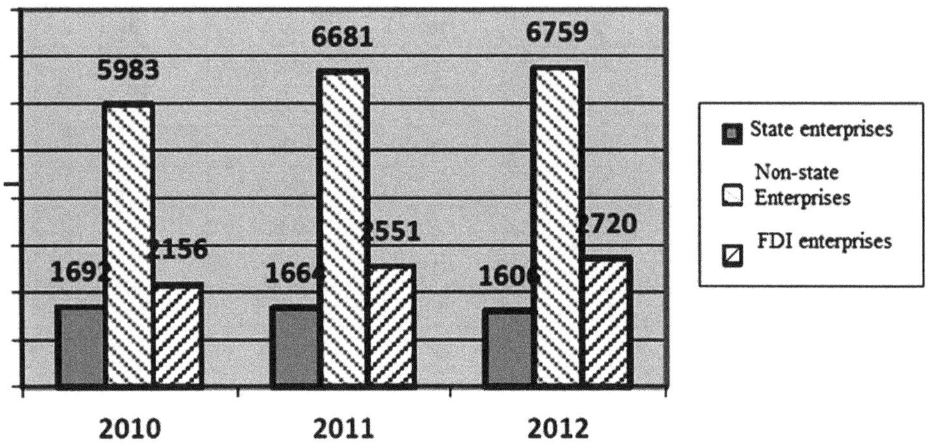

employees in 2010 (accounted for 60,86% total business jobs) and increased to 6,76 million jobs in 2012 and 6,855 million jobs in 2013 which accounts for around 60% total employment (VGSO, 2014).

In contrast, the state-own enterprise which is strategic sector of Vietnamese Government provided only 1,606 million jobs in 2012 that accounts for merely 14.49%. This asserts strongly the key role of SMEs in "contributing to the growth of the national economy, job creation, poverty alleviation and hunger eradication" (Vietnam National Assembly, 2002).

Constraints of Non-State SMEs Performance

It is really a great achievement in wide expansion that the non-state SMEs have gained over the past decades. However, according to VMPI (2014a), large number of enterprises have been doing business unprofitably since 2010 (Figure 4). The percentage of unprofitable firms increased rapidly from less than 30% in 2006 to nearly 70% in 2013. This is a raising question for policy makers in Vietnam in find-

Figure 4.

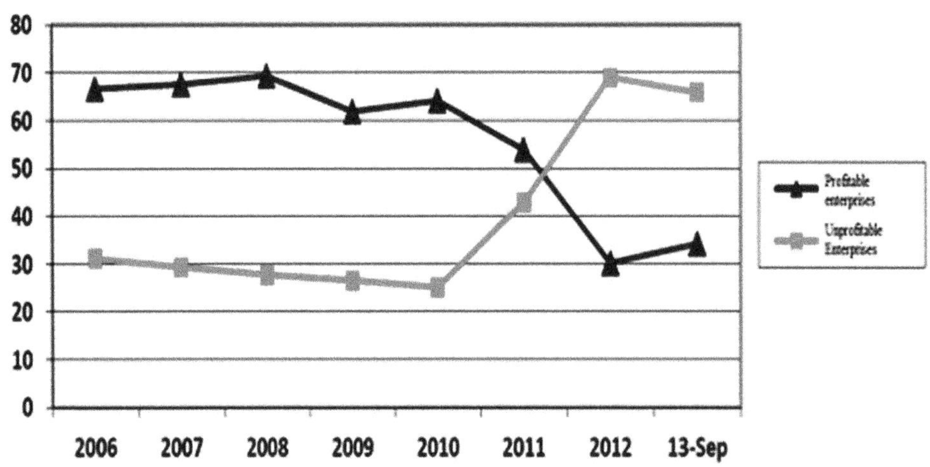

ing solutions for improving the "quality of enterprise" rather than quantity expansion (VMPI, 2014b). Along with increased number of enterprises, the health of enterprise need to be leveraged to stop the trend of bankruptcy.

Especially, Figure 5 indicates more clearly about the groups of unprofitable enterprises which mostly come from non-state enterprises. And according to VMPI (2014a), in 2010-2012, the non-state enterprises which mostly are SMEs have poorest performance compared to other groups (Figure 5). Thus, in the current context of increasing number of bankrupt SMEs, organizational performance becomes the center of growing concern among SME entrepreneurs in Vietnam. The figure also indicates that, even the total revenue of non-state enterprises was slightly increased in 2011 and 2012 but the total profit of this group fall down rapidly. This reveals the fact that the SMEs in Vietnam expanding widely but not deeply, raising number while reducing performance quality.

Subsequently, along with the increased number of new registered enterprises, the dissolved or halted-production also increased at around three forth of new registered number (Figure 6). There were up to 67,823 enterprises dissolved or halted-production in 2013, especially this enterprises are mostly non-state SMEs (VMPI, 2014a). Therefore, it is raising questions of increasing quality of non-state SMEs performance for both policy makers and business practitioners.

To explain for this slowdown, besides the effect from external factors such as the crisis in 2008, poor financial market and higher competition in Vietnam, previous reports and studies also indicated the internal weaknesses of non-state SMEs as the negative drivers for this poor performance. In the poor market of skilled labour (OECD, 2014), many constrains related to HR such as lack of management skills, poor human resource management are associated with non-state SMEs. Because the country is going deeper in global market integration, hence the external environment generated a lot of challenges besides opportunities. SMEs can earn bigger opportunities in global market but also have to face tougher competition at local market and even in attaching and maintaining competent workforce among variety of FDI firms. Less competitiveness in both attaching and retaining high skilled labour, the non-state SMEs have to deal with the low quality of recruited labours.

Figure 5.

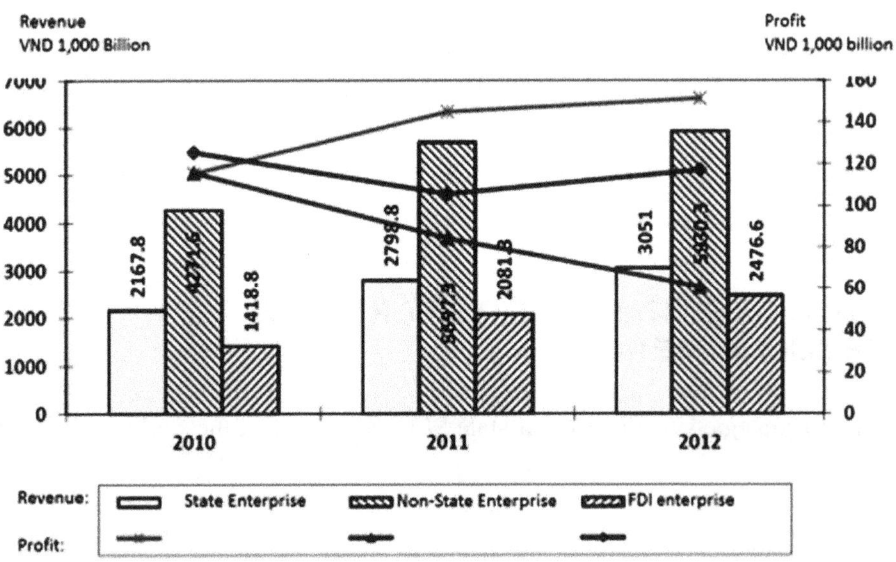

Figure 6.

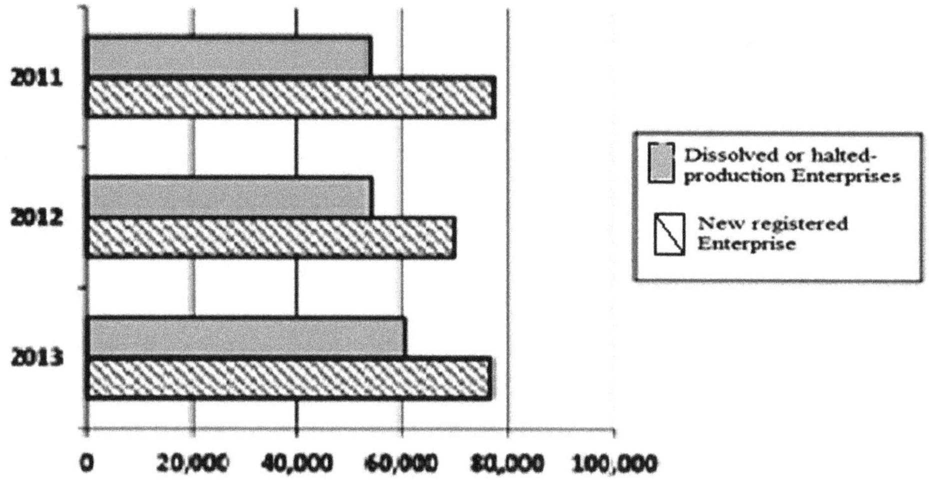

In addition, SMEs entrepreneurs in Vietnam preferred short-term net-profit indications than other development indicators (Swierczek & Thai, 2003) and now they are suffering the negative outcomes from this perception. A mass number of bankrupt SMEs recently raises the demand of strategic leadership with long- run orientation. Hence, Vietnamese scholars have focused on exploring the role of top leaders in exploring solutions leaders (Nha & Quan, 2014).

Thirdly, small scale and limited capital are other inherent weakness of non-state SMEs (OECD, 2014; Tran et al., 2008; VGSO, 2013; VMPI, 2014a; Cuong, 2007). Even the non-state SMEs in Vietnam have a significant growth over the past decades but they are still in their infant stage of development. Most of them are established after year 2000 then mostly are young and have small scale (VMPI, 2014b). According to VMPI (2014a), the average number of labor used per non-state enterprise is around 20 employees. This number is much smaller compared to other sectors such as state enterprises and FDI enterprises, those are 496 and 303 employees per enterprise relatively. In addition, in the restricted financial market, the small scale in term of capital becomes raising problem needed to be resolved.

And the last, low competitiveness, and poor absorptive technology capability and innovation (Tran et al., 2008), the shortage in efficient business linkages (N. Cuong, 2007) are also considered as the 'bottlenecks' of SMEs in Vietnam. In the modern business, business linkages can become one of competitive advantages that the firm can exploit a lot of business opportunities. When the firm has the good business linkages, they will have more chance to engage as one part of supply chain and gain more from this integration.

IMPLICATIONS FOR SUSTAINABLE PERFORMANCE OF PRIVATE SMES IN VIETNAM

Based on described strategic situation of non-state SMEs in Vietnam, the study comes up with following implications:

Implications for Policy Makers in Vietnam

Enhance National Support Programs of Leadership and HRM

Leadership with long-run orientation and HRM play important role in organizational performance of non-state SMEs in Vietnam are still very poor. While the labor market is weak in supplying skilled labor, thus the government should pay more attention in stimulating these central resources. Poor HRM could not align all resource for synergistic capacity, hence, the firm still suffer poor performance even all other resources are strong. Thus, the policy makers should firstly invest more for doing research to enrich the program of training that match with the real requirement from enterprises in term of leadership and HRM. These empirical research will provide the best background for guiding the national training program and shaping support policies, enriching training content. The empirical research result also plays important role in conveying a strong prove to wake business practitioners up in the light of management science and strategic point of view.

Complete Legal Regulation Systems

As mentioned above, Vietnam even has great effort in reforming the legal frame work and business regulations, however, the average policy index is till at lower than regional index of ASEAN. Along with strengthen central resource of human, it is truly necessary to have a favorable institutional framework and supporting business regulation. Thus, in coming year, the government should focus more on simplifying administrative procedures and legal regulations especially relating to Tax, Custom. The regulations for resolving business disputes should be clearly completed to refill SMEs communities and giving more chance for healthy firms.

Diversify and Enhance Linkages Between the Supporting Institutions and Business Associations

Being young and limited capacity and under pressures of competition from ASEAN free trade area since 2015, non-state SMEs are thirst to obtain the support from governmental institutions than ever before. Supporting in term of legal, technology transfer, market information, trade promotion, market expansion and other professional areas are really helpful for non-state SMEs in the current context. Therefore, the government should diversify the SMEs support institutions in different areas at both central and provincial levels in order to enable the non-state SMEs to be stronger, more confident and more effective in doing business.

Especially, the past decades have asserted the huge effect of information technology and internet on social and economic development. Internet is even considered as one of 10 drivers that is "flattening the world". It becomes the extremely effective tool to add more value by money and time saving. While SMEs leaders who are mostly young and active then they will be very potential to be inspired of applying internet. The government, therefore, should leverage the e-government and other online portals. The government need to diversify, modernize and upgrade the online portals in diversified fields in order to enhance the development of SMEs.

In other hand, the government should encourage the development of business associations. These associations will align the SMEs community to cooperate and consult each other in different fields such as in protecting local SMEs community against foreign competition and in penetrating foreign market.

Strengthen Assess to Finance

Capital is one of the most important resources. However, it is also can be considered as a good. If the good are sold too expensive or difficult to access then the users will have less opportunities to use. However, if the good are sold too cheap, it can be used ineffectively. The monetary policy in 2007 belongs to second case that too much money are provides to enterprises with much cheaper price than normal market price. Because at that time, the government supports up to 4% of annual interest rate for SMEs (Vietnam Goverment, 2009). Hence, a mass number of projects which include less effective and high risky ones are still invested because the enterprise can "buy the capital" cheaply. As a results, a series of projects have gone bankrupt subsequently. That is also the reason why the Vietnam government and banking system seems more careful on controlling monetary supply in recent years.

In order to support sufficiently for potential projects while sustain a healthy financial market, the government should improve the mechanism of monitoring and evaluating investment projects of SMEs or business start-up project. It also needs to leverage the role of support institutions in consulting. The support institutions can play as a mediator between banking system and enterprises. The deep participation of support institution and organization, association will enable the enterprises to access the loans timely and the bank can find more healthy projects to finance as well.

The government also needs to diversify and develop other financial source such as security market and investment funds. Then the SMEs will be more active and also have more chance to assess wider source of capital. This source of capital are normally will be very effective in selecting financed projects, hence the projects financed are normally the effective business project that contribute significantly to the enterprise development.

Enhance the Cooperation Between Non-State SMEs and Universities or Colleges and Strong Reform in All Training and Education System

In the context of poor skilled human resource that does not meet the real requirement from enterprises, the direct solution enhances the cooperation between non-state SMEs and university, college system. The governmental agency should set up the foundation that encourages them to meet each other and join in cooperation. This collaboration will directly improve the quality of workforce at both leader and employee levels. Under cooperative training program, the labor are equipped by necessary skills and knowledge that are matched to enterprise requirement.

In addition, the governmental agency and other support organizations also need to promote the cooperation between SMEs and Universities for deeper engagement in doing applied research. The young enterprises with poor workforce do need the guidance from the researchers of management science which could sustains SMEs growth for long-run.

In the other hand, for quality human resource in long-run, the Vietnamese government should take reforms strongly in education system. The quality of workforce is the outcome of the whole training and education system from primary education level to higher education level. High skilled, rich knowledge or creative workforce result from long journey of nursing habits, shaping behaviours, enriching brain since very early stage of education. Thus, the educational reforms should be systematic and meet the real requirement for development. Strong reforms in all training and education system from primary school to higher education are vital strategy to create the innovation habits, innovative culture and support higher quality labour for market.

Improving Infrastructure and Strengthen Support Industries

Infrastructure plays important role in promoting business activities. However, in Vietnam, several problem of infrastructure are needed to be resolved such as quality, progress of infrastructure project implementation. The government needs to control the infrastructure investment tightly to ensure the quality and time requirements.

The last but not least, supporting industries is indicated as the current threats for many industries in Vietnam. Thus, along with attracting FDI to strengthen these support industries, the government should encourage SMEs doing business in these fields through investment initiatives such as lower income tax or more priority in assessing to finance, supporting for R&D.

Implications for Non-State SMEs in Vietnam

Strategic Orientation and HRM is the Central Mission

As discussed above, leadership skills and HRM are the key constraints of private sector failures. Especially the short-sight of the leaders enables a lot of enterprises to go bankrupt after a few years. For long run development, SMEs in Vietnam need to improve leadership and HRM. Therefore, the SMEs should be more active in joining, cooperating with training program from support organization. It is also strongly recommended to be more active in planning and implementing the training courses at site. This solution will directly improve the workforce quality for enterprises. However, whether all opportunities and strengths are aligned to create competitive advantages or not depend on the competency of top leader. The top leader is in charge of firm success in long-run should not be short-seeing with poor skill of management. Thus, to survive successfully in current context of harder competition, the leaders themselves have to improve the leadership competency at first especially in term of strategic stand-point and leadership skills.

Pursue Differentiation-Based Focus Strategy Rather Than Cost Leadership

With limited resources and capacity, the non-state SMEs should focus on niche-market with creative way. Rather than choosing mass market and direct competing with larger enterprises, non-state SMEs should pursue differentiation-based focus strategy rather than cost leadership. The comparative advantage can be created by differentiating their product and service rather than increasing scale of production. The differentiation will be well-matched with young and active SMEs in Vietnam. Focus strategy is also strongly recommended for non-state SMEs because it is appropriate with the limited capacity of these enterprises. Thus, in light of SWOT theory, the non-state SMEs in Vietnam should pursue differentiation-based focus strategy rather than cost leadership, focus on niche market rather than mass market.

Cooperate With Universities and Colleges and Professional Associations

Business success could not be sustained for long-run in a poor skilled and knowledge enterprise. While the budget for national training program is limited and the program is designed generally to all enterprises. In this context, the entrepreneur should be more active in cooperating with universities and colleges to customize the training programs that are matched with the characteristics of their own enterprises. The cooperation should also be promoted for deeper research on finding solutions and gaining competitive advantages in dynamic market. The stronger investment in R& D through this cooperation is one of the factor contributing to the sustainability of SMEs.

Furthermore, SMEs should be more active to engage in professional associations, professional clubs, professional forums and support organizations in order to learn and support each other. Through these organizations, the SMEs leaders can improve their managerial knowledge as well as gain more market, professional and legal information. Linkages will definitely help SMEs to be more competent in leveraging their business performance.

Enhance Finance and Market Source

In the context of poor financial market and limited internal capital, the entrepreneur should be more careful in selecting the profitable projects. SMEs also can use capital more effectively by focusing on feasible projects to avoid poor performance. With limited budgets for SMEs from the current bank system, SMEs also need to be more active in calling for investment from different sources rather than rely merely on the bank. Alliance strategy is also recommended for SMEs to leverage their financial capacity.

In term of market, global integration and ASEAN Free Trade area not only bring challenges of competition but also generate the great opportunities of huge free market. Thus, instead of operating broadly in different segments ineffectively in local market, SMEs should choose suitable single segment and focus to create strong competitive advantage with creative way in that segment. Even in a small segment, but this will bring them to larger opportunities to access with regional market of ASEAN or even the global market.

Especially, E-commerce is one of the smoothest way for enterprise whose capacity is limited. Therefore, more than ever before, non-state SMEs in Vietnam should foster the application of E-commerce in doing business. E-commerce is a factor which can “flatten the world”, hence opportunities and market will not be restricted by country border to whom can take advantage of e-commerce effectively.

REFERENCES

ADB. (2013). *Proposed Policy-Based Loan for Subprogram 2 Socialist Republic of Viet Nam: Second Small and Medium-Sized Enterprises Development Program*. ADB.

ADB SMEs in Vietam. (n.d.). *Support and report*. Author.

Covin, J., & Slevin, D. (1991). A conceptual model of entrepreneurship as firm behavior. *Entrepreneurship Theory and Practice*. Retrieved from http://papers.ssrn.com/sol3/papers.cfm?abstract_id=1504448

Cuong, N. (2007). Donor Coordination in SME Development in Vietnam: What Has Been Done and How Can It Be Strengthened? *Vietnam Economic Management Review*. Retrieved from https://www.vjol.info/index.php/VEMR/article/viewArticle/585

Cuong, T., Sang, L., & Anh, N. (2007). Vietnam's small-and medium-sized enterprises development: characteristics, constraints and policy recommendations. *SME in Asia and Globalization, ERIA ....* Retrieved from http://www.vnep.org.vn/Upload/Vietnam%E2%80%99sSmallandMediumSizedEnterprisesDevelopment_Characteristics,ConstraintsandPolicyRecommendations_Sang_KimAnh.PDF

ERIA. (2014). *ASEAN SME Policy Report 2014*. Retrieved from http://www.eria.org/RPR-FY2012-8.pdf

Gaskill, L., & Van Auken, H. (1993). A factor analytic study of the perceived causes of small business failure. *Journal of Small*. Retrieved from http://search.proquest.com/openview/15dfb888bd4ed0640f72ce9860d114cc/1?pq-origsite=gscholar

Goverment, V. (2009). *Prime Minister's Decision No 131/2009/QD-TTg of January 2009*. Retrieved from http://thuvienphapluat.vn/van-ban/Tien-te-Ngan-hang/Quyet-dinh-131-QD-TTg-ho-tro-lai-suat-cho-cac-to-chuc-ca-nhan-vay-von-ngan-hang-de-san-xuat-kinh-doanh-84345.aspx

Hang, D. T. (2015). *Leader Training in Vietnam SMEs for meeting requirement of International economic Integration*. Vietnam National Univerversity.

Mahajar, A. J., Binti, J., & Yunus, M. (2006). The Effectiveness of Government Export Assistance Programs on Malaysia Small & Medium Enterprises (SMEs). *Problems and Perspectives in Management, 1*.

Nha, P. X., & Quan, L. (2014). *Response of Vietnamese private enterprises' leader under global financial crisis: From theorical to empirical approach*. Asian Social Science. doi:10.5539/ass.v10n9p26

OECD. (2014). *Structural Policy Country Notes*. Retrieved from http://www.oecd.org/site/seao/VietNam.pdf

Quan, L. (2015). Perceptions of Leadership Competencies and the Acquisition of Them by CEOs in Vietnamese Small Enterprises. *Asian Social Science*, *11*(4). doi:10.5539/ass.v11n4p17

Robertson, M., & Collins, A. (2003). Developing entrepreneurship in West Yorkshire: West Yorkshire universities' partnership and business Start-Up@ Leeds met. *Education+ Training*. Retrieved from http://www.emeraldinsight.com/doi/pdf/10.1108/00400910310495941

Suk, J. K. (n.d.). *Leadership, Organizational Culture, Knowledge Productivity and Value Creation in Four Successful Korean Companies Toward guidelines for people-oriented business leaders*. Academic Press.

Swierczek, F. W., & Thai, T. H. (2003). Motivation, Enterpreneurship and The performance of SMEs in Vietnam. *Journal of Enterprising Culture*, *11*(01), 47–68. doi:10.1142/S0218495803000044

Thang, L. C., & Quang, T. (n.d.). *Human Resource Management Practices in a Transitional Economy: A Comparative Study of Enterprise Ownership Forms in Vietnam*. http://doi.org/<ALIGNMENT.qj></ALIGNMENT>10.1080/1360238052000298362

Tran, T., Le, X. S., & Nguyen, K. A. (2008). Vietnam's Small and Medium Sized Enterprises Development: Characteristics, Constraints and Policy Recommendations. In SME in Asia and Globalization, ERIA Research Project Report 2007 (pp. 323–364). Academic Press.

VGSO. (2013). *Statistical YearBook of Vietnam 2013*. Retrieved from https://www.gso.gov.vn/default.aspx?tabid=512&idmid=5&ItemID=14080

VGSO. (2014). *Statistical Yearbook of Vietnam 2014*. Retrieved from http://gso.gov.vn/?tabid=628&ItemID=14277

Vietnam National Assembly. (2002). *Comprehensive Poverty Reduction and Growth Strategy (CPRGS)*. Retrieved from http://siteresources.worldbank.org/ImtVietnaminVietnamese/Resources/CPRGS_Vietnames_edited.pdf

VMPI. (2014a). *Report on Enterprise and Plan for Social and Economic Development 2014-2015*. Retrieved from http://business.gov.vn/tabid/98/catid/10/item/13229/t%E1%BB%95ng-quan-v%E1%BB%81-t%C3%ACnh-h%C3%ACnh-doanh-nghi%E1%BB%87p-v%C3%A0-nhi%E1%BB%87m-v%E1%BB%A5-ph%C3%A1t-tri%E1%BB%83n-kinh-t%E1%BA%BF-x%C3%A3-h%E1%BB%99i-2014-2015.aspx

VMPI. (2014b). *White Paper: Small and Medium Enterprises in Vietnam*. Retrieved from http://en.business.gov.vn/tabid/179/catid/572/item/13807/white-paper-on-vietnam-sme-2014.aspx

Xuan Nha, P., & Quan, L. (2014). Response of Vietnamese Private Enterprises' Leader under Global Financial Crisis: From Theorical to Empirical Approach. *Asian Social Science*, *10*(9). doi:10.5539/ass.v10n9p26

Yusuf, A. (1995). Critical success factors for small business: perceptions of South Pacific entrepreneurs. *Journal of Small Business Management*. Retrieved from http://search.proquest.com/openview/488b6040ba090b7262c8caf6726dc27b/1?pq-origsite=gscholar

KEY TERMS AND DEFINITIONS

Environment Scanning: This is a step of strategy formulation which includes analysis the external and internal environment in order to indicate the opportunities, threats from the external environment, strengths and weaknesses from internal environment.

Non-State Enterprises: Non-State enterprises in Vietnam include all domestic enterprises which belong to (1) Private enterprises; (2) Cooperative name companies; (3) Private limited companies; (4) Joint stock companies without capital of State (5) Joint stock companies with a maximum of 50% of charter capital shared by Vietnamese government.

Non-State SMEs: The non-state enterprises which have no more than 300 employees or no more than VND 10 billion (equivalent to USD 630,000) of registered capital.

Organizational Performance: The outcome of an organization that is measured by different perspectives such as financial performance, market performance.

Small and Medium-Sized Enterprises (SMEs): A firm that has registered capital of no more than VND 10 billion (equivalent to USD 630,000) or with no more than 300 employees of average workforce.

Strategic Orientation: This is the long-run orientation which is formulated based on the strategic situation.

Strategic Situation: This present all characteristics of firm' characteristics from both external and internal perspectives under the light of strategic standpoint. It describes not only the current characteristics but also reveals the potential factors coming in the futures.

Chapter 15
Business Incubation in Malaysia:
An Overview of Multimedia Super Corridor, Small and Medium Enterprises, and Incubators in Malaysia

Logaiswari Indiran
University Technology Malaysia, Malaysia

Kamariah Ismail
University Technology Malaysia, Malaysia

Zainab Khalifah
University Technology Malaysia, Malaysia

Santhi Ramanathan
Multimedia University, Malaysia

ABSTRACT

The purpose of this chapter is to present the importance and contribution of business incubation programmes to Small and Medium Enterprises in Malaysia. Chapter starts with a brief review of the history and transition of major economic policies in Malaysia as well as the government responses towards achieving the status of fully developed nation by the year 2020. The policy review includes the Laissez-faire Policy, New Economy Policy, National Development Plan, National Vision Policy, and New Economy Model which were set to achieve nation's rapid economic growth. This review leads the paper towards the exploration of the major drivers of current economic growth in Malaysia. This chapter identifies Multimedia Super Corridor as the most important initiative and a key driver to global Information Communications Technology development as well as the major contributor to Small and Medium Enterprises establishment in Malaysia. In addition, it outlines the significant contribution of Small and Medium Enterprises to the economic growth in Malaysia, and finally identifies business incubators as a support mechanism to accelerate the SMEs success, especially the start-up firms. This chapter provides knowledge to the researchers and practitioners on the linkages among Multimedia Super Corridor, Small and Medium Enterprises and incubators that align with the economic policy development. As a conclusion, the chapter discusses the challenges faced by the incubation programmes in Malaysia and thus, highlights the prominence of business incubators as a niche subject to be explored in depth, in terms of their growth and potentials in Malaysia.

DOI: 10.4018/978-1-5225-2165-5.ch015

INTRODUCTION

Malaysia has been making notable progress in economic development over the last century as the wave of globalisation expands across the world. Malaysia has achieved the major transformation of economic structure from being exporter of a primary commodity to an industrialized-based country. This transformation and accomplishments seems to be supported and guided by various economic policies implemented over the decades, namely, New Economy Policy (NEP), National Development Plan (NDP), National Vision Policy (NVP) and New Economy Model (NEM) which was introduced in 2010.

Vision 2020 was initiated in 1991 by Malaysia's former Prime Minister, Tun Dato' Seri Dr. Mahathir bin Mohamad, with an overriding objective which is to achieve a fully developed nation and achieve an industrialized level by the year of 2020, encompassing on the economic development, as well as focusing on other angles, including social, political, spiritual, psychological and cultural areas (Islam, 2010; Khan, Liew, & Ghazali, 2014; Vicziany & Puteh, 2004). There are nine strategic challenges outlined in Vision 2020 in order to transform Malaysia into a competitive, robust and dynamic country in the span of 30 years. Based on various strategies and initiatives, Multimedia Super Corridor (MSC) has been one of the prime project which aims Malaysia to get much insight on the development of Information Communications Technology (ICT) industry by providing a test-bed for global ICT landscape (Abdul Khalid, Gilbert, & Huq, 2012). To date, MSC has made a notable progress in ICT sectors and has been seen as a fundamental engine for becoming a fully industrialized nation by 2020.

A part from MSC, significance and development of Small and Medium Enterprises (SMEs) to the economy has been acknowledged (Husin & Ibrahim, 2014; Moorthy et al., 2012; Yeoh, 2014). In line with this, SMEs in Malaysia is recognized as the backbone for the economy development and thus paramount of SMEs business strategies were developed by government. However, the government is facing emerging challenges in shaping the future of SMEs, particularly during the start-up development phase. In order to overcome these challenges, the government has introduced the business incubators programme as an effective support mechanism to accelerate the development of SMEs (SMIDEC, 2007).

Said, Adham, & Abdullah (2012) has recently drawn attention to the paradox in MSC and incubators in Malaysia. However, the chapter will be more comprehensive if a broad range of dimension has taken into account. Therefore, this chapter aims to identify the linkages between MSC, SMEs, and incubators, align with the economic policy development, as well as conclude the importance of business incubators as a field to be explored more in Malaysia. This chapter is divided into four sections as follows. The first section presents the historical background of economy policies in Malaysia, including an overview of MSC Malaysia. The second section elaborates the SMEs contribution to economy followed by the third section that discusses the development of business incubators in Malaysia. Finally, the fourth section presents the challenges face in incubation programme in Malaysia, discussion and implication for future research.

TRANSFORMATION OF ECONOMIC STRUCTURE AND POLICY IN MALAYSIA

During the pre-independence, British colonialism tried to rebuild the export of primary commodity because Malaysia was highly dependent on the earning from exports of primary commodities; rubber, tin, timber and oil (Bekhet, 2013). Malaysia progressed impressively after it gained independence in 1957 in social and economic developments, where laissez-faire policy was pursued, with import-substituting industrialization, agricultural diversification, and rural development program (Said et al., 2012). Government strategy was to continue with import substitution strategy in the 1960s under the First Malaysia Plan 1966-1970, as to have economic diversification, which indirectly could eliminate the total dependency on primary commodities (Gunto & Alias, 2013). However, the economic expansion during this period failed to balance the inequalities exist among ethnics, which became the turning point for the introduction of the New Economy Policy (NEP) in 1970, under Second Malaysia Plan 1971-1975 (Zainal Aznam Yusof & Bhattasali, 2008). The key objective of NEP (1971-1990) was to maintain national unity through two strategies; eradication of poverty among the entire population and restructuring the society with a view to eliminate the identification of race by economic function (Menon, 2009). Along with many essential strategies, the manufacturing industry boosting with momentum in global landscape, allowed the government to regulate two programmes, including second phase import-substitution industrialization programme, and followed by export orientation programme (Said et al., 2012; Gunto & Alias, 2013). Fortunately, Malaysia holds a predominant stand, depending mainly on the high price for its primary commodities in a global market, and managed to attract industrial foreign investors, which created opportunities in economic development.

However, in the mid of 1985-86, Malaysia could not avoid the impact of global economy crisis, where the demand for primary commodity decreased dramatically (Menon, 2009; Stafford, 1997), leading Malaysia to embark widely on the privatization policy that was believed to be a remedy for the issue. The introduction of privatization policy in 1983 has proceeded as one of the multipliers to economic prosperity and enabled Malaysia to premise on the notion of new technologies and expertise through various multilevel projects, including construction of North-South Highway, Kuala Lumpur Tower, and LRT. During that period, Malaysia has emphasized a shift away from labour driven economy (assembly type manufacturing) to investment-driven economy (medium-technology manufacturing) which cultivated the growth of new technology-based entrepreneurship culture in Malaysia (Berma, 2012). Together with this paradigm, the National Development Plan (NDP) for the duration of 1990 to 2000 was introduced to replace the NEP in order to put the creation of wealth ahead of redistributing it. It was presented in the perspective of Vision 2020, which was launched in February 1991, outlining the aim of Malaysia attaining a developed-nation status by the year 2020 (The Economic Planning Unit, 2006). Thus, the transition from medium-technology manufacturing to high-technology manufacturing was accorded a vital role during this period with the government commencing on productivity-driven economy as an engine of economic development. In addition to the aim of establishing an united, progressive, prosperous, developing and competitive nation, the NVP was introduced in 2001, as an extension of NDP (1991 – 2000) (Menon, 2008). In line with this, Malaysian government has established the knowledge and technology-based industries as well as regarded Information, Technology and Multimedia (IT) industries as efficient sources of economy prosperity.

As the effect of this curve, Malaysia has begun to focus on ICT industries as an engine to accelerate the competitive advantages in global economy. As such, with the aim to promote the new economy direction, Malaysia has introduced the MSC project, an idea urged by the former Prime Minister, Tun Dr Mahathir Mohammed, in 1996. The linkages between the MSC, export orientation, the roles of multinationals and country's productivity were then spelled out in the Seventh Malaysia Plan 1996-2000.

NEM was introduced in 2010 formulated by the country's National Economic Advisory Council (NEAC) with core principles to direct Malaysia towards a developed nation by the year 2020 with its population enjoying a high quality of life, besides a high level of income resulting from economic growth that is both inclusive and sustainable (National Economic Advisory Council, 2010). NEM consists of four pillars, namely, 1Malaysia Plan, Government Transformation Programme (GTP), Economic Transformation Programme (ETP) and Tenth Malaysian Plan 2011–2015 (National Economy Advisory Counsil, 2010). Malaysia progressively continues with the Eleventh Malaysia Plan 2016 -2020 being the vital stage in the drive to achieve Vision 2020, with the theme "anchoring growth on people". In line with all the plans, policies and strategies to achieve the ultimate goal of Vision 2020, and SMEs are recognized as another major trust to economic development. SMEs are seen as an engine that will remodel Malaysia into high-income nation by the year of 2020 through knowledge-based economic approach (Abdullah & Shamsuddin, 2009; Moorthy et al., 2012; Yeoh, 2014).

MULTIMEDIA SUPER CORRIDOR (MSC) MALAYSIA

MSC as the Cluster Concept

Science parks have emerged all over the world as a mechanism to spur economic development and started to gain the impulse in the 1980's. The idea followed the steps of the successful Sillicon Valley in California, Route 128 in Massachusetts, Cambridge in the UK and the Research Park Triangle in North Carolina. Many other countries replicated the Science Park concept, including Russia, Brazil, Kuwait, China, Taiwan, India, and Israel (Ratinho & Henriques, 2010). Malaysia too, adopted science park concept and introduced MSC in 1996 (Ramasamy, Chakrabarty, & Cheah, 2004; Yigitcanla & Sarimin, 2015) that was launched officially on 27th June 1998 as a set forth to drive the county into a fully developed nation by the year of 2020 (The Economic Planning Unit, 2000). The MSC project comprises four main dimensions; (1) the development of IT and technology applications, (2) the development of IT firms, (3) the development of IT industries, and finally (4) the development of MSC region (Said et al., 2012).

MSC as a Transformation Mechanism to Knowledge-Based Economy

MSC was initiated by the Malaysian policy maker with the intention to switch the economic approach towards a knowledge-driven economy. This transformation on economic approach is incorporated in country's Third Outline Perspective Plan (OPP3, 2000-2010). It notably emphasized on the human capital development, research and development, infrastructure; science and technology, financing and equity. The emphasis believed to provide a foundation to achieve a rapid economic growth and sustain global competitiveness. The overall thrust is outlining the aim of Malaysia attaining developed nation status by the year 2020 (OPP3, 2001).

In line with this, Malaysia developed National IT Agenda (NITA), which aimed to formulate strategies and foster the utilization and development of IT, which is seen as the key to a dominant knowledge-based economy. It is followed closely by introduction of MSC in 1996 as the engine to accelerate economic development for the 21st century that has a vital signaling role as a global player in the application of ICT (Abdul Khalid, Gilbert, & Huq, 2014; Zainal Aznam Yusof & Bhattasali, 2008).

MSC as 'Multimedia Utopia': Infrastructure and Support Services

The MSC accounting a 50 x 50 km2 area, facilitated with basic telecommunication infrastructure, is a home for five emerging cybercities in the country, including Kuala Lumpur City Centre, Kuala Lumpur

Tower, Cyberjaya, Technology Park Malaysia and Malaysian Technology Development Corporation- Universiti Putra Malaysia Incubator Centre (Ramasamy et al., 2004). The vision of the MSC was ultimately to foster an IT environment through the pursuance of two strategies namely; (1) attracting world leading IT companies to move their industries within the MSC region, conducting research while developing new products and technologies, exporting, and MSC acting as being a hub as well as a global test-bed for multimedia industries in Asia; and (2) encouraging the formulation as well as the development of Malaysian IT SMEs and transforming them into world-class companies (Mohan et al., 2004).

The MSC project, covering the duration of 20 years, was divided into three phases (Said et al., 2012). Phase 1 focuses to influence world first class companies to establish their operations in the region of MSC. This is parallel to the establishment of the two cyber cities; Putrajaya and Cyberjaya. Phase 2 emphasizes on providing a platform of borderless networking among the MSC and other clusters across the country. Phase 3 aims at stemming Malaysia for future growth; knowledge-based society, on the premise of MSC as host of cities which hold the key to the global information and technology.

Along with the development of MSC, the Multimedia Development Corporation (MDeC) was established in 1996 (Earlier known as MDC) and tasked to monitor the development as well as the achievement of the MSC (MSC, 2003). Apart from monitoring, MDeC provides differing level of services within the MSC region to ensure latest intelligent cities standards are applied such as managing the infrastructure incentives and other support service; funding and granting qualified companies, eliminating red tape assistance, facilitating services, overseas market accessing, assisting developing networks with other potential local partners and financiers, and enhancing technopreneurship nurturing programmes.

As part to pursue the strategies, MSC imposed the First Wave Flagship Application; e-government, multipurpose card, tele-health, and smart schools to facilitate unparalleled collaboration between local and international companies, and to set up business incubators centres as to stem the government's approach to support the formation and development of Malaysia IT SMEs. Besides that, in order to circumvent the MSC strategies to be hosting in technology in the country, MSC Malaysia 10 Bills of Guarantee (BoGs) was introduced where all the companies that are given title MSC-status, regardless local or foreign, are eligible for it. Some of the key elements of BoGs are the companies to be entitled to receive tax benefits, including those for their income and import duties, to employ unlimited foreign white-collar workers, to get a financing and flexible ownership option, and to utilize the government-contract business which is the so-called privilege of MSC companies (MSC Malaysia, 1998). All the MSC-status companies are classified into four main ICT focus cluster namely Information and Technology (Infotech), Creative Multimedia Cluster (CMC), Global Business Services (GBS), and Institutions of Higher Education and Incubators (IHLs and Incubators).

Growing recognition on MSC Malaysia is notable and is proven by the increasing number of companies that MSC Malaysia Status as depicted in Figure 1 (MDeC, 2014). In 2014, a number of 229 new companies were awarded MSC Malaysia status which accumulates a total of 3632 companies has received MSC Malaysia status. This accounted increment 7.0% from the previous year. It shows MSC programme managed to promote the growth of creation MSC-status companies.

While reviewing the data in details, Table 1 displays the number of companies awarded as MSC-status which are classified according to the technology cluster and the number of active companies out of it, in 2014. It is apparent that the effective cluster, Infotech has the highest rate as 71%, followed by CMC and GBS with 13% and 12% respectively. IHLs and Incubators falls at the lowest rate which is 4% (MDeC, 2014). However, it shows a positive indication in the implementation as 74.6% companies are active out of the total amount of companies awarded.

Figure 1. MSC Malaysia status companies growth 2014
Source: MDeC (2014)

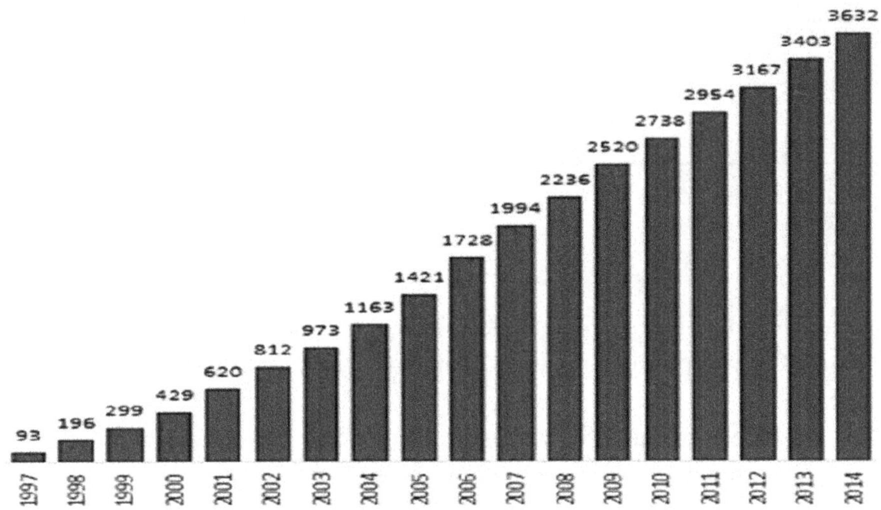

Table 1. MSC status companies awarded and active year 2014

Cluster	Number of Companies Awarded	Number of Companies Active
Creative Multimedia	436	334
IHLs & Incubators	125	111
InfoTech	2,665	1,920
Global Business Services	406	343
Total	**3,632**	**2,708**

Source: MDeC (2014)

In tandem with this growth, MSC annual industry report (2014) presented data on the number of jobs created by MSC Malaysia-status companies from 2010 to 2014 which shows a marked increase from year to year (Table 2). An increment about 7%, which is from 138,041 in 2013, increase to 147,568 in 2014 indicating MSC Malaysia experiencing an expansion on the employment growth, and it is promoting to develop high-income community by 2020.

MSC Cybercities and Cybercentre: Key Economic Focus Area

The essential strategy for promoting clustering approach in MSC region is by designating two categories; (i) MSC Malaysia Cybercity- self-centre intelligent city with the aim to build world-class business eco-system offering MSC 10 Bills of Guarantees (BoGs), (ii) MSC Malaysia Cybercentre which is a building with essential enabling environment, aiming purely to nurture, stimulate and promote the growth of ICT and ICT enabled industries, while offering partial BoGs.

MSC Malaysia Cybercity includes Technology Park Malaysia, Universiti Putra Malaysia-Malaysia Technology Development Corporation (UPM-MTDC), Kuala Lumpur City Centre-Cyberjaya, Kuala

Table 2. Number of employment from 2010-2014

Year	Number of Employment
2010	111,536
2011	119,138
2012	128,850
2013	138,071
2014	147,568

Source: MDeC (2014)

Lumpur Tower, and Kulim High Tech Park. While, MSC Malaysia Cybercentre includes Kuala Lumpur Sentral, Menara MSC Cyberport in Johor, Mid Valley City, Bangsar South City, and Melaka International Trade Centre.

As part of the strengthening the MSC strategies, there are four categories of entity eligible for MSC status, which are; (1) companies that use high level of multimedia and provide technology as well as knowledge transfer to Malaysia; (2) Institutions of Higher Learning (IHLs) or faculty of IHLs; (3) incubators that provide and share basic facilities and services, and (4) shared services and outsourcing that have to fulfil four major criteria, including headcount, export, location and investment. However, only IHLs and incubators are gaining flexibility on the location, where they are not restricted to be located in MSC cybercities or cybercentre, but still eligible for some benefits from BoGs.

Figure 2 exemplified an overview of all the national policies, even from first generation till the third generation, which consists of pre-independent laiisez-faire followed by the stages of economic approach; labor-driven economy, investment-driven economy, productivity-driven economy, innovation-based economy and finally knowledge-based economy. Along with this, snapshot of the development of economic policies includes NEP, NDP, NDV and finally NEM are clearly shown.

Figure 2. Malaysian economic development and MSC Malaysia milestone
Source: Adapted from Nordin (2002), & Berma (2012)

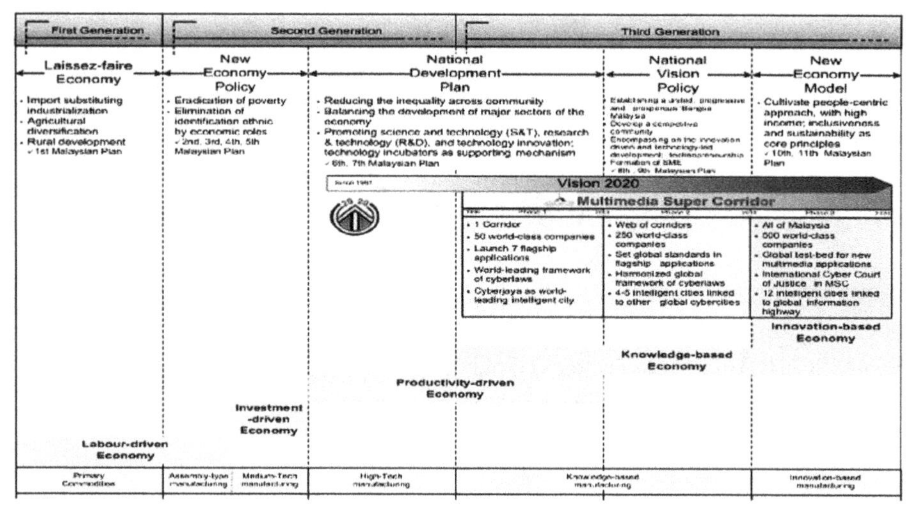

SMALL MEDIUM ENTERPRISES (SMES) IN MALAYSIA; A KEY DRIVER TO ACCELERATE MSCS' OBJECTIVES

Definition of SMEs

There is a wide range definition of SME which differs within institutions, countries, and regions. SMEs in Malaysia classified all the enterprises by the total annual turnover and number of full-time employees (SMIDEC, 2007) that resemble most of the universal characteristics. A common definition of SMEs in Malaysia which was endorsed by National SME Development Council (NSDC) since 2005, has been adapted and practiced across all the institutions, organizations, agencies, as well as the ministries.

However, the structure of economy evolved rapid changes including economy, business trend, and other structural changes, has led NSDC to introduce new definition of SME that was effective from 1st of January, 2014 (Table 3). A clear shift is observed where NSDC focused on classifying all the enterprises into two categories, which are (1) manufacturing, including transformation of materials or components, from physical or chemical component into new products, and (2) services and others including primary agriculture, construction, as well as mining and quarrying (SME Corp. Malaysia, 2013).

SMEs in manufacturing sectors are defined as enterprises with full-time employees not exceeding 200 workers and sales turnover not exceeding RM50 millions. SMEs in services and other sectors should have full-time employees not exceeding 75 workers and sales turnover not exceeding RM 20 million. The definition is applied to all the ministries, agencies and financial institutions that are involved in SMEs development programmes. Table 3 shows a clear new definition of SMEs in Malaysia by size and operation (Gopal & Mohd Sulaiman, 2013).

Table 3. New definition of SMEs in Malaysia, effective from 1st of January, 2014

<table>
<tr><th>Category</th><th>Micro</th><th>Small</th><th>Medium</th></tr>
<tr><td>Manufacturing</td><td rowspan="2">Sales turnover of less than RM300,000
OR
full-time employees less than 5</td><td>Sales turnover from RM300,000 to less than RM15 million
OR
full-time employees from 5 to less than 75</td><td>Sales turnover from RM15 million to not exceeding RM50 million
OR
full-time employees from 75 to not exceeding 200</td></tr>
<tr><td>Services and Other Sectors</td><td>Sales turnover from RM300,000 to less than RM3 million
OR
full-time employees from 5 to less than 30</td><td>Sales turnover from RM3 million to not exceeding RM20 million
OR
full-time employees from 30 to not exceeding 75</td></tr>
</table>

Source: Gopal & Mohd Sulaiman (2013)

Contribution of SMEs to Economic Development

SMEs are recognized as the backbone to economic development in Malaysia and seen as major contributor to Gross Domestic Product (GDP), export and employment. In 2011, the number of 645,136 SMEs shows a significant establishment in the development of economy, which reached 97.3% of the total enterprises indicated the importance of SMEs to the development of economy (Table 4). According to Economic/SMEs Census (2011), SMEs contribute 32.5% of GDP, 57% of total employment, as well as 19% of total exports in 2011.

While, Table 5 presents the contribution of SMEs to GDP in Asia-Pacific region where SMEs are the key drivers for both developed and developing countries. Almost all the countries within the region are considering SME as the engine for their economy development. According to Asia-Pacific SME Statistic, Index 2015, the highest contributions of SMEs to GDP is at the range of 40 to 60% from China (60.0%), Australia (55.7%), Hong Kong (54.0%), Japan (53.0%), Singapore (50.0%), South Korea (47.0%), and lastly followed by Vietnam (40.0%). Even Malaysia is in average stage, which contributed 32.7% to GDP, and still considered a good achievement. Thus, recognizing the importance of SMEs' contribution, the government has highly focused to increase the contribution to 41 percent of GDP by the year of 2020 as compared the contribution of 30% in the year of 2010, and to prepare Malaysia into a developed nation by the year of 2020, as shown in Table 6 (Hafsah Hashim, 2013).

As SMEs have a significant contribution on the economic development across the world, many researchers have look into various angle in the context of SMEs success factors. For example, innovation policies in SMEs (Wonglimpiyarat & Jarunee, 2016), motivation of SMEs entrepreneurs (Soltanian, Zailani, Azmin, & Aziz, 2016), knowledge management (Yigitcanla & Sarimin, 2015), organizational and management activities (Agostini, 2016), business-based website (Ramayah, Ling, Taghizadeh, & Rahman, 2015), network (Ing. & Ing., 2016), human capital (Onkelinx, Manolova, & Edelman, 2016) and many more.

However, in the practical perspective, critical challenges and difficulties lies ahead, particularly during the start-up phase. The failure rate of SMEs in their early stage is high and need urgent attention in most countries (Ahmad, Wilson, and Kummerow, 2011; Rasmussen, Mosey, and Wright, 2014). Therefore, many prominent researchers across the world (Aerts, Matthyssens, and Vandenbempt, 2007; Bergek and Norrman, 2008; Calza, Dezi, Schiavone, and Simoni, 2014; Hackett and Dilts, 2008; Mas-

Table 4. Number of SMEs establishment by sector

Sector	Micro	Small	Medium	Total SMEs	Total SMEs	Large Firms	Total Establishments
	Number of Establishments				% Share	Number	Number
Manufacturing	21,619	13,934	2,308	37,861	5.9	1,808	39,669
Services	462,420	106,061	12,504	580,985	90.1	10,898	591,883
Agriculture	3,775	1,941	992	6,708	1.0	2,121	8,829
Construction	8,587	6,725	3,971	19,283	3.0	2,857	22,140
Mining & Quarrying	57	126	116	299	0.05	119	418
Total SMEs	**496,458**	**128,787**	**19,891**	**645,136**	**100.0**	**17,803**	**662,939**

Source: Department of Statistic Malaysia (2011)

Table 5. Asia-Pacific SME statistic, Index 2015

Economy	Number of SMEs	SME Employment	SME Contribution to GDP
Australia	2,076,068	7,241,000	55.70
China	40,478,200	654,984,000	60.00
Hong Kong	316,432	1,296,003	54.00
India	36,200,000	101,200,000	6.20
Indonesia	56,534,591	107,657,510	23.20
Japan	4,115,830729	65,280,000	53.00
Malaysia	**645,136**	**8,460,971**	**32.70**
New Zealand	468,100	584,000	42.00
Philippines	816,759	3,872,406	35.70
Singapore	407,298	2,460,000	50.00
South Korea	3,351,404	13,059,372	47.30
Taiwan	1,306,	8,484,000	30.23
Thailand	2,913,167	10,995,997	36.60
Vietnam	242,453	32,505,242	40.00

Source: Asia Cloud Computing Association (2015)

Table 6. Actual and targeted contribution of SMEs

Category/year	Actual SME establishment 2010 (%)	Targeted SME establishment 2020 (%)
GDP	32	41
Employment	59	62
Export	19	25

Source: Hafsah Hashim (2013)

Verdú, Ribeiro-Soriano, and Roig-Tierno, 2015) have heightened the importance of business incubator programmes as key drivers to foster the development of start-up firms through job and wealth creation.

INCUBATOR AS A SUPPORT MECHANISM TO SMEs

Having the right environment is essential in ensuring the effective and efficient creation process of technology-based entrepreneurs. Research has shown that in order to encourage the formation of technology based entrepreneurs, business incubators are needed to act as catalysts (Abdul Khalid, Gilbert, & Huq, 2011; Rosa Caiazza, 2014; Wonglimpiyarat, 2016). Business incubators are generally seen as a politically attractive and widely accepted means of increasing the chances of survival for new business ventures (Dee, Livesey, Gill, & Minshall, 2011; European Commission, 2002; Lalkaka, 2003; Smilor, 1987; Tavoletti, 2013). They are also viewed incubator as one of the newest tool for promoting the growth and development of economic of a country (Al-Mubaraki & Busler, 2014; Mansano & Pereira, 2016; Marchis & Lecturer, 2011).

A systematic review was conducted on business incubation by Hackett & Dilts (2004). It was observed that most literatures agree that incubators-incubation represent a systematic method of providing business assistance to firms during the early-stages of their development. This assistance is provided with the aim of increasing firm survival rates (Mas-Verdú, Ribeiro-Soriano, & Roig-Tierno, 2015). It was also noted by earlier researcher, Allen & Rahman (1985) that while the universal purpose of a business incubator is to increase the chances of a firm surviving its formative years, the business incubator also adds value by maximizing the firms' growth potential (Rosa Caiazza, 2014).

Business incubators can be perceived to be a type of infrastructure geared to support and nurture the establishment and development of small enterprises (Bergek & Norrman, 2008; Brathwaite, 2016; European Union, 2014; Lesáková, 2012; Mas-Verdú et al., 2015; Peña, 2002). Incubators typically seek to provide a nurturing or a supportive environment by ensuring that start-up firms have access to the resources, services and assistance needed. These resources are more often than not a luxury that new ventures lack or cannot yet afford (Lee & Hunt, 2008; Trewartha et al., 2012).

Entrepreneurship in the United States thrives because of the prevalent culture of risk-taking, competitiveness, technical infrastructures, and venture capital (Adlesic & Slavec, 2012; Brathwaite, 2016; Chandra, 2009) practiced by the entrepreneurs. It must also be noted that in order to further foster the development of entrepreneurs, especially from the technology-based angle, the presence of business incubators are especially important economic development tools. A clear example of this is undoubtedly the Silicon Valley, which boasts of being the ultimate business cluster phenomenon. Results from a study conducted by Suzuki, Kim, & Bae (2002) which compared entrepreneurship in Japan and Silicon Valley showed that Japanese entrepreneurs and their counterparts from the Silicon Valley were different in four dimensions; which are motivation, risk and obstacles, growth factors and infrastructures.

In Korea and China, entrepreneurial activities are also enhanced by the emergence of science parks and incubators, which are mostly linked to universities (Lalkaka, 2002). According to Nam (2000), in Korea, the technological know-how and managerial skills could be regarded as a necessary but it is not sufficient condition to be successful ventures. As Sung, Gibson, & Kang (2003) explained that entrepreneurs in Korea have insightful evaluations about their resources and capacities as well as expectations towards the functions and features of science parks and incubators. However, it was also observed that the functions and features of science parks and incubators were generally not perceived to be a critical influence on business start-up firms or on the growth of new businesses. Contrarily, Chinese incubators not only helped to bridge the gap between government research and the marketplace, but also fostered entrepreneurial attitudes. Besides that, the incubation programs had also been effective in promoting continuous interaction and opportunities among the managers (Lalkaka, 2002).

Observations made in South East Asian countries have highlighted several initiatives which have been undertaken by various governments in order to nurture the development of entrepreneurs. Singapore's cultivation of technopreneurs as a social movement implies a fundamental shift in orientations, such as a higher concentration on innovation Foo & Foo (2000). The government has also conditioned favourable environments to encourage the blossoming of technopreneurship through the provision of a strong education system, infrastructure, and internet access. Studies have also shown a similar movement in Malaysia through the establishment of technology parks, MSC and incubators to nurture the start-up of companies. An example of this is the SIRIM Malaysia incubator hub in Sepang which aims at assisting entrepreneurs develop innovative concepts, upgrade skills and enhance their knowledge (Yunos, 2002).

Bergek & Norrman (2008) highlighted four components which bring business incubators and incubation into the limelight, namely; 1) shared office space which is rented under more or less favourable conditions to incubatees, 2) a pool of shared support services to reduce overhead costs, 3) professional business support or advice and 4) internal and external network provision. Governments have the role of providing the necessary infrastructure for the MSC, developing the human resource pool, the setting up of incubators and research agencies and councils to support SME, MSC as well as economic development. In comparison with other developing countries, Malaysia can be seen to have initiated the most integrated efforts in terms of government policies development, provision of incentives and infrastructures to support the growth of SMEs.

However, one of the challenges faced by SMEs during the start-up phase is the capability to utilize all the facilities provided by the government. One effort made by the government to reduce this problem is the increased running of programmes and policy regimes. It is hoped that through the delivery of these initiatives, SMEs will be able to enjoy further development and an escalated success rate. Six categories have been identified (SMIDEC, 2007), namely:

1. Programs on capacity building and human capital development,
2. Programs on technology development,
3. Programs on market access,
4. Programs on advisory services,
5. Programs on promotion and outreach, and
6. Programs on incubator centers and SME Industrial Sites.

Table 7. Number of business incubators in Asia Pacific region

Country	Number of Incubators	Number of Companies Incubated
China	670	45,000
Korea	279	4,700
Japan	190	2,375
Singapore	120	1,800
India	110	800
Taiwan	104	1,300
Australia	80	160
Thailand	89	412
Malaysia	**110**	**2,000**
Uzbekistan	32	488
New Zealand	10	142
Hong Kong	5	200
Vietnam	11	47
Pakistan	1	9

Source: Asia Association of Business Incubators (AABI), 2009

Malaysia is not foreign to the concept of 'business incubators', as the nation has seen the adoption of this concept in the economy since the early 1990s. The number of business incubators has been on the rise since then, and as of 2009, it was noted that there were 110 incubators in Malaysia (Association of Business Incubation AABI; 2009), and 2000 incubating companies, as is depicted in Table 7. Although Malaysia currently ranks in the mid-range levels among the 14 listed companies, the statistics are still indicative of the positive future prospects of incubation development in Malaysia.

THE NUMBER OF BUSINESS INCUBATORS AND INCUBATEES IN MALAYSIA

According to SME Corp report (2012), although there are 126 incubation centres in Malaysia, only 103 of these centres are currently active. It was also recorded that 23 of these centres are in the pre-stage status at various incubation centres (Table 8). Key information highlighted in the table with regards to the 103 active incubators indicated that there are 988 incubatee companies residing in these active incubators, and that more than 50% of these companies have already developed commercial products and are generating revenue. Less than half (43%) are actual pre seed and start-ups, with a very negligible number of virtual incubatees (3%). These figures represent a ratio of 10 incubatees to 1 incubator, which is slightly less than the average ratio of 17 incubatees to 1 incubator as was highlighted by a study conducted by infoDev in 2009. The same study found China to have the highest incubatee to incubator ratio, which stood at 67:1, while Australia was observed to have the slightest ratio at 2:1. Japan and Taiwan both have a ratio of 13 incubatees to 1 incubator, placing both countries just above Malaysia (SME Corp, 2012).

There are two ways of categorising incubation centres in Malaysia, which is either by the type of incubator or according to its industry sector focus.

- **Type:** The incubator can be of technology, business, jobs/skills and virtual (Figure 3), and
- **Sector Focus:** Agriculture, craft, manufacturing and services (Figure 4).

The following two figures provide a more detailed description of these categories.

Table 8. Number of incubators and incubatees in Malaysia, (SME Corp, 2012)

Number of Incubators	A total 126 incubation centres	
	Category	**Establishment**
	Active	103
	Pre-stage	23
	Total	**126**
Number of Incubatee	**From a total 103 active incubators**	
	Category	**Establishment**
	Pre-seed	93
	Start-up	336
	Matured	527
	Virtual	32

Figure 3. Incubation centres categorised by type
(SME Corp, 2012)

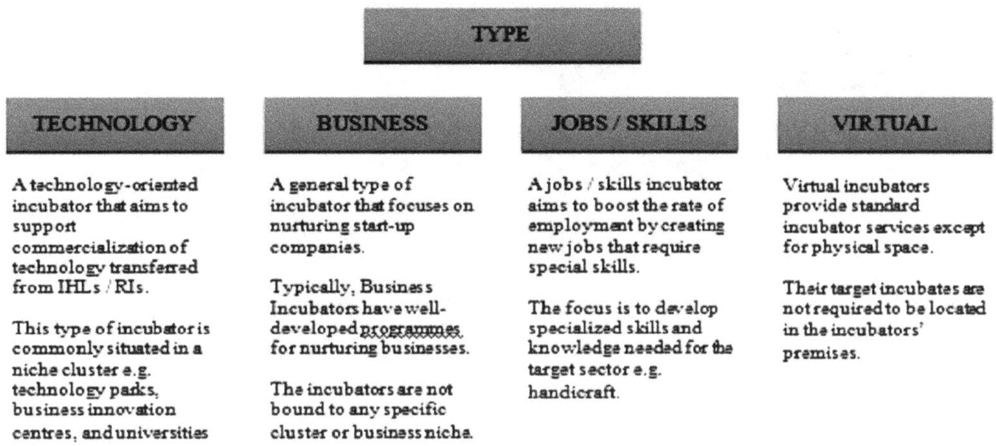

Figure 4. Incubation centres categorised by sector
(SME Corp, 2012)

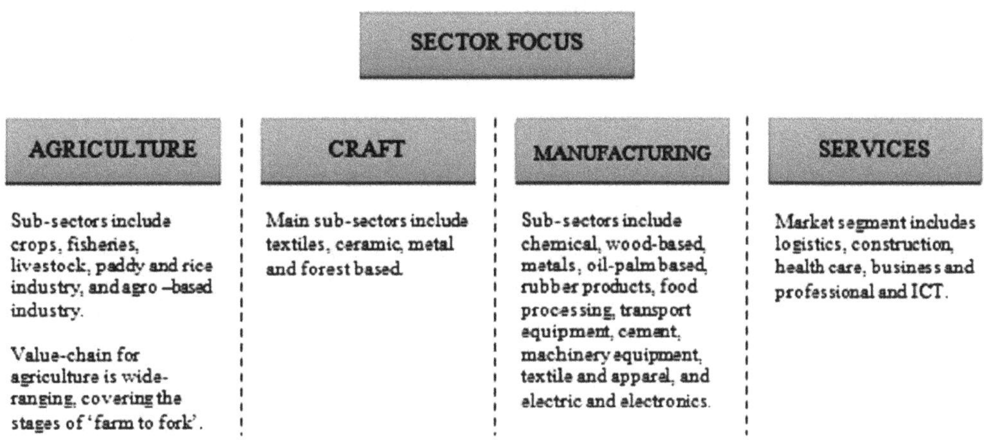

EVOLUTION OF INCUBATION MODEL

Incubation models have undergone several evolution movements over the years and can be classified into different generations based on the period of change, as is highlighted in Figure 5 (Abdul Khalid et al., 2014). 1st generation incubation models entail incubation centres that focus solely on providing real estate services and some shared physical facilities. On the other hand, 2nd generation incubation centres provide specific advisory services that are mainly based on the particular specialisation of the incubation centre. Support from the management at this stage is generally on request. 3rd generation incubation centres marked a significant change in terms of services, as these centres extended their services by providing business support (mentoring, coaching, business advisory), marketing support (market access, network, marketing services) and facilitation for access to funding sources such as grants, project financ-

Figure 5. Generation of incubation centres development
(Adapted from SME Corp, 2012 and Abdul Khalid et al., 2014)

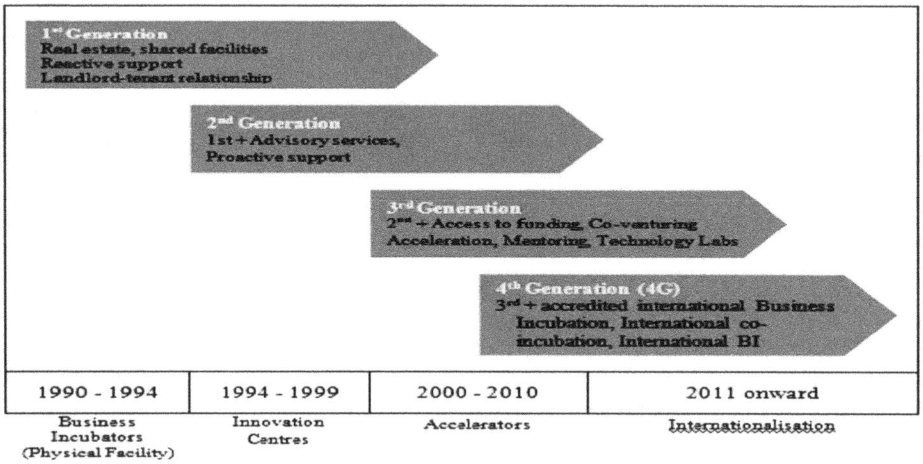

ing, loans, venture capital, and investors. Currently, incubation models are at the 4th generation phase, and the services delivered by at this phase include greater support and add internalisation value of their clients' business, seeking access to global funding, international alliances, and international markets.

CHALLENGES OF BUSINESS INCUBATORS IN MALAYSIA

It is clear that SMEs are acknowledge in literature as one of the most potential drivers of the Malaysia's economy as they are significant contributor in terms of capabilities for creating employment, contributions to gross domestic product (GDP) and exports (Ahmad et al., 2011; Bakar, Mahmood, & Ismail, 2015; Isa, Aziz, & Razak, 2011; Muhammad Wasin Jan Khan & Dr Muhammad Khalique, 2014; Ramayah et al., 2015; Sharif, 2014; Tock & Rohaizat Baharun, 2013). Thus, business incubators programmes are seen to shed light to the SMEs by providing a nurturing business environment to accelerate the development of start-up firms.

After realizing the importance of business incubation programmes, tremendous support has been given by the government. Yet, according to Mohd Saffar (2007), SME Corp (2012), and Jamil et al. (2016) there are many challenges faced in the process of incubation as:

- Lack of skilled staff to coach and monitor the incubatees,
- Weak underlying processes in incubators,
- Lack of managerial skills among the managers operating incubators,
- No standard definition and concept of business incubation modeled in Malaysia,
- Incubation programmes are parked in various ministries,
- Majority of incubators are funded by federal government, and
- Bureaucratic complexities in some of the processes.

Report from SME Corp (2012) has outlined realistic indication of Malaysia incubation scenario that 68% of business incubators in Malaysia are in first and second generation, accounted for 20% and 48% respectively. These generation incubation programmes adapt traditional landlord-tenant models (low-cost real estate), and provide basic incubation supports (office space and shared office facilities). The report also identified that 29% of business incubators are in third generation, while only 3% ended in the fourth generation. Both third and fourth generation incubators have updated their supports portfolio by offering business support services particularly coaching and mentoring, assisting the incubatees with technological upgrade, professionals, providing international market and network access, as well as providing essential support from local and global funds. This statistic infers that human, structural and network capital element need to be given attention, which will result in upgrading the level of the majority business incubators from the first and second generation to the third and fourth generation in the near future.

DISCUSSION AND FUTURE RESEARCH

Despite all the strategies and development in business incubators, little evidence on theoretical challenges was identified in Malaysia. Even developments in economics have highlighted the significance of business incubator programmes across the world, yet far too little attention has been paid on the business incubators-incubation research in Malaysia. This chapter is highlighting some of the literature research, from a range of period from 2000 to 2015 which has been conducted in both conceptual and research in Malaysia as shown in Table 9. The update clearly indicates a remarkable shortage of research in Malaysia. Thereby, this chapter suggests future researchers to explore and identify the success factors and performance of business incubator programmes which can be exploited in Malaysia particularly. It is very important for future research to close the gap by looking into the unexplored dimension. Based on the few studies conducted in business incubation, the following challenges were highlighted:

- What is the standardization of the incubation process? (Lee & Hunt, 2008),
- What is the best practise of an incubator? (Bergek & Norrman, 2008),
- What are the enabling factors for strategic management of business incubator? (Somsuk & Laosirihongthong, 2014), and
- How do business incubators use their intellectual capital? (Calza et al., 2014).

Thus, one way to explore the challenges faced by incubators in Malaysia would be exploring on the influence of intellectual capital to the performance of incubatees, as Malaysia is moving toward knowledge based economy. As intellectual capital is the major source of knowledge, Calza et al., (2014) had proposed a theoretical model to analyze the intellectual capital of new generation business incubators, where it encompasses three dimensions; human, structural and relational capital.

Therefore, moving forward, and in line with SME Masterplan 2012-2020, this chapter would like to highlight the gaps in business incubators research in Malaysia. This chapter clearly shows the urgency to carry out studies to identify the factors which influence the performance of business incubations in Malaysia, in the context of effectiveness of business incubators either during the phase of pre, during or post incubation.

Table 9. List of research in business incubators-incubation from 2000-2015 in Malaysia

Author (Year)	Title
Mohd Yunos (2002)	Building an Innovation-based Economy: The Malaysian Technology Business Incubator Experience
Jusoh & Idris (2002)	Role of Technopreneurs in Malaysian Economic
Ghazi (2006)	Growing a Vibrant ICT Incubator Industry In Malaysia.
Mohd Saffar (2007)	Malaysian Incubation Country Case Study
Sufian (2006)	Incubators as catalysts in developing high technology businesses: Malaysia's experience.
Mahmud (2003)	Seed stage venture capitalists & incubators in Malaysia: a win-win collaboration.
Mohd Saffar (2007)	Innovation and entrepreneurship policy framework: The Malaysian experience in building sustainable incubation industry (movement).
Mohd Saffar (2008)	Business Incubation and Support System in Asia-Pacific: Establishing International Cooperation among Asian Incubators
Abdul Khalid et al. (2010)	Current Practice of Business Incubation Process Elements in Malaysian ICT Incubators
Abdul Khalid, Gilbert, & Huq (2011)	Business incubation process impact on Malaysian ICT incubatee performance using multinomial logistic regression.
Abdul Khalid et al. (2012)	Investigating the underlying components in business incubation process in Malaysian ict incubators
Abdul Khalid & Gilbert (2012)	Third-generation Business Incubation Practices in Malaysian ICT Incubators – A Bridge Too Far?
Said et al. (2012)	Incubators And Government Policy For Developing It Industry And Region In Emerging
Abdul Khalid et al. (2014)	The Way Forward For Business Incubation Process in ICT Incubators in Malaysia

CONCLUSION

As part of the journey in realizing Vision 2020, MSC and SMEs have played a vital role in contributing to the economic growth. Realizing this, government has formulated and multiplied strategies and action plan to drive together the promoting of the economic growth. Taken together, the study encompass the role of business incubators as an accelerator to start-up firms, and simultaneously in line with the objectives of SME Masterplan 2012-2020 to generate greater impact to SMEs development.

This chapter reviewed the significance of MSC and SMEs in the Malaysian economy; the small but important steps taken to facilitate more effective approaches to business incubation as well as a general typology of business incubators in Malaysia. As the government is the leading stakeholder of the incubation centres and their ecosystem in the country, this is a timely moment for the nation to take key steps to regulate the incubation industry into a single governance system, with a keen focus on nurturing the incubatees and increasing their chances of survival. Undeniably, there are many drawbacks in the Malaysian incubation industry such as the fact that most of the incubation centres in Malaysia are either federal or state owned, the loose interpretation of the term incubator in Malaysia, the trend of most incubation centres in the country being placed at either 2nd or 1st generation stages, equity funding by incubation centres that is not prevalent, human capital issues especially in terms of incubation managerial skills, structural capital as well as issues with innovation. These limitations indicate that there are still many steps which must be taken by Malaysia in order to successfully achieve the status that the nations hopes to attain within the incubation industry in the near future, encompassing on the intellectual capital context of business incubation.

REFERENCES

Abdul Khalid, F., & Gilbert, D. (2012). Third-generation Business Incubation Practices in Malaysian ICT Incubators – A Bridge Too Far? *American Journal of Management, 12*, 88–107.

Abdul Khalid, F., Gilbert, D., & Huq, A. (2010). Current Practice of Business Incubation Process Elements in Malaysian ICT Incubators. In *Australia and New Zealand Academy of Management* (pp. 1–28). Adelaide, Australia: ANZAM.

Abdul Khalid, F., Gilbert, D., & Huq, A. (2011). Business Incubation Process Impact on Malaysian ICT Incubatee Performance Using Multinomial Logistic Regression. In *The Second Asian Business*. Osaka, Japan: Management Conference.

Abdul Khalid, F., Gilbert, D., & Huq, A. (2012). Investigating the underlying components in business incubation process in malaysian ict incubators. *Asian Journal Of Social Sciences & Humanities Configurations, 1*(1), 88–102.

Abdul Khalid, F., Gilbert, D., & Huq, A. (2014)... *The Way Forward For Business Incubation Process in ICT Incubators in Malaysia, 15*(3), 395–412.

Abdullah, N. H., & Shamsuddin, A. (2009). Technology adoption among SMEs in Malaysia: Development of an assessment process. PICMET: Portland International Center for Management of Engineering and Technology, Proceedings, (1), 2644–2648. http://doi.org/ doi:<ALIGNMENT.qj></ALIGNMENT>10.1109/PICMET.2009.5261819

Adlesic, R. V., & Slavec, A. (2012). Social Capital and Business Incubators Performance: Testing the Structural Model. *Economic and Business Review for Central and South - Eastern Europe, 14*(3), 201–222.

Aerts, K., Matthyssens, P., & Vandenbempt, K. (2007). Critical role and screening practices of European business incubators. *Technovation, 27*(5), 254–267. doi:10.1016/j.technovation.2006.12.002

Agostini, L. (2016). Organizational and Managerial Activities in the Development Process of Successful SME Marketing Networks. *European Management Review*, 278–293. http://doi.org/<ALIGNMENT.qj></ALIGNMENT>10.1111/emre.12069

Ahmad, N. H., Wilson, C., & Kummerow, L. (2011). A cross-cultural insight into the competency-mix of SME entrepreneurs in Australia and Malaysia. *International Journal of Business and Management Science, 4*(1), 33–50.

Al-Mubaraki, H. M., & Busler, M. (2014). Incubator successes. *World Journal of Science. Technology and Sustainable Development, 11*(1), 44–52. doi:10.1108/WJSTSD-08-2013-0030

Allen, D. N., & Rahman, S. (1985). Small business incubators: A positive environment for entrepreneurship. *Journal of Small Business Management, 23*(3), 12.

Asia Association of Business Incubation. (2009). *Asia Association of Business Incubation*. Retrieved from http://www.slideshare.net/pmtuan0/new-trends-in-incubation

Asia Cloud Computing Association (2015). *SMEs in Asia Pacific: The Market for Cloud Computing 2015*. Author.

Bakar, H. A., Mahmood, R., & Ismail, N. N. H. (2015). Effects of knowledge management and strategic improvisation on SME performance in Malaysia. *Asian Social Science*, *11*(9), 207–214. doi:10.5539/ass.v11n9p207

Bekhet, H. A. (2013). Assessing structural changes in the Malaysian economy: I-O approach. *Economic Modelling*, *30*(1), 126–135. doi:10.1016/j.econmod.2012.09.014

Bergek, A., & Norrman, C. (2008). Incubator best practice: A framework. *Technovation*, *28*(1–2), 20–28. doi:10.1016/j.technovation.2007.07.008

Bergek, A., & Norrman, C. (2008). *Linköping University Post Print Incubator best practice: A framework Incubator best practise: A framework*. Academic Press.

Berma, M. (2012). *Developing an Entrepreneurship Education Eco-System at Universiti Kebangsaan Malaysia (UKM): A Critical Analysis on Teaching*. Learning and Knowledge Development.

Calza, F., Dezi, L., Schiavone, F., & Simoni, M. (2014). The intellectual capital of business incubators. *Journal of Intellectual Capital*, *15*(4), 597–610. doi:10.1108/JIC-07-2014-0086

Chandra, A. (2009). Business Incubation in the United States, China and Brazil. *International Journal of Entrepreneurship*, *13*, 67–86.

Dee, N. J., Livesey, F., Gill, D., & Minshall, T. (2011). Incubation for Growth, A review of the impact of business incubation on new ventures with high growth potential. *Research Summary*, (September), 1–53. Retrieved from www.nesta.org.uk

Department of Statistic Malaysia. (2011). Economic Census 2011: Profile of SMEs. Author.

European Commission. (2002). Final report: Benchmarking of Business Incubators. *Personnel*, *51*(February), 47. doi:10.1086/656690

European Union. (2014). *Policy and Practice*. EU.

Foo, C.-T., & Foo, C.-T. (2000). Socialization of technopreneurism: Towards symbiosis in corporate innovation and technology strategy. *Technovation*, *20*(10), 551–562. doi:10.1016/S0166-4972(99)00171-6

Ghazi, A. (2006). Growing a Vibrant ICT Incubator Industry In Malaysia. Academic Press.

Gopal, K., & Mohd Sulaiman, S. (2013). *Circular on new definition of Small and Medium Enterprises (SMEs)*. Academic Press.

Gunto, M., & Alias, M. H. (2013). SMEs Development in Malaysia: Lessons For Libya. *Persidangan Kebangsaan Ekonomi Malaysia Ke VIII (PERKEM). VIII, JILID*, *3*, 1521–1530.

Hackett, S. M., & Dilts, D. M. (2004). A Systematic Review of Business Incubation Research. *The Journal of Technology Transfer*, *29*(1), 55–82. doi:10.1023/B:JOTT.0000011181.11952.0f

Hackett, S. M., & Dilts, D. M. (2008). Inside the black box of business incubation: Study B - Scale assessment, model refinement, and incubation outcomes. *The Journal of Technology Transfer*, *33*(5), 439–471. doi:10.1007/s10961-007-9056-9

Hashim, H. (2013). *Overview of SME Sector in Malaysia.* Presentation in SME: Global Champions, Malaysia-India SME Forum.

Husin, M. A., & Ibrahim, M. D. (2014). The Role of Accounting Services and Impact on Small Medium Enterprises (SMEs) Performance in Manufacturing Sector from East Coast Region of Malaysia: A Conceptual Paper. *Procedia - Social and Behavioral Sciences, 115*, 54–67. http://doi.org/<ALIGNMENT.qj></ALIGNMENT>10.1016/j.sbspro.2014.02.415

Ing, S. G., & Ing, G. A. (2016). Dynamic Manufacturing Cells and {SME} Network: Key Success Factors. *IFAC-PapersOnLine, 49*(12), 851–856.

Isa, W. A. R. W. M., Aziz, M. A., & Razak, M. R. B. A. (2011). Evaluating the accessibility of Small and Medium Enterprise (SME) websites in Malaysia. In *Proceedings - 2011 International Conference on User Science and Engineering, i-USEr 2011* (pp. 135–140). http://doi.org/ doi:<ALIGNMENT.qj></ALIGNMENT>10.1109/iUSEr.2011.6150552

Islam, R. (2010). Critical success factors of the nine challenges in Malaysias vision 2020. *Socio-Economic Planning Sciences*, *44*(4), 199–211. doi:10.1016/j.seps.2010.07.002

Jamil, F., Ismail, K., Siddique, M., Khan, M. M., Kazi, A. G., & Qureshi, M. I. (2016). Business Incubators in Asian Developing Countries. *International Review of Management and Marketing*, *6*(4S), 291–295.

Jusoh, M. A., & Idris, S. (2002). *Role of Technopreneurs in Malaysian Economic.* Retrieved from http://www.jgbm.org/page/1 Mohd Abdullah Jusoh.pdf

Khan, R. A., Liew, M. S., & Ghazali, Z. (2014). Malaysian Construction Sector and Malaysia Vision 2020: Developed Nation Status. *Procedia: Social and Behavioral Sciences*, *109*, 507–513. doi:10.1016/j.sbspro.2013.12.498

Lalkaka, R. (2002). Technology Business Incubators to Help Build an Innovation-based Economy. *Journal of Change Management*, *3*(2), 167–176. doi:10.1080/714042533

Lalkaka, R. (2003). Technology business incubation: Role, performance, linkages, trends. In *National Workshop on Technology Parks and Business Incubators* (pp. 20–21). Retrieved from http://egateg.usaidallnet.gov/sites/default/files/Technology BI Roles.pdf

Lee, L., & Hunt, A. (2008).*Business Incubators: Do They Matter?* Academic Press.

Lesáková, L. (2012).The role of business incubators in supporting the SME start-up. *Acta Polytechnica Hungarica*, *9*(3), 85–95.

Caiazza, R. (2014). Benchmarking of business incubators. Benchmarking. *International Journal (Toronto, Ont.), 21*(6), 1062–1069. Retrieved from http://www.emeraldinsight.com/doi/abs/10.1108/BIJ-01-2013-0011

SME Corp. (2012). *Final Report Study on Enhancing the Effectiveness of Incubation Centres as a Support Mechanism for SME Development in Malaysia.* Author.

MSC Malaysia. (1998). *Cybercity Malaysia.* Author.

Mansano, F. H., & Pereira, M. F. (2016). Business Incubators as Support Mechanism for the Economic Development: Case of Maringas Technology Incubator. *International Journal of Innovation*, *4*(1), 23–32. doi:10.5585/iji.v4i1.51

Marchis, G., & Lecturer, S. (2011). Fundamentals of Business Incubator Development. *EIRP Proceedings, 2*, 85–94. Retrieved from http://www.proceedings.univ-danubius.ro/index.php/eirp/article/download/955/874

Mas-Verdú, F., Ribeiro-Soriano, D., & Roig-Tierno, N. (2015). Firm survival: The role of incubators and business characteristics. *Journal of Business Research*, *68*(4), 793–796. doi:10.1016/j.jbusres.2014.11.030

MDeC. (2014). *MSC Annual Report 2014*. MDeC.

Menon, J. (2009). Macroeconomic management amid ethnic diversity: Fifty years of Malaysian experience. *Journal of Asian Economics*, *20*(1), 25–33. doi:10.1016/j.asieco.2008.05.005

Mohan, A. V., Omar, A. A, & Aziz, K. A. (2004). ICT Clusters as a Way to Materialize a National System of Innovation: Malaysia's Multimedia Super Corridor Flagships. *The Electronic Journal of Information Systems in Developing Countries, 16*(5), 1–18.

Mohd Saffar, A. (2007). *Asia Regional Workshop Innovation: The Role of Business Incubation Innovation and Entrepreneurship Policy Framework : The Malaysian Experience in Building Sustainable Incubation Industry (Movement)*. Forum American Bar Association.

Mohd Yunos, M. G. (2002). Building an innovation-based economy: The Malaysian technology business incubator experience. *Journal of Change Management*, *3*(2), 177–188. doi:10.1080/714042527

Moorthy, M. K., Tan, A., Choo, C., Wei, C. S., Tan, J., Ping, Y., & Leong, T. K. (2012). A Study on Factors Affecting the Performance of SMEs in Malaysia. *International Journal of Academic Research in Business and Social Sciences*, *2*(4), 224–239.

Muhammad, W. J. K., & Khalique, D. M. (2014). An Overview of Small and Medium Enterprises in Malaysia and Pakistan: Past, Present and Future Scenario. *Business and Management Horizons*, *2*(2), 38–49. doi:10.5296/bmh.v2i2.5792

Nam, Y. H. (2000). The roles of incubator organizations in hi-tech venture creation in Korea. *Asia Pacific Journal of Management*, *17*(2), 277–296. doi:10.1023/A:1015813710027

NEAC. (2010). *New Economic Model for Malaysia. Part 1: Strategic Policy Directions*. NEAC.

Nordin. (2002). *Revenue Implications of E-Commerce, Goverment and Private Sector Experiences*. Presentation at WTO Regional Seminar on Electronic Commerce, Geneva, Switzerland.

Onkelinx, J., Manolova, T. S., & Edelman, L. F. (2016). The human factor: Investments in employee human capital, productivity, and SME internationalization. *Journal of International Management*, *22*(4), 351–364. doi:10.1016/j.intman.2016.05.002

Peña, I. (2002). Intellectual capital and business start-up success. *Journal of Intellectual Capital*, *3*(2), 180–198. doi:10.1108/14691930210424761

Ramasamy, B., Chakrabarty, A., & Cheah, M. (2004). Malaysias Leap into the Future: An Evaluation of the Multimedia Super Corridor. *Technovation*, *24*(11), 871–883. doi:10.1016/S0166-4972(03)00049-X

Ramayah, T., Ling, N. S., Taghizadeh, S. K., & Rahman, S. A. (2015). Factors influencing SMEs website continuance intention in Malaysia. *Telematics and Informatics*, (June). doi:10.1016/j.tele.2015.06.007

Rasmussen, E., Mosey, S., & Wright, M. (2014). The influence of university departments on the evolution of entrepreneurial competencies in spin-off ventures. *Research Policy*, *43*(1), 92–106. doi:10.1016/j.respol.2013.06.007

Ratinho, T., & Henriques, E. (2010). The role of science parks and business incubators in converging countries: Evidence from Portugal. *Technovation*, *30*(4), 278–290. doi:10.1016/j.technovation.2009.09.002

Said, M. F., Adham, K. A., & Abdullah, N. A. (2012). Incubators and Goverment Policy for Developing IT Industry and Region in Emerging Economies. *Asian Academy of Management Journal*, *17*(1), 65–96.

Sharif, A. M. (2014). *Risk Assessment Factors for SME Software Development Companies in Malaysia.* IEEE. Retrieved from http://doi.org/978-1-4799-0059-6/13/$31.00

SME Corp. (2013). Guideline for New SME Definition. Author.

SMIDEC. (2007). Policies, Incentives, Programmes and Financial Assistance for SMEs. Author.

Smilor. (1987). Managing the incubator system: critical success factors to accelerate new company development. *IEEE Transactions on Engineering Management, 34*(4), 146–156.

Soltanian, M., Zailani, S., Azmin, M. I., & Aziz, A. (2016). Motivations of SME entrepreneurs to become halalpreneurs. *Journal of Science and Technology Policy Management*, *7*(1), 173–189. doi:10.1108/JSTPM-07-2015-0023

Somsuk, N., & Laosirihongthong, T. (2014). A fuzzy AHP to prioritize enabling factors for strategic management of university business incubators: Resource-based view. *Technological Forecasting and Social Change*, *85*, 198–210. doi:10.1016/j.techfore.2013.08.007

Stafford, D. G. S. D. (1997). Malaysias new economic policy and the global economy: The evolution of ethnic accommodation. *The Pacific Review*, *10*(4), 556–580. doi:10.1080/09512749708719239

Sufian, J. (2006). Incubators As Catalysts in Developing High Technology Businesses : Malaysia ' S Experience. *ATDF Journal*, *3*(1), 25–29.

Sung, T. K., Gibson, D. V., & Kang, B. S. (2003). Characteristics of technology transfer in business ventures: The case of Daejeon, Korea. *Technological Forecasting and Social Change*, *70*(5), 449–466. doi:10.1016/S0040-1625(02)00360-8

Suzuki, K. I., Kim, S. H., & Bae, Z. T. (2002). Entrepreneurship in Japan and Silicon Valley: A comparative study. *Technovation*, *22*(10), 595–606. doi:10.1016/S0166-4972(01)00099-2

Tavoletti, E. (2013). Business Incubators: Effective Infrastructures or Waste of Public Money? Looking for a Theoretical Framework, Guidelines and Criteria. *Journal of the Knowledge Economy*, *4*(4), 423–443. doi:10.1007/s13132-012-0090-y

The Economic Planning Unit. (2000). Malaysia: Eighth Malaysia Plan.

The Economic Planning Unit. (2006). Malaysia: Ninth Malaysia Plan.

Tock, J. M., & Baharun, R. (2013). Introduction to SMEs in Malaysia: Growth Potential and Branding Strategy. *World Journal of Social Science, 3*, 189–203. Retrieved from http://www.bnm.gov.my/files/publication/sme/en/2007/chap_4.pdf

Vicziany, M., & Puteh, M. (2004). Vision 2020, The Multimedia Supercorridor and Malaysian Universities.*Proceeding of the 15th Biennial Conference of the Asian Studies Association of Australia*, 1–21.

Wonglimpiyarat, J. (2016). The innovation incubator, university business incubator and technology transfer strategy: The case of Thailand. *Technology in Society*, *46*, 18–27. doi:10.1016/j.techsoc.2016.04.002

Wonglimpiyarat, & Jarunee. (2016). Innovation policies to accelerate SME development. *Jarunee Wonglimpiyarat, 16*(2).

Yeoh, P. L. (2014). Internationalization and performance outcomes of entrepreneurial family SMEs: The role of outside CEOs, technology sourcing, and innovation. *Thunderbird International Business Review*, *56*(1), 77–96. doi:10.1002/tie.21597

Yigitcanla, T., & Sarimin, M. (2015). *Article information: Multimedia Super Corridor*. Knowledge-Based Urban.

Yunos, M. G. M. (2002). Building an innovation-based economy: The Malaysian technology business incubator experience. *Journal of Change Management*, *3*(2), 177–188. doi:10.1080/714042527

Yusof, & Bhattasali, D. (2008). Economic Growth and Development in Malaysia: Policy Making and Leadership. *Commission on Growth and Development, 27.*

KEY TERMS AND DEFINITIONS

Business Incubation: A dynamic, interactive, and innovative process which stimulates and accelerates the discovery, validation, application of new ideas towards development and commercialization of tangible and intangible products in the market.

Business Incubator: An innovative system which is designed to accelerate the development and success of start-up firms by providing a broad range of resources and business services. Business incubators are primarily defined by nature of the incubator's promoters, their objectives, the types of projects and services, the financial model and the environment in which the incubator operates.

Economic Policy: The actions that governments take in the economic field.

Incubatee: Firms that have been registered under an incubator and had been in operation for a period of time.

Multimedia Super Corridor (MSC): MSC Malaysia is Malaysia's national ICT initiative designed to attract world-class technology companies while grooming the local ICT industry.

Small and Medium Enterprise (SME): SME definition covers all sectors, namely services, manufacturing, agriculture, construction and mining & quarrying bases on sales turnover and number of full-time employees.

Chapter 16
Corporate Social Responsibility in SMEs:
The Role of Non-Audit Services

Yuvaraj Ganesan
Universiti Sains Malaysia, Malaysia

Azlan Amran
Universiti Sains Malaysia, Malaysia

Hasnah Haron
Universiti Malaysia Pahang, Malaysia

Say Keat Ooi
Universiti Sains Malaysia, Malaysia

ABSTRACT

Given the increasing importance of the role played by small and medium-sized enterprises (SMEs) within the developing economy, this paper intends to provide further insight into corporate social responsibility (CSR) practices among SMEs. Within this context, the purpose is to propose the role of non-audit services (NAS), which contribute to the possible explanation of the SME adoption of CSR practices. A conceptual approach is taken whereby this paper is based on an extensive literature review of NAS and CSR practices in the SME context. Then, based on the knowledge-based view (KBV), this paper set to explain and highlight the role of NAS play to enhance CSR practices among SMEs. This paper provides a theoretical discussion on the importance of CSR in ensuring the survival of the SMEs. Although the proposition of NAS is relatively new, it provides an interesting and remarkable avenue for further research especially in the developing country. Overall, this paper draws attention to the importance of NAS in enhancing the survival and performance of the SMEs.

INTRODUCTION

With the growing popularity and importance of corporate social responsibility (CSR), research on CSR has grown exponentially (Carroll, 1999; Crowther & Aras, 2008; Carroll & Shabana, 2010), despite no universal definition of CSR (Dahlsrud, 2008). The notion of CSR has a long and diverse history, it proliferated and the most popular definition stated that organisations in favour of CSR typically strive to be a good corporate citizen, making profits, obey the law, and to be ethical (Carroll, 1991). Economic, ethical, legal and philanthropic, has been identified as the four important responsibilities of CSR (Car-

DOI: 10.4018/978-1-5225-2165-5.ch016

roll, 1991). As far as CSR is concerned, most of the studies were conducted on larger listed companies, instead of the small and medium-sized enterprises (SMEs) (Jenkins, 2006; Spence, 2007; Liu & Fong, 2010; Baden, Harwood, & Woodward, 2011; Vázquez-Carrasco & López-Pérez, 2012). Since there has been a lack of CSR research in the context of SMEs (Carney, Van Essen, Gedajlovic, & Heugens, 2010), this paper attempts to fill the missing gap.

Essentially, this paper focuses on CSR practices among the SMEs. Nowadays, SMEs topic has gained increasing attention among researchers and practitioners as its contribution is huge to the nation. Significantly, SMEs account for around 90% of the incorporated companies worldwide (Hsu & Cheng, 2011), generating almost 65% of employment globally (Jamali, Zanhour, & Keshishian, 2009). Moreover, SMEs contribute to the society, economy and has a significant impact on the development of the country (Ciliberti, Pontrandolfo, & Scozzi, 2008; Perrini & Minoja, 2008). According to Parker, Redmond and Simpson (2009), SMEs also play a vital role in preserving the environment as they are responsible for around 60% of all carbon dioxide emissions and 70% of all pollution. Simply put, the CSR practices among SMEs will be able to enhance the worldwide sustainable development (Morsing & Perrini, 2009). Hence, this paper intends to provide further insight into the CSR practices among SMEs, whereby the role of non-audit services (NAS) has been proposed, which contribute to the possible explanation of the SME adoption of CSR practices.

BACKGROUND

SMEs are believed to be of significantly different from the larger business organisations. The characteristic or cultural aspect of the SMEs are not the same as the large companies (Lepoutre & Heene, 2006). Apart from that, the findings from larger companies do not really reflect the SMEs' environment (Jenkins, 2004; Spence, 2007). For instance, SMEs are usually having fewer resources, governs through informal organisational structures, emphasis on survival (Parker, et al., 2009) and less likely to engaged in CSR activities (Spence, 2007), as compared to larger companies.

However, it is perceived that SMEs are in a better position and comparatively well equipped to design appropriate CSR strategies to address the needs of the local communities as they operate "on the ground", they are more aware of the local environmental risks and emerging social issues than their larger counterparts (Sweeney, 2007). Generally, SMEs have a greater understanding of the local cultural and political contexts, more partnering and links to local civil society and greater commitment to operating in a specific area (Baden, et al., 2011). Nowadays, CSR has been assumed to encompass philanthropic activities such as donation for individual or sponsorship for events. CSR has emerged into a border perspective, which include ethics and compliance, stakeholders' elements (such as employees, environment, community, customer, shareholder, and supplier) and so on (Carroll, 1999; Crowther & Aras, 2008; Carroll & Shabana, 2010). This highlights the importance and timeliness of CSR practices research among SMEs to be undertaken.

The business case for CSR has been widely discussed (Carroll, 1999; Carroll & Shabana, 2010). Some studies revealed that SMEs are actually practicing CSR without knowing that those are CSR related activities. This is normally refers to as "sunken CSR" or "silent CSR" (Jenkins, 2004; Perrini, 2006; Jamali & Tarazi, 2012; Moyeen & Courvisanos, 2012). This was proven by a study conducted by Jamali et al. (2009) on six SMEs through in-depth interviews, as the authors concluded that the benefits sought and derived from CSR activities by SMEs are clear conscience, having greater personal satisfaction and peace of mind (Jamali, et al., 2009). They highlighted that the managers of the SME tend to emphasise their preference by not publicising their CSR activities and never think about the benefits as they do not expect any benefits in return, this corresponds to a purely philanthropic / altruistic orientation (Jamali, et al., 2009). It is suggested that engagement of SMEs in the CSR activities are largely based on moral or ethical reasons (Jenkins, 2004; Longo, Mura, & Bonoli, 2005; Evans & Sawyer, 2010) and the CSR practices among SMEs do not tend to be solely a function to fulfil purely economic objectives and profit ratios (Russo & Perrini, 2010; Baden, et al., 2011). In fact, SMEs are willing to sacrifice some of their profits while serving towards a finer goal (Moyeen & Courvisanos, 2012).

SMEs involve in CSR practices for many reasons. Some contended that due to their own beliefs, values and religious thoughts, pressure and encouragement from stakeholders (Morsing & Perrini, 2009; Nejati & Amran, 2009). The study, which was conducted on ten Malaysian SMEs through semi-structured interviews, is similar to Lee, Mak, and Pang (2012), who carried out their 15 in-depth interviews and 113 web surveys with senior SME executives in Singapore. Specifically, they discovered that besides the existing regulation on environmental issues, SMEs were also pressured by customers and suppliers to adopt environmental friendly practices and hold the environmental certificates (Lee et al., 2012). The finding supports the argument that the SMEs behaviour may vary according to the demands of their supply chain (Russo & Tencati, 2009; Vázquez-Carrasco & López-Pérez, 2012). This indicates that there had been an increasing external pressure and expectation on SMEs to be engaged in CSR activities and related reporting on such activities (Fassin, 2008). Hence, CSR practices among SMEs are important as in the coming future, those SMEs that are not prepared for CSR may proscribe or struggle in the international trade (Lu & Castka, 2009).

Considerable efforts have been done to examine CSR practices among business organisations, most of the past studies focused on the outcome of CSR practices such as customers' relations, control of the firm, employees relations, supplier relations, firm image and financial improvement (Nejati & Amran, 2009); to increase the level of employee satisfaction, to increase the sales and reduce costs, to make the customer and client loyalty (Maria, 2011); decline in staff turnover, increased of customer satisfaction, increased of firm reputation (Galbreath, 2010); increased employees' productivity (Geva, 2008); product quality, improved management practices, attractiveness to investors, operational efficiencies, and enhanced demographic diversity (e.g., ethnic minorities and women) (Aguinis & Glavas, 2012). Nevertheless, not much effort was made to examine the effect of non-audit services (NAS) on CSR practices.

NAS are defined as services carried out by the accounting / audit firm that do not result in the expression of an opinion, negative assurance or any other form of assurance (Gill & Cosserat, 1996). The term of NAS used is interchangeable with business advisory services, non-assurance services, business advice, and management advisory service. The examples of NAS are taxation planning and compliance, tax incentives application business strategy and planning, HR consulting, business restructuring, budgeting, financial planning, book keeping, internal control review, risk management and others.

Most of the past NAS studies were focus on auditor independents, quality of NAS or NAS fees. While accountants are found to be the key source of advice to SMEs in terms of the frequently referred to, and their advice is rated as significant and useful (Lewis, Massey, Ashby, Coetzer, & Harris, 2007). None of the research has look into NAS provided by the accountants to improve the CSR practices among the SMEs.

Against this backdrop, this paper takes a step further by proposing and explaining the relationship between NAS and CSR practices through knowledge base view (KBV), in the context of Malaysian SMEs. The objective of this paper is to propose that the professional services provided by the external accountant to SMEs include the CSR related advices, which helps to enhance the CSR activities and strategies among SMEs.

MALAYSIAN SMEs AND CSR

In Malaysia, 98.5% of the established businesses are being the SMEs. The SMEs are defined according to employee size, sales turnover and sectors. Definitions of SMEs in Malaysia (SMECorp., 2013) fall into 2 categories:

1. Manufacturing with full-time employees not exceeding 200 or annual sales turnover not exceeding RM 50 million.
2. Services and other sectors with full-time employees not exceeding 75 or annual sales turnover not exceeding RM 20 million.

The contribution of Malaysian SMEs to employment, to export and to GDP is shown in Table 1 for the selected year (NSDC, 2012).

In Malaysia, the status of CSR is still at the infancy stage (Rashid & Ibrahim, 2002; Lu & Castka, 2009; Amran et al., 2013) and the majority of the research in CSR are related to larger companies. Rashid and Ibrahim (2002) identified that the authorities are facing challenges to understand the concept of CSR, to comprehend the understanding of CSR by the public, and to identify the type of CSR activities practiced, and the type of support that the government can offer to motivate businesses to foster CSR. Meanwhile, Lu and Castka (2009) suggested that it is important for SMEs to be ready for CSR practices, because SMEs that are not prepared for CSR may be proscribed or will be struggling in the future. Overtime, Malaysia has demonstrated an increasing awareness of CSR, nevertheless, CSR related issues are sometime overlooked, for instance, news reported that 278 companies failed to contribute to the Employees Provident Fund for their employees (The Star, 2014a), manufacturing companies failed to comply with minimum wage obligations (The Star, 2014b), companies ignored health and safety guidance at their workplace (The Star, 2014c), companies employed illegal workers (The Star, 2014d), illegal waste dumping (Singh, 2014), and unauthorised earthworks (Hafiz, 2013).

Generally, Malaysian SMEs are lagging behind the overall CSR commitment, environment policy and workplace policy compared to other types of business organisation such as government-linked organisations, local Malaysian organisations and multinational corporations (Siwar & Harizan, 2008). Some of the CSR practices by the Malaysia companies are charity donations, sponsoring art and sport

Table 1. Malaysia SMEs performance

Macro Performance of SMEs	+2003 (%)	+2005 (%)	*2010 (%)	*2020 (%) (Targets)
SMEs' contribution to GDP	31.9	32.0	32.0	41.0
SMEs' contribution to employment (excl. Govt.)	55.8	56.4	59.0	62.0
SMEs' share of total exports	18.9	19.0	19.0	25.0

Source: +SME Annual Report 2006 and *National SME Development Council 2012

event, helping single mothers (Lu & Castka, 2009), employment of handicapped individual, responsive to customer complaints, employees' welfare (facilities and benefits), and ensuring product safety (Rashid & Ibrahim, 2002).

In this context, the importance of CSR is evidenced. Companies Commission of Malaysia (CCM) has set initiatives that will raise the visibility of CSR for a large number of businesses, especially the SMEs, through developing reporting requirements and capacity building (Unicef, 2012). Furthermore, the call for SMEs to be involved is CSR is being strengthened by the chief executive officer of SMEs Corporation Malaysia (SME Corp Malaysia), Datuk Hafsah Hashim that urged all SMEs should embrace the CSR initiatives. She stresses that the sustainability of a business dependents on a good business eco-system that includes a healthy, educated workforce, adequate resources and a capable government to enable businesses to compete effectively (Hashim, 2012). The importance of CSR has been further emphasised when the Malaysian government included the CSR element in New Economic Model and Vision 2020. Additionally, this was also proven with the continued commitment to reduce carbon emissions by forming new policies for green technology and climate change concern (Zulfakar, 2014).

THEORETICAL BACKGROUND

The notion of knowledge-based view (KBV) was developed from resources based view (RBV) in order to provide emphasis on knowledge resources rather than tangible resources (Gassmann & Keupp, 2007). Although some businesses have full resources and capabilities, it is still not enough to perform well because they need knowledge to manage, combine and convert those resources in order to have a significant contribution to firm performance (Cabrera-Suárez, De Saá-Pérez, & García-Almeida, 2001). KBV suggests that knowledge is the most important resources compared to other resources, and heterogeneous knowledge is the primary determinant of differences in organisational performance (Decarolis & Deeds, 1999). The KBV is very important to provide a sustainable competitive advantage, because it is characteristically difficult to emulate, hence making it easier for sustainable differentiation (McEvily & Chakravarthy, 2002). Besides, knowledge plays a significant role in the ability of the company to become entrepreneurs (Galunic & Eisenhardt, 1994) and improve performance (McGrath, Tsai, Venkataraman, & MacMillan, 1996).

From the knowledge based perspective, organisations may source for knowledge externally if it is not available internally due to higher cost or too specialised task (Feldman, 1994). Normally, SMEs will look for external advisors to address their weaknesses and constraints. Previous studies found that external accountants are the main advisors to the SMEs (Lewis, et al., 2007; Leung, Raar, & Tangey, 2008). Likewise, Cameron (1992) stated that SMEs are unable to hire a full-time accountant, thus it is prudent to obtain services from external accountants, who offer many kinds of services to fulfil the market needs. It is common to outsource certain finance and accounting services to external auditors as the audit firm has spill over knowledge in relate to the company operational and tax issues that enable them to develop and to implement strategies (Lassila, Omer, Shelley, & Smith, 2010).

In the context of this research, knowledge is very crucial for growth and survival of the SMEs because SMEs resources are relatively limited (Mejri & Umemoto, 2010). In relate to CSR practices, Vives (2006) highlighted that the lack of CSR activities by SMEs are mostly due to lack of knowledge of the owner. This is supported by past studies (Said, Zainuddin & Haron, 2009; Khan, Muttakin & Siddiqui, 2012), whereby knowledge in CSR (of the independent director) has a positive influence on the level of CSR practices. Independent director is considered as a bundle of resources because they are able to provide advices and guidelines to management in the areas where the company has limited knowledge (Gabrielsson & Huse, 2005).

KBV attempts to explain why SMEs involved in CSR practices. In the context of this paper, knowledge based service through NAS provided by external accountants is considered as the SME's resources, whereby these accountants transfer their knowledge to the SMEs to adopt CSR practices and activities. This unique capability (knowledge based service through NAS) disseminate the CSR knowledge to ensure the adoption of CSR practices among SMEs, which will be reflected through its business performance. Hence, this paper applies the KBV as the theoretical underpinning to explain the relationship between NAS and CSR.

PROPOSITION DEVELOPMENT

Accordingly, the SMEs will look for external advisor to overcome any shortcomings in the absence of in-house expertise. This mainly happens to the SMEs due to their limited resources, challenges and constraints faced (Blackburn & Jarvis, 2010; Devi & Samujh, 2010). External advisors are refer to solicitors, consultants, external accountants, chambers of commerce, bank, academia, and government agencies (Bennett & Robson, 1999; Berry, Sweeting, & Goto, 2006; Ong, Azmi, Isa, Jusoh, & Kamarulzaman, 2008). Meanwhile, Fransen and Merk (2007) asserted that *service co-ordination firms*, such as the accountancy firms, management consultancy firms, insurance companies, debt-rating agencies, and law firms are able to coordinate the behaviour of other firms and the broader industries. These firms act as a crucial part as the foundation for decreasing unpredictability, advocating parallel practices, acting as the gatekeeper, or coordinating and to facilitate the flow logic of global production chains.

Essentially, Skouloudis and Evangelinos (2014) highlighted that services provider is able to act as intermediates for knowledge transfer and organisational change (as agents of change). These literatures provide evidence that external advisors are able to influence the behaviour of clients (the SMEs in this context). Furthermore, International Federation of Accountants (IFAC) have highlighted that accountants can be the change agents for organisations by influencing them to integrate sustainability to the organisation's mission, objectives, strategies, management and operations, stakeholder communications and definitions of success (IFAC, 2011). This is in line with Tilt (2010), who highlighted that there is evidence the accountant is able to change the behaviour of organisations to be more sustainable by changing the organisational responsibilities and routines, use of accounting techniques and tools, and the types of accounts produce by the organisations to show their performance.

Among the external advisors, the accountant was chosen by the SMEs to be their first choice business or non-audit related issue advisers (Bennett & Robson, 1999; Berry, et al., 2006; Lewis, et al., 2007) due to the already built up relationship through auditing or financial services provided to them (Spence, Agyemang, & Rinaldi, 2012). According to Tilt (2010), there are three different roles that an accountant can play in relate to CSR activities, which is as the financial accountant, management accountant and the auditor. As a financial accountant, there is possibility that its main interest is in the social and environmental aspects of assets and liabilities and to report on them in a certain standard method. As for management accountant, its concern involves cost and benefit issues, while as the auditor to provide validation or affirmation of the social account produced.

To explain further, accountants play essential role in the organisation operations, they have variety roles involving CSR activities of the SMEs such as advisor, assurance provider and reporter of factual findings on CSR performance (NBA, 2012). The accountants involve in areas such as corporate CSR reporting, ethics, transparency, risk management, communication with stakeholders, legal compliance, and resource consumption (Albu, Albu, Gîrbină, & Sandu, 2011). Besides, they also play vital role in improving social justice and contributing to the social and environmental benefits (Tilt, 2010).

The association between accountants and CSR related activities can be illustrated in many ways, such as the environment management accounting, social environmental accounting, social responsibility accounting, carbon accounting, corporate social and environmental reporting (ACCA, 2005; Albu, et al., 2011). In fact, there are a wide range of services provided by an accountant, but not limited to preparation of sustainability and integrated reports. It involves advise on the benefits of reducing energy costs and pollution, from simple behavioural changes aimed at eliminating waste, to investment in new equipment and alternate sources of energy, to developing an environmental management system (IFAC, 2012; Voghel & Thompson, 2011). According to Spence, et al. (2012), accountants could be able to contribute to environmental sustainability by:

1. Planning for the financial implication of the environmental programs which are within the budgeting process;
2. Introducing environmental performance indicators to the accounting system (for example the total materials used, direct energy used, greenhouse gas emissions, total amount of waste segregated by type and destination, environmental impacts of products and/or services and total environmental expenditures according to the type);
3. Developing new accounting and information systems, for example full cost accounting and environmental balance sheet; and
4. Incorporating environmental performance into internal management reporting and annual reports

Moreover, the International Federation of Accountants (IFAC, 2011) have pointed out that accountants may proliferate the CSR practices of an organisation through the financial functions, as follow:

1. Integrated sustainability management involves managing risk and opportunity, managing and measuring performance and provide analysis and insight to support decision making.
2. Able to improve the standard of stakeholders' communications and also the sustainability information reporting and on how it links to an organization's strategy and operations need the same strictness as the process of financial reporting. The most important qualitative characteristics information remains the same which are materiality, comparability, relevance, completeness and accuracy. Materiality, relevance, comparability, accuracy, and completeness continue to be essential qualitative characteristics of information. Professional accountants understand the need for, and how to implement quality data and robust systems to capture, maintain, and report performance. They also have the project management skills needed to put such systems in place, applying appropriate processes and controls.
3. The finance function is suitably positioned to affect the behaviour and results through incorporating sustainability considerations into strategies and plans, capital expenditure decisions, business cases, and into performance management and costing systems.

The role of accountants in relate to CSR has been further strengthened. With their knowledge in the taxes and subsidies, they can encourage their clients to get involve in CSR activities (ICAEW, 2004). For example, there are several tax incentives given by the government to companies that are involved in CSR practices in Malaysia, such as child care centre facilities at working place[1], contribution for library facilities[2], provide a scholarship to students, provisions for disabled person in terms of contribution in kind[3] (eg: facilities in public places that benefit disabled persons) or gifts of money, expenditure incurred for public amenities and contribution to community or charity projects[4] pertaining to health, education, housing, ICT, preservation or conservation of the environment, infrastructure, enhancement of income of the poor (Unicef, 2012). Additionally, grants and soft loans are also available for companies that involve in CSR activities (refer to budget 2010 where RM 100 million is allocated to CSR fund and RM1.5 billion to promote green technology). Therefore, NAS in the form of advice on CSR related practices by the external accountant to the companies about the incentives given by the government will encourage more companies to be involve in CSR activities.

Apart from that, Fraser (2005) highlighted the ability of auditors to play essential role in assessing risk and control measures associated with CSR related goals for an organisation, and the chief audit executives need to ensure that CSR is in the board agenda of corporate governance. Furthermore, internal auditor needs to advise the board on the best practices, made sure that the CSR elements are reflected in the organisation core value and code of conduct and measure the CSR performance of the organisation with international standards (Fraser, 2005). Similarly, a survey conducted by the American Institute of Internal Auditors on more than 3000 internal auditors, found that 92% of the samples opined that internal audit can add value to CSR planning and reporting for the organisation (CAI, 2007). Besides, a research conducted by the IFAC found out that, the sustainability related services provided by accounting firm to their client had increased gradually, the services related to sustainability are advisory, accounting and assurance (IFAC, 2014). Another example that depicts the influence of NAS to the extent of CSR practices through the professional advice given by an external accountant is highlighted in a research conducted on S&P companies by Huseynov and Klamm (2012). They found out that tax management services (a type of NAS) provided by the auditor, which is measured in terms of fees, is associated with the extent of CSR practices.

Based on the above discussion, it can be concluded that NAS is able to increase the level of CSR practices of the SMEs. Hence the following proposition was proposed:

Proposition: Non-audit services positively influence and level of CSR practices of the SMEs.

Figure 1 depicts the proposed model and the relationship between the variables. In this research, the dependent variable proposed is the CSR practices among SMEs which was measured through six dimensions namely environment, community, employees, shareholders, customers and suppliers (adapted from Sweeney (2009) and; Amran and Nejati (2011)). Meanwhile, the independent variable in this model is the NAS, which was measured through a score. The score will be calculated by times the services purchased from an external accountant and the extent that the firm utilised an external accountant as advisor for the particular service (adapted from Suhairi (2004) and; Ong, et al. (2008)). Additionally, previous studies indicated that firm size and industry types have an impact on CSR practices (Kamyabi & Devi, 2011; Lepoutre & Heene, 2006; Nejati & Amran, 2012; Siwar & Harizan, 2008; Sweeney, 2009). Hence, firm size and industry types were included as the control variables in this research.

Figure 1. Proposed research model

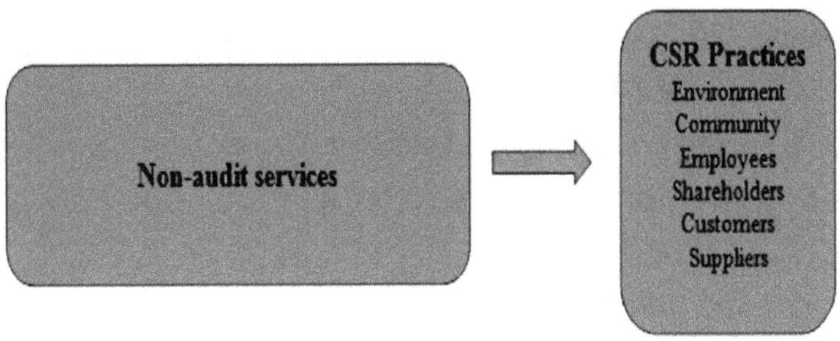

IMPLICATIONS AND FUTURE RESEARCH

This paper will benefit several parties. It will contribute to the academic world mainly for NAS and CSR researchers as it brings disseminating knowledge to the literature. As far as it could be ascertained, this research will be a great contribution as there are very limited research done previously which has examined the relationship between NAS and CSR in the context of SMEs. Additionally, this research will also contribute to the accountant profession, accounting firm, Malaysian Institute Accountant (MIA) and the government, through the understanding of whether the services provided by the accountant is able to promote CSR among their clients. For instance, if the empirical findings support the proposed proposition, it indicates the importance of NAS among the SMEs. Therefore, it helps the relevant parties to collaborate and plan related programmes with the accountants, which in turn increase CSR practices among SMEs.

Nevertheless, this paper is not yet empirically examined. This paper would propose that future researchers to investigate the proposed proposition empirically. The empirical finding would surely be an impactful contribution to the literature and increase the knowledge in SMEs and CSR.

CONCLUSION

This paper proposes the role of NAS, and highlights the relationship between NAS and CSR in the SMEs context, making possible the development of some NAS policies to promote CSR, which in turn enhance the survival and performance of SMEs.

It is important for the Malaysian government and relevant authorities to have CSR knowledge in the context of SMEs, as the SMEs makes up the largest portion of total entity companies that are available in the world, up to date, there are no publicly available data for CSR practices among SMEs, because there is no requirement for the SMEs to disclose their CSR activities yearly. Nevertheless, the importance of CSR has been long acknowledged (Amran et al., 2013), the CSR practices by SMEs are essential for Malaysia to achieve its Vision 2020 and the New Economics Model.

Due to the CSR practices research among SMEs remain rare, this paper contributes to a better understanding of the relationship between NAS and CSR in the Malaysian SMEs context. The proposition offered will be a useful insight for policy makers to have a better understanding about the extent of CSR practices by the SMEs and able to use this paper as a guide to draft the CSR plan for SMEs and some regulations or policy for accountant profession to include CSR elements in their advice to the SMEs.

REFERENCES

ACCA. (2005). Accounting Sustainability Briefing Paper 5. London, UK: Association of Chartered Certified Accountants (ACCA) & KPMG.

Aguinis, H., & Glavas, A. (2012). What We Know and Dont Know About Corporate Social Responsibility: A Review and Research Agenda. *Journal of Management*, *38*(4), 932–968. doi:10.1177/0149206311436079

Albu, N., Albu, C. N., Gîrbină, M. M., & Sandu, M. I. (2011). The Implications of Corporate Social Responsibility on the Accounting Profession: The Case of Romania. *Amfiteatru Economic*, *13*(29).

Amran, A., & Nejati, M. (2011). *Social Responsibility of Malaysian Small Businesses: Does It Influence Firm Image?* Paper presented at the IJAS Conference, Germany.

Amran, A., Zain, M. M., Sulaiman, M., Sarker, T., & Ooi, S. K. (2013). Empowering society for better corporate social responsibility (CSR): The case of Malaysia. *Kajian Malaysia*, *31*(1), 57–78.

Baden, D., Harwood, I. A., & Woodward, D. G. (2011). The effects of procurement policies on downstream corporate social responsibility activity: Content-analytic insights into the views and actions of SME owner-managers. *International Small Business Journal*, *29*(3), 259–277. doi:10.1177/0266242610375770

Bennett, R. J., & Robson, P. J. A. (1999). The use of external business advice by SMEs in Britain. *Entrepreneurship & Regional Development*, *11*(2), 155–180. doi:10.1080/089856299283245

Berry, A. J., Sweeting, R., & Goto, J. (2006). The effect of business advisers on the performance of SMEs. *Journal of Small Business and Enterprise Development*, *13*(1), 33–47. doi:10.1108/14626000610645298

Blackburn, R., & Jarvis, R. (2010). The role of small and medium practices in providing business support to small-and medium-sized enterprises. New York: International Federation of Accountants (IFAC).

CAI. (2007). Internal Auditors Can Contribute to Corporate Social Responsibility. *Accountancy Ireland*, *39*, 22.

Carney, M., Van Essen, M., Gedajlovic, E., & Heugens, P. (2010). *What do we know about private family firm performance? A meta-analytical review.* Unpublished manuscript.

Carroll, A. B. (1991). The pyramid of corporate social responsibility: Toward the moral management of organizational stakeholders. *Business Horizons*, *34*(4), 39–48. doi:10.1016/0007-6813(91)90005-G

Carroll, A. B. (1999). Corporate social responsibility evolution of a definitional construct. *Business & Society*, *38*(3), 268–295. doi:10.1177/000765039903800303

Carroll, A. B., & Shabana, K. M. (2010). The business case for corporate social responsibility: A review of concepts, research and practice. *International Journal of Management Reviews*, *12*(1), 85–105. doi:10.1111/j.1468-2370.2009.00275.x

Ciliberti, F., Pontrandolfo, P., & Scozzi, B. (2008). Investigating corporate social responsibility in supply chains: A SME perspective. *Journal of Cleaner Production*, *16*(15), 1579–1588. doi:10.1016/j.jclepro.2008.04.016

Crowther, D., & Aras, G. (2008). *Corporate social responsibility*. Bookboon.

Dahlsrud, A. (2008). How corporate social responsibility is defined: An analysis of 37 definitions. *Corporate Social Responsibility and Environmental Management*, *15*(1), 1–13. doi:10.1002/csr.132

Devi, S., & Samujh, H. (2010). *Accountants as Providers of Support and Advice to SMEs in Malaysia (No. 118)*. The Association of Chartered Certified Accountants.

Evans, N., & Sawyer, J. (2010). CSR and stakeholders of small businesses in regional South Australia. *Social Responsibility Journal*, *6*(3), 433–451. doi:10.1108/17471111011064799

Fassin, Y. (2008). SMEs and the fallacy of formalising CSR. *Business Ethics (Oxford, England)*, *17*(4), 364–378. doi:10.1111/j.1467-8608.2008.00540.x

Fransen, L., & Merk, J. (2007). *The CSR firm Emergence of service firms in the private regulation of Corporate Responsibility standards*. University of Amsterdam.

Fraser, B. W. (2005). Corporate Social Responsibility. *Internal Auditor*, *62*, 42–47.

Gabrielsson, J., & Huse, M. (2005). Directors in SME Boards: A Call for Theoretical Reflections. *Corporate Board: Role, Duties & Composition, 1*(1), 28-37.

Galbreath, J. (2010). How does corporate social responsibility benefit firms? Evidence from Australia. *European Business Review*, *22*(4), 411–431. doi:10.1108/09555341011056186

Geva, A. (2008). Three Models of Corporate Social Responsibility: Interrelationships between Theory, Research, and Practice. *Business and Society Review*, *113*(1), 1–41. doi:10.1111/j.1467-8594.2008.00311.x

Gill, G. S., & Cosserat, G. W. P. (1996). *Modern Auditing in Australia*. Wiley.

Hafiz, M. (2013, July 11). Company fined RM30,000 for illegal earthworks on Bukit Relau. *The Star Online*.

Hashim, H. (2012, October 29). SMEs, too, should embrace CSR. *New Straits Times*.

Hsu, J.-L., & Cheng, M.-C. (2011). What Prompts Small and Medium Enterprises to Engage in Corporate Social Responsibility? A Study from Taiwan. *Corporate Social Responsibility and Environmental Management*.

Huseynov, F., & Klamm, B. K. (2012). Tax avoidance, tax management and corporate social responsibility. *Journal of Corporate Finance*, *18*(4), 804–827. doi:10.1016/j.jcorpfin.2012.06.005

ICAEW. (2004). *Sustainability: The Role of Accountants*. The Institute of Chartered Accountants in England and Wales.

IFAC. (2011). Sustainability Framework 2.0: Professional Accountants as Integrators. New York: International Federation of Accountants (IFAC).

IFAC. (2012). The Role of Professional Accountants in the Sustainability of Small Businesses. Special Edition eNews.

IFAC. (2014). *Sustainability*. Retrieved 20 April 2014, from https://www.ifac.org/globalknowledgegateway/sustainability?overview&discussions

Israel, G. D. (1992). *Determining sample size: University of Florida Cooperative Extension Service, Institute of Food and Agriculture Sciences*. EDIS.

Jamali, D., & Tarazi, A. (2012). CSR: A Cost or an Opportunity for SMEs in the Middle East? CSR in the Middle East: Fresh Perspectives (pp. 72). Academic Press.

Jamali, D., Zanhour, M., & Keshishian, T. (2009). Peculiar Strengths and Relational Attributes of SMEs in the Context of CSR. *Journal of Business Ethics*, *87*(3), 355–377. doi:10.1007/s10551-008-9925-7

Jenkins, H. (2004). A Critique of Conventional CSR Theory: An SME Perspective. *Journal of General Management*, *29*, 37–57.

Jenkins, H. (2006). Small Business Champions for Corporate Social Responsibility. *Journal of Business Ethics*, *67*(3), 241–256. doi:10.1007/s10551-006-9182-6

Kamyabi, Y., & Devi, S. (2011). Use of Professional Accountants Advisory Services and its Impact on SME Performance in an Emerging Economy: A Resource-based View. *Journal of Management and Sustainability*, *1*(1), 43. doi:10.5539/jms.v1n1p43

Khan, A., Muttakin, M., & Siddiqui, J. (2012). Corporate Governance and Corporate Social Responsibility Disclosures: Evidence from an Emerging Economy. *Journal of Business Ethics*, 1–17.

Kotey, B. (2005). Are performance differences between family and non-family SMEs uniform across all firm sizes? *International Journal of Entrepreneurial Behaviour & Research*, *11*(6), 394–421. doi:10.1108/13552550510625168

Lassila, D. R., Omer, T. C., Shelley, M. K., & Smith, L. M. (2010). Do Complexity, Governance, and Auditor Independence Influence whether Firms Retain Their Auditors for Tax Services? *The Journal of the American Taxation Association*, *32*(1), 1–23. doi:10.2308/jata.2010.32.1.1

Lee, M. H., Mak, A. K., & Pang, A. (2012). Bridging the Gap: An Exploratory Study of Corporate Social Responsibility among SMEs in Singapore. *Journal of Public Relations Research*, *24*(4), 299–317. doi:10.1080/1062726X.2012.689898

Lepoutre, J., & Heene, A. (2006). Investigating the impact of firm size on small business social responsibility: A critical review. *Journal of Business Ethics*, *67*(3), 257–273. doi:10.1007/s10551-006-9183-5

Leung, P., Raar, J., & Tangey, G. (2008). *Accounting services and SMEs: An Australian Study*. ACCA Research Report No. 99.

Lewis, K., Massey, C., Ashby, M., Coetzer, A., & Harris, C. (2007). Business assistance for SMEs: New Zealand owner-managers make their assessment. *Journal of Small Business and Enterprise Development*, *14*(4), 551–566. doi:10.1108/14626000710832695

Liu, H., & Fong, M. (2010). The Corporate Social Responsibility Orientation of Chinese Small and Medium Enterprises. *Journal of Business Systems. Governance and Ethics*, *5*(3), 33.

Longo, M., Mura, M., & Bonoli, A. (2005). Corporate social responsibility and corporate performance: The case of Italian SMEs. *Corporate Governance*, *5*(4), 28–42. doi:10.1108/14720700510616578

Lu, J. Y., & Castka, P. (2009). Corporate social responsibility in Malaysia - experts views and perspectives. *Corporate Social Responsibility and Environmental Management*, *16*(3), 146–154. doi:10.1002/csr.184

Maria, S. (2011). CSR in SMEs: Strategies, practices, motivations and obstacles. *Social Responsibility Journal*, *7*(3), 490–508. doi:10.1108/17471111111154581

Morsing, M., & Perrini, F. (2009). CSR in SMEs: Do SMEs matter for the CSR agenda? *Business Ethics (Oxford, England)*, *18*(1), 1–6. doi:10.1111/j.1467-8608.2009.01544.x

Moyeen, A., & Courvisanos, J. (2012). Corporate social responsibility in regional small and medium-sized enterprises in Australia. *Australasian Journal of Regional Studies*, *18*(3), 364–391.

NBA. (2012). *Corporate Social Responsibility: CSR for SME accountants*. Nederlandse Beroepsorganisatie van Accountant.

Nejati, M., & Amran, A. (2009). Corporate social responsibility and SMEs: Exploratory study on motivations from a Malaysian perspective. *Business Strategy Series*, *10*(5), 259–265. doi:10.1108/17515630910989150

Nejati, M., & Amran, A. (2012). Does ownership type cause any difference in the perception of Malaysian SME owners/managers towards corporate social responsibility? *International Journal of Business Governance and Ethics*, *7*(1), 63–81. doi:10.1504/IJBGE.2012.046105

NSDC. (2012). *SME Masterplan 2012-2012: Catalysing Growth and Income*. National SME Development Council.

Ong, F. S., Azmi, A. A. C., Isa, C. R., Jusoh, R., & Kamarulzaman, Y. (2008). *A Report of Current Usage Patterns of Business and Professional Services Among SMEs in the Manufacturing and Distributive Trade Sectors*. MIA.

Parker, C., Redmond, J., & Simpson, M. (2009). Review of interventions to encourage SMEs to make environmental improvements. *Environment and Planning. C, Government & Policy*, *27*(2), 279–301. doi:10.1068/c0859b

Perrini, F. (2006). SMEs and CSR Theory: Evidence and Implications from an Italian Perspective. *Journal of Business Ethics*, *67*(3), 305–316. doi:10.1007/s10551-006-9186-2

Perrini, F., & Minoja, M. (2008). Strategizing corporate social responsibility: Evidence from an Italian medium-sized, family-owned company. *Business Ethics (Oxford, England)*, *17*(1), 47–63. doi:10.1111/j.1467-8608.2008.00519.x

Rashid, A. M. Z., & Ibrahim, S. (2002). Executive and management attitudes towards corporate social responsibility in Malaysia. *Corporate Governance*, *2*(4), 10–16. doi:10.1108/14720700210447641

Russo, A., & Perrini, F. (2010). Investigating Stakeholder Theory and Social Capital: CSR in Large Firms and SMEs. *Journal of Business Ethics*, *91*(2), 207–221. doi:10.1007/s10551-009-0079-z

Russo, A., & Tencati, A. (2009). Formal vs. informal CSR strategies: Evidence from Italian micro, small, medium-sized, and large firms. *Journal of Business Ethics*, *85*(S2), 339–353. doi:10.1007/s10551-008-9736-x

Said, R., Zainuddin, Y. H., & Haron, H. (2009). The relationship between corporate social responsibility disclosure and corporate governance characteristics in Malaysian public listed companies. *Social Responsibility Journal, 5*(2), 212-226.

Singh, S. (2014, July 11). Tampin company is first to be prosecuted under Solid Waste and Public Cleansing Act. *The Star Online.*

Siwar, C., & Harizan, S. H. M. (2008). *A Study on Corporate Social Responsibility Practices amongst Business Organisations in Malaysia.* Paper presented at the Annual American Business Research Conference, Dubai, UAE.

Skouloudis, A., & Evangelinos, K. (2014). Exogenously driven CSR: insights from the consultants' perspective. *Business Ethics: A European Review.*

SME Corp. (2013). *Guideline for New SME Definition.* SME Corp.

Spence, L. J. (2007). CSR and Small Business in a European Policy Context: The Five Cs of CSR and Small Business Research Agenda 2007. *Business and Society Review, 112*(4), 533–552. doi:10.1111/j.1467-8594.2007.00308.x

Spence, L. J., Agyemang, G., & Rinaldi, L. (2012). *Environmental aspects of sustainability: SMEs and the role of the accountant (No. 1859084796).* London: The Association of Chartered Certified Accountants.

Suhairi. (2004). *Personality, Accounting Knowledge, Accounting Information Usage and Performance: A Research on Entrepreneurship of Indonesia Medium Industries* (Unpublished PhD Dissertation). Universiti Sains Malaysia, Malaysia.

Sweeney, L. (2007). Corporate social responsibility in Ireland: Barriers and opportunities experienced by SMEs when undertaking CSR. *Corporate Governance, 7*(4), 516–523. doi:10.1108/14720700710820597

Sweeney, L. (2009). *A study of current practice of corporate social responsibility (CSR) and an examination of the relationship between CSR and financial performance using structural equation modelling (SEM)* (Doctoral Thesis). Institute of Technology, Dublin, Ireland.

The Star. (2014a, May 5). EPF: 278 defaulting company directors barred from leaving. *The Star Online.*

The Star. (2014b, June 3). Health product company fined over non-compliance of minimum wage regulations. *The Star Online.*

The Star. (2014c, October 1). Company linked to Penang Bridge ramp collapse fined RM40,000. *The Star Online.*

The Star. (2014d, December 3). Keeping the problem of illegal workers in check. *The Star Online.*

Tilt, C. A. (2010). Corporate Responsibility, Accounting and Accountants. In S. O. I dowu & W. L. Filho (Eds.), Professionals' Perspectives of Corporate Social Responsibility (pp. 11-32). Springer Berlin Heidelberg.

Unicef. (2012). *Corporate Social Responsibility Policies in Malaysia: Enhancing the Child Focus.* Kuala Lumpur, Malaysia: United Nations Children's Fund (UNICEF).

Vázquez-Carrasco, R., & López-Pérez, M. E. (2012). Small & medium-sized enterprises and Corporate Social Responsibility: A systematic review of the literature. *Quality & Quantity*, 1–14.

Vives, A. (2006). Social and Environmental Responsibility in Small and Medium Enterprises in Latin America. *Journal of Corporate Citizenship*, *2006*(21), 39–50. doi:10.9774/GLEAF.4700.2006.sp.00006

Voghel, S., & Thompson, P. (2011). The Role of SMPs in Greening Small Business. *Accountancy Plus*, 34-35.

Zulfakar, M. (2014, September 24,). Malaysia will continue to cut carbon emissions, Najib tells UN climate summit. *The Star*.

KEY TERMS AND DEFINITIONS

Corporate Social Responsibility: A concept that a business needs to be concerned with its impacts on the society, which calls for responsible business practices. A business needs to integrate environmental, social, and economic issues into their business decisions and activities to meet corporate social responsibility.

Knowledge-Based View: A theory that recognises knowledge as the most strategically significant resource of the organisation. It emphasises on knowledge resources rather than tangible resources.

Non-Audit Services: Services provided by external accountants to their audit clients besides financial auditing services. It is referring to any services that is beyond the related audit services or services other than the traditional Certified Public Accountant performs.

Small and Medium Enterprise: Enterprise which employs fewer than 200 full-time employees, or annual turnover not exceeding RM 50 million in the manufacturing sector; or enterprise which employs fewer than 75 full-time employees, or annual turnover not exceeding RM 20 million in the services or other sectors.

ENDNOTES

1 S 34 (6) (i) of the Income Tax Act, 1967

2 S 34 (6) (g) and S 44 (8) of the Income Tax Act, 1967

3 S 44 (9) of the Income Tax Act, 1967

4 S 34 (6) (h) of the Income Tax Act, 1967

Chapter 17
SMEs in Nigeria:
Exploring Coopetition

Sola Oni
Pan-Atlantic University, Nigeria

ABSTRACT

Research in the area of small and medium sized enterprises (SMEs) and coopetition has been ongoing for a considerable length of time. However, such studies have focused on SMEs in developed countries while there is very limited research in the same area with a focus on SMEs in Africa and developing countries. This research therefore aims to explore possible benefits and barriers that SMEs in Nigeria would experience in the adoption of coopetition. Considering the fact that it is a relatively new area of research, existing theories examining similar fields of study will be analysed with the aim of generating a theoretical framework through which factors affecting the phenomenon in the country may emerge.

INTRODUCTION

Small and medium-sized enterprises (SMEs) contribute enormously to the economy of developed and developing countries alike. According to the International trade Centre (ITC, 2015), globally, SMEs make up over 95% of all firms, account for approximately 50% of GDP and 60% - 70% of total employment, when both formal and informal SMEs are taken into account. This amounts to between 420 million and 510 million SMEs, 310 million of which are in emerging markets. In Europe, according to the European Commission (2015), they are the backbone of the economy. SMEs represent 99% of all businesses in the EU and they have created around 85% of new jobs in the past five years. They have also provided two-thirds of the total private sector in the EU and are considered key to ensuring economic growth, innovation, job creation, and social integration in the EU (European Commission, 2012). Whilst there is no doubt about the contribution of SMEs to the economy of different countries, they are very likely to lack support in terms of finances, government policy and infrastructure particularly where SMEs in developing countries are concerned.

In spite of the many benefits that they provide to the economy, there are many challenges facing SMES in developing countries. In Nigeria, such challenges include the lack of government funding,

DOI: 10.4018/978-1-5225-2165-5.ch017

inadequate infrastructure and unstable power supply. Financial constraints, management problems, lack of capital and the lack of support from financial institutions and government development agencies are issues that have also been cited as major hindrances to small business development in Nigeria (Okpara, 2011). Various studies have described Information and Communications technology (ICT) as an enabler that can aid growth and development (Hanna, 2003; Marker, McNamara &Wallace, 2002; Maier & Nair-Reichert, 2007). However, SMEs in the country are yet to take full advantage of these possibilities for various reasons. For example, a lack of power as well as the lack of skills have been identified as the two major barriers deterring the adoption of ICT amongst non-adopters in the region (Apulu, Latham & Moreton, 2011).

Additionally, SMEs in such countries unfortunately sometimes have the challenge of not being supported by government policy. For example, Okpara (2011) states that there is an inhibitive policy framework in Nigeria that discourages entrepreneurs from seeking funds to start up new or expand existing business. As a result, they have to find other means to ensure that they stay afloat. One of the ways they can achieve this is by engaging in coopetition. Coopetition, according to Levy, Loebbecke and Powell (2003) involves sharing knowledge that may be a key source of competitive advantage even though the knowledge gained by cooperation may also be used for competition. Small firms may be in a position to compete with larger firms in the area of coopetition, pooling resources to ensure that they sustain competitiveness and survive.

Recent research suggests that coopetition adds immense value to SMEs by reducing costs, improving access to research and development, and improving the innovativeness of SMEs. This research therefore aims to explore possible benefits and barriers that SMEs in Nigeria would experience in the adoption of coopetition. Considering the fact that it is a relatively recent area of research, existing theories covering similar fields of study will be examined with the aim of generating a theoretical framework through which factors affecting the phenomenon in the country may emerge.

This chapter begins by examining coopetition and considers what may make it a favourable alternative to current business practices of SMEs in Nigeria. The next section examines current literature and the context for this study. The following session analyses the issues, controversies and problems that may be experienced with coopetition. A framework that may help to resolve the issues is identified in the next session. The future research directions are then discussed in the next and finally, the conclusion of the study is presented.

LITERATURE REVIEW

SMEs and Coopetition

SME Definition

There are varying descriptions of what an SME is. The description of the term usually differs depending upon a combination of factors such as country, geographic region, level of development and business culture. Another reason why a general definition might be difficult is because SME definitions are sometimes linked to national support programmes and other regulations (ITC, 2015). In Europe, according to the European commission (2005), small and medium size enterprises (SMEs) are enterprises with fewer than 250 employees. Micro enterprises are enterprises with fewer than 10 employees while small enterprises have between 10 and 49 employees with an annual turnover and /or annual balance-sheet total not exceeding 10 million Euros. Medium enterprises have fewer than 250 employees with an annual turnover not exceeding 50 million Euros or an annual balance-sheet total not exceeding 43 million Euros.

However, in Nigeria, they are described as consisting of micro, small and medium scale industries. A Micro/Cottage Industry is an industry with a labour size of not more than 10 workers, or total cost of not more than N1.50 million, including working capital but excluding cost of land. A Small-Scale Industry is an industry with a labour size of 11-100 workers or a total cost of not more thanN50 million, including working capital but excluding cost of land. Finally, a Medium Scale Industry is defined as an industry with a labour size of between 101-300 workers or a total cost of over N50 million but not more than N200 million, including working capital but excluding cost of land (Central Bank of Nigeria, 2005). SMEs are essential to the Nigerian economy as well. They produce about 10% of total manufacturing output and 70% of industrial employment (Carpenter, 2005).

Challenges Facing SMEs in Developing Countries

Despite the fact that SMEs contribute immensely to the economic development of developing countries, they are fraught with several challenges that may prevent them from surviving. For example, according to St-Pierre, Foleu, Abdulnour, Nomo and Fouda (2015), the business environment and the lack of resources in the African ecosystem are primarily to be blamed for poor competitive capacity and business failure of SMEs. This implies that businesses are unlikely to thrive if the environment is not favourable. The authors further identify other factors that may impede the growth of SMEs in Cameroon including, corruption, financial constraints and the country's economic situation (St-Pierre et al, 2015). Similarly in South Africa, the lack of an enabling environment as well as limited access to market, finance, credit, skills and networks; poor customer relations, lack of appropriate technology, low production capacity, and the lack of a quality product (Ramukumba, 2014) are identified as factors that may have an adverse effect on the growth of SMEs. In Nigeria, there are several primary challenges identified as limiting SMEs growth, according to Mambula (2002). These include lack of funding, lack of contact with research institutes, poor infrastructure, difficulty in obtaining equipment, spare parts and raw materials, business opportunities and new product development methods. More recently, Obokoh (2008) similarly identified the following as factors impeding the growth of SMEs in Nigeria. Such factors include access to funding and inconsistency in the application of government SME development policies. Another growth inhibiting factor for SMEs is the lack of widespread ICT adoption. According to Akpulu, Latham and Moreton (2013), SMEs in Nigeria appear to have ignored the relevance of ICT in doing business and are as such, not in a position to reap the benefits.

SMEs in other countries within the region and beyond continue to face similar challenges such as rising research and development costs, high risk and uncertainty in technological development. SMEs may be unable to resolve these and those previously discussed challenges using their own limited resources and capabilities (Gnyawali & Park, 2009). In order to ensure that SMEs survive and even become more competitive, an alternative could be to establish partnerships with direct competitors who have complementary strengths and face similar challenges (Kossiva, Sarri & Georgopoulous, 2014). This phenomenon, which has been applied successfully by large firms, is known as coopetition.

Coopetition

Developed by Brandenburger and Nalebuff (1996), coopetition is described as part competition and part cooperation. This phenomenon is based on the fact that most companies can achieve more success together, than they would if they were working alone in the business environment. The authors went on to explain that coopetition allows for the real world business situation, where there can be multiple winners in the marketplace with an objective to maximize the return on investment regardless of how well or how poorly other companies perform. Challenges within the business and other environmental factors could encourage businesses to participate in coopetition. For instance, according to Walley (2007), changes in the business environment have led from a position where many firms simply competed against each other, to a situation where they had to cooperate, and now to a point where they have to both cooperate and compete to survive. In order for businesses to survive, they must be creating some sort of value. The foundation for coopetition is the assumption that there are two essential elements that make up companies' activities which include creating value and capturing value (Gnyawali & Park, 2009). Thus implying that the strategy would be beneficial not only for creating and adding value but for long term survival, it may be worth adopting a different approach.

Apart from helping to create value, there are other reasons why coopetition might be worth considering for businesses, such as ensuring customer satisfaction. Walley (2007) argued that having a combination of cooperation and competition can be an advantage to consumers because research and development activities can be pooled to provide new products that they would have been unable to on their own. Thereby serving both the needs of the business and customer adequately as a result of coopetition. This combination may also be used to generate more profits and possibly to change the nature of the business environment to favour a particular business. Being able to change the business environment within which a particular business operates ensures that one is able to shape the industry's future, which helps to create opportunities for future success (Brandenburger and Nalebuff, 1996). The authors went on to postulate that a strategic framework in necessary to actively change the game of business and that coopetition theory provides such a framework. There is also a possibility of gaining competitive advantage from coopetition. According to Kossyva, Galanis, Sarri and Georgopoulos (2014), it is a process through which organizations can seek complementary partners to promote their own resources whilst also creating and transferring knowledge and investigating further opportunities without necessarily overlooking their own interests.

Whilst it is doubtless that there are several advantages to be gained by firms choosing to participate in coopetition, the bulk of existing research covers large firms as opposed to SMEs (Morris, Koçak & Özer, 2007). There is the question of how valuable this sort of arrangement could possibly be for small businesses who already as previously discussed, have a lot of concerns that they have to deal with on a regular basis in the struggle to survive. However, Gnyawali & Park (2009) explain three critical issues that suggest the pertinence of SMEs cooperating with their competitors as opposed to making other types of alliances. Firstly, because competitors are more likely to already be in possession of resources and capabilities that are relevant since they operate within similar markets. Secondly, since large competitors present a strong threat to SMEs and they are constrained where resources are concerned, they would benefit from collaborating to combine resources putting them in a better position to compete. Lastly, SMEs who compete with each other but have similar products and technologies can work together to create a uniform voice in the marketplace (Gnyawali & Park, 2009). These and other reasons make coopetition an important strategy to consider for SMEs in developing countries. It is therefore expedient to examine precisely what sort of value SMEs stand to gain, if any, from coopetition.

SMEs and Coopetition

Although existing research covers more examples of larger firms adopting the coopetition strategy, there is some evidence that SMEs may benefit from it as well. Morris, Koçak and Özer (2007), argue that small firms should find cooperation with competitors relatively easy. They provide the following reasons to support this position. SMEs' fixed commitments are often limited and their operations are not as controlled by structure and formal policies, their image and market positioning are not well established in and their external networks may not be as well defined. This view is shared by Gnyawali and Park (2009), who postulate that SMEs are more likely to find coopetition strategy easier to pursue even though it is a complex strategy. They also argue that unlike large firms, SMEs are more able to experiment with new business models because they are less constrained by existing structure and formal procedures and policies.

SMEs are generally known as knowledge generators, but poor at knowledge exploitation (Levy, Loebbecke & Powell, 2003). They tend to exist as separate entities and information islands. By nature, SMEs in the same sector would view each other as competitors, thus implying that they would not readily share information. However, recent research suggests that there are several advantages that SMEs would benefit from, if they learned to view each other as coopetitors as well as competitors. For example, Gnyawali and Park (2009) argue that coopetition helps SMEs to develop their ability to effectively pursue technological innovations. They go on to explain that most SMEs have constraints on financial and technological resources and cannot address certain challenges using their own limited resources and would therefore have to reach out to their competitors who have the resources and are willing to collaborate to address such challenges. In addition to providing access to resources that would be otherwise unavailable, coopetition has also provided international opportunities for SMEs where such may have been unattainable. There is also the possibility of increasing competitive advantage by creating opportunities for export where coopetition is engaged by SMEs (Kock, Nisuls & Söderqvist, 2010).

Existing research covering SMEs application of coopetition explores several areas including the question of the size of the SMEs. However, according to Jankowska (2011), the size of the SMEs involved in the author's study indicates that size had no impact on the consequences of coopetiting. However, they found that companies employing less than 50 people expressed the most optimistic view of the results of coopetition for their international competitive position and internationalization, which could be explained by the fact that it is easier to develop a direct and even personal relationship based on trust when you have smaller business entities (Jankowska, 2011). Previous research has also explored various ways in which Coopetition has been applied by SMEs. It has been used as a strategy to gain market power, as a strategy in innovation processes, as a strategy in supply chain relations and as a strategy for global competition (Bouncken, Gast, Kraus & Bogers, 2013).

Whilst the benefits of coopetition among SMEs have been widely published, there could be some disadvantages as well. For instance, in a study of the effects of coopetition in knowledge-intensive SMEs engaging in clusters, Bouncken and Kraus (2013) found that coopetition negatively affects revolutionary innovation while influencing radical innovation positively. However, the majority of the SMEs interviewed pointed out the importance of competition for both revolutionary and radical innovation.

Finally, it is worth noting critical success factors that would ensure that SMEs make the most of coopetition strategy. Chin, Chan and Lam (2008), identified critical success factors which fall under three success factor categories: management commitment, relationship development, and communication management. With results indicating that management leadership and development of trust are the most important success factors.

Features and Benefits of Coopetition for SMEs

Coopetition research among SMEs has gained traction in recent years and covers a wide range of industries such as Tourism (Pease and Rowe, 2005); Information Technology (Bouncken & Kraus, 2013); Agriculture (Walley and Custance, 2010); Football (Robert, Marques & Le Roy, 2009); Aviation (Klimas, 2014)and Wine making (Dana, Granata, Lasch, & Carnaby, 2013) with each experiencing varying, though mostly positive results. Various aspects have been focused on such as the size of the firms, the nature of the firms, knowledge needs of the firms and their innovativeness as well. A key question is how can an SME be sure that is participating in coopetition? What are the key features of coopetition? Czakon, Mucha-Kus and Rogalski (2014) have identified simultaneous cooperation and competition and mutual benefits stemming from coopetition, as the key characteristics of the phenomenon of coopetition. Other features which they recognised from their analysis of previous research include complexity, dynamics, managerial challenges and industry reshaping as a trait of competition. Dagnino and Padula (2002) considered that there are four different types of coopetition that differ according to the number of firms involved and the number of activities of the values chain. These include simple dyadic coopetition, complex dyadic coopetition, coopetition in a simple network and coopetition in a complex network.

Also, according to Chin, Chan and Lam (2008) researchers have recognized in more than half of published work that coopetition strategy is a multidimensional and multifaceted concept that assumes a number of different forms requiring multiple levels of analysis. Examples of the possible forms coopetition can take include clusters, business networks, strategic alliances and short-term agreements (Jankowska, 2011). Extant coopetition literature analyses coopetition between firms. However, Walley (2007) argues that this view is limited and adopts the stance that in underpinning commercial activity, coopetition extends far beyond the interaction between firms. The author specifically considers coopetition between various strategic units within a single firm, employees of a firm, and even between a firm and its customers. Regardless of what form or structure coopetition takes, there are several benefits for SMEs as reported in current literature.

SMEs through coopetition, can look for complementary partners, as a way of promoting their own resources; transferring and creating knowledge; exploring entrepreneurial opportunities, without losing sight of their own interests (Kossyva, Galanis, Sarri, Georgopoulos, 2014). SMEs may also gain competitive advantage through knowledge sharing (Loebbecke, van Fenema & Levy, 1999). Kossyva, Sarri and Georgopoulos (2014) analysed various types of coopetition strategy as well as the implications of economic crisis on Small and Medium-sized Enterprises (SMEs) and suggested that coopetition might be an appropriate business strategy for overcoming the effect of the economic crisis. E-business success among SMEs has been identified as a feature that may increase a country's long term competitiveness and coopetition has been found to have a positive impact on e-business success, thus implying that coopetition would be beneficial on the long run for SMEs and for economic development (Eikebrokk & Olsen, 2005). Coopetition helps to increase technological diversity and combine complementary resources of rival firms in developing new technologies and products (Quintana-García and Benavides-Velasco, 2004).

SMEs can achieve multiple benefits from a coopetition network. Strengthening technological capability and capturing more business opportunities are two key benefits (Ruijun & Zhiman, 2011).

Adamik (2013) found that SMEs which cooperate with competitors more often have the resource base necessary for extension of their boundaries, they attain goals. SMEs attain by partnering with coopetitors real manifestations of extension of their business base, better satisfaction, increase business understanding, improve quality of and has a positive influence on the firm's innovativeness. According to Kossyva, Sarri and Georgopoulos (2014), the decision to adopt a coopetition strategy means that SMEs may be able to gain access to financial resources and valuable knowledge which will provide the opportunity for them to improve their core competencies, pursue large-scale innovation projects, create new products and services (in less time than it would take if they went on their own), joint innovation efforts and increase their product range. Coopetition can increase and change the competitive potential of a firm (Jankowska, 2011) and may help to manage risks effectively when SMEs use the strategy wisely (Gnyawali & Park, 2009). The table below provides a summary of these and more benefits that have been discussed in existing literature in the field of coopetition.

The benefits as listed in the table and paragraphs above are without a doubt attractive to SMEs who not only want to survive but thrive as well. However, there are several challenges to adopting this phenomenon, which cannot be ignored and are presented in the following sub-section.

Risks of Coopetition

Beneficial as coopetition may be to SMEs in both developed and developing countries alike, there are some possible downsides which have arisen over the years. For example, rivalry and conflict between firms can hamper each company's performance when they choose to collaborate (Morris, Koçak & Özer, 2007). Sharing knowledge may not be as straightforward as the SMEs think. Some may desire to share knowledge but most will not do so unless the risk of benefiting outweighs the risk of loss (Row and Pease, 2005). Considering the fact that knowledge sharing may likely occur where such a coopeti-

Table 1. Summary of the benefits of coopetition to SMEs

Benefits	Source
Competitive advantage	Loebbecke, van Fenema & Levy (1999)
Improved international competitiveness	Jankowska (2011)
Innovation	Quintana-García and Benavides-Velasco (2004)
E-Business success	Eikebrokk and Olsen (2005)
Increased understanding of the business area	Adamik (2013)
Access to financial resources	Kossyva, Sarri and Georgopoulos (2014)
Risk Management	Gnyawali and Park (2009).
New products and services	Kossyva, Sarri and Georgopoulos (2014)
Access to unique and essential resources	Spence, Coles and Harris (2001)
Access to intrinsic assets that can help to create value	Ahuja (2008)
Strengthening technological capability	(Ruijun & Zhiman, 2011).
Capturing more business opportunities	(Ruijun & Zhiman, 2011).

tive relationship or strategy exists, SMEs could therefore be at a risk of being victims of opportunists who want to steal the firm's secrets, particularly where innovation is involved (Bouncken, Gast, Kraus & Bogers, 2013).

Again, in a knowledge sharing context, some SMEs may be more involved in cooperation and therefore tend to share knowledge more openly while other SMEs emphasize the competitive aspect of the relationship and therefore may be more inclined to protect critical knowledge and also be more interested in obtaining competitive knowledge from and about the partners (Ilvonen & Vuori, 2013). Knowledge sharing would be particularly critical for SMEs who are involved in innovation. They could therefore be at risk if adopting a coopetition strategy. For example, the innovation performance of SMEs may be at risk as a result of intensified tension when there are strong contradictions and dualities inherent in such relationships (Gnyawali, Madhavan, He, & Bengtsson, 2012). Similarly, Bouncken and Kraus (2013) found that coopetition negatively affects revolutionary innovation while it positively influences radical innovation.

A blend of both competition and collaboration would imply that SMEs are likely to depend on each other. However, if some SMEs become more dependent on others, then there is the chance that their vulnerability may increase (Zineldin, 2004). They also stand to lose autonomy over decisions or circumstances where they had complete control if they choose to adopt coopetition as a strategy as this may cause firms to experience a loss of control over activities or resources. This would be the case particularly when partners become less committed to the cooperative side of the relationship or focus only on their own benefits (Morris, Koçak, & Özer, 2007). Finally, a lack of experience in working with new partners can make considerable demands on management's time, efforts and energy, which may in turn lead to an abandonment of the firm's core business objectives (Zineldine, 2004).

Combining both competition and cooperation to form a new strategy creates quite a complex type of inter-organisational relationship which sometimes have resulted in participants calling for an end to the relationship. There are many reasons why coopetitive relationships have ended among organizations. Some of which may include one party not getting enough of a return, leakage of confidential information, different objectives and intentions, general distrust, and the tendency for the competitive aspect of the relationship to become prioritized over the cooperative aspect (Walley, 2007).

Both large firms and SMEs have clearly benefited from coopetition but there remains a need to understand how to effectively manage this sort of relationship such that participating SMEs benefit from its advantages.

COOPETITION AMONG SMEs IN NIGERIA

This research handbook's theme suggests that SMEs need to consistently renew themselves in order to sustain competitiveness by revisiting their strategies and exploring innovative ideas. Coopetition among SMEs in developing countries, is one way in which they can both revisit strategy and explore innovative ideas.

Challenges and difficulties that Nigerian SMEs are faced with include lack of access to funding, lack of government funding, inadequate infrastructure, unstable power supply, financial constraints, management problems, lack of capital and the lack of support from government development agencies. These challenges also include a lack of contact with research institutes, difficulty in obtaining equipment, spare parts and raw materials, limited business opportunities and new product development methods, inconsistency in the application of government SME development policies and limited ICT adoption. Further challenges include policy incentives being tilted in favour of large scale industries, poor access to information and to markets for SME products and services, poor access to modern technology, overdependence on imported raw materials and industrial inputs, lack of patronage of SMEs' products by government departments and agencies. Additionally, low literacy levels, training and technological knowledge on the part of SME operators, poor or non-existence of preservation and storage facilities, poor implementation or non-existence of either strategic plans or business plans, lack of strategic focus including no succession plans, poor quality of products, lack of integrity, poor coordination of government policies as well as frequent changes in the policies; are also problems that Nigerian SMEs have to deal with (Mambula, 2002; Onugu, 2005; Obokoh, 2008; Okpara, 2011; Akpulu, Latham & Moreton, 2013).

To address some of these challenges and ensure that they thrive, SMEs may have to develop coopetition as a strategy, such that each SME participating in such a relationship is able to benefit mutually in a way that they are able to surmount the aforementioned difficulties. Walley (2007) argued that in many instances it is coopetition rather than competition that represents the most efficient form of inter-firm relationship. Engaging in coopetition with competitors may provide access to funding, infrastructure, equipment, new business opportunities, better access to raw materials, technology, innovative products and innovative production methods. The strategy seems to be a resolution to a lot of the challenges faced by SMEs as previously discussed. Coopetition has its strong points but there are also risks that may be involved in such a relationship. Beneficial as it may be, the question remains, what types of SMEs can benefit from this sort of arrangement and how do they draw value from such a relationship? Existing research covers SMEs in the following industries Tourism, Information Technology, Agriculture, Football and Wine making. The size of the SMEs and its effect on coopetitive relationships have also been analysed. However, current literature within the domain has focussed on SMEs in Europe with little focus on SMEs in developing areas in general and Africa in particular. Considering the fact that their challenges and opportunities may be different to those in more developed regions, this section analyses the issues, controversies and problems that may arise from exploring this phenomenon.

Influencing Factors

According to Cygler and Dębkowska (2015) coopetition belongs to the most complex types of inter- organisational relations because there are seemingly contradictory streams of relations and the attributes required from the parties involved may also be complex. They argue that not all candidates for coopetition are well suited to that kind of relationship. Similarly, Park, Srivastava and Gnyawali (2014) argued that since the basis of coopetition is the intensity of competition and the intensity of cooperation, it is expedient to examine the effects of each of them before delving into the effects of the simultaneous pursuit of both. Where inter-firm relationships between SMEs are coopetitive as opposed to being competitive, strategy for resources, capabilities and competencies will be different with the tendency to base strategy on resources, capabilities and competencies which are controlled as opposed to owned (Walley, 2007). Therefore, before delving into these kinds of relationships, SMEs must be able to address several questions. What is to be shared? Are they sharing costs, resources or knowledge?

Knowledge sharing among SMEs could carry a high risk and therefore any participating SME must understand what the value of knowledge is to the business (Ilvonen & Vuori, 2013). Risks of opportunism increase when SMEs share knowledge (Bouncken, Gast, Kraus & Bogers, 2013). As a result, any participating SME would have to develop a strategy that can help to address their knowledge sharing activities. This can be done both by recognizing better the knowledge that brings more benefits when it is shared, and by recognizing the knowledge that brings most benefits when it is kept inside the company (Ilvonen & Vuori, 2013). Whilst many SMEs wish to share knowledge this will occur only where the benefits from entering this sort of partnership exceed the potential losses. This is not the case where synergy and leverage are low (Row & Pease, 2005). Synergy refers to the additional value that cooperation and the exchange of information and knowledge generates; and leverage refers to the additional value the knowledge receiver experiences as a result from the information and knowledge exchange brought about by coopetition (Levy, Loebbecke & Powell, 2003).

Levy, Loebbecke and Powell (2003) identified three important factors that facilitate the sharing of knowledge fundamental to coopetition. These include:

- **Synergy:** The additional value that cooperation and the exchange of information and knowledge generates;
- **Leverage:** The additional value the knowledge receiver experiences as a result from the information and knowledge exchange brought about by coopetition; and
- **Negative Reverse Impact (NRI):** The deleterious effect the receiver's use of knowledge exchanged has on the sender, since the 'partners' are also competitors.

According to Loebbecke, van Fenema and Levy (1999), SMEs are poor at reaping synergies. They are poor at leverage, have limited resources and their main focus is survival. Among others, tension is another factor that may have an influence on the phenomenon among SMEs in Nigeria especially if innovation is a core part of their operations. Again, as far as innovation and coopetition is concerned, on the one hand, Bouncken and Kraus (2013) argue that empirical studies stress the positive relationship between coopetition and innovativeness but on the other hand, Tomlinson and Fai (2013) argue that coopetition has no significant impact on innovation Tensions resulting from simultaneous knowledge sharing and knowledge separation are special issues which have to be dealt with in terms of coopetitive innovation (Bouncken, Gast, Kraus & Bogers, 2015). The authors found that there are three levels of coopetitive tensions: inter-organizational level, intra-organizational level, and inter-individual level.

Kossyva, Sarri and Georgopoulos, (2014) suggested that SMEs have to build a coopetitive portfolio" consisting of different kinds of coopetitive partners; other SMEs, large enterprises as well as taking part in business networks. Developing a "coopetitive portfolio", will allow them to manage each collaborative agreement separately and try to obtain the advantages of each partnership. According to Fernandez, Le Roy and Gnyawali (2013), effective management of coopetition is not about having to choose between the principles of separation and integration. However, it is about being able to effectively combine the two principles. The strategic challenge therefore is not about making choices between integration and separation but is about how to go about doing both at the same time. As previously mentioned, coopetitive relationships are not always successful, therefore it is expedient to ensure that critical success factors are identified to ensure that participating SMEs benefit maximally with minimal risks.

This section has discussed the factors, issues and challenges that may be involved in the adoption of a coopetition strategy by SMEs in Nigeria. In the next session, this study draws from previously examined literature to develop a framework to further understand factors that are likely to be of import to SMEs who may benefit from coopetition in Nigeria and other developing countries.

A Framework for Coopetition Between Nigerian SMEs

Existing literature in the field of coopetition covers several industries which could either be large or small/medium businesses. Considering the inherent particularities that make SMEs different to large companies, it is worth considering a framework specific to SMEs to study the phenomenon. Also, there seems to be a gap in literature examining the phenomenon among SMEs in developing countries. Some level of cooperation does exist in this region, however, there is scant literature covering the research area. Nevertheless, SMEs in developed areas share several features with those in developing areas. It would therefore not be out of place to apply some of the factors identified from existing literature covering SMEs in more developed areas. Therefore, in addition to these factors, particular features of SMEs in a developing region are included in the proposed framework to provide a comprehensive view of what might be experienced in the field.

As previously discussed, researchers have recognized in more than half of published work that "coopetition strategy is a multidimensional and multifaceted concept that assumes a number of different forms and requires multiple levels of analysis" (Chin, Chan and Lam, 2008). In recognition of this fact, it is important to explain the context of the proposed framework. The framework considers the sort of relationships that SMEs currently participate in, their characteristics and how they may choose to coopete with other SMEs.

Current literature discusses some key features of coopetition which will also help to shape the proposed framework. According to Kossyva, Sarri and Georgopoulous (2014), coopetitive relationships consist of two dimensions; value creation and value appropriation. This will help to understand what sort of value the SMEs would derive and how it could help to improve their businesses. There is also the possibility of gaining competitive advantage. However, the mere adoption of a coopetition strategy is unlikely to provide competitive advantage. Instead, competitive advantage comes from an efficient management of the paradox and tensions that may be involved. (Gnyawali, He & Madhavan, 2008), pursuing integration and separation whilst comprehending the balance between the two is the key to realizing gains from competition (Bouncken, Gast, Kraus & Bogers, 2015).

According to Morris, Koçak and Özer (2007), coopetition has three key dimensions: mutual benefit, trust, and commitment. Similarly, Ruijun and Zhiman (2011) argued that a trusted relationship is the most important factor, compared with management commitment and communication management. Furthermore, holding high quality products is an important criterion for maintaining stability in the coopetition relationship. However, Zineldine (2004) argued that there are seven preconditions to developing a mutually beneficial business relationship. They are listed below:

- Organizations are willing to be engaged in an interactive exchange relationship.
- Each party possesses resources that the other party wants.
- Each party is willing to give up its some resource to receive in return the resource belonging to the other party.
- Each party is free to accept or reject terms and conditions of exchange that will leave them better off (or at least not worse off) than before the exchange.
- The parties are able to communicate and interact with each other.
- The parties recognize the ethical values and norms, interdependences, commitment and sustainable long-term relationship.
- The parties can strike a positive balance between the pros and cons of the relationship.

The Value Net, as developed by Brandenburger and Nalebuff (1996) constitutes a network of coopetitive relationships within which organizations take on multiple roles and seek complementary partners with the aim of creating value. The framework includes five players in a "business game". This players include the company in question, suppliers, customers, substitutors or competitors and complementors of that company.

The framework proposed in this study incorporates the value net as developed by Brandenburger and Nalebuff (1996). It then extends it by replacing firms with SMEs since, as discussed earlier, they are quite different to larger companies. This research argues that the characteristics which describe the particularities of SMEs depending upon the region within which they operate matter and is therefore included in the framework. The framework also includes the key dimensions and factors that have been found to be important for creating and sustaining coopetitive relationships.

SOLUTIONS AND RECOMMENDATIONS

As previously discussed, Nigerian SMEs are faced with several challenges and difficulties, some of which include; lack of access to funding, inadequate infrastructure, unstable power supply, financial constraints, management problems, lack of capital and the lack of support from government development agencies, lack of contact with research institutes and so on. To mitigate some of these challenges, coopetition has been suggested as a possible strategy.

The challenges that may be involved in the adoption of coopetition as a strategy for competitiveness of SMEs have also been discussed in the preceding sections. However, the opportunities for embarking on such a strategy are also numerous and make it a worthwhile pursuit, particularly when certain condi-

Figure 1. A framework for examining coopetition among SMEs in Nigeria

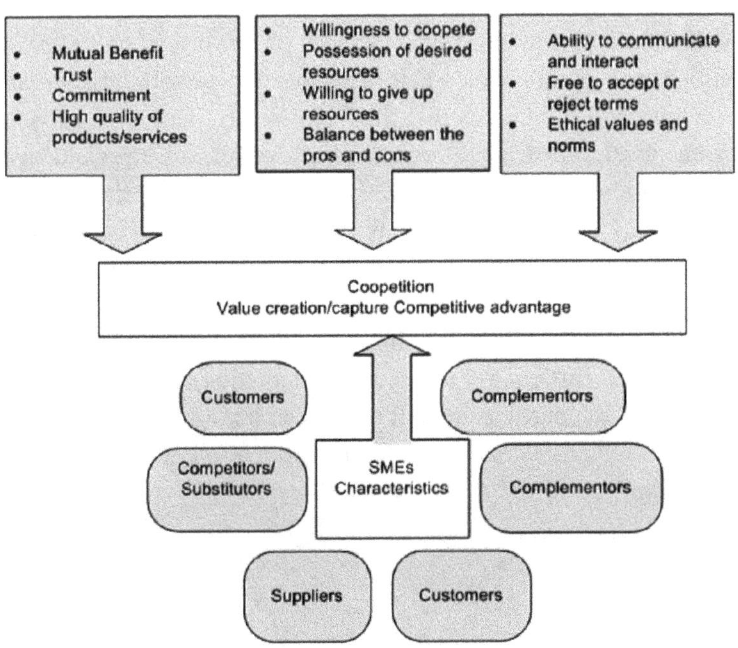

tions are met. A major question that one would have to ask is, how is value created and captured within the coopetitive inter-firm relationship? If this question is difficult to answer, then coopetition may not be a clear path for that SME. While coopetition may combine the best of both worlds of cooperation and competition, there is still an inherent paradox, given the possible tension between value creation and capture (Bouncken, Gast, Kraus & Bogers, 2015).

Some of the problems already identified from existing literature, which may stand in the way of gaining maximum benefit from coopetition include a lack of mutual trust among SMEs' business partners and a lack of integrity, which erodes confidence and trust (Onugu, 2005). If these concerns are managed, then it would be possible for SMEs to take the bold step of participating in a coopetitive relationship. They would also need to know how value is to be captured and what steps would be necessary to gain competitive advantage from coopetition. The framework that has been presented in the previous section provides a way to have a better understanding of how this process could be attempted and also lead to SMEs gaining competitive advantage and also helping to overcome the issues that prevent their growth.

This would be a relatively new territory for SMEs in Nigeria, for whom there is no clear roadmap for exploring a coopetitive strategy. Nevertheless, the proposed framework that has been developed in this research aims to fill this gap by providing a guide for SMEs willing to participate in what could be a game changer.

FUTURE RESEARCH DIRECTIONS

This chapter sought to examine the phenomenon of coopetition among SMEs in Nigeria with the aim of improving their processes and allowing them to be in a position to possibly compete against larger firms. Based on factors that were identified in existing literature, a model has been developed which could help to analyse these issues in depth. The next phase of the research would be to apply this model to SMEs in Nigeria with an ethnographic research methodology to evaluate the effectiveness of the model and the business strategy. The business strategy will be critically analysed with a view to determine if it is not only beneficial to SMEs but will provide greater chances of survival. It will also help to inform on the possibility of coopetition strategy allowing small firms to compete with large organisations.

Considering the culture and limitations that SMEs in Nigeria face, it is expected that the strategy would be met with some level of distrust to begin with. However, if some field/case studies are undertaken, this might generate more confidence and lead further SMEs to try the phenomenon and verify its appropriateness for them and whether it aligns with their business objectives.

To this end, future research directions for this study aims to carry out qualitative studies. Considering the fact that coopetition is a new phenomenon in the region considered in this study, this may also be used to follow the coopetition process. In line with Bengtsson, Eriksson and Wincent (2010), an ethnographic study will be particularly useful in this situation and it could help to unearth deeper meaning as not only do research participants tell the researcher about their experience, the researcher gets to see what the SMEs actually do and what their experiences are when they choose to participate in a coopetitive relationship.

CONCLUSION

Small and medium-sized enterprises (SMEs) contribute enormously to the economies of developed and developing countries alike and are the backbone of the economy. In spite of these, they lack support in a lot of areas which tends to result in SMEs failing to grow and sometimes failing to survive.

Research in the area of SMEs and coopetition has been ongoing for a considerable length of time and has covered both large companies and SMEs alike. It has also examined coopetition by SMEs in various industries. However, such studies have focused on SMEs in developed countries while there is very limited research in the same area with a focus on SMEs in Nigeria and other developing regions. This research therefore set out to explore possible benefits and barriers that SMEs in the country would experience, should they choose to adopt coopetition as a business strategy.

Challenges faced by SMEs in developing areas were also discussed and coopetition was suggested as a possible solution to the challenges that prevent SMEs from surviving and thriving. A framework was proposed to provide both a lens and a guide to ensure that the phenomenon may be studied in-depth and guide for any SMEs willing to participate in the process.

This study set out to examine the factors involved in coopetition and to examine benefits and risks which may make it a worthwhile venture for SMEs. It is hoped that the results from this research will inform both policy and practice. SMEs contribute a vast amount and it is time for governments in developing areas to take notice and begin to generate and effectively apply policies that will stimulate SMEs' growth and in turn stimulate their respective economies.

REFERENCES

Adamik, A. N. N. A. (2013). A partnering approach to extending the business base through cooperation with competitors (coopetition)–Is it an option for SMEs? *Recent Advances in Management, Marketing and Finances, Business and Economic Series*, *4*, 57–62.

Ahuja, G. (2008). Collaboration networks, structural holes, and innovation: A longitudinal study. *Administrative Science Quarterly*, *45*(3), 425–455. doi:10.2307/2667105

Apulu, I., Latham, A., & Moreton, R. (2011). Factors affecting the effective utilisation and adoption of sophisticated ICT solutions: Case studies of SMEs in Lagos, Nigeria. *Journal of Systems and Information Technology*, *13*(2), 125–143. doi:10.1108/13287261111135972

Apulu, I., Latham, A., & Moreton, R. (2013). Issues of ICT adoption amongst SMEs in Nigeria. *International Journal of Management Practice*, *6*(1), 58–76. doi:10.1504/IJMP.2013.052317

Bengtsson, M., Eriksson, J., & Wincent, J. (2010). Coopetition: new ideas for a new paradigm. *Coopetition: Winning strategies for the 21st century*, 19-39.

Bouncken, R. B., Gast, J., Kraus, S., & Bogers, M. (2015). Coopetition: A systematic review, synthesis, and future research directions. *Review of Managerial Science*, *9*(3), 577–601. doi:10.1007/s11846-015-0168-6

Bouncken, R. B., & Kraus, S. (2013). Innovation in knowledge-intensive industries: The double edged sword of coopetition. *Journal of Business Research*, *66*(10), 2060–2070. doi:10.1016/j.jbusres.2013.02.032

Brandenburger, A. M., & Nalebuff, B. J. (1996). *Co-opetition*. New York: Doubleday.

Chin, K. S., Chan, B. L., & Lam, P. K. (2008). Identifying and prioritizing critical success factors for coopetition strategy. *Industrial Management & Data Systems*, *108*(4), 437–454. doi:10.1108/02635570810868326

Cygler, J., & Dębkowska, K. (2015). Coopetition Effect Determinants: Competitors size, geographical scope, market and technological positions. *Organizacija*, *48*(4), 219–231. doi:10.1515/orga-2015-0019

Czakon, W., Mucha-Kus, K., & Rogalski, M. (2014). Coopetition research landscape-a systematic literature review 1997-2010. *Journal of Economics & Management*, *17*, 121.

Dagnino, G. B., & Padula, G. (2002). *Coopetition strategy: a new kind of interfirm dynamics for value creation*. Paper Presented at 2ème Conference EURAM, Stockholm, Sweden.

Dana, L. P., Granata, J., Lasch, F., & Carnaby, A. (2013). The evolution of co-opetition in the Waipara wine cluster of New Zealand. *Wine Economics and Policy*, *2*(1), 42–49. doi:10.1016/j.wep.2013.05.001

Eikebrokk, T. R., & Olsen, D. H. (2005, January). Co-opetition and e-business success in SMEs: An empirical investigation of European SMEs. In *Proceedings of 38th Annual Hawaii International Conference on System Sciences*. IEEE.

European Commission. (2005). *The new SME definition: User guide and model declaration*. Brussels: European Commission.

Fernandez, A. S., Le Roy, F., & Gnyawali, D. R. (2014). Sources and management of tension in co-opetition case evidence from telecommunications satellites manufacturing in Europe. *Industrial Marketing Management*, *43*(2), 222–235. doi:10.1016/j.indmarman.2013.11.004

Gnyawali, D. R., He, J., & Madhavan, R. (2008). Co-opetition: Promises and Challenges. In C. Wankel (Ed.), 21st Century Management (pp. 386–398). Thousand Oaks, CA: Sage.

Gnyawali, D. R., Madhavan, R. M., He, J., & Bengtsson, M. (2012). *Contradictions, dualities and tensions in cooperation and competition: A capability based framework.Annual Meeting of the Academy of Management*, Boston, MA

Gnyawali, D. R., & Park, B. J. R. (2009). Co-opetition and technological innovation in small and medium-sized enterprises: A multilevel conceptual model. *Journal of Small Business Management*, *47*(3), 308–330. doi:10.1111/j.1540-627X.2009.00273.x

Ilvonen, I., & Vuori, V. (2013). Risks and benefits of knowledge sharing in co-opetitive knowledge networks. *International Journal of Networking and Virtual Organisations*, *13*(3), 209–223. doi:10.1504/IJNVO.2013.063049

Klimas, P. (2014). Multifaceted nature of coopetition inside an aviation supply chain-the case of the aviation valley. *Journal of Economics & Management*, *17*, 96–119.

Kock, S., Nisuls, J., & Söderqvist, A. (2010). Co-opetition: A source of international opportunities in Finnish SMEs. *Competitiveness Review: An International Business Journal*, *20*(2), 111–125. doi:10.1108/10595421011029839

Kossyva, D., Galanis, K., Sarri, K., & Georgopoulos, N. (2014). Adopting an information security management system in a co-opetition strategy context. *International Journal of Applied Systemic Studies, 5*(3), 215–228. doi:10.1504/IJASS.2014.064065

Kossyva, D., Sarri, K., & Georgopoulos, N. (2014). Co-opetition: A business strategy for SMEs in times of economic crisis. *South-Eastern Europe Journal of Economics, 12*(1), 89–106.

Levy, M., Loebbecke, C., & Powell, P. (2003). SMEs, co-opetition and knowledge sharing: The role of information systems1. *European Journal of Information Systems, 12*(1), 3–17. doi:10.1057/palgrave.ejis.3000439

Loebbecke, C., van Fenema, P. C., & Levy, M. (1999). SMEs, co-opetition and knowledge Transfer. *Proceedings of 7th European Conference on Information Systems.*

Mambula, C. (2002). Perceptions of SME growth constraints in Nigeria. *Journal of Small Business Management, 40*(1), 58–65. doi:10.1111/1540-627X.00039

Morris, M. H., Koçak, A., & Özer, A. (2007). Coopetition as a small business strategy: Implications for performance. *Journal of Small Business Strategy, 18*(1), 35.

Obokoh, L. O. (2008). Small and medium sized enterprises development under trade liberalisation: A survey of Nigerian experience. *International Journal of Business and Management, 3*(12), 92–101.

Okpara, J. O. (2011). Factors constraining the growth and survival of SMEs in Nigeria: Implications for poverty alleviation. *Management Research Review, 34*(2), 156–171. doi:10.1108/01409171111102786

Onugu, B. A. N. (2005). *Small and medium enterprises (SMEs) in Nigeria: Problems and prospects* (Unpublished Dissertation). St. Clements University, Nigeria.

Park, B. J. R., Srivastava, M. K., & Gnyawali, D. R. (2014). Walking the tight rope of coopetition: Impact of competition and cooperation intensities and balance on firm innovation performance. *Industrial Marketing Management, 43*(2), 210–221. doi:10.1016/j.indmarman.2013.11.003

Pease, W., & Rowe, M. (2005). Use of information technology to facilitate collaboration and co-opetition between tourist operators in tourist destinations. Proceedings of Tourism Enterprise Strategies: Thriving-and Surviving-in an Online Era, 33-47.

Quintana-García, C., & Benavides-Velasco, C. A. (2004). Cooperation, competition, and innovative capability: A panel data of European dedicated biotechnology firms. *Technovation, 24*(12), 927–938. doi:10.1016/S0166-4972(03)00060-9

Ramukumba, T. (2014). Overcoming SMEs challenges through critical success factors: A case of SMEs in the Western Cape Province, South Africa. *Economic and Business Review, 16*(1), 19–38.

Robert, F., Marques, P., & Le Roy, F. (2009). Coopetition between SMEs: An empirical study of French professional football. *International Journal of Entrepreneurship and Small Business, 8*(1), 23–43. doi:10.1504/IJESB.2009.024103

Ruijun, C., & Zhiman, L. (2011). *Coopetition strategy management in SMEs: A case study of Nyhammers and Bäckströms Company* (Unpublished Masters dissertation). University of Gävle, Sweden.

Spence, L., Coles, A., & Harris, L. (2001). The forgotten stakeholder? Ethics and social responsibility in relation to competitors. *Business and Society Review*, *106*(4), 331–352. doi:10.1111/0045-3609.00119

St-Pierre, J., Foleu, L., Abdulnour, G., Nomo, S., & Fouda, M. (2015). *SME development challenges in Cameroon: An entrepreneurial ecosystem perspective.* Academic Press.

Tomlinson, P. R., & Fai, F. M. (2013). The nature of SME co-operation and innovation: A multi-scalar and multi-dimensional analysis. *International Journal of Production Economics*, *141*(1), 316–326. doi:10.1016/j.ijpe.2012.08.012

Walley, K. (2007). Coopetition: An introduction to the subject and an agenda for research. *International Studies of Management & Organization*, *37*(2), 11–31. doi:10.2753/IMO0020-8825370201

Walley, K., & Custance, P. (2010). Coopetition: Insights from the agri-food supply chain. *Journal on Chain and Network Science*, *10*(3), 185–192. doi:10.3920/JCNS2010.x187

Zineldin, M. (2004). Co-opetition: The organization of the future. *Marketing Intelligence & Planning*, *22*(6/7), 780–789. doi:10.1108/02634500410568600

KEY TERMS AND DEFINITIONS

Competition: The activity or condition of striving to gain or win something by defeating or establishing superiority over others.

Cooperation: The action or process of working together to the same end.

Coopetition: Collaboration between business competitors, in the hope of mutually beneficial results.

Developing Country: A country with little industrial and economic activity and where people generally have low incomes.

SME: Small and medium-sized enterprises (SMEs) are non-subsidiary, independent firms which employ fewer than a given number of employees. This number varies across countries. The most frequent upper limit designating an SME is 250 employees, as in the European Union.

Chapter 18
Social Media Strategies for Small and Medium Scale Enterprise in the Klang Valley Region of Malaysia

Donovan Chan
University of Malaya, Malaysia

Sameer Kumar
University of Malaya, Malaysia

ABSTRACT

Despite the current widespread adoption and use of social media as a marketing tool, very little empirical research focusing on local small and medium-sized enterprises (SMEs) is available. This study examines the usage of social media by small and medium-sized enterprises (SMEs) in Malaysia. The study assesses the impacts of age, educational attainment, and industry characteristics to the utilization, perceived benefits and barriers of SMEs. Results of the study indicate that social media is used by most SMEs for customer acquisition and its benefits are developing new business opportunities, reduced cost of advertising, 24 hours accessibility and decreased travelling time. The results however indicate that there is a lack of allocation of resources mainly in staffing and training when adopting the social media. Results also indicate that manager's age and educational attainment had significant impacts on social media strategies. The results did not reveal any evidence of different industry sectors relevance towards social media strategies. Implications for research are discussed.

DOI: 10.4018/978-1-5225-2165-5.ch018

INTRODUCTION

Background of the Study

In this modern era, most people spend some time of their day accessing one or even several social media networks. It is possible to say that an individual would find his day incomplete if his daily routine did not involve logging into Facebook, Instagram, Twitter and many others that are freely available. With the dawn of mobile technology, many online sites have become mobile friendly, thus further deepening our involvement in social media. Social media is an essential and necessary tool in this generation, as it has become the recent trend and preferred Internet application.

Social media does not only play a significant part for large organizations, but is also becoming increasingly important for small and medium-sized enterprises (SMEs). Researches in Germany noted that 47% of all companies use social media (Meske & Stieglitz, 2013). SMEs stand to gain a great deal by utilizing easy-to-use and easy-to-implement social media applications (Zeiller & Schauer, 2011). Furthermore, it has become less difficult and less expensive to adopt social media applications due to its wide availability and advancement in technology. As social media has become widely used by more and more SMEs, it could assist to "level the playing ground" with large competitors. (Kim, Lee, & Lee, 2011). Nevertheless, many small businesses still struggle to use social media as most of them still lack the knowledge on how to use them appropriately.

Problem Statement

As SMEs are a vital element of all economies representing 99.2% of total business establishments in the Malaysia, they are of high social and economic importance (Malaysian Business Advisory 2015). Nonetheless, SMEs are often left behind when compared to large firms in the adoption of modern technologies.

In this regard, this paper intends to discover the adoption and goals behind SMEs for using social media applications as well as to what extent are social media practices being used by SMEs specifically for marketing activities. In particular, it is important to identify social media's perceived benefits and factors behind the unwillingness of SMEs to adopt social media as marketing tool.

Research Objectives

Social Media is a relatively a new media. Studies into the commercial use of social media thus far have almost entirely been about large organizations. Although there has been increased press coverage of the use of social media by SMEs, these have primarily focused on a specific SME segment. It is therefore warranted for new research in comparing the use of social media by SMEs in different industries within Malaysia to provide a good foundation for further research in the future.

The research main objectives for this research are:

1. To investigate the adoption, goals, and social media practices, particularly the usage of social media platforms as a marketing tool in SMEs.
2. To investigate perceived added values and barriers of adoption of social media and its effectiveness as a marketing tool.

Research Questions

Based on the objectives, the main study argues that the demographic profile of an SME affects their marketing strategy. To do so, the study attempts to answer the following main research questions:

1. What are the social media usage habits and what benefits do SMEs get from using Social Media?
2. What are the barriers that SMEs perceived in using Social Media?
3. Do SMEs prioritize Social Media via the resources that they allocate to it?

Significance of the Study

This primary investigation intends to provide a deeper perspective on the uses of social media by small businesses based on characteristics (age/ education level/ industry) of owners/managers, the extent of dependency on social media and whether appropriate social media practices are being followed to when adopting this new technology. Current studies are limited and are mostly based on big companies. Till date, there is still a void on research regarding the use of social media by small businesses.

Next, the research aims at getting a deeper understanding on the main perceived values gained by small businesses using social media versus the barriers of its adoption. Lastly, this research is done in the two most booming industries of small businesses in Malaysia and a cross comparison analysis can be done to summarize the results across industries.

Scope and Limitations of the Study

The scope of this research is small businesses that only use social media as a marketing tool for their marketing activities.

Similar to other studies, this research also has several limitations. Firstly, this research focuses only on the main casual social media platforms such as Facebook, Twitter, Instagram and blogs. The social media application YouTube was not included in the research, as YouTube is not widely used by Malaysian SMEs as a marketing tool in acquiring new customers.

Next, the limitation for this study was that it targeted only two industries and specifically in the Klang Valley Region of Malaysia. According to the Malaysian Ministry of Domestic Trade, Cooperatives and Consumer Affairs as cited by the Malaysian Business Advisory 2015, Food and Beverage is the leading industry in Malaysia amounting to 36% of SME franchises. The Apparel and Accessory industry has recently witnessed a rising interest in the sector by more and more entrepreneurs accounting for about 11% of the Malaysian franchise industry. The research focuses only on the two most prominent industries accounting to 47% of SMEs in Malaysia to facilitate a smoother data collection procedure.

Operational Definitions

Consistent with prior studies in this area, the following terms will be defined as follows:

1. **Web 2.0/Social Media:** Anderson (2007) describes Web 2.0 or social media as a group of technologies that have become deeply connected contributing to a more socially linked web where everybody is capable off adding and editing content.

2. **Small and Medium Entrepreneurships (SMEs):** The National SME Development Council (NSDC) Malaysia (2013) defines SMEs in two categories. Manufacturing: Sales turnover not exceeding RM50 million OR full-time employees not exceeding 200 workers and Services and other sectors: Sales turnover not exceeding RM20 million OR full-time employees not exceeding 75 workers.
3. **Marketing Activities:** The activity, set of institutions, and processes for creating, communicating, delivering, and exchanging offerings that have value for customers, clients, partners, and society at large. (American Marketing Association, 2013).

LITERATURE REVIEW

Social Media and Businesses

Web 2.0 or social media can be described as a group of technologies that have become deeply connected contributing to a more socially linked web where everybody is capable off adding and editing content (Anderson 2007). The introduction of SixDegrees.com in 1997 sparked a social media revolution leading to the development of key sites such as MySpace and Facebook in 2003 and by 2008 it had become a worldwide phenomenon (Boyd & Ellison, 2008). The acceptance and practice of social media has grown swiftly among its users and gain much media attention but academic literature on it still lags behind.

The term "social media" means Internet-based applications that help individuals to connect and share resources and information with one another (Lindsay, 2011). Social media was initially meant to be a medium where friends could connect, communicate and share but has also been implemented as a tool for businesses (Bughin & Manyika, 2007). As social media becomes synonymous in today's modern society, the trends for it are ever changing, improving and updating to meet the demands of its users. It is difficult to define which technologies are "social media" and which are not (Alavi et.al, 2014). New advanced technologies with inventive features are constantly being introduced and are often confusing to differentiate the many variations of social media technologies available.

More and more businesses these days are shifting towards social networks in order to aid their business procedures such as marketing, customer relations' management and business networking both inside and outside the company (Kim et al, 2010). This is particularly important to small businesses or companies that have a partial or if not all of their operations in direct contact with social media. Small business owners and managers are now realizing the inevitability of being swift to adapt and change according to the technologies or stand the chance of being outdated.

Prior industry reports have shown that in 2014, 92% of small business owners seem to indicate that social media is crucial to their business (Stelzner & Stelzner, 2014). This figure had risen from 86% in 2013 whereby businesses are repositioning the investments from traditional marketing approaches to social media and other incoming strategies in advertising (Stelzner & Stelzner, 2014). Since 2013, a constant trend regarding image and video sharing has emerged compare to text-based content. Image focused social media such as Instagram, Pinterest, Tumblr and Snapchat have been on the rise but are still not a major competitor to Facebook which has a solid loyal user base (Demers, 2014). Active daily users on Facebook have increased by 8% in 2014, whereas mobile daily active users almost double that amount, an increase of 15% in the same year (Katz, 2014).

One main problem that arises though is that SMEs frequently struggle to implement this new technology because of the lack of knowledge, funds and technical expertise compared with bigger rival companies (Harris et al, 2008). With the expansion of the Internet and social media, SMEs are now given a chance to overcome these problems. The Internet has greatly lowered down the marketing costs against traditional approaches. (Harris et al, 2008). Businesses are now able to leverage of each other's connections to advertise their products, services and brands (Harris & Rae, 2009).

Challenges and Opportunities for Social Media

As with every new kind of technology being used, challenges to social media are unavoidable. Researchers have listed several challenges concerning social media. Among these challenges include the sharing of content among users or content communities and blogs (Kaplan & Henlein, 2010). These content communities can make or break any small businesses as information is spread from one user to another at rapid proportions. Any dissatisfied or disappointed clients may choose to engross in social media for complaining in the form of disapproval websites or blogs (Ward & Ostrom, 2006).

In the business arena, there is a change in tendency to opt for personalization against other businesses. While technological advancements make the world more connected, consumers seem to resist being homogenized and therefore making marketing even more localized and personalized (Dan, 2014). Big companies will now have to rethink the way they do marketing as smaller companies mainly SMEs are giving stiffer competition due to the level playing field thanks to social media.

Utilizing social media as a means for marketing or business may not be as direct as it seems. Small business owners are hesitant to get involved in social media and some even struggle with the idea of social media being used for their businesses. Most of the misconceptions regarding social media often come from the lack of knowledge on its uses and benefits to the business. Nevertheless, there is still a chance for business owners to obtain social media through free platforms that are widely available on the Internet. The most important thing for small businesses to remember about social media, is that whatever content they have it needs to be in which ever platform they decide is right for them (Nenni,2014).

Carr (2003) is one of many researchers to lead the way by questioning the value gained from investments in IT, and there is substantial literature examining the relationship between IT investments and a company's performance. Similarly, other studies focused on the "use of technology" and discovered IT payoffs can be found and measured (Devaraj & Kohli 2003). They additionally recommend cross-sectional studies with large samples in order to generalize results across different industries (Devaraj and Kohli, 2003).

A review of the literature shown above, describes the usage of social media in SMEs in general. It highlights the importance of social media platforms for marketing activities of businesses. The research paper therefore attempts to contribute through an operational model adapted from (Wamba & Carter, 2014) in Section 3 to get broader insights by analyzing the characteristics of SMEs and the use of social media.

RESEARCH METHODOLOGY

The main intent of the current study is to examine social media strategies among SMEs in Malaysia mainly in the food and beverage and apparel and accessory industry. This study particularly focused on how SMEs in Malaysia adopt and use social media, specifically for their promotion activities and marketing tasks.

Operational Framework

Three approaches had been referred to in the development of the framework of this study. The first approach was adapted from an empirical study conducted on "Social Media Tools adoption" by Wamba and Carter (2014). According to Wamba and Carter (2014) social media adoption by SMEs can be measured by manager/owner characteristics (e.g., age, and education) of the said SME. Secondly, the conceptual model of Derham, Cragg, and Morish (2011) focused on the SMEs goals and values derived from the use of social media. Finally, several aspects of the survey had been referred from a study of online marketing survey conducted by an American professor Edward Boches from Boston University (Boches, 2012).

Through the adoption of this framework, the researcher seeks to investigate the demographic characteristics of SME owners/managers in Malaysia and the values derived by SMEs from social media. To date, there are actually very limited studies on social media and SMEs in Malaysia and no single research adopting this framework specifically in the Malaysian context has been found. Therefore, this paper aims to fill the gap in the literature by providing a detailed analysis for Malaysian SME owners/managers and social media.

Figure 1 shows a framework adopting and combining all of these concepts.

Sampling and Data Collection

A quantitative research methodology was used to answer the research questions in Section 1. The implementation of a quantitative method permitted for the gathering of measurable data on SMEs and to examine the relationships between SMEs and their social media practices.

The questionnaire method or technique employed is to establish the current standing of a phenomenon (Powell & Conway, 2004). The researcher referred and adapted the questionnaire from previous study done (Edward Boches, 2012). Questions used were multiple choice, which is simple, effective and easy to complete by the respondents. The population of relevance was SME owners or managers

Figure 1. Operational framework of SME demographics and their social media strategies

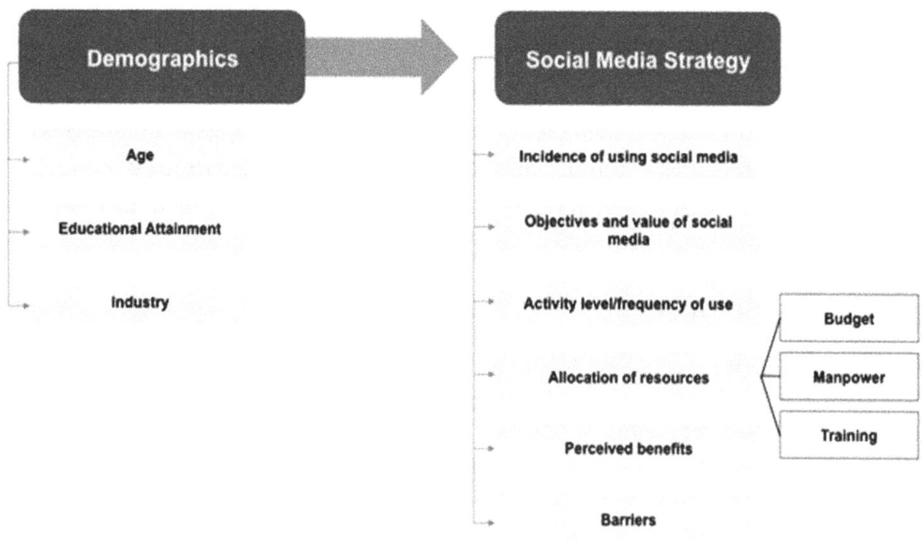

in the Klang Valley. The questionnaire was distributed to 150 SMEs in either the food and beverage or the apparel and accessory industry.

The survey was conducted in GM Klang, a shopping complex that rented out 400 places exclusively for SMEs to conduct their businesses. The survey was conducted from July 15th to 31st July 2015. Each survey required approximately 5-10 minutes to complete. A copy of the detailed survey is contained in Appendix 1.

The survey consists of three sections. The first section comprises of questions related to the demographics attributes of the respondents (age, education attainment, industry). Section two of the survey covers questions that address social media strategies of SMEs with regards to their demographic attributes. Finally, the third section covers the perceived benefits and barriers for SMES in using social media.

Data Analysis

Data analysis of the present study consists solely of quantitative data analysis. The researcher implemented an online web survey application "Typeform" to aid in the gathering, storage and analysis of the data. The researcher had chosen this particular online application due to its simple layout and support of mobile phone interactivity compared with other online surveys.

Subsequently, descriptive statistics were used to examine the data manually. Descriptive statistics are techniques of getting characteristics or summary indicators from the raw data collected from the survey. Descriptive statistics are provided for both the independent variable from the first section of the survey consisting of percentage graphs and pie charts for the categorical (e.g., age, education attainment, industry) and multiple responses from section two (e.g., incidence of using social media) and section three (perceived benefit and barriers).

This section has described the research approach taken in the current study. The quantitative (questionnaire) employed is described in detailed including the advantages and disadvantages of the approach. The next section contains a presentation of the quantitative results of the current study.

RESEARCH RESULT

This section presents the descriptive analysis of the survey. It includes frequencies and percentages for the categorical and multiple responses. It provides findings from 144 out of 150 respondents. The analysis indicated that 6 out of the 150 of the respondents' data had been corrupted and was not applicable

Demographics and Total Responses

This section aims to provide the relevant demographic background parameters of the respondents (e.g., age, educational attainment, industry) and discuss the overall responses of this study.

Figure 2 shows the percentages of the age groups of the owners or managers of the SMEs.

Individuals above the age of 50 are not found in the population. A possible explanation of this could be that, these individuals grasp of current technologies are limited and prefer to delegate the tasks of handling social media to the younger generation. The age group 20-29 had the most number of respondents totaling 53% (n= 76). The second age group 30-39 comprised of 39% (n=56) of the respondents while the age group 40-49 accounted for 8% (n= 16).

Figure 2. Age group of respondents

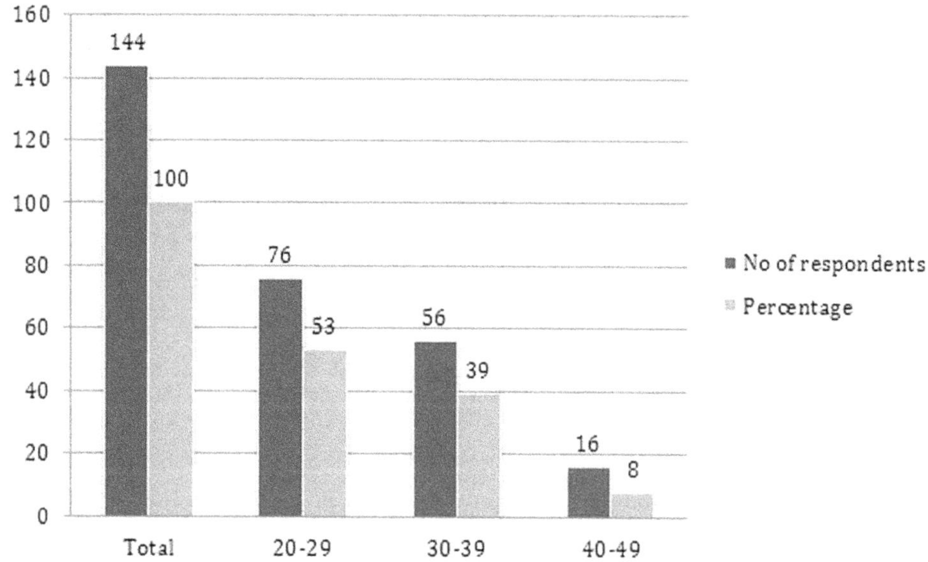

Figure 3 illustrates the educational attainment of the owners or managers of the SMEs in the survey. Educational attainment is classified into four clusters, which are, high school, certificate or diploma, Bachelor's degree, and Masters Degree or PHD. Out of the survey conducted, the majority of respondents had a Bachelor's Degree qualification amounting to 58% (n=84). The second highest was the Certificate and Diploma level accounting to 21% (n=30) respondents while 15% (n=22) of the respondents had basic high school education and 6% (n=8) had either a Masters Degree or PHD qualification. The industries of SMEs are depicted in Figure 4.

Figure 3. Educational attainment of respondents

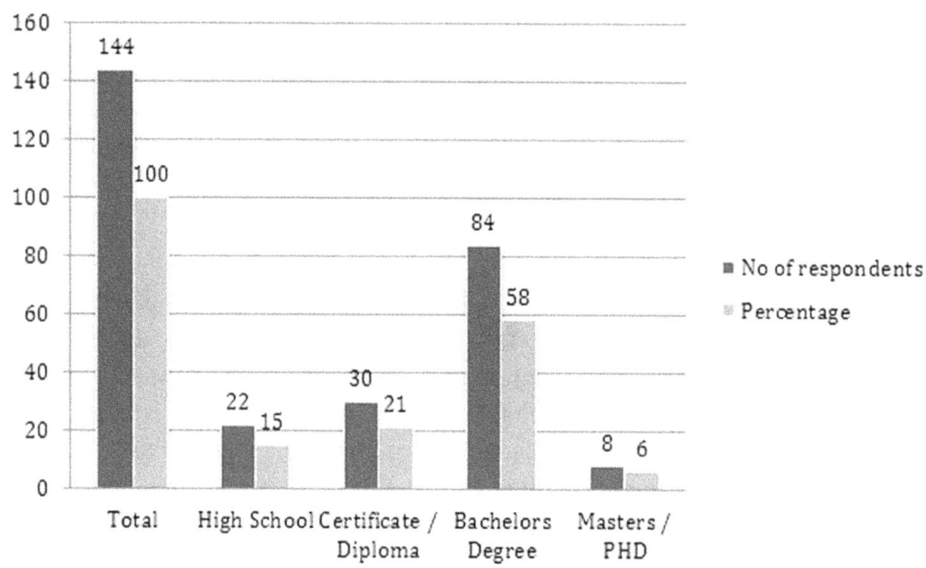

Figure 4. Industry of respondents

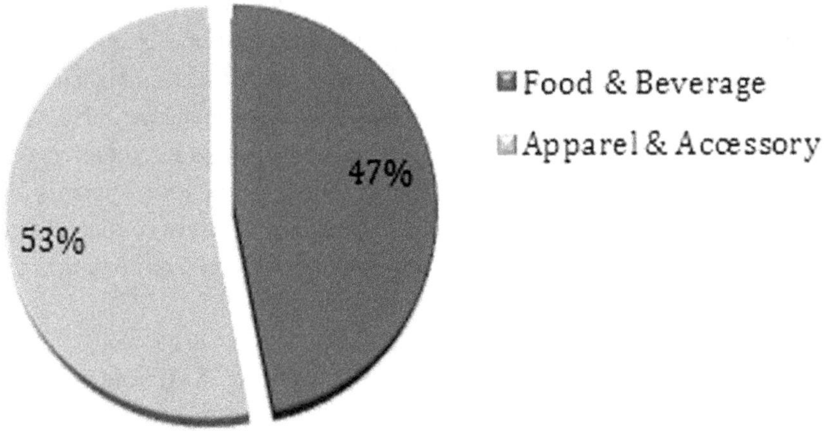

Two industries of SMEs were covered in this study namely the food and beverage industry as well as the apparel and accessory industry. Respondents from the apparel and accessory industry amounted to 53% whereas the remaining 47% were from the food and beverage industry. It is possible to say that both industries are currently thriving in the Malaysian economic scene, as the distributions of SMEs are almost similar

On the incidences of SMEs using social media, 92% of owners and managers claim that social media is incorporated into the SMEs marketing strategy while only 8% do not associate social media as part of their marketing strategies. Facebook ranked the top most used social media by SMEs with 51% of respondents using this platform while Instagram is the next choice of totaling 44% of the replies. Twitter and Blogs usage remain relatively low with only 2% and 3%. Youtube was not included, as SMEs in the survey did not use this social media application for their marketing activities. Figure 5 depicts this.

Figure 5. Social media platform usage by SMES

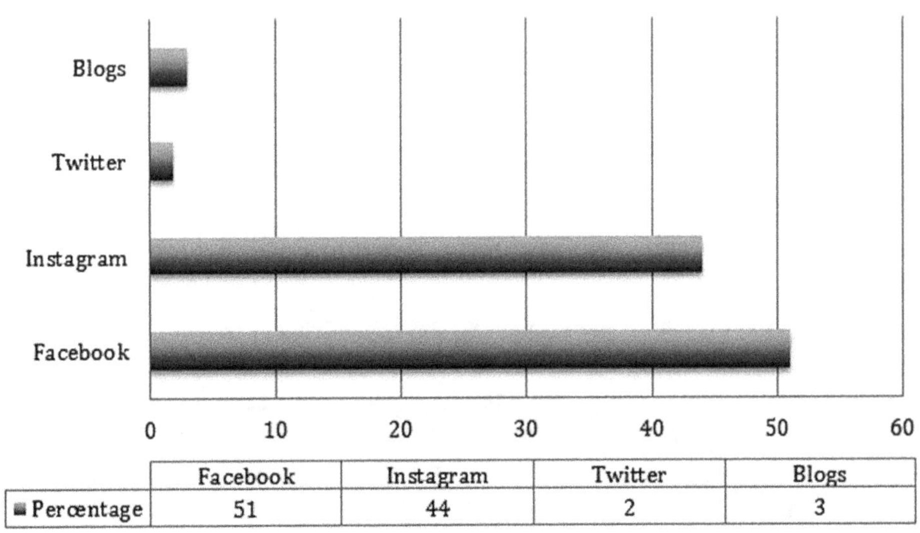

The primary objectives of using social media by SMEs in the Klang Valley tend to vary according to the individual goals of the respective owners and managers as seen in Figure 6.

The number one objective for SMEs in using social media is customer acquisition with 44%. Brand awareness is also an important objective with 33% of businesses ranking this as their end goal. Customer support and loyalty is third with 16% and only 7% of businesses use social media as a means of continuous engagement with customers. It can be implied that most businesses see social media as an advocate to help acquire more customers and in gaining customer awareness on their business

Following the objectives, the research also sought to identify the values of content that SMEs provide their customers through the use of social media. Respondents were given the option of selecting more than one value for this question. Figure 7 displays the result findings.

Out of the total responses, 88% of businesses chose "promote products and offers" while 72% of businesses "deliver updates" to their customers via social media platforms. SMEs are also actively interacting with their customers via social media as "respond to requests" is chosen by 63% of the respondents. The options of "add value to the content" and "provide utility/solve problems" were of lower interests with only 32% and 22% of respondents selecting this as values provided to customers.

Next, the research prompted respondents on the activity level or frequency of use of social media. A total of 46% of SMEs spend an average of one to two hours daily on social media related activities, 37% dedicated more than four hours, and 17% use three to four hours of their day doing online sales via social media. On uploading new social media content, 50% of SMEs create new media on a daily basis, whereas 33% do it weekly. 15% of SMEs have monthly updates and 2% who claim to update content yearly. Figure 8 and Figure 9 show this.

The next step was to discover the resources that these businesses allocated for the social media platform. On the question of allocation of budget for social media marketing activities (e.g. Facebook ads, Instagram reviews, etc.) only 26% of respondents answered that they had a monthly marketing budget set aside for social media. Those respondents who had answered this question quoted a range of RM300 to RM500 per month. From this it is possible to assume that most SMEs choose social media as a mar-

Figure 6. Objectives of social media

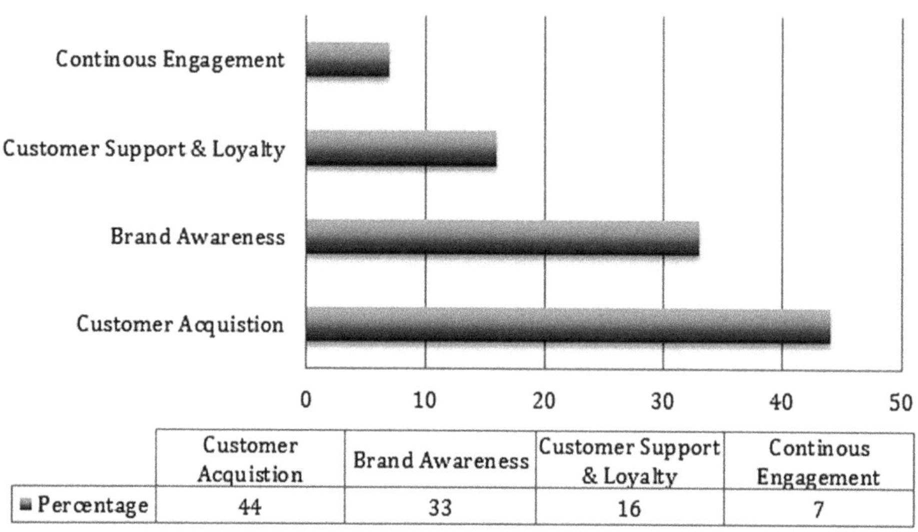

Figure 7. Values of social media

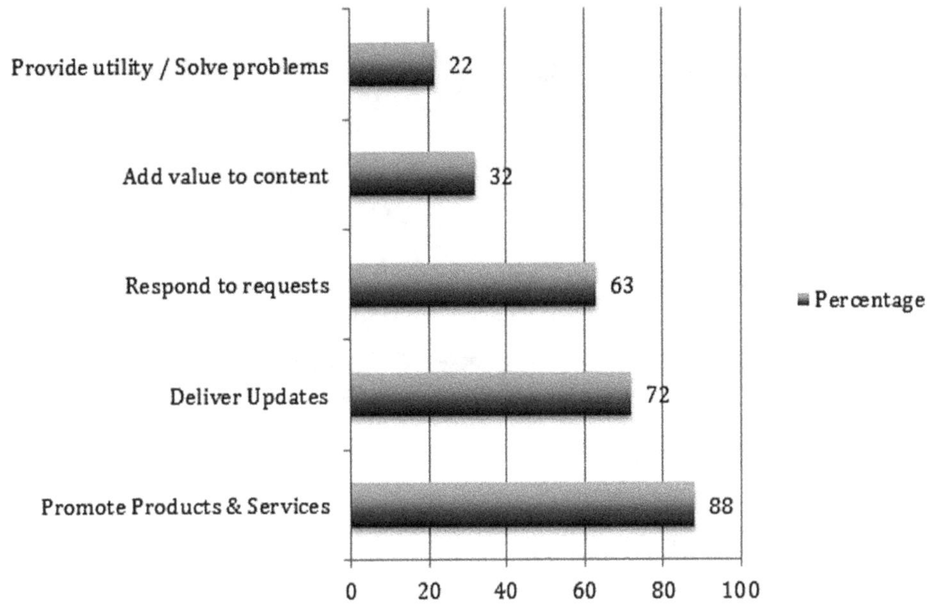

Figure 8. Daily use of social media

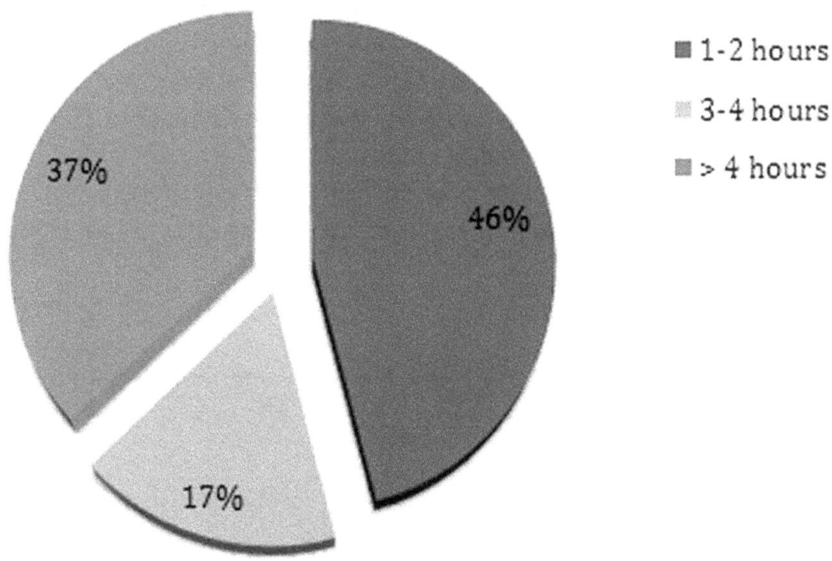

keting tool due to its "free publicity" nature. Another question on resources was whether SMEs had a designated staff to handle their social media marketing, to which only 28% of the respondents had a dedicated employee in the company assigned to this function. In the case of social media training provided to staff; only 12% of SMEs provided some sort of guidance on social media marketing to the employees.

In the final section of the research, the perceived benefits and barriers on the adoption social media by SMEs was studied. Perceived benefits by SMEs were divided into four sections, namely, market de-

Figure 9. Updating the content

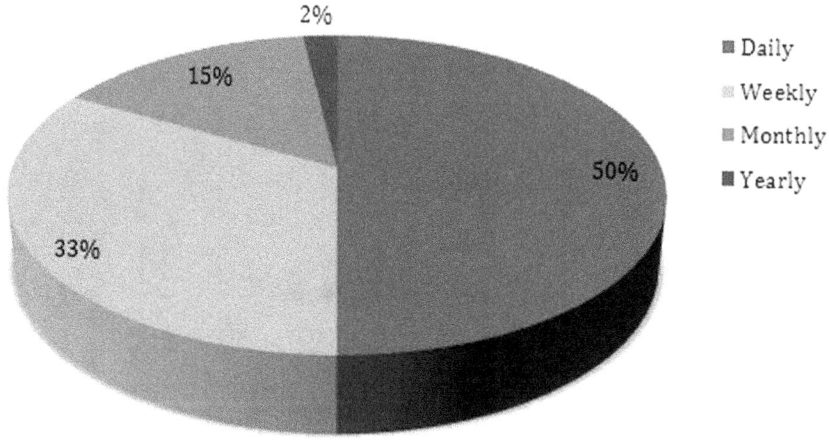

velopment, efficiency in sales and promotions, ease of accessibility, and cost reduction. In market and development, the benefits ranked as chosen by respondents were; - 1) "developing new business opportunities" (57%), 2) "providing better service to customers" (28%) and 3) "enhancing company image" (15%). For efficiency in sales and promotions, the benefits ranked as chosen by respondents were; - 1) "reduced cost of advertising" (51%), 2) "providing more effective promotions" (25%), and 3) "online sales and operations" (24%). As for ease and accessibility, benefits ranked as chosen by respondents were; - 1) "24 hours accessibility" (56%), 2) "ease of access to potential customers" (37%), and 3) "low communication cost" (7%). As for cost reduction 81% of respondents chose "decrease in travelling" over 19% of respondents opting for "savings in phone bills" as the benefit. Figure 10, Figure 11, Figure 12 and Figure 13 illustrate the data according to the sections.

Lastly, the barriers of SMEs in the adoption of social media are discussed. Among the four difficulties, the biggest difficulty for SMEs is due to the lack of knowledge and expertise of staff on social media

Figure 10. Benefits: Market development

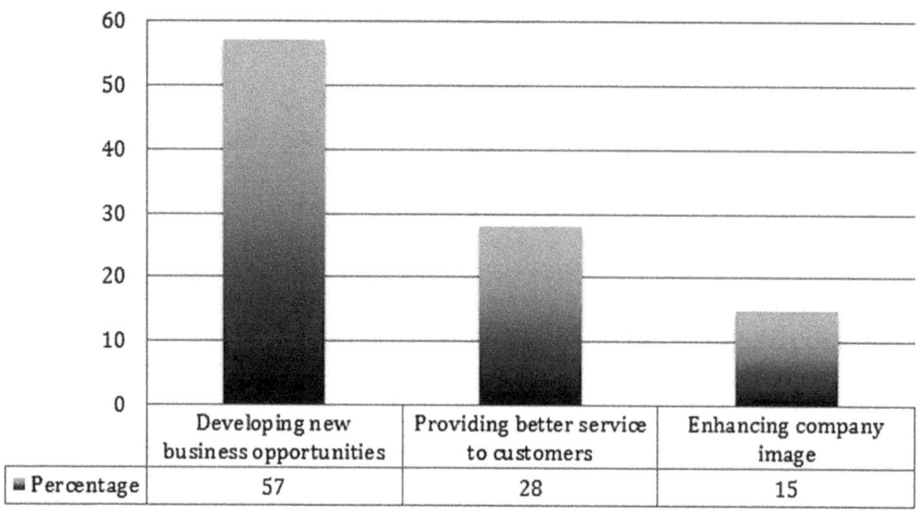

Figure 11. Benefits: Efficiency of sales and promotion

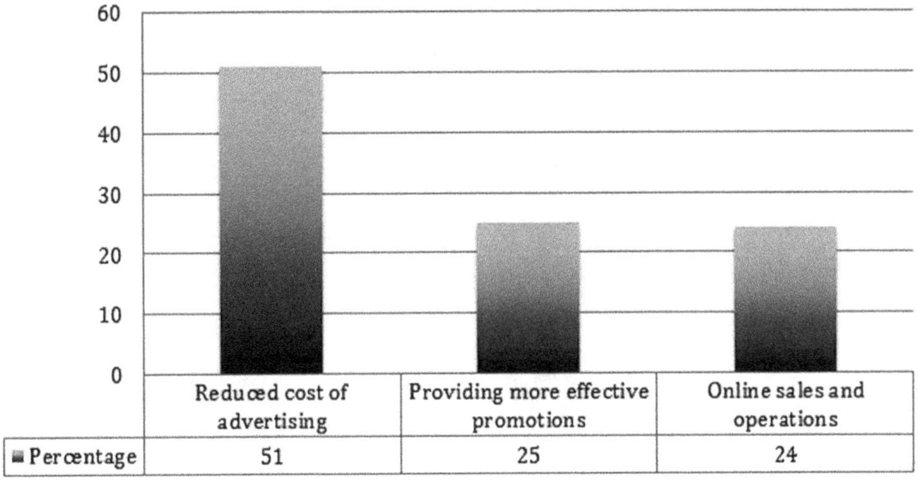

Figure 12. Benefits: Ease of accessibility

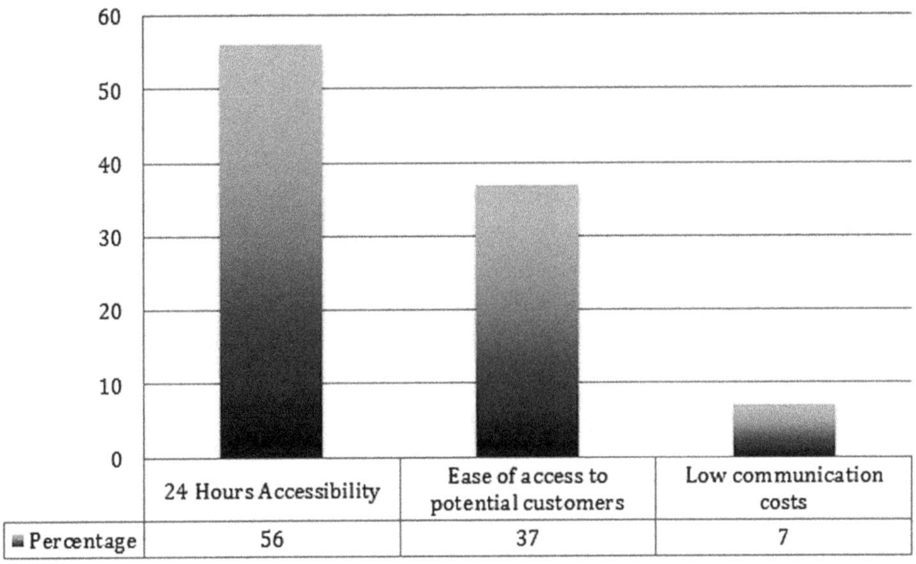

marketing with 38% of businesses stating this as their main problem. Staffs of these SMEs are usually of basic education qualifications and the outsourcing of menial jobs to foreign workers here in Malaysia maybe why this happens. Second is the uncertainty of whether or how can social media help the business with 32% of respondents selecting this as a barrier. From this, it can be presumed that although businesses use these technologies, they are unable to quantify or trust in social media strategies. The third highest ranked barrier was that social media required a big investment in time as chosen by 26% of respondents. Generally, most business managers or owners were more focused on daily operations linked directly to sales and profits. There is a small percentage of 4% of SME owners and managers that believe social media is not important for their business. These owners or managers may still prefer to do their marketing via traditional means of advertising. Figure 14 illustrates this.

Figure 13. Benefits: cost reduction

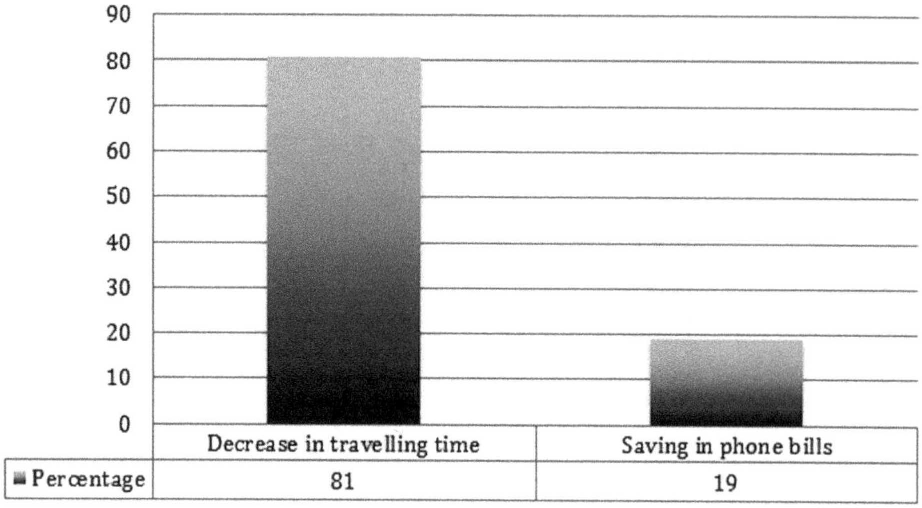

Figure 14. Barriers in adopting Social media

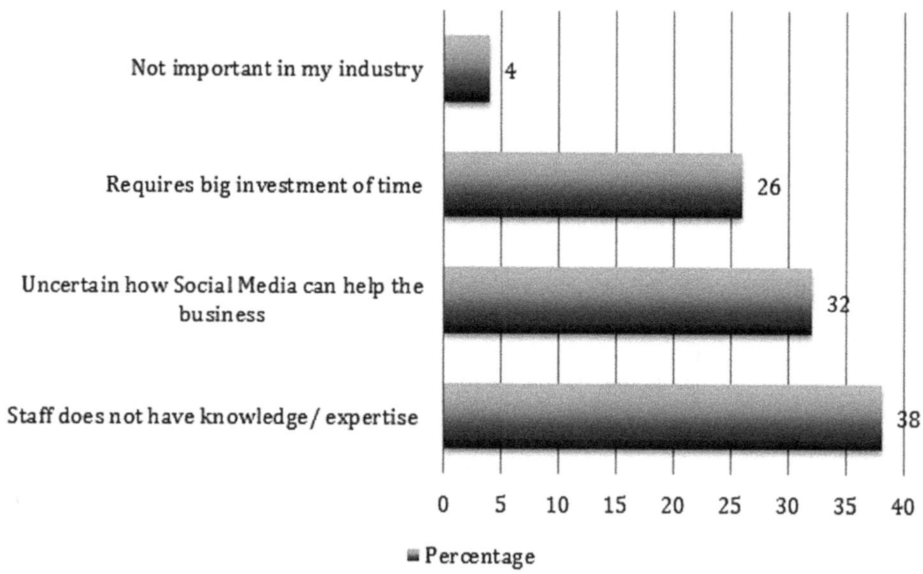

Social Media Strategies by Age

In the first comparison analysis, the research aims to relate the (age of manager/owner) with the social media strategies employed by the SMEs. The three age groups of managers or owners covered in the survey are 20-29 years, 30-39 years, and 40-49 years.

For incidences of using social media, on the question of incorporating social media strategies in the SMEs marketing plans, managers from age group 20-29 recorded the highest amount. Managers in the age group 30-39 also had social media incorporated into their marketing strategies at a lower percentage. The lowest percentage was from the age group 40-49. The results further strengthen reports of (Damanpour & Schneider, 2009) in that; older managers tend to be more accustomed to their routine and favor traditional forms of marketing. As for younger managers in both the lower age groups, it is clear that an element of social media is embedded from the very beginning and is one of the core marketing strategies.

The next comparison was the types of social media platforms that were adopted by the SMEs according to the manager or owner age level. Facebook remained the number one choice for all age groups. The adoption of this platform however was at different levels.. As with previous research (Wamba & Carter, 2014), Facebook is still the most used platform due to its widespread adoption and amount of users on the application, hence it is typical that this is the first go to for any SME adopting social media as a marketing tool. The current on-going trend or latest application that ranked second in being adopted by SMEs as conducted in the survey is Instagram. One plausible explanation for this is that Instagram uses online mobile photo or video sharing where marketers are able to promote their products.

The next comparison was the objectives and value of content based on age group of managers or owners of SMEs. Younger managers seem to be motivated towards brand awareness. For managers in the older age groups the emphasis was towards customer acquisition. Customer acquisition is preferred among older managers due to its direct correlation with profits whereas younger managers goals could be to foster better consciousness among customers as a means to separating themselves from competitors. Promoting products and offers is reflected to be most important value of content for all SMEs regardless of the age group of the managers or owner's. The importance of marketing products for SMEs remains the same for all levels of managers or owners in the hope of influencing consumers to purchase their products or service.

Following that, the activity level or frequency of use of social media was conducted. Respondents in the age group 20-29 spend the highest amount of time, committing more than four hours daily on social media marketing activities. In the age group 30-39 and 40-49, respondents were less active on social media averaging one to two hours per day. The amount of time spent on social media decreases proportionally as the managers or owners' age increases. The advent of mobile devices such as hand phones and handheld computers may support this data. As younger managers are more technology savvy hence the usage of social media is much more when compared to their older counterparts.

Subsequently, a comparison was done on the allocation of resources of SMEs. Majority of managers took on the responsibility of handling social media activities with the exception of older managers whereby the task of social media was delegated to a younger supervisor or family member in the business. Trainings for staff on social media were also very low across all age groups. It can be said that although the usage of social media is high among SMEs, the requirement for structured ways of using social media is not enforced because most SMEs do not allow staff to handle social media marketing activities.

Lastly, a comparison on perceived benefits and barriers to the adoption of social media by SMEs according to the age was examined. In Market Development, the most looked-for benefit was that of "developing new business opportunities". This benefit is more sought by older managers compared younger managers, the percentage was much lower. The cause of this is that managers in this age group also prioritized "providing better service to customers" as the main benefit. The second sub category was Efficiency in Sales and Promotions. Younger managers were of the same requirements whereby "reduced cost of advertising" was the most chosen benefit. Older managers however cited "online sales and operations" as their chosen benefit. In newer SMEs with lower capitals, social media provides an excellent way to promote the business without much cost (Harris et al, 2008). As for more experienced managers, the ambition is to use this new technology to help improve current processes and transform it into a digital form. The third benefit category was Ease of Accessibility. Among the benefits in this category, managers or owners had all selected the same benefit, which was "24 hours accessibility". As with the use of online technologies for marketing activities, most SMEs found it more convenient as they are able to access the business and potential customers at any time fitting to them. Businesses are no longer tied to the standard operating hours but are available to customers 24-7. The last benefit category was on Cost Reduction. Results for this category was similar to that of the previous one, in that all the different age groups of managers or owners had chosen the same benefit, which was "decrease in travel time". The percentages showed an increase in the amount of managers, as the age groups get older. One reason behind this could be the value of time for business owners. Established owners tend to have multiple businesses and social media helps reduce the hassle of travelling long distances for business dealings.

Finally, the research intended to understand on the different barriers by SMEs in adopting social media according to the age level of managers. Younger managers said the main barrier they faced in adopting social media was "social media marketing requires a big investment in time". Middle-aged managers noted that barriers for adoption of social media would be that "staff is unfamiliar or lacks technical skills". Older managers said the main obstacle would be "uncertain whether or how social media marketing can help the business". Through the comments, it is clear that not every individual views the adoption of social media the same. For younger managers who are more confident on using social media and tend to handle social media marketing activities themselves, the worry is that too much time is required and they will be unable to perform other tasks related to marketing. On the other hand, middle-aged managers tend to lean towards the competency of staff, as most managers may want to delegate the job of social media to their employees. Older managers however, are still used to the traditional forms of marketing.

Social Media Strategies by Education Attainment

In the second comparison analysis, the research examined the (education attainment of manager/owner) with the social media strategies employed by the SMEs. Education attainments in the survey have been classified into two groups, which are Basic Education (High School and Certificate/Diploma) and Higher Education (Bachelors Degree, Masters Degree and PhD).

For incidences of using social media, on the question of integrating social media strategies in the SMEs marketing plans, both groups of managers noted that social media strategies were incorporated into their marketing plans. The next comparison was the types of social media platforms that were adopted by the SMEs with managers from different education levels. In the basic education group, Facebook was the most widely adopted. But for the higher education group, Facebook and Instagram shared the same amount of adoption.

The next comparison was the objectives and value of content based on education attainment of managers or owners of SMEs. Managers in the basic education levels are driven by sales. For managers in the higher education group, the objectives are far less outward as customer acquisition and brand awareness are both deemed equally important. Managers with higher education may be exposed to business strategies and understand the importance of creating brand awareness for long-term profits. As for the value of content, both groups irrespective of the educational attainment had selected "promoting products and offers". In the business industry, all SMEs adopt the fundamental marketing strategy to promote products and services to customers and influence them to make purchases.

Subsequently, the activity level or frequency of use of social media by SMEs based on the different educational groups was analyzed. Managers in both the groups spent one to two hours daily on social media marketing activities. In creating new social media content, both education updated news daily. In terms of activity level and frequency, no difference is noted.

With regards to staffing, it is noted that managers or owners of different educational attainments still opted to handle social media marketing activities themselves. Trainings for staff on social media were also very low across both education groups.

Finally, a comparison on perceived benefits and barriers to the adoption of social media by SMEs according to the educational level was studied. In Market Development, the most looked-for benefit was "developing new business opportunities".. The second sub category was Efficiency in Sales and Promotions. Out of the two education groups, "reduced cost of advertising" was the most selected benefit. Social media is viewed as a cheaper alternative for promotion and publicity when compared to traditional forms of advertising (e.g. newspapers or brochures). The third benefit category was Ease of Accessibility. The benefit of "24 hours accessibility" was the number one criteria selected by both groups. Both groups agree that through social media, the businesses are able to run more efficiently and owners may access the platform at any time. The last benefit category was on Cost Reduction. Both groups selected "decrease in travel time".

Finally, the research intended to understand the barriers by SMEs in adopting social media according to the different educational level groups. In both groups, "staff is unfamiliar or lacks technical skills to use social media marketing" is deemed to be the biggest obstacle. This highlights the general view of managers concerning staff competency or lack of it in managing and using social media marketing strategies.

Social Media Strategies by Industry

For the third comparison analysis, the research intended to observe the (difference in industries) with the social media strategies employed by the SMEs. The two separate groups studied in the survey were the Food and beverage industry and the apparel and accessory industry.

For incidences of using social media, on the subject of incorporating social media strategies in the SMEs marketing plans, both groups of managers noted that social media strategies were incorporated into their marketing plans. Across industries, social media is a core component in the marketing strategies of SMEs. The next comparison was the types of social media platforms that were adopted by the SMEs. Facebook ranked the most used social media platform in the two different industries.

The next comparison was the objectives and value of content based on the different industries of SMEs. The most selected objective across both industries was customer acquisition. For the value of content, "promoting products and offers", had been chosen by both industries. The percentages for the apparel and accessory industry are slightly higher possibly due to the heavy reliance of social media to sell the continuous range of products to customers.

After that, the activity level or frequency of use of social media by SMEs based on the different industries was conducted. Respondents in the food and beverage industry spent one to two hours of the day on social media marketing activities. SMEs in the apparel and accessory industry however spent more time on social media marketing activities committing up to four hours daily. In creating new social media content, both industries uploaded new content on a daily basis. The average daily time spent on social media is higher in the apparel and accessory industry probably due to SMEs having to promote various goods across the product range to customers.

Next, a comparison was done on the allocation of resources of SMEs by industries. The research indicated that in both the industries, managers or owners of SMEs chose to handle social media themselves. Trainings for staff on social media were also minimal in both industries. In both industries, it is noted that there is low levels of training provided to staff as most managers or owners chose to carry the task of managing the marketing activities themselves.

Finally, a comparison on perceived benefits and barriers to the adoption of social media by SMEs in different industries was studied. In Market Development, the most wanted benefit was that of "developing new business opportunities". The second sub category was Efficiency in Sales and Promotions. Both industries agreed that "reduced cost of advertising" was the most sought benefit. The third benefit category was Ease of Accessibility. The benefit of "24 hours accessibility" was the number one criteria chosen from both groups. The last benefit category was on Cost Reduction. The results of percentages were nearly the same with both industries selecting "decrease in travel time" as the benefit. In this the difference in industry does not affect the outcome of the perceived benefits.

Lastly, the research intended to understand on the different barriers by SMEs in adopting social media according to the industries. In both groups, "staff is unfamiliar or lacks technical skills to use social media marketing" is deemed to be the major difficulty for SMEs to adopt social media. In the same way, barriers for adoption of social media by SMEs are the same.

Based on the results, it can be stated that successful adoption of social media practices, perceived benefits and barriers depends on the manager's age and educational level. The final section will provide the conclusion and recommendations of the study.

SUMMARY AND CONCLUSION

The study aimed to identify SMEs use of social media, their social media practices and the perceived benefits and barriers in adopting social media for marketing strategies.

In the operational model, the manager/owner characteristics (age / educational attainment) and different industries of SMEs lead to social media practices as well as perceived benefits and barriers. The research shows that use of social media has provided value for SMEs in the incorporated marketing strategies. The results of this study indicate that Facebook still holds it place as the most used social media platform by businesses in the Klang Valley region of Malaysia. However, new social media platforms such as Instagram are gaining popularity among the businesses.

The research results also indicate that the main objective of using social media strategies by SMEs is for customer acquisition but brand awareness is becoming more significant as SMEs learn to understand its importance. Besides that, the research findings highlight promoting products, delivering updates and responding to requests as the main values of content for SMEs in using social media. In terms of activity level or frequency of use, the research results point out that SMEs are indeed active on using social media as a marketing tool, spending a few hours and updating content daily

Surprisingly, the research results discovered a major flaw in the adoption of social media strategies by SMEs. Though usage of social media strategies was high, almost all of the SMEs did not emphasize on the allocation of resources to this tool. Budgets were not divulged and very few SMEs had a dedicated staff to handle the social media marketing. Besides that, there was very minimal training provided to staff on how to handle social media marketing activities.

Out of the four categories of benefits, the research results show that social media marketing helps SMEs in developing new business opportunities, reduces the cost of advertising, is accessible 24 hours and decreases travelling time. The research results also indicate that the major barrier for SMEs in adopting social media is that staff are unfamiliar or lack technical knowledge on social media marketing.

In comparison of the different attributes of SMEs, the research results indicate that managers or owners age level and educational attainment have a major impact on the adoption of social media as a marketing tool. The research results indicate that younger managers are more flexible and open to new ideas and tools and are more likely to incorporate social media into marketing strategies than older managers. Younger managers also spend more time utilizing social media as a marketing tool compared to older managers, a finding consistent to previous literature. The research results illustrate the difference in perceived benefits and barriers of social media marketing strategies amongst managers of different age groups. In addition to that, the research results also imply that a manager or owner's educational attainment has a positive affect on the use of new technologies by the SMEs. Managers with higher educational backgrounds are more supportive of using new technologies (e.g the use of Instagram) as compared to managers with basic education. Finally, in comparing different industries, the research result did not exhibit any significance in the adoption of social media by SMEs.

Implications for Research

The increasing acceptance of social media for marketing activities makes adoption very attractive for SMEs. Firms can now use social media to foster interactions with existing and new customers and to enhance sales and operations of businesses. In many cases, they can improve customer acquisition and create brand awareness by providing constant product updates and receive feedback from customers

The research has significance in that it identifies the main objectives, practices, benefits and barriers of social media by SMEs. Although research on use of social media is rising, there are currently few studies on use of social media by SMEs. Available literature on local businesses are limited and focused on larger corporations or individual companies. This study is an attempt to highlight the social media practices as well as explore the factors that significantly affect social media as a marketing tool among SMEs.

Implications for Practice

The results indicate that there is a notable relationship between the manager's age and adoption of social media. Younger managers are more probable to adopt social media strategies. SMEs should therefore consider developing young managers as this could positively influence the direction of the business to adopt social media marketing strategies. Larger companies have management trainee programs designed to groom fresh graduates for managerial positions. SMEs could gain by emulating such programs. More importantly SMEs should consider allocating more resources to the use of social media. Trainings with consultants or online advertising companies should be provided to staff as to overcome the barriers of adopting social media. SMEs could also apply "best practices" based on the trainings to better benefit from social media.

Limitations and Suggestions for Future Research

There are several limitations with this study. Similar to other survey based projects, there is a risk of bias. Sometimes, respondents may provide answers deemed to be desirable instead of reporting the normal practice. In this research, quantitative data was obtained from 150 respondents in the Klang Valley due to time constraint and limited financial resources. Future research could include qualitative data for better understanding and analysis. To broaden the coverage of the research different industries and a wider location across Malaysia can be explored further. For future research direction, analysis regarding the effectiveness of social media in leveraging competition by small businesses against big companies can provide a better insight and understanding towards this study.

REFERENCES

Anderson, C., & Wolff, M. (2010). The Web is dead. Long live the Internet. *Wired Magazine, 18.*

Agustin, C., & Singh, J. (2005). Curvilinear effects of consumer loyalty determinants in relational exchanges. *JMR, Journal of Marketing Research, 42*(1), 96–108. doi:10.1509/jmkr.42.1.96.56961

Bughin, J., Byers, A. H., & Chui, M. (2011). How social technologies are extending the organization. *The McKinsey Quarterly, 20*(11), 1–10.

Busquets, J., Kohli, R., Navarro, P., & Plana, T. (2012, July). Innovation in Banking Business Models Exploring the Emergent Customer Role in Social Networks. In *2012 Annual SRII Global Conference* (pp. 827-835). IEEE. doi:10.1109/SRII.2012.94

Constantinides, E., Romero, C. L., & Boria, M. A. G. (2009). Social media: a new frontier for retailers? In *European Retail Research* (pp. 1–28). Gabler Verlag.

Derham, R., Cragg, P., & Morrish, S. (2011, July). Creating Value: An SME And Social Media. In PACIS (p. 53). Academic Press.

European Commission. (2010). *European Commission Enterprise and Industry – Access to Finance.* Retrieved from http://ec.eu/enterprise/policies/finance/data/index-en.thm

Haenlein, M., & Kaplan, A. M. (2010). An empirical analysis of attitudinal and behavioral reactions toward the abandonment of unprofitable customer relationships. *Journal of Relationship Marketing, 9*(4), 200–228. doi:10.1080/15332667.2010.522474

Hanna, R., Rohm, A., & Crittenden, V. L. (2011). Were all connected: The power of the social media ecosystem. *Business Horizons, 54*(3), 265–273. doi:10.1016/j.bushor.2011.01.007

Kaplan, A. M., & Haenlein, M. (2010). Users of the world, unite! The challenges and opportunities of Social Media. *Business Horizons, 53*(1), 59–68. doi:10.1016/j.bushor.2009.09.003

Kim, H. D., Lee, I., & Lee, C. K. (2011). Building Web 2.0 enterprises: A study of small and medium enterprises in the United States. *International Small Business Journal, 29*, 1–19.

Latham, B. (2007). Sampling: What is it. *Quantitative Research Methods, 5377.*

Fink, A. (1995). *How to analyze survey data* (Vol. 8). Sage.

Lindsay, B. R. (2011). *Social media and disasters: Current uses, future options, and policy considerations*. Academic Press.

Meske, C., & Stieglitz, S. (2013). Adoption and use of social media in small and medium-sized enterprises. In *Practice-Driven Research on Enterprise Transformation* (pp. 61–75). Springer Berlin Heidelberg. doi:10.1007/978-3-642-38774-6_5

Michaelidou, N., Siamagka, N. T., & Christodoulides, G. (2011). Usage, barriers and measurement of social media marketing: An exploratory investigation of small and medium B2B brands. *Industrial Marketing Management, 40*(7), 1153–1159. doi:10.1016/j.indmarman.2011.09.009

Montgomery, K. C., & Chester, J. (2009). Interactive food and beverage marketing: Targeting adolescents in the digital age. *The Journal of Adolescent Health, 45*(3), S18–S29. doi:10.1016/j.jadohealth.2009.04.006 PMID:19699433

Saravanakumar, M., & SuganthaLakshmi, T. (2012). Social media marketing. *Life Science Journal, 9*(4), 4444–4451.

Wamba, S. F., & Carter, L. (2014). Social Media Tools Adoption and Use by SMEs: An Empirical Study. *Journal of Organizational and End User Computing, 26*(2), 1–17. doi:10.4018/joeuc.2014040101

Zeiller, M., & Schauer, B. (2011, September). Adoption, motivation and success factors of social media for team collaboration in SMEs. In *Proceedings of the 11th International Conference on Knowledge Management and Knowledge Technologies* (p. 4). ACM. doi:10.1145/2024288.2024294

KEY TERMS AND DEFINITIONS

Facebook: As defined by Derham, Cragg and Morish (2011), Facebook is one of the main platforms for social commerce that allows firms to harness social capital by tapping into the tremendous word-of-mouth potential of its active users.

Innovation: The Oxford Handbook of Innovation Management (2013) describes innovation as an essential means by which organisations survive and thrive.

Manager's Characteristics: A critical role of managers (age, education, and gender) in influencing behaviours in a wide variety of domains (Damanpour & Schneider, 2009).

Marketing Activities: The activity, set of institutions, and processes for creating, communicating, delivering, and exchanging offerings that have value for customers, clients, partners, and society at large. (American Marketing Association, 2013).

Small and Medium Entreprises (SMEs): The National SME Development Council (NSDC) Malaysia (2013) defines SMEs in two categories. Manufacturing: Sales turnover not exceeding RM50 million OR full-time employees not exceeding 200 workers and Services and other sectors: Sales turnover not exceeding RM20 million OR full-time employees not exceeding 75 workers.

Social Media Tools: Online platforms that provide improved communication and collaboration between the firm and its stakeholders (e.g., customers, suppliers, business partners). (Wamba & Carter, 2014).

Web 2.0: Anderson (2007) describes Web 2.0 or social media as a group of technologies that have become deeply connected contributing to a more socially linked web where everybody is capable off adding and editing content.

APPENDIX: QUESTIONNAIRE

Section 1

1. What is your age group?
   a. 20-29
   b. 30-39
   c. 40-49
   d. 50 and above
2. What is your highest level of education?
   a. High School
   b. Certificate / Diploma
   c. Bachelor's Degree
   d. Masters Degree/ PHD
3. What industry are you currently in?
   a. Food/Beverage
   b. Apparel/Accessories

Section 2

4. Is social media incorporated in your marketing plans?
   a. Yes
   b. No
5. Based on the list, what social media do you use?
   a. Facebook
   b. Instagram
   c. Twitter
   d. Blogs
6. Please indicate how focused your marketing is on the following platforms (see Table 1).

Table 1.

	Not at all focused	Somewhat focused	Very focused
Facebook			
Instagram			
Twitter			
Blogs			

7. What are your primary objectives of using social media?
    a. Customer Acquisition
    b. Brand Awareness
    c. Ongoing Engagement
    d. Customer Support and Loyalty
8. How do you measure success?
    a. Number of Fans/followers/Likes
    b. Number of Comments
    c. Number of Retweets
    d. Referrals
9. What is your daily time commitment for social media?
    a. 0 hours
    b. 1-2 hours
    c. 3-4 hours
    d. More then 4 hours
10. How often do you create new social media content?
    a. Daily
    b. Weekly
    c. Monthly
    d. Yearly
    e. Never
11. What is the value of your content? (Select all that apply)
    a. Deliver updates
    b. Promote products and offers
    c. Add value to the content
    d. Respond to requests
    e. Provide utility/solve problems
12. Do you have a dedicated employee/personnel specifically handling social media activities?
    a. Yes
    b. No
    c. I handle the social media activities myself
13. Do you have any social media training to your employees?
    a. Yes
    b. No
14. Do you have a social media-marketing budget?
    a. Yes. (Please specify amount. RM____________________)
    b. No

Section 3

15. What benefits do you think are the most important in using social media for your business?
    a. Market Development.
        i. Developing new business opportunities
        ii. Enhancing company image
        iii. Providing better service to customers
    b. Efficiency in Sales and Promotion.
        i. Online Sales and Operations
        ii. Reduced cost of advertising
        iii. Providing more effective promotions
    c. Easy of Accessibility.
        i. Low communication cost
        ii. 24h accessibility
        iii. Ease of access to potential customers
    d. Cost Reduction.
        i. Decrease in travel time
        ii. Savings in phone bills
16. What are the barriers for you to adopt social media marketing for your business?
    a. Social Media Marketing is not important in my industry.
    b. Uncertain whether or how can social media marketing help the business.
    c. Social Media Marketing requires a big investment in time.
    d. Staff is not familiar with social media marketing.
    e. Staff does not have technical skills to use social media marketing.

Compilation of References

11MP. (2016). *Eleventh Malaysia Plan 2016-2020: Anchoring growth on people.* Retrieved May 17, 2016, from http://rmk11.epu.gov.my/book/eng/Elevent-Malaysia-Plan/RMKe-11 Book.pdf

Aaker, D. (1991). *Managing brand equity.* New York: The Free Press.

Aaker, D. (1996). Measuring brand equity across products and markets. *California Management Review, 38*(3), 102–120. doi:10.2307/41165845

Aaker, D. (2003). The power of the branded differentiator. *MIT Sloan Management Review, 45*(1), 83.

Abdin, M. J. (2015). *SME cluster development key to speedy industrial growth.* The Financial Express.

Abdul Halim, M. A. S., Alias, M., Che Hamid, A., & Zakaria, Z. (2011). An inter-relationship of entrepreneurial personality, commitment and self-independent in a Terengganu agriculture industry. *International Journal of Business and Social Science, 2*(23), 274–281.

Abdul Khalid, F., & Gilbert, D. (2012). Third-generation Business Incubation Practices in Malaysian ICT Incubators – A Bridge Too Far? *American Journal of Management, 12*, 88–107.

Abdul Khalid, F., Gilbert, D., & Huq, A. (2010). Current Practice of Business Incubation Process Elements in Malaysian ICT Incubators. In *Australia and New Zealand Academy of Management* (pp. 1–28). Adelaide, Australia: ANZAM.

Abdul Khalid, F., Gilbert, D., & Huq, A. (2011). Business Incubation Process Impact on Malaysian ICT Incubatee Performance Using Multinomial Logistic Regression. In *The Second Asian Business.* Osaka, Japan: Management Conference.

Abdul Khalid, F., Gilbert, D., & Huq, A. (2012). Investigating the underlying components in business incubation process in malaysian ict incubators. *Asian Journal Of Social Sciences & Humanities Configurations, 1*(1), 88–102.

Abdul Khalid, F., Gilbert, D., & Huq, A. (2014).. . *The Way Forward For Business Incubation Process in ICT Incubators in Malaysia, 15*(3), 395–412.

Abdullah, N. H., & Shamsuddin, A. (2009). Technology adoption among SMEs in Malaysia: Development of an assessment process. PICMET: Portland International Center for Management of Engineering and Technology, Proceedings, (1), 2644–2648. http://doi.org/ doi:<ALIGNMENT.qj></ALIGNMENT>10.1109/PICMET.2009.5261819

Abdullah, A. A., & Naem Sulaiman, N. (2013). Factors that influence the interest of youths in agricultural entrepreneurship. *International Journal of Business and Social Science, 4*(3), 228–302.

Abdullah, F. A., & Abu Samah, B. (2014). Factors influencing inclination toward agriculture entrepreneurship among students in agriculture learning institute. *Asian Social Science, 10*(2), 273–278.

Abdullah, F. A., Abu Samah, B., & Othman, J. (2012). Inclination towards agriculture among rural youth in Malaysia. *Journal of Basic and Applied Scientific Research*, *2*(11), 10892–10894.

Abdullah, M. A. (1999). *Small and medium enterprises in Malaysia: Policy issues and challenges*. Ashgate.

Abdullah, N. H., Shamsuddin, A., Wahab, E., & Hamid, N. A. A. (2014). The relationship between organizational culture and product innovativeness. *Procedia: Social and Behavioral Sciences*, *129*, 140–147. doi:10.1016/j.sbspro.2014.03.659

Abernathy, W. J., & Clark, K. B. (1985). Innovation: Mapping the winds of creative destruction. *Research Policy*, *14*(1), 3–22. doi:10.1016/0048-7333(85)90021-6

Aboderin, I. (2005). Understanding and responding to ageing, health, poverty and social change in Sub-Saharan Africa: A strategic framework and plan for research. In *Research on Ageing, Health and Poverty in Africa: Forging Directions for the Future*. Oxford.

Abor, J. (2005). The effect of capital structure on profitability: An empirical analysis of listed firms in Ghana. *The Journal of Risk Finance*, *6*(5), 438–445. doi:10.1108/15265940510633505

Abu Dardak, R. (2015). *Transformation of agricultural sector in Malaysia through agricultural policy*. Malaysia: MARDI.

Abu Samah, B., D'Silva, J. L., Shaffril, H. A. M., & Uli, J. (2011). The impact of female university students' acceptance towards agriculture contract farming on Malaysian economy. *African Journal of Business Management*, *5*(15), 6625–6631.

ACCA. (2005). Accounting Sustainability Briefing Paper 5. London, UK: Association of Chartered Certified Accountants (ACCA) & KPMG.

Acs, Z. J., Morck, R. K., & Yeung, B. (2001). Entrepreneurship, globalization, and public policy. *Journal of International Management*, *7*(3), 235–251. doi:10.1016/S1075-4253(01)00046-1

Adamik, A. N. N. A. (2013). A partnering approach to extending the business base through cooperation with competitors (coopetition)–Is it an option for SMEs? *Recent Advances in Management, Marketing and Finances, Business and Economic Series*, *4*, 57–62.

ADB SMEs in Vietam. (n.d.). *Support and report*. Author.

ADB. (2013). *Asia Small and Medium-sized Enterprise (SME) Finance Monitor 2013*. ADB Publishing.

ADB. (2013). *Proposed Policy-Based Loan for Subprogram 2 Socialist Republic of Viet Nam: Second Small and Medium-Sized Enterprises Development Program*. ADB.

Adcorp. (2016). *New business start-ups slump to all-time low*. Retrieved January, 2016, from http://www.adcorp.co.za/NEws/Pages/Newbusinessstart-upsslumptoall-timelow.aspx

Adeniran, T. V., & Johnston, K. A. (2011). Investigating the level of Internet capabilities of South African small and medium enterprises in changing environments. In *Proceedings of the 13th Annual Conference on World Wide Web Applications* (pp. 5–21). Cape Town, SA: Cape Peninsula University of Technology.

Adler, P. S., & Kwon, S.-W. (2002). Prospects for a New Concept. *Academy of Management Journal*, *27*(1), 17–40.

Adlesic, R. V., & Slavec, A. (2012). Social Capital and Business Incubators Performance: Testing the Structural Model. *Economic and Business Review for Central and South - Eastern Europe*, *14*(3), 201–222.

Adnan, H. (2011, April 9). Food security policy may be extended. *The Star Online*. Retrieved from http://www.thestar.com.my/story.aspx/?file=%2f2011%2f4%2f9%2fbusiness%2f8445971

Aerts, K., Matthyssens, P., & Vandenbempt, K. (2007). Critical role and screening practices of European business incubators. *Technovation, 27*(5), 254–267. doi:10.1016/j.technovation.2006.12.002

Agba, A. M. O., Ocheni, S., & Nkpoyen, F. (2014). Microfinance credit scheme and poverty reduction among low-income workers in Nigeria. *Journal of Good Governance and Sustainable Development in Africa., 2*(1), 1–13.

Agba, A. M. O., Ushie, M. A., Bassey, A. O., & Agba, M. S. (2009). Human development trend in Nigeria: The need for concrete implementation of the seven point agenda. *Nigerian Journal of Social Development, 6*(1), 15–28.

Aghion, P., & Howitt, P. (1992). A model of growth through creative destruction. *Econometrica, 60*(2), 323–351. doi:10.2307/2951599

Agostini, L. (2016). Organizational and Managerial Activities in the Development Process of Successful SME Marketing Networks. *European Management Review*, 278–293. http://doi.org/<ALIGNMENT.qj></ALIGNMENT>10.1111/emre.12069

Aguinis, H., & Glavas, A. (2012). What We Know and Dont Know About Corporate Social Responsibility: A Review and Research Agenda. *Journal of Management, 38*(4), 932–968. doi:10.1177/0149206311436079

Agustin, C., & Singh, J. (2005). Curvilinear effects of consumer loyalty determinants in relational exchanges. *JMR, Journal of Marketing Research, 42*(1), 96–108. doi:10.1509/jmkr.42.1.96.56961

Agwu, M. E., & Murray, J. P. (2014). Drivers and inhibitors to e-commerce adoption among SMEs in Nigeria. *Journal of Emerging Trends in Computing and Information Sciences, 5*(3), 192–199.

Ahmad, N. H., Ramayah, T., Wilson, C., & Kummerow, L. (2010). Is entrepreneurial competency and business success relationship contingent upon business environment? A study of Malaysian SMEs. *International Journal of Entrepreneurial Behaviour & Research, 16*(3), 182-203.

Ahmad, A. R., Wan Yusoff, F. W., Md Noor, H., & Ramin, A. K. (2012). Preliminary study of rural entrepreneruship development program in Malaysia. *Journal of Global Entrepreneurship, 2*(1), 1–8.

Ahmad, N. H. (2007). *A cross cultural study of entrepreneurial competencies and entrepreneurial success in SMEs in Australia and Malaysia.* University of Adelaide.

Ahmad, N. H., Halim, H. A., Ramayah, T., & Rahman, S. A. (2013). Revealing an open secret: Internal challenges in creating an entrepreneurial university from the lens of the academics. *International Journal of Conceptions on Management and Social Sciences, 1*(1), 2357–2787.

Ahmad, N. H., & Ramayah, T. (2012). Does the Notion of Doing Well by Doing Good Prevail Among Entrepreneurial Ventures in a Developing Nation? *Journal of Business Ethics, 106*(4), 479–490. doi:10.1007/s10551-011-1012-9

Ahmad, N. H., Ramayah, T., & Tuan Muda, S. A. D. (2013). Unlocking the entrepreneurial propensity among prime-age Malaysians: Multi-ethnic analysis. *Journal of Arts. Science & Commerce, 4*(1), 1–6.

Ahmad, N. H., Wilson, C., & Kummerow, L. (2011). A cross-cultural insight into the competency-mix of SME entrepreneurs in Australia and Malaysia. *International Journal of Business and Management Science, 4*(1), 33–50.

Ahmad, N. H., Wilson, C., & Kummerow, L. (2011). Assessing the Dimensionality of Business Success: The Perspectives of Malaysian SME Owner-Managers. *Journal of Asia-Pacific Business, 12*(3), 207–224. doi:10.1080/10599231.2011.586855

Ahmed, T., Hasan, S., & Haneef, R. (2011). Entrepreneurial characteristics of the agripreneurs under the Scheme of Agriclinics & Agri-business Centres. *Journal of Community Mobilization and Sustainable Development, 6*(2), 145–149.

Ahuja, G. (2000). Collaboration networks, structural holes, and innovation: A longitudinal study. *Administrative Science Quarterly*, *45*(3), 425–455. doi:10.2307/2667105

Aidis, R. (2002). *Why Don't We See More Small-and Medium-sized Enterprises (SMEs) in Lithuania?* Institutional Impediments to SME Development.

Ajiferuke, I., & Olatokun, W. (2009). Sectoral Analysis of ICT Use in Nigeria. In Encyclopedia of Information Science and Technology (2nd ed.). Information Resources Management Association. doi:10.4018/978-1-60566-026-4.ch534

Ajzen, I. (1985). *From intentions to actions: A theory of planned behavior*. Springer.

Ajzen, I. (1991). The theory of planned behavior. *Organizational Behavior and Human Decision Processes*, *50*(2), 179–211. doi:10.1016/0749-5978(91)90020-T

Ajzen, I. (2002). Residual effects of past on later behavior: Habituation and reasoned action perspectives. *Personality and Social Psychology Review*, *6*(2), 107–122. doi:10.1207/S15327957PSPR0602_02

Ajzen, I. (2005). *Attitudes, personality, and behavior*. McGraw-Hill International.

Ajzen, I. (2011). The theory of planned behaviour: Reactions and reflections. *Psychology & Health*, *26*(9), 1113–1127. doi:10.1080/08870446.2011.613995 PMID:21929476

Ajzen, I., & Fishbein, M. (1977). Attitude-behavior relations: A theoretical analysis and review of empirical research. *Psychological Bulletin*, *84*(5), 888–918. doi:10.1037/0033-2909.84.5.888

Ajzen, I., & Fishbein, M. (2000). Attitudes and the attitude-behavior relation: Reasoned and automatic processes. *European Review of Social Psychology*, *11*(1), 1–33. doi:10.1080/14792779943000116

Ajzen, I., Joyce, N., Sheikh, S., & Cote, N. G. (2011). Knowledge and the prediction of behavior: The role of information accuracy in the theory of planned behavior. *Basic and Applied Social Psychology*, *33*(2), 101–117. doi:10.1080/01973533.2011.568834

Ajzen, I., & Madden, T. J. (1986). Prediction of goal-directed behavior: Attitudes, intentions, and perceived behavioral control. *Journal of Experimental Social Psychology*, *22*(5), 453–474. doi:10.1016/0022-1031(86)90045-4

Akman, I., & Mishra, A. (2015). Sector diversity in Green Information Technology practices: Technology Acceptance Model perspective. *Computers in Human Behavior*, *49*(0), 477–486. doi:10.1016/j.chb.2015.03.009

Al-Amin, M. (2013). *SMEs urged to adopt culture of innovation, boost R&D spending*. Retrieved January 10, 2016, from http:// www.smecorp.gov.my

Alam, M. M., Siwar, C., Murad, M. W., Molla, R. I., & Toriman, M. E. (2010). Socioeconomic profile of farmer in Malaysia: Study on integrated agricultural development area in North-West Selangor. *Agricultural Economics and Rural Development. New Series*, *7*(2), 249–265.

Alam, Q., Yusuf, M. A., & Coghill, K. (2010). Village Phone Program, Commodification Of Mobile Phone Set And Empowerment Of Women. *The Journal of Community Informatics*, *5*(3-4).

Alanezi, M. A., Kamil, A., & Basri, S. (2010). A proposed instrument dimensions for measuring e-government service quality. *International Journal of u- and e- Service. Science and Technology*, *3*(4), 1–18.

Albu, N., Albu, C. N., Gîrbină, M. M., & Sandu, M. I. (2011). The Implications of Corporate Social Responsibility on the Accounting Profession: The Case of Romania. *Amfiteatru Economic, 13*(29).

Aldrich, H. E., & Fiol, C. M. (1994). Fools Rush in? The Institutional Context of Industry Creation. *Academy of Management Review, 19*(1), 645–670.

Alegre, J., & Chiva, R. (2013). Linking entrepreneurial orientation and firm performance: The role of organizational learning capability and innovation performance. *Journal of Small Business Management, 51*(4), 491–507. doi:10.1111/jsbm.12005

Alex, L. (2011). *A review and analysis of policies on farmers' entrepreneurship development.* PELUM Association Retrieved from http://api.ning.com/files/mBFEJqp6LPA6uws0UOvKYJD594rw5TqjU-WCb6e5tQ*x02SZslAqcSAQN-JIAirsnn3b6LLN7QbTlhi602siwc0PPbcR26h4v/Farmerentpolicystudy.pdf

Alexander, O. S. (2014). *Unemployment In Nigeria: A Factor For Revolution!* Retrieved from http://saharareporters.com/2014/03/25/unemployment-nigeria-factor-revolution-osobu-suuru-alexander

Alkire, S. (2005). *Valuing freedoms: Sen's capability approach and poverty reduction.* Oxford University Press.

Al-Laham, A., Tzabbar, D., & Amburgey, T. L. (2011). The dynamics of knowledge stocks and knowledge flows: Innovation consequences of recruitment and collaboration in biotech. *Industrial and Corporate Change, 20*(2), 555–583. doi:10.1093/icc/dtr001

Allen, D. N., & Rahman, S. (1985). Small business incubators: A positive environment for entrepreneurship. *Journal of Small Business Management, 23*(3), 12.

Allen, F., McAndrews, J., & Strahan, P. (2002). E-finance: An introduction. *Journal of Financial Services Research, 22*(1), 5–27. doi:10.1023/A:1016007126394

AllMediaLink. (2015). *BASIS will create 23000 IT skilled man power.* Retrieved on February 2, 2016, from https://allmedialink.com/basis-will-create-23000-it-skilled-manpower/

Al-Mubaraki, H. M., & Busler, M. (2014). Incubator successes. *World Journal of Science. Technology and Sustainable Development, 11*(1), 44–52. doi:10.1108/WJSTSD-08-2013-0030

Alo, J. N. (2014, February 7). SME credit grows 18% in 2013. *Dhaka Tribune.*

Altenburg, T., & Eckhardt, U. (2006). *Productivity enhancement and equitable development: Challenges for SME development.* United Nations Industrial Development Organization.

Amason, A. C., Shrader, R. C., & Tompson, G. H. (2006). Newness and novelty: Relating top management team composition to new venture performance. *Journal of Business Venturing, 21*(1), 125–148. doi:10.1016/j.jbusvent.2005.04.008

Ambec, S., & Lanoie, P. (2008). Does It Pay to Be Green? A Systematic Overview. *The Academy of Management Perspectives, 22*(4), 45–62. doi:10.5465/AMP.2008.35590353

Amran, A., & Nejati, M. (2011). *Social Responsibility of Malaysian Small Businesses: Does It Influence Firm Image?* Paper presented at the IJAS Conference, Germany.

Amran, A., Zain, M. M., Sulaiman, M., Sarker, T., & Ooi, S. K. (2013). Empowering society for better corporate social responsibility (CSR): The case of Malaysia. *Kajian Malaysia, 31*(1), 57–78.

Anderson, C., & Wolff, M. (2010). The Web is dead. Long live the Internet. *Wired Magazine, 18.*

Anderson, B. S., Covin, J. G., & Slevin, D. P. (2009). Understanding the relationship between entrepreneurial orientation and strategic learning capability: An empirical investigation. *Strategic Entrepreneurship Journal, 3*(3), 218–240. doi:10.1002/sej.72

Anderson, B. S., & Eshima, Y. (2013). The influence of firm age and intangible resources on the relationship between entrepreneurial orientation and firm growth among Japanese SMEs. *Journal of Business Venturing*, *28*(3), 413–429. doi:10.1016/j.jbusvent.2011.10.001

Anderson, E. W., & Fornell, C. (2000). Foundations of the American customer satisfaction index. *Total Quality Management*, *11*(7), 869–882. doi:10.1080/09544120050135425

Anderson, J. L. (2006). A Structured Approach for Brining Mobile Telecommunications to the World's Poor. *The Electronic Journal of Information Systems in Developing Countries*, *27*(2), 1–9.

Anderson, J., & Billou, N. (2007). Serving the worlds poor: Innovation at the base of the economic pyramid. *The Journal of Business Strategy*, *28*(2), 14–21. doi:10.1108/02756660710732611

Ansari, N. L., Ashraf, M. M., Malik, B. T., & Grunfeld, H. (2010). *Green IT awareness and practices: Results from a field study on mobile phone related e-waste in Bangladesh*. Paper presented at the Technology and Society (ISTAS), 2010 IEEE International Symposium on. doi:10.1109/ISTAS.2010.5514618

Ansari, S., Munir, K., & Gregg, T. (2012). Impact at the bottom of the pyramid: The role of social capital in capability development and community empowerment. *Journal of Management Studies*, *49*(4), 813–842. doi:10.1111/j.1467-6486.2012.01042.x

Apéria, T., & Back, R. (2004). *Brand relations management: bridging the gap between brand promise and brand delivery*. Copenhagen Business School Pr.

Appadurai, A. (2004). The Capacity to Aspire: Culture and Terms of Recognition. In V. Rao & M. Walton (Eds.), *Culture and Public Action* (pp. 59–84). Stanford, CA: Standford University Press.

Apulu, I., & Latham, A. (2009). Information and communication technology adoption: Challenges for Nigerian SMEs. *TMC Academic Journal*, *4*(2), 64–80.

Apulu, I., Latham, A., & Moreton, R. (2011). Factors affecting the effective utilisation and adoption of sophisticated ICT solutions: Case studies of SMEs in Lagos, Nigeria. *Journal of Systems and Information Technology*, *13*(2), 125–143. doi:10.1108/13287261111135972

Apulu, I., Latham, A., & Moreton, R. (2013). Issues of ICT adoption amongst SMEs in Nigeria. *International Journal of Management Practice*, *6*(1), 58–76. doi:10.1504/IJMP.2013.052317

Argyle, M. (2001). *The psychology of happiness*. New York: Routledge.

Aris, N. M. (2007). SMEs: Building blocks for economic growth. *Journal of Department of Statistics, Malaysia*, *1*(1), 1–14.

Armitage, C. J., & Conner, M. (2001). Efficacy of the theory of planned behaviour: A meta-analytic review. *The British Journal of Social Psychology*, *40*(4), 471–499. doi:10.1348/014466601164939 PMID:11795063

Armstrong, J. S., & Overton, T. S. (1977). Estimating Nonresponse Bias in Mail Surveys. *JMR, Journal of Marketing Research*, *14*(3), 396–402. doi:10.2307/3150783

Arnould, E. J., Price, L. L., & Malshe, A. (2006). Toward a cultural resource-based theory of the customer. In R. F. Lusch & S. L. Vargo (Eds.), The service-dominant logic of marketing: Dialog, debate and directions (pp. 320-333). M. E. Sharpe.

Arshad, A. S., Rasli, A., Arshad, A. A., & Zain, Z. M. (2014). The impact of entrepreneurial orientation on business performance: A study of technology-based SMEs in Malaysia. *Procedia: Social and Behavioral Sciences*, *130*, 46–53. doi:10.1016/j.sbspro.2014.04.006

Ashley, G. M., & Bryan, A. (2009). Organizational culture and innovation: exploring the link. 11th Annual Best of Organizational Development Summit, Chicago, IL.

Ashta, A., & Assadi, D. (2009). An analysis of European online micro-lending websites. *Cahiers du CEREN*, *29*, 147–160.

Asia Association of Business Incubation. (2009). *Asia Association of Business Incubation*. Retrieved from http://www.slideshare.net/pmtuan0/new-trends-in-incubation

Asia Cloud Computing Association (2015). *SMEs in Asia Pacific: The Market for Cloud Computing 2015*. Author.

Asian Development Bank. (2013). *Asia's economic transformation: Where to, how, and how fast?* Retrived April 1, 2016, from http://www.adb.org/sites/default/files/publication/30358/ki2013.pdf

Asplund, R. (2003). *Flexibility and Competitiveness: Labour Market Flexibility, Innovation and Organisational Performance*. Helsinki: ETLA, The Research Institute of the Finnish Economy Discussion Paper, 875.

Ataman, B., & Ülengin, B. (2003). A note on the effect of brand image on sales. *Journal of Product and Brand Management*, *12*(4), 237–250. doi:10.1108/10610420310485041

Atufe, F., Okojie, G., Echenim, S., Ogunmola, T., & Bello, O. (2014). Tackling Unemployment In Nigeria. *Leadership Online Newspaper*. Retrieved from http://leadership.ng/business/379110/tackling-unemployment-nigeria

Audretsch, D. B., & Keilbach, M. (2004). Does entrepreneurship capital matter? *Entrepreneurship Theory and Practice*, *28*(5), 419–429. doi:10.1111/j.1540-6520.2004.00055.x

Aujirapongpan, S., Dungtripop, W., & Jungkivinid, W. (2005). Cost Management Strategy of Small and Medium Factory Enterprises. *Songkhlanakarin Journal of Social Sciences and Humanities*, *11*(4), 409–420.

Avlontis, G. J., & Salavou, H. E. (2007). Entrepreneurial orientation of SMEs, product innovativeness, and performance. *Journal of Business Research*, *60*(5), 566–575. doi:10.1016/j.jbusres.2007.01.001

Awang, A., Khalid, S. A., Kassim, K. M., Ismail, M., Zain, R. S., & Madar, A. R. S. (2009). Entrepreneurial orientation and performance relations of Malaysian Bumiputera SMEs: The impact of some perceived environmental factors. *International Journal of Business and Management*, *4*(9), 84. doi:10.5539/ijbm.v4n9p84

Ayyagari, M., Demirgüç-Kunt, A., & Maksimovic, V. (2008). How important are financing constraints? The role of finance in the business environment. *The World Bank Economic Review*, *22*(3), 483–516. doi:10.1093/wber/lhn018

Azer, I., Mohamad, S. A., Abdullah, N. S., & Mustapha, M. (2014). Agro-preneurial obstacles among students in the Faculty of Plantation and Agrotechnology, UiTM Pahang. *Social and Management Research Journal*, *11*(1), 1–8.

Azmat, F., & Samaratunge, R. (2013). Exploring customer loyalty at bottom of the pyramid in South Asia. *Social Responsibility Journal*, *9*(3), 379–394. doi:10.1108/SRJ-09-2011-0077

Bachmann, A., Becker, A., Buerckner, D., Hilker, M., Kock, F., Lehmann, M., & Tiburtius, P. (2011). Online peer-to-peer lending – A literature review. *Journal of Internet Banking and Commerce*, *16*(2), 1–18.

Baden, D., Harwood, I. A., & Woodward, D. G. (2011). The effects of procurement policies on downstream corporate social responsibility activity: Content-analytic insights into the views and actions of SME owner-managers. *International Small Business Journal*, *29*(3), 259–277. doi:10.1177/0266242610375770

Baden, D., & Parkes, C. (2013). Experiential learning: Inspiring the business leaders of tomorrow. *Journal of Management Development*, *32*(3), 295–308. doi:10.1108/02621711311318283

Badurdeen, F., & Liyanage, J. P. (2011). Sustainable value co-creation through mass customisation: A framework. *International Journal of Sustainable Manufacturing*, *2*(2-3), 180–203. doi:10.1504/IJSM.2011.042151

Baghai, M., Coley, S. C., White, D., Conn, C., & McLean, R. J. (1996). Staircases to growth. *The McKinsey Quarterly*, *4*, 38–61.

Bairwa, S. L., Lakra, K., Kushwaha, S., Meena, L. K., & Kumar, P. (2014). Agripreneurship development as a tool to upliftment of agriculture. *International Journal of Scientific and Research Publication*, *4*(3), 1–4.

Bakar, H. A., Mahmood, R., & Ismail, N. N. H. (2015). Effects of knowledge management and strategic improvisation on SME performance in Malaysia. *Asian Social Science*, *11*(9), 207–214. doi:10.5539/ass.v11n9p207

Bakar, S. A., Sulaiman, M., & Osman, I. (2014). Exploring the relationship between business factors and performance in the Malaysian halal biotechnology SMEs context. *Procedia: Social and Behavioral Sciences*, *121*, 243–252. doi:10.1016/j.sbspro.2014.01.1125

Baker, W. E., & Sinkula, J. M. (2009). The complementary effects of market orientation and entrepreneurial orientation on profitability in small businesses. *Journal of Small Business Management*, *47*(4), 443–464. doi:10.1111/j.1540-627X.2009.00278.x

Bakht, Z., & Basher, A. (2015).*Strategy for Development of the SME Sector in Bangladesh*. Academic Press.

Bamberger, P., Bacharach, S., & Dyer, L. (1989). Human resources management and organizational effectiveness: High technology entrepreneurial startup firms in Israel. *Human Resource Management*, *28*(3), 349–366. doi:10.1002/hrm.3930280305

Bandura, A. (1977). Self-efficacy: Toward a unifying theory of behavioral change. *Psychological Review*, *84*(2), 191–215. doi:10.1037/0033-295X.84.2.191 PMID:847061

Bangladesh Bank. (2015). *SME activities*. Retrieved from https://www.bb.org.bd/sme/

Bangladesh Bank. (2016). *Small and Medium Enterprise (SME) Credit Policies & Programmes*. Retrieved January 2016, 2016, from https://www.bb.org.bd/sme/smepolicye.pdf

Bangladesh Bureau of Statistics. (2015). *Economic Census 2013*. Retrieved from http://www.bbs.gov.bd/WebTestApplication/userfiles/Image/EcoCen13/FinalReport%20Part%201.pdf. Accessed at March 28, 2016.

Bank Negara Malaysia. (2015). Economic and financial developments in Malaysia in the first quater of 2015. *Quaterly Bulletin*. Retrieved Jun 20, 2016, from http://www.bnm.gov.my/files/publication/qb/2015/Q1/1Q2015_fullbook_en.pdf

Banu Goktan, A., & Miles, G. (2011). Innovation speed and radicalness: Are they inversely related? *Management Decision*, *49*(4), 533–547. doi:10.1108/00251741111126477

Barney, J. (1991). Firm resources and sustained competitive advantage. *Journal of Management*, *17*(1), 99–120. doi:10.1177/014920639101700108

Baron, R. A., & Shane, S. A. (2008). Entrepreneurship: A Process Perspective (2nd ed.). Mason, OH: Thomson South-Western.

Baron, A. (2011). Measuring human capital. *Strategic HR Review*, *10*(2), 30–35. doi:10.1108/14754391111108338

Barrett, M., Davidson, E., Prabhu, J., & Vargo, S. L. (2015). Service innovation in the digital age: Key contributions and future directions. *Management Information Systems Quarterly*, *39*(1), 135–154.

Basis. (2012). *Bangladesh software and IT service industry*. Retrieved on March 12, 2016, from http://www.basis.org.bd/resource/About_Industry.pdf

Bates, K. A., Flynn, E. J. (1995). Innovation History and Competitive Advantage: A Resource-Based View Analysis of Manufacturing Technology Innovations. *Academy of Management Proceedings, 1995*(1), 235-239.

Bauchet, J., & Morduch, J. (2013). Is micro too small? Microcredit vs. SME finance. *World Development*, *43*, 288–297. doi:10.1016/j.worlddev.2012.10.008

Baucus, D. A., & Human, S. E. (1994). Second-career entrepreneurs: A multiple case study analysis of entrepreneurial processes and antecedent variables. *Entrepreneurship Theory and Practice*, *19*(2), 41–71.

Baucus, D., & Human, S. E. (1994). Second career entrepreneurs: A multiple case of entrepreneurial processes and antecedent variables. *Entrepreneurship Theory & Practice*, *19*(2), 41–71.

Baum, M., Schwens, C., & Kabst, R. (2011). A typology of international ventures: Empirical evidence from high-technology industries. *Journal of Small Business Management*, *49*(3), 305–330. doi:10.1111/j.1540-627X.2011.00328.x

Baum, M., Schwens, C., & Kabst, R. (2015). A latent class analysis of small firms' internationalization patterns. *Journal of World Business*, *50*(4), 754–768. doi:10.1016/j.jwb.2015.03.001

Beck, T., & Demirguc-Kunt, A. (2006). Small and medium-size enterprises: Access to finance as a growth constraint. *Journal of Banking & Finance*, *30*(11), 2931–2943. doi:10.1016/j.jbankfin.2006.05.009

Beck, T., Demirguc-Kunt, A., & Levine, R. (2005). SMEs, growth, and poverty: Cross-country evidence. *Journal of Economic Growth*, *10*(3), 199–229. doi:10.1007/s10887-005-3533-5

Beck, T., Demirgüç-Kunt, A., & Maksimovic, V. (2005). Financial and legal constraints to growth: Does firm size matter? *The Journal of Finance*, *60*(1), 137–177. doi:10.1111/j.1540-6261.2005.00727.x

Bekhet, H. A. (2013). Assessing structural changes in the Malaysian economy: I-O approach. *Economic Modelling*, *30*(1), 126–135. doi:10.1016/j.econmod.2012.09.014

Bell, J., & Loane, S. (2010). 'New-waveglobal firms: Web 2.0 and SME internationalisation. *Journal of Marketing Management*, *26*(3-4), 213–229. doi:10.1080/02672571003594648

Bengtsson, M., Eriksson, J., & Wincent, J. (2010). Coopetition: new ideas for a new paradigm. *Coopetition: Winning strategies for the 21st century*, 19-39.

Bengtsson, A., & Servais, P. (2005). Co-branding on industrial markets. *Industrial Marketing Management*, *34*(7), 706–713. doi:10.1016/j.indmarman.2005.06.004

Benner, M. J., & Tushman, M. L. (2003). Exploitation, exploration, and process management: The productivity dilemma revisited. *Academy of Management Review*, *28*(2), 238–256.

Bennett, R. J., & Robson, P. J. A. (1999). The use of external business advice by SMEs in Britain. *Entrepreneurship & Regional Development*, *11*(2), 155–180. doi:10.1080/089856299283245

Bergek, A., & Norrman, C. (2008). *Linköping University Post Print Incubator best practice: A framework Incubator best practise: A framework*. Academic Press.

Bergek, A., & Norrman, C. (2008). Incubator best practice: A framework. *Technovation*, *28*(1–2), 20–28. doi:10.1016/j.technovation.2007.07.008

Berma, M. (2012). *Developing an Entrepreneurship Education Eco-System at Universiti Kebangsaan Malaysia (UKM): A Critical Analysis on Teaching*. Learning and Knowledge Development.

Berry, A. J., Sweeting, R., & Goto, J. (2006). The effect of business advisers on the performance of SMEs. *Journal of Small Business and Enterprise Development*, *13*(1), 33–47. doi:10.1108/14626000610645298

Bettiol, M., Di Maria, E., & Finotto, V. (2012). Marketing in SMEs: The role of entrepreneurial sensemaking. *The International Entrepreneurship and Management Journal*, *8*(2), 223–248. doi:10.1007/s11365-011-0174-3

Beverland, M., Lindgreen, A., Napoli, J., Ballantyne, D., & Aitken, R. (2007). Branding in B2B markets: Insights from the service-dominant logic of marketing. *Journal of Business and Industrial Marketing*, *22*(6), 363–371. doi:10.1108/08858620710780127

Bhaird, C., & Lucey, B. (2011). An empirical investigation of the financial growth lifecycle. *Journal of Small Business and Enterprise Development*, *18*(4), 715–731. doi:10.1108/14626001111179767

Bhaskaran, S. (2006). Incremental innovation and business performance: Small and medium-size food enterprises in a concentrated industry environment. *Journal of Small Business Management*, *44*(1), 64–80. doi:10.1111/j.1540-627X.2006.00154.x

Bhunia, A. (2010). A trend analysis of liquidity management efficiency in selected private sector Indian steel industry. *International Journal of Research in Commerce and Management.*, *1*(5), 618–628.

Bian, X., & Moutinho, L. (2011). The role of brand image, product involvement, and knowledge in explaining consumer purchase behaviour of counterfeits: Direct and indirect effects. *European Journal of Marketing*, *45*(1/2), 191–216. doi:10.1108/03090561111095658

Birley, S. (1985). The role of networks in the entrepreneurial process. *Journal of Business Venturing*, *1*(1), 107–117. doi:10.1016/0883-9026(85)90010-2

Blackburn, R., & Jarvis, R. (2010). The role of small and medium practices in providing business support to small-and medium-sized enterprises. New York: International Federation of Accountants (IFAC).

Blanchflower, D., & Oswald, A. (1998). What makes an entrepreneur? *Journal of Labor Economics*, *16*(1), 26–60. doi:10.1086/209881

Blomstermo, A., Eriksson, K., Lindstrand, A., & Sharma, D. D. (2004). The perceived usefulness of network experiential knowledge in the internationalizing firm. *Journal of International Management*, *10*(3), 355–373. doi:10.1016/j.intman.2004.05.004

Bocken, N. M. P., & Short, S. W. (2016). Towards a sufficiency-driven business model: Experiences and opportunities. *Environmental Innovation and Societal Transitions*, *18*, 41–61. doi:10.1016/j.eist.2015.07.010

Bose, R., & Luo, X. (2011). Integrative framework for assessing firms potential to undertake Green IT initiatives via virtualization – A theoretical perspective. *The Journal of Strategic Information Systems*, *20*(1), 38–54. doi:10.1016/j.jsis.2011.01.003

Boso, N., Story, V. M., & Cadogan, J. W. (2013). Entrepreneurial orientation, market orientation, network ties, and performance: Study of entrepreneurial firms in a developing economy. *Journal of Business Venturing*, *28*(6), 708–727. doi:10.1016/j.jbusvent.2013.04.001

Bouncken, R. B., Gast, J., Kraus, S., & Bogers, M. (2015). Coopetition: A systematic review, synthesis, and future research directions. *Review of Managerial Science*, *9*(3), 577–601. doi:10.1007/s11846-015-0168-6

Bouncken, R. B., & Kraus, S. (2013). Innovation in knowledge-intensive industries: The double edged sword of coopetition. *Journal of Business Research*, *66*(10), 2060–2070. doi:10.1016/j.jbusres.2013.02.032

Bouncken, R. B., Plüschke, B. D., Pesch, R., & Kraus, S. (2016). Entrepreneurial orientation in vertical alliances: Joint product innovation and learning from allies. *Review of Managerial Science*, *10*(2), 381–409. doi:10.1007/s11846-014-0150-8

Brandenburger, A. M., & Nalebuff, B. J. (1996). *Co-opetition*. New York: Doubleday.

Bransford, J. D., Brown, A. L., & Cocking, R. R. (2000). *How People Learn: Brain, Mind, Experience, and School Committee on Developments in the Science of Learning*. Washington, DC: National Academy Press.

Bremmer, I. (2010). The fourth wave. *Foreign Policy*, *183*, 53–54.

Bretherton, P., & Chaston, I. (2005). Resource dependency and SME strategy: An empirical study. *Journal of Small Business and Enterprise Development*, *12*(2), 274–289. doi:10.1108/14626000510594656

Brettel, M., Chomik, C., & Flatten, T. C. (2015). How organizational culture influences innovativeness, proactiveness, and risk-taking: Fostering entrepreneurial orientation in SMEs. *Journal of Small Business Management*, *53*(4), 868–885. doi:10.1111/jsbm.12108

Bridge, R. (2012). *How to start a business without any money?* Virgin Books.

Brodie, R. J., Glynn, M. S., & Little, V. (2006). The service brand and the service-dominant logic: Missing fundamental premise or the need for stronger theory? *Marketing Theory*, *6*(3), 363–379. doi:10.1177/1470593106066797

Brouthers, K. D., Nakos, G., & Dimitratos, P. (2015). SME entrepreneurial orientation, international performance, and the moderating role of strategic alliances. *Entrepreneurship Theory and Practice*, *39*(5), 1161–1187. doi:10.1111/etap.12101

Buckley, P. G., & Casson, M. C. (2009). The internationalization theory of the multinational enterprise: A review of the progress of a research agenda after 30 years. *Journal of International Business Studies*, *40*(9), 1563–1580. doi:10.1057/jibs.2009.49

Budget 2014: Support for SME plans. (2013, October 26). *The Star Online*. Retrieved from http://www.thestar.com.my/Business/Business-News/2013/10/26/Support-for-SME-plans-Hafsah-says-activities-will-help-to-achieve-goals.aspx/

Bueno, E., Arrien, M., & Rodriguez, O. (2003). Modelo Intellectus: medición y gestión del capital intellectual. Intellectus Model: Model for the measurement and management of intellectual capital. Madrid: CIC-IADE (UAM).

Bughin, J., & Manyika, J. (2016). *Measuring the full impact of digital capital*. Retrieved January, 2016, from http://www.mckinsey.com/industries/high-tech/our-insights/measuring-the-full-impact-of-digital-capital

Bughin, J., Byers, A. H., & Chui, M. (2011). How social technologies are extending the organization. *The McKinsey Quarterly*, *20*(11), 1–10.

Busquets, J., Kohli, R., Navarro, P., & Plana, T. (2012, July). Innovation in Banking Business Models Exploring the Emergent Customer Role in Social Networks. In *2012 Annual SRII Global Conference* (pp. 827-835). IEEE. doi:10.1109/SRII.2012.94

CAI. (2007). Internal Auditors Can Contribute to Corporate Social Responsibility. *Accountancy Ireland*, *39*, 22.

Caiazza, R. (2014). Benchmarking of business incubators. Benchmarking. *International Journal (Toronto, Ont.)*, *21*(6), 1062–1069. Retrieved from http://www.emeraldinsight.com/doi/abs/10.1108/BIJ-01-2013-0011

Calandro, E., Gillwald, A., Deen-Swarray, M., Stork, C., & Esselaar, S. (2012). *Mobile usage at the base of the pyramid in South Africa: An infoDev publication prepared by Research ICT Africa and Intelecon*. Washington, DC: International Bank for Reconstruction and Development / The World Bank.

Calza, F., Dezi, L., Schiavone, F., & Simoni, M. (2014). The intellectual capital of business incubators. *Journal of Intellectual Capital*, *15*(4), 597–610. doi:10.1108/JIC-07-2014-0086

Carney, M., Van Essen, M., Gedajlovic, E., & Heugens, P. (2010). *What do we know about private family firm performance? A meta-analytical review*. Unpublished manuscript.

Carroll, A. B. (1991). The pyramid of corporate social responsibility: Toward the moral management of organizational stakeholders. *Business Horizons*, *34*(4), 39–48. doi:10.1016/0007-6813(91)90005-G

Carroll, A. B. (1999). Corporate social responsibility evolution of a definitional construct. *Business & Society*, *38*(3), 268–295. doi:10.1177/000765039903800303

Carroll, A. B., & Shabana, K. M. (2010). The business case for corporate social responsibility: A review of concepts, research and practice. *International Journal of Management Reviews*, *12*(1), 85–105. doi:10.1111/j.1468-2370.2009.00275.x

Casaló, L. V., Flavián, C., & Guinalíu, M. (2010). Generating trust and satisfaction in e-services: The impact of usability on consumer behavior. *Journal of Relationship Marketing*, *9*(4), 247–263. doi:10.1080/15332667.2010.522487

Casillas, J. C., Moreno, A. M., & Barbero, J. L. (2010). A configurational approach of the relationship between entrepreneurial orientation and growth of family firms. *Family Business Review*, *23*(1), 27–44. doi:10.1177/0894486509345159

Cassiman, B., & Golovko, E. (2011). Innovation and internationalization through exports. *Journal of International Business Studies*, *42*(1), 56–75. doi:10.1057/jibs.2010.36

Cata, T., & Lee, S. M. (2006). Adoption of web-based applications in the financial sector: The case of online insurance. *Journal of Internet Commerce*, *5*(2), 41–61. doi:10.1300/J179v05n02_03

Central Bank of Nigeria. (2005). *CBN Bullion: Micro Finance Policy as a Strategy for Poverty Reduction*. Abuja: CBN.

Centre for Inclusive Banking. (2013). *The microfinance review 2013 - From microfinance to financial inclusion: A review of the South African microfinance sector trends, successes, challenges and policy issues*. Pretoria: University of Pretoria.

Cervantes-Godoy, D., & Dewbre, J. (2010). Economic importance of agriculture for poverty reduction. *OECD Food Agriculture and Fisheries Working Papers, 23*. doi: 10.1787/5kmmv9s20944-en

Cha, H. S. (2012). Factors influencing the adoption of location-based smartphone applications: An application of the privacy calculus model. *Asia Pacific Journal of Information Systems*, *22*(4), 7–29.

Chakravarti, D. (2006). Voices unheard: The psychology of consumption in poverty and development. *Journal of Consumer Psychology*, *16*(4), 363–376. doi:10.1207/s15327663jcp1604_8

Chandra, A. (2009). Business Incubation in the United States, China and Brazil. *International Journal of Entrepreneurship*, *13*, 67–86.

Chang, Y. P., & Zhu, D. H. (2011). Understanding social networking sites adoption in China: A comparison of pre-adoption and post-adoption. *Computers in Human Behavior*, *27*(5), 1840–1848. doi:10.1016/j.chb.2011.04.006

Chang, Y. Y., Hughes, M., & Hotho, S. (2011). Internal and external antecedents of SMEs innovation ambidexterity outcomes. *Management Decision*, *49*(10), 1658–1676. doi:10.1108/00251741111183816

Chan, K. L., Selvadurai, S., & Hamid, B. A. (2009). Malay youth entrepreneurship in Malaysia: An empirical update. *Geografia: Malaysian Journal of Society and Space*, *5*(2), 61–68.

Chartrungruang, B.-o. (2011, 25 May). *The Model of Sufficiency Economy Philosophy Application for Tourism Industry in Chiang Mai, Thailand.* Paper presented at the Sustainability and Quality-of-Life in Tourism: Tasks for Consumers, Industry, Policy and Academia, Chiang Mai, Thailand.

Chaston, I., & Sadler-Smith, E. (2012). Entrepreneurial cognition, entrepreneurial orientation and firm capability in the creative industries. *British Journal of Management*, *23*(3), 415–432.

Che Abdullah, N., & Mustapha, R. (2009). Kajian kes usahawan tani industri kecil sederhana (IKS) bumiputera di Negeri Terengganu. *Jurnal Pendidikan Malaysia*, *34*(2), 143–165.

Chen, C. N., Tzeng, L. C., Ou, W. M., & Chang, K. T. (2007). The relationship among social capital, entrepreneurial orientation, organizational resources and entrepreneurial performance for new ventures. *Contemp. Manage. Res*, *3*(3), 213–232. doi:10.7903/cmr.90

Chen, L., Marsden, J. R., & Zhang, Z. (2012). Theory and Analysis of Company-Sponsored Value Co-Creation. *Journal of Management Information Systems*, *29*(2), 141–172. doi:10.2753/MIS0742-1222290206

Chen, M. H., Chang, Y. Y., & Chang, Y. C. (2015). Entrepreneurial orientation, social networks, and creative performance: Middle managers as corporate entrepreneurs. *Creativity and Innovation Management*, *24*(3), 493–507. doi:10.1111/caim.12108

Child, J., & Hsieh, L. H. Y. (2014). Decision mode, information and network attachment in the internationalization of SMEs: A configurational and contingency analysis. *Journal of World Business*, *49*(4), 598–610. doi:10.1016/j.jwb.2013.12.012

Chin, W. W. (1998). The partial least squares approach to structural equation modeling. *Modern Methods for Business Research, 295*(2), 295-336.

Chin, K. S., Chan, B. L., & Lam, P. K. (2008). Identifying and prioritizing critical success factors for coopetition strategy. *Industrial Management & Data Systems*, *108*(4), 437–454. doi:10.1108/02635570810868326

Chirico, F., Sirmon, D. G., Sciascia, S., & Mazzola, P. (2011). Resource orchestration in family firms: Investigating how entrepreneurial orientation, generational involvement, and participative strategy affect performance. *Strategic Entrepreneurship Journal*, *5*(4), 307–326. doi:10.1002/sej.121

Chiu, S.-K., & Lee, Y.-I. (2007). Strategic resources, network competence, and sustainable competitive advantages - An empirical study on Taiwan led firms. *International Journal of Electronic Business Management*, *5*(1), 70–78.

Choudhury, T. A., & Raihan, A. (2000). *Structural Adjustment Participatory Review Initiative, Bangladesh Study Theme 2(C): Implications of Financial Sector Reforms*. Retrieved from http://saprin.org/bangladesh/research/ban_finance.pdf

Chowdhury, M. S. (2007). Overcoming entrepreneurship development constraints: The case of Bangladesh. *Journal of Enterprising Communities: People and Places in the Global Economy*, *1*(3), 240–251. doi:10.1108/17506200710779549

Chowdhury, M. S. A., Azam, M. K. G., & Islam, S. (2015). Problems and Prospects of SME Financing in Bangladesh. *Asian Business Review*, *2*(2), 51–58. doi:10.18034/abr.v2i2.304

Chow, E., Voon, S., Lim, S., Yong, Y., & Dimyati, N. I. (2014). Higher growth, less spending power. *Personal Money*, *160*, 32–47.

Ciliberti, F., Pontrandolfo, P., & Scozzi, B. (2008). Investigating corporate social responsibility in supply chains: A SME perspective. *Journal of Cleaner Production*, *16*(15), 1579–1588. doi:10.1016/j.jclepro.2008.04.016

Ciravegna, L. (2011). Social ties and technological learning in new Silicon Valley clones. *The Journal of Development Studies*, *47*(8), 1178–1198. doi:10.1080/00220388.2010.547935

Ciravegna, L., Lopez, L., & Kundu, S. (2014). Country of origin and network effects on internationalization: A comparative study of SMEs from an emerging and developed economy. *Journal of Business Research*, *67*(5), 916–923. doi:10.1016/j.jbusres.2013.07.011

Clements-Hunt, P. (2007). *Innovative Financing for Sustainable Small and Medium Enterprises in Africa, International Workshop*. Geneva, Switzerland: Meeting Report, A forward, United Nation Environment Programme.

Cohen, J. (1988). *Standard power analysis for the behavioral sciences*. Hillsdale, NJ: Erlbaum.

Coleman, J. S. (1988). Social capital in the creation of human capital. *American Journal of Sociology*, *94*, S95–S120. doi:10.1086/228943

Colombelli, A. (2010). Alternative investment market: A way to promote entrepreneurship. *Journal of Industry, Competition and Trade*, *10*(3), 253–274. doi:10.1007/s10842-010-0079-9

Commission for Africa (CfA). (2005). *Our Common Interest. Report of the Commission for Africa*. London: Commission for Africa Secretariat.

Constantinides, E., Romero, C. L., & Boria, M. A. G. (2009). Social media: a new frontier for retailers? In *European Retail Research* (pp. 1–28). Gabler Verlag.

Cook, P. (2001). Finance and small and medium-sized enterprise in developing countries. *Journal of Developmental Entrepreneurship*, *6*(1), 17.

Cooper, D. R., & Schindler, P. S. (2008). *Business research methods* (10th ed.). New York: McGraw-Hill Irwin.

Costello, A. B., & Osborne, J. W. (2005). Best Practices in Exploratory Factor Analysis: Four Recommendations for Getting the Most From Your Analysis. *Practical Assessment, Research & Evaluation*, *10*(7), 1–9.

Coviello, N. E. (2006). The network dynamics of international new ventures. *Journal of International Business Studies*, *37*(5), 713–731. doi:10.1057/palgrave.jibs.8400219

Coviello, N. E., & Cox, M. P. (2006). The resource dynamics of international new venture networks. *Journal of International Entrepreneurship*, *4*(2/3), 113–132. doi:10.1007/s10843-007-0004-4

Covin, J., & Slevin, D. (1991). A conceptual model of entrepreneurship as firm behavior. *Entrepreneurship Theory and Practice*. Retrieved from http://papers.ssrn.com/sol3/papers.cfm?abstract_id=1504448

Covin, J. G., Green, K. M., & Slevin, D. P. (2006). Strategic process effects on the entrepreneurial orientation-sales growth rate relationship. *Entrepreneurship Theory and Practice*, *30*(1), 57–81. doi:10.1111/j.1540-6520.2006.00110.x

Covin, J. G., & Slevin, D. P. (1989). *Empirical relationship among strategic posture environmental context variables, and new venture performance, Frontiers Entrepreneurship Research*. Wellesley, MA: Babson College.

Creswell, J., & Clark, V. (2011). *Designing and Conducting Mixed Methods Research* (2nd ed.). Sage Publications Inc.

Crisp, R. (2008). Well being. In E. N. Zalta (Ed.), The Stanford Encyclopedia of Philosophy (Winter ed.). Stanford University Press.

Crook, T. R., Todd, S. Y., Combs, J. G., Woehr, D. J., & Ketchen, D. J. Jr. (2011). Does human capital matter? A meta-analysis of the relationship between human capital and firm performance. *The Journal of Applied Psychology*, *96*(3), 443–456. doi:10.1037/a0022147 PMID:21244126

Croteau, A., & Bergeron, F. (2001). An information technology triology: Business strategy, technological deployment and organisational performance. *The Journal of Strategic Information Systems*, *10*(2), 77–99. doi:10.1016/S0963-8687(01)00044-0

Crowther, D., & Aras, G. (2008). *Corporate social responsibility*. Bookboon.

Cruz, C., & Nordqvist, M. (2012). Entrepreneurial orientation in family firms: A generational perspective. *Small Business Economics*, *38*(1), 33–49. doi:10.1007/s11187-010-9265-8

Cuong, N. (2007). Donor Coordination in SME Development in Vietnam: What Has Been Done and How Can It Be Strengthened? *Vietnam Economic Management Review*. Retrieved from https://www.vjol.info/index.php/VEMR/article/viewArticle/585

Cuong, T., Sang, L., & Anh, N. (2007). Vietnam's small-and medium-sized enterprises development: characteristics, constraints and policy recommendations. *SME in Asia and Globalization, ERIA ....* Retrieved from http://www.vnep.org.vn/Upload/Vietnam%E2%80%99sSmallandMediumSizedEnterprisesDevelopment_Characteristics,ConstraintsandPolicyRecommendations_Sang_KimAnh.PDF

Curran, J., Jarvis, R., Blackburn, R. A., & Black, S. (1993). Networks and small firms: Constructs, methodological strategies and some findings. *International Small Business Journal*, *11*(2), 13–25. doi:10.1177/026624269301100202

Cygler, J., & Dębkowska, K. (2015). Coopetition Effect Determinants: Competitors size, geographical scope, market and technological positions. *Organizacija*, *48*(4), 219–231. doi:10.1515/orga-2015-0019

Czakon, W., Mucha-Kus, K., & Rogalski, M. (2014). Coopetition research landscape-a systematic literature review 1997-2010. *Journal of Economics & Management*, *17*, 121.

D'Silva, J. L., Mohamad Shaffril, H. A., Uli, J., & Abu Samah, B. (2009). A review of contract farming and factors that impinge youth's acceptance to contract farming. *European Journal of Soil Science*, *11*(2), 328–338.

Dagnino, G. B., & Padula, G. (2002). *Coopetition strategy: a new kind of interfirm dynamics for value creation*. Paper Presented at 2ème Conference EURAM, Stockholm, Sweden.

Dahan, N. M., Doh, J. P., Oetzel, J., & Yaziji, M. (2010). Corporate-NGO collaboration: Co-creating new business models for developing markets. *Long Range Planning*, *43*(2), 326–342. doi:10.1016/j.lrp.2009.11.003

Dahlsrud, A. (2008). How corporate social responsibility is defined: An analysis of 37 definitions. *Corporate Social Responsibility and Environmental Management*, *15*(1), 1–13. doi:10.1002/csr.132

Dahya, J., Lonie, A. A., & Power, D. M. (1998). Ownership structure, firm performance and top executive change: An analysis of UK firms. *Journal of Business Finance & Accounting*, *25*(9), 1089–1118. doi:10.1111/1468-5957.00228

Damanpour, F. (1991). Organizational innovation: A meta-analysis of effects of determinants and moderators. *Academy of Management Journal*, *34*(3), 555–590. doi:10.2307/256406

Dana, L. P., Granata, J., Lasch, F., & Carnaby, A. (2013). The evolution of co-opetition in the Waipara wine cluster of New Zealand. *Wine Economics and Policy*, *2*(1), 42–49. doi:10.1016/j.wep.2013.05.001

Daniel, E. (2000). The provision of electronic banking services in the UK and Scandinavia. *Journal of Financial Services Marketing*, *4*(4), 319–330.

Davey, T., Plewa, C., & Struwig, M. (2011). Entrepreneurship perceptions and career intentions of international students. *Education+ Training, 53*(5), 335-352.

Davidsson, P. (1989). *Continued entrepreneurship and small firm growth*. Stockholm: School of Economics Stockholm.

Davis, P. (2011). *Escaping poverty: Patterns and causes of poverty exits in rural Bangladesh* (978-1-906433-66-6). Retrieved from UK: http://www.environmentportal.in/files/Escaping%20poverty.pdf

De Bruin, A., & McLaren, E. (2002). An Exploration of Networks of the Self-Employed. In *Proceedings of the 15th Conference of the Small Enterprise Association of Australia and New Zealand.* Adelaide, South Australia: SEAANZ.

de Clercq, D., Dimov, D., & Thongpapanl, N. (2013). Organizational social capital, formalization, and internal knowledge sharing in entrepreneurial orientation formation. *Entrepreneurship Theory and Practice*, *37*(3), 505–537. doi:10.1111/etap.12021

De Jong, J., & Wennekers, S. (2008). *Intrapreneurship; conceptualizing entrepreneurial employee behaviour*. Research Report H200802. Zoetermeer: EIM.

Deci, E. L., & Ryan, R. M. (1991). A motivational approach to self: Integration in personality. In R. Dienstbier (Ed.), *Nebraska Symposium on Motivation:* Vol. 38, *Perspectives on motivation* (pp. 237-288). Lincoln, NE: University of Nebraska Press.

Dee, N. J., Livesey, F., Gill, D., & Minshall, T. (2011). Incubation for Growth, A review of the impact of business incubation on new ventures with high growth potential. *Research Summary*, (September), 1–53. Retrieved from www.nesta.org.uk

Denan, Z., Ismail, N., & Ishak, N. A. (2009). The Impact of Environmental Dynamism on Knowledge Absorptive Capacity-Innovation Performance Relationship Amongst Manufacturing SMEs in Malaysia. *Social and Management Research Journal*, *6*(1), 63–85.

Denicolai, S., Hagen, B., & Pisoni, A. (2015). Be international or be innovative? Be both? The role of the entrepreneurial profile. *Journal of International Entrepreneurship*, *13*(4), 390–417. doi:10.1007/s10843-015-0143-y

Dennis, C., King, T., & Martenson, R. (2007). Corporate brand image, satisfaction and store loyalty: A study of the store as a brand, store brands and manufacturer brands. *International Journal of Retail & Distribution Management*, *35*(7), 544–555. doi:10.1108/09590550710755921

Department of Statistic Malaysia. (2011). Economic Census 2011: Profile of SMEs. Author.

Derham, R., Cragg, P., & Morrish, S. (2011, July). Creating Value: An SME And Social Media. In PACIS (p. 53). Academic Press.

Deshpande, R., & Webster, F. E. Jr. (1989). Organizational culture and marketing: Defining the research agenda. *Journal of Marketing*, *53*(1), 3–15. doi:10.2307/1251521

Desouza, K. C., & Awazu, Y. (2006). Knowledge management at SMEs: Five peculiarities. *Journal of Knowledge Management*, *10*(1), 32–43. doi:10.1108/13673270610650085

Dess, G. G., Lumpkin, G. T., & Covin, J. G. (1998). Entrepreneurial strategy making and firm performance: Tests of contingency and configurational models. *Strategic Management Journal*, *18*(9), 677–695. doi:10.1002/(SICI)1097-0266(199710)18:9<677::AID-SMJ905>3.0.CO;2-Q

Dess, G. G., & Robinson, R. B. (2006). Measuring organizational performance in the absence of objective measures: The case of the privately-held firm and conglomerate business unit. *Strategic Management Journal*, *5*(3), 265–273. doi:10.1002/smj.4250050306

Devi, S., & Samujh, H. (2010). *Accountants as Providers of Support and Advice to SMEs in Malaysia (No. 118).* The Association of Chartered Certified Accountants.

Dewan, A. M., & Nazmin, S. A. (2008). The opportunities and barriers of using ICT by small and medium enterprises in Bangladesh: Case of SMEs in BSCIC industrial estates. In *Proceedings of the International Conference on Computer and Communication Engineering* (vol. 1, pp. 656–661). Kuala Lumpur, MY: International Islamic University Malaysia.

Dhliwayo, S. (2008). Experiential learning in entrepreneurship education: A prospective model for South African tertiary institutions. *Education+ Training, 50*(4), 329-340.

Di Gregorio, D., Musteen, M., & Thomas, D. E. (2008). Offshore outsourcing of international competitiveness for SMEs. *Journal of International Business Studies*, *40*(6), 969–988. doi:10.1057/jibs.2008.90

Diao, X., Hazell, P., Resnick, D., & Thurlow, J. (2007). The Role of agriculture in development: Implications for Sub-Saharan Africa. Washington, DC: International Food Policy Research Institute. Retrieved from http://www.ifpri.org/sites/default/files/pubs/pubs/abstract/153/rr153.pdf

Dibrell, C., Craig, J. B., & Neubaum, D. O. (2014). Linking the formal strategic planning process, planning flexibility, and innovativeness to firm performance. *Journal of Business Research*, *67*(9), 2000–2007. doi:10.1016/j.jbusres.2013.10.011

Dickson, P. H., & Weaver, K. M. (2008). The role of the institutional environment in determining firm orientations towards entrepreneurial behavior. *The International Entrepreneurship and Management Journal*, *4*(4), 467–483. doi:10.1007/s11365-008-0088-x

Diener, E. (2009). Subjective well-being. In E. Diener (Ed.), *The science of well-being* (Vol. 37, pp. 11–58). New York: Springer. doi:10.1007/978-90-481-2350-6_2

Díez, J. M., Ochoa, M. L., Prieto, B., & Santidrián, A. (2010). Intellectual capital and value creation in Spanish firms. *Journal of Intellectual Capital*, *11*(3), 348–367. doi:10.1108/14691931011064581

Ding, S., Guariglia, A., & Knight, J. (2013). Investment and financing constraints in China: Does working capital management make a difference? *Journal of Banking & Finance*, *37*(5), 1490–1507. doi:10.1016/j.jbankfin.2012.03.025

Dobni, C. B. (2008). Measuring innovation culture in organizations: The development of a generalized innovation culture construct using exploratory factor analysis. *European Journal of Innovation Management*, *11*(4), 539–559. doi:10.1108/14601060810911156

Dobni, D., & Zinkhan, G. M. (1990). In search of brand image: A foundation analysis. *Advances in Consumer Research. Association for Consumer Research (U. S.)*, *17*, 110–119.

Dolan, P., & Metcalfe, R. (2012). The relationship between innovation and subjective wellbeing. *Research Policy*, *41*(8), 1489–1498. doi:10.1016/j.respol.2012.04.001

Dorenbosch, L., Engen, M. L., & Verhagen, M. (2005). On the job Innovation: The Impact of Job Design and Human Resource Management through Production Ownership. *Creativity and Innovation Management*, *14*(2), 129–141. doi:10.1111/j.1476-8691.2005.00333.x

Drazin, R., & Schoonhoven, C. B. (1996). Community, population, and organization effects on innovation: A multilevel perspective. *Academy of Management Journal*, *39*(5), 1065–1083. doi:10.2307/256992

DSilva, J. L., Mohamad Shaffril, H. A., Uli, J., & Abu Samah, B. (2010). Socio-demography factors that influence youth attitude towards contract farming. *American Journal of Applied Sciences*, *7*(4), 603–608. doi:10.3844/ajassp.2010.603.608

Duréndez, A., Madrid-Guijarro, A., & García-Pérez-de-Lema, D. (2011). Innovative culture, management control systems and performance in small and medium-sized Spanish family firms. *Innovar*, *21*(40), 137–154.

Durodoye, K. K. (2005). Strategic planning of information systems: Research concepts and framework. In M. A. Tiamiyu (Ed.), *Information Science concepts, models and application*. University of Ibadan.

Dutot, V., Bergeron, F., & Raymond, L. (2014). Information management for the internationalization of SMEs: An exploratory study based on a strategic alignment perspective. *International Journal of Information Management*, *34*(5), 672–681. doi:10.1016/j.ijinfomgt.2014.06.006

Economist. (2015). Hot and Bothered. *The Economist*.

Edinburgh Group. (2013). *Growing the global economy through SMEs*. Retrieved May 21, 2015, from http://www.edinburgh-group.org/media/2776/edinburgh_group_research_growing_the_global_ economy_through_smes.pdf

Eggers, F., Hansen, D. J., & Davis, A. E. (2012). Examining the relationship between customer and entrepreneurial orientation on nascent firms' marketing strategy. *The International Entrepreneurship and Management Journal*, *8*(2), 203–222. doi:10.1007/s11365-011-0173-4

Eikebrokk, T. R., & Olsen, D. H. (2005, January). Co-opetition and e-business success in SMEs: An empirical investigation of European SMEs. In *Proceedings of 38th Annual Hawaii International Conference on System Sciences*. IEEE.

Ekong, E. (2003). *An Introduction to Rural Sociology*. Dove Educational Publishers.

Ekpenyong, D. B., & Nyong, M. O. (1992). *Small and Medium Scale Enterprise in Nigeria: Their characteristics, problems and sources of finance*. African Economic Research Consortium, Nairobi, Kenya.

Eleventh Malaysia Plan 2016-2020. (n.d.). T*he Economic Planning Unit, Prime Minister's Department*. Kuala Lumpur: EPU Retrieved from http:www. rmk11.epu.gov.my/index.php/en/

Ellis, P. D. (2010). Social ties and international entrepreneurship: Opportunities and constraints affecting firm internationalization. *Journal of International Business Studies*, *42*(1), 99–127. doi:10.1057/jibs.2010.20

eMarketer. (2014). *Smartphone Users Worldwide Will Total 1.75 Billion in 2014*. Retrieved February 5, 2015, from http://www.emarketer.com/Article/Smartphone-Users-Worldwide-Will-Total-175-Billion-2014/1010536#sthash.dwESSnqk.dpuf

Emmanuel, O. O., & Daniya, A. A. (2012). Development of small and medium Scale enterprises: The role of government and other financial institutions. *Arabian Journal of Business and Management Review*, *1*(7), 16–29.

Engelen, A., Flatten, T. C., Thalmann, J., & Brettel, M. (2014). The effect of organizational culture on entrepreneurial orientation: A comparison between Germany and Thailand. *Journal of Small Business Management*, *52*(4), 732–752. doi:10.1111/jsbm.12052

EPU. (2015). *The Malaysian Economy in Figures (EPU)*. Retrieved July 25, 2016, from http://www.epu.gov.my

ERIA. (2014). *ASEAN SME Policy Report 2014*. Retrieved from http://www.eria.org/RPR-FY2012-8.pdf

Esch, F.-R., Langner, T., Schmitt, B. H., & Geus, P. (2006). Are brands forever? How brand knowledge and relationships affect current and future purchases. *Journal of Product and Brand Management*, *15*(2), 98–105. doi:10.1108/10610420610658938

Esfahani, M. D., Azizah Abdul, R., & Nor Hidayati, Z. (2015). *Influence process for practicing green information technology: Elaboration likelihood model*. Paper presented at the Pacific Asia Conference on Information Systems.

Esfahani, M. D., Rahman, A. A., & Zakaria, N. H. (2014). The status quo and the prospect of green IT and green IS: A systematic literature review. *Journal of Soft Computing and Decision Support Systems*, *1*(1).

ETP Annual Report. (2014). *Narrowing siparity*. Retrieved From July 25, 2016, from http://etp.pemandu.gov.my/annualreport2011

European Commission. (2002). Final report: Benchmarking of Business Incubators. *Personnel*, *51*(February), 47. doi:10.1086/656690

European Commission. (2005). *The new SME definition: User guide and model declaration*. Brussels: European Commission.

European Commission. (2010). *European Commission Enterprise and Industry – Access to Finance*. Retrieved from http://ec.eu/enterprise/policies/finance/data/index-en.thm

European Union. (2014). *Policy and Practice*. EU.

Evans, N., & Sawyer, J. (2010). CSR and stakeholders of small businesses in regional South Australia. *Social Responsibility Journal*, *6*(3), 433–451. doi:10.1108/17471111011064799

Evans, P., & Wolf, B. (2005). Collaboration rules. *IEEE Engineering Management Review*, *33*(4), 50–57. doi:10.1109/EMR.2005.27015 PMID:16028820

Ex-Im Bank of Thailand. SMEs' Analysis. (2012). Retrieved July 6, 2012, from http://www.exim.go.th/doc/newsCenter/38795.pdf

Farooquie, P., Gani, A., Zuberi, A. K., & Hashmi, I. (2012). An empirical study of innovation-performance linkage in the paper industry. *Journal of Industrial Engineering International*, *8*(23), 1–6.

Fassin, Y. (2008). SMEs and the fallacy of formalising CSR. *Business Ethics (Oxford, England)*, *17*(4), 364–378. doi:10.1111/j.1467-8608.2008.00540.x

Faucheux, S., & Nicolaï, I. (2011). IT for green and green IT: A proposed typology of eco-innovation. *Ecological Economics*, *70*(11), 2020–2027. doi:10.1016/j.ecolecon.2011.05.019

Federal Ministry of Agriculture and Natural Resources. (1997). Nigeria: National Agricultural Research Strategy Plan 1996-2010. Department of Agricultural Sciences, Federal Ministry of Agriculture and Natural Resources, Federal Republic of Nigeria, Nigeria.

Felício, J. A., Caldeirinha, V. R., & Ribeiro-Navarrete, B. (2015). Corporate and individual global mind-set and internationalization of European SMEs. *Journal of Business Research*, *68*(4), 797–802. doi:10.1016/j.jbusres.2014.11.031

Felzensztein, C., Ciravegna, L., Robson, P., & Amorós, J. E. (2015). Networks, entrepreneurial orientation, and internationalization scope: Evidence from Chilean small and medium enterprises. *Journal of Small Business Management*, *53*(Suppl. 1), 145–160. doi:10.1111/jsbm.12188

Fernandez, A. S., Le Roy, F., & Gnyawali, D. R. (2014). Sources and management of tension in co-opetition case evidence from telecommunications satellites manufacturing in Europe. *Industrial Marketing Management*, *43*(2), 222–235. doi:10.1016/j.indmarman.2013.11.004

Fernández-Pérez, V., Alonso-Galicia, P. E., del Mar Fuentes-Fuentes, M., & Rodriguez-Ariza, L. (2014). Business social networks and academics entrepreneurial intentions. *Industrial Management & Data Systems*, *114*(2), 292–320. doi:10.1108/IMDS-02-2013-0076

Fini, R., Grimaldi, R., Marzocchi, G. L., & Sobrero, M. (2012). The determinants of corporate entrepreneurial intention within small and newly established firms. *Entrepreneurship Theory and Practice*, *36*(2), 387–414. doi:10.1111/j.1540-6520.2010.00411.x

Fink, A. (1995). *How to analyze survey data* (Vol. 8). Sage.

Fischer, E. M., Reuber, R. A., & Dyke, L. S. (1993). A theoretical overview and extension of research on sex, gender, and entrepreneurship. *Journal of Business Venturing*, *8*(2), 151–168. doi:10.1016/0883-9026(93)90017-Y

Fishbein, M., Ajzen, I. (1975). *Belief, attitude, intention and behavior: An introduction to theory and research*. Academic Press.

Fletcher, D. (2004). International entrepreneurship and small business. *Entrepreneurship & Regional Development*, *16*(4), 289–305. doi:10.1080/0898562042000263267

Florin, J., Karri, R., & Rossiter, N. (2007). Fostering entrepreneurial drive in business education: An attitudinal approach. *Journal of Management Education*, *31*(1), 17–42. doi:10.1177/1052562905282023

Floro, S., & Yotopoulos, P. (1991). *Informal Credit Markets and the New Institutional Economics: The Case of Philippine Agriculture*. Boulder, CO: Westview Press.

Foo, C.-T., & Foo, C.-T. (2000). Socialization of technopreneurism: Towards symbiosis in corporate innovation and technology strategy. *Technovation*, *20*(10), 551–562. doi:10.1016/S0166-4972(99)00171-6

Food and Agricultural Organisation. (2006). *Better Forestry, less poverty. A practitioners guide*. Rome: FAO.

Food and Agriculture Organization of the United Nations. (2009). *How to feed the world in 2050*. Retrieved from http://www.fao.org/fileadmin/templates/wsfs/docs/expert_paper/How_to_Feed_the_World_in_2050.pdf

Fornell, C., & Larcker, D. F. (1981). Evaluating structural equation models with unobservable variables and measurement error. *JMR, Journal of Marketing Research*, *18*(1), 39–50. doi:10.2307/3151312

Francis, D., & Bessant, J. (2005). Targeting innovation and implications for capability development. *Technovation*, *25*(3), 171–183. doi:10.1016/j.technovation.2004.03.004

Fransen, L., & Merk, J. (2007). *The CSR firm Emergence of service firms in the private regulation of Corporate Responsibility standards*. University of Amsterdam.

Fraser, B. W. (2005). Corporate Social Responsibility. *Internal Auditor*, *62*, 42–47.

Freeman, S., Hutchings, K., Lazaris, M., & Zyngier, S. (2010). A model of rapid knowledge development: The smaller born-global firm. *International Business Review*, *19*(1), 70–84. doi:10.1016/j.ibusrev.2009.09.004

Frese, M., Brantjes, A., & Hoorn, R. (2002). Psychological success factors of small scale businesses in Namibia: The roles of strategy process, entrepreneurial orientation and the environment. *Journal of Developmental Entrepreneurship*, *7*(3), 259–282.

Gabrielsson, J., & Huse, M. (2005). Directors in SME Boards: A Call for Theoretical Reflections. *Corporate Board: Role, Duties & Composition*, *1*(1), 28-37.

Gagne, M., & Deci, E. L. (2005). Self determination theory and work motivation. *Journal of Organizational Behavior*, *26*(4), 331–362. doi:10.1002/job.322

Galbraith, J. R. (1982). Designing the innovating organization. *Organizational Dynamics*, *11*(1), 5–25. doi:10.1016/0090-2616(82)90033-X PMID:10256769

Galbreath, J. (2010). How does corporate social responsibility benefit firms? Evidence from Australia. *European Business Review*, *22*(4), 411–431. doi:10.1108/09555341011056186

Garcia, F., Avella, L., & Fernandez, E. (2012). Learning from exporting: The moderating effect of technological capabilities. *International Business Review*, *21*(6), 1099–1111. doi:10.1016/j.ibusrev.2011.12.001

Gargiulo, M., & Benassi, M. (2000). Trapped in your own net? Network cohesion, structural holes, and the adaptation of social capital. *Organization Science*, *11*(2), 183–196. doi:10.1287/orsc.11.2.183.12514

Gartlan, J., & Shanks, G. (2007). The alignment of business and information technology strategy in Australia. *Australasian Journal of Information Systems*, *14*(2), 113–139. doi:10.3127/ajis.v14i2.184

Gartner. (2007). *Gartner estimates ICT industry accounts for 2 per cent of global CO2 Emissions*. Retrieved on February 2016, from http://www.gartner.com/newsroom/id/503867

Gaskill, L., & Van Auken, H. (1993). A factor analytic study of the perceived causes of small business failure. *Journal of Small*. Retrieved from http://search.proquest.com/openview/15dfb888bd4ed0640f72ce9860d114cc/1?pq-origsite=gscholar

Gassmann, O., & Keupp, M. M. (2007). The competitive advantage of early and rapidly internationalising SMEs in the biotechnology industry: A knowledge-based view. *Journal of World Business*, *42*(3), 350–366. doi:10.1016/j.jwb.2007.04.006

General Economics Division Bangladesh. (2010). *Making vision 2021 a reality*. Dhaka: Government of Bangladesh.

Geva, A. (2008). Three Models of Corporate Social Responsibility: Interrelationships between Theory, Research, and Practice. *Business and Society Review*, *113*(1), 1–41. doi:10.1111/j.1467-8594.2008.00311.x

Geyzel, M. V. (2009). Working with generation. Retrieved from http//vangeyzel.com/2009/08/20working-with-gen-y/

Ghazali, Z., Ibrahim, N. A., & Zainol, F. A. (2012). Factors affecting entrepreneurial intention among UniSZA students. *Asian Social Science*, *9*(1), 85–93. doi:10.5539/ass.v9n1p85

Ghazi, A. (2006). Growing a Vibrant ICT Incubator Industry In Malaysia. Academic Press.

Gholami, R., Sulaiman, A. B., Ramayah, T., & Molla, A. (2013). Senior managers perception on green information systems (IS) adoption and environmental performance: Results from a field survey. *Information & Management*, *50*(7), 431–438. doi:10.1016/j.im.2013.01.004

Gibb, A. (2005). The Entrepreneur as the Core Competence of the Firm: Implications for Management Educators. *Entrepreneurship, Innovation and Small Business Network*, (2), 2.

Gill, G. S., & Cosserat, G. W. P. (1996). *Modern Auditing in Australia*. Wiley.

Gillwald, A., Moyo, M., & Stork, C. (2012). *What is happening in ICT in South Africa: A supply-and demand-side analysis of the ICT sector*. Evidence for ICT Policy Action, Policy Paper 7.

Gilmore, A., Carson, D., O'Donnell, A., & Cummins, D. (1999). Added value: A qualitative assessment of SME marketing. *Irish Marketing Review*, *12*(1), 27.

Gilroy, K. (2013). *The link fostering cultural of innovation and plugging the SME skills gap*. Retrieved February 14, 2016, from http: www.blogs.sap.com

Global Entrepreneurship Monitor. (2011). *Entrepreneurs and Entrepreneurial Employees Across the Globe*. Author.

Gnyawali, D. R., He, J., & Madhavan, R. (2008). Co-opetition: Promises and Challenges. In C. Wankel (Ed.), 21st Century Management (pp. 386–398). Thousand Oaks, CA: Sage.

Gnyawali, D. R., Madhavan, R. M., He, J., & Bengtsson, M. (2012). *Contradictions, dualities and tensions in cooperation and competition: A capability based framework.Annual Meeting of the Academy of Management*, Boston, MA

Gnyawali, D. R., & Park, B. J. R. (2009). Co-opetition and technological innovation in small and medium-sized enterprises: A multilevel conceptual model. *Journal of Small Business Management*, *47*(3), 308–330. doi:10.1111/j.1540-627X.2009.00273.x

Goldman Sachs Investment Bank. (2007). *Beyond the BRICS: A Look at the Next 11*. Author.

Golovko, E., & Valentini, G. (2011). Exploring the complementarity between innovation and export for SMEs' growth. *Journal of International Business Studies*, *42*(3), 362–380. doi:10.1057/jibs.2011.2

Gomes-Casseres, B. (1997). *The alliance revolution: The new shape of business rivalry*. Boston, MA: Harvard University Press.

Gopal, K., & Mohd Sulaiman, S. (2013). *Circular on new definition of Small and Medium Enterprises (SMEs)*. Academic Press.

Gopi, M., & Ramayah, T. (2007). Applicability of theory of planned behavior in predicting intention to trade online: Some evidence from a developing country. *International Journal of Emerging Markets*, *2*(4), 348–360. doi:10.1108/17468800710824509

Goverment, V. (2009). *Prime Minister's Decision No 131/2009/QD-TTg of January 2009*. Retrieved from http://thuvienphapluat.vn/van-ban/Tien-te-Ngan-hang/Quyet-dinh-131-QD-TTg-ho-tro-lai-suat-cho-cac-to-chuc-ca-nhan-vay-von-ngan-hang-de-san-xuat-kinh-doanh-84345.aspx

Grant, R. M., & Baden-Fuller, C. (2004). A knowledge accessing theory of strategic alliances. *Journal of Management Studies*, *41*(1), 61–84. doi:10.1111/j.1467-6486.2004.00421.x

Greene, F., & Mole, K. (2006). Defining and measuring the small business. In S. Carter & D. Jones-Evans (Eds.), *Enterprise and small business: Principles, practice and policy* (pp. 7–29). Harlow, UK: Financial Times/Prentice Hall.

Griffin, A., & Page, A. L. (1993). An interim report on measuring product development success and failure. *Journal of Product Innovation Management*, *10*(4), 291–308. doi:10.1016/0737-6782(93)90072-X

Grimmer, L., Miles, M. P., & Grimmer, M. (2015). A research note on the effect of entrepreneurial orientation on small retailer performance: A resource-advantage perspective. *The International Entrepreneurship and Management Journal*, *11*(2), 409–424. doi:10.1007/s11365-013-0279-y

Grönroos, C. (2011). Value co-creation in service logic: A critical analysis. *Marketing Theory*, *11*(3), 279–301. doi:10.1177/1470593111408177

Gronum, S., Verreynne, M. L., & Kastelle, T. (2012). The role of nctworks in small and medium-sized enterprise innovation and firm performance. *Journal of Small Business Management*, *50*(2), 257–282. doi:10.1111/j.1540-627X.2012.00353.x

Grossman, M., McCarthy, R. V., & Aronson, J. E. (2004). E-commerce adoption in the insurance industry. *Issues in Information Systems*, *5*(2), 467–473.

Grundling, I., & Kaseke, T. (2010). *FinScope South Africa small business survey 2010*. Retrieved May 2015, from http://www.finmark.org.za/wp-content/uploads/2016/01/FS-Small-Business_-reportFNL2.pdf

GSMA Intelligence. (2014). *The Mobile Economy: Sub-Saharan Africa 2014*. Retrieved April 20, 2014, from http://www.gsmamobileeconomyafrica.com/GSMA_ME_SubSaharanAfrica_Web_Singles.pdf

Gumbi, L. N., & Mnkandla, E. (2015). Investigating South African vendors' cloud computing value proposition to small, medium and micro enterprises : A case of the city of Tshwane Metropolitan Municipality. *The African Journal of Information Systems*, *7*(4), 1–16.

Gunto, M., & Alias, M. H. (2013). SMEs Development in Malaysia: Lessons For Libya. *Persidangan Kebangsaan Ekonomi Malaysia Ke VIII (PERKEM). VIII, JILID, 3*, 1521–1530.

Guo, H., Tang, J., & Su, Z. (2014). To be different, or to be the same? The interactive effect of organizational regulatory legitimacy and entrepreneurial orientation on new venture performance. *Asia Pacific Journal of Management, 31*(3), 665–685. doi:10.1007/s10490-013-9361-9

Gupta, J., Wilson, N., Gregoriou, A., & Healy, J. (2014). The effect of internationalisation on modelling credit risk for SMEs: Evidence from UK market. *Journal of International Financial Markets, Institutions and Money, 31*, 397–413. doi:10.1016/j.intfin.2014.05.001

Gupta, V. K., & Gupta, A. (2015). Relationship between entrepreneurial orientation and firm performance in large organizations over time. *International Journal of International Entrepreneurship, 13*(1), 7–27. doi:10.1007/s10843-014-0138-0

Gutiérrez, L. G., & Pérez, V. F. (2010). Managerial networks and strategic flexibility: A QM perspective. *Industrial Management & Data Systems, 110*(8), 1192–1214. doi:10.1108/02635571011077834

Hacioglu, G., Eren, S. S., Eren, M. S., & Celikkan, H. (2012). The effect of entrepreneurial marketing on firms innovative performance in Turkish *SMEs. Procedia: Social and Behavioral Sciences, 58*, 871–878. doi:10.1016/j.sbspro.2012.09.1065

Hackett, S. M., & Dilts, D. M. (2004). A Systematic Review of Business Incubation Research. *The Journal of Technology Transfer, 29*(1), 55–82. doi:10.1023/B:JOTT.0000011181.11952.0f

Hackett, S. M., & Dilts, D. M. (2008). Inside the black box of business incubation: Study B - Scale assessment, model refinement, and incubation outcomes. *The Journal of Technology Transfer, 33*(5), 439–471. doi:10.1007/s10961-007-9056-9

Haenlein, M., & Kaplan, A. M. (2004). A beginners guide to partial least squares analysis. *Understanding Statistics, 3*(4), 283–297. doi:10.1207/s15328031us0304_4

Haenlein, M., & Kaplan, A. M. (2010). An empirical analysis of attitudinal and behavioral reactions toward the abandonment of unprofitable customer relationships. *Journal of Relationship Marketing, 9*(4), 200–228. doi:10.1080/15332667.2010.522474

Hafiz, M. (2013, July 11). Company fined RM30,000 for illegal earthworks on Bukit Relau. *The Star Online*.

Hafiz, M. R., & Ismail, K. (2015). The propensity of adapting strategic reactiveness and entrepreneurial management amongst SMEs. *Procedia: Social and Behavioral Sciences, 181*, 356–365. doi:10.1016/j.sbspro.2015.04.898

Hagger, M. S., Chatzisarantis, N. L., & Biddle, S. J. (2002). A meta-analytic review of the theories of reasoned action and planned behavior in physical activity: Predictive validity and the contribution of additional variables. *Journal of Sport & Exercise Psychology, 24*(1), 3–32. doi:10.1123/jsep.24.1.3

Hair, J. F., Black, W. C., Babin, B. J., Anderson, R. E., & Tatham, R. L. (2006). *Multivariate Data Analysis* (6th ed.). Pearson.

Hair, J. F. Jr, Sarstedt, M., Hopkins, L., & Kuppelwieser, V. G. (2014). Partial least squares structural equation modeling (PLS-SEM) An emerging tool in business research. *European Business Review, 26*(2), 106–121. doi:10.1108/EBR-10-2013-0128

Hair, J. F., Ringle, C. M., & Sarstedt, M. (2011). PLS-SEM: Indeed a silver bullet. *Journal of Marketing Theory and Practice, 19*(2), 139–152. doi:10.2753/MTP1069-6679190202

Hair, J. F., Wolfinbarger, M. F., Ortinau, D. J., & Bush, R. P. (2008). *Essentials of marketing research*: McGraw-Hill. *Higher Education.*

Hairuddin, H., Noor, N. L. M., & Ab Malik, A. M. (2012). Why do microenterprise refuse to use information technology: A case of batik microenterprises in Malaysia. *Procedia: Social and Behavioral Sciences*, *57*, 494–502. doi:10.1016/j.sbspro.2012.09.1216

Hakala, H. (2011). Strategic orientations in management literature: Three approaches to understanding the interaction between market, technology, entrepreneurial and learning orientations. *International Journal of Management Reviews*, *13*(2), 199–217. doi:10.1111/j.1468-2370.2010.00292.x

Håkansson, H., & Snehota, I. (2006). No business is an island: The network concept of business strategy. *Scandinavian Journal of Management*, *22*(3), 256–270. doi:10.1016/j.scaman.2006.10.005

Halim, A. H., Ahmad, N. H., Ramayah, T., Hanifah, H., Taghizadeh, S. K., & Mohamad, M. N. (2015). Towards an Innovation Culture: Enhancing Innovative Performance of Malaysian SMEs. *Academic Journal of Interdisciplinary Studies*, *4*(2), 85–94. doi:10.5901/ajis.2015.v4n2p85

Halim, H. A., Ahmad, N. H., Ramayah, T., & Hanifah, H. (2014). The Growth of Innovative Performance among SMEs: Leveraging on Organisational Culture and Innovative Human Capital. *Journal of Small Business and Entrepreneurship Development*, *2*(21), 107–125.

Hall, J. K., Daneke, G. A., & Lenox, M. J. (2010). Sustainable development and entrepreneurship: Past contributions and future directions. *Journal of Business Venturing*, *25*(5), 439–448. doi:10.1016/j.jbusvent.2010.01.002

Hall, J., Matos, M., Severino, L., Sheehan, L., & Silvestre, B. (2012). Entrepreneurship and innovation at the base of the pyramid: A recipe for inclusive growth or social exclusion? *Journal of Management Studies*, *49*(4), 785–812. doi:10.1111/j.1467-6486.2012.01044.x

Hamidon, S. (2009). *The development of Malay entrepreneurship in Malaysia*. ITBM. Retrieved May 20, 2016, from http://mro.massey.ac.nz

Hang, D. T. (2015). *Leader Training in Vietnam SMEs for meeting requirement of International economic Integration*. Vietnam National Univerversity.

Han, L. (2008). Bricks vs clicks: Entrepreneurial online banking behaviour and relationship banking. *International Journal of Entrepreneurial Behavior & Research*, *14*(1), 47–60. doi:10.1108/13552550810852820

Hanna, R., Rohm, A., & Crittenden, V. L. (2011). Were all connected: The power of the social media ecosystem. *Business Horizons*, *54*(3), 265–273. doi:10.1016/j.bushor.2011.01.007

Hansen, H., Rand, J., & Tarp, F. (2009). Enterprise Growth and Survival in Vietnam: Does Government Support Matter? *The Journal of Development Studies*, *45*(7), 1048–1069. doi:10.1080/00220380902811025

Hargadon, A. B. (2002). Brokering knowledge: Linking learning and innovation. *Research in Organizational Behavior*, *24*, 41–86. doi:10.1016/S0191-3085(02)24003-4

Hashemi, S. M. K., Hosseini, S. M., & Rezvanfar, A. (2012). Explaining entrepreneurial intention among agricultural students: Effects of entrepreneurial self-efficacy, and college entrepreneurial orientation. *Research Journal of Business Management*, *6*(3), 1–9.

Hashim, H. (2012, October 29). SMEs, too, should embrace CSR. *New Straits Times*.

Hashim, H. (2013). *Overview of SME Sector in Malaysia*. Presentation in SME: Global Champions, Malaysia-India SME Forum.

Hashim, H. (2013). *Propelling Malaysian SMEs into a Higher Economic Contributor*. Saudi International SMEs Forum 2013.

Hashim, M. K. (1999). SMEs in Malaysia: Past, present and future. Malaysian Management Review, 35.

Hassan, M. S., Shaffril, M., Azril, H., Abu Hassan, M., & D'Silva, J. L. (2009). Developing agriculture in Malaysia: Internet utilization among Malaysian youth agro-businessman. *European Journal of Soil Science, 11*(2), 215–224.

Hatch, M. J., & Schultz, M. (2010). Toward a theory of brand co-creation with implications for brand governance1. *Journal of Brand Management, 17*(8), 590–604. doi:10.1057/bm.2010.14

Heeks, R. (2009). *The ICT4D 2.0 Manifesto: Where Next for ICTs and International Development?* Development Informatics, Working Paper Series, Paper No. 42, Development Informatics Group, Institute for Development Policy and Management, University of Manchester, UK.

Heinonen, J. (2007). An entrepreneurial-directed approach to teaching corporate entrepreneurship at university level. *Education+ Training, 49*(4), 310-324.

Henderson, R. (1993). Underinvestment and incompetence as responses to radical innovation: Evidence from the photolithographic alignment equipment industry. *The Rand Journal of Economics, 24*(2), 248–270. doi:10.2307/2555761

Henry, C., Hill, F., & Leitch, C. (2005). Entrepreneurship education and training: can entrepreneurship be taught? Part I. *Education + Training, 47*(2), 98-111.

Henseler, J., Ringle, C. M., & Sinkovicks, R. R. (2009). The use of partial least square modeling in international marketing. *New Challenges to International Marketing Advances in International Marketing, 20*, 277–319.

Hessels, J., & Parker, S. C. (2013). Constraints, internationalization and growth: A cross-country analysis of European SMEs. *Journal of World Business, 48*(1), 137–148. doi:10.1016/j.jwb.2012.06.014

Hewlett, S. A., Sherbin, L., & Sumberg, K. (2009). How Gen Y & Boomers will reshape your agenda. *Harvard Business Review, 87*(7/8), 71–76. PMID:19630257

Hindle, K., & Rushworth, S. (2002). *GEM Australia 2002*. Hawthorn: Swinburne University of Technology.

Hock, C., Ringle, C. M., & Sarstedt, M. (2010). Management of multi-purpose stadiums: Importance and performance measurement of service interfaces. *International Journal of Services Technology and Management, 14*(2-3), 188–207. http://newagebd.net/ doi:10.1504/IJSTM.2010.034327

Hock-Eam, L., Ahmad, S. A., & Jan, S. J. (2015). *The inferring predisposed factors for graduate agropreneur in Malaysia: Mismatch?* Paper presented at the 9th Asia-Pacific Business Research Conference, Singapore.

Hoff, K., & Stiglitz, J. E. (2000). *Modern economic theory and development*. The World Bank. Retrieved from http://www8.gsb.columbia.edu/faculty/jstiglitz/sites/jstiglitz/files/2000_Modern_Economic_Theory_and_Development.pdf

Hoff, K., Braverman, A., & Stiglitz, J. E. (Eds.). (1993). *The Economics of Rural Organization: Theory, Practice, and Policy*. New York: Oxford University Press.

Holbrook, M. B. (1999). *Consumer value: a framework for analysis and research*. Routledge. doi:10.4324/9780203010679

Homburg, C., Klarmann, M., & Schmitt, J. (2010). Brand awareness in business markets: When is it related to firm performance? *International Journal of Research in Marketing, 27*(3), 201–212. doi:10.1016/j.ijresmar.2010.03.004

Hoque, R., Saif, A. N. M., AlBar, A. M., & Bao, Y. (2015). Adoption of information and communication technology for development: A case study of small and medium enterprises in Bangladesh. *Information Development*, 1–15.

Hossain, N. (1998). *Constraints to SME Development in Bangladesh, JOBS project*. USAID.

Hossain, N. (2005). *Elite perceptions of poverty in Bangladesh*. Dhaka, Bangladesh: University Press Limited.

Hoyer, W. D., Chandy, R., Dorotic, M., Krafft, M., & Singh, S. S. (2010). Consumer cocreation in new product development. *Journal of Service Research*, *13*(3), 283–296. doi:10.1177/1094670510375604

Hsieh, M.-H., Pan, S.-L., & Setiono, R. (2004). Product-, corporate-, and country-image dimensions and purchase behavior: A multicountry analysis. *Journal of the Academy of Marketing Science*, *32*(3), 251–270. doi:10.1177/0092070304264262

Hsieh, T. (2010). *Delivering happiness: A path to profits, passion, and purpose*. New York: Business Plus.

Hsu, J.-L., & Cheng, M.-C. (2011). What Prompts Small and Medium Enterprises to Engage in Corporate Social Responsibility? A Study from Taiwan. *Corporate Social Responsibility and Environmental Management*.

Hsu, W. T., Chen, H. L., & Cheng, C. Y. (2013). Internationalization and firm performance of SMEs: The moderating effects of CEO attributes. *Journal of World Business*, *48*(1), 1–12. doi:10.1016/j.jwb.2012.06.001

Huang, H. C. (2016). Entrepreneurial resources and speed of entrepreneurial success in an emerging market: The moderating effect of entrepreneurship. *The International Entrepreneurship and Management Journal*, *12*(1), 1–26. doi:10.1007/s11365-014-0321-8

Huang, Z. J., & Cai, L. A. (2015). Modeling consumer-based brand equity for multinational hotel brands–When hosts become guests. *Tourism Management*, *46*, 431–443. doi:10.1016/j.tourman.2014.07.013

Hughes, A. (1997). Finance for SMEs: A UK perspective. *Small Business Economics*, *9*(2), 151–166. doi:10.1023/A:1007971823255

Huijts, N. M. A., De Groot, J. I. M., Molin, E. J. E., & Van Wee, B. (2013). Intention to act towards a local hydrogen refueling facility: Moral considerations versus self-interest. *Transportation Research Part A, Policy and Practice*, *48*, 63–74. doi:10.1016/j.tra.2012.10.006

Human Development Report. (2015). *Work for Human Development*. Author.

Human Rights Watch. (2016). *Country Profile- Bangladesh*. Retrieved from https://www.hrw.org/asia/bangladesh

Hunt, S. D. (1997). Competing through relationships: Grounding relationship marketing in resource-advantage theory. *Journal of Marketing Management*, *13*(5), 431–445. doi:10.1080/0267257X.1997.9964484

Huseynov, F., & Klamm, B. K. (2012). Tax avoidance, tax management and corporate social responsibility. *Journal of Corporate Finance*, *18*(4), 804–827. doi:10.1016/j.jcorpfin.2012.06.005

Husin, M. A., & Ibrahim, M. D. (2014). The Role of Accounting Services and Impact on Small Medium Enterprises (SMEs) Performance in Manufacturing Sector from East Coast Region of Malaysia: A Conceptual Paper. *Procedia - Social and Behavioral Sciences*, *115*, 54–67. http://doi.org/<ALIGNMENT.qj></ALIGNMENT>10.1016/j.sbspro.2014.02.415

Hussain, I., Farooq, Z., & Akhtar, W. (2012). SMEs development and failure avoidance in developing countries through public private partnership. *African Journal of Business Management*, *6*(4), 1581–1589.

Hussain, J., & Matlay, H. (2007). Financing preferences of ethnic minority owner/managers in the UK. *Journal of Small Business and Enterprise Development*, *14*(3), 487–500. doi:10.1108/14626000710773565

Hu, W., & Zhang, Y. (2012). New venture capability of the transformation from entrepreneurial orientation to new ventures performance: Theory model and empirical study in China. *Nankai Business Review International*, *3*(3), 302–325. doi:10.1108/20408741211264594

Hye, H. A. (1996). *Below the line: Rural poverty in Bangladesh.* Dhaka: The University Press Limited.

Ibarra, H. (1993). Network centrality, power, and innovation involvement: Determinants of technical and administrative roles. *Academy of Management Journal, 36*(3), 471–501. doi:10.2307/256589

Ibeh, K. I. N. (2003). Toward a contingency framework of export entrepreneurship: Conceptualisations and empirical evidence. *Small Business Economics, 20*(1), 49–68. doi:10.1023/A:1020244404241

Ibeh, K. I. N., & Young, S. (2001). Exporting as an entrepreneurial act an empirical study of Nigerian firms. *European Journal of Marketing, 35*(5/6), 566–586. doi:10.1108/03090560110388114

ICAEW. (2004). *Sustainability: The Role of Accountants.* The Institute of Chartered Accountants in England and Wales.

IFAC. (2011). Sustainability Framework 2.0: Professional Accountants as Integrators. New York: International Federation of Accountants (IFAC).

IFAC. (2012). The Role of Professional Accountants in the Sustainability of Small Businesses. Special Edition eNews.

IFAC. (2014). *Sustainability.* Retrieved 20 April 2014, from https://www.ifac.org/globalknowledgegateway/sustainability?overview&discussions

Igbaria, M., & Tan, M. (1997). The consequences of information technology acceptance on subsequent individual performance. *Information & Management, 32*(3), 113–121. doi:10.1016/S0378-7206(97)00006-2

Ihua, U. B. (2009). SMEs, key failure-factors: A comparison between the UK and Nigeria. *Journal of Social Sciences, 18*(13), 199–207.

Ilvonen, I., & Vuori, V. (2013). Risks and benefits of knowledge sharing in co-opetitive knowledge networks. *International Journal of Networking and Virtual Organisations, 13*(3), 209–223. doi:10.1504/IJNVO.2013.063049

Imai, K. S., & Azam, M. D. S. (2012). Does Microfinance Reduce Poverty in Bangladesh? New Evidence from Household Panel Data. *The Journal of Development Studies, 48*(5), 633–653. doi:10.1080/00220388.2012.661853

Ind, N., & Coates, N. (2013). The meanings of co-creation. *European Business Review, 25*(1), 86–95. doi:10.1108/09555341311287754

Ing, S. G., & Ing, G. A. (2016). Dynamic Manufacturing Cells and {SME} Network: Key Success Factors. *IFAC-PapersOnLine, 49*(12), 851–856.

International Institute for Sustainable Development. (1992). *Business Strategies for Sustainable Development; Leadership and accountability for the 90's.* IISD in conjunction with Deloitte and Touche and the World Business Council for Sustainable Development.

International Labour Office. (2014). *Global employment trends 2014: Risk of a jobless recovery?* Geneva, ILO: Document and Publications Production, Printing and Distribution Branch (PRODOC), ILO. Retrieved from http://www.ilo.org/wcmsp5/groups/public/---dgreports/---dcomm/---publ/documents/publication/wcms_233953.pdf

Ireland, J. (2008). Lessons for successful BOP marketing from Caracas slums. *Journal of Consumer Marketing, 25*(7), 430–438. doi:10.1108/07363760810915644

Isa, W. A. R. W. M., Aziz, M. A., & Razak, M. R. B. A. (2011). Evaluating the accessibility of Small and Medium Enterprise (SME) websites in Malaysia. In *Proceedings - 2011 International Conference on User Science and Engineering, i-USEr 2011* (pp. 135–140). http://doi.org/ doi:<ALIGNMENT.qj></ALIGNMENT>10.1109/iUSEr.2011.6150552

Islam, M. A., Agarwal, N. K., & Ikeda, M. (2015). Conceptualizing value co-creation for service innovation in academic libraries. *Business Information Review*, *32*(1), 45–52. doi:10.1177/0266382115573155

Islam, M. A., & Tsuji, K. (2011). Bridging digital divide in Bangladesh: Study on community information centers. *The Electronic Library*, *29*(4), 506–522. doi:10.1108/02640471111156768

Islam, R. (2010). Critical success factors of the nine challenges in Malaysias vision 2020. *Socio-Economic Planning Sciences*, *44*(4), 199–211. doi:10.1016/j.seps.2010.07.002

Ismail, K., Ahmad Anuar, M., Wan Omar, W. Z., Aziz, A. A., Seohod, K., & Akhtar, C. H. (2013). *Entrepreneurial intention, entrepreneurial orientation of faculty and students towards commercialization*. Paper presented at the 3rd International Conference on Leadership, Technology and Innovation Management, Istanbul, Turkey.

Ismail, W. K. W., & Abdmajid. R. (2007). Framework of the culture of innovation: A revisit. *Jurnal Kemanusiaan, 9*.

Ismail, M. Z., & Ahmad, S. Z. (2013). Entrepreneurship education: An insight from Malaysian polytechnics. *Journal of Chinese Entrepreneurship*, *5*(2), 144–160. doi:10.1108/JCE-02-2013-0003

Israel, G. D. (1992). *Determining sample size: University of Florida Cooperative Extension Service, Institute of Food and Agriculture Sciences*. EDIS.

Jaffee, S., Kopicki, R., Labaste, P., & Christie, I. (2003). *Modernizing Africa's agro-food systems: Analytical framework and implications for operations* (Africa Region Working Paper Series, No. 4). Retrieved from http://www.worldbank.org/afr/wps/wp44.pdf

Jairak, K., Praneetpolgrang, P., & Subsermsri, P. (2015). Information technology governance practices based on sufficiency economy philosophy in the Thai university sector. *Information Technology & People*, *28*(1), 195–223. doi:10.1108/ITP-10-2013-0188

Jala, I. (2013, September 30). Agriculture is a sector that is still important to Malaysia's economy. *The Star Online*. Retrieved from http://www.thestar.com.my/Business/Business-News/2013/09/30/Agriculture-is-a-sector-that-is-still-important-to-Malaysias-economy/

Jalali, A., Jaafar, M., & Ramayah, T. (2014). Entrepreneurial orientation and performance: The interaction effect of customer capital. *World Journal of Entrepreneurship, Management and Sustainable Development*, *10*(1), 48–68.

Jalilvand, M. R., & Samiei, N. (2012). The effect of electronic word of mouth on brand image and purchase intention: An empirical study in the automobile industry in Iran. *Marketing Intelligence & Planning*, *30*(4), 460–476. doi:10.1108/02634501211231946

Jamali, D., & Tarazi, A. (2012). CSR: A Cost or an Opportunity for SMEs in the Middle East? CSR in the Middle East: Fresh Perspectives (pp. 72). Academic Press.

Jamali, D., Zanhour, M., & Keshishian, T. (2009). Peculiar Strengths and Relational Attributes of SMEs in the Context of CSR. *Journal of Business Ethics*, *87*(3), 355–377. doi:10.1007/s10551-008-9925-7

Jamil, F., Ismail, K., Siddique, M., Khan, M. M., Kazi, A. G., & Qureshi, M. I. (2016). Business Incubators in Asian Developing Countries. *International Review of Management and Marketing*, *6*(4S), 291–295.

Janita, I., & Chong, W. K. (2013). Barriers of B2B e-business adoption in Indonesian SMEs: A literature analysis. *Procedia Computer Science*, *17*, 571–578. doi:10.1016/j.procs.2013.05.073

Jan, M. A., Shah, S. M. A., & Khan, K. U. (2014). The Impact of Culture on Innovation: The moderating role of Human Capital. *International Journal of Accounting and Financial Reporting*, *4*(2), 607. doi:10.5296/ijafr.v4i2.6871

Jansen, J. J., Van Den Bosch, F. A., & Volberda, H. W. (2006). Exploratory innovation, exploitative innovation, and performance: Effects of organizational antecedents and environmental moderators. *Management Science*, *52*(11), 1661–1674. doi:10.1287/mnsc.1060.0576

Jantunen, A., Puumalainen, K., Saarenketo, S., & Kyläheiko, K. (2005). Entrepreneurial orientation, dynamic capabilities and international performance. *Journal of International Entrepreneurship*, *3*(3), 223–243. doi:10.1007/s10843-005-1133-2

Javalgi, R. G., & Todd, P. R. (2011). Entrepreneurial orientation, management commitment, and human capital: The internationalization of SMEs in India. *Journal of Business Research*, *64*(9), 1004–1010. doi:10.1016/j.jbusres.2010.11.024

Jayachandran, S., Sharma, S., Kaufman, P., & Raman, P. (2005). The role of relational information processes and technology use in customer relationship management. *Journal of Marketing*, *69*(4), 177–192. doi:10.1509/jmkg.2005.69.4.177

Jenkins, H. (2004). A Critique of Conventional CSR Theory: An SME Perspective. *Journal of General Management*, *29*, 37–57.

Jenkins, H. (2006). Small Business Champions for Corporate Social Responsibility. *Journal of Business Ethics*, *67*(3), 241–256. doi:10.1007/s10551-006-9182-6

Jennings, C., & Wargnier, J. (2010). Experiential learning – A way to develop agile minds in the knowledge economy? *Development and Learning in Organizations*, *24*(3), 14–16.

Jiao, F., Wei, J., & Cui, Y. (2010). An empirical study on paths to develop dynamic capabilities: From the perspectives of entrepreneurial orientation and organizational learning. *Frontiers of Business Research in China*, *4*(1), 47–72. doi:10.1007/s11782-010-0003-5

JICA. (2015). *Finding Diamond for IT industry: Information technology engineers examination in Bangladesh*. Retrieved March 23, 2016, from https://www.jica.go.jp/bangladesh/english/office/about/story_04.html

Johannessen, J., Olsen, B., & Lumpkin, G. T. (2001). Innovation as newness: What is new, how new, and new to whom? *European Journal of Innovation Management*, *4*(1), 20–31. doi:10.1108/14601060110365547

Johanson, J., & Vahlne, J. E. (1977). The internationalization process of the firm: A model of knowledge development and increasing foreign market commitment. *Journal of International Business Studies*, *8*(1), 23–32. doi:10.1057/palgrave.jibs.8490676

Jones-Evans, D. (1996). Technical entrepreneurship, strategy and experience. *International Small Business Journal*, *14*(3), 15–39. doi:10.1177/0266242696143001

Jones, M. V., & Coviello, N. E. (2005). Internationalization: Conceptualizing an entrepreneurial process of behavior in time. *Journal of International Business Studies*, *36*(3), 284–303. doi:10.1057/palgrave.jibs.8400138

Joseph, O., Adanma, N. J., & Chinonso, E. H. (2012). Wealth allocation and determinants of venture capital among poultry agribusiness entrepreneurs in Abia State, Nigeria. *Journal of Economics and Sustainable Development*, *3*(14), 188–196.

Juscius, V., & Jonikas, D. (2013). Integration of CSR into Value Creation Chain: Conceptual Framework. *The Engineering Economist*, *24*(1), 63–70.

Jusoh, M. A., & Idris, S. (2002). *Role of Technopreneurs in Malaysian Economic*. Retrieved from http://www.jgbm.org/page/1 Mohd Abdullah Jusoh.pdf

Jutla, D., Bodorik, P., & Dhaliwal, J. (2002). Supporting the e-business readiness of small and medium sized enterprises: Approaches and metrics. *Internet Research: Electronic Networking Applications and Policy*, *12*(2), 139–164. doi:10.1108/10662240210422512

Jyoti, J., Sharma, J., & Kumari, A. (2011). Factors affecting orientation and satisfaction of women entrepreneurs in rural india. *Annals of Innovation & Entrepreneurship*, *2*(1), 1–13. doi:10.3402/aie.v2i1.5813

Kalinic, I., & Forza, C. (2012). Rapid internationalization of traditional SMEs: Between gradualist models and born globals. *International Business Review*, *21*(4), 694–707. doi:10.1016/j.ibusrev.2011.08.002

Kamyabi, Y., & Devi, S. (2011). Use of Professional Accountants Advisory Services and its Impact on SME Performance in an Emerging Economy: A Resource-based View. *Journal of Management and Sustainability*, *1*(1), 43. doi:10.5539/jms.v1n1p43

Kantabutra, S. (2007). *Development of the Sufficiency Economy Philosophy in the Thai Business Sector: Evidence, Future Research & Policy Implications*. Retrieved 7 July, 2016, from http://www.sufficiencyeconomy.org/old/en/files/26.pdf

Kantabutra, S., & Siebenhüner, T. (2011). Predicting Corporate Sustainability: A Thai Approach. *Journal of Applied Business Research*, *27*(6), 123. doi:10.19030/jabr.v27i6.6471

Kanter, R. M. (1983). *The change masters: Innovation for productivity in the American corporation*. New York: Simon & Schuster.

Kapferer, J.-N. (2012). *The new strategic brand management: Advanced insights and strategic thinking* (5th ed.). Kogan Page.

Kaplan, A. M., & Haenlein, M. (2010). Users of the world, unite! The challenges and opportunities of Social Media. *Business Horizons*, *53*(1), 59–68. doi:10.1016/j.bushor.2009.09.003

Karnani, A. (2007). The mirage of marketing to the bottom of the pyramid: How the private sector can help alleviate poverty. *California Management Review*, *49*(4), 90–111. doi:10.2307/41166407

Kasemsap, K. (2014). The role of social capital in higher education institutions. In N. Baporikar (Ed.), *Handbook of research on higher education in the MENA region: Policy and practice* (pp. 119–147). Hershey, PA: IGI Global. doi:10.4018/978-1-4666-6198-1.ch007

Kasemsap, K. (2015a). The role of information system within enterprise architecture and their impact on business performance. In M. Wadhwa & A. Harper (Eds.), *Technology, innovation, and enterprise transformation* (pp. 262–284). Hershey, PA: IGI Global. doi:10.4018/978-1-4666-6473-9.ch012

Kasemsap, K. (2015b). The roles of information technology and knowledge management in project management metrics. In G. Jamil, S. Lopes, A. Malheiro da Silva, & F. Ribeiro (Eds.), *Handbook of research on effective project management through the integration of knowledge and innovation* (pp. 332–361). Hershey, PA: IGI Global. doi:10.4018/978-1-4666-7536-0.ch018

Kasemsap, K. (2015c). Mastering entrepreneurship education in global business. In A. Szopa, W. Karwowski, & D. Barbe (Eds.), *Competitive strategies for academic entrepreneurship: Commercialization of research-based products* (pp. 1–28). Hershey, PA: IGI Global. doi:10.4018/978-1-4666-8487-4.ch001

Kasemsap, K. (2016a). Exploring the roles of entrepreneurship and internationalization in global business. In L. Carvalho (Ed.), *Handbook of research on entrepreneurial success and its impact on regional development* (pp. 481–512). Hershey, PA: IGI Global. doi:10.4018/978-1-4666-9567-2.ch021

Kasemsap, K. (2016b). Advocating electronic business and electronic commerce in the global marketplace. In S. Dixit & A. Sinha (Eds.), *E-retailing challenges and opportunities in the global marketplace* (pp. 1–24). Hershey, PA: IGI Global. doi:10.4018/978-1-4666-9921-2.ch001

Kasemsap, K. (2016c). Examining the roles of virtual team and information technology in global business. In C. Graham (Ed.), *Strategic management and leadership for systems development in virtual spaces* (pp. 1–21). Hershey, PA: IGI Global. doi:10.4018/978-1-4666-9688-4.ch001

Kasemsap, K. (2016d). A unified framework of organizational perspectives and knowledge management and their impact on job performance. In A. Normore, L. Long, & M. Javidi (Eds.), *Handbook of research on effective communication, leadership, and conflict resolution* (pp. 267–297). Hershey, PA: IGI Global. doi:10.4018/978-1-4666-9970-0.ch015

Kasemsap, K. (2016e). Advocating entrepreneurship education and knowledge management in global business. In N. Baporikar (Ed.), *Handbook of research on entrepreneurship in the contemporary knowledge-based global economy* (pp. 313–339). Hershey, PA: IGI Global. doi:10.4018/978-1-4666-8798-1.ch014

Kasemsap, K. (2016f). The roles of e-learning, organizational learning, and knowledge management in the learning organizations. In E. Railean, G. Walker, A. Elçi, & L. Jackson (Eds.), *Handbook of research on applied learning theory and design in modern education* (pp. 786–816). Hershey, PA: IGI Global. doi:10.4018/978-1-4666-9634-1.ch039

Kasemsap, K. (2017a). Professional and business applications of social media platforms. In V. Benson, R. Tuninga, & G. Saridakis (Eds.), *Analyzing the strategic role of social networking in firm growth and productivity* (pp. 427–450). Hershey, PA: IGI Global. doi:10.4018/978-1-5225-0559-4.ch021

Kasemsap, K. (2017b). Mastering consumer attitude and sustainable consumption in the digital age. In N. Suki (Ed.), *Handbook of research on leveraging consumer psychology for effective customer engagement* (pp. 16–41). Hershey, PA: IGI Global. doi:10.4018/978-1-5225-0746-8.ch002

Kasemsap, K. (2017c). Advocating sustainable supply chain management and sustainability in global supply chain. In M. Khan, M. Hussain, & M. Ajmal (Eds.), *Green supply chain management for sustainable business practice* (pp. 234–271). Hershey, PA: IGI Global. doi:10.4018/978-1-5225-0635-5.ch009

Keller, K. L. (1993). Conceptualizing, measuring, and managing customer-based brand equity. *Journal of Marketing*, *57*(1), 1–22. doi:10.2307/1252054

Keller, K. L., & Lehmann, D. R. (2006). Brands and branding: Research findings and future priorities. *Marketing Science*, *25*(6), 740–759. doi:10.1287/mksc.1050.0153

Khan, A. S. (2014). *The SME missing middle problem in developing countries and its link to lack of financing: The case of Bangladesh* (Master's Thesis). University of Ottawa, Ottawa, ON, Canada.

Khan, A., Muttakin, M., & Siddiqui, J. (2012). Corporate Governance and Corporate Social Responsibility Disclosures: Evidence from an Emerging Economy. *Journal of Business Ethics*, 1–17.

Khan, J. H., Nazmul, A. K., Hossain, M. F., & Rahmatullah, M. (2012). Perception of SME Growth Constraints in Bangladesh: An Empirical Examination from Institutional Perspective. *European Journal of Business and Management*, *4*(7), 256–272.

Khanna, T., & Palepu, K. G. (2010). *Winning in emerging markets: A road map for strategy and execution*. Boston, MA: Harvard Business Review Press.

Khan, R. A., Liew, M. S., & Ghazali, Z. (2014). Malaysian Construction Sector and Malaysia Vision 2020: Developed Nation Status. *Procedia: Social and Behavioral Sciences*, *109*, 507–513. doi:10.1016/j.sbspro.2013.12.498

Khatri, N. (2000). Managing human resource for competitive advantage: A study of companies in Singapore. *International Journal of Human Resource Management*, *11*(2), 336–365. doi:10.1080/095851900339909

Khedhaouria, A., Gurău, C., & Torrès, O. (2015). Creativity, self-efficacy, and small-firm performance: The mediating role of entrepreneurial orientation. *Small Business Economics*, *44*(3), 485–504. doi:10.1007/s11187-014-9608-y

Khor, K.-S., Ramayah, T., Ahmad, N. H., Halim, H. A., & Lo, M.-C. (2015). Bridging the Gap of Green IT/IS and Sustainable Consumption. *Global Business Review*, *16*(4), 571–593. doi:10.1177/0972150915581101

Khurshid, A., Rizwan, M., & Tasneem, E. (2014). Factors contributing towards adoption of e-banking in Pakistan. *International Journal of Accounting and Financial Reporting*, *4*(2), 437–455. doi:10.5296/ijafr.v4i2.6584

Kim, E. Y., Knight, D. K., & Pelton, L. E. (2009). Modeling brand equity of a US apparel brand as perceived by Generation Y consumers in the emerging Korean market. *Clothing & Textiles Research Journal*, *27*(4), 247–258. doi:10.1177/0887302X08327085

Kim, H. D., Lee, I., & Lee, C. K. (2011). Building Web 2.0 enterprises: A study of small and medium enterprises in the United States. *International Small Business Journal*, *29*, 1–19.

Kim, H., Kim, T., & Shin, S. W. (2009). Modeling roles of subjective norms and eTrust in customers acceptance of airline B2C eCommerce websites. *Tourism Management*, *30*(2), 266–277. doi:10.1016/j.tourman.2008.07.001

Kim, P., & Aldrich, H. (2005). Social Capital and Entrepreneurship. *Foundations and Trends in Entrepreneurship.*, *1*(2), 55–104. doi:10.1561/0300000002

Klafft, M. (2008). Online peer-to-peer lending: A lenders' perspective. In *Proceedings of the International Conference on E-Learning, E-Business, Enterprise Information Systems, and E-Government* (pp. 371–375). Las Vegas, NV: CSREA Press.

Klimas, P. (2014). Multifaceted nature of coopetition inside an aviation supply chain-the case of the aviation valley. *Journal of Economics & Management*, *17*, 96–119.

Klyver, K., & Schenkel, M. T. (2013). From resource access to use: Exploring the impact of resource combinations on nascent entrepreneurship. *Journal of Small Business Management*, *51*(4), 539–556. doi:10.1111/jsbm.12030

Knight, G. A., Madsen, T. K., & Servais, P. (2004). An enquiry into born global firms in Europe and the US. *International Marketing Review*, *21*(6), 645–665. doi:10.1108/02651330410568060

Kock, S., Nisuls, J., & Söderqvist, A. (2010). Co-opetition: A source of international opportunities in Finnish SMEs. *Competitiveness Review: An International Business Journal*, *20*(2), 111–125. doi:10.1108/10595421011029839

Kohar, U. H. A. (2013). *The factors that influence the sustainability of Malaysian Bumiputera (indigenous) new technology-based small firms* (Doctoral dissertation). RMIT University, Melbourne, Australia.

Kolk, A., Rivera-Santos, M., & Rufín, C. (2013). Reviewing a Decade of Research on the" Base/Bottom of the Pyramid"(BOP) Concept. *Business & Society*, 1–36.

Kollmann, T., Stöckmann, C. (2014). Filling the entrepreneurial orientation–performance gap: The mediating effects of exploratory and exploitative innovations. *Entrepreneurship Theory and Practice, 38*(5), 1001-1026.

Kona, O. T. (2014). *Website interface design: A study on the status quo of South African e-commerce website interfaces.* Retrieved April 2015, from http://www.web-visibility.co.za/0069-working-paper-2014-kona-weideman-interface-design-e-commerce.pdf

Koo, C., & Chung, N. (2014). Examining the eco-technological knowledge of Smart Green IT adoption behavior: A self-determination perspective. *Technological Forecasting and Social Change*, *88*, 140–155. doi:10.1016/j.techfore.2014.06.025

Korkman, O., Storbacka, K., & Harald, B. (2010). Practices as markets: Value co-creation in e-invoicing.[AMJ]. *Australasian Marketing Journal*, *18*(4), 236–247. doi:10.1016/j.ausmj.2010.07.006

Koskosas, I. (2011). The pros and cons of internet banking : A short review. *Business Excellence and Management*, *1*(1), 49–58.

Kossyva, D., Galanis, K., Sarri, K., & Georgopoulos, N. (2014). Adopting an information security management system in a co-opetition strategy context. *International Journal of Applied Systemic Studies*, *5*(3), 215–228. doi:10.1504/IJASS.2014.064065

Kossyva, D., Sarri, K., & Georgopoulos, N. (2014). Co-opetition: A business strategy for SMEs in times of economic crisis. *South-Eastern Europe Journal of Economics*, *12*(1), 89–106.

Kotabe, M., & Helsen, K. (2004). *Global marketing management*. Hoboken, NJ: John Wiley & Sons.

Kotey, B. (2005). Are performance differences between family and non-family SMEs uniform across all firm sizes? *International Journal of Entrepreneurial Behaviour & Research*, *11*(6), 394–421. doi:10.1108/13552550510625168

Kotler, P. (2001). *A framework for marketing management*. Upper Saddle River, NJ: Prentice-Hall.

Kraus, S., Rigtering, J. P. C., Hughes, M., & Hosman, V. (2012). Entrepreneurial orientation and the business performance of SMEs: A quantitative study from the Netherlands. *Review of Managerial Science*, *6*(2), 161–182. doi:10.1007/s11846-011-0062-9

Kreiser, P. M. (2011). Entrepreneurial orientation and organizational learning: The impact of network range and network closure. *Entrepreneurship Theory and Practice*, *35*(5), 1025–1050. doi:10.1111/j.1540-6520.2011.00449.x

Kreiser, P. M., Marino, L. D., Dickson, P., & Weaver, K. M. (2010). Cultural influences on entrepreneurial orientation: The impact of national culture on risk taking and proactiveness in SMEs. *Entrepreneurship Theory and Practice*, *34*(5), 959–983. doi:10.1111/j.1540-6520.2010.00396.x

Kreiser, P. M., Marino, L. D., Kuratko, D. F., & Weaver, K. M. (2013). Disaggregating entrepreneurial orientation: The non-linear impact of innovativeness, proactiveness and risk-taking on SME performance. *Small Business Economics*, *40*(2), 273–291. doi:10.1007/s11187-012-9460-x

Kreiser, P. M., Marino, L. D., & Weaver, K. M. (2002). Assessing the psychometric properties of the entrepreneurial orientation scale: A multi-country analysis. *Entrepreneurship Theory and Practice*, *26*(4), 71–94.

Krejcie, R. V., & Morgan, D. W. (1970). Determining Sample Size for Research Activities. *Educational and Psychological Measurement*, *30*, 607–610.

Krejcie, R. V., & Morgan, D. W. (1970). Determining sample size for research activities. *Educational and Psychological Measurement*.

Kristensen, K., Martensen, A., & Gronholdt, L. (2000). Customer satisfaction measurement at post Denmark: Results of application of the European customer satisfaction index methodology. *Total Quality Management*, *11*(7), 1007–1015. doi:10.1080/09544120050135533

Kuivalainen, O., Saarenketo, S., & Puumalainen, K. (2012). Start-up patterns of internationalization: A framework and its application in the context of knowledge-intensive SMEs. *European Management Journal*, *30*(4), 372–385. doi:10.1016/j.emj.2012.01.001

Kuldilok, K. S., Dawson, P. J., & Lingard, J. (2013). The export competitiveness of the tuna industry in Thailand. *British Food Journal*, *115*(3), 328–341. doi:10.1108/00070701311314174

Kunday, O., & Sengüler, E. P. (2015). A study on factors affecting the internationalization process of small and medium enterprises (SMEs). *Procedia: Social and Behavioral Sciences*, *195*, 972–981. doi:10.1016/j.sbspro.2015.06.363

Kuratko, D. F. (2005). The emergence of entrepreneurship education: Development, trends, and challenges. *Entrepreneurship Theory and Practice*, *29*(5), 577–598. doi:10.1111/j.1540-6520.2005.00099.x

Kusumavalee, S. (2010). Philosophy of Sufficiency Economy in the Large Scale Enterprise: A Case Study of Human Capital Management in the Siam Cement Group. *Human Resource and Organization Development Journal*, *1*(1), 80–90.

Kwenda, F. (2015). Investment and financing constraints: Can working capital management make a difference in South Africa? *Banks and Bank Systems*, *10*(1), 24–33.

Kyvik, O., Saris, W., Bonet, E., & Felício, J. A. (2013). The internationalization of small firms: The relationship between the global mindset and firms' internationalization behavior. *Journal of International Entrepreneurship*, *11*(2), 172–195. doi:10.1007/s10843-013-0105-1

Labonne, J. (2006). *A Comparative Analysis of the Environmental Management, Performance and Innovation of SMEs and Larger Firms*. For the European Commission, Directorate-General Environment.

Lai, K. Y. (2002). *A Study on the Relationship between Corporate Culture and Types of Knowledge Management versus Formation of Corporate Intellectual Capital Accumulation* (Master Thesis). Taiwan: Department of Accounting, National Chengchi University

Lalkaka, R. (2003). Technology business incubation: Role, performance, linkages, trends. In *National Workshop on Technology Parks and Business Incubators* (pp. 20–21). Retrieved from http://egateg.usaidallnet.gov/sites/default/files/Technology BI Roles.pdf

Lalkaka, R. (2002). Technology Business Incubators to Help Build an Innovation-based Economy. *Journal of Change Management*, *3*(2), 167–176. doi:10.1080/714042533

Lampadarios, E. (2015). *Critical Success Factors (CSFs) for Small Medium Enterprises (SMEs): An Empirical Study in the UK Chemical Distribution Industry* (Doctoral dissertation). Leeds Beckett University.

Lassila, D. R., Omer, T. C., Shelley, M. K., & Smith, L. M. (2010). Do Complexity, Governance, and Auditor Independence Influence whether Firms Retain Their Auditors for Tax Services? *The Journal of the American Taxation Association*, *32*(1), 1–23. doi:10.2308/jata.2010.32.1.1

Latham, B. (2007). Sampling: What is it. *Quantitative Research Methods, 5377.*

Laudon, K., Laudon, J., & Dass, R. (2006). *Management Information System*. Prentice Hall, Azimuth Interactive Inc.

Laukkanen, T., Nagy, G., Hirvonen, S., Reijonen, H., & Pasanen, M. (2013). The effect of strategic orientations on business performance in SMEs: A multigroup analysis comparing Hungary and Finland. *International Marketing Review*, *30*(6), 510–535. doi:10.1108/IMR-09-2011-0230

Lechner, C., & Gudmundsson, S. V. (2014). Entrepreneurial orientation, firm strategy and small firm performance. *International Small Business Journal*, *32*(1), 36–60. doi:10.1177/0266242612455034

Leek, S., & Christodoulides, G. (2011). A literature review and future agenda for B2B branding: Challenges of branding in a B2B context. *Industrial Marketing Management*, *40*(6), 830–837. doi:10.1016/j.indmarman.2011.06.006

Lee, L., & Hunt, A. (2008).*Business Incubators: Do They Matter?* Academic Press.

Lee, M. H., Mak, A. K., & Pang, A. (2012). Bridging the Gap: An Exploratory Study of Corporate Social Responsibility among SMEs in Singapore. *Journal of Public Relations Research*, *24*(4), 299–317. doi:10.1080/1062726X.2012.689898

Lee, M.-C. (2009). Factors influencing the adoption of internet banking: An integration of TAM and TPB with perceived risk and perceived benefit. *Electronic Commerce Research and Applications*, *8*(3), 130–141. doi:10.1016/j.elerap.2008.11.006

Lee, S. M., Lim, S. B., & Pathak, R. D. (2011). Culture and entrepreneurial orientation: A multi-country study. *The International Entrepreneurship and Management Journal*, *7*(1), 1–15. doi:10.1007/s11365-009-0117-4

Lee, S. M., & Peterson, S. J. (2000). Culture, entrepreneurial orientation, and global competitiveness. *Journal of World Business*, *35*(4), 401–416. doi:10.1016/S1090-9516(00)00045-6

Lehtinen, U., & Penttinen, H. (1999). Definition of the internationalization of the firm. In U. Lehtinen & H. Seristoe (Eds.), *Perspectives on internationalization* (pp. 3–19). Helsinki, Finland: Helsinki School of Economics and Business Administration.

Lei, C. F., & Ngai, E. W. T. (2013). *Green IT adoption: An academic review of literature.* Paper presented at the Pacific Asia Conference on Information System (PACIS).

Leonidou, L. C. (2004). An analysis of the barriers hindering small business export development. *Journal of Small Business Management*, *42*(3), 279–302. doi:10.1111/j.1540-627X.2004.00112.x

Lepoutre, J., & Heene, A. (2006). Investigating the impact of firm size on small business social responsibility: A critical review. *Journal of Business Ethics*, *67*(3), 257–273. doi:10.1007/s10551-006-9183-5

Lesáková, L. (2012).The role of business incubators in supporting the SME start-up. *Acta Polytechnica Hungarica*, *9*(3), 85–95.

Letsie, M., Kabanda, S., & Chigona, W. (2015). Economically disadvantaged families domesticating mobile devices: Case of South African. *Proceedings of the 9th IDIAConference*, 72–83.

Leung, P., Raar, J., & Tangey, G. (2008). *Accounting services and SMEs: An Australian Study.* ACCA Research Report No. 99.

Lévesque, M., & Minniti, M. (2006). The effect of aging on entrepreneurial behavior. *Journal of Business Venturing*, *21*(2), 177–194. doi:10.1016/j.jbusvent.2005.04.003

Levy, M., Loebbecke, C., & Powell, P. (2003). SMEs, co-opetition and knowledge sharing: The role of information systems1. *European Journal of Information Systems*, *12*(1), 3–17. doi:10.1057/palgrave.ejis.3000439

Lewis, K., Massey, C., Ashby, M., Coetzer, A., & Harris, C. (2007). Business assistance for SMEs: New Zealand owner-managers make their assessment. *Journal of Small Business and Enterprise Development*, *14*(4), 551–566. doi:10.1108/14626000710832695

Li, H., & Atuahene-Gima, K. (2001). Product innovation strategy and the performance of new technology ventures in China. *Academy of Management Journal*, *44*(6), 1123–1134. doi:10.2307/3069392

Lim, S., Trimi, S., & Lee, H. H. (2010). Web 2.0 service adoption and entrepreneurial orientation. *Service Business*, *4*(3/4), 197–207. doi:10.1007/s11628-010-0097-z

Lim, Y.-M., Lee, T.-H., & Cheng, B.-L. (2012). Entrepreneurial inclination among business students: A Malaysian study. *The South East Asian Journal of Management*, *6*(2), 113–127. doi:10.21002/seam.v6i2.1318

Liñán, F., & Santos, F. J. (2007). Does social capital affect entrepreneurial intentions? *International Advances in Economic Research*, *13*(4), 443–453. doi:10.1007/s11294-007-9109-8

Lindsay, B. R. (2011). *Social media and disasters: Current uses, future options, and policy considerations*. Academic Press.

Lindstrand, A., Eriksson, K., & Sharma, D. D. (2009). The perceived usefulness of knowledge supplied by foreign client networks. *International Business Review*, *18*(1), 26–37. doi:10.1016/j.ibusrev.2008.11.002

Lindstrand, A., Melen, S., & Nordman, E. R. (2011). Turning social capital into business: A study of the internationalization of biotech SMEs. *International Business Review*, *20*(2), 194–212. doi:10.1016/j.ibusrev.2011.01.002

Lin, Y., Wang, Y., & Yu, C. (2010). Investigating the drivers of the innovation in channel integration and supply chain performance: A strategy orientated perspective. *International Journal of Production Economics*, *127*(2), 320–332. doi:10.1016/j.ijpe.2009.08.009

Liu, H., Ding, X. H., Guo, H., & Luo, J. H. (2014). How does slack affect product innovation in high-tech Chinese firms: The contingent value of entrepreneurial orientation. *Asia Pacific Journal of Management*, *31*(1), 47–68. doi:10.1007/s10490-012-9309-5

Liu, H., & Fong, M. (2010). The Corporate Social Responsibility Orientation of Chinese Small and Medium Enterprises. *Journal of Business Systems. Governance and Ethics*, *5*(3), 33.

Li, Y., Guo, H., Liu, Y., & Li, M. (2008). Incentive mechanisms, entrepreneurial orientation, and technology commercialization: Evidence from Chinas' transitional economy. *Journal of Product Innovation Management*, *25*(1), 63–78. doi:10.1111/j.1540-5885.2007.00283.x

Li, Y., Zhao, Y., Tan, J., & Liu, Y. (2008). Moderating effects of entrepreneurial orientation on market orientation-performance linkage: Evidence from Chinese small firms. *Journal of Small Business Management*, *46*(1), 113–133. doi:10.1111/j.1540-627X.2007.00235.x

Lockett, A., Thompson, S., & Morgenstern, U. (2009). The development of the resource-based view of the firm: A critical appraisal. *International Journal of Management Reviews*, *11*(1), 9–28. doi:10.1111/j.1468-2370.2008.00252.x

Loebbecke, C., van Fenema, P. C., & Levy, M. (1999). SMEs, co-opetition and knowledge Transfer.*Proceedings of 7th European Conference on Information Systems.*

London, T., Anupindi, R., & Sheth, S. (2010). Creating mutual value: Lessons learned from ventures serving base of the pyramid producers. *Journal of Business Research*, *63*(6), 582–594. doi:10.1016/j.jbusres.2009.04.025

London, T., & Hart, S. (2004). Reinventing strategies for emerging markets: Beyond the transnational model. *Journal of International Business Studies*, *35*(5), 350–370. doi:10.1057/palgrave.jibs.8400099

Longo, M., Mura, M., & Bonoli, A. (2005). Corporate social responsibility and corporate performance: The case of Italian SMEs. *Corporate Governance*, *5*(4), 28–42. doi:10.1108/14720700510616578

Lopez, L. E., Kundu, S., & Ciravegna, L. (2009). Born global or born regional? Evidence from an exploratory study in the Costa Rican software industry. *Journal of International Business Studies*, *40*(7), 1228–1238. doi:10.1057/jibs.2008.69

Lordkipanidze, M., Brezet, H., & Backman, M. (2005). The entrepreneurship factor in sustainable tourism development. *Journal of Cleaner Production*, *13*(8), 787–798. doi:10.1016/j.jclepro.2004.02.043

Loucks, E. S., Martens, M. L., & Cho, C. H. (2010). Engaging small- and medium-sized businesses in sustainability. *Sustainability Accounting. Management and Policy Journal*, *1*(2), 178–200.

Low, G. S., & Lamb, J. C. W. Jr. (2000). The measurement and dimensionality of brand associations. *Journal of Product and Brand Management*, *9*(6), 350–370. doi:10.1108/10610420010356966

Low, M. B., & MacMillan, I. C. (1988). Entrepreneurship: Past research and future challenges. *Journal of Management*, *14*(2), 139–161. doi:10.1177/014920638801400202

Lubatkin, M. H., Simsek, Z., Ling, Y., & Veiga, J. F. (2006). Ambidexterity and performance in small-to medium-sized firms: The pivotal role of top management team behavioral integration. *Journal of Management*, *32*(5), 646–672. doi:10.1177/0149206306290712

Lucas, R. E. Jr. (1988). On the mechanics of economic development. *Journal of Monetary Economics*, *22*(1), 3–42. doi:10.1016/0304-3932(88)90168-7

Luftman, J. (1996). *Competing in the information age: strategic alignment in practice*. New York: Oxford University press.

Lu, J. W., & Beamish, P. W. (2006). SME internationalization and performance: Growth vs. profitability. *Journal of International Entrepreneurship*, *4*(1), 27–48. doi:10.1007/s10843-006-8000-7

Lu, J. Y., & Castka, P. (2009). Corporate social responsibility in Malaysia - experts views and perspectives. *Corporate Social Responsibility and Environmental Management*, *16*(3), 146–154. doi:10.1002/csr.184

Lumpkin, G. T., Cogliser, C. C., & Schneider, D. R. (2009). Understanding and measuring autonomy: An entrepreneurial orientation perspective. *Entrepreneurship Theory and Practice*, *33*(1), 47–69. doi:10.1111/j.1540-6520.2008.00280.x

Lumpkin, G. T., & Dess, G. G. (1996). Clarifying the entrepreneurial orientation construct and linking it to performance. *Academy of Management Review*, *21*(1), 135–172.

Lumpkin, G. T., & Dess, G. G. (2001). Linking two dimensions of entrepreneurial orientation to firm performance: The moderating role of environment and industry life cycle. *Journal of Business Venturing*, *16*(5), 429–451. doi:10.1016/S0883-9026(00)00048-3

Lund Vinding, A. (2006). Absorptive capacity and innovative performance: A human capital approach. *Economics of Innovation and New Technology*, *15*(4-5), 507–517. doi:10.1080/10438590500513057

Luoma-aho, V., Vos, M., Lappalainen, R., Lämsä, A.-M., Uusitalo, O., Maaranen, P., & Koski, A. (2012). Added value of intangibles for organizational innovation. *Human Technology*, *8*(1), 7–23. doi:10.17011/ht/urn.201205141650

Lusch, R. F., & Harvey, M. G. (1994). Opinion: The Case for an Off-Balance-Sheet Controller. *Sloan Management Review*, *35*(2), 101.

Lusch, R. F., & Vargo, S. L. (2014). *The service-dominant logic of marketing: Dialog, debate, and directions*. New York: Routledge.

Lussier, R., & Pfeifer, S. (2001). A crossnational prediction model of business success. *Journal of Small Business Management*, *39*(3), 228–239. doi:10.1111/0447-2778.00021

Maduku, D. K. (2013). Predicting retail banking customers' attitude towards internet banking services in South Africa. *Southern African Business Review*, *17*(3), 76–100.

Maduku, D. K., & Mpinganjira, M. (2012). An empirical investigation into customers' attitude towards usage of cell phone banking in Gauteng, South Africa. *Journal of Contemporary Management*, *9*, 172–189.

Mahajar, A. J., Binti, J., & Yunus, M. (2006). The Effectiveness of Government Export Assistance Programs on Malaysia Small & Medium Enterprises (SMEs). *Problems and Perspectives in Management, 1*.

Mahmood, R., & Hanafi, N. (2013). Entrepreneurial orientation and business performance of women-owned small and medium enterprises in Malaysia: Competitive advantage as a mediator. *International Journal of Business and Social Science*, *4*(1), 82–90.

Malaquias, R. F., & Hwang, Y. (2016). An empirical study on trust in mobile banking: A developing country perspective. *Computers in Human Behavior*, *54*, 453–461. doi:10.1016/j.chb.2015.08.039

Mäläskä, M., Saraniemi, S., & Tähtinen, J. (2010). *Co-creation of Branding by Network Actors.* Paper presented at the 10th annual EBRF conference on Co-Creation as a Way Forward, Co-creation of Branding by Network Actors.

Malaysian Department of Statistics. (2016). Retrieved 2 April 2014, from http://www.statistics.gov.my

Malhotra, N. K., Peterson, M., & Kleiser, S. B. (1999). Marketing research: A state-of-the-art review and directions for the twenty-first century. *Journal of the Academy of Marketing Science*, *27*(2), 160–183. doi:10.1177/0092070399272004

Mambula, C. (2002). Perceptions of SME growth constraints in Nigeria. *Journal of Small Business Management*, *40*(1), 58–65. doi:10.1111/1540-627X.00039

Mamun, A. A., Hossain, M. M. and Mizan A. N. K, (2012). *SME Financing: Demand Side Problems and Supply Side Responses.* Research Monograph 003. BIBM.

Mamun, A. A., Hossain, M. M., & Mizan, A. N. K. (2013). *Working Capital Financing in SMEs: Problems and Issues.* Bangladesh Institute of Bank Management.

Mansano, F. H., & Pereira, M. F. (2016). Business Incubators as Support Mechanism for the Economic Development: Case of Maringas Technology Incubator. *International Journal of Innovation*, *4*(1), 23–32. doi:10.5585/iji.v4i1.51

Manstead, A. S., & Eekelen, S. A. (1998). Distinguishing between perceived behavioral control and self-efficacy in the domain of academic achievement intentions and behaviors. *Journal of Applied Social Psychology*, *28*(15), 1375–1392. doi:10.1111/j.1559-1816.1998.tb01682.x

Manueli, K., Latu, S., & Koh, D. (2007). *ICT Adoption Models.* Paper presented at the 20th Annual Conference of the National Advisory Committee on Computing Qualifications (NACCQ 2007), Nelson, New Zealand.

Marchis, G., & Lecturer, S. (2011). Fundamentals of Business Incubator Development. *EIRP Proceedings*, *2*, 85–94. Retrieved from http://www.proceedings.univ-danubius.ro/index.php/eirp/article/download/955/874

March, J. G. (1991). Exploration and exploitation in organizational learning. *Organization Science*, *2*(1), 71–87. doi:10.1287/orsc.2.1.71

Maria, S. (2011). CSR in SMEs: Strategies, practices, motivations and obstacles. *Social Responsibility Journal*, *7*(3), 490–508. doi:10.1108/17471111111154581

Marino, L., Strandholm, K., Steensma, H. K., & Weaver, K. M. (2002). The moderating effect of national culture on the relationship between entrepreneurial orientation and strategic alliance portfolio extensiveness. *Entrepreneurship Theory and Practice*, *26*(4), 145–160.

Martin, B. R. (2013). Innovation studies: an emerging agenda. In Innovation Studies: Evolution and Future Challenges. Academic Press.

Martin, C. A. (2005). From high maintenance to high productivity: What managers need to know about Generation Y. *Industrial and Commercial Training*, *37*(1), 39–44. doi:10.1108/00197850510699965

Martinez Peria, M. S., & Singh, S. (2014). *The impact of credit information sharing reforms on firm financing?* World Bank Policy Research, Working Paper No 7013.

Martins, E. C., & Terblanche, F. (2003). Building Organizational Culture that Stimulates Creativity and Innovation. *European Journal of Innovation Management*, *6*(1), 64–74. doi:10.1108/14601060310456337

Martin, X., Mitchell, W., & Swaminathan, A. (1995). Recreating and extending Japanese automobile buyersupplier links in north America. *Strategic Management Journal*, *16*(8), 589–619. doi:10.1002/smj.4250160803

Masocha, R., Chiliya, N., & Zindiye, S. (2011). E-banking adoption by customers in the rural milieus of South Africa: A case of Alice, Eastern Cape, South Africa. *African Journal of Business Management*, *5*(5), 1857–1863.

Masurel, E. (2007). Why SMEs invest in environmental measures: Sustainability evidence from small and medium-sized printing firms. *Business Strategy and the Environment*, *16*(3), 190–201. doi:10.1002/bse.478

Mas-Verdú, F., Ribeiro-Soriano, D., & Roig-Tierno, N. (2015). Firm survival: The role of incubators and business characteristics. *Journal of Business Research*, *68*(4), 793–796. doi:10.1016/j.jbusres.2014.11.030

Mat Roni, S. (2014). *Introduction to SPSS*. Retrieved 10 August, 2016, from www.researchgate.net/publication/262151892_Introduction_to_SPSS

Mathieson, K. (1991). Predicting user intentions: Comparing the technology acceptance model with the theory of planned behavior. *Information Systems Research*, *2*(3), 173–191. doi:10.1287/isre.2.3.173

Matlay, H. (2008). The impact of entrepreneurship education on entrepreneurial outcomes. *Journal of Small Business and Enterprise Development*, *15*(2), 382–396. doi:10.1108/14626000810871745

Mc Cosker, P. (2000). *The effective management of Working Capital*. CIMA Management Accounting Magazine.

McConnell, J. J., & Servaes, H. (1990). Additional evidence on equity ownership and corporate value. *Journal of Financial Economics*, *27*(2), 595–612. doi:10.1016/0304-405X(90)90069-C

McDermott, C. M., & Prajogo, D. (2012). Service innovation and performance in SMEs. *International Journal of Operations & Production Management*, *32*(2), 216–237. doi:10.1108/01443571211208632

McDougall, P. P., Shane, S., & Oviatt, B. M. (1994). Explaining the formation of international new ventures: The limits of theories from international business research. *Journal of Business Venturing*, *9*(6), 469–487. doi:10.1016/0883-9026(94)90017-5

Mchombu, K. J., & Mchombu, C. M. (2014). *The Role of Information and Knowledge in Poverty Eradication in Africa: a case study of Namibia*. Retrieved from http://library.ifla.org/996/1/189-mchombu-en.pdf

Md Rasli, A., Khan, S., Malekifar, S., & Jabeen, S. (2013). Factors affecting entrepreneurial intention among graduate students of Universiti Teknologi Malaysia. *International Journal of Business and Social Science, 4*(2), 182-188.

MDeC. (2014). *MSC Annual Report 2014*. MDeC.

Mehrtens, J., Cragg, P. B., & Mills, A. M. (2001). A model of Internet adoption by SMEs. *Information & Management*, *39*(3), 165–176. doi:10.1016/S0378-7206(01)00086-6

Meihami, B., Varmaghani, Z., & Meihami, H. (2014). Role of Intellectual Capital on Firm Performance (Evidence from Iranian Companies). *International Letters of Social and Humanistic Sciences,* (12), 43-50.

Menon, A., & Varadarajan, P. R. (1992). A model of marketing knowledge use within firms. *Journal of Marketing*, *56*(4), 53–71. doi:10.2307/1251986

Menon, J. (2009). Macroeconomic management amid ethnic diversity: Fifty years of Malaysian experience. *Journal of Asian Economics*, *20*(1), 25–33. doi:10.1016/j.asieco.2008.05.005

Merrilees, B. (2007). A theory of brand-led SME new venture development. *Qualitative Market Research: An International Journal*, *10*(4), 403–415. doi:10.1108/13522750710819739

Merz, M. A., He, Y., & Vargo, S. L. (2009). The evolving brand logic: A service-dominant logic perspective. *Journal of the Academy of Marketing Science*, *37*(3), 328–344. doi:10.1007/s11747-009-0143-3

Meske, C., & Stieglitz, S. (2013). Adoption and use of social media in small and medium-sized enterprises. In *Practice-Driven Research on Enterprise Transformation* (pp. 61–75). Springer Berlin Heidelberg. doi:10.1007/978-3-642-38774-6_5

Michaelidou, N., Siamagka, N. T., & Christodoulides, G. (2011). Usage, barriers and measurement of social media marketing: An exploratory investigation of small and medium B2B brands. *Industrial Marketing Management, 40*(7), 1153–1159. doi:10.1016/j.indmarman.2011.09.009

Michel, G., & Rieunier, S. (2012). Nonprofit brand image and typicality influences on charitable giving. *Journal of Business Research, 65*(5), 701–707. doi:10.1016/j.jbusres.2011.04.002

Miller, J. G., & Roth, A. V. (1994). A taxonomy of manufacturing strategies. *Management Science, 40*(3), 285–304. doi:10.1287/mnsc.40.3.285

Mines, C., & Davis, E. (2007). *Topic overview: Green IT.* Forrester Research.

Ministry of Economic Development. (2004). *Digital strategy: A draft New Zealand digital strategy for consultation.* Wellington: Ministry of Economic Development.

Ministry of Finance. (2013). *Gross domestic product by kind of economic activity at constant 2005 prices (RM million) 2013-2013.* Retrieved 21 June, 2016, from http://www.treasury.gov.my/pdf/ekonomi/dataekonomi/2013/timeseries/GDPbySector2013_2014.pdf

Ministry of Finance. (2016). *Economic performance and prospects Economic Report 2015/2016. Kuala Lumpur.* Malaysia: Ministry of Finance.

Ministry of International Trade and Industry. (2006). *IMP3: Third Industrial Master Plan 2006-2020, Malasia: Toward global competitiveness.* Retrieved from http://mset.org.my/myraig/pdf/Industry/MasterPlan3/Review-MITI%20IMP3.pdf

Mintzberg, H., Raisinghani, D., & Theoret, A. (1976). The structure of "unstructured" decision processes. *Administrative Science Quarterly, 21*(2), 246–275. doi:10.2307/2392045

Modimogale, L., & Kroeze, J. H. (2009). Using ICTs to become a competitive SME in South Africa. In *Proceedings of the 13th International Business Information Management Association Conference* (pp. 504–513). Norristown, PA: International Business Information Management Association.

Moen, Ø., Gavlen, M., & Endresen, I. (2004). Internationalization of small, computer software firms: Entry firms and market selection. *European Journal of Marketing, 38*(9), 1236–1251. doi:10.1108/03090560410548951

Mohamed, Z., Rezai, G., Shamsudin, M. N., & Mahmud, M. M. (2012). Enhancing young graduates' intention towards entrepreneurship development in Malaysia. *Education + Training, 54*(7), 605-618.

Mohamed, Z., Rezai, G., & Shamsudin, M. N. (2011). The effectiveness of entrepreneurship extension education among the FOA members in Malaysia. *Current Research Journal of Social Sciences, 3*(1), 17–21.

Mohammad Nor, N. A. A., Nik Mohd Masdek, N. R., & Maidin, M. K. H. (2015). Youth inclination towards agricultural entrepreneurship. *Economic and Technology Management Review, 10a*, 47–55.

Mohan, A. V., Omar, A. A, & Aziz, K. A. (2004). ICT Clusters as a Way to Materialize a National System of Innovation: Malaysia's Multimedia Super Corridor Flagships. *The Electronic Journal of Information Systems in Developing Countries, 16*(5), 1–18.

Mohd Saffar, A. (2007). *Asia Regional Workshop Innovation: The Role of Business Incubation Innovation and Entrepreneurship Policy Framework : The Malaysian Experience in Building Sustainable Incubation Industry (Movement).* Forum American Bar Association.

Mohd Shariff, M. N., Peou, C., & Ali, J. (2010). Moderating Effect of Government Policy on Entrepreneurship and Growth Performance of Small-Medium Enterprises in Cambodia. *International Journal of Business & Management Science, 3*(1), 57–72.

Mohd Yunos, M. G. (2002). Building an innovation-based economy: The Malaysian technology business incubator experience. *Journal of Change Management, 3*(2), 177–188. doi:10.1080/714042527

Mohd Yusof, A. B., & Raja Abd Rahman, R. R. (2007). *Green lifestyle: Evaluating new business and income enhancement through agripreneurship development*. Paper presented at the The USM-UPM-PETA Conference, Penang, Malaysia.

Mohiuddin, M. (2014). Overview the e-commerce in Bangladesh. *IOSR Journal of Business and Management, 16*(7), 1–6.

Mok, H.-F., Williamson, V. G., Grove, J. R., Burry, K., Barker, S. F., & Hamilton, A. J. (2014). Strawberry fields forever? Urban agriculture in developed countries: A review. *Agronomy for Sustainable Development, 34*(1), 21–43. doi:10.1007/s13593-013-0156-7

Mokhtar, S. S. M., Yusoff, R. Z., & Ahmad, A. (2014). Key elements of market orientation on Malaysian SMEs performance. *International Journal of Business and Society, 15*(1), 49.

Molla, A., Cooper, V. A., & Pittayachawan, S. (2009). IT and eco-sustainability: Developing and validating a green IT readiness model. *ICIS 2009 Proceedings, 141.*

Molla., A., Cooper., V., & Pittayachawan., S. (2011). The green IT readiness(g-readiness) of organizations: An exploratory analysis of a construct and instrument. *Communication of Association of Information Systems, 29.*

Molla, A., Abareshi, A., & Cooper, V. (2014). Green IT beliefs and pro-environmental IT practices among IT professionals. *Information Technology & People, 27*(2), 129–154. doi:10.1108/ITP-10-2012-0109

Möller, K. K., & Törrönen, P. (2003). Business suppliers value creation potential: A capability-based analysis. *Industrial Marketing Management, 32*(2), 109–118. doi:10.1016/S0019-8501(02)00225-0

Mongsawad, P. (2009). Sufficiency Economy: A Contribution to Economic Development. *International Journal of Humanities and Social Science, 4*(2), 144–151.

Montgomery, K. C., & Chester, J. (2009). Interactive food and beverage marketing: Targeting adolescents in the digital age. *The Journal of Adolescent Health, 45*(3), S18–S29. doi:10.1016/j.jadohealth.2009.04.006 PMID:19699433

Moore, C., Boyd, B. L., & Dooley, K. E. (2010). The effects of experiential learning with an emphasis on reflective writing on deep-level processing of leadership students. *Journal of Leadership Education, 9*(1), 36–52. doi:10.12806/V9/I1/RF3

Moore, K., Berger, P. D., & Weinberg, B. D. (2014). *Issues for Exploration of Differing Values among Sub-groups of Young-Adult Consumers* (Vol. 1). Global Journal of Business and Social Science.

Moorthy, M. K., Tan, A., Choo, C., Wei, C. S., Ping, J. T. Y., & Leong, T. K. (2012). A study on factors affecting the performance of SMEs in Malaysia. *International Journal of Academic Research in Business and Social Sciences, 2*(4), 224–239.

Moorthy, M. K., Tan, A., Choo, C., Wei, C. S., Tan, J., Ping, Y., & Leong, T. K. (2012). A Study on Factors Affecting the Performance of SMEs in Malaysia. *International Journal of Academic Research in Business and Social Sciences, 2*(4), 224–239.

Moreno, A. M., & Casillas, J. C. (2008). Entrepreneurial orientation and growth of SMEs: A causal model. *Entrepreneurship Theory and Practice, 32*(3), 507–528. doi:10.1111/j.1540-6520.2008.00238.x

Morgan, G. (1989). *Creative Organization Theory: A Resource Handbook.* London: Sage Publications.

Morris, L. (2007). *Creating the innovation culture: Geniuses, champions, and leaders*. White Paper, Innovation Labs, retrieved February 25, 2016, from http://www. innovationlabs. com/innovation_culture2. html

Morris, M. H., Koçak, A., & Özer, A. (2007). Coopetition as a small business strategy: Implications for performance. *Journal of Small Business Strategy*, *18*(1), 35.

Morsing, M., & Perrini, F. (2009). CSR in SMEs: Do SMEs matter for the CSR agenda? *Business Ethics (Oxford, England)*, *18*(1), 1–6. doi:10.1111/j.1467-8608.2009.01544.x

Mostafa, R. H. A., Wheeler, C., & Jones, M. V. (2005). Entrepreneurial orientation, commitment to the Internet and export performance in small and medium sized exporting firms. *Journal of International Entrepreneurship*, *3*(4), 291–302. doi:10.1007/s10843-006-7857-9

MOSTI. (2010). *Malaysian science and technology incubator report 2010*. Retrieved April 16, 2016, from http://www.mosti.gov.my/

Movahedi, R., Latifi, S., & Sayyar, L. Z. (2013). The factors affecting agricultural students' attitude towards self-employment and entrepreneurship. *International Journal of Agriculture and Crop Sciences*, *5*(16), 1813–1819.

Moyeen, A., & Courvisanos, J. (2012). Corporate social responsibility in regional small and medium-sized enterprises in Australia. *Australasian Journal of Regional Studies*, *18*(3), 364–391.

MSC Malaysia. (1998). *Cybercity Malaysia*. Author.

Mubaraka, C. M., Momanyi, W. K., & Jibia, M. S. (2013). Integrating ICT in insurance management : Design & development of an online insurance system for E. Africa insurance company. *Journal of Information Engineering and Applications*, *3*(5), 10–20.

Mudambi, S. (2002). Branding importance in business-to-business markets: Three buyer clusters. *Industrial Marketing Management*, *31*(6), 525–533. doi:10.1016/S0019-8501(02)00184-0

Mueller, V., Rosenbusch, N., & Bausch, A. (2013). Success patterns of exploratory and exploitative innovation a meta-analysis of the influence of institutional factors. *Journal of Management*, *39*(6), 1606–1636. doi:10.1177/0149206313484516

Muhamed, K., & Haron, S. (2011). *Poverty Mapping: An effective approach in determining the poor area- Case Study of Johor.* Retrieved June 20, 2013, from http://ww.statistics.gov.my

Muhammad, M. Z., Char, A. K., Yasoa', M. R., & Hassan, Z. (2010). Small and medium enterprises (SMEs) competing in the global business environment: A case of Malaysia. *International Business Research*, *3*(1), 66–75.

Muhammad, M., Ismail, A. A., & Eh Rak, A. (2013). Competency of agriculture graduates in Malaysian public universities. *International Journal of Enhanced Research in Educational Development*, *1*(1), 1–9.

Muhammad, W. J. K., & Khalique, D. M. (2014). An Overview of Small and Medium Enterprises in Malaysia and Pakistan: Past, Present and Future Scenario. *Business and Management Horizons*, *2*(2), 38–49. doi:10.5296/bmh.v2i2.5792

Mumford, M. (2000). Managing creative people: Strategies and tactics for innovation. *Human Resource Management Review*, *10*(3), 313–351. doi:10.1016/S1053-4822(99)00043-1

Munir, K., Ansari, S., & Gregg, T. (2010). Beyond the hype: taking business strategy to the bottom of the pyramid. In J. Baum & J. Lampel (Eds.), *The Globalization of Strategy Research* (pp. 247–276). Bingley, UK: Emerald. doi:10.1108/S0742-3322(2010)0000027012

Murari, K., & Tater, B. (2014). Employees attitude towards adoption of IT-based banking services: A case of Indian private sector banks. *Competitiveness Review*, *24*(2), 107–118. doi:10.1108/CR-01-2013-0005

Murugesan, S. (2008). Harnessing green IT: Principles and practices. *IT Professional*, *10*(1), 24–33. doi:10.1109/MITP.2008.10

Musteen, M., Francis, J., & Datta, D. K. (2010). The influence of international networks on internationalization speed and performance: A study of Czech SMEs. *Journal of World Business*, *45*(3), 197–205. doi:10.1016/j.jwb.2009.12.003

Nagalakshmi, T., & Sudhakar, A. (2013). Agri-preneurs: A case study of Dharmapuri farmers. *International Journal of Science and Research*, *2*(8), 208–214.

Nahapiet, J., & Ghoshal, S. (1998). Social capital, intellectual capital, and the organizational advantage. *Academy of Management Review*, *23*(2), 242–266.

Najib, M., & Kiminami, A. (2011). Innovation, cooperation and business performance: Some evidence from Indonesian small food processing cluster. *Journal of Agribusiness in Developing and Emerging Economies*, *1*(1), 75–96. doi:10.1108/20440831111131523

Nakhata, C. (2010). The Relationship between Job Dimensions and Job Satisfaction of SME Entrepreneurs in Thailand. *Journal of American Academy of Business, Cambridge*, *15*(2), 220–227.

Naldi, L., Nordqvist, M., Sjöberg, K., & Wiklund, J. (2007). Entrepreneurial orientation, risk taking, and performance in family firms. *Family Business Review*, *20*(1), 33–47. doi:10.1111/j.1741-6248.2007.00082.x

Nam, Y. H. (2000). The roles of incubator organizations in hi-tech venture creation in Korea. *Asia Pacific Journal of Management*, *17*(2), 277–296. doi:10.1023/A:1015813710027

Nandan, S. (2005). An exploration of the brand identity–brand image linkage: A communications perspective. *The Journal of Brand Management*, *12*(4), 264–278. doi:10.1057/palgrave.bm.2540222

Naranjo-Valencia, J. C., Jiménez-Jiménez, D., & Sanz-Valle, R. (2011). Innovation or imitation? The role of organizational culture. *Management Decision*, *49*(1), 55–72. doi:10.1108/00251741111094437

Narayanasamy, K., Rasiah, D., & Tan, T. M. (2011). The adoption and concerns of e-finance in Malaysia. *Electronic Commerce Research*, *11*(4), 383–400. doi:10.1007/s10660-011-9081-5

Nasir, M. (2012, December). Innovative accountants the key to success. *Malaysia SME.*, *15*, 32.

Nasri, W. (2011). Factors influencing the adoption of internet banking in Tunisia. *International Journal of Business and Management*, *6*(8), 143–160. doi:10.5539/ijbm.v6n8p143

Nath, P., Nachiappan, S., & Ramanathan, R. (2010). The impact of marketing capability, operations capability and diversification strategy on performance: A resource-based view. *Industrial Marketing Management*, *39*(2), 317–329. doi:10.1016/j.indmarman.2008.09.001

National Agency for Information and Communication Technologies. (2008). *Cameroon national ICT Policy 10-03-2008*. Retrieved 05 30, 2009, from www.antic.com: http://www.antic.cm/IMG/pdf/Cameroun_National_ICT_Policy_10-03-2008.pdf

National Bureau of Statistics. (2015). *Unemployment/Under-Employment Watch, Q1- 2015*. Federal Republic of Nigeria.

National Economic Empowerment Strategy. (2006). The Federal Government of Nigeria.

National Encyclopedia of Bangladesh. (2015). Banglapedia. In S. Islam (Ed.), *National Encyclopedia of Bangladesh* (2nd ed.). Dhaka, Bangladesh: The Asiatic Society.

National Population Census (NPC). (1991). Federal Bureau of Statistics, The Federal Government of Nigeria.

National SME Development Council. (2012). *SME annual report 2010/11*. SME Corp. Malaysia. Retrieved April 16, 2016, from http://www.smecorp.gov.my/

National SME Development Council. (2013). *SME annual report 2013/2014: Transitioning for productivity-led and innovation-driven growth*. Sentral, Malaysia: SME Corporation Malaysia. Retrieved from http://www.smecorp.gov.my/vn2/node/1475

NBA. (2012). *Corporate Social Responsibility: CSR for SME accountants*. Nederlandse Beroepsorganisatie van Accountant.

Ndayizigamiye, P. (2014). The influence of SMMEs internal factors on e-commerce adoption: A South African perspective. *Mediterranean Journal of Social Sciences*, *5*(23), 246–253.

NEAC. (2010). *New Economic Model for Malaysia. Part 1: Strategic Policy Directions*. NEAC.

Nejati, M., & Amran, A. (2009). Corporate social responsibility and SMEs: Exploratory study on motivations from a Malaysian perspective. *Business Strategy Series*, *10*(5), 259–265. doi:10.1108/17515630910989150

Nejati, M., & Amran, A. (2012). Does ownership type cause any difference in the perception of Malaysian SME owners/managers towards corporate social responsibility? *International Journal of Business Governance and Ethics*, *7*(1), 63–81. doi:10.1504/IJBGE.2012.046105

Neneh, N. B., & Vanzyl, J. (2012). Towards establishing long term surviving small and medium enterprises (SMEs) in South Africa: An entrepreneurial approach. *African Journal of Business Management*, *6*(28), 8327–8343.

Nerkar, A., & Paruchuri, S. (2005). Evolution of R&D capabilities: The role of knowledge networks within a firm. *Management Science*, *51*(5), 771–786. doi:10.1287/mnsc.1040.0354

New Economic Model. (2012). *New Economic Model for Malaysia*. Retrieved April 16, 2016, from http://www.epu.gov.my/en/new-economic-model

Ngo, H.-Y., & Loi, R. (2008). Human resource flexibility, organizational culture and firm performance: An investigation of multinational firms in Hong Kong. *International Journal of Human Resource Management*, *19*(9), 1654–1666. doi:10.1080/09585190802295082

Nha, P. X., & Quan, L. (2014). *Response of Vietnamese private enterprises' leader under global financial crisis: From theorical to empirical approach*. Asian Social Science. doi:10.5539/ass.v10n9p26

Nonaka, I., & Takeuchi, H. (2007). The knowledge-creating company. *Harvard Business Review*, *85*(7/8), 162–171.

Nordin. (2002). *Revenue Implications of E-Commerce, Goverment and Private Sector Experiences*. Presentation at WTO Regional Seminar on Electronic Commerce, Geneva, Switzerland.

North, D. C. (1990). *Institutions, Institutional Change and Economic Performance*. Cambridge, UK: Cambridge University Press. doi:10.1017/CBO9780511808678

NSDC. (2012). *SME Masterplan 2012-2012: Catalysing Growth and Income*. National SME Development Council.

Nussbaum, M. C., Sen, A., & Sugden, R. (1993). *The quality of life*. Oxford, UK: Clarendon Press Oxford. doi:10.1093/0198287976.001.0001

Nystrom, P. C., Ramamurthy, K., & Wilson, A. L. (2002). Organizational context, climate and innovativeness: Adoption of imaging technology. *Journal of Engineering and Technology Management*, *19*(3), 221–247. doi:10.1016/S0923-4748(02)00019-X

O'Reilly, C. A., & Tushman, M. L. (2004). The ambidextrous organization. *Harvard Business Review*, *82*(4), 74–81. PMID:15077368

Obokoh, L. O. (2008). Small and medium sized enterprises development under trade liberalisation: A survey of Nigerian experience. *International Journal of Business and Management*, *3*(12), 92–101.

OCass, A., & Viet Ngo, L. (2007). Market orientation versus innovative culture: Two routes to superior brand performance. *European Journal of Marketing*, *41*(7/8), 868–887. doi:10.1108/03090560710752438

Odoyo, F. S., & Nyangosi, R. (2011). E-insurance : An empirical study of perceived benefits. *International Journal of Business and Social Science*, *2*(21), 166–171.

OECD. (2009). *Top barriers and drivers to SME internationalisation*. Paris, France: Organisation for Economic Co-operation and Development.

OECD. (2014). *Structural Policy Country Notes*. Retrieved from http://www.oecd.org/site/seao/Viet Nam.pdf

Oh, W., Choi, J. N., & Kim, K. (2006). Coauthorship dynamics and knowledge capital: The patterns of cross-disciplinary collaboration in information systems research. *Journal of Management Information Systems*, *22*(3), 266–292. doi:10.2753/MIS0742-1222220309

Ojasalo, J., Nätti, S., & Olkkonen, R. (2008). Brand building in software SMEs: An empirical study. *Journal of Product and Brand Management*, *17*(2), 92–107. doi:10.1108/10610420810864702

Oke, A., Burke, G., & Myers, A. (2007). Innovation types and performance in growing UK SMEs. *International Journal of Operations & Production Management*, *27*(7), 735–753. doi:10.1108/01443570710756974

Okezie, C. A., & Baharuddin, A. H. (2012). Risk and poverty in agriculture: Expanding roles for agricultural cooperatives in Malaysia. *Geografia: Malaysian Journal of Society and Space*, *8*(4), 1–11.

Okpara, J. O. (2011). Factors constraining the growth and survival of SMEs in Nigeria: Implications for poverty alleviation. *Management Research Review*, *34*(2), 156–171. doi:10.1108/01409171111102786

Okpara, J. O., & Kumbiadis, N. (2008). SMEs export orientation and performance: Evidence from a developing economy. *International Review of Business Research Papers*, *4*(5), 109–119.

Olejnik, E., & Swoboda, B. (2012). SMEs' internationalisation patterns: Descriptives, dynamics and determinants. *International Marketing Review*, *29*(5), 466–495. doi:10.1108/02651331211260340

Omar, C. M. Z. C., & Azmi, N. M. N. (2016). Factors Affecting the Success of Bumiputera Entrepreneurs in Small and Medium Enterprises (SMEs) in Malaysia. *International Journal of Management Science and Business Administration*, *1*(9), 40–45. doi:10.18775/ijmsba.1849-5664-5419.2014.19.1004

Omiunu, O. G. (2014). *ICT deployment, business environment information and information strategy as correlates of Women-owned SMEs performance in Oyo State, Nigeria* (Masters dissertation). Africa Regional Centre for Information Science, University of Ibadan, Nigeria.

Omiunu, O. G. (n.d.). Deploying indigenous knowledge for sustainable development. *African Journal of Sustainable Development*, *2*(1), 149-170.

Omiunu, O. G. (2014). Towards a sustainable higher education for an increasing population and information technology dynamics. *Journal of Education Research and Behavioral Sciences.*, *3*(5), 116–121.

Ong, F. S., Azmi, A. A. C., Isa, C. R., Jusoh, R., & Kamarulzaman, Y. (2008). *A Report of Current Usage Patterns of Business and Professional Services Among SMEs in the Manufacturing and Distributive Trade Sectors*. MIA.

Ongori, H. (2009). Role of Information communication technologies in SMEs: Evidence from Botswana, *Research. Journal of Information Technology*, *1*(2), 79–85. doi:10.3923/rjit.2009.79.85

Onkelinx, J., Manolova, T. S., & Edelman, L. F. (2016). The human factor: Investments in employee human capital, productivity, and SME internationalization. *Journal of International Management*, *22*(4), 351–364. doi:10.1016/j.intman.2016.05.002

Onugu, B. A. N. (2005). *Small and medium enterprises (SMEs) in Nigeria: Problems and prospects* (Doctoral dissertation). St. Clements University.

Onugu, B. A. N. (2005). *Small and medium enterprises (SMEs) in Nigeria: Problems and prospects* (Unpublished Dissertation). St. Clements University, Nigeria.

Onwumere, J., & Ukpebor, P. O. (2011). Evaluation of earning performance of female owned leather-based enterprises in Aba Metropolis, Abia State, Nigeria. *Journal of Agriculture and Social Research*, *11*(2), 120–127.

Onyeagba, J. B. C. (2008). Micro-finance and micro financing as strategy for poverty reduction in Nigeria the emerging global technology. *Journal of International Politics and Development Studies*, *4*(1&2), 160–176.

Oosterlaken, I. (2009). Design for Development: A Capability Approach. *Design Issues*, *25*(4), 91–102. doi:10.1162/desi.2009.25.4.91

Oparaocha, G. O. (2015). SMEs and international entrepreneurship: An institutional network perspective. *International Business Review*, *24*(5), 861–873. doi:10.1016/j.ibusrev.2015.03.007

Osikabor, B., Adesope, A. A., Ibrahim, A. G., Babayemi, O. F., & Olatunji, B. T. (2011). Animal-agriculture based entrepreneurship: Descriptive norms, perceived economic viability and behavioural intention among final year agriculture related students in Ibadan, Nigeria. *Asian Journal of Agricultural Sciences*, *3*(2), 87–93.

OSMEP. (2006). *Small and Medium Enterprises Master Plan (2007-2011)*. Retrieved 28 November, 2010, from www.sme.go.th

OSMEP. (2010). *The White Paper on Small and Medium Enterprises Of Thailand in 2010 and Trends 2011*. Retrieved 26 July, 2011, from www.sme.go.th

OSMEP. (2015). *Situation and Economic Indicators of SMEs in 2015*. The White Paper on Small and Medium Enterprises Of Thailand in 2015. Retrieved October 11, 2016 from http://www.sme.go.th/eng/images/data/SR/download/2015/report_year/ExecutiveSummary/Chapter%201.pdf

Osmonalieva, Z. (Ed.). (2011). *Entrepreneurship Support*. Eskilstuna-Västerås, Sweden: Mälardalen University.

Ou, C., & Haynes, G. W. (2006). Acquisition of additional equity capital by small firms–findings from the national survey of small business finances. *Small Business Economics*, *27*(2-3), 157–168. doi:10.1007/s11187-006-0009-8

Oviatt, B. M., & McDougall, P. P. (2005). Defining international entrepreneurship and modelling the speed of internationalization. *Entrepreneurship Theory and Practice*, *29*(5), 537–553. doi:10.1111/j.1540-6520.2005.00097.x

Owens, T., Hoddinott, J., & Kinsey, B. (2003). The impact of agricultural extension on farm production in resettlement areas of Zimbabwe. *Economic Development and Cultural Change*, *51*(2), 337–357. doi:10.1086/346113

Parasuraman, S., & Simmers, C. A. (2001). Type of employment, work–family conflict and well-being: A comparative study. *Journal of Organizational Behavior*, *22*(5), 551–568. doi:10.1002/job.102

Parcell, J., & Sykuta, M. (2003). *Undergraduate perceptions of the need for an agricultural entrepreneurship curriculum*. Paper presented at the Agricultural Economics Association Annual Meeting, Denver, CO.

Park, B. J. R., Srivastava, M. K., & Gnyawali, D. R. (2014). Walking the tight rope of coopetition: Impact of competition and cooperation intensities and balance on firm innovation performance. *Industrial Marketing Management*, *43*(2), 210–221. doi:10.1016/j.indmarman.2013.11.003

Park, C. H., & Kim, Y. G. (2003). A framework of dynamic CRM: Linking marketing with information strategy. *Business Process Management Journal*, *9*(5), 652–671. doi:10.1108/14637150310496749

Park, C. W., Jaworski, B. J., & Maclnnis, D. J. (1986). Strategic brand concept-image management. *Journal of Marketing*, *50*(4), 135–145. doi:10.2307/1251291

Parker, C., Redmond, J., & Simpson, M. (2009). Review of interventions to encourage SMEs to make environmental improvements. *Environment and Planning. C, Government & Policy*, *27*(2), 279–301. doi:10.1068/c0859b

Patel, P. C., Kohtamäki, M., Parida, V., & Wincent, J. (2015). Entrepreneurial orientation-as-experimentation and firm performance: The enabling role of absorptive capacity. *Strategic Management Journal*, *36*(11), 1739–1749. doi:10.1002/smj.2310

Payne, A. F., Storbacka, K., & Frow, P. (2008). Managing the co-creation of value. *Journal of the Academy of Marketing Science*, *36*(1), 83–96. doi:10.1007/s11747-007-0070-0

Payne, A., Storbacka, K., Frow, P., & Knox, S. (2009). Co-creating brands: Diagnosing and designing the relationship experience. *Journal of Business Research*, *62*(3), 379–389. doi:10.1016/j.jbusres.2008.05.013

Pease, W., & Rowe, M. (2005). Use of information technology to facilitate collaboration and co-opetition between tourist operators in tourist destinations. Proceedings of Tourism Enterprise Strategies: Thriving-and Surviving-in an Online Era, 33-47.

Peel, M. J., Wilson, N., & Howorth, C. (2000). Late Payment and Credit Management in the Small Firm Sector: Some Empirical Evidence. *International Small Business Journal*, *18*(2), 17–37. doi:10.1177/0266242600182001

Pelletier, L. G., Tuson, K. M., Green-Demers, I., Noels, K., & Beaton, A. M. (1998). Why are you doing things for the environment? The motivation toward the environment scale (mtes) 1. *Journal of Applied Social Psychology*, *28*(5), 437–468. doi:10.1111/j.1559-1816.1998.tb01714.x

Peña, I. (2002). Intellectual capital and business start-up success. *Journal of Intellectual Capital*, *3*(2), 180–198. doi:10.1108/14691930210424761

Peng, M. W., & Luo, Y. (2000). Managerial ties and firm performance in a transition economy: The nature of a micro-macro link. *Academy of Management Journal*, *43*(3), 486–501. doi:10.2307/1556406

Pérez-Luño, A., Saparito, P., & Gopalakrishnan, S. (2016). Small and medium-sized enterprises' entrepreneurial versus market orientation and the creation of tacit knowledge. *Journal of Small Business Management*, *54*(1), 262–278. doi:10.1111/jsbm.12144

Performance Management and Delivery Unit. (2010). *Economic transformation programme: A roadmap for Malaysia*. Putrajaya, Malaysia: Performance Management and Delivery Unit (PEMANDU). Retrieved from http://www.moa.gov.my/documents/10157/c65bb64f-da6c-4e83-bb51-40a1a55b9954

Perrigot, R., López-Fernández, B., & Eroglu, S. (2013). Intangible Resources and Plural Form as Drivers of Franchise Internationalization: Examination within a Two-Country Perspective. *Journal of Small Business Management*, *51*(4), 557–577. doi:10.1111/jsbm.12006

Perrini, F. (2006). SMEs and CSR Theory: Evidence and Implications from an Italian Perspective. *Journal of Business Ethics*, *67*(3), 305–316. doi:10.1007/s10551-006-9186-2

Perrini, F., & Minoja, M. (2008). Strategizing corporate social responsibility: Evidence from an Italian medium-sized, family-owned company. *Business Ethics (Oxford, England)*, *17*(1), 47–63. doi:10.1111/j.1467-8608.2008.00519.x

Pervez, T., Maritz, A., & De Waal, A. (2013). Innovation and social entrepreneurship at the bottom of the pyramid – a conceptual framework. *South African Journal of Economic and Management Science*, *16*(5), 54–66.

Peteraf, M. A. (1993). The cornerstones of competitive advantage: A resource-based view. *Strategic Management Journal*, *14*(3), 179–191. doi:10.1002/smj.4250140303

Peterman, N. E., & Kennedy, J. (2003). Enterprise education: Influencing students perceptions of entrepreneurship. *Entrepreneurship Theory & Practice*, *28*(2), 129–144. doi:10.1046/j.1540-6520.2003.00035.x

Peterson, R., & Shulman, J. (1987). Capital structure of growing small firms: A 12-country study on becoming bankable. *International Small Business Journal*, *5*(4), 10–22. doi:10.1177/026624268700500401

Phillips, T., Lyons, P., Page, M., Viviez, L., Molina, M., & Ensor, T. (2011). *African Mobile Observatory 2011: Driving Economic and Social Development through Mobile Services.* Retrieved May 10, 2013, from http://www.gsma.com/spectrum/wp-content/uploads/2011/12/Africa-Mobile-Observatory-2011.pdf

Piboolsravut, P. (2004). Sufficiency Economy. *ASEAN Economic Bulletin*, *21*(1), 127–134. doi:10.1355/AE21-1H

Pierce, J. L., & Delbecq, A. L. (1977). Organization structure, individual attitudes and innovation. *Academy of Management Review*, *2*(1), 27–37.

Piercy, N., & Evans, M. (2014). *Managing Marketing Information (RLE Marketing)* (Vol. 17). New York, NY: Routledge.

Ping, X., & Chuanwei, Z. (2013). The theory of internet finance. *China Economist*, *8*(2), 1–15.

Pitroda, S. G. (1993). Development, democracy, and the village telephone. *Harvard Business Review*, *71*, 66–79.

Plested, B. A., Edwards, R. W., & Jumper-Thurman, P. (2006). *Community Readiness: A handbook for successful change.* Fort Collins, CO: Tri-Ethnic Center for Prevention Research.

Podolny, J. M. (2001). Networks as the Pipes and Prisms of the Market. *American Journal of Sociology*, *107*(1), 33–60. doi:10.1086/323038

Pohl, H., & Elmquist, M. (2010). Radical innovation in a small firm: A hybrid electric vehicle development project at Volvo Cars. *R & D Management*, *40*(4), 372–382. doi:10.1111/j.1467-9310.2010.00608.x

Poornima, S. C. (2009). Motivating through satisfaction: An on-going effort of HR in organisations. *IUP Journal of Management Research*, *8*(5), 26–37.

Prahalad, C. K., & Hart, S. (1999). *Strategies for the bottom of the pyramid: creating sustainable development.* Unpublished Draft Paper. Retrieved June 20, 2013, from http://www.nd.edu/~kmatta/mgt648/strategies.pdf

Prahalad, C. K. (2004). The cocreation of value. *Journal of Marketing*, *68*(1), 23.

Prahalad, C. K., & Hart, S. (2002). The fortune at the bottom of the pyramid. *Strategy Business*, *26*, 54–67.

Prahalad, C. K., & Ramaswamy, V. (2000). Co-opting customer competence. *Harvard Business Review*, *78*(1), 79–87.

Prahalad, C. K., & Ramaswamy, V. (2001). The value creation dilemma: New building blocks for co-creating experience. *Harvard Business Review*, *18*(3), 5–14.

Prahalad, C. K., & Ramaswamy, V. (2004). Co-creation experiences: The next practice in value creation. *Journal of Interactive Marketing*, *18*(3), 5–14. doi:10.1002/dir.20015

Prahalad, C. K., & Ramaswamy, V. (2013). *The future of competition: Co-creating unique value with customers*. Harvard Business Press.

Prasad, V. K., Ramamurthy, K., & Naidu, G. M. (2001). The influence of Internet-marketing integration on marketing competencies and export performance. *Journal of International Marketing*, *9*(4), 82–110. doi:10.1509/jimk.9.4.82.19944

Pugh, M. (2014). Why millennials should become entrepreneurs now? *Entrepreneur.* Retrieved 28 April, 2014, from http://www.entrepreneur.com/article/230886

Puntasen, A., Premchuen, S., & Keitdejpunya, P. (2003). *Application of the Royal Thought about the Sufficiency Economy in SMEs*. Bangkok: Thailand Research Fund.

Quan, L. (2015). Perceptions of Leadership Competencies and the Acquisition of Them by CEOs in Vietnamese Small Enterprises. *Asian Social Science*, *11*(4). doi:10.5539/ass.v11n4p17

Quan, X. (2012). Prior experience, social network, and levels of entrepreneurial intentions. *Management Research Review*, *35*(10), 945–957. doi:10.1108/01409171211272679

Quintana-García, C., & Benavides-Velasco, C. A. (2004). Cooperation, competition, and innovative capability: A panel data of European dedicated biotechnology firms. *Technovation*, *24*(12), 927–938. doi:10.1016/S0166-4972(03)00060-9

Rae, D., & Woodier-Harris, N. R. (2013). How does enterprise and entrepreneurship education influence postgraduate students' career intentions in the New Era economy? *Education + Training, 55*(8/9), 926-948.

Rahman, J., & Yousuf, A. (2010). Economic growth in Bangladesh: Experience and policy priorities. *Journal of Bangladesh Studies*, *12*(1).

Rahman, S. A., Amran, A., Ahmad, N. H., & Taghizadeh, S. H. (2015). Supporting entrepreneurial business success at the base of pyramid through entrepreneurial competencies. *Management Decision*, *53*(6), 1203–1223. doi:10.1108/MD-08-2014-0531

Rahman, S. A., Amran, A., Ahmad, N. H., & Taghizadeh, S. H. (2016). Enhancing the wellbeing of base of the pyramid entrepreneurs through business success: The role of private organizations. *Social Indicators Research*, *127*(1), 195–216. doi:10.1007/s11205-015-0951-4

Rahman, S. A., Amran, A., Ahmad, N. H., & Taghizadeh, S. K. (2014). GrameenPhone: Creating a Win-Win at the Base of the Pyramid in Bangladesh. *Global Business and Organizational Excellence*, *33*(5), 41–53. doi:10.1002/joe.21562

Rahman, S. A., & Das, D. K. (2005). The Development of Small and Medium Enterprises (SMEs) in Bangladesh. *Stamford Journal of Business Studies*, *1*(1), 108–123.

Raihan, A. (2001, October). *The state of e-finance in developing countries: Bangladesh perspective*. Paper presented in Expert Group Meeting on "Improving Competitiveness of SMEs in Developing Countries: Role of Finance, including E-finance to Enhance Enterprise Development", Geneva, Switzerland.

Ramachandaran, G. (2010). Excerpts of the Government Transformation Programme (GTP) & Economic Transformation Programme (ETP): Key thrusts to power the nation towards 2020. *RSM Startegic Business Advisor*. Retrieved 22 April, 2014, from http://www.rsmi.com.my/WebLITE/Applications/productcatalog/uploaded/Docs/Government%20Transformation%20Programme%20&%20Economic%20Transformation%20Programme%20Article%205.10.10.pdf

Ramasamy, B., Chakrabarty, A., & Cheah, M. (2004). Malaysias Leap into the Future: An Evaluation of the Multimedia Super Corridor. *Technovation*, *24*(11), 871–883. doi:10.1016/S0166-4972(03)00049-X

Ramaswamy, V. (2009). Leading the transformation to co-creation of value. *Strategy and Leadership*, *37*(2), 32–37. doi:10.1108/10878570910941208

Ramaswamy, V., & Gouillart, F. J. (2010). *The Power of Co-Creation: Build It with Them to Boost Growth, Productivity, and Profits* (1st ed.). New York: Free Press.

Ramayah, T., Ling, N. S., Taghizadeh, S. K., & Rahman, S. A. (2016). Factors influencing SMEs website continuance intention in Malaysia. *Telematics and Informatics*, *33*(1), 150–164. doi:10.1016/j.tele.2015.06.007

Ramos, E., Acedo, F. J., & Gonzalez, M. R. (2011). Internationalisation speed and technological patterns: A panel data study on Spanish SMEs. *Technovation*, *31*(10/11), 560–572. doi:10.1016/j.technovation.2011.06.008

Rampersad, G., Troshani, I., & Plewa, C. (2012). IOS adoption in innovation networks: A case study. *Industrial Management & Data Systems*, *112*(9), 1366–1382. doi:10.1108/02635571211278974

Ramukumba, T. (2014). Overcoming SMEs challenges through critical success factors: A case of SMEs in the Western Cape Province, South Africa. *Economic and Business Review*, *16*(1), 19–38.

Rangan, V.K., Chu, M. & Petkoski, D. (2011, June). Segmenting the base of the pyramid. *Harvard Business Review.*

Rashid, M. M. (2012). Proposed research direction for sustainable SMEs in Bangladesh. *Bangladesh Research Publications Journal, 6*(3), 317-329.

Rashid, A. M. Z., & Ibrahim, S. (2002). Executive and management attitudes towards corporate social responsibility in Malaysia. *Corporate Governance*, *2*(4), 10–16. doi:10.1108/14720700210447641

Rashid, A. T., & Rahman, M. (2009). Making profit to solve development problems: The case of Telenor AS and the Village Phone Programme in Bangladesh. *Journal of Marketing Management*, *25*(9-10), 1049–1060. doi:10.1362/026725709X479363

Rasiah, R., & Yap, X. S. (2014). *Innovation Performance of the Malaysian Economy*. Academic Press.

Rasiah, R. (2002). Government-business coordination and small enterprise performance in the machine tools sector in Malaysia. *Small Business Economics*, *18*(1-3), 177–194. doi:10.1023/A:1015139624218

Rasiah, R., Crinis, V., & Lee, H.-A. (2015). Industrialization and labour in Malaysia. *Journal of the Asia Pacific Economy*, *20*(1), 77–99. doi:10.1080/13547860.2014.974327

Rasmussen, E. A., & Sørheim, R. (2006). Action-based entrepreneurship education. *Technovation*, *26*(2), 185–194. doi:10.1016/j.technovation.2005.06.012

Rasmussen, E., Mosey, S., & Wright, M. (2014). The influence of university departments on the evolution of entrepreneurial competencies in spin-off ventures. *Research Policy*, *43*(1), 92–106. doi:10.1016/j.respol.2013.06.007

Ratinho, T., & Henriques, E. (2010). The role of science parks and business incubators in converging countries: Evidence from Portugal. *Technovation*, *30*(4), 278–290. doi:10.1016/j.technovation.2009.09.002

Ratten, V. (2014). Future research directions for collective entrepreneurship in developing countries: A small and medium-sized enterprise perspective. *International Journal of Entrepreneurship and Small Business*, *22*(2), 266–274. doi:10.1504/IJESB.2014.062505

Rauch, A., Wiklund, J., Lumpkin, G. T., & Frese, M. (2009). Entrepreneurial orientation and business performance: An assessment of past research and suggestions for the future. *Entrepreneurship Theory and Practice*, *33*(3), 761–787. doi:10.1111/j.1540-6520.2009.00308.x

Raymond, L., & Bergeron, F. (2008). Enabling the business strategy of SMEs through e-business capabilities: A strategic alignment perspective. *Industrial Management & Data Systems, 108*(5), 577–595. doi:10.1108/02635570810876723

Razak, M. I. M., Abas, N. M., Yaacob, N. J. A., Rodzi, S. N. A. M., Yusof, N. M., & Azidin, R. A. (2015). An overview of primary sector in Malaysia. *International Journal of Economics. Commerce and Management, 3*(2), 1–13.

Raza, S. A., & Hanif, N. (2013). Factors affecting internet banking adoption among internal and external customers: A case of Pakistan. *International Journal of Electronic Finance, 7*(1), 82–96. doi:10.1504/IJEF.2013.051746

Raz, J. (2004). The role of well-being. *Philosophical Perspectives, 18*(1), 269–294. doi:10.1111/j.1520-8583.2004.00029.x

Real, J. C., Roldán, J. L., & Leal, A. (2014). From entrepreneurial orientation and learning orientation to business performance: Analysing the mediating role of organizational learning and the moderating effects of organizational size. *British Journal of Management, 25*(2), 186–208. doi:10.1111/j.1467-8551.2012.00848.x

Reijonen, H. (2008). Understanding the small business owner: What they really aim at and how this relates to firm performance. *Management Research News, 31*(8), 616–629. doi:10.1108/01409170810892172

Renko, M., Carsrud, A., & Brännback, M. (2009). The effect of a market orientation, entrepreneurial orientation, and technological capability on innovativeness: A study of young biotechnology ventures in the United States and in Scandinavia. *Journal of Small Business Management, 47*(3), 331–369. doi:10.1111/j.1540-627X.2009.00274.x

Ren, S., Eisingerich, A. B., & Tsai, H. T. (2015). How do marketing, research and development capabilities, and degree of internationalization synergistically affect the innovation performance of small and medium-sized enterprises (SMEs)? A panel data study of Chinese SMEs. *International Business Review, 24*(4), 642–651. doi:10.1016/j.ibusrev.2014.11.006

Report, G. C. (2015). The Global Competitiveness Report 2015-2016. Author.

Rezai, G., Mohamed, Z., & Shamsuddin, M. N. (2011). Informal education and developing entrepreneurial skills among farmers in Malaysia. *International Journal of Social. Human Science and Engineering, 5*(7), 146–153.

Ringle, C. M., Wende, S., & Will, A. (2005). *SmartPLS 2.0 (M3) Beta.* Retrieved from http://www. smartpls. De

Ripollés-Meliá, M., Menguzzato-Boulard, M., & Sánchez-Peinado, L. (2007). Entrepreneurial orientation and international commitment. *Journal of International Entrepreneurship, 5*(3), 65–83. doi:10.1007/s10843-007-0016-0

Ritala, P. (2012). Coopetition strategy–when is it successful? Empirical evidence on innovation and market performance. *British Journal of Management, 23*(3), 307–324.

Ritter, T., & Gemünden, H. G. (2003). Network competence: Its impact on innovation success and its antecedents. *Journal of Business Research, 56*(9), 745–755. doi:10.1016/S0148-2963(01)00259-4

Riyadh, A. N., Bunker, D., & Rabhi, F. (2010). Barriers to e-finance adoption in small and medium sized enterprises (SMEs) in Bangladesh.*Proceedings of the 5th International Conference on Qualitative Research in IT & IT in Qualitative Research*, 1–10. doi:10.2139/ssrn.1726262

Robb, A., & Robinson, D. (2014). The capital structure decisions of new firms. *Review of Financial Studies, 27*(1), 153–179. doi:10.1093/rfs/hhs072

Robert, F., Marques, P., & Le Roy, F. (2009). Coopetition between SMEs: An empirical study of French professional football. *International Journal of Entrepreneurship and Small Business, 8*(1), 23–43. doi:10.1504/IJESB.2009.024103

Robertson, M., & Collins, A. (2003). Developing entrepreneurship in West Yorkshire: West Yorkshire universities' partnership and business Start-Up@ Leeds met. *Education+ Training*. Retrieved from http://www.emeraldinsight.com/doi/pdf/10.1108/00400910310495941

Rodrigues, R. G., & Raposo, M. (2011). Entrepreneurial orientation, human resources information management, and firm performance in SMEs. *Canadian Journal of Administrative Sciences*, *28*(2), 143–153. doi:10.1002/cjas.205

Rohra, C. L., & Junejo, M. A. (2009). Strategies for developing the success of Small Medium Enterprises in Pakistan. *International Journal of Business and Management*, *4*(6), 171. doi:10.5539/ijbm.v4n6p171

Romer, P. M. (1986). Increasing returns and long-run growth. *Journal of Political Economy*, *94*(5), 1002–1037. doi:10.1086/261420

Rosenbusch, N., Brinkmann, J., & Bausch, A. (2011). Is innovation always beneficial? A meta-analysis of the relationship between innovation and performance in SMEs. *Journal of Business Venturing*, *26*(4), 441–457. doi:10.1016/j.jbusvent.2009.12.002

Rosenstein-Rodan, P. N. (1943). Problems of industrialisation of Eastern and South-Eastern Europe. *The Economic Journal*, *53*(210/211), 202–211. doi:10.2307/2226317

Rosley, F. (2015). Faster SME Growth. *The Star*. Retrieved from http://www.thestar.com.my/business/business-news/2015/10/19/faster-sme-growth/

Rothaermel, F. T., & Deeds, D. L. (2004). Exploration and exploitation alliances in biotechnology: A system of new product development. *Strategic Management Journal*, *25*(3), 201–221. doi:10.1002/smj.376

Ruenrom, G. P. (2009). Applying the Philosophy of Sufficiency Economy to Form Business Policy and Marketing Plan of Small and Medium Enterprises in Thailand. *The Business Review, Cambridge*, *13*(1), 326–331.

Rugman, A. M., & Verbeke, A. (2004). A perspective on regional and global strategies of multinational enterprises. *Journal of International Business Studies*, *35*(1), 3–18. doi:10.1057/palgrave.jibs.8400073

Ruijun, C., & Zhiman, L. (2011). *Coopetition strategy management in SMEs: A case study of Nyhammers and Bäckströms Company* (Unpublished Masters dissertation). University of Gävle, Sweden.

Rundle-Thiele, S., Russell-Bennett, R., & Dann, S. (2005). The Successful Preperation and Development of Future Marketing Professionals: A Recommended Methodological Framework. *Journal for Advancement of Marketing Education*, *7*, 27–35.

Runglertkrengkrai, S., Sirirat, J., Somboonkul, Y., Churirachaneekorn, S., & Juligpong, S. (2007). *The Characteristics of Successful Entrepreneurs in Southern Region: Service Sector*. Retrieved from http://localinfo.tsu.ac.th/jspui/bitstream/123456789/24/1/article.pdf

Runglertkrengkrai, S., Sirirat, J., Somboonkul, Y., Churirachaneekorn, S., Chulirachaneekorn, S., Samangsri, J., & Ruangsong, R. (1999). The Characteristics and Training Needs for Small and Medium Entrepreneurs in the Southern Thailand. *Songkhlanakarin Journal of Social Sciences and Humanities*, *5*(3), 233–243.

Runyan, R. C., Ge, B., Dong, B., & Swinney, J. L. (2012). Entrepreneurial orientation in cross-cultural research: Assessing measurement invariance in the construct. *Entrepreneurship Theory and Practice*, *36*(4), 819–836. doi:10.1111/j.1540-6520.2010.00436.x

Russo, A., & Perrini, F. (2010). Investigating Stakeholder Theory and Social Capital: CSR in Large Firms and SMEs. *Journal of Business Ethics*, *91*(2), 207–221. doi:10.1007/s10551-009-0079-z

Russo, A., & Tencati, A. (2009). Formal vs. informal CSR strategies: Evidence from Italian micro, small, medium-sized, and large firms. *Journal of Business Ethics*, *85*(S2), 339–353. doi:10.1007/s10551-008-9736-x

Rust, R. T., Lemon, K. N., & Zeithaml, V. A. (2004). Return on marketing: Using customer equity to focus marketing strategy. *Journal of Marketing*, *68*(1), 109–127. doi:10.1509/jmkg.68.1.109.24030

Ruth, S. (2009). Green IT More Than a Three Percent Solution? *IEEE Internet Computing*, *13*(4), 74–78. doi:10.1109/MIC.2009.82

Rutten, R., & Boekema, F. (2007). Regional social capital: Embeddedness, innovation networks and regional economic development. *Technological Forecasting and Social Change*, *74*(9), 1834–1846. doi:10.1016/j.techfore.2007.05.012

Ruzzier, M., Hisrich, R. D., & Antoncic, B. (2006). SME internationalization research: Past, present and future. *Journal of Small Business and Enterprise Development*, *13*(4), 476–497. doi:10.1108/14626000610705705

Ryan, R. M., & Deci, E. L. (2000). Self-determination theory and the facilitation of intrinsic motivation, social development, and well-being. *The American Psychologist*, *55*(1), 68–78. doi:10.1037/0003-066X.55.1.68 PMID:11392867

Ryan, R. M., & Deci, E. L. (2001). On happiness and human potentials: A review of research on hedonic and eudaimonic well-being. *Annual Review of Psychology*, *52*(1), 141–166. doi:10.1146/annurev.psych.52.1.141 PMID:11148302

Saeed, S., Yousafzai, S. Y., & Engelen, A. (2014). On cultural and macroeconomic contingencies of the entrepreneurial orientation–performance relationship. *Entrepreneurship Theory and Practice*, *38*(2), 255–290. doi:10.1111/etap.12097

Saeed, S., Yousafzai, S. Y., Yani-De-Soriano, M., & Muffatto, M. (2015). The role of perceived university support in the formation of students entrepreneurial intention. *Journal of Small Business Management*, *53*(4), 1127–1145. doi:10.1111/jsbm.12090

Said, R., Zainuddin, Y. H., & Haron, H. (2009). The relationship between corporate social responsibility disclosure and corporate governance characteristics in Malaysian public listed companies. *Social Responsibility Journal*, *5*(2), 212-226.

Saidi Kia, M. (2013). *Business management and efficiency*. Tehran: Aha.

Said, M. F., Adham, K. A., & Abdullah, N. A. (2012). Incubators and Goverment Policy for Developing IT Industry and Region in Emerging Economies. *Asian Academy of Management Journal*, *17*(1), 65–96.

Saleh, A. S., & Ndubisi, N. O. (2006). An evaluation of SME development in Malaysia. *International Review of Business Research Papers*, *2*(1), 1–14.

Salomann, H., Dous, M., Kolbe, L., & Brenner, W. (2005). Rejuvenating Customer Management. *European Management Journal*, *23*(4), 392–403. doi:10.1016/j.emj.2005.06.009

Salomon, R., & Jin, B. (2010). Do leading or lagging firms learn more from exporting? *Strategic Management Journal*, *31*(10), 1088–1113. doi:10.1002/smj.850

Salomo, S., Talke, K., & Strecker, N. (2008). Innovation field orientation and its effect on innovativeness and firm performance. *Journal of Product Innovation Management*, *25*(6), 560–576. doi:10.1111/j.1540-5885.2008.00322.x

Samad, N. A. (2007). *Positioning Malaysian SMEs in the global. Proceedings of Persidangan Kebangsaan IKS 2007*. Kota Kinabalu: Universiti Utara Malaysia.

Sánchez-Fernández, R., & Iniesta-Bonillo, M. Á. (2007). The concept of perceived value: A systematic review of the research. *Marketing Theory*, *7*(4), 427–451. doi:10.1177/1470593107083165

Sánchez, J. C. (2013). The impact of an entrepreneurship education program on entrepreneurial competencies and intention. *Journal of Small Business Management*, *51*(3), 447–465. doi:10.1111/jsbm.12025

Sandhu, M. S., Sidique, S. F., & Riaz, S. (2011). Entrepreneurship barriers and entrepreneurial inclination among Malaysian postgraduate students. *International Journal of Entrepreneurial Behaviour & Research*, *17*(4), 428–449. doi:10.1108/13552551111139656

Santos-Rodrigues, H., Pereira-Rodrigues, G., & Cranfield, D. (2013, April). Human Capital and Financial Results: A Case Study. In *Proceedings of the 5th European Conference on Intellectual Capital: ECIC 2013* (p. 384). Academic Conferences Limited.

Sapa, S. G., Phunde, S. B., & Godbole, M. R. (2014). Impacts of ICT application on the insurance sector (e-insurance). *IBMRD's Journal of Management and Research*, *3*(1), 311–320.

Saravanakumar, M., & SuganthaLakshmi, T. (2012). Social media marketing. *Life Science Journal*, *9*(4), 4444–4451.

Sarder, J. H., Ghosh, D., & Rosa, P. (1997). The importance of support services to small enterprise in Bangladesh. *Journal of Small Business Management*, *35*(2), 26–36.

Saunders, M., Lewis, P., & Thornhill, A. (2009). *Research Methods for Business Students* (5th ed.). Sussex, UK: Pearson Education Limited.

Savlovschi, L. I., & Robu, N. R. (2011). The Role of SMEs in Modern Economy". *Economia. Seria Management*, *14*(1), 278–281.

Sawhney, M., Verona, G., & Prandelli, E. (2005). Collaborating to create: The Internet as a platform for customer engagement in product innovation. *Journal of Interactive Marketing*, *19*(4), 4–17. doi:10.1002/dir.20046

Schamberger, D. K., Cleven, N. J., & Brettel, M. (2013). Performance Effects of Exploratory and Exploitative Innovation Strategies and the Moderating Role of External Innovation Partners. *Industry and Innovation*, *20*(4), 336–356. doi:10.1080/13662716.2013.805928

Schick, H., Marxen, S., & Freimann, J. (2002). Sustainability Issues for Start-up Entrepreneurs. *GMI*, *38*, 59–70.

Schmidt, J. B., & Calantone, R. J. (1998). Are really new product development projects harder to shut down? *Journal of Product Innovation Management*, *15*(2), 111–123. doi:10.1016/S0737-6782(97)00074-X

Schmitt, B. (2012). The consumer psychology of brands. *Journal of Consumer Psychology*, *22*(1), 7–17. doi:10.1016/j.jcps.2011.09.005

Schreiner, M., Kale, P., & Corsten, D. (2009). What really is alliance management capability and how does it impact alliance outcomes and success? *Strategic Management Journal*, *30*(13), 1395–1419. doi:10.1002/smj.790

Schumpeter, J., & Backhaus, U. (2003). The theory of economic development. *Joseph Alois Schumpeter*, *1*, 61–116. doi:10.1007/0-306-48082-4_3

Schwartz, S. H. (2005). Basic human values: Their content and structure across countries. In A. Tamayo & J. B. Porto (Eds.), *Values and behavior in organizations* (pp. 21–55). Vozes.

Sciascia, S., Naldi, L., & Hunter, E. (2006). Market orientation as determinant of entrepreneurship: An empirical investigation on SMEs. *The International Entrepreneurship and Management Journal*, *2*(1), 21–38. doi:10.1007/s11365-006-7087-6

Sebora, T. C., Lee, S. M., & Sukasame, N. (2009). Critical Success Factors for E-commerce Entrepreneurship: An Empirical Study of Thailand. *Small Business Economics*, *32*(3), 303–316. doi:10.1007/s11187-007-9091-9

Seen, N. Y., Singh, S. K. G., & Jayasingam, S. (2012). Organizational Culture and Innovation among Malaysian Employees. *The Journal of Human Resource and Adult Learning*, *8*(2), 147.

Sekaran, U. (2006). *Research methods for business: A skill building approach.* New York, NY: Wiley-India.

Selamat, Z., & Nasir, A. M. (2013). Efficiency measurement of Malaysian agriculture firms. *International Journal of Trade. Economics & Finance, 4*(2), 79–85.

Sen, A. (1999). *Development as Freedom.* New York: Alfred A. Knopf Inc.

Sequeira, J., Mueller, S. L., & Mcgee, J. E. (2007). The influence of social ties and self-efficacy in forming entrepreneurial intentions and motivating nascent behavior. *Journal of Developmental Entrepreneurship, 12*(03), 275–293. doi:10.1142/S108494670700068X

Sesen, H. (2013). Personality or environment? A comprehensive study on the entrepreneurial intentions of university students. *Education+ Training, 55*(7), 624-640.

Shah Alam, S., & Mohamed Sayuti, N. (2011). Applying the Theory of Planned Behavior (TPB) in halal food purchasing. *International Journal of Commerce and Management, 21*(1), 8–20. doi:10.1108/10569211111111676

Shah, D., Rust, R. T., Parasuraman, A., Staelin, R., & Day, G. S. (2006). The path to customer centricity. *Journal of Service Research, 9*(2), 113–124. doi:10.1177/1094670506294666

Shahrokhi, M. (2008). E-finance: Status, innovations, resources and future challenges. *Managerial Finance, 34*(6), 365–398. doi:10.1108/03074350810872787

Shamsuddin, A., Mohmad Isa, K. H., Aziz, M. N., Mohamed Mahfol, N. Z. N., & Alagari, T. (2013). Graduate unemployment: The awareness and perception of graduates towards government's initiatives. *International Journal of Business. Economics and Law, 3*(1), 15–24.

Shane, S., & Venkataraman, S. (2000). The promise of entrepreneurship as a field of research. *Academy of Management Review, 25*(1), 217–226.

Sharabati, A. A. A., Naji Jawad, S., & Bontis, N. (2010). Intellectual capital and business performance in the pharmaceutical sector of Jordan. *Management Decision, 48*(1), 105–131. doi:10.1108/00251741011014481

Sharif, A. M. (2014). *Risk Assessment Factors for SME Software Development Companies in Malaysia.* IEEE. Retrieved from http://doi.org/978-1-4799-0059-6/13/$31.00

Shariff, M. N. M., & Peou, C. (2008). The relationship of entrepreneurial values, firm financing and the management and growth performance of small-medium enterprises in Cambodia. *Problems and Perspectives in Management, 6*(4), 55–64.

Shariff, M. N. M., & Peou, C. (2008). The Relationship of Entrepreneurial Values, Firm Financing and the Management and Growth Performance of Small-Medium Enterprises in Cambodia. *Problems and Perspectives in Management, 6*(4), 55–64.

Sharifirad, M. S., & Atei, V. (2012). Organizational culture and innovation culture: Exploring the relationships between constructs. *Leadership and Organization Development Journal, 33*(5), 494–517. doi:10.1108/01437731211241274

Sharma, D. D., & Blomstermo, A. (2003). The internationalization process of born globals: A network view. *International Business Review, 12*(6), 739–753. doi:10.1016/j.ibusrev.2003.05.002

Siaw, C., & Rani, N. S. A. (2012). A critical review on the regulatory and legislation challenges faced by halal start-up SMEs food manufacturers in Malaysia. *Procedia: Social and Behavioral Sciences, 57*, 541–548. doi:10.1016/j.sbspro.2012.09.1222

Simanis, E., & Hart, S. (2006). Expanding possibilities at the base of the pyramid: innovations case discussion: kick start. *Innovations: Technology, Governance, Globalization, 1*(1), 43–51. doi:10.1162/itgg.2006.1.1.43

Simanis, E., & Milstein, M. (2012). Back to business fundamentals: Making " bottom of the pyramid" relevant to core business. *Field Actions Science Reports*, *4*, 82–88.

Simonton, D. K. (1999). Creativity from Historiometric Perspective. In R. J. Stenberg (Ed.), *Handbook of Creativity* (pp. 116–134). Cambridge, UK: Cambridge University Press.

Simsek, Z., Heavey, C., & Veiga, J. F. (2010). The impact of CEO core self-evaluation on the firms' entrepreneurial orientation. *Strategic Management Journal*, *31*(1), 110–119. doi:10.1002/smj.800

Simsek, Z., Lubatkin, M. H., & Floyd, S. W. (2003). Inter-firm networks and entrepreneurial behavior: A structural embeddedness perspective. *Journal of Management*, *29*(3), 427–442. doi:10.1016/S0149-2063(03)00018-7

Singh, H., Mahmood, R. (2014). Combined Effect of Competitive and Manufacturing Strategies on Export Performance of Small and Medium Enterprises in Malaysia. *Global Journal of Management and Business Research, 14*(1).

Singh, S. (2014, July 11). Tampin company is first to be prosecuted under Solid Waste and Public Cleansing Act. *The Star Online.*

Singh, A. J., & Chauhan, R. (2012). Technology challenges in e-service accessibility. *Journal of Engineering and Technology*, *2*(1), 32–40. doi:10.4103/0976-8580.93233

Singh, G., & DeNoble, A. (2003). Early retirees as the next generation of entrepreneurs. *Entrepreneurship Theory & Practice*, *23*(3), 207–226. doi:10.1111/1540-8520.t01-1-00001

Sinha, P., Akoorie, M. E. M., Ding, Q., & Wu, Q. (2011). What motivates manufacturing SMEs to outsource offshore in China?: Comparing the perspectives of SME manufacturers and their suppliers. *Strategic Outsourcing: An International Journal*, *4*(1), 67–88. doi:10.1108/17538291111108435

Sinkovics, N., Sinkovics, R. R., & Yamin, M. (2014). The role of social value creation in business model formulation at the bottom of the pyramid – Implications for MNEs? *International Business Review*, *23*(4), 692–707. doi:10.1016/j.ibusrev.2013.12.004

Si, S., Yu, X., Wu, A., Chen, S., Chen, S., & Su, Y. (2015). Entrepreneurship and poverty reduction: A case study of Yiwu, China. *Asia Pacific Journal of Management*, *32*(1), 119–143. doi:10.1007/s10490-014-9395-7

Siwar, C., & Harizan, S. H. M. (2008). *A Study on Corporate Social Responsibility Practices amongst Business Organisations in Malaysia.* Paper presented at the Annual American Business Research Conference, Dubai, UAE.

Siwar, C., Idris, N. D. M., Yasar, M., & Morshed, G. (2014). Issues and challenges facing rice production and food security in the granary areas in the East Coast Economic Region (ECER), Malaysia. *Research Journal of Applied Sciences, Engineering and Technology*, *7*(4), 711–722.

Siwar, C., Yasar, M., Ghazali, Z., & Mohd Idris, N. D. (2013). Vulnerability and sustainable livelihood of paddy farmers in the North Terengganu Integrated Agriculture Development Area (IADA KETARA), Malaysia. *Prosiding Perkem*, *8*(2), 778–789.

Skaržauskaitė, M. (2013). Measuring and managing value co-creation process: overview of existing theoretical models. *Socialnės Technologijos,* (1), 115-129.

Skerlavaj, M., Song, J. H., & Lee, Y. (2010). Organizational learning culture, innovative culture and innovations in South Korean firms. *Expert Systems with Applications*, *37*(9), 6390–6403. doi:10.1016/j.eswa.2010.02.080

Skouloudis, A., & Evangelinos, K. (2014). Exogenously driven CSR: insights from the consultants' perspective. *Business Ethics: A European Review.*

Slack, N. (1994). The importance-performance matrix as a determinant of improvement priority. *International Journal of Operations & Production Management*, *14*(5), 59–75. doi:10.1108/01443579410056803

Slotte-Kock, S., & Coviello, N. (2010). Entrepreneurship research on network processes: A review and ways forward. *Entrepreneurship Theory & Practice*, *34*(1), 31–57. doi:10.1111/j.1540-6520.2009.00311.x

SME Annual Report. (2012). Retrieved February 8, 2013, from http://www.smecorp.gov.my/v4/sites/default/files/Section1_0.pdf

SME Annual Report. (2013/2014). Retrieved 17 November 2015, from http://www.smecorp.gov.my/vn2/sites/default/files/chapter2-SME%20Development%20and%20Outlook_0.pdf

SME Corp. (2012). *Final Report Study on Enhancing the Effectiveness of Incubation Centres as a Support Mechanism for SME Development in Malaysia*. Author.

SME Corp. (2013). Guideline for New SME Definition. Author.

SME Corp. (2013). *Guideline for New SME Definition*. SME Corp.

SME Corporation Malaysia. (2011). *Financial guide for SMEs*. SME Corporation Malaysia. Retrieved from http://www.smecorp.gov.my/vn2/

SME Corporation Malaysia. (2011). *Financial guide for smes. SME Corporation Malaysia*. Retrieved March 13, 2015, from http://www.smecorp.gov.my/vn2/

SME Corporation Malaysia. (2016a). *Definition of Micro Enterprises and SMEs*. Retrieved from http://www.smecorp.gov.my/index.php/en/

SME Corporation Malaysia. (2016b). *Profile and Importance to the Economy*. Retrieved from http://www.smecorp.gov.my/index.php/en/policies/2015-12-21-09-09-49/profile-and-importance-to-the-economy

SME Master Plan. (2012-2020). Retrieved 22 April, 2014, from http://www.chinesechamber.org.my/html/themes/chinesechamber/images/content/bulletin343/SME%20MASTERPLAN%202012-2020.pdf

SME Masterplan (2013). *SME Master Plan 2012-2020: Catalysing growth and income*. Author.

SMECorp. (2015). *SME Corporation Malaysia - SME Definition*. Retrieved May 18, 2016, from http://www.smecorp.gov.my/index.php/en/policies/2015-12-21-09-09-49/sme-definition

SMIDEC. (2007). Policies, Incentives, Programmes and Financial Assistance for SMEs. Author.

SMIDEC. (2007). *SME development programme*. Retrieved March 13, 2015, from http://www.smidec.gov.my/detailpage.jsp?section=defsme&level=1

Smilor. (1987). Managing the incubator system: critical success factors to accelerate new company development. *IEEE Transactions on Engineering Management*, *34*(4), 146–156.

Smit, E., Bronner, F., & Tolboom, M. (2007). Brand relationship quality and its value for personal contact. *Journal of Business Research*, *60*(6), 627–633. doi:10.1016/j.jbusres.2006.06.012

Smith, A. J., Collins, L. A., & Hannon, P. D. (2006). Embedding new entrepreneurship programmes in UK higher education institutions: Challenges and considerations. *Education+ Training*, *48*(8/9), 555-567.

Smith, J. R., Terry, D. J., Manstead, A. S., Louis, W. R., Kotterman, D., & Wolfs, J. (2007). Interaction Effects in the Theory of Planned Behavior: The Interplay of Self-Identity and Past Behavior. *Journal of Applied Social Psychology*, *37*(11), 2726–2750. doi:10.1111/j.1559-1816.2007.00278.x

Smith, K. G., Collins, C. J., & Clark, K. D. (2005). Existing knowledge, knowledge creating capability, and the rate of new product introduction in high-technology firms. *Academy of Management Journal*, *48*(2), 346–357. doi:10.5465/AMJ.2005.16928421

Smith, L. C., Khan, F., Frankenberger, T. R., & Wadud, A. (2013). Admissible Evidence in the Court of Development Evaluation? The Impact of CAREs SHOUHARDO Project on Child Stunting in Bangladesh. *World Development*, *41*, 196–216. doi:10.1016/j.worlddev.2012.06.018

Snyder-Halpern, R. (2001). Indicators of organizational readiness for clinical information technology/systems innovation: A Delphi study. *International Journal of Medical Informatics*, *63*(3), 179–204. doi:10.1016/S1386-5056(01)00179-4 PMID:11502432

Sobhani, F. A., Amran, A., & Zainuddin, Y. (2012). Sustainability disclosure in annual reports and websites: A study of the banking industry in Bangladesh. *Journal of Cleaner Production*, *23*(1), 75–85. doi:10.1016/j.jclepro.2011.09.023

Sofowora, O. (2009). The potential of using information and communication technology for poverty alleviation and economic empowerment in Osun State, Nigeria. *International Journal of Education and Development using Information and Communication Technology, 5*(3), 131-140.

Solesvik, M. Z., Westhead, P., & Matlay, H. (2014). Cultural factors and entrepreneurial intention: The role of entrepreneurship education. *Education+ Training, 56*(8/9), 680-696.

Solomon, M. R., Bamossy, G., Askegaard, S., & Hogg, K. (2009). *Consumer Behaviour: A European Perspective* (4th ed.). Prentice Hall.

Solow, R. M. (1956). A contribution to the theory of economic growth. *The Quarterly Journal of Economics*, *70*(1), 65. doi:10.2307/1884513

Soltanian, M., Zailani, S., Azmin, M. I., & Aziz, A. (2016). Motivations of SME entrepreneurs to become halalpreneurs. *Journal of Science and Technology Policy Management*, *7*(1), 173–189. doi:10.1108/JSTPM-07-2015-0023

Sommer, L. (2011). The theory of planned behaviour and the impact of past behaviour. *International Business & Economics Research Journal, 10*(1).

Somsuk, N., & Laosirihongthong, T. (2014). A fuzzy AHP to prioritize enabling factors for strategic management of university business incubators: Resource-based view. *Technological Forecasting and Social Change*, *85*, 198–210. doi:10.1016/j.techfore.2013.08.007

Soriano, D. R., & Dobon, S. R. (2009). Linking globalization of entrepreneurship in small organizations. *Small Business Economics*, *32*(3), 233–239. doi:10.1007/s11187-008-9155-5

Sorooshian, S., Onn, C. W., & Yeen, C. W. (2013). Malaysian based analysis on e-service. *International Journal of Academic Research*, *5*(4), 62–64. doi:10.7813/2075-4124.2013/5-4/B.8

Souitaris, V., Zerbinati, S., & Al-Laham, A. (2007). Do entrepreneurship programmes raise entrepreneurial intentions of science and engineering students? The effect of learning, inspiration and resources. *Journal of Business Venturing*, *22*(4), 566–591. doi:10.1016/j.jbusvent.2006.05.002

Soumiya Devi, M. K. (2015). A study on the influencing factors for a literate youth to take up agricultural entrepreneurship. *International Journal of Management and Commerce Innovations*, *3*(1), 692–700.

Sox, C. B., Kline, S. F., & Crews, T. B. (2014). Identifying best practices, opportunities and barriers in meeting planning for Generation Y. *International Journal of Hospitality Management*, *36*, 244–254. doi:10.1016/j.ijhm.2013.09.009

Spena, T. R., Caridà, A., Colurcio, M., & Melia, M. (2012). Store experience and co-creation: The case of temporary shop. *International Journal of Retail & Distribution Management*, *40*(1), 21–40. doi:10.1108/09590551211193586

Spence, L. J. (2007). CSR and Small Business in a European Policy Context: The Five Cs of CSR and Small Business Research Agenda 2007. *Business and Society Review*, *112*(4), 533–552. doi:10.1111/j.1467-8594.2007.00308.x

Spence, L. J., Agyemang, G., & Rinaldi, L. (2012). *Environmental aspects of sustainability: SMEs and the role of the accountant (No. 1859084796)*. London: The Association of Chartered Certified Accountants.

Spence, L., Coles, A., & Harris, L. (2001). The forgotten stakeholder? Ethics and social responsibility in relation to competitors. *Business and Society Review*, *106*(4), 331–352. doi:10.1111/0045-3609.00119

Spence, M. (2003). International strategy formation in small Canadian high-technology companies: A case study approach. *Journal of International Entrepreneurship*, *1*(3), 277–296. doi:10.1023/A:1024162823079

Spowart, M., & Wickramasekera, R. (2012). Explaining internationalisation of small to medium sized enterprises within the Queensland food and beverage industry. *International Journal of Business and Management*, *7*(6), 68–80. doi:10.5539/ijbm.v7n6p68

Srivastava, A. (2014). The status and impact of e-finance on developing economy. *Golden Research Thoughts*, *3*(11), 1–3.

Srivastava, S., & Srivastava, R. (2012). Adoption of green information technology (GIT) in India-A current scenario. *Journal of Information and Operations Management*, *3*(1), 61–63.

Stafford, D. G. S. D. (1997). Malaysias new economic policy and the global economy: The evolution of ethnic accommodation. *The Pacific Review*, *10*(4), 556–580. doi:10.1080/09512749708719239

Stam, W., Arzlanian, S., & Elfring, T. (2014). Social capital of entrepreneurs and small firm performance: A meta-analysis of contextual and methodological moderators. *Journal of Business Venturing*, *29*(1), 152–173. doi:10.1016/j.jbusvent.2013.01.002

Stam, W., & Elfring, T. (2008). Entrepreneurial orientation and new venture performance: The moderating role of intra- and extraindustry social capital. *Academy of Management Journal*, *51*(1), 97–111. doi:10.5465/AMJ.2008.30744031

Starr, J. A., & MacMillan, I. (1990). Resource cooptation via social contracting: Resource acquisition strategies for new ventures. *Strategic Management Journal*, *11*, 79–92.

Statistical Centre of Iran. (2015). *Iran statistical yearbook*. Retrieved April 18, 2011 from http:// www.amar.org.ir/

Statistical Centre of Iran. (2016). *Iran statistical yearbook*. Retrieved April 18, 2011 from http:// www.amar.org.ir/

Stiglitz, J. E. (2014). The Innovation Enigma. Project Syndicate.

Stiglitz, J. (1989). *More instruments and broader goals: Moving toward the post-Washington consensus*. Helsinki: Wider Annual Lecture United Nations University—World Institute for Development Economics Research.

Stoian, M. C., Rialp, A., & Rialp, J. (2011). Export performance under the microscope: A glance through Spanish lenses. *International Business Review*, *20*(2), 117–135. doi:10.1016/j.ibusrev.2010.07.002

Storbacka, K., Strandvik, T., & Grönroos, C. (1994). Managing customer relationships for profit: The dynamics of relationship quality. *International Journal of Service Industry Management*, *5*(5), 21–38. doi:10.1108/09564239410074358

Storey, C., & Easingwood, C. J. (1999). Types of new product performance: Evidence from the consumer financial services sector. *Journal of Business Research*, *46*(2), 193–203. doi:10.1016/S0148-2963(98)00022-8

St-Pierre, J., Foleu, L., Abdulnour, G., Nomo, S., & Fouda, M. (2015). *SME development challenges in Cameroon: An entrepreneurial ecosystem perspective*. Academic Press.

Stuart, T. E., Hoang, H., & Hybels, R. C. (1999). Interorganizational endorsements and the performance of entrepreneurial ventures. *Administrative Science Quarterly*, *44*(2), 315–349. doi:10.2307/2666998

Su, C., & Yuan, H. (2013). New exploration - The role of e-finance in small business financing. In *Proceedings of the 2013 6th International Conference on Information Management, Innovation Management and Industrial Engineering* (Vol. 1, pp. 501–504). IEEE. Retrieved from www.ieee.org

Sufficiency Economy Movement Sub-Committee. (2007). *Sufficiency economy implications and applications*. Retrieved 26 July, 2011, available at: www.nesdb.go.th/Md/book/booksuffwork_eng.pdf

Sufian, J. (2006). Incubators As Catalysts in Developing High Technology Businesses : Malaysia ' S Experience. *ATDF Journal*, *3*(1), 25–29.

Suhairi. (2004). *Personality, Accounting Knowledge, Accounting Information Usage and Performance: A Research on Entrepreneurship of Indonesia Medium Industries* (Unpublished PhD Dissertation). Universiti Sains Malaysia, Malaysia.

Sui, S., & Baum, M. (2014). Internationalization strategy, firm resources and the survival of SMEs in the export market. *Journal of International Business Studies*, *45*(7), 821–841. doi:10.1057/jibs.2014.11

Sui, S., Morgan, H. M., & Baum, M. (2015). Internationalization of immigrant-owned SMEs: The role of language. *Journal of World Business*, *50*(4), 804–814. doi:10.1016/j.jwb.2015.04.002

Suk, J. K. (n.d.). *Leadership, Organizational Culture, Knowledge Productivity and Value Creation in Four Successful Korean Companies Toward guidelines for people-oriented business leaders*. Academic Press.

Sun, J., Buys, N., & Wang, X. (2011). *The Characteristics and Capabilities of New Chinese Entrepreneurs and their Emerging Small to Medium Size Enterprises*. Paper presented at the 8th SMEs in a Global Economy Conference 2011.

Sung, T. K., Gibson, D. V., & Kang, B. S. (2003). Characteristics of technology transfer in business ventures: The case of Daejeon, Korea. *Technological Forecasting and Social Change*, *70*(5), 449–466. doi:10.1016/S0040-1625(02)00360-8

Susanto, A., Lee, H., Zo, H., & Ciganek, A. P. (2013). User acceptance of internet banking in Indonesia: Initial trust formation. *Information Development*, *29*(4), 309–322. doi:10.1177/0266666912467449

Su, Z., Xie, E., & Li, Y. (2011). Entrepreneurial orientation and firm performance in new ventures and established firms. *Journal of Small Business Management*, *49*(4), 558–577. doi:10.1111/j.1540-627X.2011.00336.x

Suzuki, K. I., Kim, S. H., & Bae, Z. T. (2002). Entrepreneurship in Japan and Silicon Valley: A comparative study. *Technovation*, *22*(10), 595–606. doi:10.1016/S0166-4972(01)00099-2

Sweeney, L. (2009). *A study of current practice of corporate social responsibility (CSR) and an examination of the relationship between CSR and financial performance using structural equation modelling (SEM)* (Doctoral Thesis). Institute of Technology, Dublin, Ireland.

Sweeney, L. (2007). Corporate social responsibility in Ireland: Barriers and opportunities experienced by SMEs when undertaking CSR. *Corporate Governance*, *7*(4), 516–523. doi:10.1108/14720700710820597

Swierczek, F. W., & Thai, T. H. (2003). Motivation, Enterpreneurship and The performance of SMEs in Vietnam. *Journal of Enterprising Culture*, *11*(01), 47–68. doi:10.1142/S0218495803000044

Swoboda, B., & Olejnik, E. (2016). Linking processes and dynamic capabilities of international SMEs: The mediating effect of international entrepreneurial orientation. *Journal of Small Business Management*, *54*(1), 139–161. doi:10.1111/jsbm.12135

Tabachnick, B. G., & Fidell, L. S. (1996). Using Multivariate Statistics. New York: HarperCollins.

Taggar, S. (2002). Individual creativity and group ability to utilize individual creative resources: A multilevel model. *Academy of Management Journal*, *45*(2), 315–330. doi:10.2307/3069349

Taghizadeh, S. K., Jayaraman, K., Ismail, I., & Rahman, S. A. (2014). A Study of Service Innovation Management in the Malaysian Telecommunications Industry. *Global Business and Organizational Excellence*, *34*(1), 67–77. doi:10.1002/joe.21585

Taghizadeh, S. K., Jayaraman, K., Ismail, I., & Rahman, S. A. (2016). Scale development and validation for DART model of value co-creation process on innovation strategy. *Journal of Business and Industrial Marketing*, *31*(1), 24–35. doi:10.1108/JBIM-02-2014-0033

Talebi, K., & Tajeddin, M. (2011). The adoption of new and innovative knowledge by small and medium enterprises of Iran: Opportunities and constraints for growth. *African Journal of Business Management*, *5*(1), 39–49.

Talisayon, S., & Suministrado, J. (2008). *Knowledge for Poverty Alleviation: A framework for design and evaluation of development projects in low income countries*. Paper presented at the conference on 'Knowledge Architecture for Development', Singapore.

Tambunan, T. (2008). Development of SME in ASEAN with Reference to Indonesia and Thailand. *Chulalongkorn Journal of Economics*, *20*(1), 53–83.

Tanev, S., Bailetti, T., Allen, S., Milyakov, H., Durchev, P., & Ruskov, P. (2011). How do value co-creation activities relate to the perception of firms' innovativeness? *Journal of Innovation Economics & Management*, (1), 131-159.

Tang, G., Chen, Y., & Jin, J. (2015). Entrepreneurial orientation and innovation performance: Roles of strategic HRM and technical turbulence. *Asia Pacific Journal of Human Resources*, *53*(2), 163–184. doi:10.1111/1744-7941.12053

Tang, J., Tang, Z., Marino, L. D., Zhang, Y., & Li, Q. (2008). Exploring an Inverted U-Shape Relationship between Entrepreneurial Orientation and Performance in Chinese Ventures. *Entrepreneurship Theory and Practice*, *32*(1), 219–239. doi:10.1111/j.1540-6520.2007.00223.x

Tang, Z., Kreiser, P. M., Marino, L., Dickson, P., & Weaver, K. M. (2009). A hierarchical perspective of the dimensions of entrepreneurial orientation. *The International Entrepreneurship and Management Journal*, *5*(2), 181–201. doi:10.1007/s11365-008-0097-9

Tavoletti, E. (2013). Business Incubators: Effective Infrastructures or Waste of Public Money? Looking for a Theoretical Framework, Guidelines and Criteria. *Journal of the Knowledge Economy*, *4*(4), 423–443. doi:10.1007/s13132-012-0090-y

Teece, D. (2007). Explicating dynamic capabilities: The nature and microfoundations of (sustainable) enterprise performance. *Strategic Management Journal*, *28*(13), 1319–1350. doi:10.1002/smj.640

Tenth Malaysia Plan 2011-2015. (n.d.). *The Economic Planning Unit, Prime Minister's Department*. Kuala Lumpur: EPU.

Thailand Foreign Office. The Government Public Relations Department. (2014). *The New Theory and the Sufficiency Economy*. Retrieved June 30, 2014. From http://thailand.prd.go.th/ebook/king/new theory.html

Thang, L. C., & Quang, T. (n.d.). *Human Resource Management Practices in a Transitional Economy: A Comparative Study of Enterprise Ownership Forms in Vietnam.* http://doi.org/<ALIGNMENT.qj></ALIGNMENT>10.1080/1360238052000298362

The Daily Star. (2015). *Deteriorating air quality in Bangladesh.* Retrieved on March 12, 2016, from http://www.thedailystar.net/editorial/deteriorating-air-quality-bangladesh-197032

The Economic Planning Unit. (2000). Malaysia: Eighth Malaysia Plan.

The National SME Development Council. (2011). *SME annual report.* Retrieved from http://www.smecorp.gov.my/vn2/node/113

The New Age. (2015). *Not so digital after all.* Retrieved on March 2, 2016, from http://newagebd.net/38216/not-so-digital-after-all/#sthash.03ORQNWR.dpuf

The Star. (2014a, May 5). EPF: 278 defaulting company directors barred from leaving. *The Star Online.*

The Star. (2014b, June 3). Health product company fined over non-compliance of minimum wage regulations. *The Star Online.*

The Star. (2014c, October 1). Company linked to Penang Bridge ramp collapse fined RM40,000. *The Star Online.*

The Star. (2014d, December 3). Keeping the problem of illegal workers in check. *The Star Online.*

The World Bank. (2010). *Global economic prospects.* Author.

The World Bank. (2011). *World Development Indicators Database.* Retrieved 13 November from http://siteresources.worldbank.org/DATASTATISTICS/Resources/POP.pdf

The World Bank. (2012). *Bangladesh at glance.* Retrieved from http://www.worldbank.org/en/country/bangladesh

The World Bank. (2014). *Poverty and Equity Data.* Retrieved from http://data.worldbank.org/topic/poverty

The World Bank. (2015). *Indicators Data.* Retrieved from http://data.worldbank.org/indicator

The World Bank. (2016). *Indicators Data.* Retrieved from http://data.worldbank.org/indicator

The World Factbook. (2015). *Country Profile.* Retrieved from USA: https://www.cia.gov/library/publications/the-world-factbook/geos/bg.html

Thong, J. Y., Yap, C. S., & Raman, K. S. (1997). Environments for information systems implementation in small businesses. *Journal of Organizational Computing and Electronic Commerce*, *7*(4), 253–278. doi:10.1207/s15327744joce0704_1

Tilt, C. A. (2010). Corporate Responsibility, Accounting and Accountants. In S. O. I dowu & W. L. Filho (Eds.), Professionals' Perspectives of Corporate Social Responsibility (pp. 11-32). Springer Berlin Heidelberg.

Tock, J. M., & Baharun, R. (2013). Introduction to SMEs in Malaysia: Growth Potential and Branding Strategy. *World Journal of Social Science*, *3*, 189–203. Retrieved from http://www.bnm.gov.my/files/publication/sme/en/2007/chap_4.pdf

Todd, P., & Javalgi, R. (2007). Internationalization of SMEs in India: Fostering entrepreneurship by leveraging information technology. *International Journal of Emerging Markets*, *2*(2), 166–180. doi:10.1108/17468800710739234

Tomlinson, P. R., & Fai, F. M. (2013). The nature of SME co-operation and innovation: A multi-scalar and multi-dimensional analysis. *International Journal of Production Economics*, *141*(1), 316–326. doi:10.1016/j.ijpe.2012.08.012

Trading Economics. (2015). *Bangladesh Population.* Retrieved April 4, 2016, from http://www.tradingeconomics.com/bangladesh/population

Tran, T., Le, X. S., & Nguyen, K. A. (2008). Vietnam's Small and Medium Sized Enterprises Development: Characteristics, Constraints and Policy Recommendations. In SME in Asia and Globalization, ERIA Research Project Report 2007 (pp. 323–364). Academic Press.

Trucker, D., & Selcuk, S. S. (2009). Which factors affect entrepreneurial intention of university students? *Journal of European Industrial Training*, *33*(2), 142–159. doi:10.1108/03090590910939049

Tsai, W.-H., Huang, B.-Y., Fan, Y.-W., & Liu, J.-Y. (2006). Trends and developments in electronic lending: A preliminary research in Taiwan. *International Journal of Electronic Finance*, *1*(2), 241–259. doi:10.1504/IJEF.2006.010318

Tsunoda, J., Ahmed, M., & Islam, M. T. (2013). *Regulatory Framework and Role of Domestic Credit Rating Agencies in Bangladesh*. Academic Press.

Tung, J. (2012). A study of product innovation on firm performance. *International Journal of Organizational Innovation (Online)*, *4*(3), 84.

Tushman, M. L., & OReilly, C. A. III. (1996). Ambidextrous organizations: Managing evolutionary and revolutionary change. *California Management Review*, *38*(4), 8–30. doi:10.2307/41165852

Ulaga, W., & Eggert, A. (2006). Value-based differentiation in business relationships: Gaining and sustaining key supplier status. *Journal of Marketing*, *70*(1), 119–136. doi:10.1509/jmkg.2006.70.1.119

UNDP. (2015). *Post-2015 Sustainable Development Agenda*. Retrieved July 1, 2015, from http://www.undp.org/content/undp/en/home/mdgoverview/post-2015-development-agenda.html

UNEP. (2014). *Self Sufficiency Economy in Thailand.* Retrieved June 30, 2014. From http://ekh.unep.org/files/SELF-SUFFICIENCY ECONOMY IN THAILAND.doc

UNFCC. (2015). *195 Nations set path to keep temperature rise well below 2 degrees Celsius.* Retrieved October 9, 2016, from http://newsroom.unfccc.int/unfccc-newsroom/finale-cop21/

UNFPA. (2015). *World Population Dashboard.* Retrieved from http://www.unfpa.org/world-population-dashboard

Unicef. (2012). *Corporate Social Responsibility Policies in Malaysia: Enhancing the Child Focus.* Kuala Lumpur, Malaysia: United Nations Children's Fund (UNICEF).

United Nation Development Programme. (2004). *Unleashing Entrepreneurship: Making Business Work for the Poor.* New York: UNDP.

United Nation Environment Programme (UNEP). (2007). *Innovative Financing for Sustainable Small and Medium Enterprises in Africa.* Meeting Report presented at the International Workshop, Geneva, Switzerland.

United Nations Development Programme (UNDP). (2002). *UNDP in Africa. Supporting Africa as it Meets the Challenges of the 21st Century.* UNDP.

United Nations Development Programme (UNDP). (2004). *Human Development Report 2004.* UNDP.

United Nations Human Rights Commission. (2015). *Preliminary findings of Country Visit to Bangladesh by Heiner Bielefeldt, Special Rapporteur on freedom of religion or belief* [Press release]. Retrieved from http://www.ohchr.org/en/NewsEvents/Pages/DisplayNews.aspx?NewsID=16399&LangID=E

Unsworth, K. L., Sawang, S., Murray, J., Sorbello, T. (2009). Developing An Integrative Model For Understanding Innovation Adoption. *Academy of Management Proceedings, 2009*(1), 1-6.

Urbach, N., & Ahlemann, F. (2010). Structural equation modeling in information systems research using partial least squares. *Journal of Information Technology Theory and Application, 11*(2), 5.

Van Akkeren, J., & Harker, D. (2003). The mobile Internet and small business: An exploratory study of needs, use and adoption with full-adopters of technology. *Journal of Research and Practice in Information Technology, 35*(3), 205–220.

van Doorn, S., Jansen, J. J. P., van den Bosch, F. A. J., & Volberda, H. W. (2013). Entrepreneurial orientation and firm performance: Drawing attention to the senior team. *Journal of Product Innovation Management, 30*(5), 821–836. doi:10.1111/jpim.12032

Vanevenhoven, J. (2013). Advances and challenges in entrepreneurship education. *Journal of Small Business Management, 51*(3), 466–470. doi:10.1111/jsbm.12043

Vargo, S. L., & Lusch, R. F. (2004). Evolving to a new dominant logic for marketing. *Journal of Marketing, 68*(1), 1–17. doi:10.1509/jmkg.68.1.1.24036

Vargo, S. L., & Lusch, R. F. (2008). Service-dominant logic: Continuing the evolution. *Journal of the Academy of Marketing Science, 36*(1), 1–10. doi:10.1007/s11747-007-0069-6

Vargo, S. L., Maglio, P. P., & Akaka, M. A. (2008). On value and value co-creation: A service systems and service logic perspective. *European Management Journal, 26*(3), 145–152. doi:10.1016/j.emj.2008.04.003

Vázquez-Carrasco, R., & López-Pérez, M. E. (2012). Small & medium-sized enterprises and Corporate Social Responsibility: A systematic review of the literature. *Quality & Quantity*, 1–14.

Vega-Vazquez, M., Ángeles Revilla-Camacho, M., & Cossío-Silva, J., F. (2013). The value co-creation process as a determinant of customer satisfaction. *Management Decision, 51*(10), 1945–1953. doi:10.1108/MD-04-2013-0227

Venesaar, U., Kallaste, M., & Küttim, M. (2014). Factors influencing students venture creation process. *Procedia: Social and Behavioral Sciences, 110*, 678–688. doi:10.1016/j.sbspro.2013.12.912

Venkatesh, V., & Davis, F. D. (2000). A theoretical extension of the technology acceptance model: Four longitudinal field studies. *Management Science, 46*(2), 186–204. doi:10.1287/mnsc.46.2.186.11926

Vera, D., & Crossan, M. (2004). Strategic leadership and organizational learning. *Academy of Management Review, 29*(2), 222–240.

Verhees, F. J. H. M., Kuipers, A., & Klopcic, M. (2011). Entrepreneurial proclivity and farm performance: The cases of Dutch and Slovenian farmers. *International Journal of Entrepreneurship and Innovation, 12*(3), 167–177. doi:10.5367/ijei.2011.0039

VGSO. (2013). *Statistical YearBook of Vietnam 2013*. Retrieved from https://www.gso.gov.vn/default.aspx?tabid=512&idmid=5&ItemID=14080

VGSO. (2014). *Statistical Yearbook of Vietnam 2014*. Retrieved from http://gso.gov.vn/?tabid=628&ItemID=14277

Vicziany, M., & Puteh, M. (2004). Vision 2020, The Multimedia Supercorridor and Malaysian Universities.*Proceeding of the 15th Biennial Conference of the Asian Studies Association of Australia*, 1–21.

Vietnam National Assembly. (2002). *Comprehensive Poverty Reduction and Growth Strategy (CPRGS)*. Retrieved from http://siteresources.worldbank.org/ImtVietnaminVietnamese/Resources/CPRGS_Vietnames_edited.pdf

Vincett, P. S., & Farlow, S. (2008). Start-a-Business: An experiment in education through entrepreneurship. *Journal of Small Business and Enterprise Development*, *15*(2), 274–288. doi:10.1108/14626000810871673

Vision 2020. (2009). *Report of the vision 2020*. National Technical Working Group on SMEs, Federal Republic of Nigeria.

Vives, A. (2006). Social and Environmental Responsibility in Small and Medium Enterprises in Latin America. *Journal of Corporate Citizenship*, *2006*(21), 39–50. doi:10.9774/GLEAF.4700.2006.sp.00006

VMPI. (2014a). *Report on Enterprise and Plan for Social and Economic Development 2014-2015*. Retrieved from http://business.gov.vn/tabid/98/catid/10/item/13229/t%E1%BB%95ng-quan-v%E1%BB%81-t%C3%ACnh-h%C3%ACnh-doanh-nghi%E1%BB%87p-v%C3%A0-nhi%E1%BB%87m-v%E1%BB%A5-ph%C3%A1t-tri%E1%BB%83n-kinh-t%-E1%BA%BF-x%C3%A3-h%E1%BB%99i-2014-2015.aspx

VMPI. (2014b). *White Paper: Small and Medium Enterprises in Vietnam*. Retrieved from http://en.business.gov.vn/tabid/179/catid/572/item/13807/white-paper-on-vietnam-sme-2014.aspx

Voghel, S., & Thompson, P. (2011). The Role of SMPs in Greening Small Business. *Accountancy Plus,* 34-35.

von Graevenitz, G., Harhoff, D., & Weber, R. (2010). The effects of entrepreneurship education. *Journal of Economic Behavior & Organization*, *76*(1), 90–112. doi:10.1016/j.jebo.2010.02.015

Voon, S. (2014). Insurance. *Personal Money*, *160*, 14–15.

Vukasovic, T. (2009). Searching for competitive advantage with the aid of the brand potential index. *Journal of Product and Brand Management*, *18*(3), 165–176. doi:10.1108/10610420910957799

Wales, W. J., Parida, V., & Patel, P. C. (2013). Too much of a good thing? Absorptive capacity, firm performance, and the moderating role of entrepreneurial orientation. *Strategic Management Journal*, *34*(5), 622–633. doi:10.1002/smj.2026

Walley, K. (2007). Coopetition: An introduction to the subject and an agenda for research. *International Studies of Management & Organization*, *37*(2), 11–31. doi:10.2753/IMO0020-8825370201

Walley, K., & Custance, P. (2010). Coopetition: Insights from the agri-food supply chain. *Journal on Chain and Network Science*, *10*(3), 185–192. doi:10.3920/JCNS2010.x187

Wamba, S. F., & Carter, L. (2014). Social Media Tools Adoption and Use by SMEs: An Empirical Study. *Journal of Organizational and End User Computing*, *26*(2), 1–17. doi:10.4018/joeuc.2014040101

Wang, C. L. (2008). Entrepreneurial orientation, learning orientation, and firm performance. *Entrepreneurship Theory and Practice*, *32*(4), 635–657. doi:10.1111/j.1540-6520.2008.00246.x

Wang, C., & Kafouros, M. I. (2009). What factors determine innovation performance in emerging economies? Evidence from China. *International Business Review*, *18*(6), 606–616. doi:10.1016/j.ibusrev.2009.07.009

Wang, G. L. (2012). A Study of How the Organizational Culture of International Tourist Hotels Affects Organizational Performance: Using Intellectual Capital as the Mediating Variable. *The Journal of Global Business Management*, *8*(1), 189–201.

Wang, H. C., He, J., & Mahoney, J. (2009). Firm-specific knowledge resources and competitive advantage: The roles of economic- and relationship-based employee governance mechanisms. *Strategic Management Journal*, *30*(12), 1265–1285. doi:10.1002/smj.787

Warr, P. (2009). *The Economics of Enough: Thailand's "Sufficiency Economy" Debate*. Paper presented at the Buddhist Economics: Theory and Practice, Thailand.

Watson, J. (2003). *SME Performance: Does Gender Matter?* A paper for the Small Enterprise Association of Australia and New Zealand 16th Annual Conference, Ballarat, Australia.

Watson, R. T., Boudreau, M.-C., & Chen, A. J. (2010). Information systems and environmentally sustainable development: Energy informatics and new directions for the is community. *Management Information Systems Quarterly*, *34*(1), 23–38.

Watson, R., & Wilson, N. (2002). Small and medium size enterprise financing: A note on some of the empirical implications of a pecking order. *Journal of Business Finance & Accounting*, *29*(3-4), 557–578. doi:10.1111/1468-5957.00443

Wattanasupachoke, T. (2009). Sufficiency Economy Principles: Applications for Organisation Management Strategy. *Journal of American Academy of Business, Cambridge*, *14*(2), 263–270.

WB. (2009). Doing Business 2009. Washington, DC: Amazon.com's Publishing.

Webb, J. W., Kistruck, G. M., Ireland, R. D., & Ketchen, D. J. Jr. (2010). The entrepreneurship process in base of the pyramid markets: The case of multinational enterprise/nongovernment organization alliances. *Entrepreneurship Theory and Practice*, *34*(3), 555–581. doi:10.1111/j.1540-6520.2009.00349.x

Weber, P., & Schaper, M. (2003). Understanding the grey entrepreneur: A review of the literature. In *Proceedings of the Small Enterprise Association of Australia and New Zealand 16th Annual Conference*. SEAANZ.

Webster, F. E., & Keller, K. L. (2004). A roadmap for branding in industrial markets. *The Journal of Brand Management*, *11*(5), 388–402. doi:10.1057/palgrave.bm.2540184

Weigel, F. K., Hazen, B. T., Cegielski, C. G., & Hall, D. J. (2014). Diffusion of Innovations and the Theory of Planned Behavior in Information Systems Research: A Metaanalysis. *Communications of the Association for Information Systems*, *34*(1), 31.

Westhead, P., Wright, M., & Ucbasaran, D. (2004). Internationalization of private firms: Environmental turbulence and organizational strategies and resources. *Entrepreneurship & Regional Development*, *16*(6), 501–522. doi:10.1080/0898562042000231929

Wiboonchutikula, P. (2002). Small and Medium Enterprises in Thailand: Recent Trends. *Small Business Economics*, *18*(1), 211–224. doi:10.1023/A:1015143709196

Wibulswasdi, C., Piboolsravut, P., & Pootrakool, K. (2010). *Sufficiency Economy Philosophy and Development* (3rd ed.). Bangkok: Bureau of the Crown Property.

Wiklund, J., & Shepherd, D. (2003). Knowledge-based resources, entrepreneurial orientation, and the performance of small and medium-sized businesses. *Strategic Management Journal*, *24*(13), 1307–1314. doi:10.1002/smj.360

Wiklund, J., & Shepherd, D. (2005). Entrepreneurial orientation and small business performance: A configurational approach. *Journal of Business Venturing*, *20*(1), 71–91. doi:10.1016/j.jbusvent.2004.01.001

Wiklund, J., & Shepherd, D. (2011). Where to from here? EO-as-experimentation, failure, and distribution of outcomes. *Entrepreneurship Theory and Practice*, *35*(5), 925–946. doi:10.1111/j.1540-6520.2011.00454.x

Wills-Johnson, N. (2008). The networked firm: A framework for RBV. *Journal of Management Development*, *27*(2), 214–224. doi:10.1108/02621710810849344

Windrum, P., & de Berranger, P. (2002). *The adoption of e-business technology by SMEs*. Retrieved from http://www.merit.unimaas.nl/publications/rmpdf/2002/rm2002-023.pdf

Wong, H. Y., & Merrilees, B. (2005). A brand orientation typology for SMEs: A case research approach. *Journal of Product and Brand Management*, *14*(3), 155–162. doi:10.1108/10610420510601021

Wong, H. Y., & Merrilees, B. (2008). The performance benefits of being brand-orientated. *Journal of Product and Brand Management*, *17*(6), 372–383. doi:10.1108/10610420810904112

Wonglimpiyarat, & Jarunee. (2016). Innovation policies to accelerate SME development. *Jarunee Wonglimpiyarat, 16*(2).

Wonglimpiyarat, J. (2016). The innovation incubator, university business incubator and technology transfer strategy: The case of Thailand. *Technology in Society*, *46*, 18–27. doi:10.1016/j.techsoc.2016.04.002

Wood, R., & Bandura, A. (1989). Social cognitive theory of organizational management. *Academy of Management Review*, *14*(3), 361–384.

Woodruff, R. B., & Flint, D. J. (2006). Marketing's service-dominant logic and customer value. In R. F. Lusch & S. L. Vargo (Eds.), *The service-dominant logic of marketing: Dialog, debate, and directions* (pp. 183–195). New York: Taylor and Francis.

World Bank. (2000). *Entering the 21st century—World development report 1999/2000*. New York: Oxford University Press.

World Bank. (2005). *World Bank Report 2005: A Better Investment Climate for Everyone World Development Report*. Washington, DC: The World Bank and Oxford University.

World Commission on Environment and Development (WCED). (1987). *Our Common Future*. Oxford, UK: Oxford University Press.

World Economic Forum. (2009). *The Next Billions: Unleashing Business Potential in Untapped Markets*. World Economic Forum.

World Economic Forum. (2013). The Global Competitiveness Report 2012–2013. Author.

World Economic Forum. (2015). The Global Competitiveness Report 2015–2016. Author.

World Resource Institute. (2007). The Next 4 Billion: Market Size and Business Strategy at the Base of the Pyramid. World Bank.

World Summit for Social Development. (1995). *Report of the World Summit Social Development Copenhagen 6-12 March, 1995* (United Nations Publication, Salcs No. E. 96. Iv.8). Author.

World Wide Worx. (2013). *The time of the App*. Retrieved January 12, 2016, from http://www.worldwideworx.com/mobileinternet2014/

Wu, W. Y., Chang, M. L., & Chen, C. W. (2008). Promoting innovation through the accumulation of intellectual capital, social capital, and entrepreneurial orientation. *R & D Management*, *38*(3), 265–277.

Yaghoubi, N. M., & Ahmadi, F. (2010). Factors affecting the women entrepreneurship in industrial section. *European Journal of Soil Science*, *17*(1), 88–101.

Yang, X., Li, Y., & Tan, C.-H. (2013). *Drivers for green IT in organizations: Multiple case studies in China and Singapore*. Paper presented at the Pacific Asia Conference on Information Systems (PACIS).

Yao, X., Wen, W., & Ren, Z. (2009). Corporate entrepreneurship in the enterprise clusters environment: Influence of network resources and entrepreneurial orientation on firm performance. *Frontiers of Business Research in China*, *3*(4), 566–582. doi:10.1007/s11782-009-0027-x

Yee, Y. P. (2009). Daring adventures. *The Star*. Retrieved January 04, 2015, from http://www.thestar.com.my

Yeoh, P. L. (2014). Internationalization and Performance Outcomes of Entrepreneurial Family SMEs: The Role of Outside CEOs, Technology Sourcing, and Innovation. *Thunderbird International Business Review*, *56*(1), 77–96. doi:10.1002/tie.21597

Yigitcanla, T., & Sarimin, M. (2015). *Article information: Multimedia Super Corridor*. Knowledge-Based Urban.

Yusof, & Bhattasali, D. (2008). Economic Growth and Development in Malaysia: Policy Making and Leadership. *Commission on Growth and Development, 27*.

Yusoff, A., Ahmad, N. H., & Abdul Halim, H. (2016). Entrepreneurial orientation and entrepreneurial intention among Malaysian agricultural students: The impact of entrepreneurship education. *Advances in Business-Related Scientific Research Journal*, *7*(1), 77–92.

Yusuf, A. (1995). Critical success factors for small business: perceptions of South Pacific entrepreneurs. *Journal of Small Business Management*. Retrieved from http://search.proquest.com/openview/488b6040ba090b7262c8caf6726dc27b/1?pq-origsite=gscholar

Yusuf, A. (1995). Critical Success Factors for Small Business: Perceptions of South Pacific Entrepreneurs. *Journal of Small Business Management*, *33*, 68–73.

Yusuf, A., & Schindehutte, M. (2000). Exploring entrepreneurship in a declining economy. *Journal of Developmental Entrepreneurship*, *5*(1), 41–56.

Yu, T. F.-L. (2001). The Chinese family business as a strategic system: An evolutionary perspective. *International Journal of Entrepreneurial Behaviour & Research*, *7*(1), 22–40. doi:10.1108/13552550110385736

Zahra, S. A., & Hayton, J. C. (2008). The effect of international venturing on firm performance: The moderating influence of absorptive capacity. *Journal of Business Venturing*, *23*(2), 195–220. doi:10.1016/j.jbusvent.2007.01.001

Zahrom, B. (2012, December 13). Generasi Y digalak sertai industry tani. *Berita Harian*. Retrieved from http://www.bharian.com.my/bharian/articles/GenerasiYdigalaksertaiindustritani/Article/index_html

Zainal Abiddin, N., & Irsyad, S. (2012). The involvement of graduates youth in commercial agriculture: Issues and challenges. *International Journal for Educational Studies*, *5*(1), 15–24.

Zainol, F. A., & Daud, W. N. W. (2011). Indigenous ("Bumiputera") Malay Entrepreneurs in Malaysia: Government Supports, Entrepreneurial Orientation and Firms Performances. *International Business & Management*, *2*(1), 86–99.

Zainol, F. A., & Daud, W. N. W. (2011). Indigenous ("Bumiputera") Malay entrepreneurs in Malaysia: Government supports, entrepreneurial orientation and firms performances. *International Business and Management*, *2*(1), 86–99.

Zeiller, M., & Schauer, B. (2011, September). Adoption, motivation and success factors of social media for team collaboration in SMEs. In *Proceedings of the 11th International Conference on Knowledge Management and Knowledge Technologies* (p. 4). ACM. doi:10.1145/2024288.2024294

Zellweger, T., & Sieger, P. (2012). Entrepreneurial orientation in long-lived family firms. *Small Business Economics*, *38*(1), 67–84. doi:10.1007/s11187-010-9267-6

Zeng, X. X., & Saixing, Y. W. (2016). A theory of multi-dimensional organizational innovation cultures and innovation performance in transitional economies: The role of team cohesion", Chinese Management Studies. *Chinese Management Studies*, *10*(3). doi:10.1108/09564230910978511

Zhang, M., Sarker, S., & Sarker, S. (2007). *Drivers and effects of IT capability in "born-global" firms: A cross-national study*. Paper presented at the 28th International Conference on Information Systems (ICIS 2007), Montreal, Canada.

Zhang, M., Sarker, S., & Sarker, S. (2013). Drivers and export performance impacts of IT capability in "born-global" firms: A cross-national study. *Information Systems Journal, 23*(5), 419–443. doi:10.1111/j.1365-2575.2012.00404.x

Zhang, X., Ma, X., & Wang, Y. (2012). Entrepreneurial orientation, social capital, and the internationalization of SMES: Evidence from China. *Thunderbird International Business Review, 54*(2), 195–210. doi:10.1002/tie.21451

Zhou, L., Wu, A., & Barnes, B. R. (2012). The effects of early internationalization on performance outcomes in young international ventures: The mediating role of marketing capabilities. *Journal of International Marketing, 20*(4), 882–905. doi:10.1509/jim.12.0076

Ziggers, G., & Henseler, J. (2009). Inter-firm network capability: How it affects buyer-supplier performance. *British Food Journal, 111*(8), 794–810. doi:10.1108/00070700910980928

Zimmerman, M. A., & Zeitz, G. J. (2002). Beyond survival: Achieving new venture growth by building legitimacy. *Academy of Management Review, 27*(3), 414–431.

Zineldin, M. (2004). Co-opetition: The organization of the future. *Marketing Intelligence & Planning, 22*(6/7), 780–789. doi:10.1108/02634500410568600

Zins, A. H. (2001). Relative attitudes and commitment in customer loyalty models: Some experiences in the commercial airline industry. *International Journal of Service Industry Management, 12*(3), 269–294. doi:10.1108/EUM0000000005521

Zoppa, A., & McMahon, R. G. (2002). Pecking order theory and the financial structure of manufacturing SMEs from Australias business longitudinal survey. *Small Enterprise Research, 10*(2), 23–41. doi:10.5172/ser.10.2.23

Zortea-Johnston, E., Darroch, J., & Matear, S. (2012). Business orientations and innovation in small and medium sized enterprises. *The International Entrepreneurship and Management Journal, 8*(2), 145–164. doi:10.1007/s11365-011-0170-7

Zou, H., & Ghauri, P. N. (2010). Internationalizing by learning: The case of Chinese high-tech new ventures. *International Marketing Review, 27*(2), 223–244. doi:10.1108/02651331011037539

Zucchella, A., Palamara, G., & Denicolai, S. (2007). The drivers of the early internationalization of the firm. *Journal of World Business, 42*(3), 268–280. doi:10.1016/j.jwb.2007.04.008

Zucchella, A., & Servais, P. (2012). The internationalisation process of small- and medium-sized firms and the liability of complexity. *International Journal of Entrepreneurship and Small Business, 15*(2), 191–212. doi:10.1504/IJESB.2012.045204

Zulfakar, M. (2014, September 24,). Malaysia will continue to cut carbon emissions, Najib tells UN climate summit. *The Star*.

Zwass, V. (2010). Co-creation: Toward a taxonomy and an integrated research perspective. *International Journal of Electronic Commerce, 15*(1), 11–48. doi:10.2753/JEC1086-4415150101

About the Contributors

Noor Hazlina Ahmad, Ph.D., is a Professor at the School of Management USM. She joined the university after completing her PhD at the University of Adelaide, Australia. She teaches entrepreneurship and organisational behaviour related subjects. She also supervises PhD and MA students in the field of entrepreneurship and SMEs. Currently, she serves as the President of the Asian Academy of Management and sits on the editorial board of the Asian Academy of Management Journal. She is also actively involved with consultation programs and served as a facilitator for community, entrepreneurship and leadership projects. Her research interests are in the areas of Entrepreneurship, SMEs and Organisational Behaviour.

T. Ramayah has an MBA from Universiti Sains Malaysia (USM). Currently he is a Professor at the School of Management in USM. He teaches mainly courses in Research Methodology and Business Statistics. Apart from teaching, he is an avid researcher, especially in the areas of technology management and adoption in business and education. His publications have appeared in Computers in Human Behavior, Resources Conservation and Recycling, Journal of Educational Technology & Society, Direct Marketing: An International Journal, Information Development, Journal of Project Management (JoPM), Management Research News (MRN), International Journal of Information Management, International Journal of Services and Operations Management (IJSOM), Engineering, Construction and Architectural Management (ECAM) and North American Journal of Psychology. He is constantly invited to serve on the editorial boards and program committees of many international journals and conferences of repute. His profile can be accessed from http://www.ramayah.com.

Abdul Halim is currently an Associate Professor at School of Management, Universiti Sains Malaysia. She received her PhD from University of Malaya, Malaysia. She has been lecturing for many years on subjects such as HRM, Management, Strategic Management, Communication and others. She is also experienced in the use of modeling and application of software such as AMOS and SPSS. She currently serves as an editorial board member of the Asian Academy of Management Journal (AAMJ). She has presented her research works at various international conferences including the Australia and New Zealand Academy of Management (ANZAM), HRM conference and Global Academy of Business and Economics Research. She has also published in high impact journals such as Journal of Business, Economics and Management, Total Quality Management and Business Excellence. Additionally she also published in various journals including Journal of Human Resource Costing & Accounting, Singapore Mangement Reviews, Business Strategies Series, International Journal of Economics and Management and Journal of International Business and Entrepreneurship and received a number of best paper awards.

* * *

Theresa Nonyerem Akomode teaches Principles of Accounting and Introduction to Finance in the Pan-Atlantic University. Subsequent to her lecturing career, she engaged in industry for 10 years working with Zenith Bank, KPMG and Lagos Business School. Theresa has done some research which led to her publishing cases and journal articles. She is currently interested in sustainable finance which would lead to an effective growth of SMEs Export. Her current research is in development finance where she is looking at how financial institutions can support SMEs effectively.

Azlan Amran started his career as a lecturer at the School of Management, Universiti Sains Malaysia in 2006. He is now a Professor at the Graduate School of Business in the same University. Prior to joining USM, he worked as an accountant for several years. He has published a significant number of articles in the area of CSR in both local and international journals. He is currently supervising PhD, MBA, and Masters candidates in CSR. At present, he holds the position of Dean at the Graduate School of Business. In terms of practical experience, he has been involved in several training and consultancy projects in Accounting-related issues and Corporate Social Reporting. He is currently holding several grants to support his research on CSR-related issues. He is also a member of the editorial board for several international journals. At the national level, he is a Technical Committee member for ISO 26000.

Muruga Chinniah currently works as lecturer in Universiti Teknologi MARA Johor (UiTM Johor), Malaysia. Muruga holds a Master Business Administration (MBA) and Bachelor's degree in International Business Management from Universiti Utara Malaysia (UUM), Malaysia. He is currently pursuing his PhD at the Universiti Teknikal Malaysia Melaka, Malaysia. His field of interest is in Operation Management and Supply Chain Management/ Green Supply Chain Management.

Pei Leng Gan is a PhD student in Universiti Sains Malaysia. She is now working as graduate research student under school of management in Universiti Sains Malaysia. Her research interests are Green IT and Technology Management.

Yuvaraj Ganesan is a senior lecturer at Graduate School of Business, Universiti Sains Malaysia. He begins his career path as an Audit Assistant in an audit firm. After five years in an audit firm, he then become a Group Accountant in a commercial sector. His research interests are in auditing, service quality, non-audit services, Corporate Governance, Corporate Social Responsibility, Small and Medium Enterprises and Small and Medium Practitioner. Besides industrial experience as auditor and group accountant, he was also a Research Officer in USM in several research projects in USM, prior to pursuing his PhD. He now holds an industrial grant. He has presented in international conferences and has published articles in both local and international journals. He is a member of Malaysian Institute of Accountants (MIA) and Institute of Internal Audit, Malaysia (IIAM).

Haniruzila Hanifah is a PhD Scholar who is currently undertaking a research in the areas of Innovation and SMEs. Her research focus lies in the interplay between Entrepreneurship and Organisational Behaviour subject matters. She has published in a few international journals and presented her research works in several International conferences. Her research interests are in the areas of innovation culture, entrepreneurship and SMEs.

Hasnah Haron is a Professor of Auditing and Dean at the Institute of Postgraduate Studies in Universiti Malaysia Pahang. She was previously attached to Universiti Sains Malaysia. In 1996, she was conferred a PhD degree from the University of Hull, United Kingdom. Hasnah carries with her more than 30 years of academic experience. She was the founding Dean of the Graduate School of Business at Universiti Sains Malaysia. She is a professional member of CPA Australia, a Chartered Accountant of the Malaysian Institute of Accountant and a Fellow of the Institute of Internal Auditors Malaysia. She was a member of the Commission of the Malaysian Competition Commission (MyCC) from 2011-2013. She was also appointed as a member of Economics and Management Cluster, National Council of Professors Malaysia from 2014 to 2016. Hasnah is also involved in many consultancy projects, that include the development of the Corporate Integrity System Malaysia with Institute Integriti Malaysia and has acted as the lead consultant to examine the Effectiveness of Parole System with the Prison Department of Malaysia. Her active role in the university and in the professional accounting circle, has much shaped her publications. Hasnah has not only published in internationally refereed journals but also in Professional Accountancy Journals.

Md. Mosharref Hossain completed his MBA from Dhaka University in 2003. He joined at a private university, Stamford University Bangladesh at 2004 and left the university at 2007 for Bangladesh Institute of Bank Management. He is serving as an Assistant professor for the institute. Now he is continuing his PhD at Universiti Utara Malaysia. His research interest are on credit management, SME banking and project financing.

Yusnidah Ibrahim is a Professor of Finance in the Department of Finance, School of Economics, Finance and Banking (SEFB), College of Business (COB), University Utara Malaysia (UUM). She obtained her BA in Actuarial Science and MSc Actuarial Science from University of Iowa, US, and PhD from De Montfort University, UK. Her research and publications are in the area of capital structure, dividend policy, Islamic bonds (Sukuk), small business finance and higher education finance. She also serves as the editorial board member of the International Journal of Banking and Finance (IJBF) and International Journal of Management Studies (IJMS). Currently she is the Dean of the School of Economics, Finance and Banking (SEFB), at UUM.

Alireza Jalali has a PhD degree in the field of entrepreneurship study and managing small and medium enterprises, he has three years experience in managing projects in different industries. He teaches mainly courses in entrepreneurship, managing small business, new business creation and establishment, marketing, business statistics and research methodology.

Pravina Jayapal is currently pursuing her PhD in the field of marketing under the supervision of Associate Professor Dr. Azizah Omar in School of Management, Universiti Sains Malaysia. Her research area focuses on consumer behavior, deviant buying behavior and consumer psychology.

Kijpokin Kasemsap received his BEng degree in Mechanical Engineering from King Mongkut's University of Technology, Thonburi, his MBA degree from Ramkhamhaeng University, and his DBA degree in Human Resource Management from Suan Sunandha Rajabhat University. He is a Special Lecturer in the Faculty of Management Sciences, Suan Sunandha Rajabhat University, based in Bangkok, Thailand. He is a Member of the International Association of Engineers (IAENG), the International Association of Engineers and Scientists (IAEST), the International Economics Development and Research Center (IEDRC), the International Association of Computer Science and Information Technology (IACSIT), the International Foundation for Research and Development (IFRD), and the International Innovative Scientific and Research Organization (IISRO). He also serves on the International Advisory Committee (IAC) for International Association of Academicians and Researchers (INAAR). He has had numerous original research articles in top international journals, conference proceedings, and books on the topics of business management, human resource management, and knowledge management, published internationally.

Zainab Khalifah is Dean Faculty of Management University Technology Malaysia, Johor, Malaysia.

Melisa Koorsse is a postdoctoral fellow at the Nelson Mandela Metropolitan University, where she obtained her Ph.D. in Computer Science. Her doctoral research was focused on programming tools and software to support IT scholars in South African secondary schools. Her research interests include the use of computers and mobile devices to support education and introductory programming as well as research interests in the field of artificial intelligence and evolutionary computing, specifically related to time-series forecasting.

Sameer Kumar is a Senior Lecturer at University of Malaya, Malaysia.

Siyasanga Loleka is a Masters student in development finance at the Nelson Mandela Metropolitan University (NMMU). He obtained his undergraduate degree in Computer Science and Information Systems an Honours degree in business management at NMMU. His research interests are in the fields of computing, small and medium enterprises (SMEs) and development (with a special focus on finance).

Imran Mahmud is working as an Assistant Professor at the Department of Software Engineering, Daffodil International University, Bangladesh. At the moment he is pursing PhD in Management Information System at the School of Management in Universiti Sains Malaysia. His research interests are human-computer interaction, usability testing, software engineering measurement / models and management information systems. Imran Mahmud has published several research papers on enterprise resource planning (ERP) and information system published by Elsevier, Sage publications and IEEE. His full profile can be accessed from: http://faculty.daffodilvarsity.edu.bd/profile/swe/imahmud.html.

Haslinda Musa is currently a senior Lecturer in Operations Management at the Universiti Teknikal Malysia Melaka (UTeM). She was previously a teaching assistant and researcher at Leeds University Business School, UK from December 2006 to August 2013. Her field of interest is in Operations Management, Business Continuity Management and Green Supply Chain Management. Her current research projects (active) include Malaysian Standard (UTeM, PJP Grant), Drop-shipping Supply Chain (KPM, FRGS) and Microwave – Innovation Adoption (KPM, TRGS).

Omiunu Ojinga is a PG Student of the University of Ibadan, Nigeria.

Azizah Omar, Ph.D., is presently an Associate Professor specialising in marketing and wellness management at School of Management, Universiti Sains Malaysia (USM). She has been teaching and supervising undergraduate and postgraduate (MBA, MA, PhD and DBA) students especially in the area of consumer behavior, service quality, green marketing and web-based marketing. She has published her works in various international journals such as South African Journal of Clinical Nutrition; Journal of Telemedicine and Telecare; and Journal of Marketing Development & Competitiveness. She obtained her doctoral of philosophy from Monash University, Melbourne, Australia (2006); Master of Business Administration, Universiti Sains Malaysia (2000), and Bachelor of Health Sciences from Curtin University, Perth, Australia (1996).

Oluwasola Oni is a lecturer at Pan-Atlantic University, Nigeria. She teaches information systems at undergraduate and postgraduate level. She has been involved in research considering challenges involved in the effective diffusion of innovation technologies among individuals and Small and Medium Size Enterprises (SMEs). In addition to the study of diffusion and adoption of technologies, she is also interested in and is currently investigating mobile customer relationship management (mCRMs), mobile money, digital ecosystems and knowledge sharing.

Say Keat Ooi is a lecturer at Graduate School of Business, Universiti Sains Malaysia. Prior to joining Universiti Sains Malaysia, he worked in the pharmaceutical industry for several years. He specialises corporate social and environmental reporting, and corporate social responsibility research. His niche is in corporate climate change reporting. He has published several papers in local and international journals, and he is the co-researcher for several research grants.

Veera Pandiyan Pandiyan is an accomplished, dynamic professional trainer and a Certified International Professional Training Consultant (CIPTC) by American Certification Institute. He holds a doctorate degree in supply chain management from University of Malaya, an MBA degree and bachelor's degree in Analytical Economics. He is also a member graduate of Chartered Institute of Logistics and Transport (CILT), U.K. and Certified Purchasing Professional (CPP) from American Purchasing Society. He has more than 19 years of working experience in both military (government) and private companies. He now serves as an Associate Professor in MARA University of Technology (Malaysia) and is a freelance corporate trainer to several training providers in Malaysia, Singapore, Thailand and Vietnam.

Donovan Peter is a Masters Student at University of Malaya.

Gregor Pfajfar is the full-time professor at the University of Ljubljana.

Syed Abidur Rahman holds a PhD in entrepreneurship from Universiti Sains Malaysia. Prior joining to the OYA Graduate School of Business, he has been working as Assistant Professor in Stamford University Bangladesh. His research interests are in entrepreneurial competencies, entrepreneurial orientation, entrepreneurial event model in context of micro, small, and medium entrepreneurs. He has published some of his works in Thomson Reuters and SCOPUS indexed journals. He has also participated in national and international conferences. He was involved in research and consulting program for green entrepreneurship among selected Malaysian SMEs by Malaysian Green Technology Corporation (GreenTech Malaysia) under the Ministry of Energy, Green Technology and Water Malaysia (KeTTHA) partnering with School of Management, Universiti Sains Malaysia. Before, entering to the academia, Syed Abidur Rahman, worked in industry for four years. He served as territory manager in one of the biggest multinational company Unilever Bangladesh Limited.

Brenda Scholtz (Ph.D.) is Head of Department for Computing Sciences at the Nelson Mandela Metropolitan University (NMMU) in Port Elizabeth. Brenda has worked in the IT industry for over 15 years as programmer, systems analyst, consultant and IT manager. She was awarded her PhD in ERP skills and education in 2012. Her research interests are in the broad field of Information Systems, more specifically related to business process management, enterprise systems, business intelligence, enterprise architectures and environmental information systems. Brenda is currently serving as project manager for several industry research collaboration programmes between South Africa and Germany. Brenda is also a member of the Institute of Information Technology Professionals South Africa (IITPSA), the Association for Information Systems (AIS) as well as the Business Architecture Guild. Brenda has published over 46 papers in international journals and conferences.

Aviv Shoham is the head of Department of Business Administration at University of Haifa, Israel.

Seyedeh Khadijeh Taghizadeh is a Postdoctoral Researcher in the Centre of Social Innovation, Universiti Teknologi Petronas, Malaysia. She received her PhD from the Universiti Sains Malaysia in Malaysia. Her research interests include innovation management, social innovation, marketing and entrepreneurship. Her research has appeared in Journal of Business and Industrial Marketing, Telematics and Informatics, Management Decision, Social Indicators Research, Int. J. Mobile Communications, Business: Theory and Practices, and Global Business Organisational Excellence.

Siriluck Thongpoon is currently the Dean of Hatyai Business School. She obtained her doctoral degree from Universiti Sains Malaysia. She has published several papers in international journals and presented her research works at international conferences. Her research interests are in the area of Entrepreneurship, SMEs and Sustainability.

Nguyen Thi Uyen is a lecturer of Vietnam University of Commerce (VUC). She has completed her master program in Thailand under the Thai Government Scholarship since 2008 and conducted many courses of Strategic Management, international business Strategy, fundamentals of management, and e-marketing in both English and Vietnamese programs. She has also published several research papers in journals such as Journal of Commerce Science, Journal of Science and Technology and many international conference proceedings. She also involved in a number of research projects at both university level and ministry level in Vietnam about strategic environment scanning, strategy formulation or implementation, e-marketing mix. Her research interests are in the areas of strategic management, entrepreneurs and SMEs, leadership, strategic Human Resource Management and Organizational Behaviors.

Ali Vafaei-Zadeh is a PhD student in Operation Management at School of Management, Universiti Sains Malaysia. His research interests include information system, information security, cyber-security, information sharing, and supply chain performance. He holds MBA in production and materials management in 2010 from University of Pune, India. He has two- years industrial experience as a production manager in Iran Food Industries Noshahr, Iran.

Asliza Yusoff is currently a full-time PhD candidate at School of Management, Universiti Sains Malaysia. She is also a senior lecturer at Malaysian Polytechnic. Her research interests include agropreneurship, small business performance and entrepreneurial intentions and behavioural action.

Siti Rohaida Mohamed Zainal, Ph.D., is an Associate Professor at School of Management. She graduated with a BBA from the University of Missouri Kansas City, USA, MBA degree from the Universiti Sains Malaysia and PhD from Universiti Teknologi Mara, Shah Alam. Malaysia. Siti Rohaida is currently attached to Organisation and Work Values Section at School of Management, USM and teaches OB-related courses. Her areas of research are Leadership, Career Management Strategies, Talent Management, Work Outcomes and People Management Strategies. She has published in various indexed and non-indexed journals. She also leads numbers of research grants both internal and external. She is also very active in sharing experiences with the industry as well the community.

Index

O

P

R

S

T

U

V

W

www.ingramcontent.com/pod-product-compliance
Lightning Source LLC
LaVergne TN
LVHW060352300926
849162LV00006B/1252
* 9 7 8 1 5 2 2 5 2 1 6 5 5 *